NEW to this edition A whole chapter devoted entirely to the nature of group conflict provides insight in how to recognize and deal with unresolved conflict—an increasingly prevalent issue in group dynamics.

8 The Nature of Group Conflict

GROUPS

GROUPS

Theory and Experience

Sixth Edition

Rodney W. Napier

Matti K. Gershenfeld
Temple University

HOUGHTON MIFFLIN COMPANY
Boston New York

To Annika Zoe, the newest and smallest member of the clan. RWN

To Beryl, Howard, Richard, and Ken and their families;
each different, each a very special, caring group. MKG

Senior Sponsoring Editor: Loretta Wolozin
Associate Editor: Lisa Mafrici
Project Editor: Anne Holm
Manufacturing Manager: Florence Cadran
Marketing Manager: Pamela J. Laskey

Cover design: Rebecca Fagan
Cover image: ©Ellen Carey/Photonica

Photo Credits:
Chapter 1: Bill Aron/Jeroboam
Chapter 2: Jeff Dunn/The Picture Cube
Chapter 3: Joel Gordon
Chapter 4: Michael A. Dwyer/Stock Boston
Chapter 5: David Pratt/Positive Images
Chapter 6: Judith Canty/Stock Boston
Chapter 7: Esbin-Anderson/The Image Works
Chapter 8: Grantpix/Monkmeyer
Chapter 9: Joel Gordon
Chapter 10: Skjold Photos/Jeroboam

Copyright © 1999 by Houghton Mifflin Company. All rights reserved.

No part of this work may be reproduced or transmitted in any form or by any means, electronic or mechanical, including photocopying and recording, or by any information storage or retrieval system without the prior written permission of Houghton Mifflin Company unless such copying is expressly permitted by federal copyright law. Address inquiries to College Permissions, Houghton Mifflin Company, 222 Berkeley Street, Boston, MA 02116-3764.

Printed in the U.S.A.

Library of Congress Catalog Card Number: 98-72066

ISBN: 0-395-90417-X

123456789-DH-02 01 00 99 98

Contents

Preface

Some Strong Feelings

There are a variety of mixed feelings that we have faced as we have written our way through five and, now, a sixth edition of *Groups: Theory and Experience*. The first is a sense of gratification that so many continue to find the book enlightening, interesting, and even fun. Our hope has always been to provide a rigorous, empirically based text that is, above all, readable and, at the same time, practical. Over the years we have heard from scores of readers who have given the book a favorite place on their "not for show" bookshelves. They tell us that they use *Groups* both as a reference for information about group life, as well as a guide and tool for helping them intervene effectively in the groups they manage. By utilizing some of our designs or creating some of their own, our readers pay us the ultimate compliment.

A second strong feeling is a bit more humbling. After five editions and the desire to make the sixth better than ever, a small voice says, "Is there really anything left to say that hasn't been said? After all, groups are groups." Luckily, the reality is that there is always much more happening than we can ever capture. The research and related literature seem to expand exponentially in terms of both quantity and quality. There is no end in sight of the discoveries and understandings relating to what it is that makes groups tick. Our toughest job is to cut to the heart of what has been learned since our last edition and include the information that will have the most appeal and value to the reader.

A final strong feeling that arose before we hunkered down to the task of this latest edition had to do with our own openness to change, our willingness to listen to what our readers, teachers, and critics have had to say about our latest—now past—effort. The result is that over our twenty-five years of writing about our passion, we have had to let go some of our favorite parts—even whole chapters to which our readers somehow did not relate or found less useful than others. In a perverse way, this constraint has actually been good for us since it has kept us learning, responsive, and, we hope, improving more than we might have otherwise.

The Audience

We always find it amazing that until fifty years ago, 'groups' were not even a legitimate course of study. Now hundreds of books and thousands of articles later, it is defined as one of the very basic disciplines one must understand in order to grasp the complexities of organizational or family life. This book is used in courses on group process and dynamics in psychology, education, social work, business, and communication. To understand group dynamics in any discipline domain in which it is studied, the reader must go beyond the safety and structure of the written word and become an expert observer of the group process itself. It is bringing the words to life through systematic observation that has made the discipline so fascinating and meaningful.

For example, *educators* have learned that teaching with the students seated in straight rows and listening to talking heads is less productive, less motivating, and leads to less achievement than an effective blend of small group or cooperative group discussions, lecturing, and structured activities designed for the group. In addition, student morale is often a function of classroom norms and issues of membership, which can dominate how students relate. A failure to understand the classroom as a group limits the ability of the teacher to teach and the students to learn.

In *business,* as organizations have downsized and re-engineered themselves into more efficient units, teams and small groups have become the necessary units of choice for managers in building morale and increasing efficiencies. The only problem is that few supervisors and business leaders have ever been taught how groups function. The result is that it is often a long and arduous struggle to reach the ideal of greater efficiency and productivity. The consequence for us is that the interest in groups as 'teams' is burgeoning.

In *hospitals,* primary-care nursing demands effective teamwork. In the field of *psychology,* group therapy has moved from individual therapy in a group setting to a "process" where building trust within the community of the group is seen as essential. Only by the creative building of the therapy group as a community can the therapist gain the kind of leverage possible to establish a therapeutic process—far exceeding the more traditional approaches that, in some cases, are still being used.

At some level, the more we understand the need to work effectively in group settings, the more we become aware of just how ineffective some groups can be in actual practice. That groups can be difficult and often generate conflict and their own set of problems is all too true. But, with each passing year, and for us, each passing edition, we learn more about what to do to reduce these difficulties so that the true benefit of groups can be realized.

Our purpose is to draw together the theoretical principles and practical understanding that cut across the wide array of groups most of us face in our daily lives. To match intellectual insights with our observations will bring an increasing face validity to these daily experiences. And it is with this accumulative understanding that our readers will find the confidence to begin acting differently, and to lead those who don't understand.

Features of the New Edition

There has been an explosion of new and relevant research during the early- and mid-nineties. We have acknowledged hundreds of additional studies throughout the text with appropriate attention to the fundamental aspects of group life—communications, membership, goals, norms, and leadership. Our effort has been to identify those studies that add significantly to our understanding of a particular topic or shed new light on an area given little previous attention. In addition to this expected expansion of our empirical and theoretical research, we have added the following improvements:

DIVERSITY IN GROUPS

In our previous edition (1993), we began to focus quite intentionally on an issue that cuts across every topic and every group. We continue, in each chapter of this edition, to focus on the many faces of *diversity in groups*. Issues of multiculturalism were recognized as representing some of the greatest challenges to organizations and groups of the nineties. The initial flurry of interest in the late eighties and early nineties soon waned as leaders began to recognize how difficult the issues were, and as a result, many of them decided issues of diversity were better left alone. The problem with such a head-in-the-sand approach is that denial or avoidance will never solve the problems generated from misunderstanding, prejudice, and abuse. Our approach is to look to the long term and begin by creating awareness of the issue wherever possible.

To do this, in addition to greater focus on diversity in the chapters themselves, we have provided a new "Focus on Diversity" feature appearing in the margins at various points throughout the book. These marginal prompts and questions should stimulate discussion and awareness, and provide a starting point for rich discussions.

NEW CHAPTER ON THE NATURE OF GROUP CONFLICT

We have added a whole chapter on group conflict and its management within a group setting (Chapter 8, "The Nature of Group Conflict"). There is no question in our minds that conflict is a ubiquitous commodity and present in any group. Since most people have never had even an introductory course in how to deal effectively with conflict, it is often avoided or denied. Because of this, legitimizing dealing with conflict complements our emphasis on multiculturalism. The failure to deal with issues of diversity is partly the result of our lack of skills in dealing with conflict. Diversity by its nature relates to differences in attitude, thought, emotions, and behavior. Such differences inevitably result in conflict.

Moreover, the vast majority of organizations are averse to conflict. Having neither the skills nor the energy to enter the unpredictable world of conflict, survival, or, at the very least, the desire to maintain some semblance of comfort and control in the group becomes a goal. The result is that members often become skilled at eluding rather than resolving their conflicts—a norm of conflict aversion occurs. The outcome is something we have all experienced—a constant source of unfinished business that inevitably affects the morale, productivity, and trust within the group. How to recognize and deal with such unresolved conflict is a primary goal of this new and challenging chapter.

EXTENSIVE PRINT AND WORLD WIDE WEB RESOURCES

We often talk about the explosion of information confronting all of us as we attempt to grasp the increasing complexities of our work. Even our text, with its extensive references, will be insufficient for some. For this reason we have added at the end of each chapter a section called *For Further Information,* in which we highlight several books that expand some aspects of what is included in the chapter. Thus, someone interested in creative problem solving (Chapter 7) will find several references that will more than whet the curious reader's appetite. Some of these suggested readings delve deeper into a topic while others may provide a provocative counterpoint to a particularly complex issue. Recommended readings often expand the level of understanding in a manner we are unable to do in an introductory text. We have also identified some Internet resources that may be of interest to the Web browsers among our readers.

For faculty teaching a course relating to groups, we are offering a greatly expanded Instructor's Manual with more teaching units; a variety of exercises to promote a wide array of learning experiences; and a course guide that can provide different approaches to the teaching/learning experience.

To make room for the new research and concepts in the primary areas of group dynamics, we have dispersed content from 'The Incredible Meeting Trap,' 'Humor in Small Groups,' and 'Making Large Groups More Effective' throughout the book.

CONTENT

Our approach to presenting our content coincides with the assumption of first things first. We select and sequence the topics that tend to be present as soon as one enters any group. Clearly the most obvious issue for any group revolves around how people communicate information; how they perceive each other; and how the interpretation of such information can determine the ability of the group to function effectively (Chapter 1). In this edition, we have added a new section on diversity, which stands tall in the life of any group and, all too often, is not recognized or legitimized. It hovers over the group like a shadow, influencing the climate of the group, while usually remaining unaddressed.

Chapter 2, "Membership," faces the issue we bring into any group. It is framed around membership and questions such as: Who am I? Who are you? Who can we become together and is it worth the effort? Types of membership are explored—such as formal and informal, legitimate, and multiple memberships. Since group satisfaction and cohesion is, to a large degree, influenced by feelings of membership, we then focus on what factors gain and lose people's membership.

The factors influencing and legitimizing acceptable behaviors become evident from the inception of a group's existence. Understanding the nature of such norms by a group is a first step in the group itself being able to change or take control of their own destiny. Because norms are most often unspoken, this is easier said than done. We then explore the types of norms and how they influence the acceptance of individuals (Chapter 3). The powerful nature of norms on the life of any group is reviewed along with responses to deviance. Finally, we study how to change norms once they have been identified and how that can have a positive impact on other basic factors of group life. Particular attention, once again, is given to membership, communication patterns, goals, and leadership.

Closely associated with group norms are the goals of the group. In Chapter 4, we delve into the very real differences between group goals, leader goals, and individual goals. Further exploration analyzes goals from an operational and nonoperational perspective, and then in relation to hidden and surface agendas. The relationship of goals to group productivity and cohesion is followed closely by the changing view of the role of mission, goals, and vision and their relationship to effective strategic planning.

Chapter 5 takes a hard look at the changing views of effective leadership. Traditional Leadership (Trait, Style, and Situational) is compared to more contemporary views developed over the past ten years. Special emphasis is placed on gaining a clear understanding of the difference between Transformational and Transactional Leadership. Further clarification is gained through the review of those studies that help to clearly define the nature of each. Research exploring the universality of Tranformational Leadership is reviewed with later attention on the effort to create an intentional Pygmalion Effect (attempting to increase productivity and morale through the use of self-fulfilling prophecy within a group).

In Chapter 6, a systems perspective is applied to the complexity of organizational life. Its coverage is influenced by the recent thinking extracted from the "new" sciences and subatomic physics. Viewing the group from such an integrated and holistic perspective readies the reader to study the area of group problem solving and decision making. An important addition to this chapter is the relationship of system thinking to the family group and, in turn, its relationship to other groups and larger organizations. Relating all of this to group and organizational cultures reinforces earlier understanding of norms, membership, and goals.

Chapter 7 is designed to help the reader understand the nature of the traps that exist and, at the same time, provide some insights and tools to improve the decision-making process. Whether a group can solve its problems effectively depends on how well its members have been able to resolve issues of communication, membership, goals, norms, and leadership. Is it any wonder that problem solving and decision making are often so difficult and even painful? Fallible human beings create fallible solutions and then follow up with poor decisions. This edition adds a more comprehensive look at how the concept of groupthink influences this process. Later, an in-depth assessment of the strengths of brainstorming rounds out our exploration of tools that facilitate effective group problem solving.

The focus of our new Chapter 8, "The Nature of Group Conflict," is on how conflict arises in groups and its relation to certain historical realities. This is followed by in-depth studies of how unresolved normative, membership, and goal-related issues can cripple the ability of a group to do its work. Later, the echo of groupthink can be heard in the discussion surrounding seduction of the leader and the kinds of dysfunction that result. Finally, the concept of design is introduced to provide the reader with a means of coping with emotionally stressful conflict situations. By providing necessary structure through guidelines, ground rules, and procedures, the group leader can avoid being ruled by the emotion of the moment.

By the time readers reach Chapter 9, "The Evolution of Groups," they have the tools and experience for viewing the development of any group with greater dispassion and understanding. New insights have been added relating to the development of groups and their predictable stages and cycles. This is followed by a final chapter, "Small Group Processes," which provides sharply contrasting views of very different groups and the functions they can play in the life of an organization. With the language of groups now available to our readers, the value and difficulties of each of these structured group interventions should be readily understood.

A Final Word

Understanding groups is the result of a cumulative and progressive set of experiences. It demands the discipline to stop long enough to look—and eventually see—what is going on within the group itself. It is the interplay of intellectual concepts, theories, and empirical research with the very practical observation of human interaction that makes the study of groups so compelling. It is a never-ending kaleidoscope, a puzzle with missing pieces. Those with patience and tenacity will eventually be rewarded with insight, understanding, and influence. Those up to the challenge will be able to diagnose, intervene, and, ultimately, help change what is happening.

This edition aims to continue our effort to:

- be accessible, appealing, and engaging to our student readers.
- be comprehensive and current in our review of the literature and, yet, selective of the most pertinent information for our readers.
- be useful and applied in the tools and methods we choose to model.
- provide an accurate refection of the complexities and diversity of our society through the examples we select.
- insure a balance in our presentation of the research, theory, and practical applications.

Acknowledgments

Paula Leder has provided extraordinary help with this revision as a researcher, problem solver, typist, and project manager. Her skill and attention to detail and good humor has helped to keep us on track. Joan Reilly was an excellent researcher and tireless worker. Sheralee Connors kept our noses to the grindstone, provided excellent suggestions and, as developmental editor, maintained a sense of calm and support even as pressure mounted. To credit her being a critic without judgment is the highest of compliments. Finally, Lisa Mafrici, our editor at Houghton Mifflin, remained patient, supportive, and helpful throughout. We would also like to thank the following academic reviewers for their helpful suggestions and constructive criticism at various stages in the development of this latest revision:

Rena Krizmis, *Chicago State University*

Sonya Lott-Harrison, *Community College of Philadelphia*

J. Jeffries McWhirter, *Arizona State University*
Richard E. Pearson, *Syracuse University*
Ruth Reese, *Arizona State University West*
Corliss Thompson-Drew, *Tufts University*
Bruce W. Tuckman, *Florida State University*

R.W.N.
M.K.G.

GROUPS

1 Perception and Communication

Twenty-four people from various places and walks of life come to a remote island in Canada to learn how to become leaders and build a sense of community. They are psychologists, businesspeople, workers, students, teachers, and community leaders. They come from metropolitan centers and small towns and from all socioeconomic levels. They range in age from twenty-seven to fifty-five.

All have decided on their own to take part in the Temagami experience. They are expecting to learn leadership and community building by using parts of themselves they have never had time to focus on before.

On the first day of the program, the twenty-four participants are in a shuttle bus on the island. Somewhat self-consciously, they are preparing to follow the instructions they received before they left home: "Remain completely silent. When you arrive, decide where in the complex you want to live for the three weeks: go to the men's, women's, or mixed dorms, but do not speak. If your spouses come, do not identify them as such. They are to make their own decisions about where they want to stay."

After lunch, the group gathers in a teepee. The participants are directed to sit in a circle. As the leader begins to talk of the group's goals, the participants realize that their traditional philosophies and norms do not apply here. Not the Judeo-Christian ethics they are used to, but a Native American cultural orientation, with which most are unfamiliar, is the norm.

Imagine yourself as one of the twenty-four, alone on this faraway island with the crutches of familiar society taken away. What do you see? What do you project? What messages do you hear in the words of others? What will you learn about the group and about yourself, and how will the group respond to your presence?

We have all stood on the threshold of a new group in this way, carefully screening our own behavior and trying to communicate what we believe will be most acceptable. And, in turn, we selectively perceive information about the group facing us. We take the data we pick up from others, and after a process of filtering, sifting, and refining, we respond to our particular personal understanding of the situation—often a distortion of our own creation. The ideas and information become alloys of our own making. Thus one new member of a group may see twenty-three potential friends while another sees twenty-three sources of potential rejection. One may observe dress, tone of voice, age, sex, race, posture; another may focus immediately on evidence of influence and power, indicated perhaps in the direction of word flow or the movement of eyes toward the source of approval. Whatever the processes and needs of the individual, the view that eventually enters the mind's eye will be, to some degree, a distorted vision of what actually is taking place, reduced by some and expanded by others.

Our objective in this chapter is to dispel a stubborn, enduring myth: the myth that we see objectively, hear objectively, and speak in ways that are instantly understood and that people—if they have half a mind to—have no difficulty communicating. Not so.

We see selectively as individuals, and our culture affects how we see and what we see. Selective perception not only influences us as individuals, but it is further complicated in a group.

To be more specific, in this chapter we discuss the nature of communication that goes beyond words. We discuss factors that inhibit communication in a group even when all the members want that communication to be effective. Beyond these basics, we move on to understanding communication in groups and, finally, to examining factors that influence group communication. Expressing what you want to say and having it understood is, to say the least, a complicated, difficult process.

Selective Perception and the Individual

That we see what we need to see is not merely a psychologist's whim; it is reality. An ink blot reveals how an ill-defined or nebulous stimulus can elicit a wide range of responses from different individuals. Each perception and its interpretation of virtually any event are based on a combination of historical experiences, present needs, and the inherent properties of the scene being perceived. Because what we see is always a combination of what is actually occurring and what is happening within us at that moment, it is unlikely that two people will ever perceive the same thing in exactly the same way (Harrison, 1976).

It is necessary to base our understanding of how we perceive our experience on the assumption that we distort; then we can proceed to build on these distortions. Even with the most objective task, it is nearly impossible to keep our subjective views from altering our perception of what really exists.

Consider the experiments of Shaw and McClure (1996). They staged an interruption in a college classroom and then questioned participants about what they saw five times over five weeks. Participant-witnesses consistently reported higher levels of confidence in their responses over time yet there was no difference in their accuracy. Once we see something in a certain way, we are increasingly confident we are right.

Reader Activity

Before reading any further, look at the figure that follows. Count the number of triangles in this diagram.

Write your number here ______ before reading on.

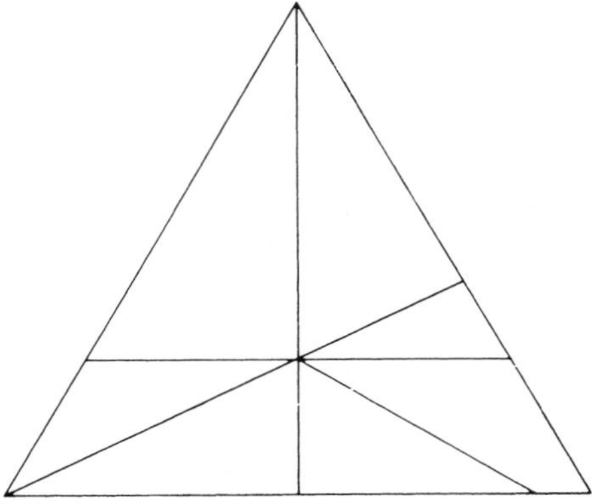

If this diagram is presented to a group of fifty people and they are asked to count the number of triangles, it is almost certain there will be anywhere from ten to eighteen different responses; at most, ten of the fifty people will agree to one number.

How is this possible among a representative group of normal, well-adjusted, intelligent people? The task is clear and easy enough (a fifth grader could handle it), yet rarely does one find more than 20 percent agreement on one response. The following are only a few of the possible reasons for the differences in the perceived realities of this group.

1. One individual vigorously defends the perception that there is only one triangle in the diagram. Somewhere in the far reaches of her memory, she sees a triangle as having to have three equal sides.
2. Another person somehow discovers forty-three by counting every possible angle as a triangle.
3. A number of people, counting from left to right around the diagram but not counting the figure in the lower right-hand corner, report six triangles.
4. Others find seven; they assume the figure in the lower right-hand corner is a triangle.
5. Some people find seven, eight, or nine triangles by combining a few of the lines to form other triangles. Others push on and discover thirteen, fourteen, fifteen, or twenty triangles.

Later, it is learned that some who stopped short of discovering all the possible combinations did not like puzzles or did poorly in geometry and still carried that fear with them. Others saw the whole thing as a game, perhaps a trick, and so felt it was a fruitless exercise. Still others felt that they were being tested and thought it wiser to find fewer triangles and be correct (as on the SATs or Graduate Record Exams, with their penalties for guessing) than to find many and be wrong. Then, of course, there were the competitors, some of whom managed to see triangles that were not even there. Some people assume that they missed some (nobody's perfect) and added from five to ten to their findings just to be on the "safe" side (thinking that, as in a jellybean contest, the number closest wins). Still others noticed who put up their hands at which numbers; if they perceived the hand-raisers as smart, they gave up their own findings and voted in accordance with the "smart" ones, for to be aligned with talent was to experience a fleeting moment of being a winner. So even in a simple, straightforward task among a responsible group of participants, one is able to ferret out unreasonable suspicion, fear of inadequacy, competitiveness, distortion of the instructions, and perhaps ten or twenty other variables that make such an enormous variety of responses predictable. (What was your own result?) Because there are so many factors involved in solving even such a simple problem, imagine what happens when we add the additional variables that pertain whenever the choice involves another human being.

INDIVIDUAL INSECURITY

One startling yet powerful insight pervades the literature on groups: when individuals join a group, they change; they are no longer the same people they were before becoming group members. Once within a group, individuals display and express behaviors that differ remarkably from their out-of-group behaviors. It seems that in a group, people's individuality—the sum of qualities that characterize and distinguish them from all others—somehow becomes warped, unsettled, and distorted. Factors operate, in both the group and the members, that distract and/or subtract from their individuality.

The most powerful factor altering people's individuality in groups is anxiety (Bennis and Shepard, 1987), a feeling of uneasiness, ranging from mild to extreme, that is brought about by a conscious or unconscious feeling of danger, not necessarily real, and a readiness or preparation to meet that danger (Holtgraves, 1991; Brill, 1972). When people enter a group, anxiety is the first apparent behavioral symptom—that is, change in their actions. Accurately or not, they feel endangered by the other members. They feel self-doubt about how the others perceive them—and about how they perceive the others—and their behavior is based on these feelings. At the base of the anxiety are internal uncertainties, such as feelings of self-doubt and fear of the unknown dangers the other members pose. Because most people feel such uncertainties in new situations involving strangers, anxiety is to one degree or another the prevailing emotion at the start of any group setting.

A second prevalent experience involves the role shift from individual to group member. This sudden role shift creates conflicts: between the person's wish to belong and his or her self-protective impulse to withdraw, between the wish to interact with others and the need to protect his or her individuality, and between the wish to contribute to the group's task and self-doubts regarding his or her *ability* to contribute (Turquet, 1978). These conflicts are experienced as ambivalence.

To sum up, then, anxiety rooted in internal uncertainties and ambivalences springing from the sudden role shift are major sources for distortions, misperceptions, and miscommunication (Bennis and Shepard, 1987; Miller and Rice, 1975; and Rioch, 1978). Our individual insecurities alter our individual behavior when we are struggling to merge countless external stimuli with often conflicting internal impulses.

LIFE POSITIONS

Often, past distortions are infused into the present and compounded in such a way that the real and imagined and the past and present intertwine and form the present reality (Nidorf, 1968; Nidorf and Crockett, 1964). Some distortions in perception stem from our early experiences with family and friends.

Transactional Analysis (TA) (Berne, 1976; Woollams and Brown, 1978) provides insight into the important influence of our past on our current behavior, both individually and in groups. It suggests that on the basis of early experiences, people decide on a *life position.* Henceforth, they are influenced by their life positions in how they think, feel, act, perceive, and relate to others.

The theory of Transactional Analysis (TA) essentially goes like this. We were all once children and, in the course of life's experiences, developed a concept of self-worth by the time we were six years old. While we were formulating a sense of our own worth, we were also formulating a sense of the worth of others, especially those around us. We did this by crystallizing our experiences and making decisions about the kind of a life we would have (sad, happy); what parts we would play (strong hero, loner); and how we would act out the parts of our life scripts (adventurously, in fear, slowly, with permission). These early days in life are our days of decision—a time when we commit ourselves to acting in ways that become part of our character. These decisions may be quite unrealistic, although they seem logical and make sense to us at the time we make them.

For example, if as children we are ridiculed and regularly called stupid, we may decide we are stupid and that other people "know it all." We will then begin to think of ourselves that way and act that way; we will base our life scripts on the conclusions that "I'm not O.K., but you (other people) are O.K." When we go to school, we may fail. As we grow older, we will further fulfill our own prophecies by constantly asking advice, doing what "they're" doing, and fearing being different. We will often make mistakes, for which we will be reprimanded, and then we will feel stupid—thereby maintaining our status quo in our chosen life positions.

According to TA theory, even as we think we are listening intently and being objective, we are screening out information that conflicts with our chosen life positions. It is not surprising, therefore, that in a group situation with a tremendous amount of incoming stimuli to be screened, we are unable to interpret the experience accurately.

PERCEPTION AND DEVELOPMENT

Developmental theory provides another way to understand how we view and interpret the world. Although people's characters are created in the early years of life, developmental theory suggests that our perception of the world continually changes throughout our life span. Piaget (1952, 1954) discovered that the views of children differ fundamentally from adult views and that cognition (thinking) and perception develop in sequential stages throughout childhood and adolescence. Each stage has certain general characteristics that determine how the individual understands and perceives the world. Consider the example of two brothers looking down from the Empire State Building. The younger brother says, "Look at the toy cars," and the older brother says simultaneously, "Look at the cars. They look like toys." The older brother has learned about the effect of distance on apparent size. The younger brother, perceiving the same scene differently, actually mistakes the cars for miniatures.

Other developmental theorists (Kegan, 1982; Kohlberg and Gilligan, 1972) have expanded Piaget's findings to include the individual's identity and relationships with other people. Constructing an identity and reality is a natural process that evolves over time in stages parallel to Piaget's stages. If you asked a young child, a high school student, and a college student what is important about the Golden Rule, you would get three very different answers reflecting three different ways of perceiving the world. The young child might say, "If he hit me then I can hit him." The high school student might say, "It's important to be a good friend or neighbor and to consider what the other person feels." The college student might say, "It's like a moral code or contract that allows the whole society to get along." The three answers reflect different constructions of "fairness" based on normal developmental stages in making meaning.

It is clear from this example that our behavior in groups is affected by our development. We perceive groups differently at different ages and as the time we spend in them goes by (Abraham, 1983–1984). As an example of how such perceptions change in our lifetimes, Selman (1980) reports on conceptions of friendship. A young child assumes that a friend thinks and feels just as he or she does. An older child realizes that other people think and feel differently but still doesn't think about the friendly interactions between two people. By adolescence, people have learned how to take another perspective and are able to think about the interaction between individuals.

Selective Perception and Culture

The culture and particular environment in which we develop also affect our perception of reality. And the cultural *context* in which the group experience takes place also has profound effects. Consider this first-person account from a college teacher of English:

> Having taught basic English to American and foreign college students for many years, I noticed something I had not witnessed before: Korean and Japanese students strictly avoided each other, even moved desks away so as to avoid any contact, particularly physical proximity and eye contact. Another time, when the class discussion focused on the pros and cons of capital punishment, students of Arabic descent clamored not only for capital punishment, but also its televising. American students, on the other hand, abhorred the idea.

Cultural factors profoundly affect how we think about groups and behave in them. When we enter a group, do we expect everyone to think as we do, based on past experience? Will we be able to understand the differing opinions and views of people from other backgrounds? Will we value and understand the group interactions as a whole, separate from our experience in the culture we grew up in? As research confirms (Varghese, 1982), we cannot understand the group experience without making reference to the cultural and personal backgrounds of the members.

UNCONSCIOUS FACTORS

Without our knowing it, a force is at work tainting our perceptions and altering our behaviors. That force is the unconscious. In the last decade of psychological research, there has been documentation that the mind reacts automatically to environmental cues before people consciously perceive them. These automatic reactions can influence our judgments and change our behavior. These findings counter the assumption that thinking and behavior are consciously controlled (Azar, 1996).

FOCUS ON DIVERSITY

Surprising finding. Knowing this, what can you do in situations with dissimilar strangers?

Psychologist Mahzarin Banaji believes that these new discoveries will change our view of human nature, giving the unconscious much more credit for behavior.

In one of their studies, for example, Banaji and Greenwald found that words trigger unconscious gender stereotypes in men and women. Research participants were shown 144 names of men and women, half famous and half not famous, and each group containing equal numbers of male and female names. Two days later, participants were shown a second list of 144 names, 72 from the original list and 72 new names of famous and not famous. Subjects were to judge each name as famous or not famous. Although there were equal numbers of famous men and women, subjects consistently identified more men than women as famous. And they most often identified male names as famous if they saw the names the first day. The researchers concluded that a stricter unconscious criterion is set for judging female fame than male fame.

These unconscious reactions are influenced by environmental cues. An example (Azar, 1996) goes like this: you meet someone, and because of his or her gender, race, or even shirt color, you have an automatic, unconscious avoidance reaction that shows up on your face. That person may notice your reaction and respond in kind with a withdrawn attitude. You wonder why he or she is so cold; yet your unconscious reaction established the *entire interaction.*

Many of us never realize that these powerful influences are at work on our perception. A group of people represents various degrees of acceptance and rejection, likes and dislikes, and pleasant and distasteful memories; it is from this complex assortment of stimuli that we conjure up a picture of our reality and respond, as we believe, appropriately to maintain our own positions and integrity within the group. We begin early. Boulton and Smith (1990) studied two classes of eight-year-olds and two classes of eleven-year-olds. Each child ranked all members of his or her class in terms of the degree to which a classmate was liked. Children consistently overestimated their own place in the hierarchy in relation to peers' perceptions.

Our personal needs remain consistently present, nearly every one of our perceptions is affected by them, and these needs affect behavior in turn. The needs are often unconscious and completely hidden from us. For example, people who have limited tolerance for ambiguity create a simple structure for reality as they perceive it, no matter how accurate or faulty that picture is (Livesley and Bromley, 1973). Those who are especially sensitive to whether they are liked and to cues regarding their acceptance are likely to be more hampered in communicating freely than those who care little about how others accept them (Winthrop, 1971).

THE HALO EFFECT

When they make decisions, most people believe their judgments are based on facts and information. They believe that in a particular situation, given specific, relevant information, they can render impartial judgments uninfluenced by their personal knowledge of the people involved.

Nisbett and Wilson, at the Institute of Social Research at the University of Michigan, were staunch believers that people could do just that until they conducted an experiment testing the psychological phenomenon known as the *halo effect* (Nisbett and Wilson, 1978). As a result, Nisbett became convinced that "one's objectivity is not to be trusted."

The experiment is an interesting one. The investigators described the halo effect as simply "the power of an overall feeling about an individual to influence evaluations of the person's individual attributes." For example, if you are usually annoyed when someone is consistently late but find lateness charming in a friend whom you like, you have experienced the halo effect.

To test the extent of the halo effect and people's awareness of its influence, Nisbett and Wilson showed college students one of two videotaped interviews with a college professor. In the first interview, the professor appeared to be quite likable, expressing warm attitudes about his students and teaching. In the other, he conveyed the unlikable attitude of distrust of his students and rigidity in his teaching. Half the students saw the warm interview and half the cold interview. The students were then asked to rate how much they liked the teacher, his physical appearance, his mannerisms, and his distinct French accent. Now, for the special part. To determine whether the subjects were aware of the cognitive processes underlying their evaluations, the researchers asked some of the students (as part of the design) whether their liking or disliking of the professor had influenced their evaluations of his personal characteristics. At the same time, they asked others the reverse question: had their ratings of individual characteristics influenced their overall liking?

Regardless of whether they had seen the warm or the cold professor, the subjects who had been asked the first question said their evaluations of individual attributes had not been influenced by their liking of the man. When the question was reversed, however, the subjects who saw the cold professor believed their negative evaluations of the individual traits had been responsible for their not liking the man. In the face of additional questioning, most of the students held firmly to these beliefs.

To summarize, the students were not aware of how they had arrived at their evaluations. This finding parallels results from similar experiments conducted by the researchers. In all such experiments, subjects' explanations differed regarding what factors affect their judgment. Nisbett and Wilson observe, "People tend to rely on their prior assumptions about the causes of behavior instead of direct introspections." Therefore, they conclude, the validity of self-reporting is questionable because people do not know why they do what they do.

We often admit to not knowing how we arrived at a judgment. But even when we think we *are* making objective judgments, research shows we are not. Given this fact, is it any wonder that opinion among many observers may differ even where "objective" evidence is available for analysis?

Selective Perception and Group Behavior

Groups as well as individuals are affected by unconscious factors and inaccurate assumptions. Consider an example involving the particularly volatile topic of AIDS, where objective information had no weight in the face of the selective perception of the group.

In October of 1986, nearly thirty fearful and disgruntled employees of New England Bell walked off the job en masse (with camera crews from the local television station there to record the event) when they discovered that one of their company workers had AIDS. Epidemics have almost always sparked irrationality and superstition, and AIDS has been no exception. Many workers react to news of a co-worker's infection with panic, anger, and cruelty. "There is something about the topic of AIDS that can cause otherwise intelligent and rational people to lose their basic common sense" (Puckett, 1988).

Public health officials, including the National Academy of Sciences, the Surgeon General of the United States, and the Centers for Disease Control, assure us that AIDS is spread only by the *direct exchange* of infected bodily fluids through sexual contact, the sharing of contaminated needles, contaminated-blood transfusions, or the exchange of maternal/fetal blood in pregnancy. It is not possible to get AIDS through casual contact, by sharing telephones or equipment, by being sneezed or coughed on, or simply by working near someone. As a result, guidelines from the Centers for Disease Control say that people diagnosed with the disease may continue on the job without endangering their co-workers.

First paragraph explains how stereotypes emerge—and problems in diversity.

However, despite extensive information and assurances, in the heat of the moment these startled and frightened New England Bell employees reacted with panic. It is within this environment of irrationality that public health officials are attempting to campaign for communication and education about AIDS. What is the likelihood of the facts being heard? Given the selective perception of groups and the many factors, unconscious as well as conscious, driving their behavior, it is likely that rumors and misinformation will continue to have much greater potency than facts, information, and data.

Problems in perception and communication cut across every group. Each group and each individual must justify its existence, it seems, at the expense of truth and reason.

THE INFLUENCE OF STEREOTYPES

In a group, individual stereotypes—preconceived notions of how individuals from certain groups think, feel, and act—feed on themselves, and as group members, we rapidly turn for support to those we believe share our own views (Levens and Yzerbyt, 1992; Kelley, 1951; Slater, 1955). We seek to affirm our personal construction of reality in any situation we fail to understand or control. Especially in a group in which our roles are not determined clearly in advance, it is natural to seek confirmation that we are not alone, that there are potential allies among the strange faces (Hattrup and Ford, 1995; Festinger, 1950; Loomis, 1959). It takes but a few minutes to scan the superficial cues and identify those with whom we can feel either safe or threatened, who have energy, anger, insecurity, power, softness, frayed nerves, or humor. We make our predictions and then spend a good part of our energy proving that we are correct (Ehrlich, 1969; Johnson and Ewens, 1971; Reid and Ware, 1972). The conclusions are used as evidence and, in the long run, can be destructive as well as helpful in the development of the group and our relationships within it.

FOCUS ON DIVERSITY

For some people, there are stereotypes of Japanese, with others blacks—with still others, pretty women. Where are you influenced? (It is not all, for all people.)

Groups of people, too, form stereotypes about the "in-ness" or "out-ness" of other groups of people. People are discriminated against or accepted because of their membership in a particular group (Locksley, Ortiz, and Hepburn, 1980). The more the makeup of a group is perceived by an outsider to be the same, or homogeneous, the more likely that outsider is to generalize one member's behavior to the whole group (Quattrone and Jones, 1980). For example, if 90 percent of all fraternity members are big, blond, and sports-minded, then an outsider to that group would be quite likely to assume that "They're all alike. They look alike, think alike, and do the same things."

People form stereotypes in this way not only about primary groups but also about subgroups within them. For example, subjects who were asked to rate decisions made by three nations (the

United States, the Netherlands, and the then U.S.S.R.) and to predict whether citizens of those nations concurred made inferences about the citizens' attitudes that were based on stereotypes of the nations (Allison and Messick, 1985).

In another study by the same researchers, subjects were asked to attribute attitudes to jurors after reading a vignette about a court case and the final decision of guilt or innocence. The results indicated that subjects attributed attitudes to jurors based on both the final jury vote and the decision of guilt or innocence (Allison and Messick, 1985).

The data of these studies indicate that people commit what the authors call *attribution error.* This they define as "a tendency to assume a correspondence between a group decision and members' preferences" even when the assumption may be unwarranted. In other words, people committing attribution error assume that the actions of the group reflect the particular attitudes of individual members and that knowing something about how a group behaves tells us something significant about subgroups or individuals within it.

Consider the relationships between Americans and Japanese. The torrent of retrospectives at the 50th anniversary of Pearl Harbor showed how Americans and Japanese still saw each other through propagandized eyes. *The New York Times* (December 1991) noted:

> In the United States, the images of Japan as sneaky, threatening, and unfair, that were flash-frozen by Pearl Harbor, resurface now in talk of Japanese as Samurai in business suits, out to do economically what they could not do militarily. In Japan, where any sense of responsibility for the aggression of Pearl Harbor is dwarfed by the horror of Hiroshima and Nagasaki, America now seems more like the decadent superpower once portrayed in Japanese wartime propaganda. . . . [B]oth countries remain trapped by history and their selective memories. In the United States, for example, the sense of treachery at Pearl Harbor and the racist depictions of Japanese continue to resonate today. . . . Many Japanese still believe racism motivates much American behavior toward Japan, from the internment of Japanese-Americans during the war to the decision to drop the bomb.

Stereotypes of more than fifty years ago persist.

The fact is that people are a thousand things, but first and foremost in our effort to understand reality, they are what we want them to be in relation to our own need for a clear, simple interpretation. We tend to see a person as fat, hostile, irrational, Jewish, lethargic, smart, African-American, paranoid, handsome, homosexual, or militant—with all that these labels connote to us. We take a very specific term with a very narrow definition and try to frame a whole, complex human being in it.

Individual Experiment

List all the stereotypes about your family background, both good and bad. What are the stereotypes about your race? About your ethnic background? About your religion? About your father's occupation? About your mother's occupation? What are your feelings about each of those stereotypes? How do they affect you? (For example, are you supposed to reach out, or to overachieve, or to work hard, given the stereotypes you cite?) How do these stereotypes affect your personality? Are they a help or a hindrance?

Reader Activity

Think back on some of your own experiences with others. How have you been labeled in a way that you did not like?

Label ____

Why didn't you like it? ________________________________

____

____

What do you wish had happened instead? ________________________

____

____

How did that label influence you? ____________________________

____

____

Individual Experiment

Choose a subgroup of people within your school, dormitory, neighborhood, or place of employment. What common characteristic do they all have? List as many attributes of this group as you can. Ask your friends how they would characterize the individuals within this group. Carefully compare your list and your actual experience with a member of the group. Is it accurate? Are some characteristics exaggerated and others minimized? Is the list of characteristics helpful in understanding the behavior of the group members or knowing how to interact with them? Does the list constitute a stereotype that is used by society to belittle, disqualify, or oppress the group as a whole? Or does it idealize, empower, and assist the group? You may find your list useful in dealing with others, or you may find it destructive because it creates negative expectations of the individuals in a group.

Take another example. In the past, many whites thought of blacks as a separate and inferior species. The word *Negro* called up images and elicited behavior among whites that caused tremendous psychological and physical suffering. Judge Leon Higgenbotham of the U.S. Court of Appeals, Third Circuit, writes of an experience during World War II:

> In 1944, I was a 16-year-old freshman at Purdue University—one of twelve black civilian students. If we wanted to live in West Lafayette, Indiana, where the university was located, solely because of our color the twelve of us at Purdue were forced to live in a crowded private house rather than, as did most of our white classmates, in the university campus dormitories. We slept barracks-style in an unheated attic.
>
> One night, as the temperature was close to zero, I felt that I could suffer the personal indignities and denigration no longer. The United States was more than two years into the Second World War, a war our government had promised would "make the world safe for democracy." Surely there was room enough in that world, I told myself that night, for twelve black students in a northern university in the United States to be given a small corner of the on-campus heated dormitories for their quarters. Perhaps all that was needed was for one of us to speak up, to make sure the administration knew exactly how a small group of its students had been treated by those charged with assigning student housing.
>
> The next morning, I went to the office of Edward Charles Elliot, president of Purdue University . . . Why was it, I asked him, that blacks—and blacks alone—had been subjected to this special ignominy? . . . Forcefully, but none the less deferentially, I put forth my modest request; that the black students of Purdue be allowed to stay in some section of the state-owned dormitories; segregated, if necessary, but at least not humiliated. . . .
>
> President Elliot, with directness and with no apparent qualms, answered, "Higginbotham, the law doesn't require us to let colored students in the dorm, and you either accept things as they are or leave the University immediately."
>
> As I walked back to the house that afternoon, I reflected on the ambiguity of the day's events. I had heard, on that morning, an eloquent lecture on the history of the Declaration of Independence, and of the genius of the founding

FOCUS ON DIVERSITY

A half century later, does it still hold that being black means being outside the system?

> fathers. That afternoon I had been told that under the law the black civilian students at Purdue University could be treated differently from their 6,000 white classmates. Yet I knew that by nightfall hundreds of black soldiers would be injured, maimed, and some even killed on far-flung battlefields to make the world safe for democracy. Almost like a mystical experience, a thousand thoughts raced through my mind as I walked across campus. I knew then I had been touched in a way I have never been touched before, and that one day I would have to return to the most disturbing element in this incident—how a legal system that proclaims "equal justice for all" could simultaneously deny even a semblance of dignity to a 16-year-old boy who had committed no wrong.[1]

Being black meant being outside the system. That perception applied to the president and the newest freshman. It was viewed as the norm, beyond change, and despite its incongruity with the Declaration of Independence, it was steadfastly upheld.

The word *black* is not the only label that elicits assumptions about a group that are untested and stereotypic. A host of untested assumptions are elicited by the words *Arab, Jew, labor, management, male,* and *female*. But in our day and age, attitudes about maleness and femaleness, about age, and about modesty and appropriateness have been uprooted. Traditional stereotypes instructing us about the "right" way to act as women and men no longer hold true. Men have learned that they can be emotional and caring. Women have learned that they can assert their opinions and rights. People are confused about what was once the most standardized and secure set of relationships.

With so many changes, even in the most fundamental areas, it can be difficult to know how to relate. A woman at a daytime meeting wearing a suit is not necessarily a businesswoman; she may just prefer to wear clothes that look "professional." A seventyish man need not be a daily golfer; he might be a full-time college student. (One author of this book, in fact, attended a Harvard graduation where a 90-year-old received his doctorate in architecture.) The essential message is that unless we are ready to challenge our own untested assumptions about individuals and groups, we can expect that there will be many breakdowns in communication. We need to force ourselves to stay open to the individual and pay attention to that person and what he or she communicates, as opposed to being in touch with our stereotypic assumptions, which are increasingly likely to be wrong.

1. From *In the Matter of Color: Race and the American Legal Process: The Colonial Period* by A. Leon Higginbotham, Jr. Copyright © 1978 by Oxford University Press, Inc. Reprinted by permission of Oxford University Press, Inc.

GESTALT THEORY

We select and organize physical stimuli in the manner that is easiest and most convenient for us, and we organize the complexities of human behavior in similar ways. A number of simple concepts developed by the Gestalt psychologists in relation to physical stimuli can help us understand what occurs when people get together in a group (Kohler, 1947). For example, we tend to create figure-ground relationships. In any one perceptual field (all the stimuli we are able to perceive at one time), certain figures are drawn forward into positions of dominance and others recede to form the background of the scene. In the following classic picture of the two profiles–goblet configuration, some viewers see a goblet in the foreground and not the people. Others see two faces and not the goblet.

Gestalt theory also helps us understand how experience organizes itself irrespective of the perceiver. In a group, for example, certain individuals will be a clear part of the foreground whose presence is easily noted (in Gestalt terms, they are figures), whereas others, for a variety of reasons, remain part of the background.

Reader Activity

People have a tendency to place objects in a natural order, thus making it easier to establish relationships in a scene. The mind struggles to achieve order by grasping similarities that appear to be present or by perceiving certain continuities in the stimuli presented. This exercise illustrates how we organize dots. Below are nine dots, arranged three dots per row in three rows. Connect the nine dots with four lines so that the end of one line is the beginning of the next. It can be done. Turn to page 19 for the answer.

Similarly, using arrangement, size, sex, race, culture, clothes, tone of voice, posture, and many other cues, we proceed to subtly break down a group of people into a variety of component groups. This ordering is how we manage to deal with complexity without being overwhelmed, a way of handling the enormous amount of data that suddenly confront us at any one moment.

Another concept discussed originally by Gestaltists concerns the tendency to take incomplete data and organize them into a meaningful whole. By that process, people more often than not see an incomplete circle as a full circle rather than a curved line. Apparently, we have a need to bring closure to objects within our perceptual field—thus we use the word *gestalt,* meaning "form" or "shape."

In looking at the participants in a group, we take the data they put forth in their skin color, culture, voice tone, verbal gestures, and dress, then add our own stereotypes, and in this way develop a complete picture of a group member. We bring closure to what is incomplete and, in a sense, fill in the missing pieces so that we can more easily be content with a previously unknown entity. By putting all the clues together into a meaningful package, we are better able to have a relationship that is consistent and comfortable for us. It provides a means of gaining a measure of safety for us in what is, perhaps, an incomplete, strange, and uncomfortable situation.

According to Gestalt theory, people have a tendency to take various stimuli and focus on one set of stimuli that appears to be "good" in terms of similarity, continuity, closure, and symmetry. According to this concept, for example, we are immediately attracted to those in a group who tend to fit our perception of a "good" group member, those who are least threatening to us and tend to create the least dissonance in terms of our own values and goals within the group.

If we were not able to impose this kind of order on the group and on certain of its members, the situation might prove unbearably tense and difficult. Thus if we are quiet and shy, we may seek order and some relief in the group by discovering those who are the least abrasive or dominating and those who show the greatest restraint. In this way, we can bring harmony to a dissonant situation; we can seek allies and support, in fact or in fantasy.

Selective Perception and Communication

Our propensity to organize a group in the manner that is most comforting to us can prove to be a distinct liability to effective communication. It often generates inflexibility, restricted routes of information, and a need to verify and then justify our initial perception. As a result, we often begin with two strikes against us in our efforts to achieve understanding and insight into group processes. Our perceptions can affect the way we communicate, as well as the messages we receive when others try to communicate with us.

Consider the importance we place on grades. We often believe that the grade someone earns is an accurate indication of that person's level of knowledge. In reality, though, grading is a result of selective perception and communication on the grader's part.

Research has shown that if twenty-five English teachers administer the same test and use the same clear criteria for grading it, the scores for that test will range along the normal distribution curve, because even with a clear set of criteria, subjectivity enters into grading. Where twenty-five *geometry,* as opposed to English, teachers administer and grade a test, there will be an even wider distribution. The reason is that math teachers give more points for effort and partial answers than English teachers do. Grading, then, is highly biased; personal needs, factors of background, and experience affect teachers' choices. Given this fact, the grades students earn in school may reveal more about their teachers than about their own levels of knowledge.

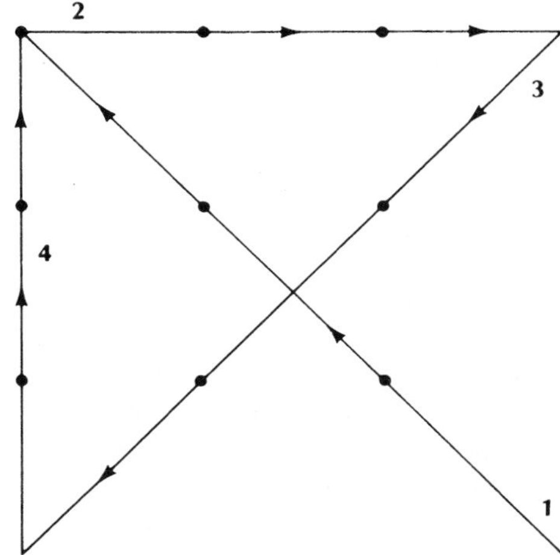

Reader Activity

When someone claims to have a 2.3 grade point average, what assumptions would you make about that person?

____

____

____

When someone claims to have a 3.9 grade point average, what assumptions would you make about that person?

____

____

____

How have grades influenced your perception of yourself?

____

____

____

Describe one situation in which a grade very much influenced your behavior. What was the effect?

____

____

____

Individual Experiment

In a group situation, such as a class or meeting, choose one person whom you do not know well and watch his or her behavior for a few minutes. Then briefly write a story about that person, including your assumptions about why he or she behaved in a certain manner, what he or she might have been feeling and thinking, and your general description of the person. Create a story about that person based on the limited information you perceive. Test the accuracy of your story by gathering information from that person about his or her intentions, perception of the situation, thoughts, and feelings.

THE NATURE OF COMMUNICATION

Verbal language is only one aspect of the ongoing communication that occurs in all human behavior. In fact, one communications theory (Watzlawick, 1977; Watzlawick, Beavin, and Jackson, 1967) postulates that "one cannot not communicate." Every action, even silence, is a communication. What that means in day-to-day life is that we are actually aware of only a small part of our communication with others. Body language, such as eye contact, gestures, posture, and proximity between individuals as they talk, is an important part of the complex process of communication of which individuals are rarely aware.

We can think of communication as having three aspects: the nonverbal aspect (which, like the verbal aspect, is determined to a large degree by the cultural and personal backgrounds of the communicator); the emotion aspect (the mood or feeling being expressed), and the content or verbal aspect. These three aspects combine to form the total message given *and* the total message received. Obviously, someone communicating anger will convey a different message from a person who delivers the same words in a very calm manner. Likewise, someone in a sad or depressed state will give a different meaning to, say, "I'd like to apply for the job" than someone excited and motivated by a career change. But emotional state has an equally potent effect on the message as it is received. Research by Bower (1981) identifies what the investigator calls the *mood-congruity effect,* whereby people tend to hear and learn information that matches their emotional states. A related phenomenon is *mood-state-dependent retention,* whereby people recall events better if their emotional states during recall match those they experienced during learning. Furthermore, when the emotional tone of a story matches the mood of the reader, the significance and memorability of events in the story increase for the reader. Sad readers thus tend to choose sad materials, identify with sad characters, and recall more about those characters.

Another, perhaps more subtle, influence shaping a communication is the particular *style* in which a message is conveyed. Style can have an important effect on what we hear and communicate. Consider a teacher inexperienced in black English who hears one boy saying to another, "You're *bad! Too* bad for this school, man." She worries that the receiver of this message might suffer from such obvious rejection and is surprised to see him grin with pleasure. The teacher is responding to the verbal message alone, but the real meaning is the product of the culture, personal style, and words of the message giver.

Another way of looking at communication is to focus on two aspects, the content aspect and the relationship aspect. The content aspect of a message conveys information of some sort or another, regardless of whether the particular information is true or false. The relationship aspect of a message includes how the content aspect should be taken. It is the attempt of the communicator to define the relationship. For example, when a mother tells her son, "This is your last warning—clean up your room or you can't go out to play," or "It's important that I get the house clean today. Please clean your room before you go out to play," the content information is the same but the relationships differ. This process of defining the relationship is an ongoing process, and the relationship gets defined and redefined with every bit of communication. In our example, if the son replies, "Come on, Mom, how come you want me to clean my room every time I have something to do? I'll clean it after," or "I wanted to see Jeffrey this afternoon. Do you think I can clean it when I come in before dinner?" he is implying two different types of relationships. In each communication there is an implicit arrangement between the individuals concerning how they mutually define the relationship and thus set up an expectation of how their next interaction will be. It is important to remember that this process generally goes on outside the communicators' awareness; that is, individuals rarely deliberately define the relationships they are in. Using Gestalt terms, the relationship aspect of communication is the perceptual ground and the content aspect is the figure.

The continual communication and interaction between individuals in a group, whether in a meeting, classroom, family, or entire school, involves an ongoing process of defining the relationships within the group and the development of a set of arrangements between group members. This set of arrangements is a system that has certain rules, norms, and regularity to it. The system of interaction and communication, like the relationship aspect of communication, exists outside of group members' awareness.

LANGUAGE EQUALS WORDS; COMMUNICATION EQUALS PEOPLE

It has often been said that today only people, and not words, have any meaning in our attempts to communicate. Unless we are able to probe behind the easily flowing façade of words that screen us from one another, we will remain confused and out of touch. So often it is gesture, tone, inflection, posture, or eye contact that holds the key to the real message, while the clear, seemingly unambiguous words merely subject the unwary listener to false starts and dead ends. Even when we think we understand the meaning behind a word, there are usually three or four possible variations in meaning that could fit nicely into the sentence. Usually, we draw on the intent we believe the speaker has in mind. It's hard to imagine that a simple word such as *hard* has more than twenty-six possible definitions (*American Heritage Dictionary,* 1973). Among other things, that one word can describe the solidity of coal, the difficulty of a test, the type of binding on a book, the ability of a person to maintain his or her position despite pressure, the penetrating power of an x ray, and the parsimony of an elderly person. Many subtle innuendos flavor language and require a personal definition before they can be translated into the context of a particular statement.

In some cases, even the dictionary may not help where an individual or a group has invented new meanings for words and phrases.

> Have you ever been to a *Valium picnic?* Or been guilty of *scoodling?* Or yearned for *warm fuzzies?* If these terms are totally bewildering, you may need a crash course in "Biz Speak," the colorful language of the business world, described by R. S. Epstein and N. Liebman (1986). These authors explain that a Valium picnic is a slow day on the stock market. Warm fuzzies are praise from the boss. And scoodling is the unauthorized duplication of prerecorded music. Wall Streeters talk about fallen angels (out-of-favor stocks at bargain prices), shark repellents (strategies used by companies to ward off takeover attempts), and fill or kill (an order to a broker that must be canceled if it cannot be completely and immediately executed). Management experts speak of tin-cupping (when one corporate division begs for management support) and dead-heading (by-passing a senior employee to someone more junior). Advertisers refer disparagingly to white bread (consumers with bland taste). Business executives try to avoid a Mickey Mouse (a major effort that produces minimum results).

And more recently there is virtual verbiage. New slang spreads quickly in cyberspace. Consider these samples from Gareth Branwyn's "Jargon Watch" column in *Wired* magazine:

Irritainment: Stuff that's annoying, but you can't stop watching—e.g., the O.J. trials.

Umfriend: A sexual relation of dubious standing. "This is Dale, my . . . um . . . friend. . . ."
Treeware: Hacker slang for printed material.
Geeksploitation: Taking advantage of twentysomething workers who are willing to toil long hours if bolstered by enough junk food, flexible schedules, and no dress code.
Elvis Year: The peak year of a thing's popularity. "Barney the dinosaur's Elvis year was 1993."

Modern Maturity (September–October 1997, p. 26)

The use of this sort of jargon—other examples of which might not be so playful as the above—has the effect of confusing and even excluding those not in the know. And yet it is commonplace for us to use words and phrases whose meaning is unclear to us, depending more on their feel and emotional tone than on their precise meaning.

Often, what we end up with is nothing more than a makeshift assemblage of words spiced with half-known definitions and a variety of feelings. What eventually transpires depends on the web created out of past experience, definitions, language skills, expectations, speed, clarity of the words spoken, and the general psychological climate that exists. How often are we led off the trail because we do not have enough information and drift further away rather than closer to the actual meaning? On the other hand, when history and experience are on our side, when we are familiar with the nonverbal communication that accompanies the words, then the group in which we are participating may respond in near unison to a message that to the casual listener may mean just the opposite.

There is an enormous tendency to disparage the idea of Americans needing another language. How will it be, not of a white middle-class American in college, but for a 10-year-old black boy who feels acceptance for once?

There are other words that, when we hear them, evoke a special meaning for us depending on our context, our experience, and our culture. One such word is *management.* To much of American labor, the word *management* is adversarial; to the union member it means "I have to get what I can get. Management is only concerned with profits and couldn't care less about me." In Japan, however, management is thought of as a caring father. Workers assume that they can trust management and can expect it to take care of them for their lifetime. These are two very different perceptions of management.

Robert Williams (Burnette, 1997), for example, the father of Ebonics (a term he coined to define black dialect) believes that many blacks are mislabeled as poor academic performers simply because the language they grew up with is considered inadequate grammar. He has demonstrated, however, that when black students take tests with questions stated in that "poor grammar" their scores improve dramatically.

"My language is an extension of me, just like my hair, my face, and my physique," said Williams. "All of these things make up my identity. So if you criticize my language, you criticize me, which lowers my self-esteem." (After study of the issue, The Oakland Unified School Board of Oakland, CA, announced its resolution to recognize Ebonics as the primary language of black students.)

COMMUNICATION: THE GENDER DIFFERENCE

It was once assumed that because boys and girls grow up in the same households and later attend the same schools, they communicate in the same way. Recent studies, however, suggest that boys and girls grow up in what are essentially different cultures, so talk between men and women is cross-cultural communication. Linguist Deborah Tannen, in *You Just Don't Understand: Women and Men in Conversation* (1990), builds a strong case for her hypothesis that boys and girls grow up in different worlds of words. Her analysis, research, and myriad illustrations had such impact that the book became a number-one national best seller.

Building on the work of Maltz and Borker (1982), she notes that boys and girls play differently, usually in same-sex groups, and that their ways of using language in their games are separated by a world of difference.

> Boys tend to play outside, in large groups that are hierarchically structured. Their groups have a leader who tells others what to do and how to do it, and resists doing what other boys propose. It is by giving orders and making them stick that high status is negotiated. Another way boys achieve status is to take center stage by telling stories and jokes, and by sidetracking or challenging the stories and jokes of others. Boys' games have winners and losers and elaborate systems of rules that are frequently the subjects of arguments. Finally, boys are frequently heard to boast of their skill and argue about who is best at what.
>
> Girls, on the other hand, play in small groups or in pairs; the center of a girl's social life is a best friend. Within the group, intimacy is key: Differentiation is measured by relative closeness. In their most frequent games, such as jump rope and hopscotch, everyone gets a turn. Most of their activities (such as playing house) do not have winners or losers. Though some girls are certainly more skilled than others, girls are expected not to boast about it, or show that they think they are better than the others. Girls don't give orders; they express their preferences as suggestions, and suggestions are likely to be accepted. Whereas boys say, "Gimme that!" and "Get outta here!" girls say,

"Let's do this," and "How about doing that?" Anything else is put down as "bossy." They don't grab center stage—they don't want it—so they don't challenge each other directly. And much of the time, they simply sit together and talk. Girls are not accustomed to jockeying for status in an obvious way; they are more concerned that they be liked.

These differences cast a long shadow into adulthood. Whereas men seek status, women seek connection. In one illustration that Tannen offers, a man and woman were standing beside the information booth at a sprawling complex of booths and displays. The man said to the woman, "You ask for directions. I don't want to ask." The woman was angry. Because asking for directions would not make the woman uncomfortable, his refusing to ask made no sense to her. For the man, asking for information sends a metamessage of inferiority. If relationships are inherently hierarchical, then the one who has more information is higher up on the ladder by virtue of being more knowledgeable and competent. From this point of view, to request information is to give up an essential part of one's independence.

More of the differences get expressed around the question of whether men or women talk more. According to the stereotype, women talk more. Throughout history, women have been punished for talking too much or in the wrong way. In colonial America, there were a variety of physical punishments: women were strapped to dunking stools and held under water, they were put into stocks with signs pinned to them, they were gagged and silenced by a cleft stick applied to their tongues.

Women are believed to talk too much, yet study after study shows that it is men who talk more—at meetings, in mixed-group discussions held in classrooms where girls or young women sit next to boys or young men. Communication researchers B. W. and R. G. Eakins (1978) tape-recorded and studied seven university faculty meetings. They found that, with one exception, men spoke more often and for a longer period of time. And not only did men speak for a longer time, but the women's longest turns were shorter than the men's shortest turns. Tannen found that regardless of the proportion of women and men in the audience, men almost invariably asked the first question, asked more questions, and asked longer questions.

Who talks more, then, women or men? The seemingly contradictory evidence is reconciled by the differences between what are called *public speaking* and *private speaking*.

Men feel more comfortable doing "public speaking," whereas women feel more comfortable doing "private speaking." To the man, talk is for information. To the woman, talk is for interaction. Telling things is a way to show involvement, and listening is a way to show interest and caring.

The Tannen theory is extensively supported in research focusing on how men and women talk. Jose and McCarthy (1988) divided 26 male and 26 female undergraduates into 4-person mixed-sex discussion groups. Each was administered the BEM Sex-Role Inventory. After each discussion, each participant rated the other group members on degree of talkativeness, quality of expressed ideas, and degree of concern for others' feelings. Those who scored highest on masculinity in the BEM Inventory were perceived to have talked more and to have had good ideas. Females and subjects with high femininity scores were judged to have had more concern about group members' feelings.

Gender differences extend to nonverbal behavior also. Research shows women to use more expressive and involved nonverbal behavior than men, and to be more skilled at sending and receiving nonverbal messages. Men are shown to be louder and more interruptive. (Briton and Hall, 1995). In another study, women were better transmitters of emotionally toned information; they were better senders of pleasantness, disgust, distress, fear, and anger (Wagner, Buck, and Winterbotham, 1993).

Is there any difference in the effect on the listener of the style of language used? Apparently there is (Frueh and Becker, 1992). Men formed more favorable impressions when the speaker, whether male or female, conformed to gender-appropriate language than when the speaker did not. Women, however, were not influenced in this way.

There are scores of examples of how men and women speak differently because they are operating within different systems; each is speaking a different "genderlect." In conversation, then, men and women need to learn how to interpret each other's messages and grasp what the other is saying so that they can understand and accept each other.

REWARD-SEEKING BEHAVIOR AND COMMUNICATION PATTERNS

People want to be liked and accepted as well as to be separate and unique. In some ways, that desire is our Achilles' heel because it leaves us vulnerable to the subtle influence and control of those from whom we seek approval. Often, the pressures pushing us toward adjustment, compliance, and eventual favor in the eyes of another are not even discernible by us or the other person (see Chapter 3 on group norms). In our efforts to be accepted, we become sensitive to the minute behavioral clues that suggest the degree of approval on the part of the other people; and as we know them better or are in a group longer, we base how we act on those clues (Greenspoon, 1955; Sorensen and McCroskey, 1977; Verplanck, 1955). Indeed, we are as keen as any bloodhound in ferreting out and following these clues to acceptance.

If the need is to be accepted by seven or eight people instead of only one, it is quite possible that we will work overtime to discover the sources of reward in the group, as well as the favored behavior. This, in turn, alters communication patterns and overt behavior within the group, as we see in the following example:

A first meeting was being held with six women college faculty and a consultant to discuss relationship problems among departments and members of the faculty. Each of the women introduced herself by her first name. They ranged in age from twenty-eight to fifty. Each was well-educated, articulate, conservatively dressed, and committed to the success and growth of the college. The consultant asked that each describe one incident that would illustrate the present problem of the college. All eyes gazed in the direction of the twenty-eight-year-old woman, the youngest of the group. She began by presenting an incident, and the others elaborated on it. No new incidents were described. The consultant then asked what was the one problem that they thought had to be resolved. This time the consultant called on the person to her left. There was a long pause, and finally she said, "I need time to think about it." A similar reply came from the next person, and the next. Again, the twenty-eight-year-old stated a problem of concern to her, and the others added information on that problem. The consultant was aware that something was happening, but what? How could the twenty-eight-year-old have such influence and, without admonishing a person or saying a word, control the group so effectively? There was an answer. The consultant looked at the youngest, most powerful member and said, "Are you the newly appointed president of the college?" She was surprised and flustered; the others were incredulous that the consultant "somehow" knew.

It was clear that members of the committee were more influenced by the impression they wanted to make on the new president than by the goal of resolving the college's problems. Acceptance was at issue, not the ostensible business of the day.

Factors That Inhibit Communication in a Group

PREVIOUS EXPERIENCE OF GROUP MEMBERS

Two of the greatest factors inhibiting communication in groups are the previous experience of members with groups and skepticism that success in a group is even possible. We remember conflicts in our families as we grew up, in which it seemed our parents represented their values and we were supposed to "be seen and not heard," and we recall our days as adolescents, when we had constant arguments with our parents and made exasperated, futile attempts to be understood. In school, we saw groups as problems as we struggled for acceptance by powerful cliques on campus.

Past experience leaves many of us with the expectation that a group experience in the present will be equally unrewarding. Unfortunately, this negative expectation creates a self-fulfilling prophecy in which we tend to perceive what we expect to perceive. As we begin to learn more about the complexities of human communication and perception, it becomes increasingly clear why we have tended to experience groups as frustrating and unsatisfying.

FALSE ASSUMPTIONS

False assumptions held by members inhibit communication in a group. Such assumptions are pervasive, and they must be brought to consciousness to be examined and, with understanding, rejected. However, they are not readily cast aside. In order to recognize these assumptions as false, we need to bring them regularly back into the glare of consciousness, and to make the decision again and again.

One faulty assumption is that we know what others mean; another is that they know what we mean.

People assume that verbal communication is straightforward. They think that all they need to do is to express what they want to say in words and that the message sent is the message received. This is not so. The meaning one person has is never identical to that another person has because meanings are in people's minds, not in the words they use. Some people readily say, "I love you." They love their friends, their dogs, their schools, certain movies, and their favorite recording stars. For them to say "I love you" to a date is an indicator of having had a pleasant evening. For another, who has been going with one woman exclusively for over a year, the words are hard to say. To him, these words reflect an intent to marry, and he is not sure he is ready for such a commitment.

READER ACTIVITY

Words evoke meaning in us in a special, very individual way. What is difficult for you to express? ______________________________

For those feelings difficult to express, how do you do it? What is your special way (a way that those who know you well may understand but that others may not)?

Anger ______________________________

Jealousy ______________________________

Unfairness ______________________________

Gratitude ______________________________

Resentment ______________________________

A terrific idea ______________________________

A ridiculous idea ______________________________

Affection ______________________________

Sadness ______________________________

What words do some people use that you think are phony? ______________

____

Overbearing? ______________________________

That stick in your throat (you don't seem to be able to say them, but you wish you could)?

____

Individual Experiment

Attend a group situation (a meeting or work group) where you know the others present. Watch for an incident—perhaps one person speaking strongly on behalf of some action, someone remaining quiet throughout a heated discussion, or someone supporting a particular person in an unpopular opinion. In writing, describe the specific incident and your assumptions about what the people involved were communicating—their intentions, thoughts, and feelings. After the meeting, ask several other participants how they perceived the people involved in the incident. Compare your assumptions with theirs.

Total accuracy in communication would require that two persons have an identical history of shared experiences, along with identical perceptual abilities. Only then could they perceive exactly the same meaning for a given message. Given the reality of different life experiences, such a situation is impossible (Chartier, 1976).

We have other false assumptions about communication (Coan, 1968; Luft, 1969; Watson, 1967):

1. That people respond to each other objectively, listening only to the information conveyed. The key to what is happening in a group or between people is not what is happening objectively but what is going on subjectively, what each person's feelings are. Subjective factors such as attitudes and values tell how people see themselves and others and how they order their world. How are women heard in a predominately male group? How are African Americans heard in a predominately white group? Older people in a college class with others in their early 20s? How are Hispanics heard, or Koreans?

   The prime aim of most people is to survive in the group and, if possible, to enhance themselves in their own eyes and in the eyes of others. Each of us is forever bound up in the issue of our own personal needs and goals within the group, but unless the group can provide a means of personal self-fulfillment, we will move from the group either psychologically, with reduced participation, or physically.

2. That what happens in a group is rational and easily understood as the group proceeds in an orderly, sequential manner to solve a problem or convey and receive information. Though some of the events in groups can be viewed as being orderly and making good sense, behavior is influenced more by emotions and by largely irrational strivings; logic and reason play relatively minor roles in human interaction. There are questions of identity: "Who am I to be in this group? What image am I going to project to these people?" and "What roles will I undertake to project this image?" In some cases, our response to these questions is very natural, but in others it is strategic and geared toward establishing an identity and a power base. Other questions relate to power, control, and influence. Who has it, and how much will be shared? Whether an individual's behavior will be facilitative or destructive to the group process will depend on that person's particular needs and the realities of that particular group.

3. That the individual, like the group of which he or she is a part, is fully aware of the sources of his or her behavior and the effects of his or her behavior on others. Parts of our behavior are unknown to us; it is often a surprise to find ourselves doing things that are difficult for us to un-

derstand or make sense of. (For example, we think of ourselves as open-minded and friendly. We recognize that the two African American women in the group hardly speak, and then in barely audible voices. We think we will sit next to them and talk to help them be more comfortable in the group. But we don't; we only think about it. Why don't we?)

We want to be accepted by other members, yet we have limited information on how they perceive us. We may be shy and frightened; they may perceive us as snobbish and aloof. We may want to be involved and see ourselves as offering suggestions that are helpful; we may be perceived as behaving in a highly dictatorial manner. We have very limited understanding of how our behavior influences others.

These false assumptions greatly reduce our ability to communicate in a group or even to understand what seems to be happening around us.

Understanding Communication in Groups

HOW TENSION AND DEFENSIVENESS ARISE IN THE COMMUNICATION PROCESS

If individuals wish to create problems in communication, there seem to be certain tried-and-true behaviors that will most assuredly help them on their way (Gibb, 1961; Rogers and Roethlisberger, 1952). A first step would be to keep other people from expressing their own ideas. People have a simple need to be heard, to have their ideas made audible. To have them accepted is desirable, yet not always possible. However, not even to be recognized or heard is an intolerable situation for most of us. Thus, there will be tension in a group if it is dominated by a few vociferous individuals while others listen passively.

Closely linked to this situation is one in which individuals respond with such certainty and force that only a full-scale verbal war would change their opinions. People naturally don't like to be pushed. Sometimes individuals in a group will attack a position in which they basically believe merely because someone has taken a "too certain" opposing viewpoint. In that situation, passive participants have just as much to do with the group tone as the active participants.

Even though we spend much time and energy evaluating people and events, if there is one thing that puts us on guard, it is the feeling that *we* are being evaluated by *others*. We are so used to judging the person along with the idea that we tend to become supersensitive to the same treatment. It is such a short step from hearing "Do you really believe that idea?" to the translation in one's mind: "How could you possibly be so stupid as to believe that idea?" In a group where our need for acceptance increases, the feeling that we are being personally judged is a sure way of developing internal friction. Similarly, if we feel someone is placing himself or herself above us in some sort of superior position, an immediate response is to prove to the world that this individual is "not that good." Quite often we find ourselves responding on the inside to the sharp but barely perceptible cues of superiority from another person.

Communication is damaged when individuals do not trust the group enough to share what they really feel or think. When we fail to express our feelings, others tend to read into this lack of expression what they *believe* we are feeling or thinking. More often than not, our need to be liked leads us to fear potential rejection, which translates this neutral behavior into a negative perception. This behavior as well as other strategies that hide one's real self from the group predictably result in defensive reactions by those on the receiving end. The outline of feelings below on this page reveals the subtleties involved in this complex process.

Bill's response to John's statement is partly the result of the selection of words, the context in which they are spoken, and his image of John, as well as of all the nonverbal cues he gets from tone of voice, gestures, and posture. Also, the nature of the statement is partly the result of John's response to Bill's particular behavioral strategy with him (in this case, neutrality). The result is a predictable increase in what Jack Gibb (1961) would call *defensive communication*. Part of the problem obviously lies in John's insensitivity to Bill and Bill's tendency to read more into the words than was actually intended. Worse than this is the fact that the underlying issues build in a cumulative fashion, which results in increased tension, deteriorated communication, greater polarization among group members, and less inclination to remove these emotional roadblocks.

Statement by John "Yes, but Bill, that's impossible. I've been here for five years, and I've never known that to work. Have you thought of the fact that . . ."

John feels:		*John as perceived by Bill*
Reasonable.	→	Evaluative, judging.
Correct.	→	Superior.
Having heard Bill.	→	Certain.
I've got him backing up.	→	Controlling.
The group is with me.		
He's probably angry; you never know with Bill.		

Bill feels:	*Bill's eventual response:*
What's he mean "yes"? ——————→	Withdrawal.
He never even heard me. ——————→	Neutrality.
If it's impossible, I wouldn't have said it. ——————→	Passive hostility.
Big deal—five years—he doesn't know everything.	
It's impossible to be right against him.	
He can sure make a person feel stupid.	
Obviously I've thought about it.	
It's always a fact coming from him.	
I'll bet everyone agrees with him.	
I should just keep quiet—that's better than looking stupid.	

Impact on Group:

Unresolved hostility.
Other members afraid to venture out against John.
Those sympathetic to Bill strengthen their protective subgroup.

Gibb found that defensiveness increases when a person feels that he or she is being evaluated or controlled or is the butt of a strategy (a plan or maneuver to accomplish an unknown outcome). A large part of the adverse reaction to many personal-growth groups is a feeling against what are perceived gimmicks or tricks to involve people and have them think they are really participating in a decision, or to make listeners think someone is really interested in them as people. Defensiveness also arises when a person feels that another is reacting to him or her "clinically" or as a case (neutrally), from a superior position, or from a position of certainty. Defensiveness interferes with communication and then makes it difficult, sometimes impossible, for anyone to convey ideas clearly or to move toward a solution.

FEEDBACK: A MEANS OF REDUCING DISTORTIONS IN THE COMMUNICATION PROCESS

We like to think that we are effective in our efforts, and it can be quite threatening to discover that often we are not. Thus, in groups we are frequently torn between a real desire to confront how we are actually perceived (at both content and image levels) and our desire to live with the image we would like to think we are projecting.

Feedback is the process by which we find out whether the message intended is the message actually received. In the simplest sense, feedback refers to the return to you of behavior you have generated. A mirror gives one kind of feedback, as does a tape recorder, a camera, or a videotape machine. Recently, researchers (Rao, 1995) have even explored feedback in telephone and computer conferencing.

However, the most powerful form of feedback is the human response. Optimal learning requires sensitivity and judgment in the feedback process, and for this reason, human response remains the most powerful instrument. In a group, honest feedback can increase accuracy, instill a sense of being understood, and promote closeness and a sense of confidence. It can also increase defensive communication and the level of guardedness.

Feedback is most effective when it is asked for (in contrast to the unsolicited "I'm telling you for your own good"); when it is descriptive rather than evaluative; when it is behavioral rather than global; when it occurs soon after the behavior occurs rather than after a long time; and when it is positive rather than negative (Campbell and Dunnette, 1968, Jacobs et al., 1973; Yalom, 1970).

What is useful feedback? Consider an example involving two colleagues at a conference. One has just given a presentation; the other rushes up to congratulate him. "You were terrific," he says with enthusiasm. "Don't give me that," retorts the other. "I need to know what exactly you liked and didn't like about what I did. What I want to know is, How did I deal with the subject? How did I come across?" He was proving (though not very tactfully) that useful feedback is nonjudgmental, descriptive information geared to the specific situation at hand.

Individual Experiment

Giving feedback is difficult; it is a skill that requires practice. Here are two practice exercises:

1. At lunch or dinner with a friend, feed back a response to something that is said. Remember, your response should be descriptive and specific. Take note of your friend's response. What did you learn from the experience?
2. At a meeting or in a group, give feedback on an incident that occurs during the session. Remember, be nonjudgmental and descriptive. Note the response and analyze its relationship to your feedback.

Besides allowing members to ascertain whether what was intended was actually received, feedback also plays a crucial role in reducing distortions in the communication process. And the impact of feedback, or how it is perceived by the members, affects members' personal and interpersonal development. Gordon (1983) studied interpersonal feedback to determine how much of it was perceived as being useful. Members of a group were asked to rate feedback as either beneficial or harmful, useful or useless, and valuable or worthless; subjects rated about 90 percent of the received feedback as beneficial, useful, and valuable.

Jacobs and her associates (1973) and Snyder and Newburg (1981) found that positive feedback was rated as more credible, more desirable, and having greater impact than negative feedback. They further found that negative feedback that is behavioral was more credible than negative feedback that was emotional. Either way, people are less satisfied with their jobs and how they perform their jobs when they get negative feedback from their peers (Denisi, Randolph, and Blencoe, 1983). We change by hearing (and seeking out) positive information on ourselves.

We are more likely to accept feedback when it's given as a consensus from a group of people (Wimer and Derlega, 1983) or when it comes from the leader of the group (Snyder and Newburg, 1981). Think about your response when another student tells you what a good job you did on that last paper, as opposed to having your professor compliment your work.

In most groups, the feedback process can be used to best advantage as a means of clearing the air, providing an opportunity to shift course or procedures, and raising important issues that could not easily be explored during the give-and-take of the meeting.

Groups do better, more effective jobs when they get feedback on how they're doing (Jorgenson and Papciak, 1981). It is possible to begin the process gently. For example, after a meeting the participants can spend a few minutes discussing what went well and what could be improved the next time in order to ensure a more effective meeting. In this way, the process can focus on future behavior and events and not just on the behavior that hindered the present meeting. It requires the participants to develop effective modes of future behavior and a constructive attitude toward their own efforts. Similarly, without becoming too personal, the participants might jot down on a piece of paper a specific type of behavior they feel was facilitative in the meeting as well as one that inhibited the progress of the group. The use of such immediate information can prepare a group to more readily accept specific information related to individual behaviors. It can also increase the members' desire to solicit information about their own effectiveness. It is out of this search for personal learning and improvement that a climate of increasing support and openness evolves. Eventually the group may develop enough trust so that the feedback process becomes an integral and unobtrusive part of the entire meeting, with members responding at both a feeling level and a content level and checking out their own perceptions with others in the group.

There is, of course, the possibility that feedback can come to be of greater importance to the members than the task facing the group. There is no doubt that the process can, if mishandled, become distorted, inappropriately personal, and an actual imposition. One way to control this situation is occasionally to appoint a member of the group as observer and nonparticipant. Examining this individual's brief descriptive report after the meeting can provide a stimulus for the group to reassess its own working goals and priorities. Another approach is to develop a clear group contract about feedback expectations. Of greatest importance is that the use of feedback not be imposed, because it will inevitably create even more tensions and divisiveness and clog the very communication channels the group is attempting to open.

POOR COMMUNICATION: THE RULE, NOT THE EXCEPTION

If we were to examine a cross section of American institutions, we would probably find that breakdowns in communication are a primary source of internal conflict and stress. Spend a day in a mental-health institution and you may observe that the administration communicates poorly with the staff, psychiatrists with psychologists, doctors with nurses, and nurses with day-care workers. Somewhere in the labyrinth of statuses, roles, job descriptions, and the multitude of internal conflicts that exist, help is given to the resident patient. There are, of course, those exceptional institutions where hierarchical power struggles are minimized, where role differentiation in terms of status is limited, and where, as a result, communication channels remain relatively uncluttered.

Perhaps nowhere is there a better example of tensions that exist because of the communication process than in our schools, particularly the classrooms. Most of us have had firsthand experience with the following problems pervading our schools:

1. Communication is one-way—from a source of information to the receiver, who can ask for clarification. The latter is seldom in a position to transfer his or her learnings to others, be they younger students or age peers.
2. In the classroom group, the goals of learning are seldom established by the participants or even with them, but by an outside power source instead.
3. Rather than being shared, leadership is usually held tightly in the hands of the "responsible" person.

4. The participants are held accountable only for content information—usually in the form of an evaluative examination that labels individuals according to performance in terms of discrete letters or numbers.
5. Although held accountable in content areas, the participants are seldom held accountable in other areas that are relevant to them, such as discipline and decision making.
6. The faculty are not held highly accountable for their performance in terms of the student participants. This lack of a two-way evaluation increases distance between student and teacher.
7. Rather than being perceived as *an* important resource to be used effectively by the classroom group, the teacher is established as the *only* resource person.
8. Often the internal climate is highly competitive and sets student against student rather than stressing the educational venture as a cooperative one.
9. The communication of information from the students to the teacher is usually, for a variety of reasons, through a relatively small number of students. Learning is passive, low-interactive communication.

With a very slight shift in titles and certain terms, the situation described here could easily be transferred to small groups within a variety of institutions. Obviously, it would be simplistic to say that changing communication patterns would change all these conditions. Nevertheless, research in the area of small groups suggests a variety of logical alternatives that could make for more open communication.

Factors That Influence Group Communication

Group leaders are often hesitant to spend (waste) time developing interpersonal relations in a group where the goals are clearly defined in terms of specific tasks (Grace, 1956; Slater, 1955). Thus a program director may have a regularly scheduled 3-hour meeting every week (150 hours over a year) for his or her staff and never spend any time strengthening the communication process or exploring ways to improve interpersonal relations within the group. Similarly, a high school history teacher may spend from 3 to 5 hours a week with the same students for an entire year, but never spend time getting to know them.

Almost any new group is charged with tension (Crook, 1961) as individuals test out their environment and observe the various personalities involved. It is in this early period when most communication patterns develop. But research has shown that time spent initially and periodically in improving the communication process will pay dividends in terms of greater work efficiency (Tschan, 1995). (See also problem solving in Chapter 7.)

Research shows, too, that when people enter into a task with a predefined need to be cooperative and interdependent, there is more listening, more acceptance of ideas, less possessiveness of ideas and, in general, more communication. Within such an atmosphere, the group also tends to create achievement pressure itself. Furthermore, there seems to be more attentiveness to members' ideas and a friendlier climate than in groups where interpersonal competition is stressed. As suggested earlier, all these conditions help to make a group more attractive to its participants and generally lead to greater group productivity.

SIZE OF GROUP

There is no exact specification of how large a group may be before it is no longer appropriate to call it a small group. The usefulness of the designation rests on the fact that size is a limiting condition on the amount and quality of communication that can take place among members as individuals. This then affects the interpersonal relations among members (Hare, 1976).

Size is a factor in group relationships because, as the size increases, the number of relationships possible among members increases even more rapidly. Kephart (1950) demonstrated how the increase in the number of relationships becomes almost astronomical with the addition of a few more people. Note in Table 1.1 on page 40 how the addition of a person vastly increases the number of possible relationships.

Because the number of potential relationships among group members increases rapidly as a group grows larger, a large group tends to break into subgroups. Communication then takes on another dimension as subgroups relate to each other. Furthermore, subgroups have the greatest chance of affecting group outcomes when members maintain regular, ongoing communication throughout discussion (Gebhardt and Meyers, 1995).

Aside from communication, group size also affects group members' self-awareness and sense of how to behave in front of the group. Mullen, Chapman, and Salas (1989) studied the effects of large and small groups on the individual. They concluded that in small groups people are more self-aware and more likely to regulate their behavior. People in large groups are less self-aware and less concerned about their behavior.

In a small work group, then, only a few possible relationships exist. Yet it is easy to understand that in a larger discussion group, when time is limited, the average member has fewer chances to speak and intermember communication becomes difficult. Morale declines as group size increases because the former intimate contact among members is no longer possible. With a larger group, there are greater

Table 1.1 **Increase in Potential Relationships with an Increase in Group Size***

Size of Group	Number of Relationships
2	1
3	6
4	25
5	90
6	301
7	966

Table, "Increase in Potential Relationships with an Increase in Group Size," from, "A Quantitative Analysis of Intragroup Relationships," by William M. Kephart, American Journal of Sociology 60 (1950). Published by The University of Chicago Press.

member resources for the accomplishment of problem solving, but the average contribution of each member diminishes and it becomes more difficult to reach agreement on a group solution.

Individual Experiment

People who talk a lot are perceived as having a lot of influence whether they say anything of value or not.

In a group of twenty people, how many people do you think would talk and dominate the conversation?

____

In a group of ten, how many would dominate?

____

In a group of eight?

____

In a group of five?

____

In a group of three?

____

In a group of two?

____

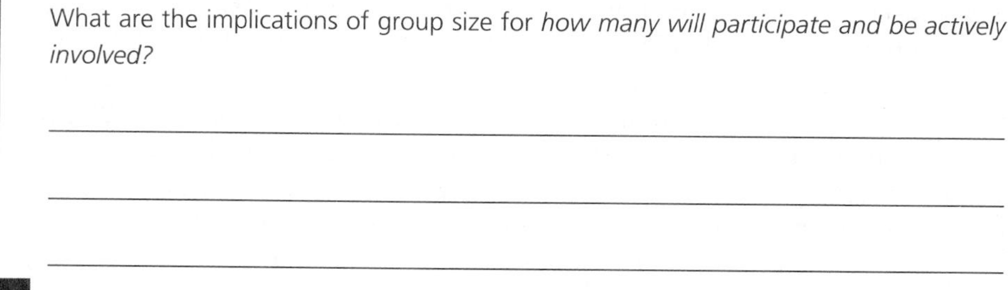

What are the implications of group size for *how many will participate and be actively involved?*

People can usually answer the questions in the foregoing experiment from experience. In a group of twenty, the number will be five or fewer. In a group of ten or eight, it will be three. In a group of five, it is likely to be two. In a group of three, interestingly, it is hard for one person to dominate, and two or all three will speak often. In a group of two, one will dominate. Thus the size of the group has a strong influence on the number of people who become actively involved in its activities. Small groups encourage proportionally more participation than large ones. It is no accident that today, with very limited time available for volunteer activities, members of large boards report minimal satisfaction with board meetings, whereas members of small task forces or small specific projects have more satisfaction (Huberman, 1987).

Size influences communication and behavior. Two-person groups often result in considerable tension, because a dominant-submissive relationship inevitably develops. When one member does not feel that he or she has power over the other, he or she will tend either to fight the other person and his or her ideas or withdraw into a passive pattern of behavior. Each member will use whatever behavior is required to balance the control component within the group. However, in the dyad, obviously the possibility also exists for the greatest degree of intimacy. Pearson (1981) found that women talk more about themselves in dyads and that men talk more about themselves in groups of three or more.

A three-person group may have less tension, but only because two people usually join forces and push their ideas into acceptance. The recognition of power through numbers decreases the resistance of the third member and allows a quicker resolution of the problem under consideration. The person in the minority may not feel good about it (in one study, the odd person out in a three-person roommate situation was dissatisfied, felt sick, and was less confident in social situations [Reddy et al., 1981]), but is better able to rationalize away his or her own impotence, given the obvious power of the opposition. Similarly, communication in odd-number groups tends to be smoother because the possibility of an equal split of opinion and the resulting struggle for power does not exist.

Above the size of five, members complain that a group is too large, and this may be due to the restriction on the amount of participation (Gentry, 1980). Beyond a certain size, groups tend to split up and form cliques (Mamali and Paun, 1982). A five-person group eliminates the possibility of a strict deadlock because of the odd number of members. The group tends to split into a majority and a minority, but being in the minority of two does not isolate an individual; the group is large enough for people to be able to shift roles.

There appears to be no magic number for a successful working group. However, in general, as the size of the group increases, the affectional tie among members decreases (Berelson and Steiner, 1964; Kinney, 1953; Schellenberg, 1959), as does motivation to do certain tasks (Kerr and Bruun, 1981). Pantin and Carver (1982) and Latané and Nida (1981) found that people were slower to respond to medical emergencies when they were part of a larger group. Much depends on the topic and on the individual personalities, motivations, and past experience of group members; nevertheless, a group of five seems to be optimal in a number of situations. It is large enough to allow for diversity of opinions and ideas, yet small enough to allow everyone to be heard (Hackman and Vidmar, 1970).

PHYSICAL ATTRACTIVENESS

What role does physical attractiveness play in interaction? On that question, debate continues (Heilman, 1980). Although people are attracted to and react more favorably toward individuals who are physically attractive, the effect of that perception is varied (Brehm and Kassin, 1993). It is not that being more attractive is an indication of greater talent or virtue (Hatfield and Sprecher, 1986). Nor is it clear that physically attractive people have greater social skills. In one study, only physically attractive *men* perceived themselves as having greater social skills than their less attractive peers (Reis et al., 1982); and in another, only physically attractive *women* perceived themselves as having greater social skills (O'Grady, 1989).

The effect of our expectations may be one of the reasons why research results on the role played by physical attractiveness in communication are so mixed. We respond in kind to the images we conjure up that relate to attractiveness. In a Yale study (Heilman, 1980), participants were asked to decide who should be hired for a management job. Attractive male applicants were considered strong and competent, and they were more likely to be hired. Attractive female applicants were judged more feminine, a quality associated with helplessness and high emotionality, and were not named to the position. The issue raises all kinds of questions about our objectivity and the relationship between physical attractiveness and our communication patterns, as well as the assumptions we have about gender-related work roles.

TIME FOR COMMUNICATION

As group size increases, the time for overt communication during a meeting of any given length decreases. Each member has a more complicated set of social relationships to maintain and more restricted resources with which to do it. In larger groups, a few members do most of the talking. Members of groups are aware of this, and an increased number of members of discussion groups report feelings of threat and inhibition about participating as group size increases. The effect of increasing size is to reduce the amount of participation per member. As the group size increases, a larger and larger proportion of members have less than their share of participation time—that is, under the group mean (Shaw, 1981; Seaman, 1981; Hare, 1982).

CROWDING AND TEMPERATURE

Crowding is another factor in communication, as are heat and cold. Crowding does not pertain just to the number of people in physical space; it is also a psychological factor. Gender seems to make a difference in the perception of crowding: females find smaller rooms more comfortable and are more likely to engage in intimate positive conversation; males prefer larger rooms (Freedman, 1971).

Raising the temperature of a room tends to create an effect of crowding, as does decreasing the distance between people conversing (Smith, Reinheimer, and Gabbard, 1981). Under conditions of crowding and increased (or varying) temperatures, people tend to react negatively to each other (Griffitt, 1970; Griffitt and Veitch, 1971).

LEADERSHIP AND CONTROL OF COMMUNICATION

A few generalizations can be made about leadership and control of communication in groups (Bavelas, 1950; Shaw, 1964).

1. Morale is higher in groups in which there is more access to participation among those involved—the more open the participation, the higher the morale.
2. Efficiency tends to be lowest among groups that are the most open. Because more wrong ideas need to be sifted out, more extraneous material is generated and more time is "wasted" listening to individuals even when a point has been made.

3. Groups that are most efficient tend to be those in which all members have access to a central leadership figure who can act as an expediter and clarifier as well as keep the group on the right track in working through the problem.
4. Positions that individuals take can have a definite influence on leadership in the group as well as on potential conflict among group members. In the process of performing communication functions—such as deciding on goals, giving directions, summarizing, and being self-assured—groups can predict potential leaders, who may be chosen for positive and/or negative qualities (Schultz, 1986).
5. Groups with centralized leadership (see item 3) tend to organize more rapidly, be more stable in performance, and show greater efficiency. However, morale also tends to drop, and this decline can, in the long run, influence their stability and even their productivity (Glazer and Glazer, 1961; Hearn, 1957).
6. Leaders in groups without strong identities (low cohesion) do best to direct and run things, but in groups that have high cohesion, leaders are more effective when they take group members' needs into account and work in a more collaborative way (Schriesheim, 1980).
7. The group leaders' gender can affect the members' perceptions of them. In an investigation of this issue, females were perceived as less competent and less potent leaders than males (Morrison and Stein, 1985). Investigating how female instructors are perceived, Gilbert, Holt, and Long (1988) surveyed 128 female and 138 male college students. In one case, students were in a same-sex group; in the other, they were the only male or female in the group. Findings indicate that the sex composition of the group affected person perception.

Groups in which the lines of communication are clear from the beginning and in which relations with authority are specified tend to be more productive in terms of completing task objectives. The price for this, of course, is a reduction in the amount of information shared and a subsequent increase in dependence on the person(s) in authority. In the short run, it is doubtful that tension and resentment in such groups would be inhibiting when the concern for completing a task is greatest. In the long run, however, such communication patterns may well create numerous problems as individual frustrations build up with no legitimate ways for venting them.

Thus, a dilemma. We may choose greater leader control and efficiency at the price of lower morale and participation. Or it is possible to choose higher morale and group satisfaction at the price of efficiency. The answer would seem to be a combination of the two, but it is the rare person who can encourage sharing and full participation and still impose the restrictions desired to help maximize the operation of the group. Playing such a role *is* possible if the individual is aware of the many difficulties and traps when, for example, some individuals demand more structure and guidance while others seek absolute freedom from restrictions.

PHYSICAL ENVIRONMENT

The physical environment, like the social environment, has a significant impact on communication and interaction in groups. In one study of the effects of different physical settings and seating arrangements, the results suggest that communication and productivity are enhanced when participants operate in a circle—for example, at circular tables (Key, 1986).

Such knowledge can help the teacher or group leader "set the stage" for the type of group interaction he or she desires.

A meeting was planned for about 40 individuals to help introduce them to one another as well as to orient them for a large convention involving 20,000 people the next day. The room was capable of seating nearly 250 people, and chairs were arranged in rows. In order to alter the sterile environment, the program director changed the chairs around in a manner that would be more conducive for informal talking and getting to know one another. Thus the chairs in the front of the room were rearranged to form loosely grouped circles of about five chairs each. Barriers were then arranged so that the chairs in the back of the room could not be reached.

When the director arrived five minutes before the meeting was scheduled to begin, he found his efforts had been futile. No one was sitting in the front of the room, and, as a result of much effort on the part of a number of individuals, the chairs in the back were now accessible and occupied. It was clear that the participants came to be talked *to* and that they felt more comfortable in straight rows and with a minimum of contact with one another. Their desires to meet and listen in straight rows, not to interact, to remain strangers in the group until drawn together by the force of a task, and to remain "comfortable" while being fed information are all the result of past conditioning. For the director to have allowed the situation to remain as it was would probably have resulted in many of the participants' leaving dissatisfied with the formal and structured nature of the program. To have moved them out of their security would have risked incurring a negative reaction as individuals became less secure and more dependent on themselves and not the authority.

STATUS AND POWER

In any group there will be both high-status members who have the power to influence others and low-status members who are less influential. Status is partly determined by a person's role in the group. It has been shown that when high-status individuals are present in a group, both high- and low-status individuals direct their communication to them (Scott and Easton, 1996; Hurwitz et al., 1968). Not only that, but Kashyap (1982) has shown that a group member who is perceived either as wealthy or as an expert on some topic exerts more influence in changing others' opinions. It is the high-status individuals who tend to be accepted more, and they find it easier and to their advantage to speak more. Group members also find that high-status people listen more (Bechler and Johnson, 1995). By contrast, because low-status participants don't value acceptance by their own status peers, they often avoid association with one another during the meeting. Rather, they wait until later to express their feelings and attitudes concerning the proceedings. Also, because there is a general fear of evaluation by those with power, those who lack power take few risks, generally speak inconsequentially, and avoid candidness in their statements. Because of this expected trend in behavior, it becomes even more difficult to contribute if one lacks power; considerably more attention is given to each contribution by a low-status person, and this increases his or her fears of intimidation and critical evaluation. The cycle is further extended by the probability that those with influence will hesitate to reveal any of their limitations or personal vulnerability among those with lesser influence, thus lending an artificial quality to the whole proceeding.

Juries are a good example of status in action. As Christian (1978) points out, "A jury is not an aggregate of twelve autonomous individuals. Leaders will emerge; some people may try to become leaders and be rebuffed; some will fit passively into the group structure, and some will become isolates."

Christian found in his study of juries that in general an individual's status and power in the jury group mirror his or her status and power in the real world. This means that men, people with higher education and prestigious occupations, whites, and older individuals will have more status than others.

Christian also found that people of similar status will form friendships and become cliques. These cliques become especially formidable. For example, in the trial of the Gainesville Eight, he found that the clustering of jury members was the most important factor in the understanding of the group dynamics and decision-making process of the jury. The key to clustering, he found, was power—the ability to convince other jurors of one's viewpoint. The person who could sway the other jury members had influence even outside the group, because the jury's decision had to be unanimous.

Interestingly, the power distribution in a group is displayed in the way the group physically arranges itself. When members of a board come into the boardroom, typically the boss sits either in the center of the short end of a rectangular table farthest from the door or at the head of the table; his or her cronies usually flank the boss on the left and right. Those either disinterested in the issue or powerless to influence the outcome generally sit at the opposite end or foot of the table and cluster together there. Where will the adversarial combatants sit? Typically they sit opposite each other on the long sides of the table—arrayed for combat.

Status and power talk to status and power, while others tend to become observers in the process. What appears to be voluntary silence may be subtly imposed by the group. Unless it is legitimate to "draw in" those pushed to the periphery by the sheer power present, they will tend to feel an increasing sense of impotence. This may not occur if the individual is able to share vicariously the ideas and influence of a person with high status. But even the individual who participates least in the group has feelings about what is going on, ideas that could contribute to the discussion, and, most of all, a desire to feel worthwhile. However, he or she may also lack the skills, trust, and energy to overcome the obstacles to his or her communication.

Reader Activity

If you wanted to enhance communication, how would you redesign the seating arrangement described above?

___

___

Predictably, if three or four high-status individuals in a group have been involved in heated discussion and someone suggests breaking up into groups of two and three, the noise level in the group goes up tenfold as individuals who have been silent up to that point realize they have a chance to express themselves. It is not that they had nothing to say before; rather, the atmosphere in the group simply did not allow free expression of their ideas. Even among individuals skilled in working with groups, it takes a concerted effort to push beyond immediate needs and sources of gratification to seek out and cultivate opportunities for participation. This process does not seem to evolve naturally—there are too many personal needs in the way.

Some researchers are exploring the possibility of using computer-mediated communication, or computer conferences, to overcome influences of a few individuals and foster equal participation in discussions. However, patterns of interaction and performance in computer-mediated groups appear not to be substantially different from face-to-face groups. Strauss (1996) created 54 three-person groups that worked on a problem-solving task either in computer conferences or in face-to-face meetings. Despite more equal participation in computer conferences, certain individuals dominated in both media. The medium had few effects on information sharing or performance, and computer groups were less satisfied.

The purpose of this chapter has been to increase awareness of the *process* underlying group endeavors. It is not necessary to print long lists of "how-tos"; awareness of what is happening is the first and largest step in correcting some of the obvious problems that exist. Awareness of ourselves at both a feeling and a behavioral level and of what is happening among other group members are most important. Communication problems that exist reflect our own fallibility and the extent of our needs whenever we get together with others. For that very reason communication is difficult, but for the same reason it is possible to improve.

Group Communication in a Diverse Society

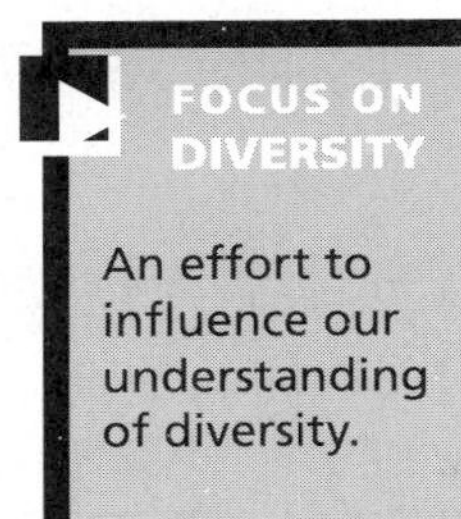

FOCUS ON DIVERSITY
An effort to influence our understanding of diversity.

Sheldon Hackney, past president of the University of Pennsylvania, recently completed a four-year term as chairman of the National Endowment for the Humanities. Asked what he had accomplished during his term, he replied that he was proud of his creation of the "Conversations with America on Pluralism and National Identity." The programs, held across the country with a broad diversity of populations in a variety of formats, were designed to encourage Americans to think about pluralism and the American character. This was accomplished by having people examine a basic text: the Declaration of Independence, the Bill of Rights, or the Constitution. In living rooms, schools, community centers, theaters, colleges, and on "call-in" radio shows, heterogeneous groups of Americans were asked to think, first, about freedom: what it meant originally and how it formed America's character. Then they examined how some concepts have broadened (citizens are no longer only white males who own property) and how some fundamental principles have remained constant (the U.S. is still a place of refuge). After initial examination and discussion, conversations turned to present implications of these ideas in a more complex, multiracial, multicultural society (Hackney, 1998). Although there is greater diversity in America than ever, it is a subject little discussed, little recognized, and even less understood.

Consider one aspect: the increasing diversity of occupational experience discussed in the Workforce 2000 report. Only 7 percent of families today fit the traditional model of a husband working outside the home and a wife at home with

FOCUS ON DIVERSITY

What would you have said has changed, and what remained the same?

two school-age children. More and more women and minorities are entering the work force, over 10 million mothers of preschoolers are pursuing careers, and more than half the mothers of children under 6 years work.

In the next couple of years, the work force is expected to become gender-balanced. It is further projected that only 58 percent of new entrants into the labor force will be "white native-born Americans." Twenty-two percent are expected to be immigrants, and the remaining 20 percent African Americans and Hispanics. But although American workers are becoming more educated on average, 65 percent of the work force reads below the 9th-grade level (Johnson and Packer, 1987).

These changing demographic characteristics directly affect organizational communication in several ways. After 3:00 P.M., for example, productivity goes down in many businesses because family issues become the focus of conversation on the work floor; and calls from home may interrupt work flow. Working parents do not forget a sick child at home, custodial fathers are aware that overtime conflicts with child-care arrangements, and workers with elderly parents recognize the potential difficulties of geographic relocation. How does communication go in a department meeting including, for example, single, career-oriented people willing to work almost any hours; single parents with child care schedules; a black woman who is head of the department; and two African-American men who are lower department members? There are myriad factors involved in any discussion, beyond the stated task. Yet often diversity is ignored, as if discussions focus only on the problem stated on the agenda.

Consider an example from family therapy.

> "I believe a couple is a couple" says John, a white family therapist who has been in practice for over 22 years in New York. John felt confident he could help Renee and Dara, a lesbian couple who came to see him complaining about bitter fights. For him the fact that they were two women, that one was black and the other white, was no more important than what they were wearing. He worked with them as he works with other couples. He started with each woman's genogram and then had them talk about how they first fell in love, practice speaking in "I" statements, and perform an exercise envisioning their future together. After six sessions, the couple told him they were ready to leave therapy and thanked him for his help. John considered the enterprise a success: he had covered all the bases, and the women had left in a happier frame of mind. A lot of therapists would have felt just as satisfied as John did—and, like John, they would have been wrong. Two days later Renee and

Dara found a new therapist. "John tried to help us, but he avoided too many issues. He never asked us about being gay, or about race."

Why hadn't they brought the subjects up themselves? "It's about confidence in the therapist. Could he handle it? Would he know what to do with it? He hadn't sent us any signals that said he could" (Markowitz, 1997).

A growing number of therapists around the country are learning that they need to broach once-unfamiliar issues of class, race, sexual orientation, and culture to help clients. By the early 1990s, special-interest groups had gathered together under the rubric of "multiculturalism," and therapists began to converse more about stepping outside usual frameworks for understanding couples and factoring in not only family patterns but also the effects of invisible yet powerful social, economic, and political stressors. These include everything from the emotional effects on same-sex couples of not being allowed to legally marry, to the way racism plays out within African-American and Latino families, to the effect of anti-Semitism on intermarried couples.

Although multicontextual therapy gives language to the larger systems that complicate clients' lives, it doesn't make problems go away. There is still poverty, discrimination, and hatred. But it does empower clients to make better choices, to stand together as a team and support each other.

One more illustration, this time from the justice system.

In a criminal case in the Washington, D.C. area, the defendant was African American and the jury consisted of six black and six white members. The jury listened to the evidence, saw the exhibits, and heard the witnesses. To eleven members it had been proven beyond a reasonable doubt that the defendant was guilty, and they were ready to vote that way. However, one African-American juror voted "not guilty" in what is known as *juror nullification*. Under this long-standing doctrine, jurors have the power to vote "not guilty" in a criminal case, even if they believe the defendant broke the law, if they consider it a "bad" law. (Jury nullification has been allowed since Chief Justice of the U.S. Supreme Court John Jay outlined the concept to the jury in *Georgia* v. *Brailsford* in 1794.) In this case, the outcome was a hung jury and mistrial. The juror thought her "not-guilty" verdict would redress the long-standing injustice of blacks being convicted more frequently than whites for similar crimes.

What did this trial portend for the future? Would there be no reasoning in juries in the future? Regardless of evidence or discussion, would African Americans vote "not guilty"? Stereotypic assumptions went into high gear.

Laura Markowitz, "The Context of Intimacy." *The Family Networker.* September/October 1997, pp. 50–58. Reprinted by permission.

At the second trial, a jury of nine blacks and three whites was selected. This jury returned a unanimous verdict of guilty. So much for multiculturalism and stereotyping.

The point is, diversity, from a wide variety of cultural backgrounds, norms, and values; to traditional and nontraditional roles for men and women; to a large non-Caucasian population; to a smaller child population and a larger aging population, makes it ever more difficult to communicate effectively. Our challenge today is to find ways to use diversity creatively—to develop more skills, to encourage new ideas, to learn more ways to negotiate differences, and to expand our horizons concerning how to work together.

REDUCING PROBLEMS OF DIVERSITY

During the past two decades, sociologists and social psychologists have directed increasing attention to the implications of language and its use in social contexts to reduce problems of diversity. Some examples and implications of this research include the following:

1. Tjosvold, Johnson, and Lerner (1981) investigated the way in which effective problem solvers discuss opposing opinions and incorporate them into their own ideas. In their experiment, men and women discussed a dilemma with a confederate, who took an opposing view. In the affirmation subgroup, the confederate positively evaluated the subject's competence. In the acceptance subgroup, the confederate made few evaluative comments but indicated that subjects were arguing in a reasonable manner. In the disconfirmation subgroup (most analogous to what happens when we communicate with someone perceived as different than or inferior to us), subjects were informed that they were ineffective. Compared to the affirmative and acceptance conditions, disconfirmation resulted in subjects' uncertainty about the correctness of their views, closed-mindedness toward opposing information, lack of interest in learning the others' positions, misunderstanding of the other's reasoning, unwillingness to incorporate the others' arguments, and dislike for the others. In short, treating others without respect and devaluing their contributions has far-reaching negative outcomes.
2. If individuals are ignored they will decrease their participation in social interaction (Geller et al., 1974).
3. The influence of prior beliefs (expectancies) about a given individual was examined with regard to three phenomena: the target's behavior, the processing of the target's behavior by perceivers, and the target's self-perception (D. T. Miller and Turnbull, 1986). The most common find-

ing was the so-called self-fulfilling prophecy. That is, people usually interpret social interaction in such a way that a target's behavior confirms their expectations. In addition, stereotypic or low expectations are likely to produce congruent behavioral responses.

4. A satisfactory exchange may help a person feel accepted and involved in a group, even if it is no more than responsiveness to a question. In general, positive behavior is exchanged for positive behavior.
5. Interpersonal communication involves skills in sending messages, but more important, in receiving messages. The skills involved in receiving messages include giving feedback about the reception, and the message, in ways that clarify and aid continued discussion. Receiving skills have two basic parts: (1) communicating the intention or desire to understand the ideas and feelings of the sender, and (2) understanding and interpreting the sender's ideas and feeling. Of the two, communicating the intention to correctly understand, but not evaluate, a message is the more important (Johnson and Johnson, 1991). The responder who evaluates the message, and either inwardly or verbally says, "I think you're wrong" or "What a dumb idea," will make the receiver defensive and cautious, and reduce the openness of communication. Furthermore, the stronger the emotions involved, the more likely group members will evaluate each other's statements.
6. Encourage a cooperative group climate that fosters equal participation of all members (Johnson and Johnson, 1991).
7. Promote group norms that hold members' ideas and views, regardless of age, gender, culture, or ethnic background, as genuinely interesting to other members of the group (Hare, et al., 1994).

Because communication is among people, anything that interferes with the relationships among them interferes with their communication. Attention must be paid to interpersonal relationships among diverse group members.

EXERCISE 1 Communication Role Reversal

OBJECTIVES

- To make group members aware of how easily they "tune out" one another
- To force people into a position in which listening becomes expected at both an emotional (affective) level and a cognitive (content) level

SETTING

A large group is divided into subgroups or sets of four or five participants. Each person is given a large name tag that is pinned on him or her or placed in his or her lap so that every other person can clearly see it. (This is to be done even if members know one another's names.) It is probably helpful if the members are not too familiar with one another, because lack of familiarity usually requires greater concentration and ensures greater involvement (unless members are voluntarily together where familiarity is one of the aims of that particular program).

ACTION

The subgroups are given a topic that ensures some involvement on the part of all the participants. If possible, the topic should be such that opposing views will be presented. After five or ten minutes—at a point when the discussion has developed to a considerable degree—the facilitator requests that each individual give his or her name tag to the person across from him or her. They are then asked to continue the discussion as if they were the person whose name tag they now have. After another five minutes, the facilitator asks the group members to begin expressing the views of the person on their right (another exchange of tags).

DISCUSSION

If the participants have really been listening to one another and the discussion is moving with most individuals participating, the exercise will not prove difficult. However, if a person has not been participating for some reason, this poses questions for the person playing him or her, and it poses questions for the group. Why was he or she not involved in a topic about which he or she must have ideas? The group is also asked to discuss whether the switch made them uncomfortable or made the task particularly difficult. Also, what was present in this situation that occurs in most group communication? Was it easy to pick up the emotional as well as the content information of the person you were playing? Did the learnings from the first switch carry over into the second switch?

The Blind Builder: A Task in Interdependent Communication

OBJECTIVES

- To observe how different individuals give direction
- To observe how different individuals receive direction
- To gain a better understanding of what happens when communication occurs under stress conditions

SETTING

This exercise is limited to some extent by the availability of materials and space. Groups consisting of four participants are established. Two of the four are to be observers. Each group must have the following materials:

A blindfold

A backsaw or other small handsaw

Odd-sized pieces of wood board (perhaps five or six)

A hammer

Ten to twenty tacks or small nails

A three-foot piece of rope or twine

The participants are told the following story:

> Two people flying across a group of islands in the South Pacific were forced to crash-land on a small, uninhabited island. The temperature is extremely hot and, although the land is quite arid, it appears that there will be rain sometime during the day. The two fully expect to be rescued in a few days, and they have enough food for five days. However, their water supply was lost in the crash and they don't even have a container for holding water should it rain. Because of the heat and their fear of dehydration, the two survivors feel it is essential to build a water container and then wait for what looks like an inevitable thunderstorm. They find some wood and tools and are ready to set about their task. The only problem is that during the crash one of the two received a heavy blow on the head and is now both blind and mute. The second person burned both hands while pulling the tools from the burning wreckage and is not able to use them at all. But together they must build the container—and before the rain comes. A few drops begin to fall.

Thus the hands of one individual are to be tied with the twine securely behind his or her back, and the other is to be blindfolded.

OBSERVER ROLES

Both observers are to take notes on the more general aspects of the activity, but each is responsible for a more detailed observational report concerning one of the people taking part. How does the second person give directions? Is it possible for the blind person to understand him or her? Do they establish a basic nonverbal system of communication so that the blind person can communicate? What signs do each of the people reveal as the task becomes increasingly difficult? How is this frustration communicated to the other, and what is the other's response? What could have been done to facilitate their communication?

ACTION

The task will take between fifteen and thirty minutes. The observers may wish to observe other groups for the sake of contrast. When the task is completed (or not completed), the facilitator consolidates the two groups of four into one group of eight for a discussion of (a) the observers' data and (b) the feelings of the two participants. He or she then has the group of eight try to pull together some general learnings and implications to be shared with the large group.

EXERCISE 3 One-Way Versus Two-Way Communication[2]

OBJECTIVES

- **To illustrate problems in communication between one person and another**
- **To show the value of clarification through a question-and-answer process**
- **To explore the feelings of the recipient of a communicated message under two conditions**

MATERIALS

Three dominoes for each person

2. A workshop demonstration of this exercise was given by Hugh Stephans of Victoria, Texas, at the National Council on Family Relations Annual Conference in Dallas, Texas (1985).

ACTION

Two group members sit in chairs with their backs to each other. Each holds three dominoes and, on his or her lap, something with a smooth, firm surface such as a book or magazine. Other group members must look on without comment.

Round 1 Person A constructs a design with the three dominoes. Person B must try to construct an exact duplicate of person A's design by asking questions that can be answered with yes or no only. When person B feels the design is complete, the participants compare and discuss the designs.

Round 2 Person A again constructs a design. This time, person A instructs person B on how to construct a duplicate design. Person B may not ask any questions. When person A believes the design has been adequately described, person B must try to duplicate it. Then the two may compare and discuss the designs.

Round 3 Person A makes another design. Now each person may give and take information. At the completion, they compare and discuss.

DISCUSSION

In a discussion following the activity, the group considers the elements needed for effective communication. Some examples are

the frustration of a one-sided dialogue

the need for clarifying questions

the importance of common terminology

the advantage of give and take

VARIATIONS

The exercise can be done in groups of two, allowing everyone to participate. Another variation is to have the leader turn his or her back to the group; in this situation, the leader is person A and the rest of the group is person B.

EXERCISE 4 A Portrait Plus

OBJECTIVES

- To observe differences in interpersonal communication between men and women
- To observe how men and women work differently

- To recognize different patterns of relationships between men and women

RATIONALE

Do men and women take the same task and work differently? Do they, in fact, communicate in a different style? Are men more achievement-oriented and women more relationship-oriented? This exercise will enable participants to answer these questions as they pertain to the objectives listed above.

MATERIALS

Large sheets of newsprint, one for each group, mounted on a wall

A set of multicolored finger paints or crayons for each group

Aprons, or some covering, to keep participants clean when using finger paints

A set of instructions for each group

SETTING

The group is divided into sets of between two and four people. One set should be all females, one set should be all males, and one set should be mixed. Depending on the number involved, there can be multiple groups in each category (male, female, or mixed). Two people are assigned to be observers of each group. Observers will focus on how the group works, how they give each other instructions, and how they divide up the task, paying attention to the words used by members doing the task.

ACTION

Each group goes to a sheet of newsprint with their paints. They are instructed to create a portrait of the class instructor (or any other person known to all), but they must include the items on the instruction sheet:

1. a ring
2. a mushroom
3. a cup
4. a flower
5. jewelry
6. a butterfly
7. eye glasses
8. an animal
9. something made from a circle
10. shoes

The groups then create their portraits. Allow about 20 minutes.

DISCUSSION

Do the men's, the women's, or the mixed group's pictures look different from one another? Can you tell which is a woman's picture, which a man's picture, and which a mixed-group picture? How?

Observers report how women's groups worked; other observers report how men's groups worked; a final observer reports on how mixed groups worked. Discussion then continues with all participants.

QUESTIONS

1. Women's Group: How did it feel to be in a women's group? How is it different from being in a mixed group?
2. Men's group: How did it feel to be in a men's group? How is it different from being in a mixed group?
3. Do men and women communicate differently?
4. Do men and women work on a task differently?
5. What are the implications?

For Further Information

McKay, M.; Davis, M., and Fanning, P. *Messages: The Communication Book.* Oakland, Calif.: New Harbinger Publications, 1983.

This book tells you what to do about communication, not just what to think about it; the emphasis is on skills. The first three chapters cover basic skills: listening, how to disclose thoughts and feelings, and how to accurately express what you want to say. The next section is on advanced skills. Following sections are more specific: conflict skills, social skills, family skills, and public skills. The emphasis is on providing information (knowledge) as the basis for the next step (practice) since communication is a skill to learn experientially. Exercises, suggestions, and myriad examples are included. A well-organized "how-to" book.

Cathcart, R. S., and Samovar, L. A. *Small Group Communication: A Reader* (3rd ed.). Dubuque, Iowa: William C. Brown, 1981.

A classic collection of forty-six essays that covers facets of small group communication from theoretical constructs about "groupness," to specific analysis of language and thought, to practical exercises that can be performed to improve group communication. There are representative articles from the disciplines of psychology, sociology, anthropology, philosophy, business, and speech communication. The basic principles of small group communication are presented by the authors of seminal works, e.g., basic encounter groups by Carl Rogers; games by Eric Berne; effective feedback by Elliot Aronson; and defensive communication by Jack Gibb. Well-presented, classic works worth reading and thinking about.

Fast, J. *Body Language.* New York: MJF Books (Fine Communications), 1970.

A classic work on nonverbal communication. Body language uses kinesics, the science of nonverbal communication, to analyze common gestures we use and observe every day. There are chapters on animals and territory and how humans handle space; on masks and touch; on positions and postures; and an alphabet of movement. There are many, many illustrations. Some of the conclusions are of doubtful validity, but the book does make readers more conscious of the crucial importance of nonverbal behavior.

Gray, J. *Men, Women, and Relationships.* Hillsboro, Oregon: Beyond Words, 1993.

John Gray is a couples therapist who wrote the best-selling book *Men Are from Mars, Women Are from Venus* to explain why men and women have such difficulty understanding each other. In this elaboration of his theme, he presents how differences in communication can be understood to build better relationships. The focus is on the meaning of words for each gender. Gray believes communication between couples can be improved and that recognition of this can make all the difference. Many "how-to" examples are included in this easy read. Although gender differences are sometimes exaggerated, there is a "truth" to them that is readily recognized.

Stohl, C. *Organizational Communication: Connectedness in Action.* Thousand Oaks, Calif.: Sage, 1995.

This book has unusual perspective. Whereas most texts and research focus on either the world of work or the world of nonwork, this one provides a link between interpersonal and organizational communication. There have been vast changes in the American family, social structures, and the global economy, which are not independent fields of experience. The author contends that neither work life nor personal life can be known, or experienced, to the exclusion of the other. Well written, and the "Making Connections" sidebars are especially vivid illustrations of the concepts being illustrated.

Fowers, B. J., and Richardson, F. C. "Why Is Multiculturalism Good?" *American Psychologist* (June 1996), 609–621. Washington, D.C.: American Psychological Association.

An outstanding article reviewing the arguments for multiculturalism. It begins with concerns of the APA and goes on to examine what multiculturalism is, the arguments pro and con, and how it can be understood. It especially emphasizes the dilemmas of working multiculturally and the necessity of continuing dialogue.

Granrose, C. S., and Oskamp, S. eds. *Cross-Cultural Work Groups.* Thousand Oaks, Calif.: Sage, 1997.

Understanding cross-cultural work groups is important for several reasons. First, they are becoming more common: many U.S. work settings include cross-cultural work groups because society itself is culturally plural, and more organizations are operating in multiple nations. Second, when cross-cultural groups are expected to act like homogeneous ones, organizations and group members are often disappointed by the processes and the outcomes. This book, from the Claremont Symposium on Applied Social Psychology, consists of scholarship from various disciplines as it applies to understanding cross-cultural work groups in organizational settings. A wide range of examples is addressed. The editors think there is already ample literature on gender differences and blacks in work groups, so these populations are omitted.

Watt, J. H., and Van Lear, A. C. *Dynamic Patterns in Communication Processes.* Thousand Oaks, Calif.: Sage, 1996.

This is a very different kind of communications book: the focus is on *dynamic patterns.* "Pattern can be recognized as a redundancy across space and across time. . . . The science of communication requires the identification of patterns across cases (people, relationships, groups, organizations, societies) and across time." The central theme is the identification and modeling of these dynamic patterns. The first part covers the methodical and theoretical significance of communication events or states that vary in some distinct pattern over time. The second part presents a variety of current theories and research based on ideas of cycling and dynamic patterns that occur in a range of communication settings. Fascinating reading complete with mathematical equations, charts, and tables.

Hale, C., ed. *Wired Style: Principles of English Usage in the Digital Age.* Compiled by editors of *Wired* (1997).

This is a book about writing (communicating) via e-mail. "It looks like writing, but it's not. It feels like talking, but it's not," write Thomas Mandel and D. Van der Leun in *Rules of the Net.* "The writing is on the fly, informal, fast-paced. The nature of e-mail changes or eliminates most of the old rules of grammar." There is a premium on brevity and direct declarative sentences. As the book says, "At *Wired,* we write geek and we write street. We insist on accuracy and literacy, but we celebrate the colloquial voice." Consider: if people frequently use e-mail and send messages in that style, what are the implications for verbal interactive communication?

2 Membership

In *Democracy in America* Alexis de Tocqueville wrote,

> Americans of all ages, all stations in life, and all types of disposition are forever forming associations. There are not only commercial and industrial associations in which all take part, but others of a thousand different types: religious, moral, serious, futile, general or limited, enormous or diminutive. . . . As soon as several Americans have conceived a sentiment or an idea that they want to produce before the world, they seek each other out, and when found, they unite.

Researcher McGowan (1987) noted that today de Tocqueville's view still holds true. Tens of thousands of clubs, societies, and coalitions, both personal and professional, exist across the nation. Currently there is an explosion of self-help groups: groups organized to help members deal with grieving, illnesses, divorce, low self-esteem, being a woman, being a man, and numerous other concerns. McGowan believed that in looking at groups he was actually seeing the "American psyche." "We are what we join individually and as a people," he wrote.

Membership is central to our thinking about ourselves. At birth we have our initiation into our first group—our families. This membership in our family of origin teaches us who we are, how to relate to others, how to express emotion, and how to resolve problems. It is so powerful that it remains a part of us and a significant influence even after our parents have died and even after we have moved to another part of the country. Beginning with that first defining membership, most of us hold myriad memberships in the course of our lives.

What gets you into the groups you join? How much does it cost? Do you have a first-class ticket or steerage? Do you even have a ticket? Consider the following situation, in which an individual attempts to become a member of a group:

Tony grew up as a minimally educated immigrant in a working-class neighborhood. He had worked since he was eleven, he knew, and maybe even before that. One summer he worked at Whitemarsh Country Club, and as he watched the cars, the clothes, the style, and the assuredness of the members, he had a dream. Someday he would be middle class, one of *them.* The dream was always there. Dues were $2,000 per year, and the initiation fee triple that. He saved, he cultivated two members who might sponsor him, he was accepted for membership—he made it, at last!

The first Sunday he dressed carefully in his expensive, casual-looking sport outfit. He entered, heart pounding. He moved into the card room. Several groups were playing, and as he walked in, a couple of people looked up and then returned to their cards in nonrecognition. He watched some of the players and listened to their talk (he knew none of the people about whom they were talking and nothing about the events they described). He moved to another table and watched. No one came near him, asked him a question, or invited him in. He walked over to the bar, where the bartender was engaged in conversation at the other end. In due time, he came over and asked Tony what he wanted to drink, and said not another word.

Tony looked at his drink, the bar, the card room, the easy ambiance the others had—the kidding, sharing, joking, talking about people they knew and a world he didn't. Suddenly—strange that it should be sudden—Tony realized that he didn't have a ticket to membership. On paper he might "belong" for twenty years, but he still wouldn't really *belong.*

FOCUS ON DIVERSITY

Ever had that experience? What did it mean to you? How do you think it affects others who have it more frequently?

Tony's experience is not unusual. We can move into small towns where families have lived for generations and thirty years after moving in, still be treated as strangers, newcomers not to be fully trusted.

In a small group, the situation is the same. Each of us enters, not knowing and fearful. How will our appearance measure up? Our religion, social status, or ethnic origin? Our mode of speaking? What we say? What expectations do those who are already members have of us? And the question we ask internally is, "Will I be accepted as a member of this group?" The uncertainty never goes away. Because membership is so important to our sense of ourselves, whenever we enter a new group the old feelings of hopefulness and anxiety return.

Reader Activity

Some tickets to membership are behavior, wealth, appearance, education, religion, and style. What are the tickets of admission in the following groups?

In your classroom ______________________________

In your club ______________________________

Among your social peers ______________________________

In your family ______________________________

Where you work ______________________________

Where don't you feel accepted that you would like to feel accepted? ______________

____

Why? ______________________________

Do you really lack the ticket, or have you simply assumed you wouldn't be accepted?

____

Sometimes we assume we have the ticket, but we may be wrong. Women attending college assume that they are equal and belong. In 1982, Hall and Sandler conducted a study of classroom climate at 120 colleges and universities. They found considerable difference between the classroom climate for men and that for women.

> **Most faculty want to treat all students fairly and as individuals with particular talents and abilities. However, some faculty may *overtly*—or, more often, *inadvertently*—treat men and women students differently in the classroom and in related situations. Subtle biases in the way teachers behave toward students may seem so "normal" that the particular behaviors which express them often go unnoticed. Nevertheless, these patterns, by which women students are either *singled out* or *ignored* because of their sex, may leave women students feeling less confident than their male classmates about their abilities and their place in the college community.**

A replication of the study (Crawford, 1986) was conducted with a random sample of 31 classes and 627 students at a state university. Students were administered a Student Perception Questionnaire that assessed the dynamics of student/professor interaction in the classroom—the "classroom climate." The most important and pervasive finding of the study was a consistently less positive classroom climate for women. Women reported that they received less praise and encouragement and more negative feedback from instructors, that they participated less than men in class discussions in spite of wanting to participate, and that male instructors were not likely to know them by name.

Reader Activity

On the basis of the Crawford study, Gershenfeld (1990) developed a number of role plays to help students and faculty become aware of the classroom climate and change it.

Is There a Place for Women?

In this role play, a male professor is lecturing on his subject (history or literature). All of the illustrations he cites involve men, and he uses the pronoun *he* generically.

One woman asks whether there were any women novelists or poets in that period (or if women had a role in history).

The professor becomes angry and says, "It seems to me you're being led down the wrong path by those angry feminists in the Women's Studies Department." He says she is "like the Russians who claim they invented the telephone and every other system. You want us to rewrite history and include women. That's revisionist, and it's hardly the truth."

This activity concerns women. Could a similar one apply to Native Americans or African-Americans?

Imagine that you saw this role play, and consider your replies to the following questions:

1. What did you think of the professor? Was he well prepared? A good teacher? What was his attitude toward students?
2. What did you think of the student who asked the question? Was she angry? Militant?
3. Why did he say she must be influenced by angry feminists?
4. Should the student have asked the question?
5. The professor raises the issues of scholarship and integrity. Should he deliberately modify his presentation to include women? Would he be justified in feeling foolish (phony) for including women merely to appease female students?
6. What is the effect of using all male illustrations on the level of aspiration and achievement found in women?
7. What do you think will be the effect of what happened in this classroom?

What could the other students in the class do to enlighten the professor? To)e supportive of the woman who asked the question?

/hat should the student who asked the question do now?

women often think they have the "ticket of admission," but do they? Is the environment the same for them as for men? Are their opportunities the same? Is communication the same? (Consider the recent Aberdeen Army hearings related to sexual harassment or the Lt. Kelley Flynn general discharge from the Air Force on adultery charges. Or the usual university policy restatement related to faculty/student relationships sent to faculty each year.)

A recent study examined whether female corporate directors hold the necessary experience-based characteristics for membership on high-level board committees or whether there is systemic, sex-based bias against them. Examination of the top 300 Fortune 500 firms indicated a pattern of bias that appears to follow traditional sex-typing; that is, committees stereotypically perceived as attending to hard governance issues favored male membership (Bilimoria and Piderit, 1994).

Today, close attention is focused on gender as an issue in work relations and on college campuses.

Relationship of Groups and Membership

We are all members of groups. If we are asked to describe who we are, most of us include information about the groups to which we belong—for example, "I'm a student at Ohio State and a member of the Management Club, Phi Delta Sigma, and hopefully the varsity tennis team" (Tajfel, 1982).

Membership is the relationship between a person and a group of other people. In fact, concepts of membership and groups are so closely related that groups are often defined in terms of members. Here are some properties of groups:

Membership is defined. (It is known who is and who is not a member.)

Members think of themselves as composing a group. (They have a shared identity.)

There is a sense of shared purpose among members.

Members communicate differently with other members than with nonmembers. (You talk differently to someone with whom you share a common identity and purpose than with a stranger.)

Members have expectations for certain ways of behaving in various situations in which the groups finds itself; members will approve or disapprove of another member on the basis of these expectations. (They let you know how you're coming across.) For example, group members always run the risk of group disapproval when they make independent decisions (Carpe[...] Hollander, 1982).

There are leadership policies and roles. (Members need to coordinate eff[...] and maintain conditions for problem solving.)

A status system emerges among members. (There is a hierarchy of worth of the individual to the group; members know how much they are valued and for what.)

No two groups are alike on these dimensions.

Types of Memberships

FORMAL MEMBERSHIP

When we say membership in a group is clearly defined, we are talking about a boundary condition. Dues-paying, card-carrying people are formally recognized as members of a group and defined as falling within the boundary condition. They perceive themselves as part of the club. They have an image of the group and its purposes that is generally shared by the other members.

ASPIRING MEMBERSHIP

Another kind of relationship is that of an *aspiring* member. For years, Tony had been an aspiring member, noting how members dressed and emulating them, trying to talk in their style, practicing golf and tennis as he was "getting ready." Aspiring members are not formally within the boundary of the group. Although they don't have a ticket of admission, they act as though they might get one, and they want to be prepared should the opportunity arise. Consider this example:

> His father had gone to Penn, his mother had gone to Penn, three cousins and an older brother had gone to Penn, and as long as he could remember, he had planned to go to Penn. The family had season tickets to the football games, he always went to Alumni Day, and he followed the news of Penn's progress in sports more avidly than his high school scores. His books had Penn covers, he regularly wore his Penn sweatshirt, and he already knew which were the best dorms on campus. He felt "his" school had made a serious mistake in cutting varsity ice hockey.

would readily admit that he is a junior in high school, not a student body, but that Penn greatly influences his dress style, his aspirations for the future. He frequently feels like a member when [illegible]d the campus in his sweatshirt with his brother, and psychologically [illegible]er. In terms of formal membership, however, he is outside the bound- [illegible] at the present.

[illegible]ARGINAL MEMBERSHIP

In contrast, consider the following situation:

> A senior at Penn is being interviewed for jobs for next year. He doesn't attend the football games or get involved in sports scores. He disdains Penn book covers and sweatshirts—for that matter, any Penn class emblems. He dashes for the train to New York immediately after his last class on Friday. He belongs, he is a member of the University of Pennsylvania student body, but neither the school nor its members influence him to any noticeable degree. He identifies much more with people making it in New York; college is already in the past. He is defined as a *marginal* member.

Consider another illustration. If a person identifies strongly with a political group—let us say, the Democratic party in Pennsylvania—and works to register voters, he or she is much more likely to prefer the Democratic candidates at the next election. This is much more likely than someone who doesn't feel a commitment to the Democratic party even if a registered Democrat (Koch, 1993). Commitment to a group is important; the registered Democrat is a marginal member.

Membership might be thought of as falling within a circle. Those who are actively involved and influenced by members can be viewed as being in the center of the circle. Conceptually, they are centrally involved as high-status members. The marginal member may be seen as within the circle (the boundary) but close to the edge (for example, the Penn senior). The aspiring member is outside the circle. Full psychological membership occurs when a person is positively attracted to membership *and* is positively accepted as a member. When this happens, our individual differences are minimized, and we tend to see ourselves and other members as interchangeable (Turner, 1981). In our earlier illustration, Tony was not a full psychological member because he was not positively accepted as a member, despite his positive attraction toward membership. The others he enviously watched were full psychological members.

Being in a group does not influence a person's entire behavior. Membership may involve only a limited investment, such as membership in a country club, a union, a church group, or a neighborhood association. However, the degree to which people are involved affects both the functioning of the group and its significance for them as members.

Reader Activity

Think of the groups with which you are involved.

In which are you a formal member? ______________________

In which are you a marginal member? ______________________

In which are you an aspiring member? ______________________

What do you understand about your memberships? ______________________

MEMBERSHIP IN THE FORMAL OR INFORMAL ORGANIZATION

Within organizations there are often two memberships: one in the formal organization, in which criteria are usually known; and another in the informal organization. Criteria for membership in the latter are often unstated, and membership rules may support or contradict the rules of the formal organization.

According to its organization chart, the director of a state hospital, the two assistant directors, the medical director, and the business manager make up the director's cabinet. The director invites the others to meet with him weekly for staff meetings. The meetings consist of routine reports of actions taken during the week and scheduling or treatment plans for the coming week.

Only the stranger thinks that decisions are made in this group. Real decisions—on strategies for dealing with various inspection boards, on promotions, on personnel problems, on training, on budget—are made by a different group. This group, which cannot be located as an entity on the organization chart, consists of the director, the director of personnel, a psychiatrist, and a physician (internist). The meetings are held in the office of the director of personnel, usually on Tuesdays in the late afternoon. How did this informal group form? How did its members obtain their power? How does the cabinet feel about this other group?

In organizations there is usually some overlap between those members who have formal membership in the formal decision-making body and those in the informal group that wields decision-making power. Frequently, political maneuverings, power plays, and other covert actions take place within this informal organization.

VOLUNTARY AND NONVOLUNTARY MEMBERSHIP

In speaking of memberships, we are usually considering participation of a voluntary nature—for example, a consumers' union, a drama club, or a professional organization. But other groups—*nonvoluntary* groups—consist of members who have no choice regarding their affiliation. For example, many individuals who are arrested for driving while under the influence of alcohol are assigned to mandatory group psychotherapy treatment programs in mental health centers. Therapy groups composed of individuals who have voluntarily chosen to attend and nonvoluntary therapy groups for individuals convicted of DWI differ sharply.

In the nonvoluntary therapy groups there is a higher level of distrust of the group leader and a lower level of personal self-disclosure and commitment to the group. Nonvoluntary group members usually put the blame for their drinking on their family, friends, or coworkers, so it's hard for them to see any value in being a group member. People who voluntarily join therapy groups, on the other hand, typically think they have a problem and see the group as having real value.

Family-of-origin households are also nonvoluntary groups. Children have no say in who will compose their families; they do not select their parents, siblings, grandparents, cousins, or even boarders. And when divorce and remarriage have occurred, household membership is even further complicated. Children may find themselves living in more than one place with stepparents, stepsiblings, and half-siblings. They may also have biological parents and siblings with whom they don't live. This illustrates how membership types can overlap; a child may be a formal member of a family household composed of siblings, but if he or she visits them only occasionally, she or he is a marginal member in terms of participation. The child is part of these families as a nonvoluntary member who has no say about the composition of the families.

There are myriad reasons aside from birth for membership in nonvoluntary groups. Examples include age and neighborhood (as in tenth-grade English class at West High), a court order (as in a drug group in a rehabilitation program or a prison group), and political turmoil (as in a group of Americans taking refuge in the American embassy prior to a hasty departure related to a government coup d'etat). Compulsory memberships may be nurturing and supporting, or they may be harsh and punitive, as in some prisons.

Why People Join Groups

There is little we can do about compulsory memberships. The real question is why people join the groups they choose to join.

Some people seem to have a stronger need to belong than others; they are joiners. Some evidence suggests that because women score higher than men on tests of sociability, they are more likely to be joiners. To date, no data have proven this hypothesis absolutely. A more predictable factor in motivating joining might simply be that joining is "good business." For example, some eleventh graders are notorious for hastily joining a broad spectrum of high school groups—a ploy for enhancing their images on college applications. In this context, if one membership is good, six are better, and ten with two presidencies will, applicants hope, gain the screening committees' favor. We see the same flurry of group joining among college seniors who will soon be job hunting.

This self-serving approach to group joining was a significant political issue in a mayoral campaign in a large eastern city. One candidate was a member of over forty organizations. The question was raised whether these memberships were for political show or represented personal interests. In the campaign, the candidate's detractors utilized the memberships to castigate him as a dilettante, and they derisively commented that his running for office was just another passing fancy to which he would not commit the time or priority necessary. His advocates used the same memberships to refer to him as a Renaissance Man, a man of broad interests and knowledge, whose familiarity with such a diversity of groups and organizations especially qualified him for the post.

Some people have more direct reasons for joining groups—for example, to meet people and share interests. Imagine a quiet, middle-aged woman not given to small talk who used to find herself alone on weekends and holidays, until someone convinced her that collecting stamps was a good hobby, a way to learn and meet people. Stamps changed her world. To be knowledgeable, she joined stamp groups—first local, then regional, then national, then international. Now there are meetings to go to, friends with whom to talk, conventions and programs on weekends, and international conventions to consider as sites for vacations.

There seem to be three major reasons why people join groups:

1. They like the task or activity of the group. O'Brien and Gross (1981) found that the more connected the individual to the task, the greater the potential for that member's participation in the group.
2. They like the people in the group. Being with people we like is not only a reason for joining social groups but also seems to be the major factor in determining whether a person finds a group experience significant. Stiles found that when a member of a group found a significant other in the group (someone special to him or her), the group experience was a positive one (1973). When we perceive a similarity, such as positive characteristics or attitudes, between us and other members, we are more attracted to that particular group (Compas, 1981; Royal and Golden, 1981). This phenomenon is colloquially known as "birds of a feather flock together."

   Keyton (1988) offers further evidence that as we perceive positive characteristics that we value in others, the attraction to become a group member is generated and bonded. Looking for specific characteristics that engender attraction to a group, she questioned (in written responses) 248 college students enrolled in a basic communication course. Prior to the questioning, the students had participated in several acquaintance activities, after which each student signed up to be a member of a particular student group. In this self-selection process, the students' choice of which group to join was based on "an individual's willingness to work, ability to get along with others, openness to communicate, and similarities of interest and personality" (Keyton, 1988). In this instance, the students joined groups that at least promised the completion of a task.

   People may join an organization initially because of an interest in the task or activity, and then find they enjoy the people as well. Often they will maintain their membership long after their task interests have waned in order to continue to participate in the pleasant personal associations. The reverse situation also occurs. A person may originally join an organization only to please a good friend who is already a member but may later become genuinely interested in the project.
3. Although the group itself does not satisfy the person's needs directly, it is a *means* of satisfying his or her needs. Some early research illuminates the reason for group membership as a means to external satisfactions. Brief observations produce numerous examples. The fledgling lawyer joins an

expensive, prestigious luncheon club because it is a good place to meet prospective clients. Funeral directors are well known for their extensive memberships, because people feel better calling in "one of their own" rather than a stranger at times of sorrow. Other examples include joining a popular activity in the hope of meeting someone to date or joining the PTA as a newcomer in order to meet others about the same age in the neighborhood.

A related reason is that people think that group experience will lead to self-enhancement, that it will be a rewarding experience for them, and they are optimistic about the benefits (Brinthaupt, Moreland and Levine, 1991). With that in mind, a recent Penn graduate may join the Alumni House in New York City. The idea is to get to know some Ivy Leaguers in New York and learn what is appropriate behavior as a fledgling business executive (learn norms for this population rather than college norms).

READER ACTIVITY

How about you? List three groups to which you belong.

1. ______________________________

2. ______________________________

3. ______________________________

For each group, explain why you joined, and why you now continue as a member. What are your main reasons for joining a group?

INDIVIDUAL EXPERIMENT

Choose a group that you belong to, such as a sports team, a club, a political organization, or a fraternity or sorority. Ask several members why they originally joined the group. What were they attracted by? Find out what they like about the group now. You may find that people joined the same group for different reasons, and that their original reasons for joining are not the reasons they continue being members. What did you learn from your interviews that helps you understand these individuals' behavior in the group?

THE BACK EXPERIMENTS

Kurt Back (1951) was intrigued by the following questions: Does *why* a person joins affect the group? Does it make any difference whether the person joins because he or she is interested in the task, because she or he likes the other people, or because the group is a means to meeting his or her needs? If it makes a difference, how? What kind of difference?

Back designed a series of experiments to get answers to these questions. He arbitrarily paired subjects but told them that, on the basis of previous tests of personality and other measures, they had a special relationship to each other. He told some pairs that their personalities were similar and that they would have a great deal in common (the "liking" condition). He told other pairs that they had common goal interests in the project (the "interest in task" condition). In the third grouping, he told each of the partners that the other would be an important person to know and could be influential (the group as a "means to" condition).

The results indicated that why a person joins does make a difference in the functioning of the group. Those primarily attracted as friends interacted at a personal level; they had long conversations, were pleasant to each other, and expected to have an effect on each other. In those groups attracted primarily by the task, members wanted to complete it quickly and efficiently. They discussed only those matters they thought relevant to achieving their goals. In those groups attracted by potential prestige from membership, members acted cautiously, concentrated on their own actions, and in general were careful not to risk their status. When there were none of these bases of attraction, members of a pair acted independently and with little consideration of each other. The Back experiments lead to the generalization that the nature of group life varies with different sources of attraction (Lang, 1977).

Multiple Memberships

As members, we bring our own interests, values, and personalities to groups. Each membership in a different group creates a unique mix of perceptions, communication patterns, and group values for the individual. Membership involves a give-and-take between the individual and the group, and because we are involved in numerous groups, the impact of multiple memberships is quite complex.

The multiplicity can carry with it a number of assets. There is the acquisition of transferable experiences based on skills obtained in different kinds of groups. For example, sitting on one university committee allows someone to learn the complicated procedures required to arrange for use of a room for a program, procedures that are thereafter simpler when making arrangements for another event for another committee. There is the possibility of expediting what someone needs to do. For example, knowing someone from one context enables one to make a phone call to check for information or possibilities for action, rather than writing a formal letter. (The often cynical comment "It's not what you know, but whom you know" is based in large part on the access we have to persons in positions of power through knowing them in another context—another example of formal and informal organizations.) A group can often accomplish its objectives more rapidly because of those contacts. There have been a number of studies pointing out that memberships on prestigious community boards are held by a small number of citizens of the community (Klein, 1968). When boards are made up of family or friends, the members find it easy to conduct business as personal relationships. Pervasive fears of acceptance have been dealt with previously and have been satisfactorily resolved. Multiple memberships can even be a source of creativity and innovation when a diverse group comes together to search for a mutually agreeable solution to a problem, as in the following example:

After decades of redevelopment, residents of a large metropolitan area stayed away in droves from a restored neighborhood with housing and quaint shops. Both the business associations and the city were frantic for a gimmick to bring people (and business) to the redeveloped historic area. One idea was to bring together representatives of the mother churches in the area, and have them plan a heritage week or festival. Each church and synagogue had spawned others in the metropolitan area, and the heritage festival might be a method for bringing suburbanites in for the activities. It was hoped that the special events (dancing, cooking, demonstrations) would also induce the nonreligious populations to have a look.

Each of the struggling groups was so delighted by the opportunity for publicity for their special quality, so encouraged by the funding for a festival, and so revitalized at the prospect of a heritage festival, which had been beyond their provincial dreams, that they vowed (individually and collectively) to produce a festival that would long be remembered. The first meeting of two representatives of each of the religious organizations began with most of them not knowing each other, but they were committed to the prospect of creating an event. Enthusiasm ran high. Diversity was the key to the excitement. Ideas tumbled over ideas as the initial meeting ran until two in the morning.

The diversity of memberships enhanced what they had to offer, and the heritage festival committee viewed themselves as creating an historic experience.

> **FOCUS ON DIVERSITY**
>
> Keep in mind that a goal to which group members are highly committed bridges major differences.

Multiple memberships coexist in each of us. We may be members of a family, a neighborhood association, a religious organization, a PTA, a tennis group, a professional association, and a faculty journal club. Usually these memberships coexist peacefully in a person's life. Sometimes, though, conflict arises among them.

CONFLICTS OF MULTIPLE MEMBERSHIP

Generally, people do not join organizations or groups with conflicting norms or values. A person is not likely to be a member of the National Association of Manufacturers and also a member of the Socialist party, nor of the Catholic church and the Abortion Rights Lobby, nor of the Ku Klux Klan and the Southern Baptist Christian Leadership. But sometimes membership conflicts are unavoidable. A businessperson who believes that survival and eventual success depend on taking advantage of every situation may be uncomfortable on Sundays in church when the minister preaches about ethical behavior. He or she may resolve this discomfort by not going to church, changing business practices, or compartmentalizing memberships—engaging on weekdays in one kind of behavior that is appropriate in the business world and on Sunday in another kind of behavior that is compatible with Christian ethics.

Some multiple memberships result in conflicts that present serious problems, where the dilemmas created cannot be resolved with satisfaction. Adolescence is a time when membership in the peer group often conflicts with membership in the family. Conflict between adolescent peers and the family has become so common that it warrants its own term, the *generation gap*. Conflicts of multiple membership can also occur within large organizations in which an individual is often a member of several subgroups. Conflicts can emerge between subgroups, or one subgroup can be in conflict with the larger organization. In college you may be a member of the baseball team, which is planning its victory celebration in the dormitory, as well as a member of the student council, which is accountable to the university for maintaining dormitory policy and rules.

Yet another kind of multiple membership conflict is common when a committee is composed of representatives of subordinate groups. For example,

> A new college moves into an old private-school campus in a quiet residential neighborhood. The college wants to add additional parking lots, arrange

zoning variances for a new classroom building, and widen roads within the campus. It holds a community meeting to discuss the changes. Present at the meeting are a minister and two members of his congregation from the church across the street, who are eager for the college to have additional parking lots so the church might use them on Sundays. Representatives of the neighbors' association come to build good relations with the new college. They are hoping to sponsor joint community lectures and programs with the college and to convince the college to create and staff a child-care facility. A group of neighbors from across the street arrives *en masse* to oppose parking changes on the street. Other community residents representing various educational and philanthropic organizations come to express support for the new college, which they see as an asset to the community.

This mixed group will argue long and loud. It embodies many conflicting interests and perspectives. The conflicts create intrapersonal dilemmas as individuals vacillate between subordinate groups and the one being forged by the current discussion.

One group of researchers (Schwartz, Eberle, and Moscato, 1973) found that "individuals with high group awareness tended to be less successful in problem solving in an *ad hoc* problem solving environment than groups of individuals with low group awareness." That is, maintaining the links took energy from the present situation.

A group expends energy in activity on the task as well as on interpersonal relations. Devoting increased activity to one aspect (interpersonal relations) means less energy remains for the task. (For further discussion, see Chapter 9 on Bales, Interaction Process Analysis.)

The resolution of conflicts generated by multiple membership is often attained at great personal cost and with much anxiety. Often these conflicts are resolved in accordance with the standards of the group that are most salient at the moment. Individuals may struggle to focus on the organization they represent at the meeting, which puts them at odds with developing opinion. Thus property owners who have come to protect their streets from overparking might hear themselves cast as the "bad guys" as the college representatives marshal support for their plans.

Reader Activity

On a separate sheet of paper, list ten groups in which you have membership. List at least one conflict each membership can produce for another membership.

How do you resolve these differences?

Individual Experiment

Talk with an adolescent about his or her group of friends. Find out what behavior, values, and attitudes are held in common by the group. Do they all dress alike? Listen to the same music? Go to the same places? Ask the young person what his or her parents expect of him or her at home. (If you don't know any adolescents, write down a list from your own experiences when you were that age.) Chances are you will see some disparities between the membership demands of these two important reference groups.

Reference Groups

Of the many groups to which people belong, which are most important to them? Which influence how they typically feel about things? To which do their attitudes most closely relate? Those groups an individual selects as his or her *reference groups* are the ones whose influence he or she is willing to accept. Consider the following illustration:

An African-American college student has pledged for fifteen weeks prior to admission to a prestigious African-American national fraternity. The final ordeal, which determines whether he is serious in desiring membership, requires that he submit to having his head shaved as a reminder of what slaves endured. There are no exceptions.

Tough dilemma. Would you want to "fit in" or hold onto your dignity?

The key issue is how much membership in the fraternity means to him. He needs to decide. Either answer is "right."

Reference groups have been described as serving two distinct functions. An individual uses such a group to (1) compare himself or herself in making judgments and evaluations and (2) set the norms to which he or she conforms. Both of these functions may be served by the same group. People's reference groups may greatly influence their attitudes toward themselves and may affect their relationships with other groups (Dolcini and Adler, 1994). If the student in the foregoing example chooses to have his head shaved in order to join the fraternity, he is acknowledging the comparison function of the fraternity as a reference group. If he joins the fraternity and over time conforms to its values and standards of behavior, he is responding to the normative function of the fraternity as a reference group.

Some recent research indicates that organizational managers and nonmanagers differ in the number of memberships they hold (Carrol and Teo, 1996). Managers belonged to more clubs and societies, and had larger core discussion networks and more people with whom they had close or intimate ties. Moreover, these membership differences between managers and nonmanagers remained significant even after differences for education, age, gender, and ethnicity were controlled. It seems that managers join groups extensively to compare themselves with other managers in making judgments and evaluations and to establish managerial norms for their organizations.

Interestingly, studies show that people with strong ties to a reference group often judge their personal situations to be satisfactory but the group's general situation to be *un*satisfactory. That is, when a group is compared to the self (rather than the self to the group), it is the *group* that suffers by comparison with respect to overall well-being. In this way, reference groups have a significant impact on the shaping of social attitudes (Crosby and Clayton, 1986).

For example, a person with a strong commitment to his or her church may feel he or she is a religious, spiritual person. If the person sees membership and attendance at the church declining, and deficits growing bigger annually, he or she may then help recruit new members, contribute more funds, and attend more meetings to help the church survive.

THE ACTUAL GROUP

In a given group, only some people function as referents, those whom individuals attempt to influence and who in turn influence them. Each member decides who "makes sense," who seems to be in touch with reality as the member sees it, and with whom he or she can identify. These few—perhaps only eight to ten in a group of thirty (and even their composition may change over time)—represent the effective, or actual, group for that person. It is they who influence him or her, and it is they to whom he or she can relate.

THE GROUP WE REPRESENT

There are two levels of reference groups in this concept. At one level are the groups that appoint or elect a member to represent them in another group. A faculty member is appointed by his or her department to represent that department on the university senate; representatives of neighborhoods are elected to sit on the community mental health advisory board; condominium owners select their representatives to the resident council. Here, the group the person represents is thought of as "his" or "her" group, which he or she must speak for, fight for, and defend. In defending his or her group, the representative believes or comes to believe that the group's approach and perspective are his or her own. The representative strives for goals that favor his or her group—these are his or her vested interests. As a member relates to the group he or she represents, it becomes a reference group.

At another level are the groups a member represents when he or she is not officially designated to do so. For example, in a classroom discussion belittling the value of fraternities, a member may feel compelled to enter the discussion in heated terms. Some say that when people defend their vested interests almost blindly, it is because these groups are important reference groups in their lives. Another theory holds that the defense occurs when people are anxious about their membership in that group; they defend the group to assure themselves that they do belong and that belonging is indeed worthwhile. In both cases, people react to the actual group as well as to the group they represent (formally or subjectively). The group they represent influences their behavior.

Who are those subjective groups that serve as our reference groups beyond those we formally represent? They are all those past and present groups of which we have been a part. We "rubberband" or flash back to them constantly. All the groups we belonged to in our past are present within us. Some are readily identifiable by skin color, sex, language, and dress, and others are revealed as a discussion or topic collides and triggers one of them. Subjective may be classified as abstracted groups, hangover groups, and fantasied groups.

THE ABSTRACTED GROUP

Abstracted groups are the groups that greatly influenced us when we still accepted our parents', teachers', leaders', and employers' words unquestioningly. For example, our experience might have left us with the notions that lenient and materially giving parents are caring and sensitive to their children's needs; that stern, "no-nonsense" teachers accomplish the most in a classroom; that verbal, articulate people tend to be charismatic leaders; and that strict, authoritarian employers are inclined to be very efficient. These are concepts that we have *abstracted* from past experiences and that greatly influence our current behavior in groups.

We run into difficulties, however, when stereotypic truths, as abstracted from our mostly forgotten models, come into conflict with the actual values of a group we are in. For instance, a senior group member may reactivate the notion of the caring and sensitive parent in a younger group member. But when that "parent" figure displays behavior that is obnoxious and callous, the younger member might feel an urgent need to vent emotions that temporarily distract and derail the group's goal. Or a member might have an abstracted sense of leadership that sharply contrasts with the group's true leader, thus generating conflict that could actually destroy the group.

When values abstracted from these forgotten groups come into conflict with the values of the current group, re-examination is necessary: How was the situation then similar to the situation at present? How is the situation now different from that earlier one? What were the objectives then? What are they now? How was the group composed then? Who is in it now?

THE HANGOVER GROUP

Unresolved membership anxieties and problems in important reference groups may be continuously dealt with in other groups. For example, the child who was the "little brother" or "little sister" in the family—the last to be heard, the most frequently disregarded, the one given almost no responsibility—may in other groups strive continually for leadership as proof of his or her competence. Or, conversely, that person may be very antileadership, rebelling against any authority in retaliation for all the times he or she could not "talk back" as a child.

Some feel that many of the problems of leadership are not legitimate problems of the actual group but are rather *hangovers* from previous groups—for example, unresolved family conflicts. A hangover group can influence the behavior of members consciously or unconsciously.

THE FANTASIED GROUP

This is the kind of group that may give a person the emotional support he or she definitely needs but is not receiving in the present actual group.

A person who has read some legal materials on an issue may fantasize himself or herself presenting the data not as a lay member to fellow members but logically and convincingly to a panel of three judges. Consultants who may know nothing about an organization sometimes come in and fantasize that they are the ultimate authorities on any problems of organization, because they have taught organizational theory in their classes for years. With just a few minutes of background, they handle a serious problem with the aplomb of a professor answering a student question. Other consultants fantasize themselves speaking with graduate students rather than with clients; they theorize or discuss situations in ivory-tower terms rather than coming to grips with the practical realities of the situation.

When people do not accept the actual group and address their behavior to it, they will use some other group or mixture of groups, or even a constructed group, to meet their needs for emotional support. Some people, when gently reminded or prodded, may recognize that they are indeed addressing their behavior to groups other than the actual persons present; to others these groups remain hidden in their subconscious.

In summary, it is evident that there are actual groups that influence us and to which we address our behavior. However, when there is a perplexing situation in the actual group, it is as though we are caught in the web of overlapping memberships. Which membership (real, past, abstracted, fantasied) should guide our behavior? Which one should we use in this instance? Memberships that overlap for us at a particular time are the ones that have special salience for us in that situation. Those cues in the present situation that remind us of another situation and affect our response give us clues about membership roles in which we are anxious.

It even seems that there is a hierarchy of reference groups, because whenever a decision is reached in an overlapping or conflicted membership situation, membership in some groups is enhanced at the expense of membership in others.

Factors Increasing Attractiveness of Membership

The lifeblood of a group is its members; they are the resources through which goals are accomplished. The satisfaction of the members, the degree to which they feel accepted, and the degree to which they want to return are critical to the survival of the group. Accordingly, one of the objectives of a group is to create cohesiveness. Cohesion is the attraction the group holds for its members; the greater the attractiveness, the higher the cohesion.

One variable that increases members' attraction to a group is a correlation between individual goals and group goals. In a study that examined these factors, Wright and Duncan (1986) found that "attraction to group and group cohesiveness were both related to individual outcome." Thus, the conformity of the group goals with individual members' goals increases the group's attractiveness and cohesiveness.

Excerpts from a graduate student's paper on her experience in a group may serve as an illustration of the growth of cohesiveness in a group.

> My first encounter with the group made me feel uncomfortable. I realized that I was older than most of the group members, and felt that I did not have too much in common with them. Because of my previous life experiences, I felt I

> had already dealt with conflict, decision making, and not being part of the "in group" more frequently than most of my peers in the class. I kept in mind, first and foremost, my purpose for being in the group—it was to successfully complete the course requirement of being in a group, nothing else. . . .
>
> My relationship with the group grew from one of skepticism in the beginning to total involvement with the group in a very short time. The skepticism was the result of fear of the unknown. Was I going to be accepted by my peers in the group? Quite early in our group relations it became apparent to me that most of the group had the same fears. It also became apparent quite early that the people in the group were warm, friendly people, although initially they didn't look that way. I found some group members more appealing to me than others, but I can say with pride that I know each member and can work with them. I also believe each of us would also say it—not one person in our group was absent all term, and several times when class ended we were the last to leave. Who would think that I would ever say I love that group? It has been one of the best experiences in my life.

Generally, we know that the attractiveness of a group can be increased if members (or potential members) are aware that they can fulfill their needs by belonging to that group. Because it is difficult to change the members' needs, the more feasible approach is to emphasize the properties that meet members' needs or the gains to be derived from belonging. Let's look at some of the properties that increase group attractiveness.

PRESTIGE

The more prestige a person has within a group, or the more that appears to be obtainable, the more he or she will be attracted to the group (Aronson and Linder, 1965; Kelley, 1951). People who are placed in a position of authority over others are more attracted to the group than those low in authority, and they show more ingroup favoritism (Vleeming, 1983). This is especially true of those in authority who expect to remain in that position. For example, the group or organization will be attractive to a principal who is appointed "for life," to army officers who may be promoted but are rarely demoted, or to chief executives who are appointed and remain in that position until a bigger executive position is available.

However, those in a position of high authority who may be demoted to one of low authority are attracted to a lesser degree. Those of low authority who expect to remain in that position are not attracted to the group. The shipping clerk, the member of the telephone squad, and the "envelope licker" are not attracted. Yet those of low authority who envision being moved up can also find the group attractive—for example, telephone squad members who see themselves as potential officers or committee chairpersons.

Imagine a questionnaire being passed around to a group in which members are asked to rank members on importance to the group. Suppose also that a questionnaire is distributed in which each member is asked how attracted he or she is to the group, on a scale from 0 (not attracted) to 10 (highly attracted). It is likely that when the data are tabulated and analyzed, results will indicate that those seen as most valued or most important in the group will be those who are most attracted to it. It follows that when we feel our ideas are listened to and acted upon, we are more attracted to the group.

GROUP CLIMATE

The more group members perceive other members as being committed to the group and compatible with one another, the more attractive the group will be (Piper, 1983; Spears, Lea, and Lee, 1990). A cooperative relationship is more attractive than one that is competitive (Deutsch, 1959; Deutsch et al., 1967). If a group works together as a team to develop a product (or outcome), and if it will be evaluated on the basis of a team effort, the members will be more friendly toward one another than in a competitive situation. However, when members are rated on the basis of individual performance, there are fewer interpersonal relationships, more withholding of information or failure to volunteer information, and fewer influence attempts.

The Deutsch cooperation studies are classic; more recently, Worchel, Andreoli, and Folger (1977) directly tested the hypothesis that cooperation leads to increased attractiveness of members for a group. The findings were significant for understanding cohesiveness. Among the groups whose members competed with each other, those who were successful found the group more attractive, and those who failed reported less attraction. For groups that cooperated, both success and failure increased intergroup attraction. Rosenfield, Stephan, and Lucker (1981) also looked at the attractiveness of cooperative and competitive groups. They found that competent group members are more valued in cooperative situations because they increase the group's chances for success. Incompetent group members fared better in competitive groups, where their performance had little effect on others' success.

DEGREE OF INTERACTION AMONG MEMBERS

More interaction among members may increase the attractiveness of a group (Herndon and Mikulas, 1996; Good, 1971; Homans, 1950). Participating in give-and-take with members, getting to know some of the others, making some good friends—these by-products of membership make a group more attractive. Being a member increases contact with people who are liked, offers an opportunity to know them better, and allows for real chances for clarification in influencing and being influenced.

Looking at the effectiveness of training psychotherapists in a group setting, Aronson (1990) reported that creative insights into the psychoanalytic process appear more often because of the presence of a leader *plus* the group members. What this means is that the leader alone doesn't effect insights. Rather, members of the group expressing their analysis of the experience promote insights, which generate more understanding. In turn, this more in-depth understanding of the psychoanalytic process raises the level of the interaction between group members and the leader, thus increasing the attraction to the group for its benefits: fuller understanding of the psychoanalytic process.

Davis (1984) found that the geographic distance a member had to travel to meetings had no significant effect on attraction to the group, but that attraction was high toward a similar-attitude group and low toward a dissimilar-attitude group. Similarly, Brown (1985) found that members were most likely to participate in an organization they considered compatible with themselves. And he stressed that an organization must embody participatory democratic principles if it is to obtain and sustain members' participation.

Although pleasing interaction increases the attractiveness of group membership, if the interaction is unpleasant (if members disregard or bore each other, or if there are members who are considered repulsive), attraction to membership will decrease (Amir, 1969; Aronson, 1970; Festinger, 1957).

Members' ethnicity also influences people's attraction to a group. Examining relationships between African-American and white sixth graders in intergroup cooperation, Johnson and Johnson (1985) reported that there was more cross-ethnic social interaction where African-American and white groups cooperated than in groups where they competed with each other. Furthermore, they found that minority subjects responded more positively to cooperative group experiences and showed more satisfaction in their group's work than did majority subjects.

SIZE

As most of us have experienced, the size of a group greatly influences our attraction to it. Smaller groups are likely to be more attractive than large ones (Wicker, 1969). In a small group it is easier to get to know the other members, discover similar interests, share dedication to the cause, and have a sense of being a significant participant. As a group increases in membership there is a corresponding heterogeneity of interests. Members' feelings toward each other become less personal, concern with the "cause" is often less intense, and there is a reduction in the degree of individual participation, intimacy, and involvement (Lindeman and Koskela, 1994; Tsouderos, 1955).

RELATIONSHIP TO OTHER GROUPS

Relationships with other groups or subgroups are also a factor in attractiveness. When groups performed several judgment tasks, for example, then were asked to evaluate members, they expressed considerable favoritism. Ratings for ingroup members were significantly more positive than those for outgroup members (Abele and Petzold, 1996). Being "one of us" influenced the evaluations.

In addition, groups are more likely to agree with an ingroup speaker than with an outgroup speaker (McGarty, Haslam, and Hutchinson, 1994).

Groups are also more attractive if their position improves with respect to other groups. A group that had been all but disregarded in its efforts to create parent awareness of alienated adolescents, for example, suddenly became valued when the governor invited the group to participate with him at a televised news conference. Not only was the group deemed more prestigious to "the outside world" (as a group), and also it enhanced individual membership, but membership also increased in attractiveness for the individual members.

Relationships with other groups are further complicated when considering ingroup and outgroup minority influences on membership (Martin, 1992). On many campuses, fraternities and sororities used to limit membership to certain categories of people—Christian, or white, or jocks or brains. Later, a "cocenter" image evolved; that is, not to be stereotyped and to add African-American members and/or Jewish members. Internally, how does the majority in the house relate to new minority members? Externally, what is the effect on coalitions with other houses or social functions with them?

SUCCESS

The maxim that nothing succeeds like success applies to groups also. People are more inclined to join groups or continue as members in groups that are successful. We even have language to express this pervasive phenomenon: BIRGing (basking in reflected glory).

When a sports team wins more games, membership on that team is more attractive. We need only briefly watch the pandemonium of a winning team after a close game to understand what winning does to enhance membership. After a big game, the hugging, champagne dousing, embracing, and dancing are all signs of being part of winning teams.

It isn't only sports teams that enjoy winning, though. A charity group whose fund raising concert was successful and who raised even more money than anticipated has little difficulty inspiring its members to "do even better" next year. They are able to recount how they were a terrific team who pulled it off against great odds. As they congratulate each other on how well they did and for what each contributed to the success, they decide again that they will continue to work for the organization; now the cause is even more important than before. Because they have been successful, they agree that they are winners. They then become more satisfied with other members and with the task. They know they have the resources in members and the skills to be successful—and consequently they are even more attracted to the group (Mullen and Cooper, 1994; Keyton, 1989; Meir, Keinan, and Segal, 1986).

Even if, in an experimental condition, members are told that their unit is *potentially* successful, the group takes on new prestige and members are more attracted to it.

It is interesting to note that if a person desires membership that is difficult to obtain, he or she will value the membership more than if it were easy (Aronson and Mills, 1959). As if to reduce internal dissonance, he or she thinks, "This membership has to be worth it for me to go through such an ordeal—of course it's worth it—it's a great group—I'm lucky to be a member" (Festinger, 1957).

There is no evidence, however, that the same situation prevails if someone does not desire membership. Then the difficulty of the ordeal simply becomes another reason why the membership is unattractive.

FEAR AND STRESS

Under experimental conditions, when group members were in a situation that made them fearful, they preferred to be with others; and the opportunity to be with others rather than alone increased the attractiveness of the group. When other subjects were also in an anxiety-provoking situation, subjects were also more likely to choose to be with the others who were anxious (or fearful) about the same thing, thus providing an opportunity for "social comparison" of their feelings (Nelson and Harris, 1995; Buck and Parke, 1972; Dutton and Aron, 1974; Morris, 1976; Smith, Smythe, and Lien, 1972).

Children in border settlements in Israel reported rushing to the bomb shelters at the first sound of attack and being comforted by seeing the familiar faces of adults and other children at the entrance. They already felt less frightened; being with the others felt good. Londoners reported similar experiences in the underground during the bombings of World War II.

And it isn't just wars and bombings. Research evidence indicates that subjects aroused by hunger, sexual stimuli, negative evaluations, or danger seek out others to be with.

Consider now the situation of Mexican-American adolescents making the decision of whether to join a gang. Schools frame gang membership as antisocial behavior, banning gang colors and the flashing of gang signs. But alternatives to gangs have not been effective; gang membership seems to be increasing. Why? One theory is that membership in gangs helps resist assimilation and retain a culture devalued by the American public school (Calabrese and Noboa, 1995; Joe and Chesney-Lind, 1995).

Sime (1983) had a rare opportunity to investigate the way people affiliate with each other in a crisis. He studied people fleeing a large public building that was on fire. On the basis of his observations, he predicted that in a situation of potential danger, individuals will not only be concerned with their safety but will also be motivated to make contact with group members with whom they have some psychological ties. In the burning building, family members sought each other and tried to adopt an optimal strategy for group survival. This finding contrasts with the panic model, which assumes that individuals in danger are concerned with self-preservation alone and will compete with each other for limited exits.

Individual Experiment

Choose a group that you belong to and ask another member the following questions in order to determine his or her level of attraction to the group. Do you find group members cooperative or competitive? Do you feel you have something in common with other group members? Do you feel that you get ample opportunity to say what you think in the group and that others listen to you? Do you feel valued by the group? Are group members generally open and trusting with each other? Is the group successful? These questions cover the general factors that make a group attractive to its members. If you receive positive replies to these questions, you can surmise that the individual likes and is attracted to the group.

Factors Decreasing Attractiveness of Membership

When does a group become less cohesive? When is membership less attractive so that people prefer to leave? Members will leave when the reasons for their initial attraction no longer exist (e.g., the people they joined to be with have left); when their own needs or satisfactions are reduced (a member of the Scout parents committee when their child leaves Scouts); or when the group becomes less suitable as a means for satisfying existing needs (a young lawyer joins a political party committee and later is appointed to the district attorney's staff; she resigns from the party committee because such membership is frowned on). Members may also leave when the group acquires unpleasant properties, such as a diminished reputation, constant fighting among members, or an activist stand with which they disagree.

Sometimes membership changes brought on by dissatisfaction with the group can actually transform the organization. The American Psychological Association, the professional association for psychologists in the United States, serves as a good example. Until about 1973, the APA was dominated by "academics," those psychologists who taught at universities; practitioners and clinicians were made to feel like second-class members. Many psychologists in clinical practice even wondered why they should bother belonging to the APA, inasmuch as it did not meet their needs. But since 1973, as the number of psychologists grew but the number of university openings diminished, practitioners came to make up the majority of the APA membership. Nowadays, the academics still want the focus of the professional association to be on research and teaching. But the practitioners want the association to deal with their problems: malpractice insurance, state licensing, and building client populations.

Similarly, Mangan reported in 1987 that academic- and research-oriented psychologists were dropping out of the American Psychological Association in increasing numbers, feeling that the group no longer served their interests. Membership in the APA was then at an all-time high, but old-time members mumbled that they didn't recognize the organization anymore, so drastically had it changed. Much effort has been spent drafting a reorganization proposal to maintain both memberships.

It is possible to be less and less attracted to the group but still to remain in it. A group can retain its members when attraction is at the zero or near-zero level. But in such situations, the group is inactive and has little influence over its members; the members in turn provide little internal support for each other or the organization. Members in this category—in conceptual terms, borderline members—are pushed over (and out) when the precarious balance is disturbed, such as when the meeting time is changed or dues are raised even a small amount.

Research findings indicate that groups can lose their attractiveness for several reasons:

1. A group disagrees on how to solve a group problem. Some will walk away from the discussion or not attend the meetings at which such a problem is on the agenda; others withdraw by working on private problems or become "turned off." Members may sense real personal frustration in such instances, and the group is viewed as a source for precipitating feelings of personal inadequacy and impotency.
2. If the group makes unreasonable or excessive demands on people, or if people feel inadequate in the group situation, the group is less attractive and they will leave (Wann, Weaver and Davis, 1992; Horowitz et al., 1953). If people are assigned a job that is too difficult for them (such as arranging a program) or if people feel inadequate in the group situation (which requires their giving verbal reports at meetings when they feel inadequate as speakers), the group will be less attractive and they will leave, often without stating or being fully aware of their reasons.
3. Groups that have members who are too dominating or who exhibit other unpleasant behaviors reduce the attractiveness of the group.
4. Staff conferences in which there is a high degree of self-oriented behavior are viewed as less attractive to the staff (Fouriezos, Hutt, and Geutzkow, 1950). Members who dominate the discussion, and thus severely limit the opportunities for participation by others, reduce attractiveness.
5. Some memberships may limit the satisfactions a person can receive from activities outside the group. For example, women in some religious groups are not permitted to drink, dance, wear make-up, or wear short skirts. Membership in such groups clearly limits satisfactions that might be derived from going to dances or being stylish. Police officers on rotating weekly shifts and nurses on night duty are also limited in their outside activities.
6. Negative evaluation of membership in a group by people outside the group (which gives the group low status) also reduces attractiveness of the group (Lee and Ottati, 1995). Being a member of the school discipline committee is not a sought-after appointment because of the reactions of peers to members of such committees.
7. Competition among groups also reduces attractiveness unless people have reason to believe they will be with the "winners."
8. People will leave one group to join another if the second is better able to meet their needs or if they have limited time for participation. For example, members may belong to an organization and then move to an-

other part of the same city, in which case they may join a branch of the organization closer to their new home. Or they may instead join a similar, but different, organization because they are moving and planning new relationships.

9. If individuals are "scapegoated" (unjustly blamed for negative events), they come to view those who attribute responsibility for failure to them less favorably. They come to see those members as less competent and less cooperative. They identify less with the group and come to feel like outsiders. This psychological process soon leads to the actual process of separation (Shaw and Breed, 1970).
10. If members in an organization are faced with stringent demands from their superiors, the members have a tendency either to seek or to establish a secondary membership within the organization's "underlife." Members retreat to a symbolic "crawlspace" within the group at large (Ingram, 1986). Furthermore, organizations that tend to lump all participants together fail to offer members enough opportunities to establish separate identities within this necessary crawlspace. Thus, both strict leadership and the failure to provide opportunities for members to participate in an institutional underlife reduce group attractiveness.

Attractiveness of Membership and Group Success

What difference does cohesiveness make? How a group functions depends on how attractive it is to its members. This is reflected in the energy members expend on reaching their goal, how easily they attain it, and how satisfying the outcome will be. There is evidence to suggest people who are attracted to membership are more likely to accept the responsibilities of membership (Dion, Miller, and Magnan, 1970). Cohesive groups that value membership status are especially productive if they are also motivated to do the task well (Hall, 1971; Landers and Crum, 1971). However, the cultural context of a group influences the members' view of its tasks.

Consider how culture can give a stronger sense of "what is right" than majority group opinion, but that groups usually aren't aware of this.

For example, Zander (1983) observed that the "Japanese work for their group's good, while Americans work for their personal good." Thus an American might be drawn to a group that provides help or autonomy for the individual, whereas a Japanese person might be drawn to the group whose purpose is to provide help and autonomy for the group (Zander, 1983). Furthermore, working for a group goal seems to be such a strong driving force in Japanese culture that group members will even deviate from majority behavior when such deviant behavior promotes a desired group outcome (Kouhara, 1990).

If a group is attractive, members are more likely to participate, which in turn increases their liking of the group (Koomen, 1988). Furthermore, attracted members will change their minds more often to take the view of fellow members.

In conclusion, increased understanding of membership factors can help us be more aware of them in groups and can thereby increase our opportunities and abilities to be more effective. It also enhances the possibilities for success of the groups with which we are concerned.

EXERCISE 1 An Experience in Building Membership

OBJECTIVES

- To build a group beginning with a dyad
- To experience the dynamics of membership building
- To understand that sharing information and our own identities is an effective way to build a group and boost commitment to it

RATIONALE

Typically we enter groups alone, feeling anxious about being newcomers. Pairing with someone we don't know reduces our sense of isolation and breaks up existing subgroups.

ACTION

(Time: 30 min.) The facilitator explains that groups will be working to solve some tasks. Then he or she asks each member to "pair with someone you don't know."

The dyads are instructed to discuss with each other the following questions, which are listed on the board:

What is your name?

What is one thing that keeps you busy?

What is one thing you are enjoying about your life?

What is one thing you are proud of in yourself?

What are two groups you identify with (gender, class, race, etc.)?

They begin by focusing on one person. At the end of fifteen minutes, the facilitator announces time, and the other person becomes the focus of attention. At the end of one-half hour, the facilitator

- asks each dyad to join two other pairs to become a group of six.
- asks one member of each pair to introduce his or her partner, adding two points about the person learned during the previous conversation.

After they are introduced in this way, the partners can comment on what was said. Then they in turn introduce their partners, making points they learned in the preceding conversation.

The facilitator asks the entire group, "What do you want from this workshop or experience?" and allows ten minutes for discussion of objectives.

DISCUSSION

The facilitator asks the dyads,

Why did the exercise begin with the discussion questions?

How do you feel about your group?

After discussing these questions, the dyads report on their answers.

VARIATION

This exercise can be done in triads as well as dyads.

Exercise 2 Reference Groups: "Who Am I?"

In social categorization people are not seen as individuals but are thought of as a "category," i.e. old, or Latino, or Catholic.

OBJECTIVES

- To understand reference groups
- To understand priorities within reference groups
- To recognize that we view reference groups subjectively

MATERIALS

"Who Am I?" sheets

SETTING

The group is divided into groups of three to five.

ACTION

"Who Am I?" sheets are distributed to each member. The facilitator asks each person to read and follow the instructions.

"WHO AM I?"

We can all describe ourselves in many ways. How would you describe yourself?

Write ten different answers to the question "Who Am I?" in the space provided below.[1]

Who Am I?

1. ______________________________
2. ______________________________
3. ______________________________
4. ______________________________
5. ______________________________
6. ______________________________
7. ______________________________
8. ______________________________
9. ______________________________
10. ______________________________

1. This exercise is adapted from an exercise in the Life Planning Workshop developed by Herbert Shepard of Yale University.

You may choose to answer, for example, in terms of the roles and responsibilities you have in life or in terms of groups you belong to and beliefs you hold. Try to list those things that are really important to your sense of yourself—things that, if you lost them, would make a radical difference in your identity and the meaning of life for you.

Silent, individual reflection is necessary while you perform this task. Continue by following the instructions in the Identity Review.

IDENTITY REVIEW

Consider each item in your "Who Am I?" list separately. Try to imagine how it would be if that item no longer applied to you. (For example, if "husband" or "wife" is one of the items, what would the end of your marriage mean to you? How would you feel? What would you do? What would your life be like?) After reviewing each item in this way, rank the items in the list by putting a number in the box to the right of each item. Put 1 beside the item that is most essential to your sense of yourself and whose loss would require the greatest adjustment. Put 10 beside the item that is least essential to your sense of yourself. Rank all items in this way; do not give any items a tying rank. Do not rank items in accordance with how much you like them but only in accordance with how great the adjustment would be if you lost them. Some aspects of yourself that you dislike might be very hard to give up!

SHARING

Group members share the experiences in these exercises with the rest of the group. No members should be forced to share their lists, and no one *can* be forced to share all their thoughts and feelings, but participants should be as open as possible. Members who are willing to share their lists can take the initiative, describing their experiences and inviting comments, questions, and comparison.

EXERCISE 3 Factors Influencing Attractiveness of Membership

OBJECTIVES

- To understand personal sources of attraction in a group
- To become aware of and experience the problems of having new members in a group
- To become aware that changed membership in a group influences not only relationships with new members but also the relationships of older members with one another
- To understand that changed membership influences sources of attraction to the group
- To understand that increasing the size of a group has disadvantages as well as advantages

ACTION

The facilitator says, "Select a partner. Get acquainted. Be aware of how you feel in this pair." Pairs talk for 15 minutes. While they are talking, the facilitator assigns each pair a number. After 15 minutes he or she tells them to stop talking and asks, "How do you feel about this dyad? Would you like to continue in this group? *Think* about your answer." Then she or he says, "Would groups 2, 5, 8, 11, and so on [every third group] split? One member go to the group on one side of you; the other go to the group on the other side of you. There will now be a series of triads, or three-person groups. Get to know one another."

DISCUSSION

One person comes alone and must develop a whole new set of relationships. How does he or she feel? How is he or she treated?

Others were in a pair that was or was not satisfying. How do they feel toward one another with a newcomer there? How do they respond to the newcomer?

How do members of the triad feel compared to how they felt in the dyad?

VARIATIONS

Discussion can be within triads rather than with the whole group, or two triads can be combined.

There can be progressions in the size of groups. Triads 2, 5, 8, 11, and so on disband. One person goes to the group at the left, the pair goes to the group at the right. The feelings of one person going into an existing group (newcomer joins trio) are examined; the same is done with a pair going into an existing group (pair joins trio).

EXERCISE 4 Increasing the Attractiveness of a Group: High Talkers–Low Talkers

OBJECTIVES

- To present an opportunity for "high talkers" and "low talkers" to develop empathy for the other
- To recognize the limitations of either behavior
- To give low talkers an opportunity to recognize that their situation is not unique
- To afford an opportunity for high talkers to practice listening and for low talkers to speak

- To experience how group membership can be determined by certain behavioral patterns

SITUATION

This exercise is appropriate after the groups have been working together for some time and usual behavior patterns are known by the members. The facilitator asks each person to categorize himself or herself as a high talker or a low talker. (This can be written down, and there can be a perception check among the members.)

ACTION

A "fishbowl" is set up with the low talkers sitting in the center and the high talkers standing around the outside observing. The low talkers discuss the problems of being a low talker. (8 minutes)

Then the groups switch. The high talkers go to the center and discuss why they talk a great deal, and what problems spring from this behavior. (8 minutes)

Both groups come together and talk about their feelings and observations.

VARIATION

Instead of action in a fishbowl setting, action occurs in mixed quartets—that is, two low talkers and two high talkers in a group. In each, there is a discussion of the problems of being a low or high talker. (20 minutes)

The entire group comes together and discusses their feelings and observations.

For Further Information

Burns, D. D. *Ten Days to Self-Esteem: The Leaders' Manual.* New York: Quill/William Morrow, 1993.

Burns's short-term, structured group program consists of ten sessions focusing on causes and cures for problems such as low self-esteem, feelings of inferiority, perfectionism, and procrastination. He uses the methods of cognitive therapy. The program's strengths are that it is not difficult to lead such a group and that it has been tested and found effective in a variety of settings (including high schools, colleges, graduate schools, and professional training programs; hospitals and day treatment programs; self-help groups; synagogues and churches; prisons; and nursing homes.) Useful to understand how a group works, how members support each other, and how individual goals are attained through a group.

Burnside, I. M., ed. *Working with the Elderly: Group Processes and Techniques.* Belmont, Calif.: Duxbury/Wadsworth, 1978.

Essentially a "how-to" book for working with the aged; weighted on operational aspects of working with groups rather than theory. There are an overview of what is involved in group work with the elderly, applicable principles from a number of theoreticians, and descriptions of the kinds of groups most effective with this population. Chapters on reminiscing groups, music and music therapy groups, group work with mentally impaired, and family groups are included. A growing field.

Galanter, M. *Faith, Healing, and Coercion.* New York: Oxford University Press, 1989.

Everything you ever wanted to know and didn't understand about cults. The author has studied cults for almost two decades. The book features a comprehensive psychological analysis of the evolution of the "Moonies" as well as a controversial account of the similarities between cults and some self-help groups like Alcoholics Anonymous. He also delineates the benefits and the dangers of such groups to members—and to the society at large.

Gilligan, C., Lyons, N., and Hanmer, T. eds. *Making Connections: The Relational Worlds of Adolescent Girls at Emma Willard School.* Cambridge, Mass.: Harvard University Press, 1990.

A series of essays continuing Harvard Professor Carol Gilligan's interest in adolescent girls aiming toward a "new psychology of adolescent girls and women." Critical times of group membership, personal development, and sense of reality converge for girls between eleven and sixteen years. The book is a result of a study by the Willard School, the Harvard School of Education, and the Dodge Foundation.

Goffman, E. *The Presentation of Self in Everyday Life.* Garden City, N.Y.: Doubleday/Anchor, 1959.

A fascinating book on human behavior in social situations and the way we appear to others. Goffman employs, as a metaphor, the framework of the theatrical performance. Everyone in everyday social relationships presents themselves to others, attempts to guide and control the impressions they form, and employs certain techniques to sustain that performance, much the way an actor does. Goffman is the ultimate observer of social interaction. A classic book.

Kavanagh, K. H., and Kennedy, P. H. *Promoting Cultural Diversity: Strategies for Health Care Professionals.* Newbury Park, Calif.: Sage, 1992.

Today's health care professionals practice in settings composed of ethnically, socially, and economically disparate populations. The book was developed to offer techniques for understanding and appreciating their differences. The authors analyze the issues surrounding cultural, gender, and experiential diversity, focusing on effective communication skills and intervention strategies. A variety of scenarios, collages, and case studies illustrate and encourage analysis in real-life situations. Although the focus is on health care, situations are easily transferable to issues of concern to members of all groups.

Reichert, R. *Self-Awareness Through Group Dynamics: Insights and Techniques for Personal Growth of High School Students.* Dayton, Ohio: Pflaum/Standard, 1970.

Although this slim volume is almost thirty years old, it raises issues that continue to be current and relevant. How can groups be utilized to help high school students develop insight that will affect their lifestyles? The focus is on groups because high school is a time when adolescents are most influenced by peers and groups. Subjects include values, freedom and responsibility, prejudice, male-female relationships, respect, and the generation gap. For each of the twelve topics, there are exercises and discussion questions.

INTREPID

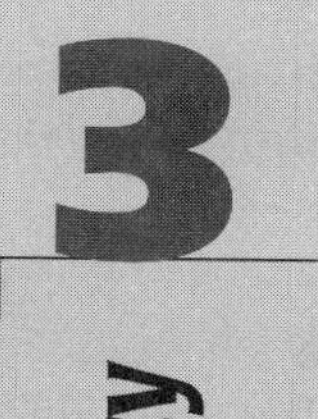

3 Norms, Group Pressures, and Deviancy

How does the Supreme Court work? How do nine justices, presumably the most brilliant legal minds in the country, make decisions that can override a president and counter a Congress—and, simply in their decision to take or not take a case, determine which laws stand and which will be changed? How do these nine justices, wedded for life to one another, arrive at their decisions?

Bob Woodward, Pulitzer Prize–winning author, and Scott Armstrong went about finding out how the Warren Burger Court functioned between 1969 and 1976. In the course of their investigation, they interviewed more than 200 people, including several Supreme Court justices, more than 170 of their law clerks, numerous employees, and assorted savants. Their object was not to illuminate the problems of the Court or to press for better justices. Their object was to understand and report on the process in a book they called *The Brethren.*[1] (The subject had fascinated them, and they hoped it would also intrigue a curious nation and produce a best seller.)

One after another, reviewers of *The Brethren* expressed incredulity. To quote from John Leonard's review in the *New York Times,*[2]

> The Supreme Court behaves like any other committee with which I've had any acquaintance. Its scruples are relative; its personalities clash; its many pairs of eyes are on the main chance, the good opinion of posterity, the boss, the clock and sometimes the Constitution. One imagines that, even in the Agora, Socrates was hustled. . . .
>
> An associate justice of the Supreme Court is allowed to be ordinary. . . . We are advised that Chief Justice Warren Burger is most ordinary. He delays voting until he can be in the majority or finagle the assignment of the writing of an opinion; that he is no stranger to tantrums . . . and that he holds a grudge.

The reviews continued, noting that one justice doesn't do his homework and delays decisions because he is ill-prepared; another, on the slightest provocation, launches into one of his favorite ideological sermons as others tune him out and impassively wait for him to finish. One justice was almost blind, and the group had to make special concessions in working with him; another, of high status as a liberal and a favorite with the press, was an "unpleasant man for whom and with whom to work."

The reviewers expressed shock that these men, esteemed for their fine logical minds and ability to think through enormously complicated legal issues, act like any other committee. It seems impossible that *they* are frustrated with a leader who is not viewed as the most brilliant; that they subtly coerce and are coerced; that they

1. Bob Woodward and Scott Armstrong, *The Brethren: Inside the Supreme Court* (New York: Simon & Schuster, 1979).
2. John Leonard, *New York Times Book Review,* December 16, 1979, p. 1.

know what they can and cannot expect of each of the others; and that their way of functioning is quite different from that of the Warren Court, which preceded them.

One of the fundamental properties of groups is that each group has norms. Simply put, norms are the unspoken rules and standards that guide a group and define acceptable and unacceptable behavior by the group's members. Norms emerge from the participants who work together, at a given time, to accomplish a task. These norms emerge whether the groups are in high places or low ones. Norms are probably the most difficult group concept to convey and to understand. We somehow think that when *they* work together, their brilliance and erudition produce an interaction that is of a rarified form, with which we can in no way identify. How can it be that *they* interact like other committees?

This fundamental idea of group norms is a crucial one for understanding what is happening in a group. The main reason why we don't "see" group norms is that we have never looked. We like to think that we act moment by moment, spontaneously and appropriately. We think any problems are somehow related to "difficult" personalities or some kind of unchangeable situation in which personalities as different as oil and water don't and won't mix. We think that we march to our own drummer and are not conformists to a group. Not true. For the most part, we are conformists.

Without acknowledging the impact that group norms have on our behavior and on the interaction of the group as a whole, we have great difficulty exercising individual control over reaching our goals. It is literally the difference between merely looking at a group and actually seeing it. Even highly trained psychologists can miss seeing a group, as in the following example:

A talented, well-trained Ph.D. clinical psychologist became a member of a university department that had a strong group focus. As part of his familiarization with this departmental emphasis, he participated in a group led by another member of the faculty. He emerged from the experience shaken. In response to a casual, "How was it?" he raged, "She saw everything, everything. She is a witch; that's the only way anybody can see all that. She saw all these things happening; she predicted what would happen—and it did. It was one of the scariest experiences of my life. There are only two explanations possible. Either I am totally uneducated, and I sure felt that way, or—the more plausible one—she is a witch."

One year later, this individual ran the same group. "Today," he boasts, "I am a witch, a seer. After looking at and becoming aware of the group in its interactions, understanding its norms and its environment, I can *see*. I can predict, and amaze people who are probably thinking, "How does he do it? Either I am terribly uneducated or he is a witch."

The Concept of Group Norms

Consider this example, reported by C. Haberman in the *New York Times* (1988),[3] of the power of norms:

All this week, Japan's Parliament was brought to a standstill because an influential member rejected one of this country's most cherished social graces, an apology.

Japanese are expected to say they are sorry when things fly off-kilter, whether they are right or wrong, whether they mean it or not.

They do it because it is expected of them. The apology is an indispensable, all-purpose device for insuring a social harmony.

Everybody here knows that.

Except, apparently, Koichi Hamada, chairman of the powerful Budget Committee in Parliament's House of Representatives, who uttered public remarks widely judged to be offensive and then refused to retract them. He is a man who means what he says, Mr. Hamada declared.

When Japanese heard that, many of them were dismayed. Where would the country be, they asked, if everyone felt that way?

So serious was Mr. Hamada's breach of decorum that opposition parties refused to attend critical hearings of the Budget Committee, effectively preventing the entire Parliament from doing any work all week. What had begun as a seemingly small episode mushroomed into a major political crisis, the first to strike the three-month-old administration of Prime Minister Noboru Takeshita.

3. Excerpt from "Straight Talk Down Japan House" by Clyde C. Haberman, *The New York Times,* February 14, 1988. Copyright © 1988 by The New York Times Company. Reprinted by Permission.

With the pressure upon him intense, Mr. Hamada finally gave in at the end of the week, apologizing publicly and resigning his committee post. Nevertheless, his tale underlined the importance of social imperatives here, and how even the mighty may not escape them. . . .

It was not clear why, but, whatever the reason, he went before television cameras Friday and said, "People of the nation, please forgive me."

He was stone-faced as he spoke. To many Japanese he did not seem the least bit contrite. But that was not important.

The point was that he had come around and behaved the way a proper Japanese should, and that was enough for the Parliament, and the rest of Japan, to feel it could go about its regular business once more.

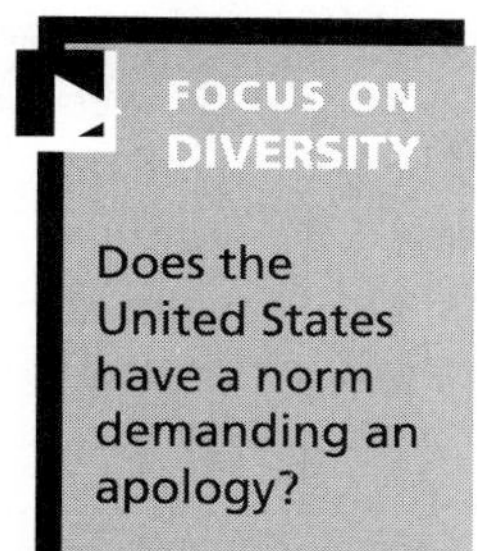

FOCUS ON DIVERSITY
Does the United States have a norm demanding an apology?

Apology is a significant national norm in Japan. In this case, the pressure to behave in accordance with this norm galvanized the attention of the entire nation and distracted the population from its routine business. We might even say that one highly visible man's temporary failure to conform to the national norm nearly brought the country to a halt.

Again, norms are the *rules of behavior,* the proper ways of acting in a group that have been accepted as legitimate by the members of that group. They are accepted as legitimate procedures of the group as a system, as well as of each member within the system. Group norms regulate the performance of the group as an organized unit.

When individuals first enter a group, their conduct appears to be constrained: their feet shuffle and their hands twitch or become rigid; their eyes flit or are directed at inanimate objects; their conversation is forced and superficial or nonexistent; and their laughter is loud and boisterous, tinny, or lacking. When they enter groups, people manifest behaviors that express anxious or uncertain feelings and thoughts about who they are in relation to others, who the others are in relation to themselves, and who the others are in relation to each other.

This confusion is made worse by the absence of a code of conduct, or rules of behavior. Suddenly, out-of-group behavior is inapplicable, and questions arise: "What may others do to me here?" "What may others do to each other here?" and "What may I do to others here?" These and similar thoughts race through a member's mind. As the group functions over time and members come to behave in ways that prove acceptable or unacceptable to individual group members, group agreement is shaped. Initial anxious feelings and thoughts are supplanted by firm, accepted ideas about personal security, safety, and membership status. Members come to feel comfortable in the group. This process of reaching agreement on behavior in the group is called *norming* (Tuckman, 1965).

NORMS AT THE INDIVIDUAL LEVEL

At an individual level, group norms are ideas in the minds of members about what should and should not be done by a specific member under certain specified circumstances. They are learned by members. Usually, norms provide one of the most important mechanisms for social control of individuals' behavior within society.

It is important to understand that norms are not only rules about behavior in a group but also ideas about patterns of behavior. Rarely can the ideas be inferred directly from behavior; rather, they must be learned. For example, one student in a group project may want to do a considerable amount of reading in preparation for a class presentation. However, she can see from the disapproving looks she receives from the others that it would be wiser to do a project that can be developed on class time so that other members can do an equal amount of work. The group will now redefine its project to mean one that they can complete in class. Or, despite instructions from the director of the counseling center that all records must be updated weekly, staff members may learn that as long as their records are current at the time of a record review, twice a year, leaving records undone is accepted. Or a scientific team member learns that attire is of little importance to other members. Dress can be as informal and casual as the individual prefers. However, at monthly report meetings with the divisional managers, members wear business suits or dresses.

Through such experiences, group members learn that the significance of an act lies not in the act itself, but in the meaning the group gives to it. They learn that the meaning may change according to who performs the act and the circumstances under which it is performed. This experience results in what are called *shared ideas* among members about what a specific member should and should not do under certain circumstances. A shared idea means, in the previous examples, that although a class presentation should be well done, it should not occupy personal time; that incomplete records are permissible in that clinic, despite the director's stern speech; and that scientific team members are sometimes expected to dress for a more traditional business setting.

When norms are expectations for the behavior of a particular person, they are called *role expectations*. For example, if someone asks who will take notes at a meeting, and all eyes turn to one member who has unofficially taken notes at several previous meetings, this is a role expectation that has become readily visible.

Reader Activity

Below are two activities to help you understand the concept of norms.

1. One way to understand norms is to understand the difference between the "green" you and the "veteran" you. Select one of these situations, and using the situation you selected, list five things you found difficult (or were fearful of) as a new member.
   a. Being a first-year student and being a senior
   b. Being a new employee and being that employee a couple of years later
   c. Being a member and being an officer in the same group

____

____

____

____

____

____

2. As you became experienced in the group or organization, you learned what the real rules are. How do you handle these situations now?

____

____

____

____

____

For example, first-year students are very concerned with what to wear and often read magazines on the current college fashions; they are apprehensive about looking phony or too new and are eager to cultivate the "right" look. Seniors ridicule reading such magazines; they know what to wear.

Consider dealing with registration, meeting people, making friends, having a "crowd," picking the right teachers and the right courses, and, in the college situation, even getting the right hours. Think of yourself then (not knowing the norms) and later (when you knew). The difference is understanding how the system operates; when you know, you can invest much less energy and suffer much less anxiety.

INDIVIDUAL EXPERIMENT

Choose a group of which you are a member, such as a class, club, sports team, committee, work group, or political organization. Make a list of the norms and informal rules of the group. Include such details as

Dress: formal, informal, or uniform

How people are addressed: title, last or first name, or nickname

Language: jargon, intellectual and formal, informal, or street language

Content of the meetings: serious and always work-related, mostly serious but a lot of socializing, mostly socializing and humorous but work gets done, intimate and personal discussions along with more superficial socializing and work

Process of the meetings: Who talks most and who talks least? Do people tend to agree and keep opposing opinions to themselves? Are different opinions debated openly? Who seems to influence the decisions of the group most often? Are decisions made strictly by the hierarchy of who is in charge or by the group leader? Who informally influences decisions?

Ask two other group members what they think the group's norms are. You will probably have to ask specific questions to help people think about the norms, because they probably have not consciously thought about them or talked about them before. It will be interesting to see what similarities and dissimilarities emerge in your lists.

NORMS AT THE GROUP LEVEL

At a group level, norms (or more accurately, the so-called *normative system*) are the organized and largely shared ideas about what members should do and feel, how they should be regulated, and what sanctions should be applied when behavior does not coincide with them (Mills, 1967). Group norms function to regulate the performance of a group as an organized unit, keeping it on course toward its objectives. They also regulate the functions of individual members of a group.

A culture is, from one perspective, a specific kind of group. Social psychologists have shown that "all of us inhabit numerous local cultures and adopt hundreds of small-scale cultural roles within the large-scale culture" (Hirsch, 1987, p. 97). For example, a variety of cultures exist within a given high school or college. One study (Louis et al., 1989) revealed that local cultural norms at various research universities had more influence than broad social values in determining whether scientists became involved in entrepreneurship. There are thus subcultures within cultures and norms that exist independently at each level.

Cultural norms can also exist at a broader level. In the Hausa tribe of northern Nigeria, children are expected to take the role of buying and trading in public while women, who produce the goods for sale, are constrained by other cultural norms to remain in the house (Spradley and McCurdy, 1990). In this case, both the roles of children and those of women are influenced by a set of larger cultural norms.

Norms in some cases specify particular behavior, and in other situations merely define the range of behaviors that are acceptable. In some cases, no deviations from expectations are permitted; in others, wide variability may be practiced. This range of acceptable behavior is very often apparent in religious groups. For instance, among Muslims, not all women wear the *hijāb,* the veil and sheath that cover all but a woman's face and hands (Coffman, 1991). Similarly, some groups of Jews do not keep kosher.

THE INVISIBILITY OF GROUP NORMS

Whenever we enter a strange or new group, we are uncomfortable. We need to know how it operates and how we will fit in. Until we know, until we get "the lay of the land," we utilize all the strategies that have worked in former groups. We are dressed in the way we think they will find acceptable. We scan for clues—who is "in," who is "out"; what the leader is like; who is popular; how people talk; how one gains acceptance. For new members, there is constant strain in scanning, learning, watching, imitating. In order for new members to feel as though they have gained the group's acceptance, they need to know the "rules of the game."

To insiders, the long-term members, the idea that there are rules within the group is viewed as ridiculous. They say they just act naturally and are accepted. They feel acceptance; they are not under any recognizable tension. They can't understand what this talk of tension is about—it must be something that psychologists dreamed up. Insiders are so familiar with group expectations and rules that they don't know these norms exist. This is what social psychologists call *cultural relativism,* and the phenomenon James Merrill may have referred to when he aptly stated that "life is translation and we are all lost in it" (Geertz, 1983).

In real-life groups, then, norms are invisible. They are taken so much for granted that they are given little thought. The invisibility of norms is analogous to the classic figure/ground gestalts in that norms are often the undifferentiated ground rather than the figure that emerges. We see the task, membership, and problem-solving methods, but we don't see the process of interaction, the ways members conform or influence—these are the background.

Too often, when we try to understand the functioning of individuals and groups, we ignore "invisible" norms. Sometimes norms are difficult for us to discuss openly in a group, especially when there are important decisions to make, when membership is changing, or when emotions are running high. Talking about norms at such times may make us feel more vulnerable or fearful about the group accepting us. Thus groups often collude to keep their own norms out of conscious awareness.

This collusion to keep norms invisible is most pronounced in family systems, where some norms or myths literally go unrecognized (and thereby unchallenged) for generations (Boszormenyi-Nagy and Spark, 1973; Ferreira, 1963; Laing, 1972). Every family, after all, is an independent, defined organization with common characteristics within a given culture. Each can be either functional or dysfunctional, often as a result of such invisible norms. (For more on the family as a microcosm, see Chapters 6 and 10.)

According to a study of invisible norms within organizations (Blake and Mouton, 1985), pressure to conform within the group maintains the norm. Once the invisible norms are exposed, however, the group or organization can become involved in changing repressive norms. One requirement for organizational change is the acknowledgment and identification of silent norms.

How Group Norms Develop

In a culture in which independence, equality, and being able to "pull yourself up by your own bootstraps" are highly valued, being influenced by a group does not seem very likely. Yet despite the cultural emphasis on individualism, we are all affected by group norms, even though we may believe in free will and self-determination. How does this happen? There are a number of interpretations.

A SOCIOLOGIST'S VIEW

Sociologist Erving Goffman devoted his life to seeing, cataloguing, and attempting to understand the interaction rituals performed by people in the physical presence of others. Such contacts may be so fleeting and informal as to be unrecognizable as social functions—an elevator ride, a dash for a bus. They also include such major events as weddings and funerals.

> More than to any family or club, more than to any class or sex, more than to any nation, the individual belongs to gatherings, and he [or she] had best show that he [or she] is a member in good standing. Just as we fill our jails with

> those who transgress the legal order, so we partly fill our asylums with those who act unsuitably—the first kind of institution being used to protect our lives and property; the second to protect our gatherings and occasions." (Goffman, 1963)

Whether behavior occurs in public or private places, the rule of behavior that seems to be common to all such encounters, and exclusive to them, is the rule obliging participants to "fit in."

In his classic *Presentation of Self in Everyday Life* (1959), Goffman views social contact in theatrical terms. Every scene develops as an interaction between the actor and the audience (observers). Goffman is especially interested in "thespian technique": How is it that the actors develop their performances to look real? How do they present their behavior as acceptable to the audience while they are in the "front region" (on stage, before the observers) and act very differently in the "back region" (off stage, not before the observers)? Goffman notes that the audience knows the actors are giving a performance that is not real, but it colludes with the performers to act as though the performance were authentic, spontaneous behavior. Both the actors and the audience seem to desire a good show.

Think of a restaurant with a dining room and kitchen, waiters, and customers. The dining room is softly lit and has immaculate tablecloths and place settings. The waiters move from table to table quietly and slowly, speaking with others in low, well-modulated voices. When waiters go through the doors into the kitchen, however, they yell out orders, dashing around to assemble the necessary glasses and plates, salads or soups—very different from the elegant reserve displayed in the dining room. From a sociological perspective, the dining room is where the waiters are on stage, seeking to create a certain ambience, and the kitchen is off stage, the back region.

For Goffman, learning the rules of social contact—the rituals and then the more difficult "acts"—is necessary to avoid an asylum. It is a basic condition of social life and social survival that occurs even in the most tenuous contacts. The basic rule in social contact is to fit in. Norms thus develop from an individual's learning to fit in.

A BEHAVIORAL INTERPRETATION

Learning theorists have advanced relatively straightforward explanations for what appears to be conformity to group norms. They extend the law of effect; that is, people behave in ways that win them rewards and avoid or suppress behaviors that are punished.

Simply put, people learn to identify cues that signal what behaviors will be reinforced and, especially upon entering a new group, are extremely sensitive to cues signaling punishment. For the most part, establishing or retaining membership in a group (itself a reinforcing condition) is a consequence that results only from choosing to conform to these standards—deriving appropriate reinforcements from appropriate behavior. As a pattern of reciprocity appears in this exchange of behavior-for-reinforcement, the phenomena called *group norms* take shape.

Because individuals differ in the consequences they find reinforcing, nonconforming behavior also can be found in groups. Expulsion is the most severe form of punishment. If individuals are to retain membership without conforming, then they must either find a way to change the norms so that deviant behavior becomes redefined as socially appropriate and reinforceable, or be permitted to formulate a role that permits deviance and reinforces other members' tolerance of that deviance (for example, an authority above the law or a lovable class clown).

In fact, in American culture, both conformity and autonomy are considered "desirable qualities in a person. . . . One should be autonomous, but one should also conform to the expectations of society" (Hewitt, 1989).

This behavioral interpretation is most frequently applied to the practice of group psychotherapy, where it is hoped that clients will establish socially adaptive norms and that their behavior can be shaped to the desired behavior. In such situations, norms are made explicit and highly visible so that expectations are clear, and coaching is directed to conformity. For example, clear expectations that group members treat each other with respect and share their feelings with one another, rather than talk about other topics, establish norms about self-disclosure and trust (Bandura, 1977; Heckel and Salzberg, 1976; Liberman, 1970; Rose, 1977).

In real life, group norms are often established through a process that is largely outside our conscious awareness. Behavioral research offers evidence for such a subliminal, though potent, social learning process:

1. Stimuli that are outside conscious awareness (such as subliminally presented pictures of popcorn in a movie theatre) can influence behavior (getting up to buy popcorn). Visual perception studies have shown that pornographic pictures presented too quickly to be consciously recognized nonetheless can cause male college students to become sexually aroused.
2. Reinforcement can increase the performance of desired behavior and punishment can discourage undesired behavior, even though the target individual (whose behavior is being modified) remains consciously unaware of the manipulation. Consider two examples.
   a. In many cases, when teachers apply behavior modification principles to reinforce sitting still and to decrease the incidence of acting inappropriately, such manipulations can be successful without the student

even being informed or consciously recognizing the teacher's intervention (Martin and Lauridsen, 1974).

b. In individual psychotherapy studies, active listening responses, such as saying "um hm" and smiling, increased the client's tendency to talk about certain subjects or themes, or even show certain emotions, without being aware of or able to verbalize the therapist's subtle manipulation.

Thus group norms may develop through a process of *subliminal conditioning* as, through trial and error guided by past experience and preconceptions, we learn to identify the criteria by which reinforcements and punishments are meted out in a group. Social behavior, as the norm to which we conform, is situation-specific; it is based on the features and norms of a particular group.

COMMUNICATIONS THEORY

Communications theorists build a somewhat different rationale for the formation and acceptance of group norms. The Palo Alto Group (Watzlawick, Beavin, and Jackson, 1967) suggest that all behavior is communication. In fact, it is impossible not to communicate, because even the act of choosing not to communicate is conveying a message. The following principles, according to the Palo Alto Group, occur in all communication:

1. The command component implicit in any act of communication is the communicator's proffered definition of the relationship between self and other(s) involved in the act of communication.
2. In response to the first person's act of communication, the second communicates acceptance of the protagonist's definition of the relationship between them—or offers a counterproposal, an alternative definition of the proferred relationship.
3. Successive acts of communication represent a negotiation or bargaining process until, in accordance with social learning principles, a mutually acceptable quid pro quo—a satisfactory exchange of social reinforcements from complementary points of view—is established.
4. If the negotiation process is not successful, the participants will terminate their relationship. That is, the quid pro quo agreed upon will be the end of further communication between them. This bargaining process is largely subliminal as participants learn of each other's criteria for social reinforcement and preferred reinforcers as givers and receivers.

Communication has inherent in it an aspect that is concerned solely with establishing norms between communicating individuals. A father talks to his adolescent differently than to his grade school child, and he talks to his wife in a qualitatively different way than to either of his children. In a university some professors teach courses and communicate in a manner that encourages questions, differing opinions, and direct intellectual challenges, whereas other professors communicate to students their dislike of being questioned or challenged. The first type of professor communicates in both what he or she says and how it is said that "I am the professor and you are the student; part of my job in teaching you is to encourage independent and critical thinking." The second professor communicates "I am the professor and your job as a student is to learn the material I teach."

Especially in groups that have a history as groups, the give-and-take that leads to the establishment of a quid pro quo is ongoing. The beginning or end of an interaction episode is an arbitrary marker, an act of punctuation that determines how the participants will understand (or misunderstand) what has transpired during the course of their interaction. (Watzlawick gives the example of the experimental rat who "has the experimenter trained to issue food pellets whenever he presses the bar in the cage"—a form of punctuation in their interaction that differs from the experimenter's understanding of the relationship.)

A major controversy in education today is whether language should be made culturally uniform, that is, strengthen its similarity among individuals and groups of people. In his speculative book *Cultural Literacy,* Hirsch states that "effective communication requires a shared culture." Therefore, by not providing minority children with access to the language of the mainstream culture, we are reinforcing the quid pro quo in education (Hirsch, 1987). A current test of the controversy was the recent decision in Oakland, California, to approve Ebonics as the primary language of African-American children. The theory is that it will help these children learn standard English and improve as students.

Once established, the quid pro quo pattern of the relationship is resistant to change. *It is in the exchange of command components and the subsequent quid pro quo that social reinforcers come.* Information rarely, if ever, has this strong interpersonal impact.

In summary, norms exist in all social contacts. We pick them up in the course of living, even as we go about learning content or information. Norms develop through our communications with others, but not directly and straightforwardly for the most part. Rather, norms develop by subtle, subliminal, beyond-awareness processes of inference; we note raised eyebrows, hear supportive "uh-hums," and watch how others gain approval. They may evolve through an interpersonal process of negotiation as we attempt to follow the rules of fitting in. Within each group there is a history of what is and what is not acceptable behavior. This history has developed over time in that situation, and members learn and understand it well.

Classification of Norms

If it is understood that norms are a set of standards that groups develop for themselves, is there a way to classify these standards? Are there dimensions along which these norms develop? Is there a way to understand a group in terms of its norms, and can this method also be a means to contrast groups? Sociologist Talcott Parsons (Parsons and Shils, 1951) thought so. He thought that norms in any society or group had to provide answers to questions related to at least four dimensions.

1. *Affective relationships.* How personal are the relationships? Are relations among members to be based on the expression of feelings they have toward each other, or are feelings to be suppressed and controlled? Is an expression of emotion considered legitimate and appropriate, or is it understood that any expression of emotion is too personal and will hamper the movement of the group? For example, in a school situation, teachers are not supposed to express their feelings of dislike for a particular student or even another teacher. Hospitals often set aside a separate section in the cafeteria for doctors to ensure their not being too personal with other members of the staff or with patients. In a family, on the other hand, the norm is for eating together, sharing personal experiences, being expressive of feelings, and vocally approving and disapproving of members.
2. *Control, decision making, authority relationships.* Is the involvement with another to be total and unbounded by time constraints (as with a parent and a child), or is it to be restricted and specific (as with a swimming instructor and a pupil)? Parents have almost total decision-making control over their children, yet the swimming instructor's control over the pupil is limited to the time of the lesson.
3. *Status-acceptance relationships.* Does the relationship with the other person exist because he or she represents a type or a class (a servant, a client, a teacher) or is it due to the personal uniqueness of the relationship with the other (a brother, a cousin, a friend)? In some groups, the norm is to leave the minute the session is over, without even a goodbye. In others, a personal relationship among colleagues develops as they become friends and regularly "do lunch" together.
4. *Achievement-success relationships.* Is the person valued for his or her personal qualities (intelligent, trustworthy) or for his or her professional skills (as a researcher, as an athlete)? Within the faculty of a college department,

some people are respected for their professional contributions, and others are valued because they sit on administrative committees that benefit the whole department. To all, rank is a significant factor.

One way to compare norms across groups might be with regard to answers members give to the foregoing questions. A great variety of combinations is possible. It may prove a simple, meaningful way to contrast groups. It may clarify the difference between members' wishes for norms and the actual existing norms. It may also make it possible to reduce stress for the members or to precipitate action toward changing the norms.

As noted earlier, Deborah Tannen has written extensively on the differences between the ways in which men and women communicate. In her book *You Just Don't Understand,* Tannen characterizes conversation between men and women as "cross-cultural communication." In keeping with their normative behavior, "women speak and hear a language of connection and intimacy," one that stresses affective relationships. Men, on the other hand, "speak and hear a language of status and independence," which stresses status-acceptance relationships. By understanding the differing norms that govern women's and men's communication patterns, we may begin to break down the gender barriers.

Kinds of Norms

Understanding norms is not a simple matter; there are many norms, and it is difficult to determine which take precedence over others, which are time-specific and which are general, which apply to all members and which to some members, which must be strictly adhered to and which are to be totally ignored.

WRITTEN RULES

Some norms are codified, as in bylaws and code books. They may be formal, written statements intended to be taken literally as group rules, and they are enforced by organizational sanctions (that is, actions to ensure compliance). They are stated and presumably available to members who are willing to examine the constitution or corporate policies. But there are complications.

Sometimes statements in code books are not adhered to as stated. For example, it may be stated with regard to procedures for promotion for university faculty that teaching skill, service, and publication will be weighted equally. However, because publication is easier to measure and more prestigious, it in fact takes on greater weight. The norm, then, is that publication is most important; teaching skill and service become secondary factors.

Sometimes there is a tacit understanding that formal laws can be ignored, much like old statutes that remain on the books but are no longer enforced. A classic example is an old Connecticut statute that makes taking a bath on Sunday unlawful.

The distinction between norms and written documents is an important one, for as some of the formal rules are weighted differently than perceived, as some are adhered to and others are not, a new set of rules is established. Those unfamiliar with this distinction might examine a copy of the group's bylaws and believe these are the procedures by which that group functions, but there may be a world of difference between such official pronouncements and what actually occurs.

EXPLICITLY STATED NORMS

Some norms do not appear in codifications or formal written form, but may be explicitly stated verbally or easily be recognized by members. In being hired, an employee may be told, "Everyone gets here by 9:30," an explicitly stated norm being that you're late if you arrive after 9:30. However, as previously stated, explicitly stated norms may not be the actual norms practiced.

NONEXPLICIT, INFORMAL NORMS

Within each group there may be nonexplicit, informal, or silent norms that influence member behavior. For example, a stated norm may be that all members of a team are expected to be present at weekly hospital rehabilitation staff meetings. However, what happens is that the physician, nominally the team leader, calls just before the meeting stating that she is tied up and asking that they meet without her. The nonexplicit, informal norm that develops is that the entire team is to be present except the physician, who will call to say she won't be there. After weeks of this practice, the team makes assignments to members knowing that they do not have to clear them with the physician. She is informed by reading the weekly staff-meeting minutes.

NORMS BEYOND AWARENESS

Some norms are created as if by accident, in a gradual, unconscious pattern. We conform without even knowing that we feel these pressures. We automatically raise our hands when we want to be recognized; we say hello to those we know when entering a room; we expect a certain order at a meeting: an opening, the minutes, the treasurer's report, old business, then new business. We expect paid-up members to be notified of meetings.

Individual Experiment

Norms are related to a variety of behaviors of group members, one of which is communication within the group. In some groups, strict parliamentary procedures provide rigid norms; in others, communication is informal and more flexible. Choose a group you participate in that has a fair amount of discussion and interaction among members. Discreetly take notes about the interaction of the group, noting such things as how often each individual talks, who seems to talk after whom, which members agree or disagree, who talks about irrelevant and unrelated events, who cracks jokes and when, who talks just about the task or work of the group, and who tries to make decisions in the group. You may notice some patterns in who talks to whom and so on, or you may not. In about one month, take the same kinds of notes about the group interaction again and compare the two sets of notes. The similarities you discover will represent some of the informal norms about communication in the group.

Forces That Induce Acceptance of Group Norms

The process by which a group brings pressure on its members to conform to its norms, or by which a member manipulates the behavior of others, is the process of social influence. It is recognized that some groups may legitimately exert pressures for uniformity of behavior and attitudes among members—for example, church groups, political parties, and professional societies. Others exert influence on members without their awareness that it is happening. This occurs among office associates, teachers in a given school, and lunch groups—those who interact frequently, though they have not created any formalized structure. They exert influence through their informal group standards and may have an important effect on members' behavior.

If the norms of the group are compatible with an individual's norms and goals, that person will conform to the norms of the group. However, if an individual finds that his or her behavior deviates from the group norms, he or she has four choices: to conform, to change norms, to remain a deviant, or to leave the group.

Why do people bother to learn the norms of a group so that they can conform? Is it worth the effort? How do members induce other members to conform?

Seeking answers to such questions, Feldman (1984) examined the enforcement and development of group norms. With respect to norm enforcement, he found that "groups are likely to bring under normative control only those behaviors that (1) ensure group survival; (2) increase the predictability of group members' behaviors; (3) prevent embarrassing interpersonal situations; or (4) express the group's central values." Feldman found that group norms develop through "(1) explicit statements by supervisors or coworkers; (2) critical events in the group's history; (3) primacy, and (4) carry-over behaviors from previous situations."

Basically, the forces that induce an individual to conform can be classified in one of two categories: internal forces, those based on intrapersonal conflict; and external forces, in which others attempt to influence the person directly.

INTERNAL FORCES BASED ON INTRAPERSONAL CONFLICT

One of the major early studies in group dynamics sought to demonstrate how a group influences individuals to conform. In the classic Sherif experiments (Sherif, 1935, 1936, 1961), each subject is placed in a darkened room and asked to judge how far a dot of light moves. (Although the light appears to move, it actually does not. The phenomenon is known as the *autokinetic effect.*) The subject sees the dot of light and makes a series of individual judgments. Then the subjects are brought together in twos and threes to again judge how far the light moves. In this situation, their judgments tend to converge to a group standard. Later, when they view the light again as individuals, they retain the group standard and give that answer.

This experiment has been replicated with variations for almost five decades, and the results are so predictable that it is even conducted as a classroom experiment (Hare, 1976; Martin, Williams, and Gray, 1974). The essential finding is that when a situation is ambiguous and there is no external reality for determining the "right" answer, people are especially influenced by the group. They look at the light and have no objective way of determining how much it moves; they make a judgment as best they can. When they are in a group, they hear one another's judgments, a clarity develops for them, and they adjust their answers to fall within the range of the others. Generally, the greater the ambiguity of the object, the greater the influence of other group members in determining the judgment of the subject (Sorrels and Kelley, 1984; Keating and Brock, 1974; Luchins, 1963; Mills and Kimble, 1973).

In an extension of the Sherif experiments, Stassen and Hawkes (1995) found that, even when a group is later asked to make a judgment on another task, they remember the group discussion and are influenced by it.

In real life, then, membership in a group influences individuals in many of the things they will see, think about, learn, and do. Given a change in the price of gold or in unemployment statistics, union members will hear a different set of "facts" to clarify that situation than will chamber of commerce members. College students at Berkeley or San Francisco State will understand student involvement quite differently from students at a small midwestern college.

How an event or situation becomes less ambiguous is to a large extent determined by the group memberships of the person. Because of the limited range of events in a group, there evolves a common set of perceptions and convictions among members. Discussion groups, bull sessions, and rap groups all serve the function of helping an individual develop clarity in an ambiguous situation. The process of each member of a group giving his or her own opinion, even without attempting to influence an individual, can be highly influential in developing what the members consequently think.

A second classic and ingenious series of experiments was designed by Asch (1951, 1955, 1956). Asch was interested in understanding when individuals would be independent of the group and when they would conform.

In his experiments, the stimulus materials were two sets of cards. On one set, each card had a single black line (the standard). Each card in the other set had three labeled lines; one of these was the same length as the standard, and the other two were easily recognizable as different from the standard. Individuals from psychology classes who volunteered for the experiment were arranged in groups of seven to nine. They were seated at a table and asked to state in turn, starting at the left, which line was closest to the standard.

Reader Activity

Pretend you are one of the students in the Asch experiment. You are seated in a position to give your opinion sixth in a seven-person group.

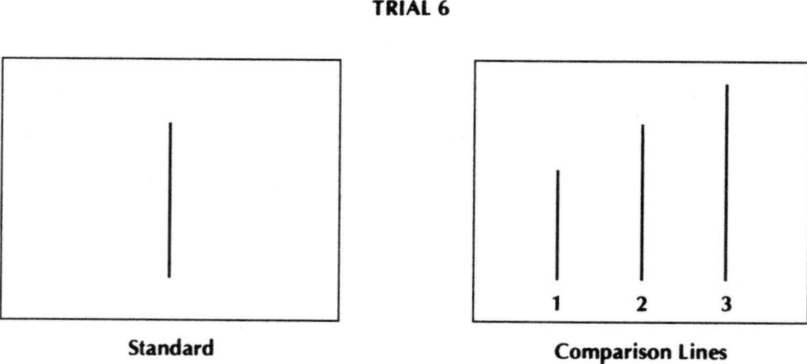

Which of the comparison lines is closest in size to the standard line? Person 1 says line 2, the next person says line 2, the next person says line 2, the next person says line 2, and

the next person says line 2. It is now your turn. What do you say? ____________
Then person 7 says line 2.

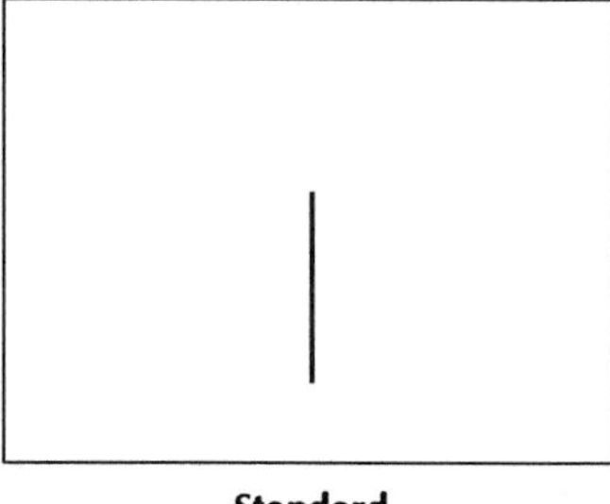

Standard

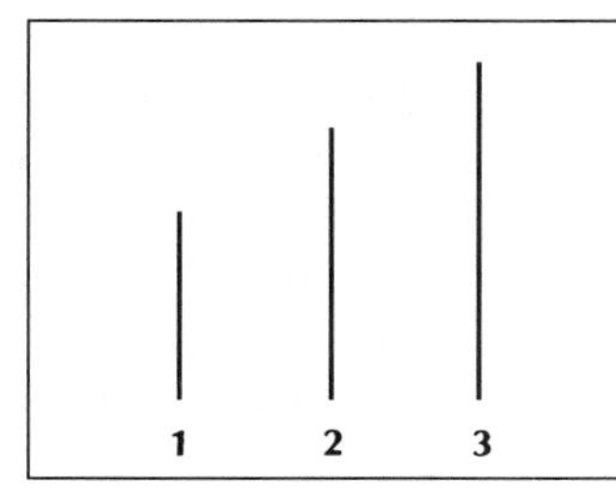

Comparison Lines

What would you say if you were actually at a table with six others? You look at the lines at the same time they do; they see what you see. How is it that sometimes all of you see the lines the same way and agree, as in trial 6, and at other times they all agree but you see it differently? This is an issue not of opinion but of perception. It is simple to see which line is closest to the standard. What is happening to you? What would you do?

____

____

____

____

What Asch did was to coach six of the seven to give the same incorrect reply on twelve of eighteen trials. In each group, there was 1 naive subject. The experiment was conducted with 123 naive subjects altogether. The findings were overwhelming: nearly 37 percent of the subjects' responses were in error, compared with almost no errors in the control trials. On one trial, less than 50 percent gave the correct answer. Remember, the subjects did not know each other, there was no overt group pressure to conform, each had the solid information of his or her senses to rely on, and the situation was not ambiguous. There was no promise of future favor or advancement, nor was there any threat of ostracism or punishment. How did it happen that so many (over a third) gave the wrong response?

Asch explains the situation as follows: Individuals come to experience a world they share with others; events occur that they and others see simultaneously. They understand that an environment includes them as well as others and that they are in the same relation to the surroundings as others. If it rains, it rains on them as well as on those standing beside them. If an automobile in which they are passengers stops suddenly, they as well as other passengers will be shaken. They know (in the basic internal sense of knowing) that they and others are in a similar experience and that each responds to certain identical properties (they all are wet as a result of the rain, the smoothness of the ride is interrupted for all because of the sudden stop). Because individuals are aware of similarity of experience and similarity of response—which seems to be the inevitable direct response to an identical experience—an intrapersonal conflict arises for them under the experimental conditions Asch set up.

Although a person was likely to give an incorrect answer when responding in a large, unanimous group, especially over time, it should be noted that if even *one* other person gave the correct answer, the person trusted his or her own sensory information and gave the correct answer. No matter what the size of the majority, even one supporter encouraged the subject to trust his or her own senses—an important understanding for anyone attempting to lead or change norms.

Khoury (1985) tested the Sherif and Asch experiments. He asked how strongly assessments are influenced by the urge toward social conformity. First, he had group members judge the number of coffee beans in a jar and found mild agreement, as in Asch's study. Next, he asked subjects to rate two jokes in terms of humor—a task involving much more ambiguity than guessing the number of coffee beans in a jar.

The results of Khoury's experiment confirmed the hypothesis that the convergence of opinion regarding humorousness would be greater than in the unambiguous, coffee-bean problem—in fact, the convergence of opinion regarding the jokes was *twice* that regarding the beans. Generally, individuals are more likely to conform to group opinion when the object to be judged is ambiguous and the individual must make his or her opinion public. Individuals are highly sensitive to social forces in norm building, and humor is a formidable social force.

Even more recently, in a 1989 study that sought to further verify some of the variables in Asch's experiment, Campbell and Fairey found that the larger the group, the greater its normative versus informational influence. In other words, as a group increases in size, information from individuals becomes redundant and therefore declines in influence. They also found, however, that the normative influence varied as the "norm changed from one that might be correct to one that is clearly wrong" (Campbell and Fairey, 1989). Thus the degree to which a group can influence an individual may depend on how extreme the group's responses are.

These results have wide implications in terms of social influence. The Asch findings continue to be powerful testimony to how a group influences its members and how members conform (Ross, Bierbrauer, and Hoffman, 1976; Lamb and Alsikafi, 1980; Mugny, 1984).

In each of these studies, the group's influence on judgment occurs only when there is internal conflict, not when the judgment is based on personal preference. Here, individuals do not perceive themselves as being in a situation similarly experienced by others; they perceive themselves as having idiosyncratic preferences that are theirs alone. If, for example, they were sitting in a group with others and a researcher asked for each person's favorite flavor of ice cream, internal conflict would not occur. The first person might answer "chocolate," the next might also say "chocolate," and even if the next three reply "chocolate," the sixth will answer "coffee" or "burnt almond" or whatever his or her favorite flavor is. Personal preference replies are in a different category from judgment replies, in which each person is aware of being in a common situation.

TENDENCIES TO CREATE A SOCIAL REALITY

Internal forces can also lead individuals to conform as they seek a social reality. Festinger (1954) proposed that there is a basic drive within each of us to evaluate our own opinions and abilities. It is potentially dangerous, or at the very least embarrassing, to be incorrect or to misperceive how well we can do various things. To avoid that, we constantly seek relevant evidence. For some opinions and abilities, the evidence is directly available to us in our contacts with the physical world. If we are not sure of the time, we can check our watch. If we are not sure whether we can jog two miles, we can go find out. However, for most of our opinions and abilities, there is no objective, nonsocial way to evaluate ourselves. All we can do is turn to other people. If we are not sure how well we speak, we find out by observing how others respond to our talk. If we are not sure how we should relate to the opposite sex (to open doors, light cigarettes, pay for meals), we listen and look for others like us to help us develop a *social reality.*

In addition to other individuals' influences, much of our social reality is constructed through the kinds of institutions we establish. Within our institutions there develops a normative order that enables us to criticize and ultimately transform the existing order (Swidler, 1991). In other words, the mere establishment of norms within our various institutions provides us with the mechanism to change our social reality (Roggenbuck et al., 1991). For example, in a 1989 study of news reporting and its role in the formation of public opinion, Vincent Price points out that the media's depiction of how groups of people are responding to issues actually

> **FOCUS ON DIVERSITY**
>
> What, then, is the effect of news media playing up a murderer as African-American?

influences individuals' opinions on those issues. According to Price, "the media perform the key role of linking separate members of the mass to wider trends in public debate" (Price, 1989). For better or for worse, they create a new social reality.

In another study (Kahn et al., 1982) individuals were interested in maximizing the social rewards in a situation and making a positive impression on other group members regardless of their own monetary gain. In fact, situations in which subjects focused on social rewards resulted in their loss of rewards as part of the experiment. In other words, our motivation to join groups, create social realities, and feel accepted by others is a common need we either underestimate or minimize. Therapy groups and self-help groups rely heavily on the process of social comparison and perception of similar experience and feelings in others. In groups this universality of experience and the development of a social reality are primary factors in helping people feel good about themselves and increase self-esteem (Brothen and Shovholt, 1981).

In evaluating ourselves, we have a tendency to seek fairly similar others as a comparison group. We seek a similar, attractive reference group and use these individuals as a basis for comparison (a further illustration of Festinger's social comparison theory).

When there are vast changes in social norms, styles, morality, taste, criteria of beauty, child-rearing practices, divorce, and myriad other aspects of our lives, our reactions to the changes are primarily based on the evaluations of those around us. For that reason, friends or members of our peer group have greater influence than others.

Just as there is pressure to establish the correctness of an opinion, there are pressures to establish the appropriateness of an emotional or bodily state. And because emotion-producing situations are often novel and outside the realm of our past experience, it is not surprising that emotions are particularly vulnerable to social influence. Consider an example:

> Each weekday morning, year in and year out, there were, with few changes, the same people standing on the suburban station platform waiting for the 7:40 train to take them into the city to work. As each arrived, he or she nodded "good morning" or perfunctorily commented on the cold or the rain. For the most part, they got their papers or their coffee and waited in small clusters where they thought the doors would be when the train stopped.

There were a few women, and they boarded first; then the older men boarded, and then the others. On the train they read, worked, or slept. There was almost no conversation. It was just another morning, except on October 15 it wasn't.

In an incredible accident, the 7:40 crashed into a stopped train in front of it with such force that over 300 people were knocked unconscious and strewn about the cars, thought to be dead. Bloody noses and bleeding heads were commonplace as the crash stop hurled passengers into the seats in front of them. Broken glass from the windows spattered all within range. Smoke darkened in the cars.

It could have led to a stampede for safety through the broken windows. It could have created a trampling horde concerned only with reaching a door and getting out. It could have produced a caged mob regressed to the basic instinct of personal survival. It was the first commuter accident in fifty-two years. No one could have been prepared for it or have known how to act, given the nature of the catastrophe, the early hour of the morning, and the fact that most were half asleep as well.

But the norms of the station platform prevailed. The first concern was for the women, as people next to them helped them with their injuries while they themselves were bleeding. Then passengers shouted for the older men and rushed to their aid; one who was knocked unconscious was picked up by three men who moved him to a bench, covered him with their overcoats, and attempted to revive him. Not one person left; those who were not visibly injured were helping others.

Even when the police arrived, people who had been helping others stayed with them on the trip to the hospital so that they would not be frightened by being injured and alone. People on the train emerged supporting others who were unable to walk and remained at their sides, helping them to phone booths to call their relatives and waiting with them until a family member arrived.

Police, newspaper reporters, and hospital workers alike commented that they had never seen anything like it. No looting or robbing, no pushing or crushing, no abandoning others for the police to care for in due time. Over and over, those injured reported, "I can't believe strangers can be so caring." A woman whose nose had been crushed and head badly lacerated reported, "The man who had been seated next to me and to whom I had never said more than 'good morning' held my arm and kept telling me that I would be all right. He would stay with me in the hospital. He would call my husband and daughter. I was so frightened and bloody and hurting, I don't know what I would have done without him. And it was like that throughout the car."

One possible explanation is that the daily routine and copresence had subtly conditioned the riders to each other and that some positive—though subconscious—relationship had developed over time.

Reader Activity

Now that you have read about this incident, how do you explain the norms that were expressed after the train crash? How do you explain people's caring, altruistic response?

____

____

____

____

Imagine yourself on that train. How do you think it happened that train group members influenced each other and were able to get such conformity?

____

____

____

____

EXTERNAL FORCES BASED ON DIRECT INFLUENCE OF OTHERS

Coming into a group means interacting, which means influence attempts. From the simplest "Why don't you sit here with us?" to "John is by far the best candidate. How could you consider anyone else?" we influence each other. When we persuade a person to act in a certain way under certain circumstances, we are using direct influence.

There are a number of reasons why people attempt to influence others to comply to certain norms. One is that it will help the group accomplish its goals; another is that it will help the group maintain itself. Both these functions must be developed with strong supporting forces if the group is to succeed.

TO ACHIEVE GROUP GOALS Pressures toward uniformity among members of a group may occur because uniformity is necessary for the group to achieve its goal (Festinger, 1950).

When a group is attempting to raise funds, for example, it develops norms for standardizing pledge cards, assigning members to districts to be solicited, turning in money, and reporting results. All of these procedures develop because they will help the group achieve its objective of successfully raising the money needed. Consider how members will respond to the member who turns in pledges on the corner of a menu or the back of a shopping list. How will they respond to the member who solicits people in someone else's territory? How will they respond if the campaign ends and a member doesn't turn in the money? People exert pressures on others to follow approved procedures that are directed toward achieving the group goal. These are sources of uniformity that are seen as legitimate.

Sororities and fraternities often provide classic examples of how norms develop as part of the process of achieving a group goal. In a 1988 study of binge eating in sororities, Crandall found clear evidence of group norms about appropriate binge eating and its relationship to popularity. Because of the social importance of body size and shape for this group, it is likely that physical attractiveness is one of the group goals sought by maintaining these norms (Crandall, 1988).

If a football team is to win, members are expected to learn and execute the plays. The maverick who disregards the rules (pressures toward uniformity) often will be ridiculed—"So you thought you were the whole team, or better than the whole team?" The norms may allow one superstar on the team, but even he must play within the limits set by the group norms.

In sum, members are expected to adhere to the norms viewed as necessary to help the group achieve its goal. Any member who does not adhere will be seen as a threat to that end, and efforts will be made to induce him or her to return to the group procedures—or to leave the group.

FOR GROUP MAINTENANCE Some group standards are sustained to help the group maintain itself. Procedures for paying dues, pressures for attending meetings regularly, and norms of delaying the start of a meeting until enough members are present are all norms that are conducive to maintaining a group or an organization.

Frequently, other norms develop in an effort to sustain a group. For example, members may avoid areas of conflict in discussion for fear that conflict may evoke anger or loud voices and cause some members to leave as a result of the unpleasant experience. (Outward display of harmony as necessary for group survival is a common norm.)

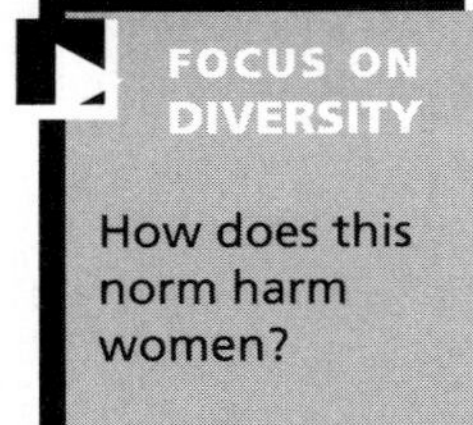

FOCUS ON
DIVERSITY
How does this
norm harm
women?

One study showed that the norms present in fraternities tend to emphasize a stereotypical concept of masculinity. The behaviors exhibited (such as competition over new members, sports, or women) encouraged a "context in which the use of coercion in sexual relations with women is normative" (Martin and Hummer, 1989). These behaviors seem to reinforce the emphasis on masculinity and therefore help to maintain the group.

On the other hand, norms of announcing honors to the group also develop. Whether a member is named in the newspaper, makes the varsity team, or is included in a prestigious representative council, groups brag because doing so boosts their image of being winners and enhances the desirability of membership. These norms will be enforced as members are solicited to report such honors as an invitation to speak, a publication, or a promotion; members may even be reprimanded for not letting others know. The group is thereby maintained by pressures to "let everyone in on" individual achievements.

A Preliminary Theory of Norm Development

A major work on how norms develop emerged from research by Bettenhausen and Murnighan.[4] Initially, these researchers focused on decision making in small groups and were not concerned with norms. However, they noticed that norms developed when their five-member groups came together and that norm development had a major impact on the decision-making process. They, like Feldman (1984), found that in new groups the meanings attached to action were based on members' prior experiences in what they believed were similar situations. These findings led to the formulation of a preliminary theory of norm development. The figure below illustrates four possible ways members can interpret the situation in a new group.

The first propositions use this scheme of interpretative possibilities and indicate the directions different groups might pursue.

- *Proposition 1.* In new groups, uncertainty over appropriate behavior leads group members to anchor the current situation to what they perceive as similar, previously experienced situations.
- *Proposition 1a.* If all members use similar scripts and define the situation in the same way, interaction is easy (cell I).
- *Proposition 1b.* If group members use different scripts but respond in similar ways, initial interaction may not be problematic, but latent discord may eventually lead to conflict that is then difficult to resolve (cell III).

4. This discussion is based on the work of Bettenhausen and Murnighan (1985).

GROUP MEMBERS' SCRIPTS

MEMBER'S DEFINITION OF THE NEW SITUATION		Similar to Each Other's	Different from Each Other's
	Similar to Each Other's	**I** Interactions confirm each member's interpretation and are not problematic.	**II** Initial interactions proceed smoothly but latent disagreement may require subsequent development of a group-based understanding.
	Different from Each Other's	**III** Initial interactions trigger the development of a group-based understanding of the situation; members must work toward a common definition of the current situation.	**IV** Initial interactions either frustrate the group or trigger the development of a group-based understanding of the situation; elaborate discussions are necessary.

- *Proposition 1c.* If group members do not adopt common interpretations of the novel situation, they must develop a group-based understanding of the situation (cells II and IV). If they have different scripts, they must build understanding without the aid of past references.

Initially, one member's action may be incompatible with another member's interpretation of the situation. When this occurs, the group must negotiate (sometimes tacitly) to determine which interpretation is appropriate.

- *Proposition 2.* As group members interact, their shared experiences form the basis for expectations about future interactions.
- *Proposition 2a.* When other members' actions are compatible with the meaning a member has attached to the task, the interpretation is legitimized and confidence in applying the interpretation increases.
- *Proposition 2b.* When some members' actions are incompatible with other members' conceptualizations of the task, the nonacting members may revise their original interpretations, or

- *Proposition 2c.* They may attempt to persuade the group to accept their conceptualization, defining the observed actions as inappropriate.

In trying to persuade the group to accept a point of view, a group member challenges the prevailing interpretation of the situation and what constitutes appropriate action within it.

Although norms can develop without them, threats are crucial to understanding the formation of a norm, because they allow the group to consider its own evolving, taken-for-granted activity publicly.

Threats may be easy or extremely hard to resolve. When a single, unsupported group member makes a threat, the situation is often quickly resolved. Just as the conformity pressures of a group break down when nonconformists are supported by other group members (Asch, 1951), so too are *supported* threats expected to provoke discussion and resolution. Successful threats demonstrate that the group's previous behavior may have been due to ignorance (Krech and Crutchfield, 1948) rather than an accurate understanding of appropriate behavior.

- *Proposition 3.* Challenges to the group's evolving pattern of behavior can reveal the subjective meanings the members attached to the group's interaction.
- *Proposition 3a.* Quickly accepted threats indicate general approval of the action expressed in the threat.
- *Proposition 3b.* Quickly dismissed threats indicate general agreement expressed only implicitly in the group's actions.
- *Proposition 3c.* Threats not quickly resolved (major threats) indicate that members attached incongruent meanings to the group's actions.
- *Proposition* $3c_1$. Groups that resolve major threats become more immune to subsequent ones.
- *Proposition* $3c_2$. Groups that have not experienced major threats may be particularly vulnerable when one surfaces.

At some point, the group begins to base its actions on the meanings that have developed *within* the group rather than on the meanings the individuals used initially to anchor and understand the task. At that point, we would say that a norm unique to the interacting members exists. Opp (1982) and others proposed that norms are gradual and evolutionary. However, although norms certainly can change over time, the observations of Bettenhausen and Murnighan suggest that norm formation is subtle but swift.

The test of any norm is its ability to control behavior. When group members impose sanctions on behavior that violates the group's precedents, a norm can be considered fully operative.

- *Proposition 4.* Once a norm has formed, any further attempts to alter the behavior it controls will be met with sanctions.

The Power of Groups

What is the power of groups to make people conform? How does it happen that people can be induced under the pressure of a group to commit unusual acts? Social psychologists, incredulous about what they see about them, have sought to understand and theorize how it happens that people conform, comply, and obey.

Kelman (1958) sought to understand how officers had been brainwashed as prisoners during the Korean War. Jahoda (1956) was aroused by the civil liberties issues, loyalty oaths, and outrageousness of Joseph McCarthy's congressional hearings in the 1950s.

Galenter (1980) addressed the upsurge of charismatic religious sects in the last several decades and members' abrupt abandonment of earlier social ties. The power of the group to induce people to conform is a continuous source of questions, speculation, and wonder. Consider the following now-legendary further examples:

Patty Hearst, the abducted heiress daughter of the San Francisco publishing family, was photographed robbing a bank with an ultra-radical group after only two months of being with the group. She later testified that she was forced to conform to the group's demands out of fear for her life.

In late March 1997, the San Diego Sheriff's office startled the country when they reported finding thirty-nine men and women dead in a mansion on a hill in a plush San Diego suburb. They were all wearing white shirts, black pants, and identical new sneakers; and lay on neatly made beds. Part of the Heaven's Gate cult, they had committed mass suicide in an attempt to link up with a UFO they believed was passing by earth in connection with the Hale-Bopp comet.

Cults like the "Moonies," Scientology, Hari Krishna, and others are able to convince typically white, middle-class, college youth to forgo their families, education, career goals, and material possessions.

Another tragic example is the experience of a Vietnam veteran[5] who called a Boston radio station on Labor Day, 1972:

> I am a Vietnam veteran, and I don't think the American people really, really understand war and what's going on. We went into villages after they dropped napalm, and the human beings were fused together like pieces of metal that had been soldered. . . . I was there a year, and I never had the courage to say that was wrong. . . . A lot of guys had the guts. They got sectioned out, and on the discharge it was put that they were unfit for military duty—unfit because they had the courage. Guys like me were fit because we condoned it, we rationalized it.

In fact, during the Vietnam War era, the questioning of authority by youths was transformed into what was perceived as anti-American behavior. During periods of nationalism, norms often became "facts."

Each of these incidents is incredible and almost impossible to understand. How do groups induce people to conform to this extent?

In thinking of how people respond to group pressures, three concepts have been helpful. They are conformity, compliance, and obedience (Baron, Roper, and Baron, 1974).

CONFORMITY

It is hard to resist explaining conformity through an old joke. It goes like this: A person is standing on a corner intently looking at the sky. Another person comes by, sees the first person looking at the sky, and also looks up. After a while there is a small crowd clustered around the original person, all looking at the sky. After looking for a while, and waiting, someone finally asks the first person what he is looking for. "Oh," he replies, "I'm not looking for anything. I have a stiff neck and I'm waiting for my friend to pick me up and take me to the doctor." That's conformity! It involves the way we are influenced by others simply on the basis of what they do. Our implicit assumption is that similar behavior will elicit approval and that dissimilar behavior will bring censure.

READER ACTIVITY

When you were in high school, how were you supposed to look?

Hair ____

5. Excerpt from *Time,* "Human beings fused together" in *Time,* October 23, 1972, p. 36. Copyright 1972 Time Inc. Reprinted by permission.

Clothes ____

Shoes ____

Cosmetics ____

Jewelry ____

Do you remember people who didn't look that way? What happened? How were they treated? ____

____

____

Although clothes are readily evident illustrations of conformity, they were not the only example. Which activities were "in"? ____

____

Which activities were "out"? ____

____

Why? ____

What did you want to do but chose not to do because it would be "uncool" (or whatever the derisive expression was in your day)? ____

____

____

____

Conformity occurs because we internally decide to go along with the group (Moorman and Blakely, 1995). It may be because we are ignorant of the subject, they are more knowledgeable, and we listen to the experts.

A study by Campbell and associates (1986) showed greater conformity where pressure and self-doubt were high and the existing norm was more extreme. Also, conformity increases as the size of the group grows; the larger the number, the larger the group with whom we compare ourselves, and the more likely we are to conform (Gerard, Wilhelmy, and Conolley, 1968).

The more conforming behavior is reinforced, the more likely we are to continue (Endler, 1966). And of course, the more we want others to like us (ingratiating behavior), the more we search for cues to what they want and give it to them (Jones, 1964). In general, the more we like a group, the greater the conformity (Kiesler, 1963; Savell, 1971).

Similarly, the more our values resemble those of some reference group, the more likely we are to conform to that group's norms.

When women identify strongly with a reference group (for example, a health group), they know what the norms are and what is expected of them (the perceived norms). They also "know" there will be consequences if they don't follow the norms: they are less likely to be part of the high-status groups made up of those losing weight, becoming thinner, and admired by the others. Terry and Hogg (1996) found that if the women identified closely with the group, their intentions to engage in regular exercise and sun-protective behavior increased. This perceived group norm influenced the women's attitudes, and was predictable.

Fisher suggests that "with respect to AIDS, relevant group norms may reject using condoms . . . or promote engaging in other risky sexual practices" because people may fear sanctions for not conforming. One example is that in many cultures, being concerned with AIDS may not be consistent with "machismo" values (Fisher, 1988). Thus, conforming to group norms may even take precedence over life-preserving behavior such as AIDS prevention. Yet it is important to note that if a person has a different reference group, he or she will conform to that group's norms. Currently, adult gay men rebounding from the AIDS tragedies they have witnessed among their gay friends, for example, have strong norms of using condoms (Joseph et al., 1987).

COMPLIANCE

Although in the *conformity* situation there is no overt pressure on a person to behave as others do, he or she responds as though there were pressures to comply. In the Asch experiments, each person responded as he or she saw the line, but when there was unanimous group agreement, it created an internal pressure on the individual to conform. By contrast, in *compliance* situations, the request is direct. A person asks you to do a favor, to vote for a particular candidate, to contribute to a fund, or to do an unpleasant job. In conformity, the pressure is invisible; in compliance, it is obvious.

Compliance seems to arouse resistence. We are bombarded by requests, from being asked to do a colleague a favor by covering a class for him or her to being solicited to buy tickets to help a cause; from taking minutes at a meeting to being asked to chair a committee. When a request comes, we pause as we think, "Now how can I get out of it and still have them like me?"

For some, a request almost automatically induces compliance. For them, there is now a whole world of literature on assertiveness training (Fensterheim and Baer, 1975) and learning how to say no. Of course, at different times in our lives our need to be accepted by others has a profound effect on our ability to say no. For example, when we're teen-agers it's nearly impossible to say no to friends with whom we strongly identify. Yet when we're older and involved in a career or family, saying no to friends has a different meaning and may be easier to do than before. Ward and Wilson (1980) found that motivational orientation and stage of moral development affect whether an individual will acquiesce to social pressures toward conformity.

Compliance research has focused on how, despite resistance, a person can be induced to comply. One way to get people to do so is to do them a favor so that they are indebted to us. If someone has borrowed your class notes, an unequal relationship exists in terms of costs and rewards. The relationship is no longer equitable. The borrower will feel more comfortable, and equity will be restored, if she or he does something nice for you.

Regan (1971) designed a simple experiment to test the hypothesis that doing someone a favor induces compliance later. In the experiment, subjects waited in groups of two (however, one of the two was a confederate). In half the situations, the confederate was pleasant and amiable as they chatted, waiting for the "experiment" to begin; in the other half, the confederate was purposely unpleasant. In one condition, the confederate then bought sodas for the two of them; in the other, the two just sat and waited. Then the confederate asked the subject to buy raffle tickets to help the confederate's home town high school build a gym, saying that the person who could sell the most tickets would win a $50 prize. The results overwhelmingly indicate that whether the confederate was pleasant or unpleasant, the subject was most likely to buy the raffle tickets if the confederate had performed a favor for him or her. Thus compliance is strongly increased when a person feels obligated to the one making the request.

The foot-in-the-door technique is another method to get a person to comply. First, ask the person to comply with a small, innocuous request, then ask for a big one (Freedman and Fraser, 1966). In a fascinating field experiment, researchers asked subjects to place a large sign on their front lawns that said "drive carefully,"

FOCUS ON DIVERSITY
African-Americans and Latinos usually do not join cults?

but less than 17 percent were willing to do so. Another group of subjects were first asked to place a small sign saying "drive carefully," and then at a later time a large sign on their lawns. Now, over 76 percent were willing. And interestingly enough, a small initial request seems to be a better technique for inducing compliance than a moderate one (Baron, 1973).

Margaret Singer, whose interest in brainwashing and cults led her to interview every prisoner of war who returned from North Korea and Southeast Asia, developed an understanding of how cults operate. Singer believes that members of religious cults are victims of this foot-in-the-door technique.

> In many cults, when people join they don't realize what it is they are joining, and they are lured a step at a time by very persuasive and deceptive practices. Middle-class Caucasian kids, in particular, are not very street smart. They are trusting and naive and they believe people who approach them with offers (of a dinner, a place to stay, a weekend away, instant companionship) much more than lower-class kids, who are wise to the fact that no one gives you anything without expecting something in return. (Freeman, 1979)

What starts as a response to friendship, or an invitation to dinner, insidiously moves with each step of compliance to a greater act of compliance, until after years of being in a cult, leaving is almost unthinkable. The gradual, foot-in-the-door technique escalates to the point where compliance becomes automatic and decision making as an individual extremely difficult.

OBEDIENCE

In compliance, people can say yes or no; there are options and alternatives. They may feel compelled to say yes, but they can be resistant. They don't have to accept the invitation to the group meeting, attend the dinner, or acquiesce to the first request. There will not be severe consequences.

Obedience is different. If one person has power over another person, obedience can be demanded. If the second person fails to obey, power is exercised in the form of negative sanctions such as demerits, demotions, fines, imprisonment, even death. Those who refuse to follow orders are labeled bad, rebellious, uppity, even psychopathic. Here, the social influence is very direct and very explicit. There is a sense of "Do it, or else. . . ."

Obedience is instilled in us as children, first when we are expected to obey our parents and later when we hear, "Listen to the teacher. Do what you're told." Enlisted men and women are expected to obey their officers, no matter what the personal consequences or moral concerns, as in the incidents the Vietnam veteran reported, mentioned above. But whether in Vietnam, Nazi Germany, or elsewhere, how is it that otherwise moral, ethical, sympathetic people can be induced to be obedient to commands that inflict great harm on others?

Stanley Milgram (1963, 1964, 1965) at Yale designed a series of experiments that are among the most important in social psychology. He sought to understand how it could be that people would actually harm one another. This was behavior, not words, and called *action conformity.* The supposed intent of his research design was "to test the effects of punishment on memory." The question Milgram really raised was whether individuals who received a command from a legitimate authority would obey, even though the authority figure had no real power to compel obedience. In the experiment, subjects were ordered to give a confederate an electric shock whenever he or she got a word wrong. The more words wrong, the greater the intensity of the shock. (In fact, no shock was given; confederates were trained to writhe in pain and pound on the wall). Despite apparent pain, the intensity of the shocks was to increase whenever he or she was wrong. There are serious questions about experiments that use human beings. These are dramatic experiments and need to be understood correctly.

When a group of college students was asked to predict how subjects would respond, the majority guessed that they would refuse to administer extremely strong shocks to an innocent victim. However, most subjects did, in fact, obey the command to continue shocking the victim up to the maximum level. After watching the confederate pound on the wall and refuse to do the next task, only 13 percent of the subjects defied the experimenter and stopped. Even when the intensity of the shock reached the danger level and beyond, well over half the subjects were still administering shocks to the victim.

How did the subjects react as they were carrying out an order to deliver painful shocks to an innocent victim? They were not indifferent or cold-blooded torturers. Rather, they seemed to be very nervous, and their tension appeared to be extreme. Subjects perspired, trembled, stuttered, bit their lips, groaned, and dug their fingernails into their palms. Over a third engaged in nervous laughter. Subjects afterward were embarrassed about the laughter and explained that it was not under their control; it did not indicate that they enjoyed the task.

This experiment puts subjects in a conflict situation—conflict between their moral values about harming others and their tendency to obey an authoritative command. What is frightening about the results is that, in this case, the authority figure had no real power over the subjects. They would never see the authority figure again. Presumably, obedience would be even higher if the commands came from someone who had some control over the subject's life.

Milgram, in a modification of the original experiment, wondered whether subjects could be induced to perform acts in response to group pressure that they would not perform individually (Milgram, 1964). The same general experiment was used, but now the subject administering the shock was joined by two associates (confederates). The level of shock to be administered was suggested on each trial by the subject and his or her two associates; the learner received the lowest of the three suggestions. If he or she wished, the subject could administer the mildest shock simply by naming the lowest (15-volt) level each time. The assistants proposed increased shock levels each time.

As a control condition, to determine how individuals respond without group pressure, some subjects had no assistants and each was told that he or she could select any shock level he or she wished on the various trials.

The group pressure led to much more intense shocks being given than the subject-alone condition. When subjects were by themselves, only 5 percent went past the 150-volt condition, in which the learner asked to be released because of a heart condition. Better than two-thirds of the subjects went past this shock level when the confederates urged them on. Once again, it was shown that subjects can rather easily be influenced to inflict pain on an innocent victim.

Although individuals said they would not harm someone and knew it was morally wrong, they did so on command of the experimenter or at the suggestion of the associates in the group condition. If group pressure can induce the subject to continue to give shocks and intensely harm an innocent person, what will encourage the subject to defy the experimenter?

In yet another revision of the Milgram experiments (Milgram, 1965), in the group condition the two confederates went along with the experimenter until the 150-volt shock level. At this point, one of them indicated an unwillingness to participate any further because of the learner's complaints. Despite the experimenter's insistence, the associate got up and went to another part of the room. The experiment was then continued, but after 210 volts the second confederate also decided not to continue, saying, "I'm willing to answer your questions, but I'm not willing to shock that man against his will. I'll have no part of it." With defiant peers for support, 90 percent of the subjects were able to defy the experimenter and stop shocking the victims. Without such support, only 35 percent did so.

Milgram suggests that in the regular experimental condition, moral pressures probably lead many individuals to come near to defiance, but the moral pressures are not quite enough for them to take the final step. Additional pressure from fellow group members who are defiant is sufficient to push them over the threshold of disobedience. As one subject said, "Well, I was already thinking about quitting when the guy broke off." For others, it was as though the defiant peers had suggested something new. "The thought of stopping didn't enter my mind until it was put there by the other two."

Not surprisingly, most subjects denied that the confederates' behavior had anything to do with their defiance; the data, however, clearly indicate that the confederates exerted a powerful influence.

In real-life situations, if only a few individuals speak out and refuse to engage in acts they consider wrong, their influence can be surprisingly powerful. People have greater freedom to defy immoral standards than they realize, and the defiant behavior of someone else can make that fact obvious.

Collusive Behavior: Maintaining the Status Quo of Norms

Butler (1987) examined the anatomy of another kind of collusion: "cooperating with others consciously or preconsciously to reinforce prevailing attitudes, values, behaviors, or norms." The *effect* of such collusion in a group is the maintaining of the status quo; the *goal* is self-protection.

Conscious collusion is easy to recognize and understand. A consultant, for example, witnesses a meeting in which a boss seeks subordinates' commitment to his proposal. The subordinates suppress their true feelings and say only positive things, believing their boss does not want to hear negative feedback. The consultant senses that the subordinates did not respond honestly and confirms this suspicion in private conversations with them. Nevertheless, he still tells the boss, "You ran a good meeting," fearing that the truth will cause the boss to cancel his contract. The boss wants support for his ideas and uses much rhetoric about team work; he neither sees nor looks for subordinates' reservations.

Everyone at this meeting knows what game is being played. The norms are against telling the truth, and all present act out of socially programmed ignorance (Argyris, 1982). This is a clear example of conscious collusion.

Preconscious collusion occurs when a person does not simply hide his or her feelings but actually remains unaware of them. When people feel threatened, which means they face a loss of power, they may exhibit preconscious collusion. A key motivation for collusion is not losing—and perhaps even winning.

Have you ever become angry at being interrupted while making a point—and then pleasantly denied being upset? Such behavior not only reflects our parents' admonitions against expressing negative feelings but has a self-protective function as well. Admitting to anger gives people important information about us, increasing our vulnerability.

Messages from Childhood Leading to Collusive Behavior

Message	Alternative Internalizations	Possible Collusive Behaviors
Be nice	I should mask negative feelings.	Saying "yes" when you mean "no"
	I am a bad person because I am not nice.	Devaluing yourself
You must work harder than white men (a message for women and minority groups).	I am not as good as a white man.	Acting in ways fulfilling the "inferior" label
	I will never be appreciated.	Feeling bitter and resentful toward white men
Do not question adults.	I must defer to those in power and authority.	Not saying what one feels
	Those in power and authority may be ignorant, despotic, uncaring, easily embarrassed, or the like.	Not threatening or challenging those in power and authority
It is not nice to fight.	I must manipulate people to get what I want.	Acting passive-aggressively
	I must avoid disagreeable situations.	Making superficial agreements
Put others first.	What I want is not important.	Devaluing yourself

Much collusive behavior is preconscious. Typically, when a supportive observer points it out, people can see their collusion and acknowledge it. Because it is preconscious, however, and likely to stem from deep socialization messages reinforced consistently by past collusion that successfully protected us (see preceding chart), we are likely to continue to behave collusively in similar situations.

Janis's work on "groupthink" (1982) has shown how socialization pressure leads to collusive behavior at high levels and how organizational difficulties arise because people withhold honest feedback. Researchers have also demonstrated that after groups are required to make a unanimous decision but then could make decisions by majority rule, they continue to decide by unanimity. The conclusion was that the homogeneity of members' opinions at the outset created a strong, continuing norm (Kameda and Sugimori, 1993). Certainly, to live in any society one must play the collusive game to some degree. But the important phrase here is *to some degree.* More understanding and deeper recognition of our collusive tendencies may enable us to reduce the frequency with which we harm ourselves through such behavior.

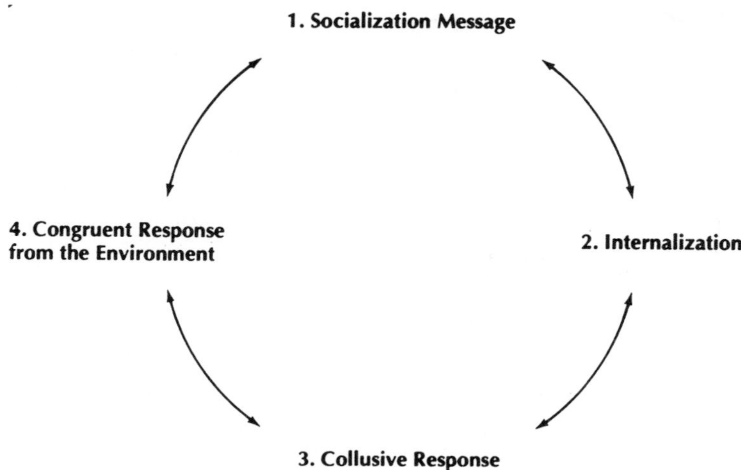

THE CIRCLE OF COLLUSION

Accepting Group Norms: Under What Conditions?

Under what conditions does a member act like other members and conform to the norms of the group? He or she is most likely to conform when one or more of the following circumstances are a factor.

CONTINUED MEMBERSHIP IS DESIRED

If membership is desired, people are more likely to be influenced by other members of a group. If the group is a reference group for a person, he or she will be especially influenced by its norms (Buchwald, 1966; Gould, 1969). It is because we want to "fit in" that we look for dress cues on a campus, listen to others and let their opinions mold ours, and withhold our views when they disagree with those of the majority (Singleton, 1979).

LOWER STATUS IS PERCEIVED

In group-pressure conformity experiments, women tend to conform more than men (Cooper, 1979; Eagly, 1978; Eagly and Carli, 1981; Maccoby and Jacklin, 1974). A possible interpretation of this sex difference is that sex functions as a *status*

FOCUS ON DIVERSITY

What can women do to change others' perceptions of their low status? What about Latinos, or the elderly, who may be perceived that way?

cue in newly formed groups (Berger et al., 1977; Berger, Rosenholtz, and Zelditch, 1980). According to this interpretation, people who enter groups are identified by others in terms of cues, or attributes, that convey information about their status. Sex is a status cue, because—despite women's efforts to overcome these conditions—men generally have higher status than women in both organizational hierarchies and families. Age, race, and physical attractiveness are other examples of status cues.

Social interaction is affected by these status characteristics, because the cues lead to expectations about performance. In particular, men who manifest higher status characteristics than women are expected to contribute more effectively to a group's task. Consequently, they are usually given more opportunities to participate.

Eagly and Chrvala (1986) found that age carried an even stronger status message than sex, and that younger members of both sexes were more likely to conform than older members or female members as measured alone.

SALIENCE OF MEMBERSHIP IS HEIGHTENED

Imagine a research experiment designed to acquire information on attitudes toward birth control. Let us assume the population to be studied is divided into two groups. One group will be asked their opinion on birth control. For the second group, the design will be changed slightly. One additional question will be asked prior to the central one; each person will be asked his or her religion. How will the responses differ? The question on religion heightens the salience or cues of membership, and the respondent is more likely to remember "how one of us is expected to feel."

When a member receives cues that he or she has been named, for example, a member of the administrative staff of a hospital, a member of a professional organization, a Christian, or a member of Amnesty International, he or she is more likely to accept pressures toward uniformity for that group than if membership is unconfirmed.

THE GROUP IS COHESIVE

A cohesive group is one that members find meets their needs or one in which they desire to remain for some other reason. The more cohesive the group, the greater the likelihood that members will conform to the group norms, and the greater the pressure members exert on others to conform (Festinger and Thibaut, 1951; Janis,

1971). It is often said that managers or administrators should help their lower staffs or employees become cohesive units. A highly cohesive work group might develop group pride and produce at a high level. Worker participation often results in production innovations and higher-quality output. Several studies indicate the impact of cohesiveness and subsequent norms on group members' behavior. Baird (1982) reports that prior sharing between individuals produces greater cohesion and cooperation in later problem situations. In a study by Norris and Niebuhr (1980), cohesion was significantly correlated with increased performance. Furthermore, greater cohesion alleviates social pressure on deviants. It's as if cohesiveness induces such norm acceptance that there is little need to halt deviant behavior (Barnard et al., 1992).

SANCTIONS ARE EXPECTED

Norms exist for specific purposes, and if these purposes are valued by members, those who are deviant can expect to be sanctioned. The sanctions may be fines (for lateness, swearing, and so forth), a negative comment, sarcasm or ridicule, or even exclusion from the group. In some situations, the sanctions may be even more severe, such as being dishonorably discharged, fired, banished, or imprisoned, or even put to death.

In the book *One Flew over the Cuckoo's Nest,* the cocky hero, McMurphy, arrives at a state mental institution, which is his lazy man's alternative to the chain gang at the state prison. He becomes interested in the patients and involves them in basketball, watching the world series, even reviving their interest in sex and women—all the while defying the rules of the head nurse, which are expressed as the "community norms."

The patients know the system and the obedience expected; group therapy is a farce. Briefly there is renewed hope that McMurphy will defy the system. As the others marvel at his questioning and noncompliance when it doesn't make sense, they are exhilarated.

It becomes increasingly clear, however, that the system will prevail in the end. It will take away McMurphy's identity (he has defied the rules) and make him and the others dependent on the authorities (who stand futilely by or must punish infractions no matter what). The tragedy unfolds, from electric shock treatments to the ultimate sanction for defying the rules and the authority, a lobotomy.

Sanctions are powerful mechanisms to force members into compliance. When patients, clients, or students are the involuntary members, sanctions can enforce conformity beyond belief. Although the term *sanction* generally has a negative connotation, it is important to note that sanctions can be used for positive reinforcements. Sanctions may also include our name on the honor roll, the designation "good citizen of the week," a raise, a bonus (to the person with the best safety record in the plant), and a promotion.

Another aspect of sanctions is that they carry two messages, one about present behavior and another about future behavior. For example: "That was quite a mistake (present); that had better not happen again (future)"; or, "You're doing a great job (present). At the rate you're going, you'll be a vice-president in no time (future)." Sanctions can be expected to influence both present and future conformity.

Deviance from Norms

What about those who do not conform to norms? An act that violates a shared idea about what should or should not be done at a particular time (or by a particular person) is called a *deviant act.* It is deviant to disagree with Nurse Rachett in *One Flew over the Cuckoo's Nest,* to sit on the table during a board meeting, or to arrive at class in a bathing suit. However, not every behavior that departs from the expected is deviant. A quiet member may become more active; an active member may take an unpopular position in the course of discussion; one member may change his or her feeling toward another member. None of these are deviant acts unless the group has norms that quiet members remain quiet, that no opinions other than the traditional may be discussed, and that members maintain the same relations with others. What happens when a person is deviant?

Interaction with a deviant increases when a group first recognizes a member's deviancy. There will be efforts directed toward amplification and clarification of his or her position, and opposing information will be directed toward him or her in an effort to lessen the deviancy. If the pressure induces the deviant to return to the norms of the group, the discussion will continue, with the deviant in his or her usual role. If, however, the deviant continues the behavior, the group may redefine its boundaries to exclude him or her, ignoring him or her in discussions. This is most likely to occur in a cohesive group and when the area of deviance is relevant to the purpose of the group (Schachter, 1951).

However, if the member is respected and valued, the situation may be different. There is a theory (Hollander, 1960) that prestigious members have "idiosyncrasy credits"—that is, a kind of credit for helpful behavior in the past that allows them leeway in following the norms of the present. It is as though their previous work for the group entitles them to some rewards in the form of increased flexibility of behavior and immunity from punishment for deviance. A prestigious member who deviates from the norm may be dealt with in a number of ways. One is that he or she may be purposely misinterpreted or "not heard." Another is that his or her behavior may be perceived as idiosyncratic ("You know he has these bad days. Disregard anything he says; he doesn't mean it"). Or nonconforming acts are now approved rather than disapproved. (A successful, grant-getting physician and corporation president continues to wear green scrub suits to staff meetings when other staff members are stylishly dressed in designer suits. No one comments on the green scrub suit.)

Until recently, deviance from norms was regarded only as a negative function, behavior requiring reinterpretation and individual or group pressures to return to accepted norms. But Hanke and Saxberg (1985), who studied isolates and deviants in both American and Japanese workplaces, found evidence that members who are constructively deviant, raising questions while coworkers remain silent, can be productive workers rather than costly troublemakers. Thus deviance can serve a positive function.

Piers (1994), by contrast, studied the scapegoat phenomenon. He found that deviance early in the life of a group was perceived as threatening, while at a later time in group development differences were embraced as the "art of the team spirit." Scapegoating can occur for a number of reasons: constitution and temperament, personal inclination, or group selection. But the scapegoat is ultimately a nonconformist. However, if nonconformist behavior is not too self-destructively expressed, the group can utilize it to move away from a simple dual opposition between the leader and the led. This sort of change can move a group from compliance and suggestibility to initiative and social responsibility, and a scapegoat can facilitate such a transition.

Deviance also helps members to master norms (it is a demonstration of what should not be done) and helps them to be more articulate about these norms. In addition, it helps them to comprehend what their group is and what their group is not (to be offended by an act and to see others similarly offended provides information on ourself and on the group that could be gained in no other way). Often, the individual perceives his or her social identity only when it has become problematic (Hewitt, 1989), so in a sense, deviant behavior provides a social identity.

A number of studies call attention to the importance of distinguishing true independence (indifference to the normative expectations of other people and groups) from rebellion (direct rejection of the normative expectations of other people and groups). Although both represent nonconforming behavior, it is important to recognize that they are very different in both the attitudes they represent and the resulting behaviors. *Conforming behavior* (to norms) is a consequence of a person's awareness of expectations held for him or her by others of a group, coupled with a decision to adhere to these expectations. *Rebellion* against norms is a consequence of awareness of the norms, coupled with a decision *not* to adhere to them. True *independence* represents indifference to the norms and expectations of others; personal criteria for behavior, rather than expectations of others, are seen as motivators of behavior.

A provocative way to think about deviance, conforming behavior, rebellion, and independence can be illustrated by the behavior of Michael Bloomberg.

> Michael Bloomberg is a Wall Street legend; over 75,000 investment bankers, bond traders, and money managers pay him $1,000 monthly to receive his news reports and market data. His Bloomberg Information Channel broadcasts on four continents, and his empire has annual revenues of $1 billion.
>
> With a newly minted Harvard M.B.A. in 1966, he signed with a New York investment company at a salary of $9,000 and left to start his own company fifteen years later with a severance check for $10 million (Bloomberg, 1997; Taylor, 1997). How did he rise so fast? "I came in every morning at 7am getting there before everyone else except [the president]. When he needed to borrow a match or talk sports, I was the only other person in the trading room, so he talked to me." And he not only came in before everyone else but he stayed later than everyone except the managing partner. "So when he needed someone to make an after-hours call to the biggest clients, or someone to listen to his complaints about those who had already gone home, I was the someone."
>
> Bloomberg doesn't ever attend going-away parties for his employees. "Why should I? I don't wish them ill, but I can't exactly wish them well either. I wouldn't mean it. We're dependent on each other and when someone departs, those of us who stay are hurt. . . . We have a loyalty to *us.* Leave us and you're *them.*

How do you see Bloomberg as he deviates from work "time" norms? As he deviates from group "leaving" norms? Is his deviance destructive? Will others negatively respond to his behavior? Is he rebellious from norms, deviant, or independent?

Yet another way to think about conformity and independence is the recent phase model developed by Tarnow (1996). He presents the idea that conformity and independence may be due to collective phenomena analogous to those producing different physical states like solid, liquid, and vapor. There are two phases in his model: relatively individual and relatively conforming. In the first phase, group members are free to move in any direction, like water vapor. In the second phase, members conform their behavior, like the water molecules in ice that are all lined up in the same direction. What happens within a phase can change while the phase remains the same. It explains the apparent contradiction between crowd suggestibility and difficulty in controlling a crowd. This model provides simple explanations for some large-group characteristics, such as sudden decision making and rigidity.

Individual Experiment

When you broke a rule as a child or adolescent at home, who talked with you and how? By whom and how were you punished? These experiences represent how your family managed deviance. Groups often respond to deviance in less explicit ways, but usually just as predictably. In a group in which you participate, write a list of minor deviant behaviors, such as not raising your hand before you talk, coming late to a meeting or leaving early, talking about completely irrelevant events, or being too adamant in a disagreement. Take your list to the next group meeting and notice how the group responds to the deviant behavior. Does the leader openly scold you? Does the leader indicate that he or she would like to talk to you after the meeting? Does the leader give you a certain look or make a disapproving face? Do other members communicate nonverbally in some way with you? Is a joke made of the behavior? Will a member talk privately to you after the meeting? Will the behavior be tolerated and not commented on? Or will the behavior be tolerated until it occurs too often and then some formal action be taken by the leader, such as a written warning or a failing grade?

Norms as Inhibiting, Preserving, Institutionalizing, and Stagnating Groups

Group norms can have powerful effects on a group's productivity, goals, and expectations. To illustrate the debilitating functions of norms, John Kenneth Galbraith (1970), in a *Time* article, referred to regulatory bodies, but the phenomenon he described is familiar: "the fat cat syndrome."

> Regulatory bodies, like the people who comprise them, have a marked life cycle. In youth they are vigorous, aggressive, evangelistic and even intolerant. Later they mellow, and in old age—after a matter of ten or fifteen years—they become, with some exceptions, either an arm of the industry they are regulating or senile (p. 88).

After examining the effects of group norms and goal setting on productivity, Lichtman and Lane (1983) suggested that the effects of goal setting are regulated or moderated by the presence of group norms.

Also, group norms tend to preserve the status quo. Procedures that at one time were appropriate and helped the group achieve its purposes may still exist long after their appropriateness has diminished.

Yet the resistance to change that promulgates increased difficulties and problems in a differentiated society is one of the group's prime assets as well. Norms and pressures toward uniformity create security and order in interaction. Members know the rules and procedures for working in that group; they know what is expected, and they hope to be rewarded for conforming to group norms.

It is pointless to ask whether group norms are good or bad. But there are fruitful questions to ask: Which norms help a group achieve its purposes, and which are harmful or inhibiting? Which norms are compatible with the goals and values of the group, and under what conditions? How can the norms be changed or reconsidered to permit a group to achieve its purposes and maximize its resources (Bonacich, 1972; Ford, Nemiroff, and Pasmore, 1977; McGregor, 1967)?

Changing Group Norms

How many people are giving up smoking or going on a diet? Why is it that every year there is a new fad diet book that enough people buy to produce a best seller for the authors? How many people make New Year's resolutions about how they are going to change—this year, definitely!

If an individual who is convinced of a need to change (he or she reads the diet books or throws away the pack of cigarettes) has such difficulty, imagine how hard it is for a group to change—at least ten times as hard. Once norms, which are the group's procedures or expectations for its members, are developed and agreed upon, they are exceedingly difficult to change.

The military umbrella situation is a simple but hard-to-believe illustration (Sciolino, 1997). The Army and the Marines have a policy that male soldiers may not carry umbrellas while in uniform. (However, in a kind of reverse discrimination, female soldiers in the Army and the Marines are allowed to carry umbrellas. The Air Force and the Navy have an "umbrellas-for-all" policy.)

The *Army Times* published a cover story in June 1997 on the umbrella question and, in an editorial, advocated a change of policy. The article elicited more letters than any other subject in recent memory. Neither the Army nor the Marines can explain exactly why the policy exists. The Marine Corps commandant rejected, without public comment, a recommendation by the Marine Corps Uniform Board to change the policy. And the Army chief of staff recently rejected a lifting of the umbrella ban, when he decided not to decide: "The regulation is clear, and we follow regulations in the Army."

The arguments for lifting the ban are many: men wear civilian clothes to the Pentagon (with umbrellas) and change to uniforms at work; being wet coming to work lowers morale; male soldiers can better look out for security concerns when not soaking wet; and they can see through their glasses when there are not rivulets on them. It is also ludicrous when it rains at the Army-Navy football game, and the Navy men sit under their umbrellas while the Army men get very wet. Yet the policy has not been changed.

Communication theorists (Watzlawick, Beavin, and Jackson, 1967) describe a homeostatic balance, which any group or organization has, between new and traditional practices. Communication theory also describes two kinds of change: first- and second-order change. First-order change is just more of the same—when you press down on the gas pedal you go faster. Second-order change is a fundamental rule or norm change, such as when you shift gears in your car in order to go faster. It's something qualitatively different from what you were doing before. It can be an "aha" experience of insight, a significant change in how a group does business and interacts, or a structural change in the roles played by people in a group or organization.

"A chief goal of cultural politics is to change the context and values of the culture," according to Hirsch in his controversial book *Cultural Literacy.* What has been controversial, however, is that what he suggests is *not* a second-order change (Hirsch, 1987).

In a recently posited theory (Galam and Moscovici, 1994), change occurs after a group has determined its norms, when it moves on to the challenge of including and stabilizing internal conflicts.

In a series of experiments where half the groups worked cooperatively and half worked competitively, groups developed norms according to their experiences. The groups were then challenged, some interpersonally, as when two groups with different norms had to reach a joint decision. The other groups were challenged structurally, by a new task altering their incentives for cooperation. Interpersonal challenges were found to be more successful when the norms were cooperative; structural challenges were more successful when the norms were competitive (Bettenhausen and Murnighan, 1991).

Even a change that promises positive results can cause people to be doubtful and threatened by the unknown. For example, in recent years many companies have been changing their computer programs or versions of software for key tasks, but workers have been reluctant to cooperate, even in the interest of the company. Many groups and organizations involve people in planning new changes, making sure that information is clearly communicated. This diffuses some of the resistance to change that maintains status-quo norms.

The classic illustration of resistance to group norm change is the 1954 *Brown v. School Board* Supreme Court decision, which stated that segregated education was, by definition, unequal education. Thirty-five years later, in a reexamination of integration of the schools, it was evident that counterforces had prevailed. The primary method for maintaining the status quo (nonintegration) in the South was for whites to send their children to a newly organized system of private schools rather than to the public schools. In the North, white families moved to suburban areas, where there were almost exclusively other white families. More than three decades later integration was limited, especially in the North. (It had been assumed that the South would oppose integration but that there would be no such problems in the "liberal" North.)

Changing norms is not easy. However, there are a number of ways to do so.

Through "contagion," as in dress style or patterns of speech.

Through influence on the group from the external environment. Examples here relate to reexamination of values about the family: sexuality, relationships to children, and the effects of divorce. For example, a mother's asking for time off to attend a conference with her child's teacher would once have been viewed as evidence that she was not committed to a career, and it would have been unimaginable that an executive father would ask for such time. Similarly, divorce would have seriously impaired a man's career, and a working wife would have been viewed with suspicion.

Through high-status members, who have earned *idiosyncrasy credits*. As mentioned earlier, Hollander (1958, 1960, 1964) offers the hypothesis that those who have reputations for demonstrating competence or living up to the expectations of the group have accrued idiosyncrasy credits. These credits are like a bank account of favorable impressions built up over time. They may be exchanged for freedom from criticism or rejection following nonconforming or individualistic acts. A high-status member can attempt to change norms by playing devil's advocate or offering a "wild idea" or the suggestion to "try this on for size." However, even high-status members may be viewed as deviant if the changes they are suggesting are too drastic. This hypothesis would indicate that a new member of a group who has not had time to build up idiosyncrasy credits would be accorded less freedom for nonconformity than a senior member who has had ample time to build up good will. In a sense, senior members have "paid their dues" and are rewarded with increased freedom from censure.

By groups diagnosing their own norms and modifying them, so that they are compatible with goals and resources.

By an outside consultant. Outside consultants, who are behavioral scientists and experts in organizations, bring an objective perspective to the organization. And because they are not part of the hierarchy, they can influence changes in norms without the same fear of sanctions. They may offer a variety of alternatives and methods for examining change that may be acceptable to the organization.

By trained internal consultants. In this situation, members of the organization are specifically designated to review procedures in light of organization goals.

Through group discussion. Norms formed through interaction can be changed by interaction. Group discussion is generally found to result in more change than other forms of persuasion, such as lectures or directives (Lippitt, Watson, and Westley, 1958).

By those with high self-esteem (Constanzo, 1970; Stang, 1972) and those who are willing to take risks.

Change involves not only increasing the forces in the direction of the desired change but also holding resistant forces constant or reducing them. How can that be done?

Lewin describes three stages in the change process. First, there must be a *disequilibrium.* People need to reexamine the present system, or feel a tension or dissatisfaction with it, or experience themselves in new ways (for example, shop for clothes and be shocked at the size that fits). There need to be "ripples," or incidents, or crises in their lives. As a result of disequilibrium, people experience a sense of urgency, feel off balance, and acquire a different perspective—all leading to the beginning of a process for change. The women's movements of the late sixties stirred organizations to reexamine their norms concerning women. Declining enrollments induced universities to reexamine their admission and recruitment procedures. A deficit in a city budget induces concern about RIFS (reductions in force) and employee morale.

Sometimes heads of organizations say, "We can't change now. Wait until the crisis is over. Then we'll look at what needs to be changed, but not now." However, the greatest inducement for change occurs when there *is* a crisis, an urgency for change.

At the second stage in the change process—behavior changes—people act in a way different from the previous norm, or they come from the disequilibrium (being off balance) to the third stage (behavior) in what is called *freezing*. Some examples of the famous Lewin "action research" during World War II may illustrate these concepts.

Americans were used to eating meat in the 1940s and especially enjoyed red meat. However, there was a war and meat was in short supply. The question became, how could families be induced to try low-priority meats like sweetbreads, kidneys, and liver (Lewin, 1947)? How could their food habits be changed so that they would buy them?

The war effort and the desire to be loyal Americans were the factors that created the disequilibrium; the next step was to produce behavior change. Lewin determined that women were the "gatekeepers"—the major influence on which foods were brought into the house—and he set about changing the behavior of their families through them. Two methods were used to convince them to buy and serve the unfamiliar, unpopular foods. Some women were given lectures on the values of eating the new foods (information); others participated in discussions (which involved information and social comparison).

After discussion, the women reached consensus about what they would do, which was stated and agreed to publicly. Once this public standard existed (for example, "We believe loyal Americans will agree to substitute low-priority meats for high-priority meats once a week"), it was easier to change individual behavior in accordance with the new standard. Lewin found there was greater change among the women who had participated in the group discussion, and that more of these women continued the new behavior. Tjosvold and Field (1983) support the importance of discussion and participation in their study, which states that group decisions meet greater acceptance when they are achieved by consensus rather than majority vote. Falk (1982) similarly found that unanimous decisions created less task conflict in group situations than decisions made by majority rule.

There is extensive research to support the finding that discussion leading to consensus can create a new group norm. In attempting to understand why group discussion seems to be an important element in change, researchers have found evidence pointing to a number of factors. One area of research indicates that breaking down an old value system prior to adopting a new one (creating the disequilibrium stage first) is a crucial element in changing norms (Rokeach, 1971).

Skinner and Cattarello (1989) found that, for marijuana smoking, once a behavioral commitment was made, group norms had a much greater effect on continuing the behavior than attitudes about marijuana smoking. Thus it may be that in any attempt to alter habitual behavior, examining how the peer group operates in constraining its members' behavior is as valuable as, if not more valuable than, merely attempting to change individual attitudes.

Similarly, what produces the changed behavior is not so much the public decision as actual group consensus (Bennett, 1955). The pressure for conformity is greater when there is consensus, as in the Asch experiments, in which a person was most likely to conform when there was not a single dissenter.

In the third stage of change, *refreezing* or stabilization of the behavior change occurs. This is often the most difficult aspect of change. Participants can go through a laboratory experience or be in a personal-growth group and learn about themselves in different ways. Under these special circumstances, they can try a variety of new behaviors and be quite proud of how they have changed. Often, they are convinced that when they return to their organizations they will make major changes there (Luke, 1972). What a disappointment! They return only to find that the behaviors that were so appropriate in the laboratory are discrepant with the norms of the organization. They learn that individual change is very different from organizational change. Although trust and open communication are norms in the laboratory, there are norms of competitiveness, secret information, and distrust in the organization. It is only a matter of weeks before they revert back to the prelaboratory behaviors—often with redoubled frustration: although they were able to make some personal changes, the newly recognized restrictiveness of the organizational norms is even more confining.

Pilot projects are often developed with high hopes. Behavior is changed, but then at the end of the project, the system reverts back to its initial norms. Educators in public schools become wary of innovations; they have become enthusiastic, worked hard, seen projects come and go, and watched the system revert back to where it was before the project began. Some businesses have hired corporate "gurus" to increase productivity by converting work apathy into worker allegiance.

A report in the *Wall Street Journal* (Waldman, 1987) described a typical effort involving expensive training programs designed to change corporate norms by fostering such feelings as teamwork, company loyalty, and self-esteem.

> Workers, however, have had decidedly mixed reactions to the attitudinal training, creating, in many companies, bitter conflicts between employees who embrace the new concepts and those who don't. Younger employees, especially, are more apt to praise the sessions for addressing productivity problems and for attempting to make jobs more meaningful. But many older employees say the seminars—and management—are simply paying lip service to serious concerns in the workplace.

The article made clear that while such training may accomplish some transient changes, negative forces increase owing to resistance to the efforts. The training created ripples but failed to change the culture of the organization.

Perhaps more difficult still is actually playing the role of mover and shaker—effecting change on an individual level. For example, increasing numbers of women have moved into middle- and upper-management positions in many industries, yet most organizations remain predominantly male. Women in these situations often find their options within their work group limited. J. Paaluzzi, in *Savvy* magazine, (1984) shared this revealing anecdote:

> While attending a chamber of commerce luncheon not long ago, I sat next to our city treasurer. Because I was involved in developing a grant application for the city, I took the opportunity to ask her about such issues as tax programs, residential changes, and industrial development.
>
> We had been involved in several minutes of intense conversation when the board member sitting to her other side turned to us, grinned, and said, "Enough of that girl talk. Let's get down to business!" (p. 80)

A woman's actions are evaluated differently from male group members' actions because she is a woman. However hard she may try, she still may not be seen as a legitimate agent of change.

In many areas, we have witnessed enormous societal changes, and these have had an impact on norms that would have been difficult to even fantasize.

An order of nuns was founded in the middle of the last century and remained virtually unchanged for 130 years. It had 1,000 women dedicated to treating the poor and the sick. Women who entered the order knew that they could be sent home for even the simplest disobedience. They wore long black habits made from fifteen yards of material held together with seventy-two tiny buttons that had to be closed with a button hook. They wore immaculate, heavily starched bonnets with attached veils. The convents housed fifty or more nuns. Inside there were no visitors, not even family, and conversation was frowned upon as frivolous or gossip. At dinner, each had her seat at a large table; seating was by longevity in the order. Those who were novices sat at the foot of the table, served, and washed the dishes. No one spoke. Each evening was spent in work or prayer in the chapel. They were not permitted to attend family functions—not even a sister's wedding.

Contrast that description with that of the same order today.

Members are still committed to the poor and the sick, but now they may live in a small house in an urban neighborhood where they can be close to those they serve and share the lifestyle and community of their people. In small groups of four to six, they become a family for each other. All work, cook, and serve on community committees, and they can go to the movies or lectures or classes. They are dressed in clothes typical for women their ages. Discussions on how the community should be conducted are essential elements in their planning for the future of the order, and they vote on many issues. They are consulted rather than ordered. Visitors are welcome, and the nuns are regularly in touch with their families.

Who would have believed all of this could have occurred in the last twenty years?

New members will enter a group confused; the group norms will be unseen or will feel ambiguous. They will feel restrained in their behavior until they can determine what is appropriate behavior and what is expected of them. As they interact with others, the rules become less absolute and more flexible. They appear not only as constraints but also as guides. Newcomers are then better able to see the norms as outer limits within which they are free to operate. When they learn what is allowed, they gain both a sense of confidence and a greater latitude in their behavior—they have options to conform, to deviate, to change, or even to leave.

Multinational Teams and Cultures[6]

Multinational executive teams are coming of age. It is becoming increasingly unlikely that major multinational corporations can operate complex organizations from an unambiguous cultural base of their home country. And the traditional practice of separating national organizations of the same company is quite limiting.

6. The discussion in this section is derived from Maznewski, M. and M. F. Peterson, *Cross-Cultural Work Groups*, pp. 61–89, copyright © 1997 by Sage Publications, Inc. Reprinted by Permission of Sage Publications.

> **FOCUS ON DIVERSITY**
>
> Consider multicultural, multiracial, and multi-ethnic teams as you read this section.

The trend is toward multinational corporations that know how to use multinational teams as business conditions require.

The concept of multinational teams can be greatly expanded to mean multinational teams within the United States, or multicultural teams both here and abroad. Because the United States is, and always has been, a multicultural society, multinational/multicultural work teams influence work in totally domestic organizations.

However, multinational executive groups present a serious paradox for managers. Multinational teams offer the potential for more creative and higher-quality solutions to global business problems than do monocultural teams. They bring more information about global business problems; they view the problems from a variety of perspectives; there is a dynamicism in multicultural group processes which forces an immediate awareness of different viewpoints. Paradoxically, multinational executive teams can also present challenges to effective group interaction that can eradicate potential advantages. Cultural differences can mean different expectations for group processes, and managers from different cultures can lead in ways that produce major conflict and confusion. Lack of agreement on action can mean no action at all. More often than not, multinational teams do not achieve their potential.

Culture systematically influences how team members notice, interpret, and respond to events. *Culture* here means a set of assumptions and deep-level values concerning relationships among people and between people and their environment, shared by an identifiable group of people (Maznewski and DiStephano, 1995; Kluckhohn and Strodtbeck, 1961). Cultural assumptions and values begin very early in life, and then we are socialized in families and institutions within a particular society. These cultural assumptions (norms) are deeply held and a significant influence on individuals and their social behaviors.

Kluckhohn and Strodtbeck (1961) believe that there are five basic questions to which each society must develop answers if its members are to interact effectively. They are:

1. What is our relation to nature?
2. What is our orientation to time?
3. What do we assume is the basic nature of humans?
4. What are the most essential relationships among people?
5. What is our preferred mode of activity?

Although people do not always follow the norms of their culture, culture is particularly relevant to understanding norms and consequently the effectiveness of multicultural work groups. With little information on a person, culture provides a good first interpretation of that individual. We assume others are like us; but if we understand that a person is from another culture and know something of that cultural background, we have more realistic expectations of how to interact. Finally, cultural assumptions and values describe the nature of relationships between people and their environment.

Culture influences all aspects of work in a multinational work group. It affects what events are noticed and how they are thought of in relation to the task. Are they noticed for task-related implications, process implications, or both? Culture affects the processes of individual deliberation and social discussion through which events are more fully examined. It affects preferences for responding. Not only does culture influence which events are noticed, but how they are noticed. Some are highly aware of the process implications—if missing, they will not work well on the task. For other cultures, it is the task; nothing else matters.

Although Maznewski and Peterson (1997) present an excellent analysis of cultural responses to the five questions listed above, a full examination of these responses is beyond the scope of this book. However, discussion of the *relationships among people* may be helpful in understanding how a cultural norm influences a multinational work group.

RELATIONSHIPS AMONG PEOPLE

Relationships among people can be described by three basic patterns. If a society's members think of their prime responsibility as to themselves, or themselves and their nuclear family, the relationship is described as *individualistic.* Societies that see their primary responsibility as to a much larger group, as an extended family or peer group, are called *collective.* And in some societies, relationships among people are arranged in a hierarchical pattern; those higher in the hierarchical order are responsible for those below them, and those lower are expected to obey those higher. Levels of power can be held either individually or by a group.

The implications of these orientations will be greatest for those working within the team itself. For example, a team may be discussing a controversial issue. Members socialized in individualistic cultures expect each member to express his or her ideas and will not notice those who do not speak, assuming they have nothing to say. Members from collective cultures tend to engage in "face saving" in group settings, or ensuring that others are not offended. They are more likely to notice members who are more confrontational. People from hierarchical cultures will be sensitive to hierarchy within the group, notice what senior members of the team say, and respond only if asked.

The relationship orientation influences the norms drawn on when interpreting events. Members of individualistic cultures will go to the person considered the most expert, disregarding hierarchy or group membership. Members of collective cultures will go to others only if it causes neither party to lose face. If asking a question implies that the questioner should have known the answer, or the "expert" should have given the answer without being asked, the question will not be asked. Instead he or she will seek an indirect way to find the answer so that harmony will be maintained. Members of hierarchical cultures are most likely to go to their supervisors or team leaders when trying to understand events.

Group members from each of the different orientations to human relationships, with their different norms, can make important contributions to multinational teams. Those who have grown up in an individualistic culture will fully use their background(s) as they relate to events and expect others to do the same. Members from a collective culture will listen carefully to others, make full use of their contributions, and expect group members to ask others for their ideas. And members socialized in a hierarchical culture will bring the group's attention to senior members and their contributions, and personally make the most use of information communicated by them.

Effective multicultural teams develop synergistic approaches to their work, by integrating and building on the different perspectives brought by members. Two critical processes for achieving such synergy are known as *decentering* and *recentering* (DiStephano and Maznewski, 1996). Decentering is taking the perspective of others and explaining problems in terms of differences in perspective rather than blaming other group members. Recentering calls for identifying or building a common view of a situation and a common set of norms. Both the view and the norms must be acceptable to all work group members. The processes are closely interrelated. Decentering provides information necessary for recentering; recentering provides a basic foundation to build on using the different perspectives.

In multicultural work groups, people accept new ways of thinking, but their prior way of interpreting situations is not erased. The social experiences of their youth will retain a key place regardless of later experiences with other cultures. Culture matters; it is necessary to take into account different cultures as people interact. Thus, managers and multinational work teams face a complex, dynamic reality in which cultures intersect with greater frequency than ever before. They must learn how to work effectively with groups from many cultures, each with their own long-established norms.

EXERCISE 1 Toward Changing Group Norms

OBJECTIVES

- To understand what is meant by group norms
- To recognize the difficulty in changing norms
- To offer an opportunity to examine and change norms at various levels
- To develop insight into how norms can be changed in organizations

When appropriate, this exercise can be used after a group has been working together for some time. It can be a work team, a task group, an organization, segment of a class group, or a seminar.

ACTION

Phase 1 *The facilitator presents a short lecture on norms—what they are, their influence on a group, and so forth. The material in the first part of the chapter might be the basis for development of such a talk. (Approximately 10 minutes)*

Phase 2 *The groups are asked to examine their norms. They list on paper as many as possible (dates, times, seating arrangements, order of meeting or work, typical behaviors, and so on). (Approximately 20 minutes)*

Phase 3 *The group is then asked to change some of its norms. The facilitator says, "Which norms can be changed?" He or she has the group change them and holds a brief session under the new conditions.*

Typically, groups change superficial norms: they will sit on the table instead of in chairs, they will shout rather than talk to one another, or they will attempt to conduct the session nonverbally. This encourages laughter and a reduction in inhibitions—perhaps even a party atmosphere. (Approximately 20 minutes)

(Usually a break is indicated here.)

Phase 4 *The groups are asked to examine which norms they changed and how relevant the changes were in helping to accomplish their goals. What impeded changing norms? What norms need to be changed? The group then goes into its work session on this basis. (The ensuing discussion is very different from the party atmosphere of the first change; it raises difficult issues and involves members in high-risk behaviors.) An observer might be assigned to watch for behavior that changes norms.*

Phase 5 *Later (perhaps the next day, the next week, or at the next group meeting) the group should discuss what norms were changed, which were difficult to change, and why. Who was most influential in changing or proposing changes in norms? Who has the highest status and role in the group? What are the problems involved in changing norms to increase movement toward the group's stated goals?*

EXERCISE 2 Observations and Gender[7]

OBJECTIVES

- To observe gender as a characteristic of communication
- To determine how, if at all, the speech of men and women differ
- To determine how, if at all, interaction among men and women differ

ACTION

(Time: 30 minutes) The exercise can be done in three conditions.

In condition 1, four men speak and are observed by others using the Observing and Gender sheet.

In condition 2, four women are observed, again using the Observing and Gender sheet.

In condition 3, two men and two women interact. The remaining members observe them, using the Observing and Gender sheet.

Observers are instructed to tally behaviors on their sheets and take notes on the interactions that occurred. The facilitator gives each group a topic to discuss. Some suggested topics:

1. What do you consider the state of communication in the United States?
2. How did the stock market rise to over 9,000 affect people?
3. How do you think the educational system should be changed for greater effectiveness?

7. The "Observing and Gender" sheet was first presented by Janine Roberts, of the University of Massachusetts at Amherst, at the National Council on Family Relations Annual Conference, Atlanta, 1987.

OBSERVING AND GENDER

Time Observing ________________

Place ______________________

Name	Number of Times Talks (Code with Tallies)	Amount of Talk Time (Code in Minutes)	Talk After Whom (Code in Initials)	Who Responds to Their Talk (Code in Initial & A—Affirmation B—Disqualification C—Neutral)	Body Language Communicates What to Whom (Code with Brief Notes)	Content Is More Socioemotional or Task Related (Code in S or T and Brief Notes)

Each group speaks for 10 minutes. Round 2 goes on for 10 minutes, and Round 3 goes on for 10 more minutes. Observers should use a different sheet for each set of observations. After the three rounds, observers review their notes and report on the following:

1. How did groups 1, 2, and 3 differ?
2. What was the communication pattern?
3. How does gender affect communication?
4. Do you see a relationship between gender and status?
5. What are the implications of these observations?

FOR FURTHER INFORMATION

Hochschild, A. *The Second Shift: Working Parents and the Revolution at Home.* New York: Viking Press, 1989.

Already a classic, often-quoted book about the contemporary roles of women who work full-time and then come home to child care, household care, cooking, and other family responsibilities (the "second shift"). Addresses the question: Have traditional role/norms changed for women due to their increased employment, or are they expected to take on an additional eight-hour work day?

Kotlowitz, A. *The Other Side of the River: A Story of Two Towns.* New York: Nan A. Talese/Doubleday, 1998.

The story of two towns in Michigan, St. Joseph and Benton Harbor. Although only separated by a river, the towns are worlds apart. St. Joseph is white and prosperous, Benton Harbor is impoverished and 95 percent African American. When the body of a black teenage boy from Benton Harbor is found in the river, it stirs suspicions and unhealed wounds between the two towns. Especially potent in revealing attitudes, styles, and misperceptions of the people in the two towns; challenges readers to think about assumptions about race.

McGrath, J. E., ed. *Social Issues and Social Change: Some Views from the Past.* New York: Plenum, 1983.

An interesting and provocative set of twelve past *Journal of Social Issues* articles which span five decades. Dealing with social change from many different angles, the articles are arranged in six pairs, first with an older article and then its current social-change focus. A second section deals with group processes involved in social change, some of which we are hardly aware, others with group process and social integration, education, and law.

New Games Foundation. *The New Games Book: Play Hard, Play Fair, Nobody Hurt.* San Francisco: New Games Foundation, 1976.

So-called *new games* started as a reaction to the Vietnam War and the counterculture of the late 1960s. Founder Stewart Brand wanted people to understand war through fairly intense physical activity and competition in which no one gets hurt and the groups of players have fun. His first game was "Slaughter," and New Games Tournaments were organized. In this book, however, the norms of playing games have been changed. Although they may include competition, players also act cooperatively, and enjoy the activities and being together. New games have been used in schools, workshops, retreats, professional conferences, and national parks, both here and on other continents. A classic book that explains the origins of new games and presents about sixty games for groups of all sizes.

Peters, T. J., and R. Waterman Jr. *In Search of Excellence. Lessons from America's Best Run Companies.* New York: Warner Books with Harper & Row, 1982.

A well-known, very popular book that invokes the question, How do they do it? The authors studied forty-three successful firms in service industries, consumer goods, and technology to develop eight principles of management, which they believe are transferable. Lots of anecdotes and examples to get a feel for organizational norms and ways of operating.

Thernstorm, S., and A. Thernstorm. *America in Black and White: One Nation Indivisible.* New York: Simon and Schuster, 1997.

Prominent researchers look honestly at the history of racism in America and how to change norms to become a more just, cohesive, and ultimately color-blind society. They argue strongly for color-blind policies as the surest route to a society where people are judged by what they do, not the color of their skin. Much to think about.

Yalom, I. D. *The Theory and Practice of Group Psychotherapy.* 3rd ed. New York: Basic Books, 1985.

Yalom is the author of the standard text in the field. He understands group concepts well and working with groups well, and he is an outstanding writer. The book deals extensively with group concepts, from forming a group (membership), to norms, to cohesiveness, to conflict, to stages of development. There is also a chapter on groups with therapeutic components but not labeled therapy groups. Though written for therapists, it is valuable reading for anyone working with groups.

4 Goals

Imagine that, at the end of a long search, we finally find the oracle. We ask the ultimate question: What is a happy person? What does a person need for happiness?

Here is the simple answer. The things you really need to be happy are

- a dream, to lead you.
- a direction, to give you a sense of purpose.
- a good friend or lover to be intimate and comfortable with.
- meaningful work that is a source of gratification.
- a source of fun, to keep the child in you alive.
- a belief in a force beyond yourself, be it truth, justice, or a universal goal.

If you analyze this advice, you will see that it is *goal-directed*. Goals are defined as internal representations of desired states. The study of goals is ubiquitous in psychological research and spans the history of psychology (Austin and Vancouver, 1996). This is because human beings are doers, and happiness comes to those who pursue dreams beyond their day-to-day reality. Dreams give purpose to life, and people who have lost their dreams have lost their energy and youth as well.

Shorter-term goals are important too. They give life meaning on a day-to-day basis. Examples of long-term goals are to buy a house, become a lawyer, and move out of our parents' house. Short-term goals might be to finish a project, lose five pounds, or pass an exam. Setting up such objectives gives us energy to make use of our time. Without goals, we might drift aimlessly.

Though goals are important to our happiness, life is not about the *attainment* of money, material things, or anything else. Rather, it is about goals *in process*. It is not the ends we strive for, but the process of striving itself that is essential to our satisfaction.

As a nation, we are ever willing to acknowledge and work toward short-term goals but unwilling to concern ourselves with process. Thus we face situations that bring us anger and pain. In an old joke, a passenger asks the driver how far they have to go. The driver replies, "The good news is that we're proceeding at full speed with no obstacles. The bad news is—we're lost." As a nation, we need to understand our goals within the context of their consequences for the overall quality of our lives.

Power of a Goal

Goals have an enormous motivating power, as at least one aspect of the war in Vietnam exemplified. The North Vietnamese had a motivation in the fight that the

FOCUS ON DIVERSITY

Do differences related to diversity (gender, race, or ethnic origin) produce differences in motivation to succeed?

U.S. forces never had. For decades, they had succumbed to the rule of foreign nations. For them, the war was an effort to reclaim their country. Our service people, on the other hand, were no match in terms of will. In fact, they often understood little about why they were in the jungles of Vietnam or why our country was involved in the fighting. In terms of goals, the North Vietnamese were highly focused, whereas U.S. troops were vaguely and poorly motivated.

Distinguishing Between Individual Goals and Group Goals

As individuals, we are constantly concerned with fulfilling our personal goals, but group goals have a different place in our lives. What is the relationship between individual goals and group goals? What proportion of our goals are individual goals? group goals?

Actually, early social scientists debated the very existence of group goals. Allport (1924), an early social psychologist, would have said there is no such thing as a group mind and there could not be a group goal. He argued that

> Alike in crowd excitements, collective uniformities and organized groups, the only psychological elements discoverable are in the behavior and consciousness of the specific persons involved. All theories which partake of the group fallacy have the unfortunate consequence of diverting attention from the true locus of cause and effect, namely the behavioral mechanism of the individual. . . . If we take care of the individuals, psychologically speaking, the groups will be found to take care of themselves.

Kurt Lewin (1939) argued to the contrary. He noted that groups were different from individuals and that groups as systems could not be explained solely as aggregates of individuals. For example, person A has the goal of marrying Jane, and person B has the goal of marrying Jane, but it is absurd to say that the group goal is to marry Jane. Clearly, individual goals are distinct from group goals. Although the raging controversy is over, there continues to be confusion in this area (Quey, 1971; Janssens and Nuttin, 1976; Shaw 1981).

To arrive at a group goal, we must first conceive of the dyad, or a two-person group, and then ask what present or future state of this unit is thought to be desirable to the pair. Clearly, a desirable state cannot be "to win," because the dyad as a unit is not a contestant and has no opponent; the dyad itself can neither win nor lose. Consequently, to refer to the goal of a unit as "to win" is meaningless. What is the goal of the unit?

READER ACTIVITY

Consider the illustration of two tennis players. Each has an individual goal—to win, or perhaps not to lose badly. They meet the criterion of a group, which is usually stated as two or more people interacting with a common goal. They will be interacting.

Are they a unit (two or more individuals)? _____ Yes _____ No

Why? ____

Is there a *common* goal? _____ Yes _____ No

Explain. ____

____

If yes, what is their common goal? ____

____

There are a number of common goals possible, but in connection with tennis, the goal of the players is to play a high-quality game, where they can land and receive some good shots, and where superior play wins. The group goal, as distinct from any individual goals, is to have a good match.

We need to understand two levels of goals: an individual goal, which is to win; and a group goal, which is to have a high-quality contest. Of course, the two are interrelated. The individual needs to be motivated to win to help produce a good contest; the rules of play and the process of selecting contestants are designed to stimulate good play.

For another example, let's look at courtship at both the individual and group levels. An individual's goals in courting are primarily to sell himself or herself, to express a romantic impulse, and to convince the other person that the relationship has a future. The group goal of courtship, on the other hand, might be simply to perpetuate the family. Similarly, in marriage an individual's goals may be to transform the partner into the ideal husband or wife, whereas the group goals might be to satisfy expectations for raising a family.

Two points need emphasis. First, a group goal is not the simple sum of individual goals, nor can it be directly inferred from them. It is the desirable state of the group, not just of the individuals. Second, the concept of a group goal is not a mental construct that exists in some mythical group mind. What sets a group goal apart is that, in content and substance, it refers to the group as a unit—specifically, it is a desirable state of that unit. The concept resides in the minds of individuals as they think of themselves as a group or unit. Remember the saying "The whole is greater than the sum of its parts"? A group goal is the interaction of individual goals, which produces a single goal that is distinctly different from the individual goals.

How Are Individual Goals Formed?

We recognize that we are motivated, and we move with direction, but how is this motivation formulated into a goal? How is it that we keep working in a chosen direction? Some of the most imaginative research was conducted very early in the history of the social sciences by Zeigarnik (1927). According to Zeigarnik's theory, when we set goals for ourselves, an internal tension system is aroused that is correlated to each goal. That tension system continues to motivate us until the goal is actually achieved, or until there is a psychological closure so that we feel it has been achieved.

In the experiments on which the theory is based, subjects were given a long series of tasks to do (typical experimental tasks such as putting pegs in holes or crossing out a given letter on a page). On some of the tasks, the subject continued until completion; on others he or she was interrupted prior to completion. A significant finding was that subjects remembered the uncompleted tasks more frequently than those they had completed. This finding showed that there is a tension system connected to a goal and that it continues until the goal is met. This theory has been tested and verified with a wide variety of subjects.

For example, students have a goal to do well in a course, and a subgoal to pass a midterm examination. They review the texts, study their notes, and apprehensively submit themselves to the ordeal of taking the examination. At the end of the test period, is the tension system reduced? Certainly not. They wait anxiously in the hall and query others on their responses to difficult or ambiguous questions; they enter the next session of class eager to know whether the papers have been marked. Someone can be depended upon to ask at the beginning or end of each session, "When will the papers be back?"

The tension system subsides only when the students have their papers returned and they know more about their progress toward their goal. They then can determine what their next goal will be—with a new tension system modified by the new information.

Horwitz (1954) wondered if tension systems would also apply to group tasks. In his variation, he had teams of two go through the series of tasks. In some, he interrupted one person, but the other member was allowed to complete the task. In other tasks, the individual who started the task completed it. A group tension system did emerge. Members feel a closure when a task is completed, whether they themselves perform the final stages of a task or another member of the group does.

How Are Group Goals Formed?

How do goals change from individual goals to goals for a group? In the transmittal, what are the problems, the implications?

Cooper and Gustafson (1981) suggest that groups, in a manner analogous to the unconscious planning process of individuals, have the capacity to work collaboratively and plan unconsciously for their collective goal attainment. Goals in groups are sometimes consciously planned and established by the group itself or by the environment in which the group exists; at other times, they appear to develop naturally from the interaction of the members.

INDIVIDUALS HAVE GOALS FOR THE GROUP: PERSON-ORIENTED AND GROUP-ORIENTED GROUP GOALS

Basically, we participate in groups because we believe that in doing so, we will derive more satisfaction than if we did not participate or belong.

Individual motives may be characterized as *person-oriented* or *group-oriented.* Although reasons are roughly classified in one category or the other, these motives should be viewed as a mixed bag—a percentage of each will motivate an individual's behavior.

Some people belong to a group for a group-oriented motive; that is, they accept and conform to the group objective even though accomplishment promises no immediate personal benefit to them individually. They are satisfied by results favorable to the group as a unit. For example, people may be active in a political party although they do not personally know the candidates, are not anticipating a job in government, and do not expect any direct rewards. They are motivated to act because they believe their party represents the better choices in the forthcoming elections; they will be satisfied if their party wins and especially pleased if their party "wins big."

Another illustration involves members of a community center board who recognize that facilities at the agency are inadequate and antiquated. They recommend the establishment of a committee to raise funds for a new center. They are fully aware that their children are grown and will not utilize the new center, and that spearheading a building campaign will mean they have less time to spend on their businesses and will cut into their already limited free time. It will entail the onerous task of asking people for money, and it will be a thankless job. Yet they vote for the establishment of the fund-raising committee, knowing full well that if it is approved, they will become members.

On the other hand, an individual whose primary motive is person-oriented is likely to consider a suggested group goal in terms of alternatives for himself or herself. Which of the alternatives will be most satisfying? Which offer the greatest benefits at the least personal costs? The individual whose prime concern is the group-oriented motive will consider which goal, if attained, will be most beneficial to the group, even when the consequences may not benefit him or her.

Although the terms used here are *person-oriented* and *group-oriented,* you are aware of their similarity to other, more familiar terms. Person-oriented goals are sometimes referred to as "selfish" motivations or "ego orientations," and the person is said to be thinking in terms of "what's best for me." Group-oriented goals are often thought of as "altruistic" motivations or "task orientations," and the prime concern of such people is how well the group achieves its goals.

Does it really make a difference for which reasons a person helps a group achieve its goals? Isn't the real issue that he or she be willing to accept the group's goal and move in that direction? It seems it does. In an experiment where students could set individual goals or group goals on a task, their group goals were of lesser difficulty. Thus social factors may have an important role in goal-setting situations (Hinsz, 1991). Furthermore, groups with more self-motivated behavior had longer meetings yet covered fewer items on their agendas. Also, they reported being less satisfied with both the decision making and the leadership in their meetings than those groups having more group-oriented members (Rieken and Homans, 1954).

Studying the processes that mediate the relationship between a group goal and group member performance, Weingart and Weldon (1991) report that group members who had a common group goal felt that more satisfaction was gained from the group's process because it was viewed as a personal challenge to work through difficulties to achieve the goal. By contrast, person-oriented group members did not feel satisfaction with the process or resolution of interpersonal difficulties.

The impact of person-oriented and group-oriented motives of group members has been the subject of recent research (Welden and Weingart, 1993). One object of special interest is the goal-setting conditions, or the conditions imposed by outside-the-group sources, such as researchers. For instance, one study examined the effects of four different goal conditions: (1) an individual goal condition, (2) no specific goal condition, (3) a group goal condition, and (4) an individual plus group goal condition. These goal conditions were analyzed in terms of their impact on group members' performance on an independent task. Performance on that task was worse in the individual goal condition than in any of the other three.

Furthermore, research indicates that person-oriented group members—that is, people who are working under their own goal condition—tend to be more competitive and less cooperative than those working under the other three conditions. Although the categories of person-oriented and group-oriented denote two separate entities, they really overlap such that individual motives, be they person-oriented or group-oriented, vary over time and therefore fluctuate. Thus goal conditions, or the condition(s) imposed on a group by outside-the-group individuals or group members, do affect group members' performance to achieve goals.

INDIVIDUAL GOALS ARE CONVERTED TO GROUP GOALS

There are certain limitations on the determination of goals. First, there are the limits set in the purposes of the organization. A United Fund committee does not decide that its goal will be whether to raise money but, rather, how much money to raise. The organizational purposes determine the goal in this case, and it is the subgoal (how much money this year) that is discussed and agreed upon. A second limitation concerns changes in the group or its environment that may necessitate reevaluation of its goals (Elliot and Harackiewicz, 1996). Within these limitations, groups develop goals by applying the criteria of fairness, effectiveness, or some combination of the two.

There seems to be a sustaining myth that groups arrive at goals in a manner reminiscent of a New England town meeting. Each person speaks and makes his or her point of view known. The others listen, consider the information, and arrive at a decision that represents the most effective method for dealing with the situation, or at least the best decision possible. The group decision arrived at is assumed to be compatible with the individual interests of the majority. In reality, the picture is usually quite different. Although ideally each member should have an equal say in the determination of goals, it rarely happens. Some, by their personalities, are more verbal and forceful than others. Some speak eloquently on many subjects, others only in an area in which they disagree. Still others do not participate at all.

On another level, some group members are excluded from even an opportunity to speak, because decisions are made by the executive board or the planning committee. The criterion of fairness—that is, full participation—in setting of goals is not met. Frequently decision making or goal setting by a select few or even one person is justified in terms of effectiveness. It is assumed that the head of a company knows best what a group can achieve; the expert is most knowledgeable in setting a goal for the whole group. The argument frequently goes, "If we had unlimited time, we could allow all members to participate, but it becomes such a long and frustrating procedure that it is more effective to have goals set by one person or a few people."

For some, an attempt at fairness means reduced efficiency; they believe time expended in arriving at goals could be better expended in progress toward achieving the goal. However, it is possible that the preceding two criteria may be compatible. That is, it may be possible to widen member participation in setting goals and direction for the group (increasing the fairness criterion) *and,* through this increased participation, arrive at goals that are also most effective. A problem-solving method of arriving at group goals involves discussing alternative choices, examining the resources of members for developing each of the alternatives, considering the time available, and assessing the probability of success.

In terms of the previous discussion of person-oriented (individual-oriented) and task-oriented (goal-oriented) motives of participants in setting goals, some differences in behavior may be discernible (Kelley and Thibaut, 1954). If task-oriented motives are dominant, members are more likely to arrive at group goals through problem-solving approaches—that is, through exchange of information, opinions, and evaluations. If person-oriented motives are dominant, goals are apt to be determined only after arguments, negotiations, bargaining, and forming of coalitions (Fourezios, Hutt, and Guetzkow, 1950).

Reader Activity

Our membership in groups is not random. We join groups for a number of reasons, and we are committed to the group's goals in different ways. Consider two situations:

1. Think of the group you most want to be associated with.

   What do you want from this group? ______________________

   ____

   What are you prepared to give to it? ______________________

   ____

   What does the group want from you? ______________________

   ____

   What does it give to you? ______________________

   ____

2. Think of a group you recently left or are considering leaving.

What do you want from this group? ____________________

____

What are you prepared to give to it? ____________________

____

What does the group want from you? ____________________

____

What does it give to you? ____________________

____

3. How do these different situations influence you in working for the group's goals?

____

Individual Experiment

Pick a group of which you are a member. It could be the student council, a sports team, a class project group, or a fraternity or sorority. Interview two group members, one who is centrally involved in the business of the group and one who is minimally involved. Find out from each what his or her personal goal is in being a group member, as well as what he or she sees as the goal of the whole group. Can you identify points of similarity or difference between the group and individual goals of the two people you interviewed? How do you think similar or different viewpoints affect how the group works?

Classification of Goals

In addition to understanding goals from both an individual and a group perspective, we can also understand goals in terms of a number of classifications. We can classify goals as formal or informal and as operational or nonoperational. And we can describe the movement on goals as action on a *surface* agenda or a *hidden* agenda (Bradford, 1961). These concepts are illustrated in the following example:

The dean of students at a suburban college was concerned about lack of involvement, even among heads of campus organizations, in school activities. It is a predominantly commuter school where students come to their classes and then immediately leave for their jobs. In a move to build cohesiveness, college officials decided to subsidize a weekend retreat and encourage campus leaders, as well as those interested in becoming more active at school, to sign up to learn leadership skills.

Following the retreat, the student newspaper reported that a very successful, productive weekend had taken place.

So much for the myth! The very next issue of the student newspaper carried a banner headline: "President of student government resigns." The article noted that the vice-president of the student body and the president had resigned before the end of the weekend.

It turned out that under a plan fostered by the dean of students, a coalition was created in which all student organizations would be subsumed under a new head. This plan in effect demoted the student council a layer; now it was just another of the student organizations on campus. Also, it had been determined that there was a need for a student center building and that getting one would be the goal of the new organization.

The president and vice president resigned ostensibly because they objected to the way the coalition was formed. The president also attributed her resignation to a lack of support: "We've plodded along with no positive or negative feedback. . . . I didn't get support at the weekend retreat, and if you don't get support when everyone is 'up,' when do you get it? Half the student body doesn't know we exist. Why should we even be there?"

At a formal level, the purpose of the retreat was to teach leadership skills to existing and potential leaders and show them how to have an impact on campus. At an informal, or implicit, level, the group goal was to take power as a group. It was on this level that actions were taken (coalition formed, plan for a student center drawn up, resignations submitted). The formal goals had little meaning in this context, and the actions that took place were hard to interpret in the context of those formal goals. In short, action on goals is understood in terms of the dynamics at the *informal,* not the formal, level.

OPERATIONAL VERSUS NONOPERATIONAL GOALS

Operational goals are goals for which clear, specific steps to achievement are discernible. *Nonoperational goals* are abstract; steps to their accomplishment may be difficult, if not impossible, to discern, and achievement may take a tremendous amount of time—if it occurs at all. The coalition's goal to create a new student center was a nonoperational goal, because the college had its own long-range building plan for the next five to ten years that did not include such a building. The odds were small that students would have sustained interest in a building that, even if constructed, would never benefit them. (Most present students would be long gone before such a center could even be built.) Also, the college, always short of funds, was unlikely to allot several million dollars to a building for student leaders when there was little interest in student activities or student government on campus anyway. We might conclude that the president, despite her *stated* reasons, resigned solely because the other leaders had voted to adopt a nonoperational goal.

Nonoperational goals are broad and vague (for example, supporting motherhood, working for full employment, and favoring a separate building for student activities). There is fundamental agreement among members, and the subject is safe. There are words, but few actions other than vague recommendations and general resolutions.

Operational goals, on the other hand, are specific. They have well-defined targets, action plans, and evaluations set for specific times. A six-month campaign to gain fifty additional members for the organization is an operational goal, as are strategies to increase the organization's income. An operational goal in the context of our example might be to hold a series of meetings to decide whether students wanted representation by the student government. The commission would hold hearings on how students wanted to be represented on campus. The hearings and a process for arriving at a conclusion would represent active steps to be taken in the achievement of an operational goal. It was further found that when goals are clear (explicit and operational), the result was a gradual but steady improvement in complex task performance (DeShon and Alexander, 1996).

Operational goals are specific and carry with them clear direction for movement and recognition of what will constitute a solution or goal attainment.

An analysis of faculty career goals suggests that faculty share a common core of goals specifically geared to their professional advancement (Mann, 1989). In turn, this suggests that common goals breed operational goals that are manifested in decisive action plans, such as clearly delineated targets, professional steps to be taken, and time management to allow for goal evaluation, revision, and resolution. Bantz (1993) found that in work with culturally diverse, cross-cultural teams over ten years, the most effective tactic for managing the impact of differences was identifying clear, mutual, long-term goals. However, operational goals can involve conflicts, as individuals discuss different ideas about steps to be taken and desired outcomes. Operational goals also entail concepts of success and failure, time limits and evaluations, and responsibility and achievement.

Surface and Hidden Agendas

In addition to classifying goals, we can describe movement on goals on two levels: the surface level, or *surface agenda,* and the below-surface level, or *hidden agenda.*

In our weekend-retreat example, the surface agenda was to bring students together to learn leadership skills. Student leaders would get to know each other through extended contact over a weekend—this is a straightforward goal. Though others on campus might have been apathetic, these students were interested in student organizations and had some commitment to the goals of student government. Their tasks over the weekend were predictable: participants would practice leadership skills, team building, and diagnosis of simulated or real organizational problems.

However, on a hidden level much more would happen. When the dean of students suggested that a coalition structure would help students have a greater impact, what was his goal? Was it simply to establish the coalition, or was it to facilitate his own dealings with student leaders by consolidating them into one group? Or was he perhaps suggesting the coalition in the hope that its head would be a student he favored over the current president of the student association?

When the student president initially accepted his suggestion with enthusiasm, what was her goal? Was it perhaps to simplify the way students were heard through an existing structure? Or was her goal to increase the power of the student government association? Or to counter the growing power of the administration over student organizations and ensure that students retained their power?

Perhaps some leaders accepted the dean's suggestion simply because many of their friends would be in the coalition. Perhaps one agreed because he or she saw a chance to be elected head of the new coalition. And dissenters might have opposed the idea merely because they resented the fact that the dean of students could further his ideas without conferring with them.

As we reflect on this situation, it may seem that logical thinking had been foregone and that emotionalism had become the norm. But we need to realize that groups work simultaneously and continuously on two levels. One level is formally labeled. Whether confused or clear, simple or difficult, this is the obvious, advertised purpose for which the group meets. Unlabeled, private, and covered, but deeply felt and very much the concern of the group, is another level (Bradford, 1961). On this level are all the conflicting motives, desires, aspirations, and emotional reactions of the group members, any subgroups, and the group as a whole that cannot be fitted legitimately into the accepted group task. Here are all the problems that, for a variety of reasons, cannot be explicitly acknowledged. These are called *hidden agendas.*

Hidden agendas are neither better nor worse than surface agendas. Rather, they represent all of the individual and group problems that differ from the group's surface task, and therefore get in the way of the orderly solving of the surface agenda. They may be conscious or unconscious for a member or a group.

Both groups and individuals can have hidden agendas. In essence, hidden agendas represent what people want as opposed to what they say they want. Albert Ellis, the founder of rational-emotive therapy, notes that neurotic goals can dominate these agendas, but hidden agendas need not be neurotic. They represent a wide variety of "reasons" not to focus on the present situation. Such goals interfere with our ability to focus on group needs and group goals in the present. Instead, they keep us functioning at the level of our impossible-to-meet needs. Such needs include

- the need to be perfect.
- the need to be liked and cherished by every living human being.
- the need to appear sure about everything.
- the need to have complete control.
- the need to appear neutral by concealing feelings.
- the need to avoid conflict owing to an inability to confront and work things through.
- the need to defend oneself and resist feedback with defensiveness.
- the need to project onto others what one does not want to see in oneself.
- the need to judge oneself and others.

Remember, leaders as well as members can have hidden agendas.

Each agenda level affects the other. When a group is proceeding successfully on its surface agenda with a sense of accomplishment and group cohesiveness, it is evident that major hidden agendas have been settled, are being handled concurrently with a surface agenda, or have been temporarily shelved. Let the group reach a crisis on its surface agenda, however, and hidden agendas that have not been resolved may emerge.

Groups can work diligently on either or both agendas. A group often spends endless time getting nowhere on its surface agenda, seemingly running away from its task, and yet, at the end, gives the impression of a successful, hard-working group. Often group members leave a meeting saying, "Finally we're getting somewhere." When asked what they have accomplished, they might mention some trivial aspect of the surface agenda. What they are really saying is that an important issue on the hidden agenda has been resolved.

A group may have been working vigorously without visible movement on its assigned task. Suddenly, it starts to move efficiently on its task and in a short time completes it. The group had to clear its hidden agendas out of the way before it could work on its assignment.

Let's return to our retreat example. On this college campus, apathy about involvement in student organizations may have prevailed for years, if not decades. However, the retreat changed all that. The first newspaper article, which presented the surface agenda for the retreat, seemed to indicate that the weekend had gone well and that the surface agenda was in fact followed. The second article, however, exploded the myth and brought the hidden agenda to the surface. Real issues—whether students or administrators would really run student activities, conflicts between the president of student government and the office of student services, and conflicts between the student president and coalition—all came to light and became the focus of discussion. This sparked more interest in student government than the campus had seen in years.

Hidden agendas can block the progress of a group. If they are not recognized and understood, a great deal of the organization's energy will be wasted in frustration and feelings of powerlessness. Hidden agendas can be dealt with in the following ways:

Consider that hidden agendas can be present. Recognition of hidden agendas at individual and group levels is the first step in diagnosis of a group difficulty.

Remember that a group is working concurrently on two levels. Recognize that the group may not move so quickly on the surface agenda as the more impatient might wish.

Not all hidden agendas can be brought to the surface; they may hurt group members' feelings if discussed openly, and create an atmosphere of distrust. Other hidden agendas can be talked about and do become easier to handle. It is important to know which can and which cannot be faced by the group.

Don't scold or pressure a group because there are hidden agendas. They are legitimate; each of us is constantly working out individual needs in the group as well as group needs. It is a legitimate part of group life that we see things differently and want different things accomplished.

Help a group work out methods of solving hidden agendas just as they develop methods by handling surface agendas. Methods may vary, but basically they call for opening up the problem, gathering data on it, generating alternatives for a solution, and deciding on one. Data from people, and feelings, are important.

Help the group evaluate its progress on handling hidden agendas. Each experience should indicate better ways of more openly handling future hidden agendas. There may be short evaluation sessions (ten minutes) at the end to review progress. Are members able to talk more freely in areas that were previously difficult? Is there a greater feeling of comfort?

Groups can deal with hidden agendas via careful planning, perhaps by facilitators or a steering committee. Answering these five questions at the planning stage will help counteract the blocking power of hidden agendas:

1. What are the advertised goals of the program?
2. Do the leaders have any covert or hidden goals?
3. Do the participants have any covert or hidden goals?
4. What do participants expect will be the outcomes of the program?
5. What do participants actually want from the program?

There are several techniques a leader can use within meetings themselves to bring hidden agendas to the surface. Suggesting a quick "go-around" is one. The leader asks each person to express his or her feelings about a proposal before the group votes as a whole. Another technique is to ask directly, "What seems to be blocking us?" Yet another is to separate participants into small groups of three or four and ask them to determine what must happen before the problem at hand can be solved. Small group discussions sometimes yield answers that are blocked from surfacing in the larger group (Rohde and Stockton, 1992).

READER ACTIVITY

Think of a group of which you are a member. What blocks the group's movement toward its objectives? Why do things seem to "go off on a tangent"? List as many things as you can think of.

____

____

____

Who has the hidden agenda? (A member? A subgroup? The leader?)

____

____

____

Think about each of these hidden agendas. Given your knowledge of your group, what are some things that could be done about one of the hidden agendas?

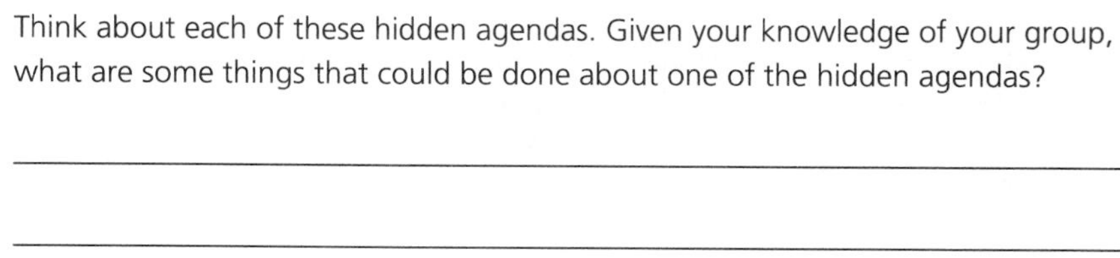

As a group increasingly deals with hidden agendas, it becomes possible to see with greater clarity what the group's goal really is. From the viewpoint of members, goals are sometimes classified as "clear" or "unclear." When clear goals exist, each member, if polled, could respond with a statement of the goal and the steps for its attainment. Clear goals are more likely to be operational goals, more likely to be stated formally, and more apt to be on the surface agenda. When unclear goals exist, members, if polled, would give a variety of replies depending on their personal interests, and they would have a variety of ideas about how these goals should be attained.

Generally, a successful group has clear objectives, not vague ones, and members have personal objectives that are compatible with the group's objectives. The more time a group spends developing agreement on clear objectives, the less time it needs to achieve them, and the more likely members' contributions are to converge toward a common solution. Lane (1982) found that making group goals explicit improves the chances of a group to achieve the stated goals.

Relationship Between Group Goals and Group Activities

Goals themselves are powerful inducers of action (O'Leary-Kelly, Martocchio, and Frink, 1994; Locke, 1996).

What the goal is and what kind of goal it is influence relationships among members (Korten, 1962). For example,

In a recent book (Benjamin, 1997) an anthropologist reports on sending her children to school in Japan. She writes that besides mastering a curriculum set by Japan's Ministry of Education, "children were expected to absorb what Japanese consider the key lesson: that people are happiest and most productive in groups." Classes are large and heterogeneous, with one teacher for forty children of varying abilities. The primary instructional method is division into *han,* small groups in which students devise answers together and affirm or correct one another's ideas. Teachers mostly interact with *hans,* but not individuals. In this system, substitute teachers are rarely used; when a teacher is sick, even first graders can run the class themselves.

FOCUS ON DIVERSITY

Does understanding their culture have a bearing on teaching immigrant children? Or working with immigrants in any way?

Given the key lesson that people are happiest and most productive in groups, note how activities are structured all day, every day. How do students communicate? How do they solve problems? How do they deal with individual differences? And especially note the role of the teacher. It is almost impossible for many in the United States to imagine such a large class where children can conduct the class when the teacher is sick. This system is totally unlike the American individually-oriented one, but it does help us understand how each system produces very different outcomes, and that group goals are a prime influence on group activities.

Now think about sports teams. What are their goals? In practice sessions process goals predominate—how teammates will work the plays, how consistent are they at getting the ball into the goal. However, in competitive games, the focus is on outcome—how well are they scoring, whether they are winning (Brawley, Carron, and Widmeyer, 1992).

Goals also have a powerful impact on the interdependence between goals and resources. When goals are mutually dependent on resources (such as available information given by a computer to aid in a problem-solving task), positive goals promote higher individual achievement and group productivity in problem-solving success (Johnson, Johnson, and Stanne, 1989). When the goal is positive (such as gain in scholastic status) and the resources are readily available, then the group goal encourages group activities that promote success.

CONTENT OF THE GOAL AFFECTS THE GROUP

Let us assume that the goal of a correctional institution is the rehabilitation of prisoners (Zald, 1962). Staff members might be given a great deal of autonomy and might be encouraged to be creative. There would be great emphasis on programs. There might be a reading program or even a college program on the premises. There might be lectures, plays, and special speakers brought in to keep members informed. There might even be group activities such as an orchestra, chorus, or dramatic group that performs for community groups outside the prison. The goals would be to encourage prisoners to develop their vocational and artistic skills and to become more competent in the outside world while serving time.

Contrast these activities with another correctional institution where the goal is custody of prisoners—holding them so they cannot inflict damage on citizens of the community. In this situation, there would be fewer professional staff and more custodial staff (guards). Authority would be centralized, and rules and penalties would be the basis for relationships.

The difference in content of goals will result in a difference in relationships among staff and prisoners, as well as a difference in activities.

DIFFICULTY OF THE GOAL AFFECTS THE GROUP

Suppose that in a twelve-game season, a college football team won eight games. What will be the team's goals for the next season? Will it set a goal of winning two games? To win only two games would be regarded as a disaster; it would be too easy. Will it set a goal of winning all twelve games? This seems too difficult and would probably doom the team to failure.

Assuming none of the key players graduates or sustains serious injuries, the group would set an aspiration level of perhaps nine or ten games. To win this number would be regarded as a successful season, a fine performance by the team.

This example is meant to illustrate the aspiration level of a group; that is, when a group confronts a set of alternatives ranging from easy to difficult and selects one, this is referred to as the group's *aspiration level.* Performance above this level will be considered successful; performance below this level, failure. The level of aspiration will influence members' self-evaluations, group activities, attractiveness of membership, and subsequent group cohesiveness. Groups that are successful tend to be realistic about their aspirations (Waung, MacNeil, and Vance, 1995; Atkinson and Feather, 1966).

Failure to reach group goals can undermine the attractiveness and cohesion of a group. Taylor, Doria, and Tyler (1983) conducted a study of an intercollegiate athletic team that experienced repeated failure but was able to maintain a high level of cohesion, however. Two factors were responsible for this. First, responsibility for performance was spread over the entire group, rather than being given to specific individuals or subgroups. Also, group members tended to attribute failure more to themselves and less to other group members, yet they did not attribute more than an equal share of success to themselves. In general, though, more committed and more cohesive groups were found to outperform less committed and less cohesive groups under difficult goal conditions (Whitney, 1994).

TYPE OF GOAL AFFECTS THE GROUP

Whether goals are competitive or cooperative greatly influences the activities toward the goals and the relationships among members. We are a highly competitive society. We play games in which there are winners and losers; in fact, we speak of people as "winners" or "losers" even outside the context of games. Tennis is an example of a competitive game; baseball is another. If one team wins, the other loses; there is never a tie at the end. However, baseball also has cooperative goals. Each member of the team can attain his or her goal of winning only if the entire group also attains its goal—the team must win as a unit. Members therefore attempt to cooperate with one another, coordinate their efforts, and use their resources jointly. Observers report significant differences between groups working under competitive conditions versus cooperative conditions.

Where there were competitive goals, members would seek to "one up" each other, withholding information and displaying hostile feelings and criticism (Klein, 1956). For example, in schools where grade-point competition is keen and colleges will accept only a limited number from one high school, competition is unbelievable. High-ranking students push to become presidents of obscure clubs, thus gaining one more degree of status to edge out competition. It comes as no surprise that a student will remove the notice of a prospective visit by a prestigious college representative or information on scholarships from the bulletin board to reduce competition. And the competitiveness induces hostility and criticism toward those who figure out the best "angles."

The classic work on the effects of cooperative and competitive conditions in attaining group goals was done by Deutsch (1949). Deutsch explained that in a cooperative situation, group goals are homogeneous—that is, group members hold the same goal for the group. In a competitive situation, group goals are heterogeneous—that is, group members hold differing goals for the group.

In a competitive situation, when one person reaches a goal, others will, to some degree, be unable to obtain their goals. Each person is out for himself or herself. In a cooperative-goal situation, if one person reaches a goal, all other members are helped in reaching their goals. Whether the situation is cooperative or competitive influences a wide variety of group processes, including attitudes and willingness to work with others as well as the attractiveness, cohesiveness, and effectiveness of the group. Regarding the latter characteristic, Deutsch (1949), in another classic experiment, determined that productivity per time unit was greater in cooperative than in competitive groups and that the quality of both the products and the group discussions were higher in the cooperative groups.

The relationship of cooperation and competition in groups to achievement and productivity is still a much-debated subject. Johnson (1981) compared the effectiveness of four types of goal structures in groups: cooperation, cooperation with intergroup competition, interpersonal competition, and individualistic goal orientation. He reports that cooperation is considerably more effective than interpersonal competition and individualistic efforts. Cooperation with intergroup competition was also found to be superior to interpersonal competition and individualistic efforts. Kramer and associates (1986) looked at cooperative and noncooperative responses of undergraduates reacting to a simulated resource-conservation crisis. As predicted, cooperatively oriented students responded to the resource depletion with greater self-restraint (that is, greater concern for others) than did the noncooperators.

What are the dynamics of cooperation? Johnson and Johnson (1991) reviewed more than 520 experimental and more than 100 correlational research studies conducted over the last ninety years. After comparing cooperative, competitive, and individualistic efforts in their own twenty-five years of research, they concluded that "working together to achieve a common goal increased effort, yielded higher achievement, and greater productivity than working alone." (p. 88)

They found three broad outcomes of groups working cooperatively together.

1. *Effort exerted to achieve.* Working together in a situation where groups can succeed in reaching their goals results in members encouraging and facilitating each other's efforts. Members search for and receive more information from each other, use members' information, and influence each other's attitudes and conclusions. Group members become intrinsically motivated to succeed and have continuing motivation to complete the task successfully. The superiority of working cooperatively is most clearly seen in conceptually complex and problem-solving tasks as members share information, examine alternatives, and influence each other in discussions of vexing problems.

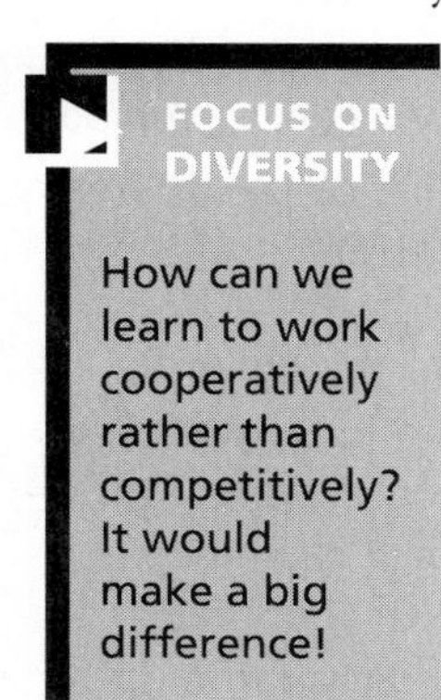

FOCUS ON
DIVERSITY
How can we learn to work cooperatively rather than competitively? It would make a big difference!

2. *Quality of relationships among participants.* An important factor not sufficiently recognized is that individuals care more about each other and are more committed to each other's success when they work together cooperatively. These results hold even when group members are of different sexes, ethnic groups, social classes, or ability levels. The more frequently cooperation occurs, the more positive relationships become. Members become friends; they even have more positive attitudes toward supervisors and organizational superiors. And it

spreads further: They like their tasks more, as well as even the organization within which the cooperative group works.

3. *Participants' social skills and competence.* Social skills and competencies tend to increase more within cooperative groups than in competitive or individualistic groups (Johnson and Johnson, 1989).

Yet another recent study (Chatman and Barsade, 1995) raised a different question. If someone is disposed to work cooperatively, does it continue when the organizational culture is individualistic? Participants in the study were assessed as to their dispositions to cooperate, then they were assigned randomly to simulated organizations that either emphasized collectivistic or individualistic cultural values. Cooperative participants in collectivistic cultures were rated by coworkers as the most cooperative. They could work well with more people, evaluated others by contribution to the group, and were more responsive to collectivistic or individualistic norms. Cooperative people exhibited greater differences in their behavior across the two cultures than did individualistic people; that is, being cooperative produced a greater ability to work cooperatively in different organizational cultures.

GROUP GOALS THEMSELVES ARE INDUCING AGENTS

Previously, we discussed the tension systems linked to a goal. It seems that when a group accepts a goal, those who most strongly do so display a strong need to have the group achieve its goals. Acceptance of the goal is for them an inducing agent (Martin and Manning, 1995; Horwitz, 1954).

However, if a group goal is not accepted by a significant section of a group, there is likely to be a high incidence of self-oriented and resistant behavior rather than group-oriented behavior, with activities being coordinated to personal rather than group goals. In a study that examined the motivational effects of feedback and goal setting on group performance, Watson (1983) found that explicit goal setting improved group performance and was a significant factor even where no feedback was given.

In a study of the role of goal setting and its influence on self-efficacy, or the individual's power to produce an effect on group goals, Lee (1989) found that the performance of a female college field hockey team was related to the team's winning percentage. It seems that setting an explicit group goal elicits significant motivation to reach the group's goals: to win.

Further supporting the hypothesis that goal setting is a major factor in inducing better group performance, Harlow (1989) reports that groups with specific goals outperform those who are asked simply to do their best.

GROUPS AS TOOLS FOR CREATING GOALS

Given that goals are important group motivators, it is important to know how groups themselves can set goals. A good model was suggested in 1985, when a symposium of applied and academic scientists proposed to improve relations between the two groups. The first symposium was attended by eighteen applied scientists and eighteen academics representing thirty colleges and business firms. Four topics for small group discussion were specified: research and development, education, management of practice, and technical applications. Each group agreed on five goals for improving relations between academics and practitioners. Smith and Culhan (1986) reported that "the high priority recommendations for the four [small] groups agree to a significant degree [and] every group identified faculty internships in industry as a key to improving relationships." This agreement established goals for further action.

Group Productivity

Group goals are meant to be a guide for action. However, structure of a goal can affect group productivity, and there has been recent interest focused on this subject. In a series of experiments with preexisting groups, researchers established four different goal structures: egocentric individual goals, group-centric individual goals, group goals, and group goals in combination with group-centric individual goals. The results indicate that goal structure does make a significant, consistent difference. Performance in groups having both group goals and group-centric individual goals was superior to all other combinations of goal conditions (Crown and Rosse, 1995).

An obvious measure of a group's productivity is its success in achieving its goals. Were goals clear enough and operational enough to be measured? At what costs? Are members disillusioned and are relationships strained? Are members glad the project is over so they can terminate their associations?

Some might question the validity of raising the question "At what costs?" For them, the productivity question is the most important one. Did they accomplish the goal—raise the money, develop the recommendations, increase membership, or resolve the situation between the executive director and the staff—in the best way?

Nonetheless, it has become standard (Barnard, 1938) to describe the adequacy of group performance in terms of both concepts: *effectiveness* (task orientation), the extent to which the group is successful in attaining its task-related objectives; and *efficiency* (maintenance orientation), the extent to which a group satisfies the needs of its members.

Each factor can be examined independently of the other. It is possible to examine task accomplishment alone, and frequently that is the only factor considered. It is also possible to examine only relationships among members and the degree of satisfaction each feels as a member of the group, although this is much less frequently considered by itself. Yet it is important to remember that a group expends energy on both aspects of performance, and the effectiveness and efficiency of a group set upper limits on each other. Some illustrations will clarify this relationship.

COHESIVENESS OF THE GROUP AFFECTS PRODUCTIVITY

If members spend their time strictly on business—the surface agenda—and ignore interpersonal relationships and hidden agendas, misunderstandings can increase. Communication may be severely limited, subjects to be discussed are highly controlled, and members rely on the "grapevine" and other informal systems to meet their personal needs. In this situation, each individual does his or her job but steadfastly remains uninvolved with other members as people.

On the other hand, if members spend a great deal of their work time getting acquainted, building personal relationships, and developing increased listening skills and influence on each other, there may be high personal satisfaction, at least for some, but no time or energy invested in the task. High personal involvement may mean high morale but little effort on task activity and consequently, low productivity. The dilemma of whether to sacrifice productivity or member relations is ever present.

However, there is evidence (Thelen, 1954) that if a group spends more time initially on interpersonal relationships, there will be greater long-run efficiency. If, during the initial phases of the group, members talk to each other, discuss their personal goals, and get to know each other, they build a common frame of reference, a step toward problem solving.

Elias, Johnson, and Fortman (1989) found that when group members disclosed information about themselves, they later reported a significantly higher "group cohesiveness, commitment to task, and productivity." Furthermore, these researchers suggest that the function of self-disclosure may be to evoke cooperative behavior in task-oriented groups for resolving problems, reducing stressful conflicts, and enhancing positive communication among individuals.

Consider the following example:

An affluent community was having difficulty coping with drug problems among its youth. To develop strategies, the pastor of the leading church invited heads of six organizations concerned with youth to meet with him: the head of youth services in the township, the head of the juvenile division of the police force, the executive director of the YMCA, the principal of an elementary school, the principal of a high school, and the executive director of a rehabilitation center. All agreed to serve, but none was really clear about how to proceed, how they should organize, and what they could do to reduce the influence of drugs on young people. Two of the seven members knew each other. The others had met at various public functions but had at best a nodding acquaintance. Although each was committed to the goal, all were busy and could commit only two hours per month to this group. Even deciding on a meeting time agreeable to all had been a major accomplishment. Although members were willing and committed, they were frustrated by the first two meetings and questioned why they had agreed to serve. Very, very little was happening.

Because the meetings occurred from 8:00 to 10:00 a.m. (to reduce the amount of time taken from work), the group then decided to meet at 7:00, have breakfast together, and then proceed. That should have produced horror at getting up and to a central location at such an early hour. Instead, the group, in its first enthusiastic decision, agreed.

The effectiveness of the committee markedly changed after that first breakfast meeting. While eating their eggs, the members socialized and developed a knowledge of one another that greatly enhanced their ability to make decisions on how they would proceed with their task. Members came to like each other in the process and became committed to becoming a "terrific" task force. One member jokingly said that he enjoys the breakfast meetings so much that he eats breakfast at the restaurant *every* Thursday morning so that he won't miss the meetings (the group met the second Thursday of the month).

Members learn over time that some issues are to be avoided whereas others can be readily discussed. They learn which subjects are special favorites of particular members and in what areas members agree. They develop a clearer view of their roles and where they fit into the group.

Frequently, more cohesive groups are more productive than less cohesive groups (Norris and Niebuhr, 1980). The more attractive a group is to members, the more membership is valued, and the more members can influence each other. There seems to be a general circular relationship between group solidarity and efficiency. Group solidarity, satisfaction, quality of interaction, and goal attainment have all been shown to be positively correlated (Wheeless, Wheeless, and Dickson-Markman,

Socializing is often viewed as a waste of busy people's time, but is it? How can it be helpful with a diverse population?

1982). As members work together and come to see one another as competent, they are drawn even closer together, and this relationship increases the likelihood of successful performance.

However, increased cohesiveness does not always mean increased productivity. Increased cohesiveness means that members are able to influence one another more. If they decide to use this influence for increased productivity, they could be very effective. However, low productivity may have several related causes within a group or organization, in which case simply increasing the cohesiveness of the group will not solve the productivity problem.

When groups seem bogged down in movement on their goals, one way of understanding the difficulty is to examine the relationships between time spent on task and time spent on interpersonal relations (task and maintenance behaviors). Or, to put it differently, study the relationship between effectiveness and efficiency.

PERSONALITIES IN THE GROUP AFFECT PRODUCTIVITY

How is productivity related to personality? Which is better, people who are all task-oriented—who want to get the job done and leave—or members who want warm, intimate personal relationships? Which will be more productive? Or is it better to have a mix so that they can complement each other?

The prime consideration is the nature of the task. If the group has a purpose that emphasizes problems of expressing emotions in relationships (an alcoholics recovery program), members should not have difficulty being close or expressing emotions. On the other hand, a project that emphasizes problems of control (procedures for conducting a census) should not be composed of members who have difficulty following directions or working on an ordered task.

If the task involves the major steps in problem solving, persons who have high individual scores on intelligence tests or problem-solving ability reflected in higher levels of education usually form a more productive group than those who are less able (Tuckman, 1967; Turney, 1970).

"Interdisciplinary research teams are faced with special coordination and productivity problems different from those faced by individual scientists in organizational settings," reported Fennell and Sandefur (1983). The Laboratory for Social Science Research at Stanford University studied several such research teams from 1975 to 1978. The data indicated that individual scientists seemed to be hampered by formal organization but still required structure for effective communication and interaction. In fact, they suggested that where a clear, formal structure was lacking, team members were likely to spend extra time and energy constructing a workable informal structure. Furthermore, clear authority and evaluation processes were necessary for the smooth functioning of a team.

Findings in general indicate that groups composed of those who prefer more formal relationships when working on a task were most productive (Berkowitz, 1954), but groups composed of members who prefer closer and more intimate personal relationships were also productive (Schutz, 1958). That is, groups made up of similar types, either task-oriented or relationship-oriented, were more productive than groups made up of some who preferred closer relations and others who wanted more distant interpersonal relations. This last group was characterized by recurring personality clashes and lower productivity (Reddy and Byrnes, 1972; Roethlisberger and Dickson, 1939).

According to Jungian personality theory, two personality factors related to the way people gain information affect group productivity. Some gain information by what Jung called *sensing;* others are *intuitive.* Sensing types acquire data through their senses—by seeing, hearing, smelling, reading, and touching. Intuitives acquire data from their inner sense of what is happening. Jaffe (1985) found that sensing types focus on regulations, step-by-step explanations, and facts, whereas intuitive types focus on outwitting regulations, supplying theoretical explanations, and ignoring details. Conflict between these two types can account for lower group productivity.

Compatible groups were found to be more productive, presumably because they were able to agree in the social-emotional areas and, in so doing, freed themselves to work on the task.

For the same reasons, groups tend to be more productive when they are made up of members of the same sex (Gurnee, 1962), and groups of friends are usually more productive than groups of strangers (Weinstein and Holzbach, 1972).

These are only a few of the personality factors that affect productivity. Stress, lack of interest, and self-oriented behaviors might also influence productivity. It is important to recognize that productivity can be understood only by examining both the nature of the task and social-emotional factors.

PRODUCTIVITY AFFECTS THE GROUP

Consider under which of the following conditions a group will be most productive.

1. the group is given a task, but no goal. They are simply asked to do their best.
2. the group is asked to select their own goal.
3. the group is assigned a goal.

Studies have found that groups who set their own goals were more positive about the goal-setting situation and about their commitment to the goal. However, these groups selected goals that were less difficult than the assigned goals. The groups with assigned goals attained higher levels of performance than self-set or no-goal groups (Hinsz, 1995; Mone and Shalley, 1995; Sagie, 1996).

READER ACTIVITY

In an experimental situation, where a group would be meeting for the first time, why would it set a less difficult goal?

____

____

____

Having ensured their success with a goal that they were confident they could meet, what would happen if they met a second time and could set their own goal? What kind of a goal would they select? Would it be at the same level? Why?

What is the difference between a long-term group and a short-term (one-session) group in regard to self-setting goals and satisfaction with the goal-setting situation? What are the implications?

____

____

____

____

In related research, Brawley, Carron, and Widmeyer (1993) found that the amount of perceived participative goal setting and group cohesion were the most reliable predictors of group goal satisfaction. Their results support the idea that participation in goal setting is strongly related to member perceptions describing "groupness." If a group is more participative, cohesion increases. But the properties of groups (or teams) are not static, and they vary in their influence as a group develops over time.

What happens to a group in the process of achieving a goal? How are members influenced as they work together to determine their goals, to integrate personal goals into a group goal, to synchronize a series of activities with specialized roles for members, to evaluate the outcomes, and perhaps to modify or change their goals? How is the group different after this process?

First, groups have real, practical knowledge of their resources. After a group has worked together, the members know one another and what can be expected of each.

Second, they have increased experience in working together as a group. They now know how to determine a goal, how to get information they may need, and what skills are required to complete a task.

Especially if they were successful at the first task, members have increased confidence in the resources of the group. The first time is the hardest and the most uncomfortable. The initial floundering lessens, the reluctance to make a decision diminishes, and the early inexperience is replaced by growing experience and confidence. Members may begin to feel more comfortable and express themselves more freely and clearly.

Third, new group procedures and norms may emerge. Working together, members may realize that they could be more effective if they revised some of the procedures. They may even have changed some of the patterns of working relationships. Based on experience, they may decide to modify their methods of arriving at goals; they may modify the aspiration level based on their previous experience; they may even develop different criteria for success and failure.

Also, the emotional level of the group changes. The initial surface politeness is gone. Members get to know one another, and friendships develop. There may be greater flexibility in role behaviors; people who were too shy or fearful to volunteer for certain roles may now feel free to volunteer. Members may feel more comfortable in the group and so may say what they are thinking more spontaneously.

Then again, it might mean just the opposite. There may be a small status group, and others may feel less acceptance. The high-status members may speak only to each other, and most may feel outside the ruling clique. There can be increased hostility among members (as each may blame the others for failure) and reduced willingness to accept group goals or to work together.

Successful productive groups seem to make a fuller commitment to the group goal through increased effort, planning, and working cooperatively. They also communicate more openly, and there is even morale-building communication due to better personal rapport. (Weldon and Weingart, 1993). Work on one task influences the next, leading to a greater likelihood of success in pursuing goals in each subsequent task.

Mission, Goals, and Objectives

A set of terms that are goal-related but vague have become popular in current organization parlance. These terms are *mission, goal,* and *objective.* Too often in planning a course of action, organizations misuse these terms, and their semantic confusion reflects a more fundamental confusion about how to execute the plan. For clarity, we define these terms here.

The *mission* is the organization's vision of its fundamental work. It should express the *heart,* not the mind, of the system. It is the mission that gives the organization its energy to move. The mission statement is the wide-ranging goal that reflects the values and direction of the organization.

Goals are the means of achieving the mission. They are measurable, outcome-oriented, relatively short-term products.

Objectives, or subgoals, are steps to achieving the goals.

As an example, the *mission* of a business organization might be to become the central identifiable firm in the field, one perceived as having quality and integrity. The *goal* of the organization may be to acquire a 50-percent share of the market by 1995. *Objectives* might include placing the product in a particular chain of supermarkets, doubling the number of salespeople in the western region of the United States, and creating production plants in the South, the Chicago area, and the West.

The Strategic Plan

Businesses frequently work on their goals through a strategic plan. The word *strategy* is from the Greek *strategos* and has its roots in military parlance. Literally it means "the art of the general," and the term was originally used to describe the grand plan behind a war or battle.

Business has adopted the term and applied its concepts to long-range plans and management of the resources needed to achieve the goals and objectives of such plans. Often short-term decisions that may have long-term effects are described as strategies.

Of course, goals need to be more specific than general, long-range plans expressed in nonoperational terms. But the opposite mode—crisis, "seat of the pants" decision making—is also recognized as insufficient. Nor can organizations achieve their goals on "automatic pilot" by following an inflexible set of rules. A meaningful plan needs both overarching goals and specific strategies to achieve them.

The traditional definition of *strategy,* adapted by business leaders and academicians from its military roots, is "the broad plan for operating in a competitive environment to achieve organizational goals." The strategic plan provides for implementing a successful campaign to realize goals, and it serves as the backdrop for tactical decisions that are made in pursuit of an ultimate goal. Tactical decisions, in contrast, are the short-term actions designed to implement strategy, the plays that drive the game plan to success (Carnevale, Gainer, and Villet, 1990).

For most organizations, there are at least two levels of strategies. "Umbrella" or organization-wide strategies are the long-term plans the business has for achieving success in the marketplace; functional or divisional strategies are the operating plans that concern the day-to-day activities performed to implement the overarching strategy.

To create a strategic plan, an organization defines its objectives and then sets about developing a broad game plan to pursue its goals. From this plan flow operational, strategic, and tactical decisions that move the organization toward those goals. The overarching plan provides the organization with a well-thought-out and clear picture of its basic approach to gain the competitive edge. It also gives the organization the flexibility to modify its tactical approaches without losing sight of the overarching plan.

The marks of a strategic decision are that it is future-oriented and that its implementation affects the long-term prosperity of the organization. It involves the allocation of large amounts of company resources and influences many or all of the organization's divisions or departments. It hinges on the involvement of top management in the planning processes and considers both the multiple (and frequently inconsistent) goals of the organization's various components, as well as the impact of such external factors as the state of the economy and the labor market (Pearce and Robinson, 1985).

A successful strategic plan can be built only on a broad base of knowledge about the organization and its capabilities. It draws on the insights and creativity of people throughout the organization. Its centerpiece must be the collective input of employees, supervisors, and managers at varying levels of the organization.

Small groups from the organization are usually assigned to develop parts of the strategic plan. An executive board, heads of departments, or other management groups will work to ask the following key questions:

1. Where is the corporation now?
2. If no changes are made, where will the corporation be in one year, two years, five years, ten years? Are the answers acceptable?
3. If the answers are not acceptable, what specific actions should the corporation undertake? What are the risks and payoffs involved? (Wheelan and Unger, 1986).

The Relationship Between Norms and Goals

Norms, or understandings about the roles we are expected to play in groups, are intimately related to group goals, sometimes directly and sometimes unconsciously. When norms are incompatible with a group goal, the group is unlikely to achieve the goal. For example, if a chairperson of a meeting indicates that he or she would like to hear ideas about how the company can expand its markets but the norm of the organization is to take cues from the chair, no ideas will be forthcoming. The normative structure or creative environment that would foster the expression of ideas does not exist. Thus norms may affect the attainability of goals.

But goals may also influence norms, which in turn will influence future goals. Consider a situation in which there is great pressure to achieve certain difficult goals. These goals may engender norms that are competitive and reduce the organization's ability to achieve successes in the future. Consider this example.

A computer organization has been struggling with declining sales and the possibility that it may have to close. In a last-ditch effort to spur sales, the company offers an extraordinary bonus to the salesperson who can produce delivered sales of $3 million within the next six months. Suddenly salespeople begin taking leads from newspaper ads and even from each other's desks. They begin bribing the secretary to send future leads to them, rather than waiting their turns as policy dictates. They solicit in each other's territories and stop sharing tips and strategies on how to close with particular clients. In short, war erupts in the sales force. Each seller is now out for "number one," and the norms of the organization have changed dramatically. Even after the six-months cutoff date, the norms of the work group are still competitive and secretive.

High school teenagers offer a clear illustration of the relationship of norms and goals. They have strict dress norms—the goal is to be attractive and noticed. Clothes are not simply a means of appearing attractive but become the end. The goal becomes to always have the latest styles; having the new look guarantees being noticed. The need to have new things leads to a norm of dressing in "outrageous" current fashion. In this way a norm becomes a goal that reinforces the norm.

To use another example, consider partners in a marriage who fear divorce and set a goal of remaining married at all costs. Within that context, conflict comes to

> **FOCUS ON DIVERSITY**
>
> Does this norm also prevail among some racial and ethnic groups? What is the goal there? the outcome?

mean "bad marriage." Therefore, the partners establish a norm of suppressing conflict and eschewing arguments. This leads in turn to a norm of speaking only about noncontroversial subjects. Alienation and boredom result, spurring a new goal: to have an affair for the excitement and closeness missing from the marriage. Thus norms shape goals that may then affect the norms and influence the outcome of the original goal.

The reciprocal influences between norms and goals reveal the fact that norms, our unstated rules, evolve. We need some drive or consensus to adhere to them. If we look closely enough, we see that norms are really subtle goal behavior. Individual goals are more frequently expressed overtly, but group goals often remain unstated norms. Sometimes these normative goals are eventually stated outright, but often they remain the unidentified motivators of a group.

Changing Group Goals

Goals in the broadest sense include a future-oriented perspective. Sometimes group goals are inappropriate and should be re-examined and changed, but goals, like norms, are difficult to change. However, it is more likely that new goals will be supported, with concomitant implementation, if there is active discussion in their creation. If those to be involved at a later date in carrying out new policies or procedures are also involved in setting them, it is more likely that they will integrate the new goals into their personal goal structures. Where behavior change is desired, setting goals through group discussion is more effective than separate instruction of individual members, external requests, or imposition of new practices by a superior.

Erez, Earley, and Hulin (1985) tested the hypothesis that the level of group acceptance increases as the level of participation increases and that increased participation in goal acceptance in turn increases performance. In one study, they asked college students to work on a simulated scheduling task under four conditions. In another study, they used animal caretakers to determine whether involvement in goal setting would increase goal acceptance. Findings in both studies supported the hypothesis: "Participative and representative goal setting significantly increased individual goal acceptance, and individual goal acceptance significantly contributed to performance."

The paradox, however, is that because of the very support members receive from one another, it is difficult to change the group's goals. A number of steps have been suggested (Lippitt, 1961) to help a group be more productive.

1. The group must have a clear understanding of its purposes.
2. The group should become conscious of its own process. By improving the process, the group can improve its problem-solving ability.
3. The group should become aware of the skills, talents, and other resources within its membership and remain flexible in using them.
4. The group should develop group methods of evaluation, so that the group can have methods of improving its process.
5. The group should create new jobs and committees as needed and terminate others when they are no longer compatible with the goals.

Group Goals and the Individual Member

In many graduate classes, an objective of the course is to have students develop group skills in preparation for working well in teams, departments, or committees. A frequent means for achieving this end is to divide the class into groups. The groups are assigned a group task (for example, to design an advertising campaign for a new product or to create a program to stop teen-age smoking) and spend a portion of the class working in their groups. At the end of the semester, they submit their products; the grade they receive is the grade for each member of the group. It sounds fair enough, but who hasn't been in a group where three people do 90 percent of the work and the others freeload?

Recently there has been considerable research interest in what is termed *social loafing* (Green, 1991; Harkins and Szymanski, 1987; Williams, Karau and Bourgeois, 1993). This is defined as "a reduction in individual effort when working on a collective task (in which one's outputs are pooled with those of other group members) compared to when working either alone or coactively" (Williams et al., 1993). Why social loafing occurs is a basis for considerable study. It is found to occur when a group is larger, when individual roles are not clearly identified, when a group feels "involuntary" and there is little cohesion, when some members feel less competent than others, when tasks are not divided among members, when decisions are made by a few, and when there is a desire to avoid conflict.

Obviously, if social loafing becomes contagious, a project may never be completed, or at least much less than it could have been. It may leave people convinced that working in groups is a disaster and that there are some people they don't want to work or be with in the future. Countering the forces that encourage social loafing is a subject of increased awareness as individual members are encouraged to identify with group goals. If there is a desire to discourage social loafing (riding on the work of other group members and not being detected), there needs to be action (by leaders, committed members of the group) to have each person in the group identify with the group's goals.

Usually, there is another situation that emerges when members enter a new group. Initially, members act in a new group as they acted in others (Mills, 1967); there is for them an undifferentiated membership role. They scan others for guides to norms and expected behaviors. As they become familiar with the processes of the new group, they learn which behaviors are rewarded and which are deviant. They widen their understanding of what is acceptable behavior in this group. Their personal goals are no longer the only considerations.

They begin to operate at a higher level. They come to understand the group's goals and accept them. They commit their personal resources to accomplishing the goals, and give them higher priority than their own goals. They eventually come to evaluate their performances and the performances of others in terms of accomplishment of the group's goals. They even modify their behavior to help the group become more effective.

Goals are such a central concept of groups that the most common definition of a group is "two or more people interacting with a common goal." Social scientists agree that group goals influence all aspects of group behavior.

EXERCISE 1 A Series of Skill Exercises

OBJECTIVE

- To increase skills in goal areas

RATIONALE

Goal setting seems obvious; participants often feel they have no difficulty setting goals or agreeing on them. Frequently, any difficulties that arise are seen as "personality conflicts," which is another way of saying that nothing can be done. These exercises give participants an opportunity to check out their perceptions of and movement toward goals. They also enable members to build skills in goal setting or in stating the problem. These exercises focus on the group problem rather than on inducing individual defensive behaviors. They should be used individually as appropriate.

1. Setting Up the Problem Usually, when defining a problem, we do so in a way that implicitly suggests a solution. This may cause some people to become defensive and work on their private or personal goals rather than the group goals. This exercise attempts to help participants overcome that difficulty.

ACTION

Participants are divided into groups of six to ten. The facilitator introduces the exercise by saying, "Though all of us publicly state that we want the group to make a decision, we behaviorally don't mean it even when we think we do. For example, we say that the office secretaries use the phone too much and ask what we can do about it. But this question does not allow the group to make a decision based on determination of the situation. Rather, it puts the secretaries on the defensive. We do this all the time. How can we state the problem in such a way that some people do not begin to feel guilty and in which there is no implied solution? This will be an exercise to practice these skills."

The facilitator may state one or several problems that have occurred in the life of the group (one is preferable). In each case, the facilitator asks each participant to assume the appropriate position for asking the question (in the illustration cited, he or she could be the office manager). Each person writes the problem so as not to make anyone feel guilty and not to imply a solution. Then each member reads his or her statement, and the others critique it for meeting the criteria. The group suggests improvements, and the next person is heard. As the analysis goes on, some general principles of stating the problem emerge. Each group reports its best statement of the problem and the general principles. As additional skill building, groups make up a problem and submit it to the next group. The same procedure is used, and there is a testing of the general principles.

This exercise is cognitive, but members find the experience interesting in that they come to appreciate the difficulties of avoiding predetermined solutions as they refine their skills. Here are some problems for restatement, if the group does not create its own:

1. A bus driver reports that students in the buses are destroying property, using abusive language, and picking on younger children. The high school buses especially have this problem on the morning run, at 7 a.m.
2. Shortly, we will be electing class officers. I believe that they should be truly representative of the class. In the past, this has not been so.
3. Ms. Brown, from the American Federation of Teachers, came to visit me yesterday, and she urges us to affiliate. Last year Bill and John led the opposition, and we did not join.

2. CLARITY OF GOAL SETTING Here the objective is to increase observer skills in goal setting and awareness of various aspects of goal setting. The facilitator introduces a role-playing situation (the hidden-agenda example in this chapter is appropriate, or another that involves a current group issue). Depending on the facilitator's objectives, he or she may have one group role play and all others observe, or divide the total membership into a number of role plays with two observers for each role-playing group. The first method builds common skills in observation and goal setting; the second develops an understanding of personal and group goals via observation.

Observers are instructed to note whether behaviors are person-oriented or group-oriented, which behaviors helped to clarify the problem, and which impeded movement on the problem. The facilitator cuts the role playing when a decision is reached or if it becomes evident that a decision will not be reached. Role players report how they feel, especially with regard to movement toward a goal. How did their private agendas help them? Or did they impede them? Was there a group goal? What would have helped them become involved in the group goal?

The observers also report. In the hidden-agenda role play, there are usually so many more individual behaviors that it becomes obvious that a decision cannot be reached until these factors are dealt with. Some might be brought out into the open, some consciously ignored.

After the exercise, members begin to understand both the problems with and pervasiveness of work at several levels on goals. They also develop increased awareness of the behaviors needed to help groups focus on group issues rather than personal goals.

3. DIAGNOSIS OF GOAL CLARITY AND GOAL MOVEMENT If groups are to work efficiently at goals, at both task and maintenance levels, it is essential that they become aware of their own processes. It is important to gather data on the current state of the group and use this information to help set goals, clarify them, and learn the degree of involvement of its members.

SIMPLE REPORTING One method is to stop each session 10 minutes before the end. The members of the group then discuss their answers to these two questions: How much progress do you feel we made on our goals today? What would help us?

This can be done in a workshop at the end of each session, and it can be used effectively in ongoing groups. Initially there is resistance to the concept as well as the process. But if it is begun at a routine session or becomes part of an ongoing process, it loses much of its threat and becomes a simple, effective device for helping the group get feedback on its movement toward goals.

INDIVIDUAL—GROUP REACTION, REPORTING The design here is similar to the one above. It is used about 20 minutes before the end of the session. Sheets with the following questions are distributed to each group member:

1. What did you think the explicit goals of the group were?
2. What do you think the group was really working on (implicit goals)?
3. What was helpful?
4. What hindered movement?

Each person replies to these questions privately and individually. Members then share their replies and consider actions based on the data collected.

This method is also initially threatening to members, but if it becomes routine, it develops increased skills in diagnosing group problems and allows for greater group productivity.

FEEDBACK ON GOALS, INSTRUMENTED Another method for achieving clarity of goals, as well as movement on a goal, is to use a chart that is distributed and scored, and the results fed back to the members. Because it has a more objective, statistical format, it sometimes encourages members to be more open to the findings and less defensive. It takes more time, and perhaps a half-hour should be allowed. The group is rated on the following three dimensions:

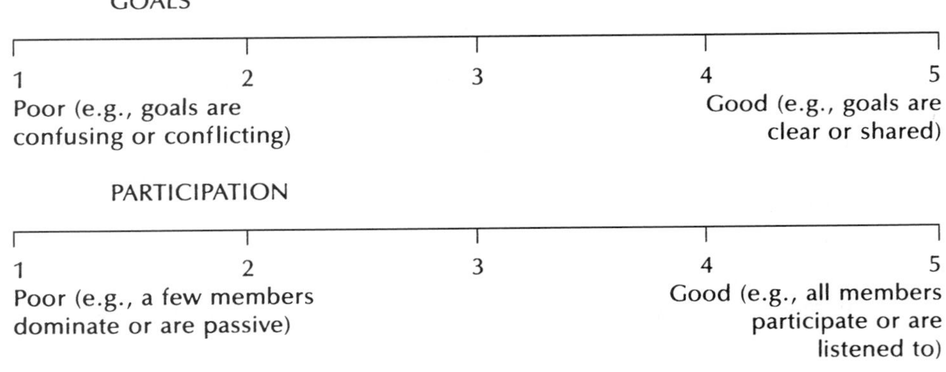

FEELINGS

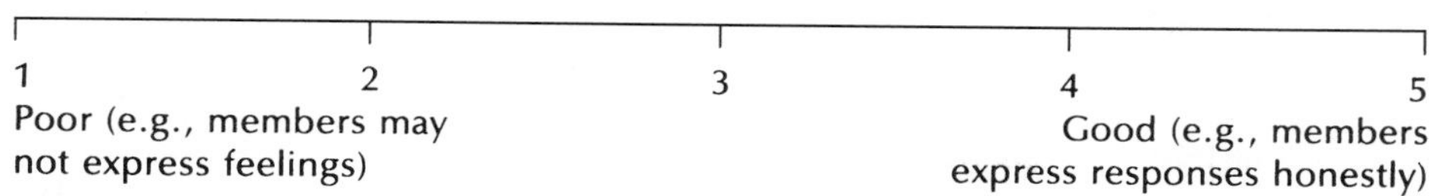

The sheets are collected. One member tabulates the data. A check is scored at its numerical value on the scale (a check between 3 and 4 is scored 3.5), then the numbers are totaled for each question. The findings on each dimension are reported in terms of highest and lowest scores as well as average. The higher the score, the closer the group is to the objectives of goal clarity, group participation, and openness in response. Members then discuss the findings.

Although these techniques may meet with some initial resistance (this is why the simple, open-ended discussion is the first recommended), each helps the group diagnose its own situation and modify its behaviors toward increased productivity.

EXERCISE 2 Setting Individual Goals and Reassessing Them

OBJECTIVES

- To increase understanding of what is meant by setting goals as an individual
- To develop skill in stating goals clearly and specifically
- To recognize that goal setting is an ongoing process
- To periodically re-evaluate goals and determine whether any changes or modifications are needed
- To increase understanding and skill in giving and receiving help

RATIONALE

We participate in many group experiences with only a vague idea of what we expect to derive. This exercise is designed to help the participant formulate goals specifically and realistically, and then re-evaluate them at regular intervals. It is hoped not only that you will develop skills in formulating goals in the course of the experience, but also that once this has been brought into consciousness, you will be motivated to pursue these goals in your activities. As we move toward a goal, we encounter new insights, new obstacles, new understandings. Thus, as a result of increased understanding at time A, we can make revisions of goals and move into time B. At this time we again reassess goals for time C, and so on.

TIMING

Phase I of the design should take place early in the program. It might be used after an initial "microlab" or "getting to know each other" opening session. It is appropriate for a workshop or course that will continue over a period of time. Phase II should occur about the middle of the program, Phase III at the end. Each phase takes approximately one hour.

ACTION

The facilitator announces the exercise and may informally state some of the objectives. The group is divided into trios. These trios become a support system for each individual, helping to redefine his or her goals as well as analyze the forces that help or hinder him or her. Each helps and receives help from the others. The facilitator reads and explains Phase I, Steps 1 and 2, and when these are completed, suggests the group continue with Step 3. Discussion questions may be considered at this point.

Phase II is scheduled midway through the learning experience. The groups form into their original trios. The facilitator reads and explains Phase II. The trios work. If there is time, a discussion similar to the one after Phase I occurs; however, the exchange will be very different from the first one. Trio members will be much more comfortable with one another; there will be much less anxiety and more willingness to share and to help. More time should be allowed.

Phase III should be scheduled at the end of the learning experience. It will be conducted similarly to Phase II, but there will be a marked change in atmosphere. Trio members will feel closer and will honestly discuss their feelings and reactions to the workshop. The prospect of continuing in a home setting produces mixed responses. There are those who "can't wait" to continue on the goals, and others who are apprehensive about whether their situations will permit even tentative movements in the directions they would like to go. However, Phase III cannot be eliminated. It must be continued in "real life" if developing skills in individual goals is to have any permanent value. A discussion following Phase III might enable participants to discuss the aids and hindrances they expect to encounter, and to show how they may find alternatives for dealing with these factors.

GOAL-SETTING PROCEDURE

PHASE I INITIAL GOAL SETTING

Step 1 Take five minutes to write one to three responses to the following question: *What do I want to learn most from this workshop* (or course or laboratory experience)?

Step 2 Take turns going through the following procedure: One person starts by reading one of his or her responses from Step 1. All discuss the response (goal). The following guideline questions may be helpful to clarify and amplify the goal under discussion:

Is the goal specific enough to permit direct planning and action, or is it too general or abstract?

Does the goal involve you personally—that is, something you must change about yourself?

Is the goal realistic? Can it be accomplished (or at least progress made) during the period of this program?

Can others help you work on this goal?

Is this the real goal, or is it a "front" for a subtle or hidden goal?

During or following the discussion, the person whose goal is being discussed revises his or her goal so that it is specific and realistic. This procedure is used for each goal listed. Allow about 20 minutes per person

Step 3 Discuss in turn the barriers you anticipate in reaching your goal(s). Write them down as specifically as you can. Take a few minutes to list ways in which you individually, or with the help of others, can overcome these barriers. Discuss your lists with your trio.

PHASE II REASSESSMENT

Earlier this week (day, month, session) you prepared your initial assessment of goals for this workshop. One purpose of this session is to re-examine your goals in light of your experience so far. Refer to your earlier responses. Look at the goals stated there. Also look at the helping and hindering factors you listed earlier.

Step 1—Goal Reassessment Within your trio, take turns reassessing and discussing your goals. As you discuss them, one of the other members should enter your modified or reconfirmed goal on the list of goals. These statements should be checked out to your satisfaction.

Step 2—Analysis of Helping and Hindering Factors After your goals have been reformulated or reconfirmed, discuss in turn your perception of the present helping and hindering forces—in yourself, others, and the setting—and make a list.

PHASE III REASSESSMENT

We are now in the concluding period of this workshop. Within your trio, re-examine your goals as modified and the helping and hindering forces you listed. How much progress did you make? What still needs to be done?

Step 1—Evaluation of Progress on Goal In turn, discuss how much you feel you accomplished on your goals. What helped you most? What hindered you?

Step 2—Goal setting for the Home Discuss how you could continue on your set goals at home. What forces will help? What will hinder? As you discuss these questions, another member of the trio should enter the new goals on the lists.

DISCUSSION

For some people, revealing personal goals and inadequacies is extremely difficult. Attempting to verbalize expectations is a formidable task for others because they lack practice in doing it. Giving help and accepting help may also be new and difficult experiences. Some of the following questions give participants an opportunity to discuss their feelings in these areas and thus reduce anxiety:

What problems did you encounter in first stating your goals? Why?

How did your goals change after discussion?

How do you feel about help on your goals?

Are these your real goals? How honest do you feel you were in stating them?

What is the relationship between your goals and the goals of this workshop?

Are they compatible? Where is there conflict?

EXERCISE 3 Skills in Goal Setting

OBJECTIVE

- To demonstrate how individual behaviors affect action on goals

- To demonstrate how characteristics of group goals affect group behavior
- To build skills in goal setting through observations of behavior in two conditions

SETTING UP THE SITUATION

The facilitator discusses the general nature of group goals ("a place the group members want to reach in order to reduce some tension or difficulty they all feel") and how these goals are made explicit through the coordination of individual motives and needs.

The class is divided into subgroups of five or six persons. The facilitator explains that each of us has our own way of dealing with problems related to goals.

ACTION

PHASE I

Members receive sheets listing three problems of goal setting:

1. When I am a member of a group that does not seem to have a clear awareness of its goals or how they are to be achieved, I usually . . .
2. When I am a member of a group that has a clear understanding of its goals but seems to have little commitment to accomplishing them, I usually . . .
3. When I am a member of a group that has conflicting opinions on what its goals should be, or that has members with conflicting needs and motives, I usually . . .

Members fill out the sheets and then discuss problems with goals and their individual solutions. (Allow 15 minutes.)

Groups are asked to report their conclusions about how to deal with certain group problems. The facilitator then reviews the conclusions as indicators of proper procedures in goal setting.

The facilitator briefly reviews proper procedures in goal setting.

PHASE II

The facilitator asks a volunteer from each group to be an observer. The observers are briefed (by the facilitator, outside) to pay attention to (1) the number of times members attempt to clarify a goal, (2) disruptive, ineffective behavior by members, and (3) general productivity.

Observers return, and the facilitator gives the groups a short time to accomplish a vague, abstract, complex task.

Task 1 (time: 7 to 8 min.): Reach agreement on this statement: What are the most appropriate goals for maximizing social development in a democratic society? After the time is up, the facilitator gives the groups a concrete, clear, simple task.

Task 2 (time: 7 to 8 min.): What are your goals in taking this course and how will they be met?

ANALYSIS

Observers report to the whole group on what they have noticed (for example, "The first task evoked long silences, considerable anger, many calls for clarification, and long, vague, intellectual comments. The second task produced an initial burst of laughter and very rapid discussion, and nearly everyone took part, which was very different from the first task").

The class members generalize about characteristics of effective types of goals (for example, "attainable, clear, challenging") and examine the reasons for the negative, disruptive behaviors appearing in the first task (which involved an ineffective goal).

EXERCISE 4 Implementing Goals

OBJECTIVES

- **To illustrate goals that initially seem clear but are in fact unclear**
- **To demonstrate how goals change in implementation**

SETTING UP THE SITUATION

The facilitator assigns participants to groups of four to six.

ACTION

(Time: 15 min.) The facilitator instructs the groups to choose themes for pictures that each will draw on paper.

He or she gives each group a large piece of newsprint or shelf paper and a colored marker of a distinct color.

The facilitator then instructs the groups that at the word *begin* they are to draw the picture they decided on. However, there are two restrictions: (1) as of the signal to begin, no one is to speak or influence each other in any way, and (2) members will work on the drawing one by one until everyone has had a turn. The finished pictures are to be hung on the wall.

DISCUSSION

The groups then discuss the following three questions (time about 10 minutes):

1. What helped you come up with a theme? Which approaches or behaviors were helpful?
2. How did you feel when you heard that the project was nonverbal and that you could draw only once? How did you feel when someone added to what you did? How did you feel about your group before drawing? How do you feel about your group now? If your feelings have changed, what produced the changes?
3. Do you think your group solved the problem adequately? Are you satisfied with the result?

One person is to do a presentation for each group, explaining the group's theme, how members feel about it, and how their feelings about the group changed. This person should address these questions:

1. What could group members have done differently in arriving at their theme to make their drawing successful?
2. What are the implications of this exercise for goal setting and implementation?

For Further Information

Feinstein, J. *A March to Madness.* Boston: Little, Brown, 1998.

Feinstein follows all nine ACC basketball teams through the 1996–1997 season. It was the year in which Dean Smith broke Adolph Rupp's all-time record in coaching victories, and Carolina fought its way into another Final Four after a dismal start. The book brings to light the hidden world of college basketball—the bitter rivalries between coaches, the competition between marriages and careers, and the difficulties coaches have with NBA-bound players. According to a *Kirkus* review, "What Feinstein does better than anyone else is to make you understand the complex mix of psychology, group dynamics, and political pressures that make athletes tick."

Green, R. G. Social Motivation. *Annual Review of Psychology,* 42 (1991), 377–399.

Harkins, S. G., and K. Szymanski. Social loafing and social facilitation: New wine in old bottles. *Review of Personality and Social Psychology: Group Processes and Intergroup Relations,* 9 (1987), 167–188.

Silberman, M., ed. *Twenty Active Training Programs.* San Diego: Pfeiffer, 1992.

How do trainers/facilitators/leaders achieve goals through the use of groups? This source book includes program directives, program resources, and even program forms for one-day designs. It covers twenty topics ranging from productive group skills to stress management, from cross-cultural training to meeting management, and from performance review to strategic planning.

Tarkenton, F. *What Losing Taught Me About Winning.* Needham, MA: Simon and Schuster, 1997.

Tarkenton is remembered as the losing quarterback in three Super Bowl games and was tagged a loser at the time. Determined to be a winner, he went on to found twelve companies and made millions. The book is about creating a small business, his anecdotes about his own triumphs and setbacks as well as his stories about others who defied the odds, and who had their "eye on the goal."

VanDerveer, T. *Shooting from the Outside: How a Coach and Olympic Team Transformed Women's Basketball.* New York: Avon, 1997.

A remarkable story of how a three-time National Coach of the Year guided the U.S. Women's Olympic Basketball Team to the gold medal, and how she molded twelve individuals into a powerful unit. The story is a watershed event for female athletes, because it led to the formation of the two women's professional basketball leagues. A riveting behind-the-scenes look at the making of the team.

Williams, K.; S. Karaw; S. and M. Bourgeois. Working on collective tasks: Social loafing and social compensation. In *Group Motivation: Social Psychological Perspectives.* Ed. M. S. Hogg and D. Abrams. London: Harvester Wheatsheaf, 1993, 130–148.

5 Leadership

A few years ago, a young army captain in one of Africa's newly emerging nations became disenchanted with the progress of social and economic reform in his country. At that time, his nation was plagued by a failing economy, public disillusionment, and a poorly paid military. Working within a seedbed of discontent with the support of other young officers, and making full use of his considerable personal charm, idealism, and charisma, the captain led a coup and took over the reins of power. His immediate popularity was tremendous, and the future of the country suddenly seemed bright.

Now, only a few short years later, the country is on the brink of financial ruin, the new leader's popularity is declining, and he is scrambling to maintain his precarious base of power and influence. One thing he recognizes is that the leadership skills that enabled him to take control are not what he needs currently to maintain his position and move the country ahead. That flamboyant, dictatorial, and very personal leadership style was well received at first, but it rapidly lost appeal as promises were left unfulfilled and hopes evaporated into the parched African air. Meanwhile, the young leader's style and approach changed—he is now more subdued, more eager to listen, and more willing to reach out to his own constituents for help. Furthermore, he seeks more dialogue with those who must respond to his decisions, and he realizes that the success of change depends on the acceptance of those who must live with it. This leader has become acutely conscious of the fact that power can be a short-lived illusion if hope, expectations, and realism are not carefully balanced.

Gone suddenly are this leader's brashness, irreverence, and distaste for politics and bureaucrats. Today, he knows that both politics and bureaucrats are part of his reality and essential to his success. Charisma and promises are not enough. He recognizes the tenuousness of his situation and realizes that in all likelihood another young, disillusioned officer somewhere is plotting his demise.

Six Theoretical Views of Leadership

This chapter looks at the evolving nature of leadership theory and practice, and its implications for small groups and organizations. Leadership is a concept that has a chameleon's ability to take on a new appearance with every new occasion. Even the definition of leadership varies with the circumstances. One study (Kraus and Gemmill, 1990) found that the subjects' own definitions of leadership greatly influenced how responsible they believed the leader was for the outcome of the group. How we define our leaders, therefore, may be related to how well they lead. It has been estimated that this word *leader,* not even coined until the middle of the nineteenth century, has more than 100 definitions.

Robert Terry, of the Center for Advanced Leadership at the Hubert H. Humphrey Institute of Public Affairs, has attempted to bring clarity to the muddle by identifying six theoretical views of leadership: (1) leadership as power, (2) organizational leadership, (3) trait theory, (4) situational theory, (5) vision theory, and (6) ethical assessment. In the following sections, we explore the notion of leadership from each of these theoretical perspectives in turn.

LEADERSHIP AS POWER

Where leadership is viewed as power, the term is actually synonymous with *action.* Here, *leadership* means getting things done or making things happen that, without the intervention of a leader, would not occur. Whatever the style, position, or behavior utilized, in this context the leader acts as a central catalyst that moves the group toward action.

In some cases, the leader may attempt to lead by creating the desire for action within the followers themselves. The focus is still on making something happen, but there is a shift toward *empowering,* or enabling, followers to take responsibility for the resulting action. A good example of such empowerment occurs in a typical community action program in which a leader mobilizes support to address critical problems that influence the lives of his or her constituents.

In this context then, where leadership is power, *leadership* can be defined as how often and with what success an individual is able to influence or direct the behaviors of others within a group. The crucial question here is this: What allows power to occur in the first place? Simply put, when one person does what another wants him or her to do, we say that the influencer has *power* over the other. Leadership clearly involves power—that is, the ability to influence other people by whatever means necessary (McDavid and Harari, 1968).

Fairhurst and Chandler (1989) revealed that people identified as leaders speak differently to subordinates than they do to other identified leaders. From our earlier study of norms, it is easy to understand how a consistent and quite clear expectation of these rather obvious language patterns can influence existing relationships. Predictable, patronizing, and condescending behavior can subtly reinforce old stereotypes and attitudes.

A person may be very influential and have a great deal of power in one group, and he or she is considered the leader because the group frequently accepts his or her direction. In another group, she may have little power; her suggestions are infrequently accepted by the group, and she would not be identified as one of the leaders. It is not unusual for a person who is a clerk in a business to be a powerful board member in a Girl Scout council. The reverse also occurs, though less often.

The chairperson of a university department—high power in the department—may only be window-dressing (low power) in a community association. *Power is not a universal: it is limited by the person being influenced. A powerful person has power over only those whom he or she can influence in the areas and within the limits defined by the person being influenced.* In other words, we have only the power those being influenced let us have. Even when people feel powerless, ultimately, only they can give it to someone else.

Discussions of leadership sooner or later evolve into a discussion of power. The word itself evokes visions of manipulation, the omnipotent "big brother," and personal feelings of powerlessness. We think of Machiavelli's *The Prince* and his strategies of power; we recall the dictum of Lord Acton, "Power corrupts, and absolute power corrupts absolutely," in relation to the centralization of power; and politics is defined as the ultimate power game.

Machiavellian politics can easily be transferred to encompass modern concerns. Machiavelli was, of course, the "first management thinker to actually bring power out of the closet" (Clemens and Mayer, 1987). Even so, power is rarely addressed and seldom is addressed among leaders in management. What do we personally think of power? Would we rather be powerful or powerless?

Reader Activity

In what situations do you perceive yourself as having power and influence?

____

____

____

What are the behaviors you use when you are being powerful and influential?

____

____

What do people whom you consider powerful do to convey that image?

____

____

____

Can you imagine exercising power with others in that way?

____

____

____

Perhaps it is the influence of American history, with its ideal of egalitarianism, that is the basis for our ambivalence about power. Perhaps we are fearful of being thought deranged—to need power can be viewed as "sick." We want power—to be decision makers, to be controllers, to have things go our way—yet we are often ashamed to admit, even to ourselves, that we desire power. According to John W. Gardner, former Secretary of Health, Education and Welfare and author of extensive leadership papers, most of us want leaders who are not hungry for power, but ironically enough we have created a system in which only those hungry for power will stay the course (Gardner, 1989).

And why wouldn't we want to be powerful (except for our confusion on the subject)? The more powerful members of a group tend to be more popular than low-powered members. They speak to, and are addressed by, the other higher-powered members more than are lower-powered members (Stogdill, 1974). They participate more, they make more influence attempts, and their influence is more accepted (Gray, Richardson, and Mayhew, 1968; Hoffman, Burke, and Maier, 1965; Mulder, 1971; Rubin et al., 1971; Rubin and Lewicki, 1973). Groups tend to be better satisfied when more powerful members occupy leadership positions (Stogdill, 1974), and those in positions of power enjoy being in the group more (Kipnis, 1972).

Furthermore, being in a position of power correlates with positive self-concepts. In an experiment with groups of Harvard undergraduates, Archer (1974) found that those with high power changed in the direction of more positive self-concepts over the experimental period, and that those with low power changed in the direction of more negative self-concepts.

What determines who has power? One conceptual scheme (French and Raven, 1960) that holds continued interest distinguishes five different kinds of power.

1. *Referent power.* We all have people to whom we look for guidance, to whom we listen because we identify with their ideas, their style, their humor or popularity. They have influence or *referent* power over us. We may not question their ideas because we like or admire their status, position, or even personal charisma. The disadvantage is that we may be

hooked by some characteristic that can cloud our ability to be rational when listening or interacting with them. They possess the kind of attraction that can breed dependency and reduce our ability to discriminate.

2. *Legitimate power.* Contrast this to the person who has *legitimate* power over us. Such individuals tend to have authority that normally cannot be denied. Our boss is the best example. Even in the most democratic organization, if "the boss" says something with certainty, the feeling is we'd better listen. Such power may be derived from a legal role, being elected to an office, or simply having status gained from a higher "level" of the organization. Unlike referent power, where influence is gained only in terms of the power we give someone, here the role comes with authority and determines, in part, the nature of the relationship (Goldman and Fraas, 1965; Julian, Hollander, and Regula, 1969; Spillane, 1983).
3. *Expert power. Expert* power is just that: experience, knowledge, special skills, or information that sets an individual apart from other resources. Style, status, and authority become less relevant if a leader has expertise that is needed. As with referent power, a person will hold it as long as what he or she offers is appreciated by others. For example, someone's credibility, and thus power, can be lost if a response is perceived as reflecting ignorance, or lack of forethought or relevance.
4. *Reward power.* If I have something you want and the ability to give it to you, I immediately have power over you, *reward* power. Rewards can be derived from teachers (grades), bosses (pay raise or promotion), friends (entry into a group or clique), or anyone simply appreciating a job well done. They can be positive and affirming, or manipulative. In most instances, they relate to somebody who has a position that can control how we feel about an outcome. Although rewards can be positive, they can also increase dependency, create fear, and be used to manipulate. Such power, however, can only hold sway over those who care about the nature of the reward being offered.
5. *Coercive power.* Finally, *coercive* power reflects either a threat or the reality that something can be taken away if we don't act a certain way. Or it can suggest a negative consequence for certain actions; it can lead to abuse and punishment. The recipient often feels impotent, totally unable to do anything about it.

Now, imagine the power evoked if an individual incorporates more than one type of power in his or her ability to influence another person. A boss, for example, may combine the use of referent, legitimate, expert, and coercive power together. The person may be admired for past achievements, and an employee desires to be respected by him or her. Add to this the legitimate authority the role itself carries, the expertise the boss has, and a reputation for punishing those who don't do as he or she suggests, and there is an enormous amount of power that can be brought to bear on an individual employee. It is little wonder that it takes a strong person to speak his or her mind in the face of such formidable influence.

Another example:

> Students mechanically attend the first session of class in a required course. They carefully scrutinize the teacher for clues as to how much reading will be required, how much work they will have to do, how often examinations will be given, and how interesting the lecturer sounds. They also look for clues on attendance requirements and possibilities for getting a good grade. Simultaneously, they acquire data on how expert the instructor seems to be and, over time, determine how they feel about the instructor as a teacher, a scholar, and a human being.
>
> The university gives the instructor legitimate power to teach the course and administer rewards or punishment in the form of grades. Students also perceive the legitimacy of this power. The students, however, determine the degree of expertness they attribute to the instructor; that is, the students determine the extent of their being influenced by the instructor as someone to emulate or relate to. How much influence the course will have on the students will depend to a large degree on how much power the students attribute to the instructor. It may be only coercive power, and in a hostile environment the students "get by." Or the course may have a profound influence; the students may relate to the instructor as a personal model, consider him or her genuinely knowledgeable, and find the course personally rewarding in adding to their insights or skills. Although legitimate power is the basis for the influence of an instructor, and some students may even question this and drop the course, other bases of power develop and determine the extent of influence.

For some, legitimate power is enough. The right to be in a position to make decisions that affect others is everything. Wielding power gives them enormous satisfaction and a sense of prominence. There is something about being able to control others that is overwhelming. Consider an example:

The lobby corridor was wall-to-wall with about twenty elevators. As the woman came around the corner, she noted one with the door open and the "up" light on; she immediately darted in, pleased that she didn't have to wait. Then, she "caught it." From someplace down the hall she heard, "Hey, where do you think you're going? I'll tell you which elevator is going up; I'll tell you where you stand to get the elevator. You want to stand there? Fine. But it isn't going up—not 'til I say so." It was incredible; in just seconds the woman felt like a bad child. She meekly got out, waited until the man told her which one was going up, and got on feeling intimidated (he might not have liked her, and then she would never get to the thirty-second floor). All the while the woman was thinking, "Can you believe it? I got into a power hassle over getting into an elevator! His bit of legitimate power is determining who gets into which elevator. He's power mad."

For some, wielding power in the form of rewards or sanctions is everything. Being liked is unimportant or, at best, secondary to having power. Being in a position of legitimate power, being able to influence decisions and the "lives of others," is the insatiable quest. This can lead to corruption, manipulation, and loss of a sense of purpose and vision.

Individual Experiment

Think of two separate groups of which you are a member. Identify one individual in each group whom you think of as powerful. Make a list of the specific behaviors he or she uses in exercising that power. What type of power is he or she using? Compare the types of power used in each of the two groups. Is one type of power more effective than others?

ORGANIZATIONAL THEORY

In organizational theory, someone's power is defined by his or her *position influence* and role within a bureaucratic/hierarchical structure. A person's influence stems from his or her role, clearly defined in terms of function and position, within the hierarchy. Complex organizations require control, order, and discipline to ensure some degree of efficiency and predictability in what might otherwise be chaos. Thus, clear paths of authority and an understanding of where one must go for help, information, or direction emerge. Except where revolution or internal reorganization take place, leaders are those who wear the cloak of authority at each level in the organization; it is position alone that gives the occupant power to influence (Abrahamson and Smith, 1970).

In all bureaucracies, be they in the military, business, or educational world, the roles and functions of members are clearly defined, so in theory at least, no questions need arise regarding authority and responsibility. Unlike theories of power in which need, timing, and personal charisma all contribute to a person's influence without regard to formal structure, here the structure itself affords legitimacy of authority. Thus, an assistant principal responsible for discipline in a large urban school has a clearly defined role and unquestioned authority. Similarly, a captain in the military and a vice president of marketing are guided by clearly defined roles. Subordinates may provide information and ideas, but each knows his or her place in the organization and thinks twice before challenging the authority of those in higher positions in the hierarchy.

The values of such an approach to leadership are the order, predictability, and consistency created in complex systems wherein it is necessary to minimize confusion and inefficiency. But the price paid is often the creation of dependency and an attitude of unquestioning obedience to superiors in those waiting docilely for the opportunity to move up the ladder. Such groups can demoralize personnel and reduce efficiency within the organization. Because bosses wield preordained influence over the lives of subordinates, real openness, free expression of feelings, and other truths are often limited to the safe haven of the informal system and are conspicuously lacking in the formal structure where they might be most useful. Superficial concerns—looking good, keeping a clean record, and *apparent* loyalty—often replace honesty, creativity, and risk taking as employees' values with respect to their work. Consider the following example:

A few years ago, a colonel in the United States Army Corps of Engineers was faced with deteriorating morale and efficiency at the large military base he ran in Germany. This man was scheduled to retire the following year without having been promoted to general. His personal goal was to leave his post in the best condition possible and to end a distinguished career with pride and honor.

His key staff was composed of both military and civil service officers, both German and American, who were responsible for maintaining the base. These top aides had, like the colonel himself, been rotated into their positions from other bases for two- or three-year tours of duty; staying anywhere much longer was a sign that one's career advancement was in trouble. Given that time frame, it was clear to all personnel that identifying problems was useless, because there would never be enough time to solve them. Furthermore, problems, as everyone knew, stuck to one's name like honey sticks to fingers, so trying to solve them was considered "making waves" and was therefore avoided. The abiding norm, then, was to look good at all times, maintain the status quo, and *never* have any problems.

At this base, years of such avoidance had resulted in a facade of normalcy covering a caldron of inefficiency, low morale, and corruption. The colonel, who had no more steps to climb on the organizational ladder and nurtured a desire to end his career with a flourish, had the "nerve" to hire a management consultant to look under the lid into this long-brewing organizational stew.

It took the consultant only two days to discover the problem. The pattern had existed for years and was obvious to anyone who cared to observe. What the consultant found horrified the colonel. As a result of the short-term orientation of the top-level supervisors, many of whom could not even speak German, the civilian work crews and their first-line German supervisors had developed a routine of "work" that included

1. the addition of unnecessary men on almost all work crews.
2. extensive travel times to and from work sites that were often double and triple what was actually required.
3. up to an hour of prework briefings of crews that required only a few minutes.
4. the general practice of quitting early several times a week for regular beer drinking and card parties at the equipment barn.

Top-line staff and supervisors knew about the rampant inefficiency but chose not to take action that might call blame down on themselves. They simply bided their time, waiting to be transferred to their next tour of duty. Lower-level supervisors, not wishing to incur the wrath of the German workers, colluded with the perpetrators and became part of the problem.

The colonel submitted a report. Instead of exploring a potential solution, the colonel's boss—a highly respected lieutenant general—threw a banquet to celebrate the good work of the consultant, thanking him for his effort and sending him home on the next plane. He then sent the colonel to headquarters to take a soft desk job pending his retirement. He shelved the report to avoid embarrassment and the possibility that similar conditions were rampant at other bases. The final results were these: The colonel retired with honor, the workers remained happy, the general's record remained unblemished, and the consultant left frustrated.

Although many hierarchical bureaucratic organizations are efficient, well managed, and have high morale, their rigid system of promotion by position often results in the tendency among personnel to deny problems, develop norms of self-protection, and avoid conflict with ongoing attempts to please the leader. Over time, this tendency can result in inefficiency, mistrust, and dishonesty among even the best-intentioned participants in the organization.

Bailey and Adams (1990) suggest a strategy for nonbureaucratic leadership whereby concerns within an organization become, for example, innovation versus stability, efficiency versus accountability, and empowerment versus control. This would help minimize the formation of powerful, informal subgroups that often develop within troubled organizations and in which frustrations are vented.

The foregoing example raises a logical question: Can we say that a high-status position automatically implies leadership in the person holding that position? History is replete with actions of kings of very limited intelligence who had tremendous influence and whose whims were law. Does the organizational theory of leadership suggest that such behaviors are appropriate? We all know from experience that there have been position leaders whom we saw as excellent or outstanding and others who were failures and about whom we raised questions about their qualifications.

It is necessary to draw a distinction between leaders and leadership (Holloman, 1968). A leader may be a person in a position of authority; he or she is given the right to make decisions for others—as a teacher is given the right to teach the class, or a foreman the authority to assign work for his or her unit. From that position, the leader may influence others who look to him or her for clues or seek to emulate him or her.

From another perspective, it might be said that whoever influences a group is the leader; that is, any person who influences the group (whether in a formal position of leadership or not) exhibits leadership behavior. Leadership behavior is distinguished from the leader position; leadership behavior has to do with influence on the group regardless of the position.

One study of emergent leadership (Myers, Slavin, and Southern, 1990) found that leaders emerge according to the needs of the group. These results imply that we may be able to foster environments wherein different leaders emerge once we decide what kind of leadership is lacking.

Finally, there is the issue of the "power behind the throne." We are all aware of people who occupy this position. Well-documented accounts of boss rule in politics are generous in their details of mayors or governors who were once handsome, mellifluous-voiced errand boys for the "boss," who himself held no official position. Each of us knows of occupants of positions who are given name-on-the-door trappings of office but who in reality must check almost everything with someone in a higher position, or even someone who has retired from office but must be consulted prior to any move. Study limited to actual occupants of positions obscures who influences the decision making, the processes in that group, how they develop, and with what consequences.

TRAIT THEORY

Perhaps the oldest and the most popular theory of leadership over the years has to do with the belief that leaders are born, not made—that is, that they are genetically determined. The words "she is a natural leader" convey the sense that a particular individual's rise to power and glory is inevitable and that no amount of education and training will enable "nonleaders" to experience such a rise. Thus, trait theory views leadership as part of personality, a characteristic that differentiates those who have it from the pack. As might be expected, this view is controversial, given the evidence that training *can* be beneficial in developing leaders.

Leadership became a prime subject of social science research at about the time of World War I. With increased knowledge of testing and new statistical tools, there was strong impetus to accumulate data and determine what traits leaders shared. If these could be identified, perhaps those who exhibit them could also be identified, and leaders could be selected quickly and efficiently. The usual procedure in studies on leadership has been to select certain personality attributes and relate them to success or lack of success in certain leaders.

READER ACTIVITY

Think of people you know who are leaders of groups. What traits do they possess?

____

____

____

Do you think those traits apply to leaders generally?

____

____

____

Implicit in much of the research on personality traits and leadership is the belief that the qualitative components that make for effective leadership are consistent. Simply put, you have it or you don't. The leader might have been born with these traits (one theory) or have acquired them (another theory), but in either case, the person possesses the traits of leadership. The only problem, it would seem, is that personality traits are still poorly conceived and unreliably measured. Proponents think that as they refine the methods of measuring personality traits, they will be able to determine what traits groups need to find or teach. In this theory, the ability to create leadership effectiveness is just around the corner.

Results of this approach, however, have been disappointing. There is some evidence that leaders tend to be a bit taller, more intelligent, more enthusiastic, and have greater self-confidence and social participation than nonleaders (Berleson and Steiner, 1964; Smith and Cook, 1973; Sorrentino, 1973; Zigon and Cannon, 1974). However, it is impossible to predict and use this information in selecting and training leaders. For example, it has been repeatedly demonstrated that a person who does most of the talking (greater social participation) becomes a leader, *unless* he or she talks so much that he or she antagonizes other group members (Stang, 1973).

After extensive surveys of the literature seeking to identify leadership traits, researchers are increasingly coming to the weary conclusion that leadership does not emerge from some combination of traits (Stogdill, 1974). Rather, "in every instance, the relation of the trait to the leadership role is more meaningful if consideration is given to the detailed nature of the role" (Gibb, 1954, p. 878). Since traits of an effective leader are so closely related to the functions that the leader performs, the most general rule would be to focus on what task needs to be performed and to select those who are willing to perform it and have the skills to do so.

The sorting out of leaders with various leadership traits from those without them has been notoriously ineffective, then. One early study (Bird, 1940) extensively reviewed the relevant research and compiled a list of traits that seemed to differentiate leaders from nonleaders in one or more studies. However, only 5 percent of the traits listed appeared in four or more studies; many of the other traits listed appeared in only a single study. Mann (1959) reviewed 125 leadership studies searching for a relationship between personality and performance in small groups. His search yielded 750 findings about personality traits, but no traits as conclusions. He found a lack of consistency among traits described as significant for leaders and further found that some traits listed as significant were diametrically opposed to significant traits listed in other studies. Researchers continue to search for the behavioral scientists' (if not the alchemists') gold, and with similar results. In studying discussion leaders, Guyer (1978) found no statistically significant relationships among traits of discussion leaders, student evaluations of them, and the grades received by students. His conclusion: "Attention to personality traits . . . would have been of limited value in the selection of discussion leaders" (p. 697).

An interesting new line of inquiry has begun during the past five years, however. It suggests that although a small degree of a leader's success can be predicted from a trait analysis, and even more can be predicted by considering past performance (grades, test scores of achievement and aptitude), new variables supporting the views of Peter Senge and others are gaining prominence. These variables have to do with the degree to which leaders (in this case, business leaders) appear open to learning from the ideas of others or from personal feedback about their own performance. The more open they are to such information, the greater their success as leaders. Research by McCauley, Lombard, and Usher (1989) suggest that their emphasis is increasingly on helping leaders assess their own effectiveness and compare their behavior patterns to those of leaders identified by their peers as particularly effective. Such an approach is bound to make leaders more conscious of their impact on individuals and their own organizations (McCauley et al., 1989).

STYLES OF LEADERSHIP

Because social scientists have been unable to find consistent evidence that particular traits are related to leadership, they have shifted focus in recent years to leadership "styles." Plato was perhaps the first to deal with the idea of leadership style. In *The Republic,* he provides an analysis of leadership powered by "self-serving individualists," "benevolent tyrants," and of course the dialectic style of leadership (Clemens and Mayer, 1987, p. 39). The term *dialectic style* suggests an open dialogue among individuals seeking positive change through a rational discussion of opposing arguments. It was the seedbed of a more open and "democratic" approach.

Style is simply another word for a collection of behaviors in a particular situation. Many contend that people with the broadest range of leadership-related behaviors are the most effective leaders—as long as they have the ability to choose the right behavior for the situation. Conversely, in this view, individuals with a limited range of leadership behavior (styles) have a limited ability to influence. People who are inclined to be nice, gentle, and solicitous and cannot confront or deal openly with conflict are seen as handicapped in their ability to lead. Likewise, those who are overly serious, directive, and in need of control may have difficulty in such areas as delegating, motivating, or being playful—all useful leadership behaviors. In this way, leadership becomes a function of particular modes of behavior.

Today, it is generally acknowledged that leadership qualities are intimately linked to our personalities—which in turn are the products of our upbringing plus our inherited traits. At the same time, social scientists widely believe that training and education *can* have an impact and that, with experience and practice, people are capable of altering their behaviors and developing effective leadership styles.

DOES LEADERSHIP STYLE MAKE A DIFFERENCE? Classic research by Lewin, Lippitt, and White (1939; White and Lippitt, 1968) investigated the following questions: What effect does style of leadership have on a group? Is a group more productive if the leader is autocratic, democratic, or laissez-faire? Does it make a difference in how members relate to one another? Is there a difference in the social climate?

In each experimental situation, three leadership types were established: the autocratic leader, the democratic leader, and the laissez-faire leader. Each leader had legitimate power as he worked with ten-year-old boys on basically similar craft projects. The findings were dramatic. Results indicated that demonstrably different group atmospheres developed. Furthermore, in each experimental group, there were readily perceived differences in relations among members and their ability to handle stress, as well as in their relations with the leader. The findings convincingly demonstrated that in that particular situation, the best leader was the democratic leader.

CHOOSING A LEADERSHIP STYLE Which leader is "best" depends on how we perceive that label. Describing a person as an *autocratic leader* conjures up an image in which he or she is allied with demagogues, dictators, and coercive administrative processes. Yet the term *autocratic* can also describe a person who is directive, who stands firm in his or her convictions, and accepts the responsibilities of supervision and ultimate responsibility for his or her decisions—in short, one who has the necessary attributes of leadership.

Clearly, it is the ability of leaders to first identify the most appropriate behavioral response called for in a particular situation and then to actually use it as needed that separates those who are successful from the rest. The dance of leadership is dependent upon the ability to choose the exact dance step (behavior) to fit the exact need of a group at any given moment. And it is the particularity of the choice that makes predicting an effective leader such an extraordinarily difficult thing to do.

PERSONALITY AND LEADERSHIP: HOW DIFFICULT IS IT TO LEAD? People can teach others to organize, solve problems, use their time effectively, and plan. They can educate them in management by objectives, meeting design, and the qualities of transformational leadership. But it is extremely difficult to teach someone how to translate knowledge, experience, and their unique genetic history into what we might call *effective leadership*. Hogan, Curphy, and Hogan (1994), in a thorough review of the literature, estimated that leadership incompetence is rampant—as high as 60 to 75 percent—and that our hiring practices are so flawed that well over

50 percent of leaders hired by organizations are doomed to fail. It is the researchers' contention that the problem is not so much related to what we don't know as it is to our unwillingness to apply knowledge we already have.

For example, they point to evidence that a combination of cognitive measures, personality tests, structured interviews, simulations, and other assessments can enhance typical selection processes and reduce what are called *false positives,* or candidates who appear talented and qualified but ultimately fail to perform well. Yet, for a variety of reasons, there appears to be an inclination to short circuit what might be a more rational process. Instead, other criteria less related to behavioral success gain influence over the decision. Thus, engineers with great technical skill may be promoted into supervisory positions as a form of reward for good work. However, it is not uncommon for some of these individuals to be ineffective supervisors, with little patience and few interpersonal skills. Or, just as bad, someone may be promoted into a leadership role because he or she is likable and "good with people." Yet that same person may be indecisive and avoid conflict. Finally, some individuals are promoted because of their ability to work easily with those above them. The problem is that the majority of their time is spent with people below them in the hierarchy, where they may have difficulty delegating, sharing authority, or coaching.

DERAILED LEADERS Numerous studies have begun to hone in on the factors that tend to derail leaders. For example, Lombardo, Ruderman, and McCauley (1988) and others (Hellervik et al., 1992) agreed that derailment is related less to technical skills and intellectual capacity than to much more personal factors relating to relationships. The inability to develop trust and the tendency to micromanage are two common factors. Other characteristics of ineffective leaders include difficulty disciplining employees, being indecisive, unwilling to exercise authority, or being just plain irritable. Apparently being bright and technically competent is often insufficient to compensate for arrogance, selfishness, or insensitivity. But the patterns are clearly idiosyncratic and difficult to generalize across individuals.

CONCEPTIONS OF OTHER PEOPLE A leader's conception of human beings has implications for his or her leadership style (Mastow, 1954; McGregor, 1960, Schein, 1969). Two theories of how to lead have held sway for forty years. In the first (Theory X according to McGregor; rational-economic man according to Schein), people are seen as having little ambition, a reluctance to work, and a desire to avoid responsibility. People are motivated by economic competition, and conflict is inevitable. Without managerial effort, men and women do virtually nothing. The leader operating under these assumptions must motivate, organize, control, and coerce. He or she directs; people under him or her accept and even prefer it, because they have little ambition or desire for responsibility. The leader bears the responsibility and burden of his or her subordinates' or followers' performance. This represents the traditional theory of management, especially business management.

Another theory (Theory Y for McGregor; self-actualizing man for Schein) holds that people are motivated by a hierarchy of needs. The assumption in this theory is that as basic needs are met, new emergent needs become motivating forces. Each of us has a desire to use our potential, to have responsibility, to *actualize* ourselves. The theory assumes that men and women enjoy work as well as play or rest. Thus, individuals will exercise self-direction and self-control toward the accomplishment of objectives they value. Furthermore, they can be creative and innovative. They will not only accept responsibility but also seek it. That potential for imagination, ingenuity, and resourcefulness is widely distributed within the population but poorly utilized in modern society. In this theory, the leader creates challenge and opportunity for subordinates to use their abilities to a greater extent. There is no need to control or motivate; the motivation is waiting to be unleased.

A leader's conception of men and women greatly affects his or her style of supervision and the bases of power he or she will implement. The first theory is more likely to use money as a motivating reward and coercion to compel compliance. The second theory is likely to promote intrinsic rewards of self-satisfaction and pride in achievement; coercion is used infrequently.

Familiar labels of leadership styles do not necessarily provide the clarity we might like.

To be labeled a *laissez-faire leader* is to be viewed as in a fog, incompetent, fearful of making a decision, and shirking responsibilities. This is clearly an offensive label. Yet on the other hand, "Creativity must be given free rein" and "He who rules least, rules best." Shall the leader supervise closely, or "trust his or her people"?

To be labeled a *democratic leader* usually suggests that the person is well liked. As for his or her behavior, does it mean that he or she shares all decisions with others regardless of the consequences? Does it mean that staff members are one big happy family, that they talk in terms of *we* rather than *I,* and that all relationships are collaborative rather than competitive? Do all decisions have to be group decisions? Is giving up power the price of popularity? Is the "big happy family" the goal to strive for no matter what? Is any aspect of competition to be avoided at all costs?

At one time this labeling was important, as theorists sought to understand the continuum that went from the laissez-faire leader, who was minimally involved, to the autocratic leader, who arbitrarily made decisions based solely on his or her own style. At that time, the democratic leader stood for a middle-of-the-road view, neither the "abdicrat" who avoided being decisive or assertive, nor the autocrat, who demanded adherence to personal dictates, and there was a desire to reinforce the conviction that democracy is "best." The entire concept of experimentally inducing three different leadership styles, analogous perhaps to governments, was powerful. The results generated increased understanding of the problem and of the limitations of each style.

The studies have been so effective that they continue to be replicated (Bernstein, 1971; Koch, 1978; Sargent and Miller, 1971; Scontrino, 1972; Sudolsky and Nathan, 1971); researchers find the early hypotheses continue to be valid. In fact, there has been quite a bit of research on style of leadership. Sanders and Malkis (1982) found that leaders who were categorized as Type A (coronary-prone who work hard, rest little, and are impatient) did not do so well with problem solutions as Type B people (who pace themselves, relax at regular intervals, and manage stress better). Drory and Gluskinos (1980) studied personality styles they characterized as either high or low "Machiavellian" (after the Italian prince who wrote about power). They found that "high Machs" tended to give more orders and were less supportive when in group leadership positions than "low Machs."

Yet today, the question of whether one is democratic or autocratic, or whether a high-pressure personality makes a better leader than a low-pressure personality, is less meaningful. We have come to look at effective leadership as the relationship between the individual leader and the rest of the group. We no longer view leaders as being in a box that can be labeled, whether by their detractors, their friends, or even their own dilemmas. Even so their style does affect how group members communicate (Barlow et al., 1982).

PREDICTING SUCCESSFUL LEADERSHIP The delicate task of attempting to synthesize the findings of widely varied research in the area of personality resulted in five areas of general agreement, called the "big five" taxonomy (Hogan et al., 1994). These characteristics appear to be especially consistent among emergent leaders—those who appear leaderlike even when there is little information available upon which to judge them. The five qualities are as follows:

Surgency. This refers to the outgoing, charismatic, social behaviors exhibited by individuals who have the capacity to dominate a situation with their behavior and be liked while doing it.

Agreeableness. Here are behaviors that help define a person as easy to work with—perhaps cooperative and diplomatic in style.

Emotional stability. This quality means consistency, steadiness, self-control, and in control in any situation. It applies to someone who can be counted on, who does not fold under the pressure of the moment.

Conscientiousness. This describes a person who is achievement-oriented, responsible, and goes about his or her business with great integrity. Being highly motivated to do the right thing is an essential quality.

Intellect. This refers to being bright, active, open to new ideas, and willing and able to ask penetrating questions.

These five qualities are rarely, if ever, found in a single individual. However, they provide an interesting road map of different types of behavior that have proven successful in leaderless groups as well as in assessment center activities, where the goal of skilled observers is to isolate the behaviors of the most effective leaders in a variety of challenging situations.

The value of these predictors was shown to overlap substantially with behaviors found in leaders who were able to build effective teams (Hallam and Campbell, 1992). Since building an effective team is increasingly valued in the current downsized and re-engineered work world, such findings take on great significance. Thus, leaders with high surgency behaviors tend to communicate more, which increases the likelihood of clarity of goals and expectations. High levels of conscientiousness suggested greater trust, with higher degrees of strategic planning and organization. Similarly, emotional stability resulted in a willingness to deal with conflict and negative feedback in a timely way. Finally, a high degree of agreeableness related to the presence of greater trust, morale, and generally better communication.

Reader Activity

What follows is a well-known instrument, the Leader Preferred Coworker Scale (LPC), used by Fiedler (1967) in his early research on leadership style.[1] Taking this test will help you understand your own style and allow you to relate more personally to the research discussed in this chapter.

THE LEAST PREFERRED COWORKER SCALE

Think of the person with whom you can work *least well.* This person may be someone you work with now or someone you knew in the past. This person need not be the person you *like* least well but should be the person with whom you had the most difficulty working to get a job done.

1. "A Contingency Scale for Effective Leadership" from *Theory of Leader Effectiveness* (p. 41) by F. E. Fiedler. New York: McGraw Hill (1967). Copyright 1967 by McGraw-Hill Publishers. Reprinted by permission of the author.

Please describe this person by putting an *X* in the appropriate space on the following scales:

Pleasant									Unpleasant
Friendly									Unfriendly
Accepting									Rejecting
Helpful									Frustrating
Enthusiastic									Unenthusiastic
Relaxed									Tense
Close									Distant
Warm									Cold
Cooperative									Uncooperative
Supportive									Hostile
Interesting									Boring
Harmonious									Quarrelsome
Self-assured									Hesitant
Efficient									Inefficient
Cheerful									Gloomy
Open									Guarded

To score yourself on this exercise, identify the favorable pole for each item—for example, *relaxed* versus tense; *cooperative* versus uncooperative; *supportive* versus hostile; *cheerful* versus gloomy, the italicized words being the favorable poles in these pairs. An *X* closest to the favorable pole is an 8, in the next space is a 7, in the next a 6, and so forth, to 1 in the least favorable spot. Total your marks to get your score. There are 16 items, so the highest score you could receive would be 128. This would mean that you would have scored 8 points for each of the items. Similarly, your lowest possible score would be 16; for this you would have placed a 1 in the least favorable place for each item. Your score, then, will fall somewhere between 16 and 128. The higher your LPC score, the more "relationship-oriented" you are. A very low score would indicate that you are a "task-oriented" individual.

SITUATIONAL THEORY

A far cry from the rigidly traditional trait theory is the theory of *situational leadership.* This notion rests on the assumption that human beings are ultimately able to learn the techniques of leadership and that virtually anyone can become a more effective leader by mastering certain skills and knowledge.

This point of view was espoused by Reddin (1970), Blake and Mouton (1969), and others in the late 1960s and was popularized by Hersey and Blanchard as their life-psycholeadership theory (1969, 1975, 1977). The latter created a framework that attempts to explain why the results of leadership training have been mixed and why efforts to produce effective leaders have been limited, even though training can be effective in teaching new behaviors. The essential point is knowing *which* behaviors to use *when.*

TASK AND RELATIONSHIP DIMENSIONS As scoring for the LPC scale suggests, there appear to be two central dimensions of any leadership situation: that involving a *task,* or a goal or project; and that involving a *relationship,* or social-emotional issues, consideration for others, and interpersonal relations (see accompanying figure[2]).

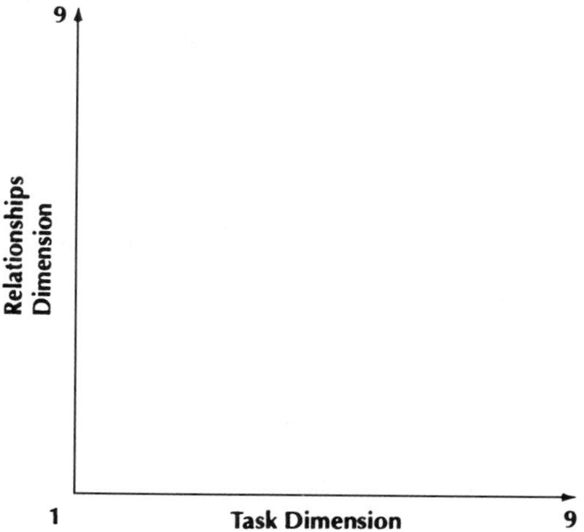

In this formulation, task behavior is illustrated on the horizontal axis. Task (production) becomes more important to a leader as his or her rating advances on the horizontal scale. A leader with a rating of 9 has a maximum concern for production.

2. Figures on this page and page 236 from *Training and Development Journal,* May, 1969. Copyright 1969 by the American Society for Training and Development, Inc.

Do the male and female leaders you know conform to this general trend?

Concern for people is illustrated on the vertical axis. People become more important to the leader as his or her rating progresses up the vertical axis. A leader who has a rating of 9 on the vertical axis has a maximum concern for people.

In one study of situational variables and gender, Petzel, Johnson, and Bresolin (1990) found that male participants spoke more and were selected as leaders more frequently than female participants in a situation where an impersonal task was presented. In a "personal" group, however, women spoke more and were also chosen as leaders more often.

As shown in the figure below, the four quadrants produced by the grid describe leader behavior. (There are five in the Blake-Mouton formulation, the fifth being at the cross of all four quadrants). Quadrant I represents a leadership style that is high on task and low on people; quadrant II represents a style high on both task and people; quadrant III is high on people with little concern for the task; quadrant IV is a style low on both task and people.

After identifying task and relationships as the two central dimensions, some management writers have suggested a "best" style. Most of these writers have supported an integrated leader behavior style (high task and high relationships) or a people-centered, human relations approach (high relationships).

Relationships		
	High People Low Task **III**	High Task High People **II**
	Low People Low Task **IV**	High Task Low People **I**

Task

However, there is convincing evidence that there is no single "best" style (Korman, 1966). Both directive, task-oriented leaders and nondirective, human relations-oriented leaders are successful under some conditions (Fiedler, 1967). Different leadership situations require different leader styles. Differences in leadership effectiveness that were once attributed to a traditional personality trait may instead involve the ability to perceive the needs and goals of a group and then to adjust one's personal approach to meet them (Kenny, Zaccaro, and Stephen, 1983). Thus, the ability to move between the task and relationship dimensions as called for by the changing situation is essential.

THE EFFECTIVENESS DIMENSION To measure more accurately how well a leader operates within a given situation, Hersey and Blanchard (1979) added a third dimension—effectiveness—to the two-dimensional model (see figure below). The effectiveness dimension cuts across the two-dimensional task/relationship factors and builds in the concept of a leader's style, integrated with the demands of a specific environment. When a leader's style is appropriate to a given environment measured by results, it is termed *effective;* when her or his style is inappropriate to a given environment, it is termed *ineffective.*

If a leader's effectiveness is determined by the interaction of his or her style and environment (followers and other situational variables), then any of the four styles defined by the grid quadrants may be effective or ineffective, depending on the environment. Therefore, there is no single ideal leader behavior style that is appropriate in all situations. In an organization that is essentially crisis-oriented, such as the police or military, there is evidence that the most appropriate style is high-task orientation; under riot or combat conditions success may depend on immediate response to orders. Studies of scientific and research-oriented personnel show that they desire or need only a limited amount of social-emotional support. They know what they are doing and "want to get on with it." They view meetings as "wasting time." Under these conditions, a low-task and low-relationship style (leaving them alone for the most part) may be the most appropriate.

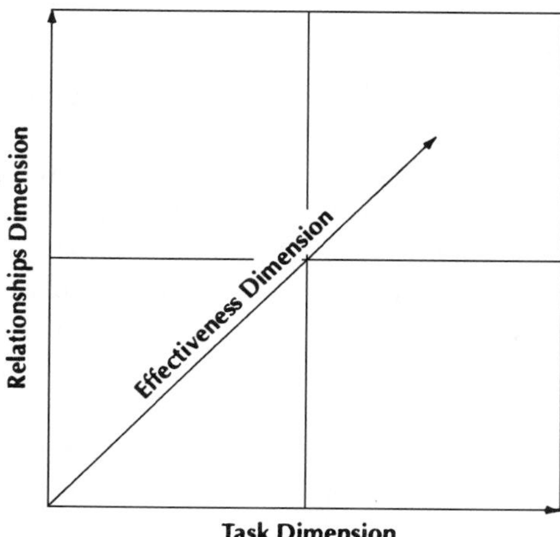

In summary, an effective leader must be able to *diagnose* the demands of the environment and then either adapt his or her leadership style to fit these demands or develop the means to change some or all of the variables.

THE MATURITY FACTOR In their situational leadership theory Hersey and Blanchard (1969) have, in response to the vague concept of *situational determinants,* sought to conceptualize them and how they relate to leadership behavior (task and relationships). The primary element in the theory is that an effective leadership style is related to *the level of maturity of followers.*

According to what Hersey and Blanchard call the *life-cycle theory,* as the level of maturity of one's followers increases, appropriate leader behavior requires not only less structure (task) but also less social-emotional support (relationships).

Maturity, in life-cycle theory, consists of several components. First, mature people have the capacity to set high but obtainable goals and a desire for task-relevant feedback (how well am I doing?) rather than task-irrelevant feedback (how well do you like me?). Second, they are willing to take responsibility, which involves willingness (motivation) and ability (competence); the highest level of responsibility would be taken by those high on ability and competence. Third, maturity can be thought of as involving two factors: (1) job maturity, the ability and technical knowledge to do the task; and (2) psychological maturity, a feeling of self-confidence and self-respect as an individual. These two factors seem to be related; high task competence leads to feelings of self-respect, and the converse also seems to be true.

Finally, although the maturity concept is useful, we must remember that diagnostic judgments may be influenced by other situational variables such as a crisis, a time bind, or one's superior's style.

According to the theory, as level of maturity of followers increases in terms of accomplishing a specific task, leaders should begin to reduce their task behavior and increase their relationship behavior, beginning at quadrant I with immature, inexperienced followers, moving to quadrant II and then III as the individual or group moves to an average level of maturity (see figure on p. 239). As an individual or group reaches an above-average level of maturity, it becomes appropriate for leaders to decrease not only task behavior but also relationship behavior (moving now to quadrant IV). Now, members are not only task-mature but also psychologically mature and can provide their own psychological reinforcement. They need much less supervision. An individual at this level of maturity sees a reduction of close supervision and delegation of responsibility by the leader as an indication of trust and confidence. This theory, then, focuses on the appropriateness or effectiveness of leadership styles according to the task-relevant maturity of the followers.

This cycle is illustrated by the bell-shaped curve going through the four leadership quadrants in the figure.

DETERMINING APPROPRIATE LEADERSHIP STYLE What does the bell-shaped curve mean to a leader with a specific task to accomplish with a given organization or group? It means that the maturity level of one's followers develops along the continuum from immature to mature—and that the appropriate style of leadership moves accordingly.

To determine what leadership style is appropriate in a given situation, a leader must first determine the maturity level of the individual or group in relation to a specific task he or she is attempting to accomplish through their efforts. Once a leader identifies this maturity level, he or she can determine the appropriate leadership style. If the followers are low in maturity, the leadership style of quadrant I would be most effective, the style of quadrant II second most effective, quadrant III next, and quadrant IV least effective.

The theory has broad applicability to leadership not only in organizations but in other groups, even families.

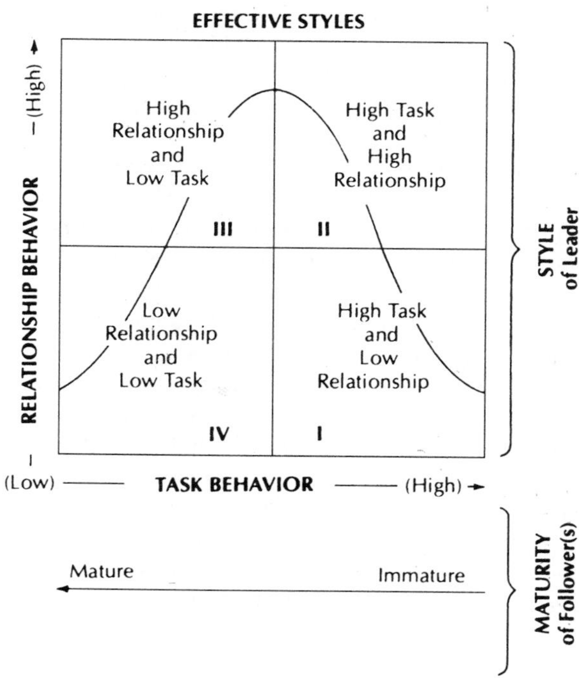

AN ORGANIZATIONAL EXAMPLE

Let's look at a detailed example of leadership operating in a business context.

Combining the two medium-sized printing companies representing two different regional markets seemed to be a logical move that would ultimately reduce overall business expenses. Both companies were profitable, and the two presidents had been friends for many years. The president of the northern company was a quiet, warm, personable former political science professor whose leadership style centered on client satisfaction and harmonious human relations both within and outside the company. Walking into the company's offices, one found large, open spaces with few visible barriers to separate the different organizational levels. Shirt-sleeve informality was the rule, and office relationships spilled over easily into the social realm.

The other company, equally successful, was run by a dynamic, hard-driving, charismatic individual who, though engaging and personable in nature, was a stern taskmaster with little tolerance for incompetence. Stepping into the southern company's office, one found executives in the latest Brooks Brothers suits sitting in plush, paneled offices. Unlike the family feeling in the northern company, here there was an air of tough competition marked by locker-room humor, sarcasm, and liberal use of four-letter words, balanced by pride, efficiency, and a certain rugged confidence.

The management styles in these organizations differed markedly also. The northern president prided himself on involving his coworkers in the decisions that affected them and on delegating as much responsibility as possible. He saw himself mainly as an agent of public relations and support. In contrast, the southern president was clearly a hands-on boss, involved directly in most of the activities in his firm. Personnel went to him for advice and counsel before making critical decisions.

As a result of the merger, the popular, easy-going northern president became the CEO responsible for daily operations of the new company. The southern president moved up to become chairman of the board, and took responsibility for long-range planning and development.

Trouble began almost immediately. One of the leaders from the northern division depicted his southern counterparts as aggressive sharks, interested only in the bottom line and caring little about relationships or concepts of modern participative management. He characterized them as abrasive, quick to act, and often insensitive to those around them. Disgruntled leaders in the southern division complained that the northern division was inefficient and unprofessional. They saw the new CEO as only barely competent and as relying more on his own personality than on hard-nosed business practices.

During the year following the merger, antagonism between the two organizations became so profound that meetings often had to be held in a neutral setting. Threats of quitting and retaliation were commonplace, and although dollar profits remained reasonable, employees constantly evaluated and criticized the new CEO. The problem was further exacerbated when the new CEO continued to delegate authority and therefore did not meet the southern group's needs for counsel, feedback, and direction. The response of the latter was to turn to their former boss, who, in spite of his new role, still made himself available to hear questions and complaints. The outcome appeared to be a stalemate, each group setting up roadblocks for the other and blaming the other for any failures that occurred.

The situation seemed hopeless, and in fact there was talk of ending the merger. However, at a critical time one of the most powerful executives in the southern division resigned, leaving a vacuum in the company and creating the opportunity to hire someone with a philosophy more consistent with that of the northern division. In addition, the CEO finally recognized that he had to become more directive during what was to be a long transition period. He suddenly "took charge," which allayed some of the fears of the southern group.

In this example, even though both organizations showed bottom-line success, the different management styles resulted in very different levels of organizational maturity. The new CEO had failed to recognize that the southern division's dependency, created by the hands-on management style of the former president, required a slow weaning process. Without such a transition, the leaders of the southern group felt abandoned, left to flounder; and they became resentful as well because their tough, businesslike attitudes would not let them admit their need for support and direction. Their immature organization was matched with a new CEO who proved inflexible in adjusting his own style to their needs, and this in turn almost resulted in the CEO's overthrow. In the end, he had to reach beyond his "natural style" and adopt new behaviors—ones he had intentionally discarded years before. In sum, his short-term inflexibility and inability to see the quadrant-I needs of his southern counterparts almost proved disastrous for the entire organization.

INDIVIDUAL EXPERIMENT

Identify a group in which you participate that is not working very well. Write down a list of adjectives that describe the style of the group leader. Write down your description of the group members' ability to set reasonable goals, degree of motivation, and willingness to take responsibility to make sure the work of the group gets done. Does the leadership style match the group members' maturity? If not, how should the group leader change? How should the group members change?

VISION THEORY AND ETHICAL ASSESSMENT

Vision theory and ethical assessment are the last two of the six theoretical positions presented by Terry (1987) in his effort to explain leadership in small groups or organizations. *Visionary leadership* involves purposefully exploring societal needs and drawing public attention to the future. Unlike situational leadership, which focuses more on current concerns and daily operations (and is seen by some, such as Bennis and Nanus [1985], as "management rather than leadership"), visionary leadership focuses on identifying future needs and mobilizing resources to reach projected goals. By capturing the imagination of followers around the issue of "what could be," a leader mobilizes idealism and hope. Obviously, turning such a vision into action requires other aspects of leadership discussed previously, but the visionary must be able to ignite the flame and set the direction. Such leaders attempt to find effective managers to handle the problems of day-to-day operations so that they can focus on the bigger picture, including the strategies and planning necessary to drive the organization toward realizing the vision.

Most organizations start with a dream that becomes translated into a vision and then into a specific, obtainable goal. Landing a person on the moon and garnering support for the civil rights movement were goals set by visionary leaders who also helped provide the energy and focus needed to mobilize people into action. On another level, but equally visionary, is a factory supervisor's goal of fostering cooperation and efficiency in his plant or a coach's dream of building team spirit that goes well beyond the winning of any single game. According to Rouche, Baker, and Rose, in their 1989 book *Shared Vision,* historical visionary leaders such as Thomas Jefferson and Martin Luther King, Jr. shared dedication to achieving a goal; but even more significantly, they influenced others to share their vision with them. In short, "a vision is more than any one individual's perspective". . . . It is the cultivation of followership (p. 111).

Burns (1978, p. 19) defines *ethical assessment,* the final view of leadership, identified by Terry as follows:

> Some define leadership as leaders making followers do what the followers would not otherwise do, or as leaders making the followers do what they want them to do; I define leadership as leaders inducing followers to act for certain goals that represent the values and motivation—the wants and needs, the aspirations and expectations—*of both leaders and followers.*

Such leaders are driven by a conscious awareness of the public good and a desire to serve the interests of their constituencies. Both Burns and Terry agree that, in tapping followers' will and interests and mobilizing them to serve those interests, this form of leadership transcends many of the others in importance. For leaders of this sort, a keen sensitivity to moral and ethical considerations is essential, and often their first task in leading a group is raising the group's consciousness. Calabrese (1988) states the guidelines for ethical leadership as including "respect for all members of society, tolerance for divergent opinions and cultures," among other things (p. 1).

To clarify, the quality of the ethical vision and its relationship to the public good set them apart from the dream of the visionary leader. Both kinds of leaders are conscious of needs, trends, and the future. Both focus on increasing their followers' awareness. But the leaders who set goals with respect to their *ethical* assessments raise both followers and themselves to higher levels of performance and achievement.

Functional Leadership

The functional perspective defines leadership as those acts that help the group achieve its goals. Finding the right leader for the moment is the key. Thus, leadership can, in principle at least, be performed by any group member. Leadership acts are those that help the group set goals, that aid in movement toward the achievement of goals, that improve the quality of interpersonal relationships among members, or that make needed resources available to the group. When leadership is considered in terms of behavior that furthers the goals of a group, it is difficult to distinguish leadership from followership. Chris Lee argues that because we tend to view leaders in isolation, followers are often viewed as "empty vessels waiting to be filled" (Lee, 1991, pp. 27, 28). But effective organization needs to alter these conceptions, for "effective followers are partners in creating the vision in the first place."

This approach recognizes the uniqueness of each group. Actions required by one group may be quite different from those of another, so the nature and traits of the people having influence differ in each group. For example, a pilot may be the acknowledged leader of his or her group while in the air. But what if the plane crashes and the crew is faced with the goal of surviving in the wilderness and finding its way back to safety? The skills needed are now very different. Who knows the terrain on the ground? Who knows about "survival training"? Who can calm the others and reduce squabbling? The person who will be the crew leader on the ground may be very different from the leader in the air. The functional approach recognizes that a variety of behaviors by any member may be helpful in the achievement of the group's purposes. It stresses behaviors that influence the group. If a group is threatened by conflicting subgroups, members who engage heavily in mediating functions may be expected to be influential. If, however, a group is faced with low prestige in the community and members are leaving, quite different behaviors will be required to be influential.

TYPES OF FUNCTIONAL ROLES

Leadership is basically the execution of a particular kind of role within an organized group, and this role is defined essentially in terms of power or the ability to influence others. Conceived of as a role, leadership may be more or less specific to the particular structure of a particular group (McDavid and Harari, 1968). A leader in one group does not automatically emerge as the leader in another group. As membership changes, the leader may change; or if the purpose or activities change, the leader may change then too. Leadership implies followership. One person exerts influence or social power, and others are influenced. Leadership is defined as the frequency with which an individual in a group may be identified as one who influences or directs the behaviors of others within the group. Murphy (1988, p. 658) states that very often, however, "leaders can . . . achieve results by acting like followers and depending on followers to act like leaders."

Early studies by Bales (1950, 1970) and others (Benne and Sheats, 1948; Rieken and Homans, 1954) have identified three types of leader-member behaviors, hereafter referred to as *member roles* because they can be performed by any member. Each is worth examining closely.

GROUP TASK ROLES Roles of members here are to help a group select and define the common goals and work toward attainment of those goals.

Suppose representatives of school and community groups decide to work together to "do something about the drug problem." Members whose actions would be categorized in the task realm may *initiate* discussion of what could be done or how the problem might be approached, or they may suggest different methods for getting teenagers involved. Someone else may offer *information* on what other groups in the city are doing and what official agencies are available for further help.

Another may offer *opinions* on the subject. With this variety of opinions and suggestions, some can *coordinate* or clarify the various suggestions in terms of which are appropriate for this group to work on. An *energizer* may prod the group to reconsider its potential and stimulate members to greater activity.

These are some of the functions members undertake to help a group accomplish its task. The group member who acts in some of the above ways is exercising leadership by moving the group toward its goal. He or she is not necessarily the designated leader, yet he or she displays leadership behavior by influencing the group.

GROUP MAINTENANCE ROLES Although task roles focus on the rational problem-solving aspects of achieving movement toward a goal, equally important but at a different level are the roles that focus on the personal relationships among members in a group. These are known as *group maintenance roles*.

Just as task roles help a group to achieve its explicit goals, maintenance roles help a group to work together. These behaviors help a group maintain itself so that members will contribute ideas and be willing to continue making progress on a group task. Both kinds of roles are needed, and each complements the other. The chapter on problem solving (Chapter 7) examines these relationships in greater detail, but briefly note here that the relationship is not only complementary but also spiraling: successful work on the goal increases members' sense of the attractiveness of the group and liking for each other. Liking each other and having worked out interpersonal relationships free energy to put into the task and its accomplishment.

Let's return to the illustration of the group studying the drug problem. As opinions are given, the *encourager* may ask for additional examples or inquire whether others have similar opinions. The *supporter* may agree with suggestions of others and offer commendations. The *harmonizer* may attempt to mediate differences among members or points of view, or relieve tension with a joke. Someone who previously felt that public health agencies and not citizens' groups should work on the drug problem may, after hearing the discussion, come around and agree to a compromise, whereby the coordinating group sponsors a series of meetings in which public health officials describe their efforts. A *gatekeeper* may notice that representatives from one community group have not spoken and ask if they have any ideas on the subject. These roles help a group maintain itself so that work on its task can proceed without becoming immobilized by inappropriate social behaviors and so that individuals are brought effectively into the emotional sphere of the group's life.

INDIVIDUAL ROLES Another set of behaviors has been identified in which members act to meet individual needs that are irrelevant to a group task and not conducive to helping it work as a unit. Such individual-centered behavior frequently induces like responses from others. An attack on one person leads to a response of personal defense; a joke may escalate to an hour of "I-can-top-that" jokes; and blocking by one member may lead to retaliatory blocking. The goal and the group are forgotten; the individual acts primarily to satisfy his or her personal needs.

In the representative citizens' group, the *aggressor* may question, with thinly veiled sarcasm, the competence and veracity of the person giving his or her opinion. The aggressor may imply that the speaker does not have the foggiest notion of what he or she is talking about. Or the aggressor may sneer that this "half-baked" committee hasn't the competence to solve a serious problem; why not sponsor a day for the kids at the ball park and accomplish something? Similarly, it might have been agreed that drug addicts would be referred to the local community mental health center. However, the *blocker* persists in stating that unless a center is opened especially for addicts, the committee is useless. Further, they may turn every request for suggestions into a renewed attack on present plans or a renewal of advocacy for a treatment center. The *self-confessor* may use the audience to express personal problems and gain sympathy through catharsis. The self-confessor may reveal the problems he or she is having with a son who is disrespectful, shocks the neighbors with his late hours, and is a disgrace in general to a parent who has worked hard all his or her life in order that the children may lead better lives than the parents did. In an emotional voice, the self-confessor despairs that family relations and respect are not what they once were. The *recognition-seeker* may respond with his or her personal advice and describe in glowing detail how it was successful in numerous other instances, or remind the group of a paper he or she has just delivered at a convention, or of other important committees on which he or she has served. The *dominator* attempts to take over with an assortment of strategies such as interrupting others, flattery, and asserting superior status.

Integrating the Six Dimensions of Leadership

Although we can identify the six distinct types of leadership described here (power, organizational, trait, situational, visionary, and ethical assessment) in our daily lives, there is a growing case for the argument that the most powerful and effective leadership involves the integration of most or all these types. Terry (1987) sees leadership on a continuum from transactional, or means-oriented, to transformational, or ends-oriented. Put simply, *transactional leadership* focuses on the business of getting things done. Here, reciprocal negotiations result in an ever-changing relationship between leaders and followers ("I'll vote for you if you give me a job"). Such leadership is basically rooted in the here and now, where reaction, conflict, and crisis drive us more than thoughts of ethics, responsibility, and morale.

However, life consists of more than reacting to crises and fulfilling basic needs. Satisfaction and effectiveness are partly related to issues beyond our own self-interest; they depend on our accomplishing tasks in a way that improves or contributes to the world. In this context leadership is perceived as a *transformational* process focusing on the mutual needs, aspirations, and values that produce positive social change. Howell and Higgins (1990) examined transformational leadership behaviors in champions of technological innovations and found that these behaviors were used to a larger extent by such champions than by others. More specifically, the champions' abilities to stimulate a shared vision, as well as to display and motivate others to display innovative actions, were what enabled them to achieve their goals.

ISOLATING THE FACTORS OF TRANSFORMATIONAL AND TRANSACTIONAL LEADERSHIP

In their efforts to argue in favor of the universality of these concepts, Bass and Avolio (1993) reviewed the literature and found that transformational statements fell into four rather clear but somewhat interrelated components. Their summarized definitions of these components provide added clarity to the sometimes ambiguous descriptions of transformational leadership. Instead of idealistic generalizations, each category incorporated relatively specific, observable behaviors. In a similar fashion, the four factors of transactional leadership can be easily compared to each other as well as to the transformational components (Guastello, 1995).

TRANSFORMATIONAL LEADERSHIP Basically, transformational leadership is about believing in certain attitudes, values and ultimately, behaviors that will help keep a group in a work mode that motivates and supports necessary/ongoing change. Thus, *idealized influence* aims to establish positive attitudes among employees toward each other and the process of work itself. *Inspirational motivation* helps a group focus on a valued vision and the standards required to reach it. The process is supported by the group's value of *intellectual stimulation,* where striving for the best practices and keeping ahead of the competition on the learning curve of new ideas and products is constant. Finally, *individualized considerations* reflect the knowledge that individual motivation to change is grounded in respect for group members, their needs, and their development. Transformational leadership incorporates all four of these factors and consists of the following:

Idealized influence (charisma). The leader takes risks, takes stands, is value driven, believes in and builds trust, considers purpose and commitment important, and promotes ethical considerations.

Inspirational motivation. The leader presents an idealized future, sees framing of a clear vision as important, models a high level of support, and encourages high standards.

Intellectual stimulation. The leader tests all assumptions as well as traditions and beliefs, encourages new approaches, reviews cultural norms, and explores differences openly.

Individualized considerations. The leader considers individual needs and interests, considers individual abilities and aspirations, and supports personal development, teaching, and mentoring.

TRANSACTIONAL LEADERSHIP Transactional leadership focuses on the immediate situation and some specific leadership action to get the job done as easily and quickly as possible. The most positive and useful of the accompanying leadership approaches espoused here is *contingent reward,* in which positive outcomes are rewarded. *Active management by exception* represents close observation of employees and proactive intervention whenever performance lags. *Passive management by exception* is a "reactive" response to ineffective performance. *Laissez-faire leadership* is the traditional hands-off approach to the leadership process. The four types of transactional leadership can be summarized as follows:

Contingent reward. The leader establishes clear goals, rewards for goal achievement, negotiates resources, bases support on an implicit contract, and rewards effort by support and help.

Active management by exception. The leader monitors performance and, if necessary, takes corrective action or remediation; and maintains control by enforced rules.

Passive management by exception. The leader waits to act until a problem is brought to his or her attention and intervenes only if a problem is recognized as serious.

Laissez-faire leadership. The leader avoids responsibility, is often absent when needed, and fails to respond to requests for help.

In an early study, Bass (1985) found that when he combined measures of the four transformational categories they were more critical to successful leadership than the four transactional behavioral components. This was confirmed in later studies (Avolio and Bass, 1990). On his research, Bass commented, "Transformational leaders are more effective than those leaders practicing contingent reward; contingent reward is somewhat more effective than active management by exception, which in turn is more effective than passive management by exception. Laissez-faire leadership is least effective." (Bass, 1997, p. 134)

Thus, it appears that transformational leadership is measurably more effective than transactional leadership. However, it would be misleading to represent the transformational and transactional approaches as being independent or polar opposites of one another. Instead, there is increasing evidence that in the right combination, the two approaches can be complementary (Guastello, 1995).

TRANSFORMATIONAL LEADERSHIP AS A STATE OF MIND The old paradigms relating to task/product dimensions versus process/maintenance dimensions are no longer sufficient to explain success when using transformational thinking. Thus, it is conceivable that successful leaders can be quite autocratic and directive while still being transformative. As noted earlier, it is the ability to inspire, to raise the level of play, and to think and act in a selfless and idealistic manner that can be compelling. Similarly, collaboration and democratic methods will not necessarily result in motivated, efficient, or innovative workers. It is leaders who are able to integrate the best of the task/process dimensions along with process/maintenance behaviors who appear to be the most effective.

THE UNIVERSALITY OF TRANSFORMATIONAL LEADERSHIP

Recently, Bass (1997) has built a strong case that, in an increasingly global economy, the advantages of transformational leadership are becoming more apparent. In a work world that increasingly demands adaptability and responsiveness to quickly changing realities, the rule-based, competitive, and regulation-driven transactional organization, which centers on individual incentives, lacks flexibility. Organizations espousing a transformational approach to management are more likely to be team-based, cooperatively-focused, and participative in nature.

People from vastly different political and social realities admire transformational leadership qualities, but few societies practice these beliefs. Why?

Furthermore, transformational leadership, with its bent toward open communication, fits nicely into the communications revolution currently taking place. Access to information via the Internet has never been easier, and the more universal use of English has leveled the playing field and spawned an interest in sharing information across cultures. The visioning and mutual goal-setting processes allow for rapid adoption of new methods and strategies. These in turn can translate into greater responsiveness and more rapid change.

Bass and Avolio (1993), reporting the results of factor-analytic studies, identified what appear to be a number of universal propositions in that they hold up across countries with markedly different cultures. For example, there is a distinct hierarchy of correlations among the various leadership styles and outcomes in effectiveness, effort, and satisfaction. And these findings have been replicated in countries as diverse as New Zealand, Austria, India, Spain, and China.

A second correlation supporting the universality of transformational leadership is that, regardless of country, "When people think of leadership, their prototype and ideals are transformational" rather than transactional (Bass, 1997, p. 135; Bass and Avolio, 1989). It seems to matter little whether someone is from a collective culture or one supporting greater individualism; the principles of transformative leadership are of value in both. In fact, transformative values are not dependent on being either democratic or autocratic, participative or directive. In more individualistic societies, greater participation will often prevail, while in more directive societies, greater control is often utilized and higher degrees of conformity required (Jung, Bass, and Sosik, 1995). Nevertheless, in both, leaders attempt to motivate workers by encouraging them to transcend their own needs and look toward the interests of the organization. In addition, leaders foster a vision of what Burns called *higher-order outcomes,* such as providing quality service, meeting certain value-based standards, and perhaps providing measurable customer satisfaction (Burns, 1978).

BLENDING TASK AND PRODUCT DIMENSIONS FOR GREATER PRODUCTIVITY In a related study, which supports Bass's view that transformational leadership is indeed cross-cultural, Misumi (1995) used performance and maintenance dimensions (drawn from Kurt Lewin's original experiments) in an effort to explain differences in productivity among Japanese work environments. He found that a sensitive blend of what American theorists would label transformative and transactional leadership was most effective.

This conclusion is consistent with a third correlation hypothesized to be universally true by Bass (1997), which he refers to as a "one-way augmentation effect." That is, clear transformational behaviors blended with a contingent-reward approach, appear to create effective leadership. Although considerably more research must be conducted, the belief is growing that a balance between traditional yin/yang (masculine–feminine) or task/process behaviors can greatly benefit efforts to increase work productivity as well as improve employee morale. Just thinking in these terms has increased the complexity of the management equation significantly while at the same time providing a wide range of new strategies for influencing employee performance.

THE PYGMALION EFFECT Part of the role of the transformational leader is to motivate, support, and help each worker become the best he or she can be in a given work situation. As long as forty years ago Likert (1961) and McGregor (1960) promoted the view that leaders who expect more from their workers' performance will inevitably reap the benefits of their greater achievement. This assumption is at the heart of the so-called *Pygmalion effect* (Merton, 1948), which suggests that raising a manager's expectation of subordinates' work will result in their actually achieving more. Eden (1992), elaborating this notion, devised a Pygmalion leadership style, in which intentional use of self-fulfilling prophecies can result in higher performance.

Typical of the research conducted in this area is an early study by King (1971). He first identified four pressers, five welders, and five mechanics who were part of a training program for disadvantaged workers and labeled them as "high-aptitude personnel." In fact, the individuals were chosen at random and were no better or worse than others in the program. However, having been identified as high performers, the chosen workers lived up to expectations with higher test scores, higher supervisor and peer ratings, shorter learning times, and a lower dropout rate. Further research confirmed that if leaders communicate expectations of high performance from their followers, it will occur.

Similarly, Eden's research with the Israeli military found that when a leader's direct reports are expected to do well, it tends to bring out superior supervisory behaviors on the part of the leader, and this translates into better performance on the part of subordinates. As Eden noted,

> The sarcastic adage that 'managers get the subordinates they deserve' should be replaced by one that has greater fidelity to what it is that we know about leader-expectation effects: *Managers get the performance they expect.* The practical upshot is that we need to develop ways of getting managers to expect more. (Eden, 1994, p. 279)

THE GOLEM EFFECT We know that creating a positive self-fulfilling prophecy can stimulate higher production and higher morale. However, as Livingston noted (1988), there are more negative Pygmalions than positive Pygmalions in U.S. business and industry. Often the great potential of people is placed in the negative shadow of low expectations based on stereotypes and poor past achievement. This so-called *Golem effect,* or the result of negative conditioning, can be turned around by simply altering the expectations of leaders of their workers. Eden (1992) provides the example of a packaging plant in Israel. New immigrant labor from Eastern Europe was highly valued and so expectations of excellent performance were high. In contrast, no such high expectations were held for local Israeli employees in the same jobs, who had the reputation for being less efficient and less motivated. Over time, the Golem effect occurred, and the local employees continued to lose respect.

The plant manager, familiar with the notion of self-fulfilling prophecies, decided to alter the situation. For the next group of local hires, he told one of his floor supervisors that they were a special group; they had been hand-picked. He indicated that he expected no problems and that they would achieve full production quickly. This group exceeded all expectations, in record time. The supervisor later praised the manager for his better hiring decisions. Thus, there remains little doubt that there are countless opportunities for conscious application of the Pygmalion effect in the workplace.

BUILDING CONFIDENCE AND INSPIRATION Part of an effective supervisor's role is diagnostic in nature. After assessing the uniqueness of each worker, the leader can design interventions using self-fulfilling prophecies as part of a larger strategy to help motivate and build the confidence of each individual. One goal here is to create a *high-expectancy culture,* which entails the leader helping individuals, and the organization as a whole, to envision possibilities at both the individual and system levels. Integral to this is raising the leader's expectations of his or her own behavior, as well as that of others.

A FINAL NOTE ON THE PYGMALION EFFECT The power of suggestion also has an effect on behavior that is opposite the Pygmalion effect, and this is often overlooked. Palich and Hom (1992) have shown that workers convinced that their leaders are especially competent tend to cause fewer problems and "give" the leaders "more permission" to lead. This establishes its own self-fulfilling prophecy: the leaders feel more accepted and increasingly competent. The implications of this effect for leadership development are obvious. That is, how new leaders are brought into an organization and provided legitimacy may have a telling impact on their eventual success. Likewise, how upper management talks about—whether in praise or discredit—lower-level leaders can have a major influence on worker attitudes and their willingness to follow these leaders.

FOCUS ON DIVERSITY

How do you account for the differences between male and female leaders? Are they due to the expectations of followers or gender differences?

What Women Bring to the Workplace

It will not be long before the numbers of women graduating from professional schools of medicine, law, and business equal or surpass men. Few will deny that women bring different attitudes, needs, and interests to the table. Almost a decade ago Rosener (1990) provided evidence that women have differing views of leadership than their male counterparts. Men tend to favor a predominantly transactional, carrot-and-stick style, whereas women apparently favor a more transformative approach. It may not be coincidental that during the intervening years, the more balanced transformational approach has found a business climate increasingly conducive to its views.

Will the male leaders who dominate positions of leadership in business and the professions be threatened by such views? Will the leaders/teachers of management in our professional schools, who also tend to be predominantly male, give legitimacy to these new views? The jury is still out.

What we do know is that women who are measured as being successful also view the reasons for their success as different from the responses traditionally expected by men. For example, successful women tend to:

- encourage a high degree of participation in the management process.
- when possible share information and power.
- attempt to enhance the self-worth of those with whom they work.
- attempt to excite people about their work.

Such a positive, collaborative view has also found support in the theories of management promoted by the likes of well known modernists such as Agyris, Senge (1990b), and Covey. It will be a decade or more before we will know whether the rhetoric of greater cooperation and less competition, more open communication, shared leadership, and self-understanding—all qualities traditionally characterized by women—prove to flourish within the male dominated organizations.

What transformational leadership provides is a greater balance between the traditional male and female approaches. The future holds the distinct possibility that the differences in style and attitude, which distinguish men and women so that the best of both required at a given moment in time, can be utilized to enhance the effectiveness of the work force (Berdahl, J. L., 1996).

Corporate Culture and Performance

Kotter and Heskett (1992), in a sixteen-year study of over 200 firms from twenty-two different industries, have attempted to identify cultural values and behaviors that separate high-performing and low-performing organizations. What was striking in the results was that the low-performing organizations had cultures with many qualities opposite those found in Bass's composite of transformational leadership behaviors, discussed above. Thus, they found that the most successful cultures were those that were also the most adaptive. Furthermore, leaders were

- free to take risks.
- openly cooperative.
- proactive in their search for problems.
- continually open to new ideas and innovation.
- attentive to all stakeholders (clients, employees, owners).
- enthusiastic.

Contrast this description to the behaviors and attitudes found in unhealthy cultures, in which leaders tended to be

- know-it-all and defensive—self justifying.
- inconsistent in their treatment of different stakeholders.
- relatively risk-averse, with management (control) replacing leadership and innovation.
- little inclined to seek data feedback and often inclined to ignore the resulting information.

Thus, the less successful organizations became more insular, less proactive, less vision-directed, and more concerned with maintenance of the status quo.

What Transformational Leadership Is Not

An organization's values, philosophy, and image are easily discernible in how a leader and key associates communicate and position their vision. Conversely, these same factors can reveal insensitivity to or ignorance of the organization's principles, which in turn can lead to failure. The following story reveals the latter: here arrogance and insensitivity overrode a firm's vision and spelled disaster.

Ten years ago, few had ever heard of this tiny midwestern advertising agency. But the bold, creative, and even brash challenge it made to the New York goliaths was soon to be reckoned with. Always willing to push to the edge of propriety, this audacious little firm adopted trendy and often assertive views of the world and blended humor, sarcasm, sex, and outrage in a way that titillated the buying public and created an increasing demand for its services. Clients and revenues multiplied, and million-dollar accounts became commonplace. The firm's leaders were in demand, the future was bright, and opportunity continued to knock.

At a statewide annual conference on the marketing for representation of higher education services, this company was represented by one of its top designers, who provided the audience with a taste of the agency's upbeat, unconventional, and irreverent attitudes and practices. One woman in the audience, a Ph.D. who had represented her university at the conference for ten years, took offense at the sexist language and the general tenor of the presentation. After the conference, she sent what she felt was a reasonable letter to the presenter, indicating that she had been impressed by the creative level and quality of the work but had been annoyed and offended by the negative stereotypes of women in the presentation. "I appreciate the personal apologies you made at the time for the tone of that material," she wrote, "but they didn't make up for those negative stereotypes or for your company's obvious interest in perpetuating what I can't help thinking of as a macho style of doing business." She concluded by expressing disappointment that a company on the cutting edge had to resort to such shopworn ideas to convince people of its creativity.

Although such criticism is not easy to take, there are certainly many ways of responding to it and of acknowledging its usefulness as feedback. But the firm's presenter took a different route. He sent the woman a letter thanking her for her "deeply thoughtful and perceptive letter." That done, he suggested she might find it interesting to visit the East African home of the Dinka tribe to study a custom used in tribal initiations, which appeared explicitly lewd and distasteful and left the professor shocked and dismayed.

Her response to this offensive and bizarre form of male humor was to send her letter and his response to a woman's consortium that acted as a clearing house for 170 women's groups. Two staff members of the consortium sent a letter to the president of the company asking whether the reply of the presenter represented company policy. The letter from the consortium stimulated two replies from the company, neither sent to the consortium itself—both were sent to the writer of the first letter. The letters of the CEO and the chairman both included profuse thanks for interest and then continued the "joke." One offered her a one-way ticket to Dinka land for the opportunity to study the ritual first hand. The other sent her a mosquito net and pith helmet for the trip.

The monumental arrogance, rudeness, and bad taste that somehow eluded the men resulted in the members of the consortium sending copies of all the transactions, without comment, directly to selected clients of the agency, several potential clients, and local newspapers and a number of trade journals. The company was deluged with letters of outrage, criticism, and some support. A week after the materials were made public, the company sent a conciliatory letter to the professor. By then, however, the company had experienced $10 million in canceled accounts and was threatened with the loss of an estimated $20 million in new ones.

Though the leaders of this firm had created a monster, similar mistakes, perhaps on a smaller scale, happen every day. Therefore, it's worth studying the reasons for these leaders' enormous gaffe.

1. Though conscious of the changing norms of society that allowed them to push the boundaries of propriety, they failed to realize how sharply their attitudes conflicted with that very society's changing views of women.
2. Perhaps because of their success and the rewards they had received for their brazen advertising style, the leaders had allowed themselves to become isolated from external feedback—a critical error, because many of their clients, as well as many of their own staff members, were women (Davies and Kuypers, 1985).
3. Complacency, fear, and ignorance kept internal feedback from reaching the leaders. Even the women within the organization were either unaware of changing views or unable to express their own outrage at the course of events. This would suggest that other information was inaccessible to the leaders as well.
4. Arrogance and old-boyism created nonfunctional individual goals and roles (protecting egos, getting even, using scapegoating and humor at other people's expense).
5. The leaders' response was cause for particular concern, because it represented a studied response to a small problem. The punitive and hostile attitudes expressed there could only be symptoms of how other issues would strike these leaders personally and how they would be handled within the agency.

Summary

Because this chapter has covered a great deal of complex material on leadership, let us conclude with a summary of the key points.

- Leadership is not a rare commodity, nor is it an inborn gift. Almost everyone can be trained as a leader at any level of society.
- Leadership originates in people's willingness to organize and commit themselves to goals and visions to which they have applied themselves. Though leadership skills can be learned through training and practice, the success of the leaders studied in this chapter resulted largely from their goals and attitudes toward themselves.
- Leaders attempting to effect change must be conscious of the need to work *with* those who are to live with the impact of that change. Often, creating and communicating a vision will succeed only insofar as others are able to internalize and pursue the vision with the leader.

- Collaborative problem solving and the development of creative design strategies (see Chapters 7 and 8) can enhance the leader's ability to lead while involving others in action (Terry's term).
- At the simplest level, leadership is a *transaction* between a leader and an individual or a group of people. The transaction is based on each receiving something of importance from the other, such as a vote for a political promise or money for a job.
- Leadership can also be a more complex phenomenon, extending into the domains of power, visionary thinking, and ethics. In its most integrated form, leadership is *transformational.* In this process, individuals and groups are drawn into action by a clearly communicated vision that fulfills specific needs. When the followers internalize that vision, its values, and the process of change, and in turn become leaders and inspirers of further change, the transformational process has been completed.
- Finally, regardless of how clearly a goal or vision is communicated or how well organized a plan of action is, ineffective or insensitive behavior on the part of leaders can result in failure. Thus open channels of communication, feedback, and leader flexibility are all critical. Furthermore, initial success can breed arrogance, distance, and limited access to critical information, which in turn can result in a deterioration of morale and performance within the group or organization.

EXERCISE 1 A Series of Nonverbal Experiences in Leading and Being Led

The following exercises focus on our feelings of leading and being led, and provide data to examine both our behavior and our attitudes in being a follower and being a leader. The exercises are appropriate as a beginning microlab in a longer workshop. They are also useful to members as a means of examining their typical roles and understanding areas in which modification or reevaluation may be needed. The exercises lead to nonintellectualized discussions of leadership in terms of personal satisfactions or conflicts, areas of skill and ineptness, and enjoyment of authority or fear of responsibility. They also allow participants to see the complementary nature of leader–member relationships in trust, openness, spontaneity, communication, and dependence–independence.

The exercises are of varying lengths and, depending on the purposes, can be expanded or reduced. They involve varying degrees of risk and should be used with an understanding of both the purpose of the exercise and the type of group involved. For some groups, any touching is beyond the bounds of propriety, so certain exercises should be eliminated. Because touching is counter to the norms of the group, much tension is generated and effectiveness in examining leader–follower relationships is severely curtailed. Some groups who consider themselves serious and work-oriented may frown upon games that call for a childlike spontaneity; they may consider games contrived and not regard them as a legitimate basis for learning. The values and resistances of the group should be taken into account so that the exercises used will help members achieve their purposes.

The procedure is as follows: the exercise is named, as illustrated below, and the facilitator gives instructions so that participants have a feel for the exercise and how it is to be carried out.

1. CONNECTEDNESS BY RUBBER BANDS

The facilitator begins by saying, "Pick someone. Put your hands out in front of you. Almost touch the hands of your partner. Pretend now that your hands and his or hers are connected by rubber bands. Move—feel what happens" (5 min.). "Pretend your feet are also connected by rubber bands" (5 min.). "Talk about what happened" (10 min.).

The objectives of the exercise are to increase awareness among participant pairs of their own boundaries and those of others; and to increase body awareness, control of self, and control of another person. It also presents a leadership–followership situation. Did one person lead all the time? Did the participants reverse roles? When? At what signals? Which role was more comfortable, leading or following? Did one partner see the other as being more comfortable leading or following? Did it make a difference whether it was hands or feet that were connected?

Not all of these questions have to be asked. A few may be suggested, depending on what clues the facilitator observes. He or she may mention these as a basis for discussion, but it is important not to spend too much time in discussion. Rather, participants should express their response to this experience and let their impressions build with subsequent exercises.

2. COMMUNICATION BY CLAPPING

The facilitator gives the following instructions: "Pick someone who has not been your partner previously. Clap a message. Then let the other person respond." (The facilitator should select a member of the audience and demonstrate. The two stand facing each other, and the facilitator claps the phrase "How are you?" The other person claps back, "fine," or "angry," or whatever.) "You see how it is done. Remember that it involves restructuring meaning from familiar sounds. Now try having a conversation through clapping" (10 min.). "Between you, discuss what happened. What was expressed?" (5 min.). Then the entire group discusses what they experienced (5 min.).

At one level, this exercise allows participants to experience expression through tactile and auditory senses, to create and hear rhythm and sound as expressive of emotion and sequence. At another level, communication is seen as a process requiring a sender and a receiver; one side is insufficient for communication. At yet another level, it is essential to recognize who initiated the "conversation," who "talked" more, who led, who followed, who was frustrated and withdrew. The exercise can also be used to examine functional roles of members.

3. LEADER–FOLLOWER TRUST WALK

The facilitator begins: "This exercise focuses on being a leader or a follower. Half of you will be blindfolded. Those who are not blindfolded will select a partner. This is a nonverbal exercise, so you may not speak to your partner to tell him or her who you are. Let's begin by counting off in twos." (Participants count off "1, 2, 1, 2," etc.) "Will all of the ones come to this side of the room? Here are handkerchiefs to use as blindfolds. Put them on and adjust them so that you cannot see." (The ones arrange their blindfolds and wait.)

Now, the facilitator talks to the twos quietly so that the others cannot hear. "Each of you will select a partner from the group of ones. Stand beside the partner you choose so that we can determine who still needs a partner. Remember, you and your partner may not speak, but by all means try to develop a nonverbal language between you. You will be the leader. How can you help your partner experience his or her world? Can you enlarge his or her world? Be aware of how you see your role. Is it to protect him or her, to get him or her through safely? Is it to be with a minimum of effort on your part? Is it to be serious; is it to be fun? (Pause) Now select your partner."

"Explore your world, nonverbally of course. I will see you back here in 15 minutes." (If this occurs in a building, 15 minutes is adequate time. If it is outdoors and time permits, allow up to an hour. It is frequently a moving experience to see the partners develop their own signals, increasing sensitivity to each other, a trusting relationship.)

The facilitator alerts the group two minutes before time is up. If the setting is outdoors, he or she simply hopes that they will straggle back reasonably on time.

When they return, the facilitator has the "blind" remove their eye covers to see who their partner is. (This produces tension, anxiety, even fumbling, as the "leader" wonders whether his or her follower will be disappointed when identities are revealed. There is also the anxiety of returning to the "real world," which does not encourage the closeness and trust some of the partners felt. Now the mood changes; the "uncovering" produces laughter and squeals of recognition or surprise.)

The facilitator proceeds: "Would you share your feelings in the experience? What did you find out about yourself that was new? What did you find typical of yourself? How did you feel about your role as a leader or a follower?" (15 min.).

"I am sure each of you wants to experience the other role. Will all of the twos come to this side of the room? Now, it is your turn for the blindfolds. You know what to do."

He or she then talks to the ones as previously to the other group. Although they have been through the experience and know what they want their partner to experience, nevertheless it seems helpful to remind them, through the questions, of a variety of possible relationships they may have with their partner in the leader role. Once more, those not blindfolded select a partner and stand beside him or her. Frequently, the choosing partner will select his or her former partner in order to "repay" his or her felt interest. For a variety of reasons, a person may prefer to select a new partner. After selections are made, the exercise continues as in the first pairing. The groups return, see each other, and share their feelings.

Sometimes the participants feel their reactions are significant and relatively private; they may want to share only with their partners. Sometimes participants are quite eager to share their new understanding of themselves with the whole group. If there is a group sharing, one of the questions the facilitator should ask is how it felt to be a leader and how it felt to be a follower. What was learned?

This exercise has usually been considered primarily an experience of trust; however, it is striking how often members report on their relationship with authority. Students frequently note that it helps them understand their parents or gives them insight into what kind of parent they would like to be. Men and women discuss their societal sex roles, in which a man is expected to be the leader, and their feelings when those roles are reversed. Some who usually see themselves as leaders are surprised at their reactions to being followers and gain a different perspective on the relationship; those who are usually followers give similar reports. Participants also talk about clues they pick up from each other—being tired, bored, excited—which greatly influence the other person and the relationship; new insights are reported on complementary relationships.

As an aside, if a supply of handkerchiefs is difficult to obtain, paper towels as they come from a dispenser and masking tape are equally effective as blindfolds.

4. FOLLOW THE LEADER—A MUSICAL VARIATION ON THE CHILDREN'S GAME

Select an instrumental record with a diversity of moods, tempos, and sounds (Vivaldi's *Four Seasons,* for example). Participants are divided into groups of eight to ten and stand in a circle facing each other; in some groups, participants take off their shoes to enhance a feeling of movement.

Then the facilitator says, "I'm going to play a record. Listen to it, get a feel for the mood. If it reminds you of something, or if you want to express what you feel, come into the center of the circle and do it. Those of us who can feel it with you will follow you in our places. When the mood of the music changes, return to your place. Someone else, who is feeling something he or she would like to share, will go into the center. O.K.?" (10–15 min.).

"How was it? How did you feel about what happened?" (10 min.).

One of the questions to be raised is "Who initiates leadership?" It is someone who knows what is needed, feels he or she has the skills or resources to do it, and feels it is safe to try. Discussion encompasses all these issues. Some will say they could not even think in terms of what music could mean in a public place; their minds went blank immediately. Others had a mental image of what the music evoked but did not seem to have the skill or resources to transfer that image into body movement. Still others hesitated to come into the center for fear of appearing clumsy, childish, or not very original. Another area for brief discussion is how the situation changed. When did you start to feel comfortable, or enjoy it? What happened?

5. BUILDING A GROUP BY MUSIC

This exercise is done with an instrumental record that has an easily discerned tempo, rhythm, and mood; ethnic folk dances are especially suitable (African dances and Irish or Israeli folk dance records work well).

1. *Pair.* The facilitator gives the following instructions: "Select a partner. When the music starts, one of you move to the music, as you feel it. The other person will be your mirror image; he or she will do what you do. If it helps to be more realistic, pretend each of you is touching a mirror with the palms of your hands. The person who is the mirror will try to follow facial expressions as well as body movements. Change who is mirroring when you want to." The record begins. (About 3 min.).
2. *Quartet.* "Add a pair to your group. Continue to move to the music but do it as a group." (About 3 min.).
3. *Octet.* "Add a quartet to your group. Continue to move to the music as a group of eight." (About 3 min.).
4. *One more time (a group of sixteen).* "You're right. Add an octet to your group. Stay with the music. Move to the music as a group." (About 3 min., preferably to the end of the record so that there is a natural feeling of closure.) This produces exhilaration but also a good supply of creaking joints, and a surge of business for the water fountain. There should be no discussion for at least 15 minutes.

The objectives of this exercise are to examine leader–member relationships in varying group sizes. Who follows, who leads? Is it easier to lead in a small group than a large one? Do some leadership patterns remain? Why? How is leadership determined? What role do members play? Do they have inputs that are listened to? Who was the leader (or leaders) at the end? How did he or she get influence? On what was it based? The facilitator asks how some of the members felt in this experience. He or she expands on some of the answers given to the foregoing questions or raises a few new ones. Once more, the discussion should be brief and informal.

CONCLUSION

The facilitator might close by reminding the group that they have been through a battery of nonverbal experiences that explore leader–member relationships. They may consider what new understanding they have about themselves—for example, how they acted when they were asked to pick a partner. Did they choose or wait to be chosen? Why? What new insight do they have on the subject of leaders, members, and followers?

Participants may be asked to write a log, or self-report, verbalizing what they have learned. They can be divided into small groups to discuss some of their experiences. A large group discussion leaves too many as listeners without an opportunity to participate; at best, it might be used briefly to begin the discussion.

The facilitator should be particularly sensitive to norms of the group with whom he or she is working. These exercises should be used only where appropriate. As noted earlier, they should not be used with groups who consider touching inappropriate, nor should they be used unless they will enhance the goals of the training.

EXERCISE 2 A Task-Maintenance Exercise

OBJECTIVES

- **To increase understanding of task-maintenance roles**
- **To increase skills in observing a group; to learn to categorize by functional roles of members**
- **To increase learning about the difference between intended behavior and perceived behavior**

RATIONALE

This exercise permits participants and observers to understand that intent is not enough. Attempting certain behaviors does not mean that a person will be perceived in the role he or she intends. In addition, intending to behave in a certain way does not indicate a person's skill in this role, factors that may interfere with his or her intentions, or the fact that more conscious behaviors are called into play. Participants come to understand some of the complexities in the interpersonal and group processes that go on in meetings.

This exercise is not appropriate unless the members have become familiar with the task-maintenance concept and functional roles and are willing to consider the implications of what they have learned. It can be followed by skill sessions in practicing each of the task and maintenance roles. The role play may be repeated after discussion or skill session, with members attempting to be more congruent or skillful in their roles and observers attempting to focus more clearly on behaviors.

MATERIALS

The following materials are needed: two copies of the role-play situation described below and six role-play names; six copies of the Explanation Sheet of Task and Maintenance Roles, to be given to role players only; newsprint, felt-tip markers, and tape; and a table and six chairs.

DESIGN

The facilitator introduces the design as a role play. He or she explains that in a role play, a situation is concocted that is not real but could be. Participants enact not their usual roles but rather, the roles they are instructed to play. The role play permits an examination of behavior without embarrassing anyone and helps develop increased skills in the situation.

The facilitator asks for six volunteers to participate in the role play, selects six people and briefs them in private, and then distributes six pieces of paper (usually holding them face down and having the role players select one of the papers). The papers should read as follows:

> *Association President—assume number 1 task role and number 1 maintenance role.*
>
> *Teacher Representative—assume number 2 task role and number 2 maintenance behavior.*
>
> *Association Negotiator—assume number 3 task role and number 3 maintenance role.*
>
> *Superintendent of Schools—assume number 4 task role and number 4 maintenance role.*
>
> *School Board Representative—assume number 5 task role and number 5 maintenance role.*
>
> *School Board President—assume number 6 task role and number 6 maintenance role. You are somewhat hostile to the teachers and their position on the salary increase.*

The association negotiators, the board, and the superintendent are given a few minutes to discuss as individual groups what they plan to do. While they are doing this, observer sheets are distributed to others in the group.

The facilitator instructs observers to tally every time any of the role players' behavior falls under either Task or Maintenance, as described on the Explanation Sheet. He or she asks them to record words or acts that will help recall and support their observations and also to write the names of the role players at the top of the sheets. The facilitator answers any questions observers may have. Then he or she calls the role players back into the room, seats them at the conference table, and reads the role play to the entire group. He or she gives one copy to the role players to keep before them.

THE ROLE-PLAY SITUATION

A negotiations impasse over salaries between the Teachers Association and the school board is imminent. The association's original proposal called for a beginning salary of $19,000, with a $2,000-per-year increment for 12 years. This would have given the association the highest beginning and ending salary in the country.

The first counterproposal by the board maintains the existing salary of $19,000, but with $1,000-per-year increments for 12 years. This was refused by the association. A second counterproposal by the board maintains the existing salary increment of $2,000 per year for 20 years but begins at $12,600. This would give the association the lowest starting salary in the country but the highest maximum salary. A special levy has already been called for, and the amount, which includes no salary adjustment, has been earmarked. As the scene opens, the board members say that they cannot change the earmarking of the special levy funds and that no other funds are available. The teachers say that they cannot accept the last proposal, maintaining that it will decimate the professional staff of the district. The association negotiators have agreed that if they cannot get the board to utilize the reserve funds (7½ percent of the total budget), they will declare an impasse at the present meeting.

The facilitator continues the role-play situation for 10–15 minutes. He or she ends it when it appears that there will be no further movement, before interest lags. Then he or she asks observers to meet in trios and compare their perceptions and tallying. The trios do this and arrive at a joint report indicating what role each player was primarily playing (about 10 minutes). The facilitator returns to the general session and places the names of the role players on newsprint. He or she asks for reports from trios, and next to each name he or she writes the role the trio thought each person was taking. Then he or she asks each role player to reveal the role assigned to him or her and what he or she was attempting. That information is written next to his or her name on the newsprint. The prediction is that there will be a discrepancy between the way the role player understood his or her role and the way he or she actually acted it out. Also, it is predictable that the observers will vary in their reports of how the role players were acting.

EXPLANATION SHEET Of TASK AND MAINTENANCE ROLES[3]

(To be given to role players only)

Task roles

1. *Initiating:* Proposing tasks or goals: defining a group problem; suggesting a procedure or ideas for solving a problem.
2. *Information or opinion seeking:* Requesting facts; seeking relevant information about a group concern; asking for suggestions and ideas.
3. *Information or opinion giving:* Offering facts; providing relevant information about a group concern; stating a belief; giving suggestions or ideas.
4. *Clarifying or elaborating:* Interpreting or reflecting ideas and suggestions; clearing up confusion; indicating alternatives and issues before the group; giving examples.
5. *Summarizing:* Pulling together related ideas; restating suggestions after the group has discussed them; offering a decision or conclusion for the group to accept or reject.

Maintenance roles

1. Encouraging: Being friendly, warm, and responsive to others; accepting others and their contributions; rewarding others by giving them an opportunity or recognition.
2. *Expressing group feelings:* Sensing feelings, mood, relationships within the group; sharing own feelings with other members.
3. *Harmonizing:* Attempting to reconcile disagreements; reducing tension through "pouring oil on troubled waters"; getting people to explore their differences.
4. *Compromising:* When own idea or status is involved in a conflict, offering to compromise own position; admitting error, disciplining self to maintain group cohesion.
5. *Gate-keeping:* Attempting to keep communication channels open; facilitating the participation of others; suggesting procedures of others; suggesting procedures for sharing opportunity to discuss group problems.

3. Based on Benne and Sheats, 1948.

Task roles (cont.)

6. *Consensus testing:* Sending up trial balloons to see if the group is nearing a conclusion; checking with the group to see how much agreement has been reached.

Maintenance roles (cont.)

6. *Setting standards:* Expressing standards for the group to achieve; applying standards in evaluating group functioning and production.

DISCUSSION

Role players are asked how comfortable they were in their roles. Was it like their usual roles? Which players enacted their roles most faithfully—were they perceived by others as being in their assigned roles? Which players had the greatest discrepancies? Why? Which behaviors caused difficulties in attempting to attain observer agreement? Are there generalizations that can be made about the observations?

The facilitator might briefly dwell on the several factors that influence the interpersonal and group processes going on at meetings. At least two factors appear prominent as a result of this role play.

1. *A perceptual factor.* Not all of us perceive the same thing when we are watching the behavior of another person. Some perceive a person giving feelings, while others hear him or her giving information or expressing opinions.
2. *Our intentions are different from our behavior.* Participants might have intended to play a given role but might have given out mixed messages. Their words said one thing, but their nonverbal behavior in body or tone emitted another message.

Sometimes we intend to play roles at which we are not skilled; we mean to behave in a certain way but get "off the track." Sometimes cues from another person evoke responses we have not intended. We sense that the person does not like us, and we become defensive or see the person as an opponent rather than, as previously assumed, a friend. How we feel about others personally affects our behavior.

EXERCISE 3 Functional Roles of Membership

OBJECTIVES

- To increase the understanding of functional roles of membership
- To see leadership emerge
- To practice observing types of behavior
- To develop an increased understanding of leadership requiring followership

MATERIALS

The materials needed are the same as for the role play above. Also needed are copies of Group Building and Maintenance Roles and Group Task Roles (included with this exercise).

RATIONALE

Any of the role-play exercises in this book or the problem-solving exercises in this chapter are appropriate as a situation to examine functional roles of members. The goal is to develop skills in observing types of behavior and increasing awareness of the functional roles.

DESIGN

The facilitator establishes the role play included with this exercise or uses Tinker Toys and asks each group to create a symbol of its group. Or he or she can use newsprint, crayons, and other materials and ask each group to create a collage. Two observers are assigned to tally for functional roles. Each time someone behaves in a role, a tally is made. One person can tally for task roles, the other for maintenance roles. A better procedure is to have two observers for task roles and two for maintenance roles so as to check reliability. Following the activity, the observers feed back their findings in the emerging roles.

Sometimes a questionnaire can be distributed to participants immediately following the situation, in which each person is asked to state who he or she felt was the leader of the group, who was most influential, and with whom he or she would like to work again. These results are determined. There is discussion about the amount of agreement or variety of responses. This discussion gets at the various bases of power. Following the administering of questionnaires, the observers feed back their findings. The group examines how these results support or are different from their ratings on the questionnaires.

GROUP BUILDING AND MAINTENANCE ROLES

Categories describe the types of member behavior required for building and maintaining the group as a working unit.

Usually helpful	*Usually destructive*
1. *Encouraging:* Is friendly, warm, and responsive to others; accepts others and their contributions; is giving to others.	Is cold, unresponsive, unfriendly; rejects others' contributions; ignores them.
2. *Expressing feelings:* Expresses feelings present in the group; calls attention of the group to its reactions to ideas and suggestions; expresses own feelings or reactions in the group.	Ignores reactions of the group as a whole; refuses to express own feelings when needed.
3. *Harmonizing:* Attempts to reconcile disagreements; reduces tension through joking, relaxing comments; gets people to explore their differences.	Irritates or "needles" others; encourages disagreement for its own sake; uses emotion-laden words.
4. *Compromising:* When own idea or status is involved in a conflict, offers compromise, yields status, admits error; disciplines self to maintain group cohesion.	Becomes defensive, haughty; withdraws or walks out; demands subservience or submission from others.
5. *Facilitating communication:* Attempts to keep communication channels open; facilitates participation of others; suggests procedures for discussing group problems.	Ignores miscommunications; fails to listen to others; ignores the group needs that are expressed.
6. *Setting standards or goals:* Expresses standards or goals for group to achieve; helps the group become aware of direction and progress.	Goes own way; is irrelevant; ignores group standards or goals and direction.

Usually helpful (cont.)	*Usually destructive (cont.)*
7. *Testing agreement:* Asks for opinions to find out if the group is nearing a decision; sends up a trial balloon to see how near agreement the group is; rewards progress.	Attends to own needs; does not note group condition or direction; complains about slow progress.
8. *Following:* Goes along with movement of the group; accepts ideas of others; listens to and serves as an interested audience for others in the group.	Participates on own ideas but does not actively listen to others; looks for loopholes in ideas; is carping.

GROUP TASK ROLES

Categories describe the types of member behavior required for accomplishing the task or work of the group.

Usually helpful	*Usually destructive*
1. *Initiating:* Proposes tasks or goals; defines a group problem; suggests a procedure or ideas for solving a problem.	Waits for others to initiate; withholds ideas or suggestions.
2. *Seeking information:* Requests facts; seeks relevant information about a group problem or concern; is aware of need for information.	Is unaware of need for facts or of what is relevant to the problem or task at hand.
3. *Giving information:* Offers facts; provides relevant information about a group concern.	Avoids facts; prefers to state personal opinions or prejudices.
4. *Seeking opinions:* Asks for expression of feeling; requests statements of estimate, expressions of value; seeks suggestions and ideas.	Does not ask what others wish or think; considers other opinions irrelevant.

Usually helpful (cont.)	*Usually destructive (cont.)*
5. *Giving opinion:* States belief about a matter before the group; gives suggestions and ideas.	States own opinion whether relevant or not; withholds opinions or ideas when needed by the group.
6. *Clarifying:* Interprets ideas or suggestions; clears up confusion; defines needed terms; indicates alternatives and issues confronting the group.	Is unaware of or irritated by confusion or ambiguities; ignores confusion of others.
7. *Elaborating:* Gives examples; develops meanings; makes generalizations; indicates how a proposal might work out if adopted.	Is inconsiderate of those who do not understand; refuses to explain or show new meaning.
8. *Summarizing:* Pulls together related ideas; restates suggestions after the group has discussed them; offers decision or conclusion for the group to accept or reject.	Moves ahead without checking for relationship or integration of ideas; lets people make their own integrations or relationships.

ROLE PLAY TO PRACTICE OBSERVING FUNCTIONAL ROLES

Second Observation—Role Play—Preliminary Negotiations Between Union and Management

1. *Mediator from Chamber of Commerce.* You want both sides to be happy. Your goal is to arrive at a solution that satisfies both sides. It would look bad for business in town if there were a strike; on the other hand, if word goes around that labor gets everything it wants, business will not be attracted to this city.
2. *Union Representative.* The workers must have a raise: too many are beginning to question why they pay dues. If you can't get a raise, get an equivalent. The president of the company is a nice guy if you treat him with respect (he goes for that), but you don't like to kowtow. You will if things get bad; the most important part is to come out with something.
3. *Shop Steward.* You want a raise for the workers. It makes you feel important to sit down with the president of the company and feel that you are his equal. You want to be sure he treats you as his equal. You are easily hurt by any slight; your voice must be heard. Remind them you can cause a strike, make trouble for them, and so forth. You want to show the workers in your plant how important you are and to get them a big "package."

4. *Company President.* You are head of a large company. You are in the midst of modernizing your equipment, which will mean more automation and laying off workers. Possibly workers can be shifted to other places in the plant but not at the same level. A small raise wouldn't be bad (profits have been substantial), but how about the layoffs next year and the possibility of a strike then? Perhaps something can be worked out, but you want them to understand that you are considering such alternatives. You are a leader in the community; you are not the equal of the working person in intelligence, education, or standard of living—you are superior.
5. *Independent Businessperson.* You are a small businessperson. An increase in this industry means an increase for every worker. You are just barely making ends meet; you can't afford a raise; you would be faced with going out of business. You like being on a par with the president of the large company, a prominent person in town. You certainly see his point of view better than that of the workers, who care only about their earnings; they are unconcerned with yours.

DISCUSSION

What did you learn about your behavior in a group? Which roles do you usually play? Which do you wish you could take on more frequently? These questions can be listed in a short questionnaire and fed back as data to participants. There could then be sessions allowing participants to build skills in the roles with which they have difficulty.

What kind of leadership is helpful to the group? What blocks movement? These questions usually lead into a discussion of clarity—or lack of clarity—of goals. It becomes obvious that we are open to the influence of only some members. Frequently, we have difficulty in putting out needed behavior for fear of its not being accepted.

EXERCISE 4 Decision Making Along a Continuum—Problems

OBJECTIVES

- To experience some of the roles people play in decision making
- To experience ambiguity with a leader and note how it affects both the process and the product

- To understand the choice-of-leadership continuum and its implications for members
- To increase understanding that a leader–member relationship is a dynamic one, each previous relationship affecting the present one
- To increase observational skills of a dyad in change

RATIONALE

This exercise yields very dramatic learnings. It becomes obvious that the leader–member relationship is a fundamental one in understanding group process and organizational functioning. The leader and member roles are defined much as they frequently are, and the leaders have more direct access to instructions from the top than the members. The information members receive is based on how the leader decides to transmit it—whether limited, ambiguous, or honest. Although the leader becomes more member-oriented in his or her decisions, the member may not perceive himself or herself as having a more significant role. He or she may be reacting to previous behaviors of the leader and may have developed a lack of trust and an apathetic response. Participants become aware of the dynamic relationships in a group. That is, they recognize that members' trust of the leader influences the degree of work in decision making and that clarity in decision making is an important factor in leader–member relationships. It also permits members to understand the effectiveness of multilateral versus unilateral decision making.

MATERIALS

There should be three lists of innocuous items to be rank-ordered. (The lists are not important in themselves; they are simply a basis for discussion and decision making.) Some examples: What are the most important qualities of a good teacher? Ten qualities are listed, with a dash as a place for ranking before each item. The qualities listed might be education, initiative, creativity, persistence, fairness, a sense of humor, diligence, love of teaching, interest in travel, and experience. Other similar questions: Rank these 10 presidents in order of their importance in history. Then the names of ten presidents are listed. Another example: Rank these people in order of the importance of their contribution to mankind: Charlemagne, Julius Caesar, Socrates, Martin Luther, Galileo, Darwin, Shakespeare, Queen Victoria, Karl Marx, and Adam Smith.

Three different lists are required, and there should be two copies of each list, preferably on different-colored paper. One color (let us say green) should always be given to the leader; the other color (white) should always be given to the member. There should be enough lists for two-thirds of the participants. There should also be sheets printed for observers. The sheet is headed Observer's Sheet and should list questions to direct the observer's attention to the data to be gathered (see the sample Observer's Sheet included with this exercise). These sheets are needed for one-third of the group.

ACTION

The group is divided into trios. One person is the leader, one the member, and one the observer. Each trio will be asked to perform three ranking tasks and to turn in their decision on each, according to specific instructions. Following the third exercise, observers report their findings, and leaders and members respond with their feelings on the situations. This is followed by a general discussion.

The group is again divided into triads and told that they will be asked to perform three tasks, each of which involves reaching a decision. In the tasks, the participants are to maintain the same roles throughout; that is, the person who is the leader will continue in his or her role as leader in all three tasks, the person who is the member will occupy that role for all three tasks, and the observer will maintain that role throughout.

Instructions are given at the beginning of each task, but the members are asked to leave the room first. Only the leaders receive instructions, as frequently happens in many groups and organizations. Instructions are then transmitted from the leader to his or her member or subordinate. It is important that the members leave prior to instructions so as to avoid the psychological effect of feeling left out, and because they should not know the changed rules for each task.

Task I Instructions are given to leaders; members are not in the room. The leaders are instructed that they and their paired member will each be given a list of items to rank-order. (The leader is given the green sheet, the member the white sheet.) Each person will rank the items individually. Then the leader and member will discuss the lists between them. No attention is to be given to the member's list. At the completion of this task, the leader will turn in only the list he or she made. No mention is made of the member's list. Members are not told about the special instructions. The leader may discuss his or her list with the member in any way he or she likes, but only his or her list represents the final selection. Observers will not participate. They will be concerned with gathering observational data. Members are called back in. The leaders and members take their sheets and rank the items individually. The facilitator announces that the group has 20 minutes to work before each group is asked to submit a list. The groups work on the task; at the end of 20 minutes, the leaders turn in their sheets.

OBSERVER'S SHEET

Pay particular attention to the following:

How does the leader act toward the member (friendly, cordial, patronizing, and so forth)? Attempt to note specific behaviors—verbal or nonverbal.

How does the member act toward the leader?

How open are they to each other's influence in this situation?

How is this situation different from the previous one for the leader? For the member?

Task I:

Task II:

Task III:

DISCUSSION

The facilitator should be aware of how members feel when they are asked to leave the room and how they feel about only the leaders receiving instructions. They feel left out, apprehensive. They feel that "this is how it always is"; the members are given the information secondhand and only to the extent that the leader wants to relay information to them. They also feel "used" because the leader paid no attention to their suggestions and submitted only his or her own ranking. Leaders often feel that they should discuss issues with members, frequently leaving members with expectations of influence. It is a disillusioning experience to find that members' suggestions were not considered. This discussion is not brought before the group. It is outlined here so that the facilitator may understand some of the dynamics developing in the relationship.

Task II Members are asked to leave the room; instructions are given to the leaders. The leaders are instructed that they and their paired member will each be given another list of items to rank-order. However, this time they are to use a fair and equitable decision-making process. They are told to consider the member's list adequately so that a collaborative ranking is developed. They are told not to mention their special instructions to the members. The members are called back in. The leaders and members take their sheets (a new listing but maintaining the same colors for leaders and members) and again rank the items individually. The facilitator announces that the groups have 20 minutes to work before each group is asked to submit a list. The groups work on the task; at the end of 20 minutes, joint sheets are submitted.

DISCUSSION

The member once more feels left out but feels it more acutely following the unilateral decision making just experienced. This person's feelings about the leader may range from strong anger at being manipulated to "you can fool some of the people some of the time, but you won't fool me again." This member will be more guarded and less willing to be involved in the task and may feel the leader is pressuring him or her. This person may be verbally antagonistic to the leader, may see the leader turn in a joint list, or may still feel the leader is turning in his or her own list. It is important to note that the member's subjective reality greatly influences the climate of the group as well as his or her relationship to the leader.

Task III The members are again asked to leave the room; as previously, instructions are given only to the leaders. The leaders are again instructed that they will be given a list of items to rank, as will the members. Once more the new lists are distributed on the same colored and white paper. The instructions to the leaders now are, "The list you turn in really does not matter, because we will throw it away. Let the members turn in whatever they want; their list will be the one representing the group. Once more, do not tell the members of these instructions."

Members are asked to return. The members and leaders take their lists and rank them. The facilitator announces that each group will work on its task and will be asked to submit a list for the group. Usually this takes about 10 minutes. The members submit their lists.

DISCUSSION

The members become even more annoyed at being left out of the instructions. Attitudes toward the leader are mixed. In some groups they are beginning to reconsider their relationship, partially and somewhat grudgingly. In other groups, the relationships are strained and viewed as a "personality clash." However, now the leader either acts apathetically or seems to be pressuring the member in order to influence his or her list. The relationship is ambiguous. The level of involvement is low, effort on the task is greatly reduced, and the climate is characterized by minimal communication and maximal suspicion. The member has more influence in making the Task III decision, but neither he or she knows nor is involved at this point. The actions of the leader leave this person confused and increasingly less sure of his or her own role.

GENERAL DISCUSSION

Following the three tasks, the group observers report on the behaviors they have seen. Leaders and members respond with their feelings on each of the situations. There can be a discussion with the entire group related to their reactions in each of the situations, the level of involvement, and their feelings about the group as a whole. Discussion can be in terms of how participants felt after each task, and perhaps they can generalize some of the learnings.

The following questions might be the basis for general discussion: How do people feel about multilateral versus unilateral decision making? Both the leader and the member experienced a task in which each made decisions irrespective of the other; they also experienced a time when they shared the decision making. How does it affect both the process (the degree of involvement) and the product (how good the participants think their list was)?

How did the members feel when they were asked to leave? Why? (Allow time here; feelings are generally quite strong.) How did members feel about the leader? Why? What are the implications for working with ongoing groups? What are the implications of this exercise for decision making in a group? What behaviors are helpful? Which hinder progress?

For Further Information

READING

The Study of Kurt Lewin, Father of Field Theory and Modern, Strategic Leadership. Lewis is one of the two or three most influential scholars in the field of group dynamics. He provided the social sciences with the eyeglasses for understanding how groups and, later, organizations function. Perhaps his greatest contribution was his ability to apply complex principles and theories in practical ways. In many modern studies of organizational life (e.g., Senge and Peter, *The Fifth Discipline,* New York, Doubleday, 1990), one can hear the voice of Lewin echoing throughout their pages. He provided a strategic, systems way of thinking that many believe was the first step in modern organizational development where planned interventions in groups and organizations are intended to bring about meaningful change. For further reading in this fascinating area consider the following:

Lewin, K. *Principles of Topological and Vector Psychology.* New York: McGraw Hill, 1936.

Lewin, K.; R. Lippitt; and R. K. White. "Patterns of Aggression in Experimentally Created Social Climates." *Journal of Social Psychology,* 10 (1939) 271–299.

Lewin, K. "Frontiers in Group Dynamics: Channels of Group Life: Social Planning and Action Research." *Human Relations,* 1 (1944) 143–153.

Lewin, K. *Field Theory and the Social Sciences.* New York: Harper & Row, 1951.

The New Sciences and Modern Leadership. One of the remarkable contributions to leadership in the 1990s was spearheaded by Margaret Wheatley. She explored the relevance of the "new" sciences of biology, physics, and chemistry with special attention to quantum physics, self-organizing systems, and chaos theory. She, and now others, have attempted to apply some of the insights in the arena of organizational dynamics. Just as the brilliant views of Sir Isaac Newton held the minds of our best thinkers captive for 200 years before Einstein and a handful of other explorers of the mind had the courage to challenge the old, intractable ways, so she has opened new doors for organizational thinkers. Those interested in a challenging new dimension of group and organizational life will want to read:

Capra, Fritjof. *The Web of Life.* New York, Doubleday, 1996.

Kaufman, Stuart. *The Origins of Order: Self Organization and Selection in Evolution.* Oxford: Oxford University Press, 1993.

Sheldrake, Rupert. *Seven Experiments that Could Change the World: A Do-It-Yourself Guide to Revolutionary Science.* New York: Riverside Books, 1995.

Weisbord, Marvin. *Productive Workplaces: Organizing and Managing for Dignity, Meaning, and Community.* San Francisco: Jossey-Bass, 1988.

Wheatley, Margaret. *Leadership and the New Sciences: Learning About Organization from an Orderly Universe.* San Francisco: Berrett-Koehler, 1992.

Wheatley, Margaret, and Myron Kellner-Rogers. *A Simpler Way.* San Francisco: Berrett-Koehler, 1996.

Zohar, Danah, and Ian Marshall. *The Quantum Society: Mind, Physics, and a New Social Vision.* New York: Morrow, 1994.

The Notion of Servant Leadership. Almost every intelligent book on leadership in the past twenty years at least makes note of the wisdom provided by Robert Greenleaf. His views came from four decades of work within the world of American business. Based on his experience and ability to integrate the views of others, he created a book that lies outside of the bounds of most theoretical or applied books on leadership and organizational life. It provides a view of work life that has only grown stronger over time and that needs to be considered by anyone who desires to work and provide leadership within an organizational context.

Greenleaf, Robert K. *Servant Leadership: A Journey into the Nature of Legitimate Power and Greatness.* Mahwah, N.J.: Paulist Press, 1997.

The Leading of Change through Participation. Historically, meaningful change has been tightly controlled by a few with the ability to influence a group or organization. Those with the necessary power have been reluctant to give it up. The dilemma of this point of view is that whether talking about changing norms in a small group or large system, if those expected to implement the change fail to buy the "process" of change or the product of the change effort, it will inevitably fail at the point of implementation. The past decade has provided new insights as to how to accomplish change more effectively. Readers interested in this area of group and organizational work should find it useful to explore samplings of writings of three of the movement's leaders:

Emery, F. E., and E. L. Trist. "The Causal Texture of Organizational Environments." *Human Relations,* 18, 1 (1965) 21–32.

Emery, F. E. "Searching for Common Ground." In *Systems Thinking.* Vol. 2. Ed. F. Emery. Harmondsworth, Eng.: Penguin, 1981.

Trist, E. L. *Towards a Social Ecology.* London: Plenum Press, 1975.

Weisbord, Marvin. *Productive Workplaces* (see 2 above).

Weisbord, Marvin. *Discovering Common Ground.* San Francisco: Berrett-Koehler, 1992.

Popular Books in the Field. The two authors who have had the widest popular appeal over the past decade are Stephen Covey and Peter Senge. Both have a practical/applied view of leadership and provide information that many find useful to translate theory into language that can be used by those working within the context of a group or organization. Following are several books which have proven to be best sellers, along with two important books on applied leadership.

Block, Peter. *Stewardship.* San Francisco: Berrett-Koehler, 1993.

Covey, Stephen R. *The 7 Habits of Highly Effective People.* New York: Simon & Schuster, 1990.

Covey, Stephen R. *Principle-Centered Leadership.* New York: Simon & Schuster, 1991.

Pozner, Barry, and James Kunzes. *The Leadership Challenge.* San Francisco: Jossey-Bass, 1994.

Senge, Peter M. *The Fifth Discipline: The Art and Practice of the Learning Organization.* New York: Doubleday, 1990.

Senge, Peter M.; A. Kleiner; C. Roberts; R. B. Ross; and B. J. Smith. *The Fifth Discipline Fieldbook: Strategies and Tools for Building a Learning Organization.* New York: Doubleday, 1994.

THE INTERNET

Anyone interested in the broad area of leadership will find plenty of material on the Internet. Two that provide useful quotes about different aspects of leadership can be found at:

www.leaderx.com/managers versus leaders.html

www.sba.oakland.edu

6

A Systems View of Small Group Behavior

Groups, like people, are fascinating because of their diversity, their lack of predictability, and the variations they play on so many themes. Despite these variations, though, people seem naturally to seek order and simple, understandable interpretations of complex phenomena. We feel more comfortable with the familiar and easily recognizable. As a result, we are forever creating theories to make sense of our experience.

To Friesen (1985), a theory is a mental model or map to help us perceive reality. Theories provide structure that helps us bring order to the information we take in. Most often, especially in the social sciences, a theory evolves gradually and is based on values, experience, goals, empirical research, and, of course, other theories. A theory is not necessarily "true" but is taken as a well-intentioned effort to explain events. Two theories may explain the same phenomenon in two entirely different ways and may exist side by side for years until one is finally accepted over the other. The origin of the universe, for instance, has given rise to many and diverse theories, as has the movement of land masses and the causes of depression in human beings.

To be useful, a theory must relate the basic concepts, assumptions, and hypotheses associated with the phenomenon it addresses in a manner that is both logical and consistent. As Friesen notes, a theory must be applicable to many situations while still maintaining internal consistency. And a theory must be testable in accordance with the scientific method. It must help make sense of a phenomenon—an event or behavior we have observed—by helping us sort out and categorize our observations and come to some conclusion.

General systems theory provides a structure and vocabulary that illuminate much that happens in small groups. It is useful in helping us comprehend the nature of certain events at the national, organizational, and individual levels.

General Systems Theory and Behavior in Organized Settings

Cause-and-effect relationships have preoccupied Western scientists since the beginning of the scientific age. The result of this dominant view has been a rather "mechanistic" approach to science that has had a powerful influence on our understanding of both the physiology and the psychology of human beings. In medicine, for instance, this approach would lead a doctor to treat a particular symptom (such as pain or nausea) by removing it in the simplest, most direct manner possible. The removal of the symptom would signify the cure of the patient. Nowadays, with cause-and-effect giving way somewhat to more holistic perspectives on illness, we consider such a view simplistic and sometimes even counterproductive to determining the real problem. We know that a tumor in one part of the body can create stress or pain in another, chemical imbalances, or sleep disturbances.

Furthermore, we have learned that physical and emotional stress can induce a wide range of physical ailments, and that eliminating a symptom in such a case in no way addresses the cause.

Not until the 1940s was any attempt to change our purely mechanistic thinking taken seriously. It has not been easy to wean ourselves from our simplistic causal mentality and to adopt a more holistic approach. After all, viewing the whole and acknowledging the possibility of multiple causes of phenomena render human behavior much more complex. At the same time, however, focusing on interrelatedness makes life much more understandable.

Ludwig von Bertalanffy (1968), a biologist, was the first to create a theory that enabled us to see the significance of interrelationships in the functioning of the total organism or system. He summarized his remarkable approach this way:

> The basic assumptions of our traditions and the persistent implications of the language we use almost compel us to approach everything we study as composed of separate, discrete parts or factors which we must try to isolate and identify as potential causes. Hence, we derive our preoccupation with the study of the relation of two variables. (p. 16)

He went on:

> While, in the past, science tried to explain observable phenomena by reducing them to an interplay of elementary units investigated independently of each other, conceptions appear in contemporary science that are concerned with what is somewhat vaguely termed with "wholeness," i.e., problems of organization, phenomena not dissolvable into local events, dynamic interactions manifested in the difference of behavior of parts. (pp. 36, 37)

Von Bertalanffy opened gates in all the sciences, but in the social sciences he triggered a revolution in thinking that continues today. The mode of thinking he described was called *systems theory.*

For the purposes of this book, a *system* is a set of interrelated elements or units that respond in a predictable manner and where the nature of the interaction is consistent over time. Thus, a change at any one point will eventually have an impact on the total system and upon its various subparts.

DEVELOPING A SYSTEMS PERSPECTIVE

There is nothing difficult about thinking and observing from a systems point of view. But systems thinking does demand that we ask questions of consequence about the impact of a given event on the parts of any group. It is common knowledge that people who are able to predict the consequences of an action make the best problem solvers and that this skill, in turn, can increase their effectiveness as leaders.

In a group, a keen awareness in both members and leaders of the predictable consequences of a particular action will yield an array of alternatives from which an effective response can be chosen. For example, when Michelle is depressed or sullen, her group's natural response is to try to cheer her up with upbeat talk and positive conversation about the weather or life in general. If over time the members had realized, however, that this particular system response seemed to generate in Michelle a feeling of inadequacy ("If everything is so great, why do I feel so miserable? I must really be a mess.") and actually *reinforced* the downward emotional spiral, they might have chosen a response that had a more positive system impact.

Though it would not be difficult to notice the impact of Michelle's depression on herself and the group, it would take discipline for the group to avoid making the one-cause/one-effect response and to choose one based on a full awareness of the system. Systems thinking demands that groups sharpen their observations and quite often become more creative and sensitive.

APPLYING "SYSTEMTHINK"

One of the authors recounts the following story to demonstrate the impact of systems theory:

> Some years ago, while attending a training program, I met Jim, a likable, articulate professor from a major western university who, like myself, had come to learn more about the nature of group dynamics. As members of an intense support group, Jim and I and the other participants were encouraged to learn as much as possible about each other, our family backgrounds, and our personal ambitions, goals, strengths, and weaknesses. Once we gained knowledge and began to trust each other, the stories that each member told were touching, humorous, sad, and joyous. The fact that barriers began to slip away and we each allowed ourselves to be "known" gave the group great energy and a sense of significance.
>
> One evening, Jim took a deep breath and said, "The truth is that even after all we've shared and been through together, you don't know me at all, and it's important that you do if this process is not going to be a farce and a lie for me and you." To say that we were shocked and curious is an under-

statement, since by this time we had all shared an enormous amount of information. Jim went on to tell us about his loving childhood on a Pennsylvania Dutch farm, where his mother had devoted her life to nurturing, supporting, and feeding her family. Eating her luscious homemade breads, cakes, and pies was one way people had of expressing their thanks and appreciation for her devoted love. And feed them she did, with joy and abundance. By the time the six-foot-tall Jim left home for college, he weighed more than 350 pounds.

We gasped, since before us was an athletically fit 175-pounder. Jim went on to say that barely six months ago he had weighed 320 pounds even though he had dieted for years. Part of the problem, he told us, was that whenever he began to lose weight and returned home, his mother would shriek that her poor boy was wasting away without her home cooking, and she would feed him "back to normal." Jim also discovered that he used food as a source of personal affirmation when he doubted himself or felt lonely.

Though he had not been able to lose weight, Jim had become quite successful as a professor and research fellow and had a satisfying professional life. He was also happily married and had a thriving social life. In fact, many of his most endearing qualities were those of the stereotype—the jovial, good-natured, compliant fat man, a well-liked encourager who was always there when needed.

Still, Jim knew that his obesity was a threat to his physical health. It kept him tired and played havoc with his own self-concept, especially since he believed he suffered not from a physical problem but rather from a lack of discipline and will power.

Finally, Jim met a health specialist who guaranteed him weight loss if he changed his "eating-for-affection lifestyle" and combined a normal diet with regular daily exercise for six months. The Jim we saw was the product of this agreement. We in the group were awed and filled with questions when he passed around a picture of his "old self," showing some embarrassment at the uncomfortable laughter with which each person responded. How did he like his new self? What did his wife and friends think? Were there consequences for his work and social life? He tackled each question patiently as if carefully protecting a still-tender wound.

To our surprise, the results of his effort had been nearly catastrophic. It was only the valiant support of his wife and his personal desire for physical health that kept him from returning to his old fat-and-happy self. In fact, he had just resigned his position at the university and was about to begin a new job several thousand miles from his old home. Somehow he had lost the support of his colleagues and many of his friends, and at this point he wasn't even sure whether he liked himself or not.

The information did not match our expectations at all. We thought he would report joy and affirmation at his obvious success and were aghast that this thoroughly witty, energetic, intelligent, and supportive person could have experienced such devastating consequences just from losing weight.

Reader Activity

Consider major changes you have experienced at various times in your life. What unanticipated consequences resulted that influenced your family or work "systems"?

THE COMPLEX CONSEQUENCES OF SYSTEM CHANGE

Jim's need to alter *his own* system (his body) resulted in a variety of unanticipated consequences. First, his "soft," compliant image was replaced by the image of a handsome, athletic man who was attractive to many and had become a threat to some. Second, Jim suddenly had considerably more energy and drive than before; he needed less sleep, was able to work longer, and as a result could produce more. He responded more efficiently to challenges and generally felt more motivated and enthusiastic about his work. His increased desire to publish altered the delicate balance between competitiveness and personal achievement in his department, and some of his colleagues became annoyed and even jealous of his newfound confidence. He became aware of a constant stream of such statements as, "I just don't know who you are anymore," or "You're so driven lately, it's almost as though you've become a workaholic," or "What happened to the old happy-go-lucky Jim?" Quite simply, Jim had disrupted the balance in the work group system of which he was a part, or subsystem. He was generating unwanted competition and resentment while reducing the amount of humor, goodwill, and support available to the group. The emergence of his new, slimmer self was like the sudden appearance of a new and unwanted rival on the scene. Everyone had to adjust whether they liked it or not—and many did not.

The work system was in turmoil, and many individuals within it made strong efforts to return it to the old levels of comfort and expectation by somehow attempting to sabotage the new Jim. This was difficult because Jim was less compliant now, less easily manipulated. He had spent years "feeding his colleagues" by supporting them and complying with their wishes in order to gain their acceptance;

it was the style he had learned in his family. His mother would feed the family in order to gain appreciation, and Jim would obediently eat whether he was hungry or not. In his work system, he himself would feed the group—with humor, service, and support—for which he was given love and acceptance in return. But his tolerance for this behavior vanished along with his excess weight. Needless to say, his new impatience—with his old ways and those of the group—left him increasingly alienated and isolated in the group.

Jim felt himself being rejected from the group almost as though he were a transplanted heart being rejected by a body. What appeared to be a rather simple and positive isolated event (the loss of 145 pounds) had created disruption not in one system alone but in a multitude of systems: his body, his work group, his social community, his nuclear family, and his extended family.

At the new university—where he was hired for his energy, assertiveness, and leadership, the very qualities that were threatening to his former peers—he was accepted easily and adjusted without problems. In this case, the old system was not thrown out of balance (*equilibrium* in systems terminology) by his arrival, because his presence filled a critical gap in the organization that had prevented its effective functioning and had created a certain imbalance (disequilibrium). Jim's troubles and his eventual resolution of them might seem mystifying from the single cause–single effect viewpoint, but a systems approach accounts for all the consequences he related.

General-systems-theory thinking—the mode of thinking that involves viewing a particular problem not in isolation, but as the problem is connected to, and therefore interrelated with, other problems—is new and complex. When Jim recounted his successful weight loss, the group members' expectations were shattered. Jim's weight loss, instead of resulting in joy and self-satisfaction, led to his resigning from his job, moving far away from his home, losing his colleagues' support, and doubting himself. While viewing causes as a whole, systems theory specifically necessitates thinking about the individual as a part of many systems and about the emotional–cognitive process as a system. General systems theory can greatly enhance our understanding of the diversity that people and groups exhibit. It encourages the explanation, description, and clarification of individual and group dynamics. Thus, the systems theory approach may represent the expansion of our concept of group dynamics to include complex social interactions, such as meetings of political heads of state (Konigwieser and Pelikan, 1990).

The Family as a Small Group System

One of the most productive areas of work in systems theory has originated in family therapy and from the study of families as self-contained groups. Nowhere has

FOCUS ON DIVERSITY

Keep in mind that families, besides being systems themselves, are part of larger community and cultural systems.

the emphasis moved more dramatically and more conclusively away from the simplistic cause–effect relationship.

Over the last thirty-five years, a wealth of theories and practices have yielded creative insights into this most common of all groups.[1] Goldenberg and Goldenberg (1980) sum up the relationship between the individual and the system as follows:

> Family therapy offers a broader view of human behavior than does individual therapy. The "identified patient," the person sent initially for help, does not remain the central focus of therapy for long. Rather, the family begins to understand that his or her problems or symptoms are an expression of the entire family's system. Problems get related within a family framework as relationship difficulties. Within such a system's perspective, the locus of pathology is not the individual but rather the individual in context, and the individual's experiences and subsequent behavior patterns begin to change. The focus of family therapy is in changing the system—the family's characteristic pattern of interacting with one another, their style and manner of communication, the structure of their relationships—so that each member experiences a sense of independence, uniqueness, and wholeness while remaining within the context and security of the family relationship. (p. 9)

It is possible to learn much about small groups in general by looking at the family. Most of us are naturally fascinated by families because most have been part of these intense nuclear groups and can readily perceive their impact on ourselves and others close to us. The bridge from family systems to those of groups we encounter in business, education, and religious and social organizations is a short one.

THE ULTIMATE SMALL GROUP

Our responses to the dynamics of virtually any group originate in our personal family experiences. In other words, our attitudes about leaders, coworkers, partners, and subordinates are shaped by our attitudes about and behavior toward our parents, siblings, spouses, and children. Sadly, just as parents are ill-trained in understanding the enormous complexities of family development, so leaders are often ill-equipped to understand their own groups as they evolve.

1. A sample of these authors and their work includes Ackerman (1958, 1970), Beavers (1977), Bell (1978), Bodin (1969), Foley (1974), Friesen (1985), Goldenberg and Goldenberg (1980), Haley (1976), Minnchin (1974), Satir (1967), and Smith and Schwebel (1995).

Furthermore, how group members, both leaders and nonleaders, cope with the process of family life will have direct implications on how they go about solving problems in other groups. For example, the ability to handle conflict among our children, plan a trip, conduct a family meeting, or deal with in-laws whose values diverge from our own, and our ways of budgeting our time, handling financial problems, dealing with religious differences, and developing social relationships are all reflected in our ability to handle related issues within the workplace. For this reason, in the following subsections we will compare dysfunctional and functional family groups and explore their implications for other group settings. From a systems perspective, we are seeking to determine what throws a family or other group out of homeostatic equilibrium. Thus, some of the problems that dominated family therapy a few years ago, such as infidelity, the acting-out child, sexual impotence, and the abused child or spouse, have come to be treated as elements of a more comprehensive exploration of the family scene.

In more recent times, issues of different family structures (after divorce or remarriage), changes in family size (no children or one child), and racial differences among children's living arrangements have come to the fore. Scott (1993), studying families, thinks that a developmental systems perspective is a useful tool for understanding these recent changes. In a similar fashion, strikes, low quality and productivity, absenteeism, low morale, and even sexual harassment tend to be symptoms of larger, more complex problems that can block the development of a government, military, business, or educational system.

NATURAL CYCLES AND BLOCKS TO DEVELOPMENT IN FAMILIES

Despite their plans for a happy future, many couples lack the skill and understanding to realize their dreams. The need for conflict-resolution skills usually surfaces with recognition that the individuals hold values and expectations that differ greatly despite their love for each other and their mutual desire for an exceptionally good relationship. How the two resolve the differences that arise in the formative year of their relationship will set the tone and often the structure of the entire relationship.

EXPANDING THE FAMILY UNIT

For many couples, having a child may seem to be an "enabling" experience that allows full expression of marital respect, sharing, cooperation, and all the other family virtues. More often, however, this period represents a major trauma, a disturbance of the sensitive balance created in the earliest stage of the relationship. Suddenly all the carefully developed rules change again, and the new third party puts stress on the fundamental relationship of the couple. How this stress is handled becomes critical. Good problem-solving skills may well turn the imbalance into a chance for growth and self-discovery, but weak problem-solving skills can lead to serious schisms.

If a family system is open to new ideas, positive energy, and feedback, and if clear channels of communication exist, then the arrival of a new baby will stimulate the system to new levels of effectiveness (steady state). But if, as often happens, communication breaks down, then new ideas are shut out, problem solving becomes entangled with issues of power and influence, and issues of membership (usually never articulated) arise. Any discord that originated in the formative stage will widen, and the family's overall vulnerability will increase. In each of these cases, the analogy between family and small group holds true.

FURTHER DISRUPTION

Clearly, critical events in the life of a system, be it family or small group, disrupt the temporary balance and force members to change. How they adapt to changing demands will determine whether an event will initiate a stimulating and engaging stage of growth or result in a divisive and debilitating response. Any organization consciously aware of a critical impending event would be misguided not to give time and attention to potential consequences. Such a proactive approach will stimulate growth and differentiation of the family group. Yet people often sit back and avoid asking the hard questions and anticipating the consequences of predictably traumatic events. This almost always ensures some degree of failure because the resulting "crisis reactive" approach to change inevitably reduces choices and contributes to later problems.

Certainly parallels exist in other groups, where a decision to expand (arrival of new staff/children, issues of membership, roles, goals), the appearance of a new CEO on the scene, the reorganization of a business, the death of a critical employee, or a strike can affect every part of the organization. These major events generate life energy of their own and can have long-lasting implications for the group. Simply trying to muddle through, acting as though such powerful occurrences were "business as usual" is to give in to the forces that can break a group apart from within.

THE DEVELOPMENT OF A HEALTHY FAMILY SYSTEM

Trying to define an "ideal" or "perfect" group is to walk on very thin ice. Nevertheless, it is worth the risk, because it allows us to explore certain dimensions of group behavior that can result in a productive work climate where both emotional and task needs are addressed. Furthermore, such a discussion can, at the very least,

How can we focus and build on the strengths of diversity?

yield a basis for comparison in the evaluation of working groups. Special circumstances and particular demands apply to specific groups, but certain conditions appear to operate in *all* successful groups.

In families in particular, because they are so diverse and complex in their backgrounds, any qualities that can be isolated as characterizing health and good function are important. And, again, such characteristics have value in the analysis of other small group systems.

In 1986, Stinnett and Defrain published their book *Secrets of Strong Families*. They began by identifying 130 families, recommended by state extension agents, who scored high on the Family Strengths Inventory. These were families who scored high on "marital happiness" and on good parent–child relations. After the pilot group, 3,000 additional families were studied, 10 percent extensively. The study included a wide range of economic and educational levels; many religions; African Americans, Hispanics, and Caucasians; and people ranging in age from the twenties to the mid-sixties.

What are strong families? The authors explain that family strength is "more than being without problems; strong families have problems. It is the presence in the family of important guidelines . . . and the ability as a family to surmount life's inevitable challenges when they arise."

As might be expected, the researchers did not isolate any single quality as more important than any other. Rather than a "single thread," the authors suggested a tapestry of qualities that distinguish strong families. The same qualities are equally useful in describing any well-functioning small group or organization. The following are the distinctive qualities in the "tapestry":

Commitment. Members of strong families are dedicated to working together and promoting each other's welfare. In a group, this means working cooperatively to achieve a goal and recognizing each person as having resources that contribute to the group.

Communication. Members have good communication skills and spend a lot of time talking to each other. At a group level, this means talking about interpersonal matters as well as task issues. It means the open sharing of information in a direct and specific manner. Differences of opinion seem welcomed, and bringing clarity to these differences seems crucial.

Appreciation. Members show appreciation and support of each other. Members are encouraged to express their feelings and emotions, and this authenticity and supportiveness are important.

Coping Ability. Members view stress and crisis as opportunities to grow. They see something positive in a crisis and focus on the positive elements. They unite to face the challenges of a crisis and ask how they can help. They work to minimize fragmentation, set priorities, and simplify. Groups too must cope with challenges, stressors, and problems. Working together to achieve a goal or overcome obstacles can generate new energy and forge a stronger group. People are working as part of a whole while maintaining their individuality.

Other studies of healthy families (Lewis et al., 1976) add that parents (leaders) model clear roles of authority, although their "power" is not used in an arbitrary or rigid manner. Quite the contrary: they solicit ideas and opinions of other family members, and a healthy sense of negotiation and compromise emerges as members share their interests and concerns. In dysfunctional families, by contrast, there is less differentiation among individuals, less flexibility, and a greater sense of control for its own sake. In functional families, family members share responsibilities, individuals have a relatively clear understanding of their places in the family community, and both authority and individuality are honored. In general, strong families express warmth, caring, and commitment to working together and dealing with problems. They have stress and conflict, but they tend to deal with these experiences openly and promptly, looking at alternatives and solutions that make sense to all members.

Some families recognize that they have not been "strong" only when a major problem arises. Because the pattern of family interaction has gone on for so long, it is not easy for them to implement a solution. For example, when parents have a substance-abusing adolescent and are willing to go to family therapy, the adolescent frequently refuses. But a recently developed model shows promise for helping families change their patterns and deal with such problems (Selekman, 1991). Offered by the Solution-Oriented Parenting Group, it teaches techniques of healthy families, builds on families' strengths, and teaches parents how to set small, realistic goals for themselves and their adolescents.

As is discussed later in the chapter, successful family systems are able to maintain their equilibrium and not become dysfunctional by keeping communications open, appreciating members' good works, and handling conflict when it arises. Furthermore, by maintaining effective feedback among individual family members, the family system remains open. In classic system terms, it also avoids the ultimate dysfunctional state of *entropy* in which family members act in rigid, defensive, often angry ways which shuts out the possibility of healthy change and adaptability.

The Invisible Group and Its Life Space

If you have ever attempted to build a house of cards, you know that no matter how patient you are, how careful your effort, or how stable the house may appear, it could collapse at any moment for a wide variety of reasons. The more complex the house, the more possible causes of collapse. Many such reasons will not be observable to the naked eye—a sudden draft or breeze, for instance, or an unanticipated vibration, a misplaced card, a slight imbalance, even a loud noise. In a similar fashion, what appears to the untrained eye to be going on in groups may have nothing to do with the actual success or failure of the group.

For years, small groups were seen as nothing more than a collection of individuals, and a group's success or failure was viewed as related to the impact of certain individuals on the group. If a problem existed, the usual mode of operation was to find the "problem individual" and "fix" him or her. This approach is still used in classrooms, office groups, families, and on sports teams. The group ignores the impact of individual behavior on the *system,* because the participants and leaders are simply not trained to observe in that manner. Thus, in the case of Jim, above, his weight loss was not perceived as a problem, even though it was the inability of the group to deal effectively with its consequences on many of its established norms, goals, and membership issues that was generating the difficulties.

Agazarian and Peters (1981), in their fascinating book *The Visible and Invisible Group,* explore in depth group phenomena that commonly occur in any group and are lost to observers who focus exclusively on individuals. Their work reinforces the idea that the system of a small group is much more than individual behaviors coming together at one point. By understanding systems, we are much better able to understand the impact of norms, membership, goals, communication patterns, and leadership (authority and influence) on the behavior and expectations of the group. Sorting through the activity that goes on in this "invisible group" yields clues to what is really happening at any given time. It also gives us some understanding of what must occur for the group to mature.

Kurt Lewin (1951) developed a goal-oriented systems view of a group, in which he literally "mapped out" a group's progress toward a particular goal, showing the barriers that had to be overcome for success to be possible. To Lewin, there were many paths to the same goal, some where resistances or barriers to success were increased and some where they were minimized. As Lewin saw it, the job for any group is to discover the most efficient and productive route to the goal. In the language of Agazarian and Peters's "invisible group," this means some understanding of such potential barriers as

- individual goals versus group goals.
- norms blocking effectiveness.
- individuals feeling lack of membership.
- ineffective communication patterns.

Because solving one problem could create others, Lewin showed that it is necessary to perceive a group in the context of the *whole*. (This is one of the underlying principles of Gestalt psychology, discussed in Chapter 1.) Lewin's point of view also fits nicely with von Bertalanffy's general systems theory, which stresses the interrelationship of all parts to the total system and the impact of any act on all of those parts. In Lewin's terms (Agazarian and Peters, 1981), an observer must grasp the total *life space* of a group to understand fully the events that occur in that group.

Reader Activity

Identify a life goal you currently have. Explore the "barriers" in your life space that could keep you from achieving your goal. Pay particular attention to how the barriers are related to each other and how addressing one barrier could affect the others.

Lewin's view of life space can be applied to a maturing individual, or a small group, or even a nation attempting to move toward some set goals. A story drawn from the history of China's early contact with the West offers a good example of how the systems approach can clarify understanding. In 1840, shortly after the British presence was first felt in China, a British merchant became convinced that there was a potentially huge market for nightcaps among the Chinese. Even if he convinced only a small percentage of the 200 million men of the merits of sleeping with a nightcap, he believed, he could easily become very wealthy. As a good entrepreneur, he saw a scarce supply of a proven product as the key to his fortune. Thus, he sold his personal assets, borrowed from friends and relatives, and shipped a large supply of nightcaps to his "waiting" population. The poor man's dream crumbled when he sold nary a one. He had failed to identify the barriers in his own life space to his goal of wealth and good fortune. These included

1. the lack of words to even explain the concept of *nightcap* in Chinese.
2. no easily explainable benefits for people who had slept capless for thousands of years.
3. no established network for selling nightcaps (or, for that matter, anything else) in China.

A more recent example was Chevrolet's attempt to sell the Nova in Spanish-speaking countries, where *no va* means "doesn't go."

Had this man understood the system and the barriers to reaching his goal, it is likely that he would have arrived at a different goal.

Background of Organizational Culture as a Concept

The idea of an organizational culture is fairly new. In fact, it has been largely ignored in psychoanalytic literature; roles, norms, and values in the social psychology of organizations have received much more attention. But in the 1950s and 1960s, the study of organizational psychology began to distinguish itself from industrial psychology by focusing on groups instead of individuals (Bass, 1965; Schein, 1965). As focus shifted from individuals to groups, whole organizations emerged. Now the focus was on groups and entire organizations, which were viewed as a system. This system was understood to encompass a total social unit: individuals, individuals in groups, and individuals in groups within organizations. Katz and Kahn (1966) developed their analysis of organizations around systems theory, and the new term *systems dynamics* was coined. This provided the important theoretical foundation for thinking about organizational culture.

DEFINITION OF ORGANIZATIONAL CULTURE

The concept of an organizational culture rests on the assumption that people, living together, have had time to form common traditions, rites, and history. Out of these commonalities, a culture has emerged. That culture is binding in the sense that it determines how people learn to survive, learn to live together, and learn to solve problems in such a way that their culture is upgraded (in their minds) and maintained. This learning is continually occurring, whether consciously or unconsciously, and regardless of the quality of the problem-solving decisions being made to uphold the culture. And, of course, the machinations it takes to form and preserve a culture may or may not be viewed as right or just by other people. The term *organizational culture* denotes whatever ideations are dominant and operating in any given group or nation, for it is these ideations that continuously feed and sustain the ever-emerging organism called culture.

Not long ago, an executive came to us with a problem. He had been hired by a unique board to help develop a new manufacturing organization that was to create several high-tech products and introduce them into competitive world markets. The board was creating this small company of perhaps 300 people by drawing on some of the best product developers and researchers working at two huge high-tech conglomerates that considered the new products potentially beneficial to themselves. The anticipated lag time between concept and production was short, given the energy, talent, and simplicity of the small new company.

The president and his key managers sincerely wanted to incorporate the best that was known about "new management" so that productivity (task efficiency and quality) and the morale of the workers (the maintenance or process dimension) would reflect the latest information on effective management. They also appeared to have a realistic understanding of the amount of time and the depth of commitment such an ambitious goal would require of them.

For us, this was a rare opportunity to bring together, at the very beginning of an organization's life, much of what we had spent years learning. It was agreed that our first step would be to gather information from those already in the organization concerning their view of their new organization and what their ideal might be like. Accordingly, we gathered information regarding the organization's culture from the 100 or so individuals who had come together at a common work site (50 from one parent organization, 30 from the other, and 20 hired from the outside). The views of these individuals were quite consistent with those of the key leaders. Their areas of agreement included the following:

AREAS OF AGREEMENT

1. *Open communication.* They desired open communication. This encompassed an interest in having important information, data, and events available to members of the organization and not held in secret, as was often the case in the large bureaucracies from which many had come. Furthermore, they expressed a desire for two-way communication, which suggested that they hoped their ideas, feelings, and concerns would be actively solicited by those in positions of authority and that management would make timely responses to them.

2. *Nonhierarchical organization.* They hoped to maintain a rather "flat," or nonhierarchical, organization in which people would be respected for their contributions and treated as equals. Furthermore, they wanted few titles or other means of making "class" distinctions within the system.

3. *Problem solving with participation.* Many expressed the hope that problems influencing their lives in the organization would be solved with their participation—at least their input, but ideally their active involvement. They suggested that whenever possible, problems should be solved at the point in the organization where those having to live with the consequences would be the most highly involved.

4. *Desire for real "community."* There was a desire for a sense of real "community" and for the development of teams around projects in the work setting, wherever possible.

5. *Balance between work and family.* The employees hoped that a balance could be found between work time and family time.

Although those interviewed mentioned other conditions, this handful of desires stood out. Management agreed that such goals were certainly in its best interest and promised to promote them actively during the coming year.

From the Lewinian point of view, the life space of the organization was to be framed by these fairly specific goals, and steps would be taken to help make them a reality. However, a life space involves much more than goals; it also encompasses potential barriers to reaching them. It took several months of our consultancy for us to realize that the new organization was *already* a complex system and that efforts to reach one of the goals created new barriers to the achievement of others. What appeared to be simple, straightforward, and ultimately reachable goals turned out to be a mine field of norms, personal goals, authority issues, and communication habits that posed huge problems on the road to solution. This is how various elements of organizational culture can confound the accomplishment of what appear to be logical goals.

The following is a list of some of the barriers we identified within the life space of the new organization:

BARRIERS

1. *Tension resulting from divergent leadership styles.* It became readily apparent that the two cultures from which most of the members of the organization had come were very different and clashed in many ways. Though both firms were successful in their own fields, one had democratic/participative management, and the other was run as a conglomeration of project-based benevolent autocracies, where responsibility, control, and leadership were held tightly by specified leaders. It is not surprising that these two divergent views of leadership created tensions from the outset.

2. *Differing personal motives and ambitions.* The idealistic view that everyone was there as part of a team to develop a new community was shattered almost immediately. People came from the two parent organizations for an array of different reasons. Some came simply to escape the complex bureaucracies. Feeling "lost in the line" was common to many, and they were drawn by the opportunity to identify with a small, community-

based organization. Others came in rebellion at the authority of the large system and were dedicated to the idea that decision making and problem solving would be shared. A good number simply wanted to be left alone to work in peace, not burdened by the responsibilities and expectations of a more complex system. A few simply couldn't get along with their bosses or had somehow dug a hole in the organization that was difficult to climb out of and found it easier to start afresh somewhere else. Finally, some saw the small organization as a source of real opportunity for advancement and creativity. Common to all these individuals was the fact that they had volunteered for their new positions and had been competitively selected. The result was a highly heterogeneous organization driven by the energies of individuals who had quite different personal motives and ambitions as well as different views of what the organization should be.

3. *Predictable burnout.* By the time the organization was six months old, a view of its place in the world of work had already been established. Within the firm, success seemed to be defined as everyone pitching in and solving one crisis situation after another. Loyalty and recognition were both seen as the measures of people's willingness to put themselves out for the organization. Because one of the norms was not to complain—certainly never about the time spent in fulfilling work responsibilities—the predictable burnout of talented and well-motivated people was already clearly etched on the horizon.

4. *Failure to achieve desired balance between work and family.* Because no boundaries were placed on people's time, and success was partly measured by the degree to which people were willing to give time, the desired balance between family and work life was never achieved. Obviously, a gap existed between people's expressed values and the behavior the organization rewarded.

5. *Nonhierarchical organization only an ideal.* People professed a desire for a nonhierarchical organization, but developing rules were already differentiating people on the bases of type of job, amount of pay, special privileges, the distribution of profit sharing, and other rewards. Equality in concept but not fact was fast becoming the reality.

6. *Despite promises, arbitrary decisions.* The fast pace of the developing organization had already shut down lines of communication and resulted in what appeared to be arbitrary decisions made by the very people who professed a desire for collaboration and participation. This set poorly with those who had left their parent organizations because they sought in-

volvement in the issues that affected their lives. Signs of open hostility toward some of the leadership were already surfacing.

7. *Norm against formal supervision reexamined.* A strong norm in the organization existed from the beginning against specific and formal supervision. Somehow the expectation arose that employees (many of whom were engineers or other specialists) hired for their technical competence and maturity could be expected to accomplish their work without much hands-on supervision. This compelling argument clashed with considerable differences in the quality of performance and failed to acknowledge such indirect aspects of supervision as performance standards, career development, education, and training.
8. *Negative attitude toward training.* The two parent organizations had spent enormous amounts of time and money on leader and management training over the years, but the concepts espoused in the training were not often modeled in the organization itself. As a result, participants came away with a negative attitude toward almost any kind of training at all. In the new firm, an assumption prevailed that people had the requisite skills because at one time they had taken the training. But few had had the opportunity to practice or internalize the skills they had learned, and their expertise existed more in name than in substance. Thus, the organization tended to act as though it were humane, collaborative, and open as a result of good leadership training—when in fact it modeled a limited amount of these behaviors.
9. *"Communities" versus time spent on production.* Finally, communities evolve through participants' hard work and willingness to devote time and effort to both the task/product and the process/maintenance dimensions. In this organization, time was spent on production only, and as a result any sense of community was a long way from reality.

These were but a few of the barriers created by the evolving organizational culture. Addressing any one proved to have consequences for the others. In such a system, solutions are possible, but a naive belief that intelligent people, good intentions, and clear goals will eventually lead to success spells certain failure. The complex and interrelated issues in such a system must be choreographed as carefully as any complex dance. Planners must anticipate these realities and map out resistances and barriers. Leaders must educate themselves in the complexity of their own system and the need for integrated strategies. As in any successful therapy, taking possession of the problem is the first big step required; next comes forging a clear understanding of the implications of the problem for all parts of the system. Only then can effective problem solving begin.

The Vocabulary of General Systems Theory[2]

As stated earlier, the goal of this chapter is to present a new way of thinking about groups by reducing dependence on cause-and-effect relationships and emphasizing the relationship of the parts to the whole. To help in this effort, it is important to introduce a number of concepts here that allow for the description of systems with some consistency. To bring concrete meaning to these terms and concepts, a real-life small group attempting to define itself within the context of a larger group system appears below.

Most systems, in addition to existing as a collection of interdependent parts, are also parts of larger systems in which they are necessary units or subsystems. Thus, any individual in a system is also usually part of a number of group systems, which in turn are parts of large organizations, and so on. The interrelationships among multiple system organizations can be complex indeed. One primary purpose of management is to create a workable and utilitarian structure in which various systems can operate smoothly, harmoniously, and efficiently.

THE CASE OF "NO WAY, NEW WAY"

The large parent system in this case is an insurance company directed by a distant group of senior officers whose primary concerns are bottom-line profits and maintaining a corporate image of beneficent paternalism. At the time described, the company was in a period of high growth, related to both sales and fiscal belt tightening, and every dollar spent had to be justified by more than a dollar earned. As in many organizations of this type, support services never quite caught up to the increase in growth, so those in the trenches (such as underwriters, clerks, and secretaries) seemed to be forever overworked, underpaid, and unappreciated. At the same time, those generating sales and direct services to the client were paid well and recognized as heroes of the organization.

One primary goal of those directing any large system is finding ways to make the subsystems more cost-effective. In this particular organization underwriters had to handle, rate, and bill every policy sold, so they, along with ancillary, secretarial, and clerical staff, represented a constant-cost factor. The underwriters worked in a "Dickensian" pool of more than one hundred desks where they pushed paper in a work environment that permitted their supervisors to oversee and control them

2. This section represents an effort to integrate the views of many contributors to the field of systems theory, including Agazarian (1981), Alderfer (1986), Friesen (1985), Goldenberg (1980), Prochaska (1984), von Bertalanffy (1975), and Wilden (1980).

easily. They had no privacy in the confines of their huge work "bin," and received little affirmation or support. Rather, they were under constant pressure to complete the never-ending flow of paperwork generated by sales. As one might expect, the morale of the underwriters was low, and this was reflected in less than satisfactory productivity, considerable absenteeism, and rapid turnover.

The director of the underwriters had been asked to cut costs in the recent cash flow crunch and had attended a training program exploring the benefits of autonomous work groups. These were simply small, interdependent teams of individuals who had related responsibilities for certain product goals. The idea was to give them specific goals and responsibilities and to allow them to direct themselves in most areas of their work lives, as long as specified standards regarding both quality and productivity were maintained. Quite often, groups of this type are more productive, have a greater sense of purpose, and show lower rates of turnover, absenteeism, and down time than individuals working in isolation.

As in the case of the Chinese nightcap merchant, the director rushed home from his training with visions of the extraordinary benefits his department would reap from the new organizational structure. With little to lose, he immediately established an experimental group to test the concept. From a pool of volunteers, he selected a group of six underwriters, three clerks, and a secretary. He also matched them with a supervisor and assigned two days for team building. The supervisor had no formal instruction in autonomous work groups, team building, or group dynamics, but the manager arranged for her to have a brief orientation and private screening of a film on the subject. The team, which was to be called the New Group, was given a separate work space marked off by portable six-foot cubicle walls. This thirty-by-thirty-foot alcove was about one hundred feet from the other ninety or so underwriters, who remained in their "bin."

During their orientation, the New Group spent considerable time defining their own goals, ways to use each other, and ways to create a work flow process that would maintain productivity and ensure that they met the quality standards established for them. Management believed that if the New Group maintained the same standards as the larger group and if the experiment resulted in higher morale (and, as a result, in less turnover and absenteeism), then the program would be a success. Any increased efficiency would be considered a bonus.

The team members discovered immediately that they liked each other's company and that work was becoming "fun" again. The supervisor recognized this and gave them plenty of free rein while providing support, minimal direction, and the clarification of policies, standards, and work expectations. Other than that, the group created its own roles, relationships, policies on the use of space, and work schedule.

Systems Note: In relation to general systems theory, the new autonomous work group fulfilled the definition of a *system* because it remained associated with but independent of the other underwriters. It was a subsystem of the total organization, but its internal roles and functions were clear and interdependent, with each of its own subunits having a clear relationship to the whole. This meant it could operate with relative independence.

The New Group fulfilled the definition of an *open system.* Although it was predictable and consistent in how it managed its work and functioned with respect to the total organization, it remained responsive to the larger environment. It maintained a constant flow of information and kept its production free-flowing and functional with a clear goal-directed emphasis.

The members of the New Group were highly motivated and had an increasing desire to be effective for their own sakes. But they also realized they were a test case for the organization and wanted to prove that the small group atmosphere, with its focus on *team,* was a much better means of operating than the old bin system. Thus, they were highly conscious of their own efforts. They monitored their own performance in daily meetings and constantly adjusted their work flow to increase their efficiency. In any such dynamic and open system, new influxes of energy, increasingly differentiated roles resulting in higher levels of performance, and a tendency toward increasing complexity and specialization may all be apparent. We might liken the group to a basketball team that, over the years, develops intricate patterns of play that the team members could not have even conceived during their initial work together. The New Group, with its growing abilities to communicate, give mutual support, and accept each other, showed increasing productivity even though its members were working at their own pace during hours they themselves chose. The group found itself with ever more free time while it still maintained high levels of productivity and quality.

Systems Note: Compare the New Group with a *closed system,* which tends to exhibit low levels of energy and be static, lacking in innovation, and highly resistant to change. In theory, closed systems eventually shut down and die, because the ability to adapt—which they lack—is crucial whether in nature, business, or social systems. The concept of *adaptability* is useful. We know that nonadaptive human organizations become restrictive, inflexible, and resistant and that trouble inevitably ensues. Symptoms of such groups or organizations are often decreasing productivity and low morale. In this example, the ninety remaining underwriters in the bin had many symptoms of low morale. New ideas were virtually nonexistent, energy was low, conformity rather than innovation was the norm, and individual roles were much more isolated than in the New Group, where interdependence was the norm. Also, caution was much more the rule in the bin, where there was always more work than time available and little recognition for effort. Still, the larger system—the parent organization—was more open than some; it sought new ideas (for example, the autonomous work group) in order to increase efficiency and allow differentiation (as occurred in the New Group).

It is clear that it was the open communication channels and feedback mechanisms that enabled the New Group to achieve its high level of organization and sophistication. These, in turn, created a natural state of awareness, which enabled members to view adaptability as positive. Such a natural and highly productive mode is referred to as a *steady state* in systems terminology. It suggests the presence of a dynamic tension that allows for a healthy *disequilibrium* so that positive input and change beneficial to the system can occur with minimal disruption.

As the New Group became increasingly efficient, it allowed itself to take longer than "normal" breaks, hold small celebrations, meet to discuss members' problems and work relationships, and take exercise breaks to maintain their physical health and high energy during the work day. Simultaneously, the supervisor, careful to keep too much of a good thing from ruining the group, distributed increasing amounts of work to the New Group—far surpassing the normal expectations of the underwriters performing laboriously in the bin. Group members received this additional work without complaint because it was clear to everyone that the New Group was thoroughly enjoying its autonomy and would never voluntarily return to the bin.

Systems Note: When a system is *closed,* there is a tendency for a certain degree of chaos or disorder to occur. In human systems, this results in a breakdown of communication, loss of information, role confusion, and a general increase in organization. We might assume that an old, habituated system would exhibit fewer such conditions, but without new energy and ideas and healthy adaptations, this state of *entropy,* as it is called, tends to increase naturally. In organizations where tenure is prevalent and personnel turnover rare, intellectual stagnation is common. Individuals tend to isolate themselves and pay increasingly less attention to the needs of the whole system. In such a context, entropy becomes a sort of "noise" that reduces the system's ability to function efficiently and with optimal morale.

There was little entropy in the New Group. More characteristic, owing to the continued influence of new ideas and energy, was the state of *negentropy,* typified by growth and development. In a state of negentropy, people are rewarded for new ideas and the sharing of information, which in turn reinforces the healthy steady state of the system.

Systems Note: In theory, most groups and organizations show some signs of entropy and move over time toward some level of disorganization. In human organizations this process can be arrested, thanks to the human capacity to use new information and ideas and to respond to feedback. Removing *all* "noise" is difficult, but efforts to reorganize, sensitize, and integrate can have positive benefits, and ongoing sources of feedback can keep the system in a healthy balance. Quite simply, giving *feedback* is the process of providing specific information concerning the consequences of a particular action. Such information allows reaction to a particular event to return to the system to be studied and acted on. The physical body is full of feedback mechanisms—for example, too much heat triggers the onset of perspiration, which cools down the system.

In human groups, giving feedback sensitively is a challenge. Too often, the task is undertaken without sensitivity or skill; as a result, group members feel blamed or judged negatively, which can trigger defensiveness or denial rather than openness and acceptance. Still, feedback is our primary source of information on "how we're doing" (see Chapter 1). In theoretical terms, feedback is the information that permits the adjustments necessary to bring a system into *homeostasis*—that is, balance. All systems periodically get out of adjustment, and feedback is the built-in cycle or loop of information that allows for continual realignment. In organizational life, a lack of useful, descriptive feedback inhibits the ability to solve problems effectively and, if necessary, to reorganize.

For a time the New Group prospered. In systems terms, it was a healthy, open system, existing in a dynamic steady state with an overall homeostatic balance. The presence of negentropy proved that the system was responsive to its internal and external environments. The group received and appeared to be using feedback when necessary. In fact, the New Group seemed to be succeeding beyond anyone's wildest expectations, and two more autonomous groups were planned for the near future. Then disaster struck.

Systems Note: A system such as the New Group may run smoothly within its own sphere of influence, but if it creates conflict or stress in the life of the larger system, its own life may be threatened. In systems terms, if it throws the parent system out of homeostasis, that larger system will do anything necessary to return to its state of balance or comfort, including getting rid of the problematical subsystem.

One winter morning at 10:00 A.M., a vice president far out of his territory was making his way toward the underwriter bin. As he passed the New Group area, he nonchalantly peeked over the top of the cubicle and was astonished at what he saw. There, six people were performing some kind of aerobic dance to music while two others casually read magazines and another put the finishing touches on a small model airplane. The executive's initial astonishment turned to outrage, and he burst onto the New Group scene demanding an explanation of what he deemed totally inappropriate behavior. Before receiving a response, he launched into a lecture on professional behavior within the organization. The more he talked, the more angry he became. It was clear to the group members that they had broken a basic if unstated law of the organization against having fun, "wasting" time, exercising on work time, or simply taking a break from desk work on the job. Intuitively, the members knew their efficiency and productivity would mean nothing to the executive; it would not assuage his anger at their "inappropriate" behavior. To the uneducated vice president they had sinned, and he would make them pay. As he left, he let it be known that they would be hearing from him again.

It did not take long for him to make good on his promise. Both their supervisor's supervisor and their own supervisor quickly read them the riot act. Productivity, efficiency, and morale suddenly weighed little against their having broken a basic rule. Although no one threatened the New Group with dissolution or firings, it was clear that members were to shape up and straighten out. In pursuing their fitness break on the job, they had clearly gone too far.

Systems Note: The vice president who reacted so strongly was concerned about the well-being of the entire system. In his eyes, the group's behavior threatened all parts of the organization. Also, the New Group had, in their isolation, lost touch with some of the basic organizational realities. Though it had been meeting organizational goals, the group was fast becoming an uncontrolled maverick. As the table shows on page 311, the New Group, without being conscious of it, had developed a work ethic that conflicted with many traditions and expectations of the large system. Such words as *fun, sharing, the whole person, participative management,* and *autonomy* were seldom heard in the benevolent autocracy of the company at large. Thus, when the vice president glanced over the cubicle wall, he knew it was his responsibility to stop such behavior immediately, before the "disease" spread and endangered the organization.

In most large, hierarchical bureaucracies, a powerful reprimand from a powerful vice president would have put the matter to rest. But because of the group members' camaraderie and ability to talk through problems, they called a meeting to discuss the situation. They concluded that they were being treated unfairly and decided to draft a letter to their supervisor on stationery sporting their own "new way" logo. It should be noted that they had been explicitly told ten days earlier that such individualized logos were unacceptable because they ran counter to the feeling of "community" in the organization. The New Group had been irritated at this affront to their individuality but had accepted it as a small price to pay. Now, however, things had changed, and they considered it necessary to take a stand for what to them seemed right and just. The letter below addressed a variety of concerns that the group had previously been unwilling to put on the line but were ready to deal with now because of the vice president's insensitivity. The issues included the possibility, under discussion, that one of their senior underwriters would have to be shared with another autonomous team being created. Another plan also bothered them. Jan, the manager, would be expected to manage both their team and another. And management's habit of increasing their workload fueled disillusionment. Here is the letter they sent.

Dear Management:

WAIT A MINUTE!!!!!

Whatever happened to job satisfaction?

We've really worked hard at making this team work—what is the limit? We've really slugged our guts out to satisfy your expectations with very little feedback from management, except Jan! Now you expect even more from us. We're only human . . . slow down!!

Our Concerns Are:

1. Bruce being senior underwriter for both our team and the proposed new team:
   - We expect the majority of his time will be spent with the other team.
   - What happens to us?
   - We need him for his knowledge, training, leadership qualities, positive personality, and the work he does as part of our workload.
   - Will he be able to divide his loyalty between the two groups?
2. There is going to have to be too much of an adjustment made when we lose Jan's "hands-on manager" influence.
   - She's our support and a large factor in our morale.
   - Will the other team resent her "favoritism" to the New Group?
   - We expect morale will suffer—even when she's just there physically, we feel her support and it aids in our production.

- Out of all of management, she's the only one who knows what we're going through and cares about our feelings and concerns—we're scared!!
- We're concerned not only about the pressures on us, but also those on Bruce and Jan themselves. We can see it—can you???

3. Workload: we're overworked compared to others doing our same job.
   - Our volume is considerably more than that of people doing the same type of work.
   - There is a proposal to take away 1.5 people—strong people—from our team because we're being so productive. Isn't that punitive?
   - What about self-administration? It takes time and planning, which for some reason is not legitimate in the organization.
   - Group dynamics: we're not willing to give up our sessions, which help us work together as an effective team.
   - Our fitness break is an important factor in keeping up morale, energy, and even productivity.
   - Where do we find time for all of these??
4. Recognition:
   - There is none.
   - We do more work and assume more responsibility, and keep getting better—all without appreciation.
   - We're trying all of these new ideas—we were the test team—but who uses our ideas?? Anybody?? Does management really know what it takes to create the team we've so successfully managed to do?
5. Productivity:
   - Quality and production are suffering because of all the extras being put on us.
   - Management always looks at statistics and always wants more rather than trying to understand why we've been successful in increasing our output.
   - We can't do more—that is, produce more and take on all the extras management would have us do.

Because of all these things, you are really asking a lot of us, and we really feel the pressure. We've put a lot of personal effort into our work, but we do have our own personal lives—not everybody will do this. We are extremely frustrated and are starting to revert to our old ways, which we know are the "pits." Morale is dropping.

We came into the team trusting management to make things better. What are you doing to us? We feel used!

We're willing to continue to make an honest effort to make it work. We need time and support. At the present we feel pushed against the wall.

<u>You're</u> asking too much . . . too soon!

Signed: ________________ ________________

________________ ________________

________________ ________________

The letter was personally signed by all the members of the New Group, and copies were sent to their supervisor and her supervisor in the expectation that one would find its way to the vice president who originally criticized them. Though the language was not in formal "corporate" style, it was quite specific, and the expression of real feeling was clear. If the larger system really was "open," as it defined itself, it would take the information as an indication of problems that needed prompt solutions—in short, as a feedback loop.

However, management read the letter as an attack on its own integrity and as expression of the New Group's desire to step out of its subordinate role and influence the management process through intimidation. One executive described its tone as "childish petulance." Even though the larger system professed to support the idea of independently thinking work groups, because of its inexperience with them it failed to anticipate the consequences of loosening its firm grip on its employees.

The letter served only to outrage management as much as the exercise break had angered the vice president. With this letter, the New Group had broken three organization norms that were never discussed but always adhered to:

1. No employees would join together to increase their influence.
2. No group would question management's decisions or process. These were traditionally management functions, not to be interfered with by "line" workers in the organization.
3. No one would, with emotion and feeling, complain about their treatment in the organization, because management prided itself on "fairness" and taking care of its own. The very idea that people were treated unfairly was simply unacceptable.

A Conflict in Values

	The Large System View	The New Group View
Norms	• Time on the job is for work, not play.	• Work is to be distributed over job time to maximize effort and efficiency and to maintain morale.
	• Play is frivolous.	• Play keeps people fresh and invigorated and able to do more work.
	• Task and product, not maintenance or process, are of concern to the organization.	• Maintenance is critical to a healthy working environment.
Goals	• Treat everybody the same, and expect the same behavior in return.	• Treat groups and individuals in unique ways as long as they remain productive.
	• Keep busy all the time.	• Maintain a balance of work and relaxation to maximize both productivity and morale.
	• Produce as much as you can in the time available.	• Produce what is consistent with a healthy work environment.
Membership	• Full membership means putting in a fair day's work for a fair day's pay.	• The well-rounded, whole person who contributes fully to the New Group through support, sharing, efficiency, and enjoyment will have the fullest membership.
	• Members gain acceptance by obeying the spoken and unspoken rules of the organization.	• As long as it follows organizational policies and meets expected goals, the autonomous group has the right to develop its own rules of operation within some proper limits.
	• People can gain membership by participating fully in the numerous "extra-curricular" activities available after work.	• People spend the greater part of their lives at work, so fun should be incorporated into the workday.
Leadership	• Keep on the troops, stay attentive to their performance, and maintain control.	• Individuals work more effectively when they have the opportunity to govern themselves and establish their own work rules and responsibilities within production guidelines.
	• As much as possible, treat everyone the same or you will be seen as playing favorites; this pertains both to individuals and to separate work groups.	• Individuals work differently because they have different needs and styles. These differences should be encouraged as long as productivity is maintained and the group functions effectively.

A Conflict in Values (cont'd)

The Large System View	The New Group View
• Too much autonomy is by definition threatening to any large system. It encourages the expectation of exceptions to the rules and values individual differences.	• Group autonomy leads to teamwork and a sense of ownership and responsibility in the work process. As long as people's individual styles do not impede group effectiveness, diversity should be encouraged; it will increase individual morale.
• All efforts should focus on creating as much product of the highest quality as possible.	• Work and productivity must be seen in a long-range context in which maintaining high performance over time is always a delicate balance between task and process.

Systems Note: For years, management had discouraged real collaboration among subordinates in the organization, believing that meetings of concerned individuals would give people a sense of power in numbers. Several years previously, a local union had attempted to organize workers in the firm. This so frightened management that it came to see any organized disagreement on the part of the workers as a hostile act. The New Group's expression of opinions and feelings was seen not as a natural outcome of the more creative and independent group process but as a veiled threat to organize.

By its nature, the autonomous group rewarded independent thinking, collaboration, shared decision making, and a sense of equality among workers. As a result, members' loyalty to the team was greater than to the total organization. Paradoxically, the group's higher-level steady state and its own homeostatic equilibrium had triggered the need for a new relationship with the larger system, and this need itself had resulted in a struggle with the organization. The larger system, mixed in entropy, immediately came down hard on the New Group and attempted to influence it in every area, including its *goals* (focus on product, not process), *membership* (team loyalty and commitment are always subordinate to those of the total organization), *communication* (problem identification, the sharing of information, and the seeking of solutions are management functions and of little concern to subordinates), and *leadership/authority* (control, dependency, and the resulting passivity are the true promotable qualities). These underlying truths were woven into the very fabric of this company's life, and the challenge to them in one angry confrontation was felt at every level within the New Group system. The consequences of that encounter, given its fundamental nature, had the potential to affect the entire large system as well. Note that viewing this incident from the point of view of simple cause and effect would have failed to acknowledge the complexity of the relationships involved.

As a result of the letter, the "autonomous work group experiment" was put on hold for six months until management could gain a "greater understanding" of its impact and could form a comprehensive set of expectations and training plans that would be consistent with the philosophy and values of its system.

Reader Activity

Using your own family as an example of a system, describe it by using the system terminology introduced in the "No Way, New Way" case. The following guidelines may prove useful:

1. Is your family an open or a closed system? Explain.
2. Provide examples of entropy or negentropy in your family system.
3. Feedback is essential to the development of an open system. Does your family provide opportunities for regular feedback? Give specific examples of recent feedback you have given or received—in your family or other groups to which you belong.

Summary

A healthy system is one that has the ability to remain in a state of *dynamic equilibrium*. The two words may seem antithetical, but they clearly reflect the facts that most systems are alive with activity and that the question is not *whether* change is occurring but rather *how* it is occurring and what the consequences will be. Stopping the free flow of communication and blocking the paths of necessary feedback will result in the breakdown of information, role and goal confusion, and/or the setting of unattainable objectives. Such a state has characteristics of entropy rather than the more dynamic, creative, and progressive condition of negentropy.

In small groups and human systems, entropy—system breakdown—is not inevitable. Both members and leaders can inhibit it by identifying the nature of the complex relationships in their system and acting with an awareness of consequences. By asking hard questions and using the language of group dynamics, participants can gain a true understanding of the complex system in which they are involved and learn to intervene in a positive manner.

For Further Information

Weisbord, M. A. *Discovering Common Ground.* San Francisco: Berrett-Koehler, 1992.

This is an applied systems book dealing with the issues of change management. Focuses on the organization and all its stakeholders, and how to deal with systemic issues that can block the possibility of change.

Wheatley, M. *Leadership and the New Science: Learning About Organizations from an Orderly Universe.* San Francisco: Berrett-Koehler, 1992.

The author makes a valiant effort to relate the phenomena of systems and the new physics in terms that apply to organizations.

Capra, F. *The Web of Life: A New Scientific Understanding of Living Systems.* New York: Doubleday, 1996.

The author explores the relation between various breakthrough theories that are challenging conventional views of evolution and the organization of living systems. Covers the new thinking at the root of Gaia theory, chaos theory, and complexity theory; and how they relate to organisms, social systems, and ecosystems.

Capra, F. *The Tao of Physics.* Rev. ed. Boston: Shambhala, 1991.

A good beginning point for anyone interested in the new physics and a systems view of the universe.

Emery, F. E., ed. *Systems Thinking: Selected Readings.* New York: Penguin, 1969.

Ideas on systems by experts before the concept fully came into vogue.

Senge, P. M. *The Fifth Discipline.* New York: Doubleday, 1990.

A multidirectional exploration of organizational life and why new views of the organization must be learned if breakthroughs in productivity and morale are to occur. Draws on the wisdom of many disciplines, integrating psychology, physics, philosophy, and mysticism into an understandable view of modern leadership in corporate life.

Senge, P. M.; A. Kleiner; C. Roberts; R. B. Ross; and B. J. Smith. *The Fifth Discipline Fieldbook.* New York: Doubleday, 1994.

The authors weave in practical approaches to change management, with special attention to systems thinking. Written to be a practical guide to real organizational problems.

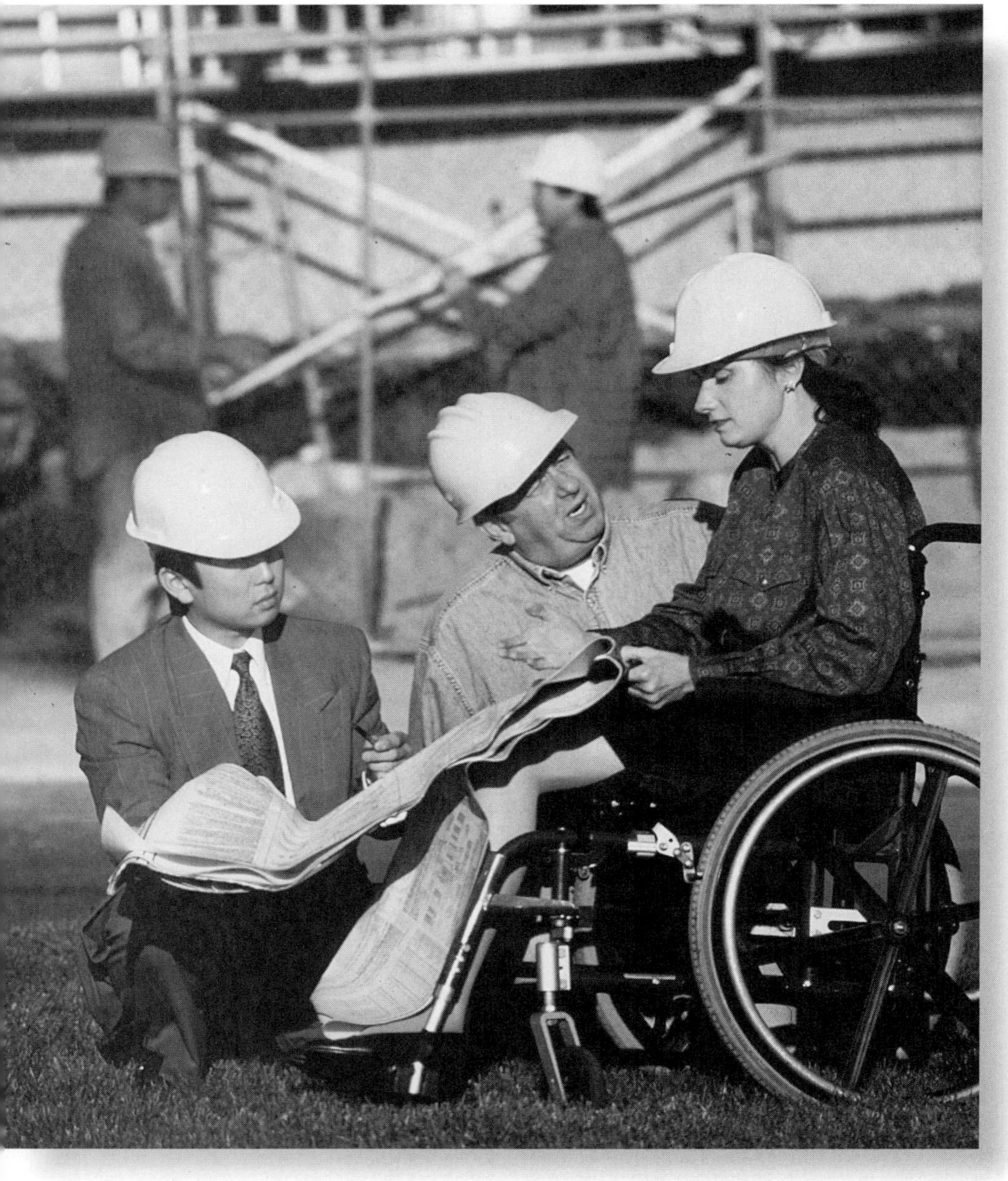

7 Group Problem Solving and Decision Making

Decision making is at the center of our very being. A thousand times each day we make decisions, sometimes casually, almost without thought, responding to long-established routine. Who we are as decision makers is no more or less complex than who we are as people. The web of factors influencing us can be incredibly complex: our cultural backgrounds, parents, schooling, feelings of attractiveness, social status, religion, and general level of achieved success. Add to this mix our willingness to risk, our dreams, goals, fears, biases, and a hundred other variables, and you begin to have some idea of how complex even our most casual or spontaneous decisions might really be.

Now place five or six, or ten or twenty such complex individuals together, attempt to develop an agreed-upon decision, and the potential differences seem almost beyond comprehension.

Reader Activity

Take a sheet of paper and make two columns. On the left-hand side, list the qualities and characteristics of the last group you attended in which members successfully solved a significant problem together. In the right-hand column, list the characteristics of the last group-solving session you attended that ended unsuccessfully. Extend this list to include specific behaviors or events that worked against success. Thinking in this manner should bring perspective to the following pages and help you relate to the common patterns that exist in many groups.

Group Decision Making: Disadvantages and Advantages

Any problem solving implies the possibility of change and the exploration of alternatives to the status quo. Using a group can compound the difficulties of problem solving beyond those resulting from the volatility created by a roomful of different personalities, with all of their individual needs, biases, and personal agendas.

Let's look at the disadvantages of group decision making as well as its advantages and benefits.

DISADVANTAGES Group decision making does have its "downside."

1. The results of group decision making are often dismissed by those in positions of influence, who are unwilling to give credence to a process few of them have experienced as positive.
2. All too often, participants learn that what appears to be a fair, democratic process is really a charade. That is, decisions have already been made, and group participation is provided as a means of placating those who have to live with the ultimate decisions.

3. Unless well designed, a group effort at problem solving can be a colossal waste of time, money, and effort.
4. Few group leaders are trained in the effective utilization of group members, which can result in a deterioration of both the process and task dimensions of group life.
5. As a result, instead of morale and team spirit improving because of a group approach, it may degenerate.
6. If the selection of group members is not related carefully to the task at hand, the technical and experiential components simply will not be available when needed.
7. It is common for members of a problem-solving group either to be briefed inadequately prior to a meeting or to fail to do premeeting work that enables the group to begin with clearly defined goals.
8. A few individuals may take over a group and dominate its process or inhibit the participation of members whose contribution represents the reason for the group in the first place.

ADVANTAGES With so many possible pitfalls for groups, questioning their use is justified. Assuming that groups are not always the best vehicle for problem solving, why and when should they be utilized?

1. A group solving problems together will provide those participating with a baseline of common understanding and information that cannot be replicated in a memo or other less personal means. Such involvement inevitably results in greater sympathy toward the complexities of the problem and lays the groundwork for the group's acceptance of the eventual solution. Theorists increasingly understand how critical to any solution is its acceptance by those who must live with it. Thus, effective communication, understanding, and eventual acceptance of a solution are tied closely together.
2. As indicated earlier, it is only natural for individuals to enter into a problem-solving situation with personal biases, needs, and perspectives. A group setting offers an environment that legitimizes a variety of viewpoints. Usually, provided that good information is translated in an intelligent manner and a climate exists in which individuals are not compelled to defend their positions, a group, like any individual, will move toward the best ideas.
3. Given even a minimal level of trust and good will, a group is capable of producing a greater quantity and variety of ideas than the average individual.

4. A good experience in a group can generate enthusiasm and be contagious. The commitment toward eventual action can be born out of the teamwork, arguing, building of alternatives, and movement toward choice. Individuals can feel good about their contribution to the group and their relationship to it.
5. The give-and-take of open and free discussion in a group can bring new ideas into play that might never have been considered by an individual. Different from the formal presentation of new ideas in a group setting, open discussion enables members to be irreverent, to question even the unquestionable, and to challenge old absolutes. This process can tap the group's natural creativity.
6. Problem solving is a multidimensional process. It is quite possible to involve large numbers of people (fifty, one hundred, five hundred, or more) during the problem identification, diagnostic (clarification), and ideational (generating alternatives) phases. As suggested earlier, people feel better about the solution they have to live with if they have been given a fair opportunity to participate and are aware of all the factors underlying an issue.

It is true that many problems can be solved more easily and efficiently and with less conflict and stress individually. On occasion, such individual problem solving can be justified because of the special expertise of the problem solver, limited time, or the nature of a crisis that might exist. However, when we realize that the decision itself is in many ways only half the battle, group participation makes more sense.

A study done in one factory clearly demonstrates how participation in decisions raises morale and increases production (Fox, 1987). In one group, changes affecting members were imposed by management; three other groups were allowed to participate in the decision-making process that led to changes. In the first group, members resisted the decision, production and morale dropped, and a few group members even quit. In the other groups, which all decided to make the changes imposed on group 1, work enthusiasm and production rose.

Group problem solving and employee involvement in decision making have tended to be viewed as a luxury in which corporations indulged when times were good. In a surprising turnaround, there has recently evolved a trend toward utilizing employees in group decision making when times are bad.

According to an article published in *Time* magazine, "Is Mr. Nice Guy Back?" some companies realize that worker morale has been shredded by layoffs, with the elimination of some six million jobs since 1983. There is a further recognition that restoring competitiveness to American industry will require serious collaboration between workers and management. The resulting acknowledgment is that people need to be empowered.

> One manager who is emblematic of this shift in approach is GE chairman John Welch. Known in the '80s as "Neutron Jack" for zapping 100,000 employees—25% of the company's work force—Welch now stresses the importance of teamwork. Says he: "To get every worker to have a new idea every day is the route to winning in the '90s."
>
> To help bring good ideas to life, GE holds "workout" sessions in which groups of workers and managers spend three days in shirt-sleeve meetings on anything from gripes to pitches for new products. The high point comes on the third day, when employees pepper their bosses with scores of suggestions that the brow-mopping managers must accept or reject on the spot. Most turn out to be keepers. In a session at an aircraft-engine plant last September, one team pitched a plan that cut the time needed to produce a jet-combustion part nearly 90%. And an electrician proposed a design for an aluminum reflector that has cut the plant's light bill in half. Over two years, the grueling workouts have spawned dozens of innovations, ranging from improved light-bulb packaging to the elimination of reams of paperwork.[1]

DISSONANCE: THE NATURAL OUTCOME OF DECISION MAKING

Decisions, by their very nature, suggest alternatives, argument, and conflict. Basically, a decision represents the termination of a controversy with a particular course of action. However, conflict and tension do not end with the decision. How the individual or group copes with the doubts, suspicions, and skepticism generated during the discussion has important implications (Festinger, 1957; Festinger and Aronson, 1968). The longer and stronger the discussion, the more ambivalence will be created (whether it is overtly recognized is another question), leading to a state of *cognitive dissonance.* This dissonance is a continuous source of tension, and the individual or group attempts to reduce it in a number of ways. For example, once a decision is made, there is a tendency to begin valuing it even more than before (Brehm, 1956). As with a religious convert, many of the old questions and doubts are forgotten and the decision is constantly reinforced. If it took so long to reach a decision, it must be the "best."

The trouble is that a decision may become overvalued, and an intransigent attitude may develop that closes the door on future discussion of alternatives or even

1. From *Time,* "Is Mr. Nice Guy Back?" by John Greenwald, January 27, 1992, p. 42–44. Copyright © 1992 Time Inc. Reprinted by permission.

a fair evaluation of the decision at a later date. A subtle process of rationalization and justification may evolve. This is particularly true if the decision turns sour and must still be lived with (a leader is chosen who proves inept, a tax is imposed to curtail inflation and unemployment increases, a surplus is guaranteed and a deficit is incurred).

Similarly, people are inclined to make the best of a bad thing when the decision is out of their control. Thus, even though it can be proved that most school grades lack objectivity and validity, students and parents alike still defend them. Outwardly they may go through a long and involved defense of the system, noting the value of the grading process, whereas inwardly their desire to perpetuate the system lies in the more clouded area of "I've suffered and so should you." This rationalization has nothing to do with the questions surrounding the legitimacy of grades. Still, such internal justifications tend to reduce dissonance and constitute the major source of support for maintaining the status quo. Therefore, people need to justify their expenditure of time, energy, and hope in a decision that is a matter more of image than of principle but that will shape future behaviors and accompanying decisions (Festinger and Aronson, 1968; Festinger and Carlsmith, 1959).

Constructive Controversy and Conflict

FOCUS ON DIVERSITY

Is an aversion to conflict universal? Can you think of some people or groups who do not avoid conflict?

In recent years, conflict has been allowed out of the proverbial closet. Perhaps because our society has always equated conflict with pain, dissonance, and destructive behavior, until recently most groups have avoided it at all costs (Wall and Nolan, 1986). Alternatively, it may have been a lack of experience in turning conflicts in group settings into something more positive that inhibited most of us from allowing them to surface. Whatever the reason, nowadays conflict is increasingly seen as useful and sometimes even necessary to effective group problem solving (Goddard, 1986; Jacobs, 1983; Tjosvold, 1985). Research now indicates that groups with dissenters as members can accomplish more than those whose desire for agreement is high. Where dissent is supported, teamwork comes to be valued over competition, individual participation is encouraged, and diversity of ideas is actually promoted (Goddard, 1986). Mutual goal setting, along with a clear understanding of problem-solving and decision-making strategies, results in increased trust and cohesion, not negativity or a critical attitude. And the decisions reached are more easily implemented, and with less resistance, than in a no-conflict group.

When an effective design makes it possible to define expectations clearly and to understand safe avenues of participation, conflict can be viewed as a means of expression. Dissent and controversy become assets to creative problem solving rather than blocks and sources of tension. This is not to say that inappropriate, hostile, or insensitive personal behavior will not pose problems. But in groups such behaviors often reflect frustration and disillusionment at the problem-solving process itself and, being symptoms, actually disappear when the problem—repressed conflict—is solved.

One of the real issues that emerges in the life of a problem-solving group isn't whether there is or should be conflict, but whether healthy conflict is allowed to emerge. The notion of "groupthink," something each of us has experienced, continues to be a provocative source of discussion among individuals interested in sorting out the underlying reasons group members withhold crucial information or are unduly influenced by unresolved authority issues within the group itself.

THE CONTINUING CONTROVERSY SURROUNDING GROUPTHINK

Irving Janis (1982), in the most recent edition of his book *Groupthink,* raised an important concern related to the use of groups as vehicles for problem solving and decision making. He asked what norms formed in a group where unanimity and conformity were valued and where disagreement, argument, discord, and dissent were equated with disloyalty, even infidelity, to the group. The pressure on members, he argued, was to agree not to disagree—especially regarding the ideas of the leadership. He called this insidious process *groupthink.*

There is increasing evidence that such was the mentality in the White House during the days of the Watergate cover-up (Cline, 1983). All the classic signs of groupthink were present: President Nixon and his staff were isolated and defensive and found strength in strategies that built a sense of cohesion—for example, "stonewalling." They increasingly isolated themselves from the criticism of the press and even from colleagues, and they excluded dissent—along with impartiality and objectivity—from the decision-making process. They stopped critically discussing and carefully considering particular consequences of immediate decisions, and as each of their decisions in turn created controversy and intensified their need to justify their actions, their exclusivity as a group increased.

Another extreme example of such social conformity was the mass suicide that took place in "Jonestown," Guyana, at the instigation of Reverend Jim Jones (Ulman, 1983). It might seem easy to attribute this and the Watergate example to a "siege mentality" resulting from unusually great stress. But the pressure to conform can be overwhelming where loyalty to the group is so strong that members censor their own doubts and blindly follow the leader.

A final and more recent example occurred in 1997 when a religious cult committed a mass suicide. Pool (1997) refers to such extreme acts as "induced psychosis," which he defines as occurring when someone who is psychologically stronger gets weaker members to change their belief systems. Often the control increases over time. In the Heavens Gate situation restrictions became policy beyond discussion (celibacy and castration) and established a climate of permissiveness that eventually led to death as acceptable (Ferris et al., 1997).

The implications of groupthink are serious not only for prestigious, high-level presidential advisors but also for more mundane committees. It might be useful to examine the conditions that spawn groupthink and to therefore understand when groups are most vulnerable to it. Janis (1977) emphasizes that great cohesiveness (here defined as attractiveness of belonging) and a directive leader who makes known early what course he or she favors are the two most significant preconditions. But for full-blown groupthink there need to be others: the group should be under stress, facing a crisis situation, and should not have established procedures for considering a variety of viewpoints. Janis's analysis of groupthink by policy-making groups has helped clarify the antecedent conditions, the symptoms of groupthink, and those of the defective decision making that results (see table on page 325).

It is frightening to think that committees can make vital decisions that affect all our lives while they are victims of groupthink. But it also helps us to recognize that everyday committees who could develop better decisions might be mired in groupthink.

REDUCING THE THREAT OF GROUPTHINK One interesting study undertaken with 19 four-person student groups in a college setting had leaders randomly distributed among the various teams. Some of these leaders were told to withhold their opinions, while others were encouraged to state their opinions at the beginning of the discussion. Those groups in which the leaders did not express their opinions were significantly more diverse in their solutions. The researchers' conclusion was that these members were less cautious (Anderson and Balzer, 1991).

Familiarity among group members and leaders resulting in subtle influence on how free people feel to express their opinions has been the subject of other interesting studies. For example, in one study of 213 M.B.A. students placed in groups of three to solve a murder mystery, the researchers formed three different types of groups (Gruenfeld et al., 1996). In the first type, all the individuals knew each other. In the second type, two of the individuals were familiar to one another and one was unfamiliar. In the third type, all the members were unfamiliar to each other.

Analysis of Groupthink by Policy-Making Groups

Antecedent Conditions		Symptoms of Groupthink	Symptoms of Defective Decision Making
1. High cohesiveness 2. Insulation of the group 3. Lack of methodical procedures for search and appraisal 4. Directive leadership 5. High stress with a low degree of hope for finding a better solution than the one favored by the leader or other influential persons	CONCURRENCE-SEEKING → TENDENCY →	1. Illusion of invulnerability 2. Collective rationalization 3. Belief in inherent morality of the group 4. Stereotypes of out-groups 5. Direct pressure on dissenters 6. Self-censorship → → 7. Illusion of unanimity 8. Self-appointed mind guards	1. Incomplete survey of alternatives 2. Incomplete survey of objectives 3. Failure to examine risks of preferred choice 4. Poor information search 5. Selective bias in processing information at hand 6. Failure to reappraise alternatives 7. Failure to work out contingency plans

Analysis based on comparisons of high- and low-quality decisions made by policy groups.
Source: Reprinted with permission of The Free Press, a Division of Simon & Schuster, Inc. from *Decision Making: A Psychological Analysis of Conflict, Choice, and Commitment* by Irving L. Janis and Leon Mann. Copyright © 1977 by The Free Press.

In some groups, some clues were provided to all the members; in others, the information was given only to certain individuals. The results were that the "stranger" groups were most likely to solve the mystery when information was shared among all the members. However, in the groups with all-familiar students or part-familiar students, there was a greater likelihood that they would solve the mystery when the clues were not shared. Results might reflect that the students who were most familiar to each other were more inhibited, less willing to risk sharing ideas that may have differed with the strong opinions of one or two other members. Creativity is often stifled when individuals are fearful of how nonconforming ideas will be received. In stranger groups, there may be less concern about repercussions in relation to status or acceptance.

Results of this nature are hardly consistent, however; the jury appears still to be out on the subject. For example, some studies (Watson and Kamalesh, 1992; Bantel, 1993) suggest that homogeneous groups are *more* effective in problem solving than those of greater diversity. But it has also been shown that where time and effort are taken to blend diverse members into a group, then outcomes can be markedly more positive (Maxnevski, 1994). (This phenomenon and the impact of brainstorming techniques on the quality of decision making and problem solving are explained further later in the chapter.)

Reader Activity

In random groups of four or five, consider the following question alone, then compare your experience and the overall group response with the research on the phenomenon of groupthink:

What factors cause you to hold back information or feelings in a group? Are you more or less able to risk in a group of strangers or a group of friends? In which will discussions be deeper and more relevant?

Share your findings with the other small groups in the class and attempt to determine if there are patterns of responses that seem to corroborate one of the points of view taken in the research. (Keep in mind that research on group dynamics is a "work in progress" and so will continue to provide considerable controversy.)

Janis (1982) identified some of these concerns when he made a number of suggestions designed to reduce the impact of groupthink. These include the following:

1. The leader can assign the role of critical evaluator to each member, making clear that it is critical examination, not agreement, that is valued.
2. The leader should avoid stating his or her personal preference among the alternatives being considered.
3. At intervals the group should break into subgroups, each studying the same problem. They should then reconvene, report their recommendations, and negotiate a resolution to their difficulties.
4. As appropriate, outside experts (including those who disagree with the plan) should be brought in and heard.
5. Once a plan (decision) has emerged, there should be a "second chance" review of the alternatives.

Just as some committees have a well-earned reputation for creating abysmal decisions, there are also committees that work productively—even extraordinarily well. Groups can harness the efforts of members to greatly enhance individual performance, or they can fall very short of it. Which it will be depends on how effectively the group's organization and norms exploit members' skills and apply them to the task. The more we understand fundamental group processes, the better we can design groups to work at their full potential.

THE STEPLADDER APPROACH—A NEW EFFORT TO CONTROL GROUPTHINK A new problem-solving strategy introduced by Rogelberg and Lowe (1992) demonstrates how a small structural change in the ways a group works can contribute to a desired outcome and reduce the influence of groupthink. In this strategy, called the *step-ladder technique,* two people begin a problem-solving task by exploring the nature of the issue and the possible alternatives. After some time, the two are joined by a third person, with the notion of educating the new participant about the issue but intentionally holding back any specific solutions developed by the original two participants. The new contributor proceeds to explore his or her own point of view and what his or her own solution(s) might look like. Then the solutions of the first two are added to the mix and full discussion ensues among the three. Finally, after a predetermined amount of time, a fourth person joins the group. Once again this new person attempts to explore the background of the problem along with any assumptions or givens and then is encouraged to add his or her perspective before hearing the determinations of the other three. The intent is to have a new pair of ears and eyes added to the discussion, and new insights they may add to the effort.

Rogelberg and Lowe found two particular benefits from this design strategy. The first was a reduction in social loafing (see Chapter 3) since members tend to focus on communicating information and remain attentive to the issue at hand, rather than taking time for unnecessary social amenities or "shooting the breeze." Second and more important, participants feel less pressure to conform to the opinions of others. In fact, individuals are encouraged to add original thoughts independent of the biasing conclusions of other members. With each individual feeling supported for his or her own point of view, the final discussion tends to incorporate the rich perspectives of all four contributors.

SOME FINAL THOUGHTS ON GROUPTHINK A recent evaluation of groupthink by Aldag and Fuller (1993) suggested that although the concept has captured the imagination of group theorists, it may be more the result of "allure" than of substantive research evidence. They do, however, conclude that the topic warrants more research.

It's the authors' belief that anyone who has ever experienced a heated discussion among colleagues where individuals sway to the pressure of the group or individual members has witnessed the impact of groupthink. The classic study of individual conformity in a group setting, conducted over forty years ago by Asch (see Chapter 3) was the first time groupthink gained notoriety. And who has never sheepishly left a meeting upset with him- or herself for having withheld a strongly held opinion to avoid appearing stupid or perhaps incurring the wrath of the boss or others? The concept of seduction by a group leader (see Chapter 5) demonstrates that leaders are continually faced with the potential of deceit because of members' fear and the perceived possibility of repercussions for disagreement. There is an enormous amount of face validity to the concept of groupthink. Thus, we are awaiting research to reveal in an organized fashion what most of us have experienced in the groups in which we all participate.

OPEN-ENDED VERSUS CLOSED-ENDED PROBLEMS

Now let's explore a major reason why problem solving often fails. The issue is one of attitude and perceived opportunity. Many of us, as individuals or as part of a group, enter a problem-solving situation with a predisposition toward the problem itself and the range of solutions open to us. Quite often we establish what might be called *premature boundary conditions* for problems that, by their very nature, restrict our ability to see creative alternatives. Traditional education does not encourage active, creative thinking but instead emphasizes learning rote answers. Too often, well-intentioned teachers turn out students who know the "right" answers but do not even know how to begin to use creative reasoning to solve an unfamiliar problem. Of course, children have more limited cognitive capacities than adults, so learning universal "shoulds" is a reasonable place to begin. However, as adults we know that most problems have more than one solution, so in that sense answers are relative.

In addition to becoming dependent on what Rickards (1974) calls the *defining authorities* for the boundaries of solutions and on the accompanying reluctance to challenge those boundaries, many people feel impotent within their institutions and, lacking real power, believe it does little good to look for creative alternatives. More likely than not, we suspect that additional effort will result in embarrassment or rejection. Thus, there is little perceived payoff for extending ourselves. The fact is that there are few problems that are closed and not open to a variety of creative solutions. It is the job of problem solving to draw out the best alternatives and to break down artificial barriers, including those that psychologically bind the problem.

Groups themselves, when composed of a variety of individuals, often provide the different perspectives necessary to push boundaries away. Most of us have experienced situations in which our own close proximity to a problem reduced our ability to see a logical or creative solution. Marriages are particularly prone to this, as predictable patterns of behavior come to establish a very limited vision of what is possible. One purpose of therapy is to reduce boundaries and help us reframe problems (Watzlawick, 1978).

RATIONAL VERSUS INTUITIVE WAYS OF THINKING[2]

Most of us are more comfortable using one of two ways of thinking. Whether this is based on family upbringing, some genetic attribute we inherit or perhaps reinforcement of a favorite teacher, over time we tend to become more inclined toward one over another.

> **FOCUS ON DIVERSITY**
>
> What are some cultural factors that might cause people to think more in the rational or the intuitive style?

At one end of the spectrum, we often hear of individuals referred to as being intuitive, free-spirited, able to think "out of the box," and likely to deal comfortably with both feelings and ideas. At the other end of the spectrum are those who feel most comfortable with orderly, rational, linear thinking and to whom logical thought provides intellectual stimulation and reward. In the eyes of linear thinkers, people who think more intuitively are disorganized, undisciplined, and overly emotional. They believe that more than one intuitive thinker in a group will most certainly make it degenerate into chaos at worst and waste precious time at best. Those of an intuitive bent may find their more rational friends to be excessively rigid, inflexible, and tied to what is known—unable to feel comfortable in the world of the imagination, fantasy, and the arational.

Both extremes of these types exist, as do all shades in between. Problems, however, tend to arise when groups comprising representatives of both approaches come together to solve problems. Without useful strategies for legitimizing and involving the strengths inherent in both types of thinkers, tensions and misunderstandings often arise. More often than not, in a bottom-line, time-conscious world, the intuitive types give way. This tendency may raise different issues for a group because it is common for those most comfortable with the linear approach (or traditional yang behaviors) to be men and those more comfortable with intuition (or traditional yin approach) to be women. Suddenly, what appeared to be stylistic differences in thinking are tied into gender issues, with all the tensions that often accompany them.

In fact, both approaches are important, and skilled leaders have the ability to work comfortably in both arenas. When to utilize intuitive approaches versus more linear ones is not a gender issue. Here is an example of a situation when use of a more intuitive approach appeared "logical":

2. This discussion is drawn in part from the thoughtful studies and application of research by such writers as Richard Bandler and John Grinder (1979), Henry Mintzberg (1976b), Robert Ornstein (1975), Paul Watzlawick (1978), and Benjamin Young (1979).

The art department of an advertising agency is assigned a new project to work on. On the first day of the project, the department is given a description of the product—what it does, who might use it, and how long it lasts—and is told what other similar products are already being sold. A meeting later in the week draws the group together in one room, and they toss out ideas that might sell the product—everything from slogans to vignettes for commercials and logos for sportswear. To an observer, the meeting is chaos: people all talk at the same time, there are excited interruptions as one person uses what someone else has just said to generate another idea, and someone across the room says, "Yes! What about . . . ."

Two weeks later the bare bones of the advertising campaign are sketched out, and the planning to clarify, coordinate, and expand the design is begun. It is only after this point that all that "necessary" information given to the team on the first day is dug out from under the drafting table. Group members can now look at their product and begin to figure out how it fits in with the budget, what the client expects, and the market the product is aimed at. It is only near the end of the process that the art department finds rational reasons to substantiate the creative work it has already completed.

Once "creative juices" have drawn out the best ideas without many imposed constraints, then is the time to establish some order and necessary boundaries to a situation. The following sections will provide a variety of tools and ways of thinking that will facilitate both more-intuitive and more-linear ways of approaching problem solving.

Individual Experiment

Choose a problem that you have thought about recently. It may be a problem concerning other people in a group setting; it may be a question concerning career direction, job choice, or living arrangements. Sit in a comfortable position in a quiet place where you will not be disturbed. Relax for a few minutes by letting your mind wander or concentrating on your breathing. Imagine a picture of yourself once your problem has been solved. What will you be like? How will you be different? Fill in your picture with as much detail as you can, such as how you will be feeling, what you will be doing, saying, wearing, and so on. Your picture can be one snapshot or several frames, as in a movie. In this process your right brain has been working, projecting you into the future. It has gone through an intuitive problem-solving process that tends to go on unnoticed. Now evaluate your picture. Are there any surprises? Is the picture realistic? If you took a more logical, planned route, do you think you would have arrived at the same solution?

Rational Problem Solving

The study of problem solving by social scientists has shown the process to be not the straightforward one dictated by the scientific method, but rather a nightmare of complexity—something so tortuous to use that few people have the time, energy, inclination, or know-how to do it right. The reason is that people initiate the process and are affected by many other factors, including the organizational environment and their own personal needs. The fact is that no one model can account for all the complexity and richness of the human spirit and behavior.

The purpose here is to provide a general overview of rational problem solving, integrating insights drawn from systems theory, communications theory, group dynamics, and organizational development. Then a more comprehensive model elaborating the more general perspective and its potential for use in a group setting is presented.

THE SIX STAGES OF RATIONAL PROBLEM SOLVING

For the most part, the steps we move through in solving a problem are quite simple. First come the identification and clarification of an issue. There follow the development of alternatives, selection of one or more of these, an implementation phase and, finally, evaluation of the outcomes. It is a wonder, then, that a process so straightforward and so lacking in complexity can result in so many problems and pitfalls. (See the exercises at the end of this chapter for examples of how to implement these six stages of problem solving.)

STAGE 1: PROBLEM IDENTIFICATION We can recognize that a problem exists either by chance or as a result of systematic inquiry. More often than not, it seems that problems arise naturally, announcing their presence through increasing tension and conflict, or perhaps inefficiency. Conditions worsen if the presence of such tensions is not confronted or if they are denied or covered over so that accompanying frustrations become a breeding ground for other problems. This is too often the case in groups in which a little internal festering is preferred over dealing directly with issues as they arise.

In some cases, there is simply no mechanism available to help bring problems into the open. Something as simple as a suggestion box (if there is evidence that it is being used) can be a direct line to sources of individual, group, or organizational problems. Occasional questionnaires or small group discussions can be helpful in drawing problems into the open before they become destructive. Such problem sensing, of both task and emotional issues, can help keep communication channels open. Other problems will arise, however, if a group or individuals are encouraged to identify specific problems, and those problems are then avoided or minimized by people in positions of influence. Problem identification is just the first step of a process, not an end unto itself.

STAGE 2: THE DIAGNOSTIC PHASE Once symptoms have been recognized and brought to the attention of others, several steps seem to follow quite naturally. First, the problem must be clarified and relationships identified. Too often the symptoms are little more than a generalized recognition of discomfort or stress and reveal little about the underlying factors creating the disturbance. At this point it must be discovered how much the problem is shared by others as well as its degree of urgency. A second step in the diagnostic process is to gather supporting evidence on the nature of the problem. Third, with this new information, the problem should be restated in terms of a condition that exists and that, to some extent, needs to be changed.

Quite often, problems are stated simplistically in terms of an "either-or" situation or "good" or "bad," which immediately polarizes potential problem solvers into win-or-lose camps. If a condition can be shown to exist that is less than optimal, then the problem of the decision-making group becomes one of identifying the factors that keep the condition from being optimal. Energy can then be directed toward isolating specific causal factors, such as a single person dominating the discussion, lack of time, or the need for clear goals. Thus, arguments become limited to the relative strength of such factors, not to whether they exist. This approach encourages compromise and multiple solutions.

Finally, having gathered as much data as possible concerning the problem, stated it as a condition to be changed, and isolated the various causal factors, the group must make a determination regarding its own ability to solve the problem. This involves looking squarely at the group's own power to influence the prevailing condition, what kinds of resources are going to be necessary, and how much impact their efforts will have on others.

For change to occur, those involved must see the problem as "their own"; it cannot be imposed on them. This principle has important implications for who takes part in the diagnostic process and which people are kept closely informed about what is happening. Developing solutions proves to be nothing more than an academic exercise if those who will be affected have not even admitted that a problem exists.

STAGE 3: GENERATION OF ALTERNATIVES Groups and individuals seek quick and easy solutions. This is one reason why the problem-solving process so often breaks down. As we fasten onto what we perceive as a logical and resourceful solution, we automatically screen out numerous other possibilities, some of which (difficult as it is for us to believe) may be more appropriate. We commit ourselves to one idea and are then compelled to defend it. This may be particularly true in a group in which some of us have a need to convince others of our wisdom and skill.

However, formulating solutions before ideas have been thoroughly explored not only reduces the potential quality of the eventual solution but also inhibits open communication. Thus, it is a major pitfall to evaluate solutions at a time when the intent should be merely to explore every potential solution. Done effectively, this process can reduce the tendency for groups to polarize around answers that are comfortable, and it may also help them look toward new approaches.

After the ideas have been generated and explored in relation to specific causal factors (isolated during the diagnostic stage), then there should be a general screening process to integrate and synthesize the solutions into a smaller number. Again, the goal here is not to select a "best" solution, because the problem is likely to be multifaceted, with a number of possible alternatives. Before any final decision is reached, a period of weighing and testing of the alternatives should be undertaken. If time and resources allow, an effort should be made to gather data about the various solutions reached up to that point. This could range from establishing a pilot study to seeking the opinions of other individuals, such as experts.

STAGE 4: SELECTING SOLUTIONS Along with gathering new data and taking time to think about the alternatives, it is ideal to consider the consequences of each alternative in relation to the problem. Many times a group, anxious to get under way, fails to explore the unanticipated consequences and focuses only on the obvious benefits to be gained. Thus, it is at this stage that each potential solution should be carefully evaluated in terms of its possible limitations as well as its strengths.

STAGE 5: IMPLEMENTATION Many participants of decision-making groups, after being successful in developing a useful decision, have watched helplessly as the ideas so carefully designed and agreed on are never implemented. Part of the problem often can be traced to an early stage of the process and the failure to involve, or at least to keep informed, those with the power to kill the idea and those who will be influenced by the final decision. Equally damaging is the failure to build accountability into the action or implementation phase. Too often, interest is not developed in the decision-making group. Accountability must be carefully cultivated so that individuals feel responsible for the outcome and are answerable to the others involved.

STAGE 6: EVALUATION AND ADJUSTMENT One reason why people are resistant to new ideas is that they believe that once change occurs, the new status quo will be just as impervious to change as was the previous one. Building in a mechanism of evaluation as well as flexibility to make adjustments once the data are analyzed can keep the entire problem-solving process flexible and open to new alternatives. Most important, it gives those being influenced by the decision the recourse to alternative procedures and a feeling of some potency in the process. Also, the notion of accountability is tied directly into the evaluation and adjustment. Thus, evaluation becomes more than a superficial exercise and tends to be used as an integral part of an ongoing problem-solving process.

Rational problem solving is designed to keep us making sense, to productively manage irrational biases and limit customs and habits, to expand our vision, to look at the consequences of our choices, and to make sure that ultimate decisions result in constructive action. The orderly, stepwise process that follows is designed to draw participant(s) along in a systematic manner. It takes time; it should not be done in a hurry. "Quick-and-dirty" problem solving inevitably leads to quick-and-dirty solutions that simply mirror preconceived notions we wish to sell. In fact, Hirokawa (1980) found that groups who spent more time on procedural matters were better able to reach agreement and make effective decisions.

Problem solving is a circular process that continues in an ongoing fashion (see accompanying figure). Individuals and groups are self-adjusting and self-maintaining organisms in which the evaluation and adjustment stage feeds back into the initial problem-identification stage. In fact, Koberg and Bagnall (1981) suggest that the

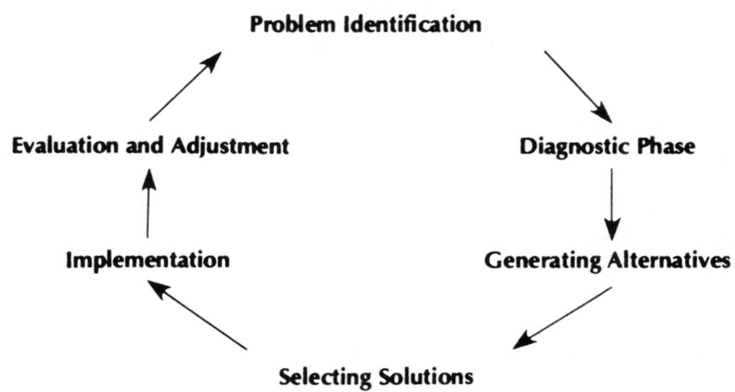

stages occur simultaneously as well as progressively. We gain constant feedback by checking the previous steps as we proceed in solving a problem.

Note, as an aside, that one reason why we fail to invest enough time and energy in problem solving is that it forces us to admit that there is a problem in the first place, that we are less than perfect, and that change is likely to be called for. These are difficult pills to swallow. Change is usually uncomfortable at best and painful at worst. Who needs it? With that in mind, let's take an excursion into rational problem solving.

Reader Activity

Consider thoroughly a problem you have, and then generate as many alternatives as you can discover. Whether you decide that change is not worth the price or choose a conservative or even radical alternative is up to you.

Identify three problems that play important parts in your life—problems that have been with you for a while and that you would like to resolve. In this instance, a problem is defined as a state or condition in your life that you believe probably requires changing. Now, think of a friend you respect and trust and who knows you rather well. Ask this person to take an evening with you to problem-solve one of the conditions you have indicated. (Promise to do the same for that individual if he or she believes the process is worthwhile.) The purpose of the friend's involvement is to provide you with a different perspective, help "turn over stones" you might not see, push you further, and ask tough questions you might not be willing to ask. The friend will represent another side of reality.

You can also perform this activity with a small group. Because a group represents more ideas, concerns, and points of view, a bit more time is required to do justice to the problem-solving process.

Follow the problem-solving process outlined in the following section a step at a time. Don't hurry. Probe each explicit question and then ask yourself other questions that come to mind. Your goal is to find a better way. But be warned that problem solving is serious business, because it should influence you and your life. One reason we fail to take such activities seriously is that many of us have spent time doing just this with inconsequential problems. If there is nothing important you wish to explore in order to enjoy the stimulation of the search, then move on and read through the process with the thought that it may prove valuable later.

A MODEL FOR RATIONAL PROBLEM SOLVING

Step 1. Make a general description of the problem condition as you see it. What seems to be the crux of the problem? How does it influence you? Where's the rub? Talk the problem over in general terms, trying to outline its parameters.

Step 2. Describe what the defined condition would be like in an ideal but reachable state. Here we are trying to establish a sense of the changes that would have to occur by looking hypothetically at, for example, how production operations in a factory might differ, how the attitudes of people might change in certain working relationships, how discipline in a classroom might change, how a group might solve problems differently. Again, it is important to talk over the ideal condition and obtain a feel for it. This in itself will often help sharpen the focus on the real problem. The concern is *what* could be, rather than *how* to achieve it.

Step 3. Identify the specific discrepancies that exist between the present view of reality (step 1) and the ideal state (step 2). The problem(s) should begin to take on a different shape as a result of this analysis.

Step 4. Analyze the nature of the condition more thoroughly. Do this by asking a series of critical questions.

1. Does there appear to be more than one problem, each of which warrants individual attention? Although the relationships between certain problems must be recognized, the more concretely a problem can be defined, the less difficult will be the task of problem resolution.
2. What benefits does the present condition hold for the individual, group, or organization that is defining it as a problem? One reason why problems don't just disappear is that very real satisfactions have to be given up to solve them. Consider for a moment the benefits a smoker who "wants" to quit must give up, the benefits an obese individual will have to sacrifice, the benefits that accrue to a person with a volatile temper who would "really like to stop blowing up all the time," the benefits realized by a "talker" even though the individual knows his or her talking alienates some people, and the benefits to a group that constantly complains about starting a meeting late or members arriving late. Until a group or individual is willing to look such benefits squarely in the face, the chance of significant change occurring will be slight. If we are not somehow compensated for these lost benefits, it might be crazy to change, even though we'd be the last to admit it.
3. What are the blockages that have been thrown up in the face of previous attempts at change? Underlying a blockage may be a hidden benefit that subtly supports the existence of the status quo.
4. What solutions are currently being attempted unsuccessfully? By taking a hard look at our unsuccessful efforts, we often gain a clearer understanding of the problem. For example, one supervisor would procrasti-

nate in getting corrected work reviews back to her subordinate, who often needed the information but would "simply make do." The subordinate hated conflict and couldn't confront his boss. Not only that, but he couldn't stand the feeling of being a nag. Thus, instead of mentioning his need, the subordinate withdrew from the problem and never faced up to the difficulties being created. The boss, on the other hand, was being subtly reinforced (not being accountable meant not having to do the work). Thus, part of the problem was the subordinate's attitude toward the problem.

Step 5. Now, in light of all the new information about the problem condition, redefine it as clearly and succinctly as possible. It is not uncommon to discover that there are several problems. But in order to ensure that the time invested will be put to good use, it is necessary to isolate the one problem that is most important to solve and whose solution might have the greatest impact on other existing conditions. Several examples of clear, succinct problem conditions follow. Note that a problem condition simply describes a state that needs changing; there is no implication of good or bad and no implied solution.

1. The present level of shared participation in our meetings.
2. My ability to state my personal opinions in a group.
3. The present level of productivity by team A.
4. The present level of absenteeism in this department.
5. My ability to assert myself in conflict situations in which I wish to make my point.

Step 6. Without considering the implications of a particular solution, generate as many alternatives as possible. Potential solutions might result from reflection on any of the previous steps. The key in this stage is not to worry about implementation or consequences but simply to develop real, concrete choices that presently are not available.

Step 7. Screen the various alternatives by changing them into specific objectives that suggest direction and quantity and where and when they will occur. Also make an effort to determine which of the resulting objectives will have the greatest impact at the least cost to you or the organization and which objectives, for whatever reason, seem impractical. This is a preliminary screening step; more will occur later. Taking the first condition used as an example in step 5—the present level of shared participation in meetings—possible objectives might include

1. to provide each participant with ten chips at the beginning of each meeting. They must give up a chip each time they speak. Once a person's chips

are gone, he or she has no opportunity to speak again unless more chips are negotiated from other members.

2. to establish the rule that during periods of discussion an individual can make a second point only after each other person in the group has been given the opportunity to speak.
3. to have a person appointed prior to each meeting to the role of "participant observer." This person is responsible for pointing out, through various means (for example, a chart of how often each person speaks), how effectively the group is communicating.
4. to identify the leader as primarily responsible for gaining the input of all members.

An objective for the fourth condition above—the present level of absenteeism—might be to use the last six months as a baseline for absenteeism and to provide a paid day off every two weeks when team members have, as a group, averaged 30 percent below that baseline for a month. Recipients of the paid day off would be rotated throughout the team over time.

The most effective objectives are those that are specific enough to be measured in some manner. At this point we are less concerned with practicality than we are with clarity and specificity. Once clarity has been ensured, we can discuss other considerations related to the value of a particular objective.

Although someone may not necessarily agree with the objective for attacking absenteeism, it is clear, specific in intent, and provides information about what would occur, when, to whom, and under what conditions—and that is the aim during step 7.

Step 8. Consider the consequences, the price to be paid, the impact on the individual, organization, or group if each of the selected objectives were implemented. Then decide whether to alter the objective, either to improve its effectiveness or to reduce its negative consequences. This hard-nosed step of anticipating consequences is often overlooked because of the enthusiasm and blush of success that often surround the generation of solutions. As shown previously, there are numerous attempts at change and many reasons for their failure. Thus, the surrender of chips as individuals talk might initially be seen as fun but later be resented as a game and tossed off as impractical. Assigning a process observer the legitimate role of keeping participation high and communication open seems not only appropriate but feasible. Even this idea has its limitations, however, because most observers must be trained, given time in the group, and supported.

This step is down-to-earth and ultimately practical. Its purpose is to make an objective workable or to discard it. Questions need to be raised about such issues as

- motivating people to accept a particular idea.
- ensuring that the group has the necessary skills to facilitate success.
- overcoming cost factors.
- educating people to the value of a new idea.
- exploring issues of timing and pace of implementation of a new idea.
- overcoming previous failures as well as the "we've-done-it-before" syndrome.

These and any number of other factors could render a potentially good idea, as translated into an objective, ineffective. This step, then, explores not only consequences but also the strategies necessary to overcome potential resistances and polishes the objective into something that will work.

Step 9. Develop and monitor appropriate support systems to ensure the stabilizing of most change efforts. Generating alternatives is the easiest part of problem solving; getting those alternatives into action often proves impossible. Looking at consequences and building support strategies (step 8) are helpful. But equally important is establishing the means of effective accountability. The reasons why New Year's resolutions are seldom kept are that there is no accountability built into the process, not to mention the problem of consequences we don't consider at the time we commit ourselves. Increasingly, we find that for change to work, groups and individuals need to know that some time in the future, the results of their promise to act will be assessed. Viewed in this light, we can utilize monitoring as a means of support and development rather than punishment and control. Monitoring suggests adjusting and adapting a process to ensure success. Thus, it should occur early enough to be motivating and helpful, before mistakes are made that cannot be corrected and prior to guilt setting in.

Support systems are vital to most monitoring processes. For example, legitimizing all the talk about the process of change with people who have been through it before (AA, Weight Watchers, new students, ex-convicts) or with people who are undergoing similar experiences in the present can be gratifying, reassuring, and profitable. It is always helpful to learn from others' experience. In addition, making public our own objectives tends to have a positive impact; our commitment is supported by others who now expect action to occur and will reinforce it.

Step 10. Evaluate problem-solving efforts to decide what steps should be taken next. There are several ways in which a relatively simple evaluation can occur. First, at a designated time in the future, assess the degree to which the discrepancies between the present situation and the ideal have increased or decreased from the period of original assessment. A second approach is to take the objectives established in step 7 and compare them to specific outcomes.

Further problem solving can occur at this point. It is ill-advised to consider problem solving, as many do, a one-shot operation. Most problem solving is a jerky, inconsistent process that results in success and failure and, we hope, an overall sense of accomplishment. But as long as all are willing to continue looking at the process of change, there is a good chance that the mistakes that inevitably occur and the natural resistance that accompanies virtually any efforts at change will disappear.

Some of you may be wondering how a "simple" problem became so complicated. It is we humans who are complex, along with a multitude of factors that impinge on us. The problem-solving process described here is, in fact, rather simple compared to some (Easton, 1976; Kepner and Tregoe, 1968). The problem is that it is rare for individuals to have the time, patience, endurance, or courage to expend the kind of energy required to tackle some of these creative and technically sound approaches to problem solving and decision making. The issue is further complicated by the question of who should be present during the problem solving. Sound and highly structured problem solving can take literally thousands of hours of time; and with many problems, it is difficult to measure whether a complex or a simplified process is preferable. Perhaps it is most important to help people adopt a tough-minded view of problem solving that they can bring to bear, without requiring a cumbersome and time-consuming procedure except in special situations.

The Pareto System

Another tool for rational problem solving is the Pareto analysis and diagram, which is being used increasingly in organization management and with organizational work groups.

PARETO ANALYSIS

Much advice on decision making appears in management literature, but only rarely does one find any reference to the *Pareto system* (also known as the *80/20 rule* and the *ABC method*). Nevertheless, the Pareto principle can be a significant decision-making aid.

Pareto analysis takes its name from the Italian economist Vilfredo Frederico Damaso Pareto (1848 – 1923). In the course of his studies on the unequal distribution of income, Pareto found that 80 percent of the wealth was controlled by only 20 percent of the population. The essence of the Pareto method of inspection and analysis, then, is identifying that vital few to which corrective action can be applied where it will do the most good, the most quickly.

DEVELOPING A PARETO DIAGRAM

The steps in developing a Pareto diagram are as follows:

1. List the condition(s) or cause(s) you wish to monitor—for example, absenteeism. (In the list, discussion, and illustrations that follow, we draw on an example suggested by Dr. Gloria Bader, president of the Bader Group.)
2. Collect the raw data (names, numbers of days absent, and so on.)
3. Rank the various conditions or causes from highest to lowest (most absent to least absent). (See table below.)
4. Under a horizontal axis, write these causes in descending order (the most important cause to the left and the least important to the right). As an example, in the figure on p. 342 we find John on the left, with nine absences and Don on the right, with only one absence.
5. On the left-hand vertical axis, note the measurement scale (total number of days absent).
6. On the right-hand vertical axis, note the percentage scale (the total number of absences must equal 100 percent).
7. Plot the data and then the cumulative frequencies.

Absenteeism

Name	Days Absent	Percent of Total Days Absent
John	9	30.0
Alice	7	23.3
Bob	6	20.0
Mark	3	10.0
Kim	2	6.7
Diane	2	6.7
Don	1	3.3
Totals	30	100.00

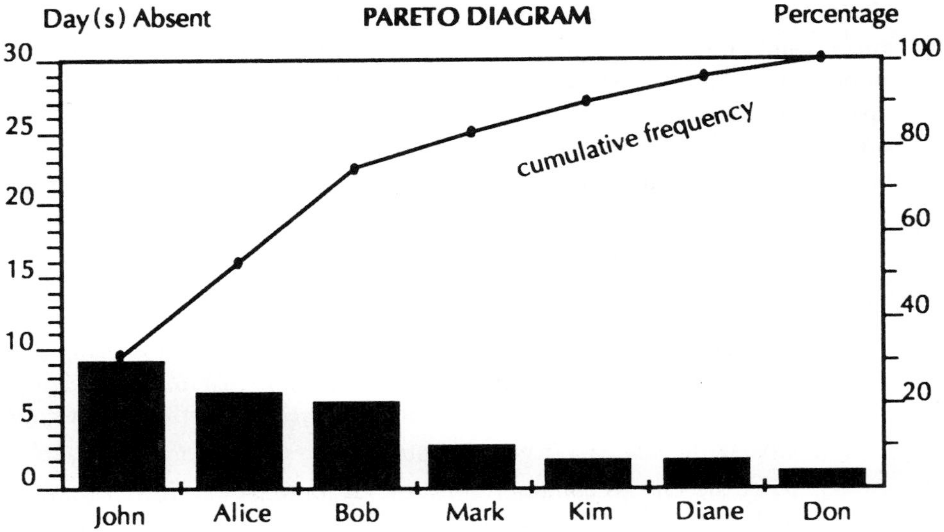

Comparison of Day(s) Absent from Work per Person

In a hypothetical example, consider a group of fifteen workers. The table gives data for the employees who missed at least one day of work in October. It shows that John, Alice, and Bob are the worst offenders. A member of the group could have anticipated that these three would be somewhere near the top. However, he or she would not have guessed that between them, they would account for nearly 75 percent of all absences. Confronted by these results, the organization may feel that it has been too tolerant—especially in the case of John.

It would be easy to explain to John in an objective fashion what the data mean and then simply ask him two questions. First, "John, what does this suggest about your behavior in relation to the others?" Second, "If you were I (the administrator), what would you tell John?" It would be very difficult for John to deny the vivid reality. Such data can be well utilized as a first step in many change processes.

ADVANTAGES AND A DISADVANTAGE

A Pareto diagram can be particularly helpful to problem solving since it shows how often something occurs, as well as the relationship between different parts. In the absenteeism table, it is easy to identify the "high" absentees, the days absent for each, and the percentage of days absent in relation to all other absences. With this information it would be difficult for John to make excuses or deny the situation.

The possible applications of a Pareto diagram are almost infinite. Because cost, quantity, and quality are the three main concerns of management, the Pareto diagram is a powerful tool that should be familiar to every decision maker or group of decision makers. It can be used as a motivator, and it is easy to implement and understand.

The main disadvantage of a Pareto diagram is that only quantifiable data can be used in constructing it.

Intuitive Problem Solving

The only problem with an orderly, systematic, linear approach is that it overlooks the important intuitive aspect of problem solving. Many of us would like to believe that the product of a rational approach will be the most reasonable, appropriate, and qualitatively best response possible. But anyone who has undertaken serious problem solving realizes that many of the most creative decisions result from some unexpected thought, an aside tossed off in jest, a moment when defenses were down, or at a point of exhaustion, frustration, or exasperation that could never have been programmed or anticipated.

Thus, effective problem solving is not just providing order and a tough-minded approach to viewing causes and consequences. The key involves bringing to the surface as many of the existing solutions as possible. This means overcoming our personal predispositions, defenses, and habits in order to give ourselves as many choices as possible. So it is that serious problem solvers are forever looking for ways of becoming "unstuck," of taking a new and different look, of redefining the problem in a manner that may provide a new perspective and freedom to consider alternatives not yet accessible to them.

BECOMING "UNSTUCK"

Opening the floodgate to new ideas may occur in many ways. Some of these are created by rephrasing a question, or posing one that gives permission to look outside the psychological boundaries we often subtly impose on a problem. One approach is simply to step back and take the time to redefine the problem in several different ways, using totally different words. Legitimizing new words and pushing ourselves to other definitions often uncover a useful approach to the solution, because many answers fall too neatly out of the problem statement itself.

Another approach to uprooting one's mind-set is to discuss the problem via analogies, which forces us to think about a problem in terms of its similarity to other, unrelated situations or objects. This approach is based on the assumption that if two things are similar in some respects, it is very likely that they are similar in others. A stubborn person standing in the way of progress, seemingly intransigent, may be likened to a boulder or tree stump, for example. Pausing to consider ways of removing the boulder or uprooting the stump may open up the discussion. Pushing the boulder in the direction opposite to forward progress may free it and then allow rapid forward movement. Similarly, an individual may be insisting on a point of view simply because others have refused to recognize its legitimacy. Giving due credit is often difficult in arguments, but it may be the key to inducing the individual to give up a cherished—though impractical—position. Saving face seems a long way from the pushing of a boulder, but they may be similar indeed.

Another, related approach is to have problem solvers think metaphorically. Talking about retirement and old age conjures up fear and resistance in many individuals. For some it suggests the end, giving up, relinquishing our sense of potency, and becoming dependent. But if a discussion by people about to retire is framed in terms of how to enjoy the "freedom years," then resistances might be reduced.

A route that is a bit more unusual is to have people take apparently very different situations and ideas and probe for similarities. Such an exercise forces another look at the givens, at the reality of a problem, which in turn opens up the possibility of new insight.

In addition, stopping a discussion and injecting one of the following open-ended statements may be all that is needed to discover new entrances into the problem:

This situation or problem is just like . . . .

A different way to describe this is . . . .

The only time anything like this happened before was . . . .

This feels like a . . . .

This situation reminds me of . . . .

Reader Activity

Consider any recent open-ended problem you or your group have had or still are concerned about. Now take at least two of the methods suggested here and reconsider the problem. Try to use different words to describe it, perhaps developing several definitions of the same problem. Utilize a metaphor or develop an analogy to try to uncover every possible similarity between the problem and that to which you are making the comparison. You will be surprised at the number of insights that result from being forced to stretch your thinking in this simple approach to problem assessment.

BRAINSTORMING

The first real break away from strictly rational, linear, and highly controlled approaches to problem solving came nearly half a century ago, when Alex Osborn (1953) introduced the concept of *brainstorming*. He discovered that by establishing a few simple rules and utilizing a limited amount of time in a novel manner, he could dramatically alter the atmosphere in a problem-solving session. In his estimation, the approach could create more and often better ideas than might otherwise occur. Needless to say, such innovation is always a source of controversy, and the real value and significance of brainstorming have been subjects of heated debate for years. For example, whether brainstorming groups are actually more productive than individuals working alone is a question that needs investigation. There is no question, however, that his procedure opened the gate to more creative approaches to problem solving.

Brainstorming is a technique designed to do two separate things simultaneously, that is,

1. to make sure that the creativity of each individual is not limited by various influence processes that occur in groups, such as fear of social embarrassment, pressures for conformity, and status systems discouraging low-status members from participating.
2. to take maximum advantage of whatever creativity-enhancing forces exist in groups: social support, reinforcement for contributing, cross-stimulation, and the positive norms of working together.

GROUND RULES FOR BRAINSTORMING Used at the right time, brainstorming can break open a stuffy and inhibited group. Research has shown that even when a group knows it is vulnerable to criticism, the use of brainstorming techniques can have a positive influence on productivity (Maginn and Harris, 1980). If a leader has effectively read the need of the group and successfully educated them about the brainstorming approach, there is a good chance that the productivity of the group will be enhanced. To accomplish this, the group and leader should be familiar with the following ground rules:

1. Usually a preliminary practice is called for, to make sure the rules are understood. The subject should be a basis for having fun and getting creative juices flowing. Men's canes have gone out of style. What could you do to repopularize them? In what ways might graduation exercises be improved?
2. One person agrees to serve as "secretary" and record each idea.
3. A time limit is set—anywhere from one minute to perhaps fifteen.

4. Ideas are presented and placed before the group as rapidly as possible with no discussion, clarification, or comment.
5. *Criticism or evaluation of ideas is not permitted.*
6. Quantity is very important. Individuals should not screen their ideas. Each person can piggyback on ideas he or she has heard in order to generate more ideas.
7. When moving around the group, it is often helpful to limit members to one idea at a time to encourage less vocal members to get their ideas out.

After a list of ideas has been generated, those most obviously impractical or ridiculous are eliminated from the list. The substantial number of ideas that remain are then subjected to serious scrutiny.

It is important to follow the ground rules for brainstorming. Otherwise, participants often criticize ideas and dominant individuals exert too much influence. Research reveals that this damages the essential rationale for brainstorming and gives creative problem solving a bad name (VanGundy, 1984).

ADVANTAGES OF EFFECTIVE BRAINSTORMING What are some ways in which brainstorming might benefit a group, beyond simply generating a large quantity of ideas for solving problems? The fact is, we are living in a time when people are demanding to be heard and involved. People are using group decision-making procedures for an ever-widening variety of problems. How is it possible to facilitate the work of these groups? Brainstorming, given the proper exposure and a relatively nonjudgmental climate, has much to offer a decision-making group, particularly during the diagnostic and generating-of-alternatives stages. For example, brainstorming

- reduces dependency on a single authority figure.
- encourages the open sharing of ideas.
- stimulates greater participation within a group.
- increases individual safety in a highly competitive group.
- provides for a maximum of output in a short period of time.
- helps to ensure a nonevaluative climate, at least in the ideation phase of a meeting.
- provides participants with immediate visibility for the ideas that are generated.
- develops some degree of accountability for ideas among the group because they have been generated internally, not imposed from outside.
- tends to be enjoyable and stimulating.

Reader Activity

After all the discussion of brainstorming, you probably want to try it on for size. What follows might be used as a warm-up activity for a group involved in serious problem solving. Like anything else, brainstorming requires participants to be in the right mood if the benefits of the process are to be gained. Thus, the following could be used with a group of fifty or with as few as two or three people. It helps if a large sheet of newsprint is available to write down the ideas as they are generated.

We live in a highly critical society in which competition and a win – lose atmosphere are often the rule. It is not uncommon to see people getting ahead by putting someone else down. Brainstorming is a means of reducing this inclination. Still, it requires practice to overcome the tendency to be negative and overly evaluative. With this in mind, get ready to brainstorm. Read the following brief story:

> A small wholesaler, Señor Gomez, in the hinterlands of Mexico had called his buyer in Vera Cruz and asked him to obtain an order of pipe cleaners from the United States. The buyer, Señor Gonzales, agreed. He also agreed to advance Señor Gomez a substantial sum to finance the deal. A month later, just as the ship was arriving in Vera Cruz, Señor Gonzales received a frantic phone call from Señor Gomez. Apparently the warehouse and outlet store had burned down and there simply was no more business. Gonzales was suddenly faced with somehow selling 200,000 pipe cleaners.

You and your group have exactly three minutes to generate as many creative alternatives as possible. Don't think, don't hold back; anything goes.

After three minutes, your list may include as many as twenty, thirty, or even forty items. Depending on how far you wish to go, the next step would be to take the five or six best ideas and spend time creatively developing them further. Usually the screening process is based on criteria that are developed by the group and that incorporate parameters important to the problem solvers.

DIFFICULTIES OF BRAINSTORMING Hardly a meeting goes by these days in which brainstorming is not used. The problem is, it appears that brainstorming, regardless of how ubiquitous and popular it is, can have some serious flaws.

For many people, brainstorming is a strange sort of experience, creating an initial sense of discomfort (Collaros and Anderson, 1969; Hammond and Goldman, 1961; Vroom, Grant, and Cotton, 1969).

In addition, many recent studies have revealed that traditional brainstorming can be quantitatively less productive than brainstorming with nominal groups (see pp. 349–350 or by breaking into smaller subgroups (Camacho and Paulus, 1995;

Paulus and Dzindolet, 1993; Poletes and Comacho, 1993; Mullen et al., 1991; Van de Ven and Delbecq, 1971; Hill, 1982). Apparently, many leaders fail to follow the carefully detailed rules of brainstorming identified earlier.

Stroebe and Diehl (1991) found that procedural factors are the biggest contributor to lower than expected productivity in brainstorming groups. More specifically, how answers are given and recorded, people's not being able to provide all their input, interruptions, and side conversations can all reduce the free flow of information.

Paulus and Dzindolet (1993) agree with this assessment, but they believe that a variety of social-psychological factors can also pose potential difficulty for groups attempting to brainstorm. For example, some individuals may become "dependent" on the fast talkers in the group and withdraw from participating. Or the status of some in the group may inhibit the participation of others. Subgroups and cliques may also affect the group's productivity. Thus, what people often envision as a "no brainer" activity can be limited in effectiveness by a variety of factors.

IMPROVING THE SUCCESS OF BRAINSTORMING

1. *Overcoming Criticism and Discounting.* Smith (1993) has taken a hard look at factors he says inhibit psychological freedom in groups, which ultimately influence the creativity of group members and their willingness to risk. As a result of his research, he contends that the judgment or "discounting" of people's ideas represents the single most inhibiting factor to group productivity. Discounting can be subtle, including such tactics as rolling eyes at a suggestion or "yes, butting" an idea, and have a minor impact. Or it can include more overt nonverbal behavior, such as the "thumbs down" signal or stronger words such as "That's a stupid idea" that have a major impact on the production of further ideas (Smith, 1993). Brainstorming was originally established to help combat just such behaviors, but the subtle and not-so-subtle behaviors can still occur. If a group has a history of personal criticism and nonsupport, imposing a boundaried brainstorming process will not necessarily free people psychologically from their fear of criticism.

   Smith's (1993) research indicated, however, that the debilitating influence of discounting behaviors on a group's problem-solving performance can be mediated by training. Groups in which discounting occurred were the least productive and generated fewer ideas when compared to groups educated in how to avoid discounting. The fact that training in how to control judgmental behavior can actually increase group performance is a crucial finding.

2. *Raising Standards.* Paulus and Dzindolet (1993) performed a series of five studies to test social influences on group brainstorming. These studies concluded that if groups were provided standards with which to com-

pare their performance, the productivity of the groups would rise. Higher standards generally meant higher performance. This result reflects the same outcome as when individual expectations are raised artificially, resulting in increased productivity—or the Pygmalion effect (discussed in Chapter 5). As shown earlier, for a variety of reasons the very process of interacting with a group often has a positive impact on attitudes of participants. Thus, although the process itself may not be more productive than other techniques (nominal technique, for example), interactive brainstorming groups perceived their ideas to be better and thought they had generated more of them than they actually did (Paulus and Dzindolet, 1993; Stroebe et al., 1992). It appears that many brainstorming groups simply feel good about themselves and their product. Other things being equal, if a process of work can help people to feel better about their work, it is not far-fetched to assume that they will also feel better about themselves, their group, and their potential. Purposeful strategies that improve morale without raising costs or reducing productivity appears to have few downsides.

OTHER METHODS OF GENERATING IDEAS

Brainstorming is meant to reduce inhibitions, encourage new ideas, legitimize the unthinkable, and push participants past the bounds of their normally restricted thinking. Over the years, a variety of methods related to brainstorming, which can be used with small groups, have been developed (Gordon, 1961; Phillips, 1948; Prince, 1970; Rickards, 1974).

NOMINAL GROUP TECHNIQUE It has been noted that groups that use conventional interactive techniques tend to pursue a limited train of thought (Dunnette, Campbell, and Jaastad, 1963; Taylor, Berry, and Block, 1958); confer undue influence on high-status people (Dalkley and Helmer, 1963; Hare, 1976; Torrance, 1955; and Tuckman and Lorge, 1962); and generate group pressure for conformity (Hoffman, 1979). There also arise dysfunctional hidden-agenda effects (Collaros and Anderson, 1969) and an amount of time required for the group to maintain itself (Maier and Hoffman, 1962).

The nominal group technique (NGT) (Delbecq, Van de Ven, and Gustafson, 1975) was developed to gain the benefits of group participation and improve group participation while minimizing competition, domination by a few individuals, and the pressure of time constraints. The nominal group technique is most frequently used to generate goals and choose among alternative goals or policies.

In an impressive series of eight studies—involving 228 groups—that compared NGT with conventional interactive techniques, NGT was found to be superior in every instance (Carr, 1975; Chung and Ferris, 1971; Frederick, 1976; Gustafson et al., 1973; Nemiroff, Pasmore, and Ford, 1976; Van de Ven and Delbecq, 1974; and White, Blythe, and Corrigan, 1977). As a result, it is being used with increasing frequency. NGT is a two-stage process. Individuals work separately in the first, or elicitation stage, then work as an interacting group on the evaluation (choosing) stage. The first stage involves generating alternative means, generating alternative goals, or deciding on the best answer. The second stage involves the group collectively listing and then evaluating the plans, ideas, or judgments that were generated in the first stage (McGrath, 1984).

Fox (1989) has since introduced some modifications to arrive at an improved nominal group technique (INGT). This consists of communicating the purpose of meeting in advance to participants, and inviting them to submit any ideas they have on 3 × 5 cards. The cards are duplicated and sent to each participant in advance. Participants are asked to bring the full list, and their suggested changes or combinations, to the meeting. To reduce further the power of personality or status at the evaluation stage in the meeting, Fox recommends that each participant use a 3 × 5 card to state his or her concern, suggestion, or modification. The facilitator reads the cards to the group.

INGT is appropriate for identifying and evaluating options, positions, or problems; solving a problem when no standard is available; and reviewing and refining written proposals or other documents. Typically, an INGT is designed to address one purpose in a 1½-to-3-hour session. For example, a meeting might be devoted to identify and then to order the most pressing problems confronting a group. Then a second meeting is used to solve one of the top-priority problems identified.

Either type of nominal group technique can be powerful because it allows individuals to generate ideas independently (the creativity of brainstorming) and then brings them together to evaluate those ideas. Some feel it offers the best of both worlds.

COMPUTER-INTERACTIVE GROUPS What happens to productivity when we are able to remove the social inhibitors that often accompany interactive groups? Early on (Osborn, 1957; Maier, 1963), the notion of synergy evolved in relation to the natural piggybacking that occurred when it was discovered that individuals would build on the ideas of others, often in a manner that helped create new concepts and ideas. With the synergy, however, also came competition, and certain negative behaviors such as blocking and discounting. Dennis and Valacich (1994) thought that some of these negative consequences would disappear if a computer were introduced into the equation. True to their hypothesis, their fully-connected, intact computer groups outperformed face-to-face groups in both quantity and quality of work performance. The computer groups, given the same tasks, apparently were not distracted by the "noise" of their personal interactions and could focus more directly on the task at hand. Evidently the groups dependent on verbal interaction were more linear and unable to engage in the "simultaneous conversations" that could occur in computer-generated problem solving (Dennis and Valacich, 1994). Thus, it appears that part of the computer group's success could be attributed to "multiple monologues." Such an interactive process, in other words, fosters multiple conversations appearing on the screen at the same time and, as a result, stimulates more ideas and overall productivity with fewer blocking behaviors. Similar studies (Aiken and Riggs, 1993) have confirmed that both the idea generation and consolidation process can occur via computers, without verbal communication, at a higher level of both productivity and satisfaction. We are in an interesting time of learning and adaptation as we attempt to combine the advantages of face-to-face groups with the benefits of computer-generated brainstorming. The next decade will provide new breakthroughs in the blending of technology, distance learning, and face-to-face problem solving.

One can easily imagine a number of creative variations on this theme. For example, a group of seven or eight people is asked to develop perhaps 10 ideas around a particular theme in a brainstorming fashion. The ideas are then discussed openly in terms of the strengths of various items. A second group, which has been watching the activity quietly from outside the group, is then asked after 10 or 15 minutes of discussion to switch places with the first group. They are requested to develop 10 new ideas, considering the strengths discussed by the first group. They then discuss their ideas, again focusing on strengths. Finally, after 15 minutes or so of discussion, clusters of four are formed by two members from each group. These clusters (approximately four or five) are then asked to develop two or three of the best ideas that seem to incorporate as many as possible of the strengths suggested in both of the large groups. These finely tuned ideas are then presented to the entire group perhaps an hour later. A group that is representative of the whole then determines which idea or combination of ideas best suit their requirements. The advantages of such a design include

- the generating of ideas in a nonthreatening atmosphere
- a relatively nonjudgmental screening process
- the opportunity to build on one set of ideas after listening to benefits, thus reaching beyond ordinary limits or boundaries
- the development of competition in the best sense of the word as individuals in the second group of eight try to generate new and even better ideas, and the

groups of four attempt to develop the best idea or combination of ideas knowing that three or four other groups are doing the same thing

- full participation by a large number of individuals
- the utilization of individual resources, both in the development of ideas and in the important critiquing and selecting phase
- the efficient utilization of time itself

ROUND ROBIN GROUPS Another creative means of generating ideas involves a small group of perhaps five individuals (simultaneous groups of five can be working on the same problem at the same time). Five problems that need solving and are recognized as open-ended are selected by the group. Generally, these are operational problems—those that influence people who work together, are hindering a particular task, or are seen as within the purview of the group working on them. They should be problems that do not depend on some outside authority for determination. Each individual writes the problem he or she has been given on the top of three 5-by-8-inch cards and then proceeds to write a different idea or solution on each card. After perhaps five minutes, each individual passes his or her three cards to the next individual, who then writes a new solution or idea on each of the three cards. Ideas can be original or simply constructive additions to what is already there. After each individual has had the opportunity to respond to all the problems, each original problem is summarized by one person, integrating the ideas from each of the three cards onto newsprint. These are then considered by the whole group of five, whose job is to discuss the pros and cons of the various ideas and determine whether a creative and operationally viable idea emerges. Obviously, such an approach assumes that the group has the necessary time (from one to two days) to work effectively on the various ideas. If less time is available, a variation of the design would be to develop only one or two ideas and use a slightly different manner of passing the various cards through the group.

THE WILDEST IDEA Strange as it seems, one reason why creativity is minimal in a group of creative individuals is that permission is not given to be "wild and crazy." Telling individuals in either a brainstorming group or nominal group to generate the wildest ideas they can imagine in relation to a particular problem elicits thoughts that never would be considered in the normal course of events, when most people are usually worried about their image or what is appropriate. Thus, when a group is bogged down, ideas are not coming, and frustration is mounting in a problem-solving effort, the simple request to drop all pretense and let go for five minutes with the most outrageous ideas possible will inject fun, energy, and new interest into the group. In addition, it is very likely that among the "wild and crazy" ideas lie the seeds to some creative new approaches to a solution.

SYNECTICS

William Gordon (1961) worked for years with methods for expanding the vision and creativity of people in problem-solving situations. Dissatisfied with the constructive yet limiting approaches of brainstorming and nominal groups, he experimented with a variety of methods that would release some of the restricted capacity we have for creative problem solving. Gordon saw our ability to speculate as the key to removing normal resistances and the stereotypical and predictable traps we often fall into while solving problems. From this assumption, Gordon developed his *synectics* theory:

> The word *synectics,* from the Greek, means the joining together of different and apparently irrelevant elements. Synectics theory applies to the integration of diverse individuals into a problem-stating, problem-solving group. It is an operational theory for the conscious use of preconscious psychological mechanisms present in man's creative activity (Gordon, 1961, p. 1).

PREREQUISITES OF A SUCCESSFUL SYNECTICS GROUP In their study of problem solving with groups, Gordon and Prince and their colleagues discovered a number of elements that must be present. Just as a synectics excursion must evolve out of the needs of a group and cannot be "canned," although we can provide some productive guidelines, there are no easy formulas for helping a group work more effectively together. Following are some critical areas that merit attention in any problem-solving approach but are of particular importance to those using synectics in a group context[3]:

1. It is necessary to maximize participation and convince individuals that their ideas are valued, which will increase feelings of trust, openness, and willingness to risk. Destructive competition and the developing of win–lose attitudes are the aspects of traditional problem solving that must go. Thus, a prerequisite to any synectics group is paying attention to the need to develop effective group process, with members aware of their impact on the group, and a willingness of the group to monitor its own behavior.
2. A critical factor in any problem-solving group is the willingness and ability of group members to listen. People are so busy selling their own ideas, proving themselves, and reacting to personality rather than words that it is a wonder we hear as much as we do. There are so many intrusions into our listening that something needs to be done that legitimizes "hearing" others and that protects us from our own inclinations to "yell and sell." Active listening (see Chapter 1) is one of the central themes of synectics.

3. See Rickard's discussion (1974, pp. 71–73).

Basically, it means being aware of both the verbal and the nonverbal messages being communicated, as well as the feelings that often carry the real information. By rephrasing, paraphrasing, or in some manner feeding back what we hear another saying, we can make speakers less defensive because they realize they have been heard. Individuals who know they have been heard are less inclined to say it one more time. Thus, if active listening can be built into the problem-solving process and individuals know that it is part of the game, an immediate change in climate can be detected. When we feel understood, it matters less whether the idea itself is eventually adopted because we personally feel accepted.

3. A rather simple pattern that occurs in many groups is created out of our desire to protect ourselves and to put responsibility or, on occasion, blame onto another individual. The pattern is one of asking questions. You might respond to this "wondrous" revelation by shouting back at the page, "Of course, problem solving is all asking questions, probing reality, testing the value of an idea." True, but the trap is that behind nearly every question an individual asks is a statement—often an implied answer. The question, then, often incorporates a message we are trying to give with minimal risk, putting the individual who responds on the spot and absolving us from responsibility for the implied statement. Thus, by asking questions, we often shift attention and a sense of blame or guilt onto the person being asked. Questions tend to corner the individual, leaving him or her feeling trapped and vulnerable—and likely to justify or rationalize his or her response with much more vigor than might otherwise be necessary.

   Individuals using synectics attempt to reduce the number of questions being asked and instead encourage participants to make statements that provide new meaning or clarification to a problem or another idea. In addition, statements provide information about one's own point of view, indicate alternatives, or request additional information. Statements are direct, and they tend to establish ownership immediately. This leads to a sense of integrity in the group and, again, helps to build a climate of trust.

4. One of the crucial differences between a synectics-type meeting and others is that individuals with special influence or power are requested not to run the meeting. It is assumed that their ideas are crucial but their influence is not. All too often the leader is also the boss, with his or her own agenda, whose style and status can create a sense of intimidation, resistance, fear, dependency or even anger that can corrupt the open problem-solving approach that is being attempted. As long as thirty-five years ago, Gordon recognized the seeds of groupspeak (see Chapter 5) as well as the idea of "seduction of the leader," as reflected in his recom-

mendation that leaders participate and not lead in synectic groups. Turning facilitation over to a neutral party, the synectics process "neutralizes" the influence of the boss. Selecting a group leader who can lead the problem solving from a position of neutrality and take an objective view of the process boosts the group's chance of success. Of course, such a leader should be acceptable to the group, should not be easily manipulated, and should have skills in active listening, goal setting, and group maintenance.

5. Perhaps one of the most insidious factors that undermine productive group problem solving stems from the natural inclination of group members to be overly critical of each other. Most of us have cut our teeth on a view of group participation that encourages criticism. The problem is that such criticism is often born out of a desire to minimize someone else's success and has little to do with a desire for group success. If we can make someone's ideas appear inadequate, perhaps our own will grow in stature. A simple rule developed in synectics meetings—focusing at first on the strengths of an idea—is validating of the giver and reduces the inclination to defend. In addition, focusing on the positive aspects of an idea often reveals that part of a solution can be used. Even when the idea is clearly inadequate, the first effort is directed at finding ways of improving the idea so that it may be workable. This method reflects the conviction that the more good choices a group has, the better will be the quality of the final product.
6. A synectics viewpoint encourages effective group process. Many of the suggestions would be useful even in more traditional, well-ordered, rational approaches to problem solving. But they are absolutely critical for synectics participants, because at the center of their approach is the *excursion*. There are many ways for an excursion to occur, but all have the common theme of pulling the problem solver away from premature solutions, from patterned, expected, or predictable thought. The excursion is designed to relax the group, to build a sense of purpose with the added dimension of fun so that participants will be inclined to move beyond the tried and true, away from any preconception of "the right way." The excursion is a trip away from reality and the constraints of expected thought into a realm where unrelated, untested, and creative ideas are valued. Clearly, for participants to allow themselves the freedom to try on totally different, often outrageous, and absurd ideas requires a climate of trust and openness in which there is no fear of being judged and there are no recriminations.

   An excursion might be a metaphor, scrutinizing an object and fantasizing about its qualities, or visualizing being shipwrecked on a raft with a few implements of survival. By taking the group "away" and freeing them to think outside the proverbial box, the leader lubricates the thinking process. Having accumulated new, apparently unrelated information, the facilitator will ask a question such as, "Think of as many ways as possible our metaphor (or example) can be used to solve our problem." The group is given permission to abstract from the excursion the seeds of ideas which can then be planted into the real situation. Thus, a fishhook from the survival excursion may bring to light an idea concerning how to "hook" the support of labor in a management–union disagreement.

Though ample evidence attests to the effectiveness of synectics, the method is used relatively rarely. Perhaps the benefits are not great enough to warrant the cost in time, the expense of an outside facilitator (few organizational trainers have the necessary skills), and the trust required to complete the process successfully. A study by Thamis and Woods (1984) reviewed a longitudinal study within the research-and-development arm of a large multinational organization, where synectics are used along with other creative problem-solving techniques aimed at stimulating innovation and creative thinking. To the investigators' surprise, even though synectics was fairly effective, it apparently lost ground to a less successful technique and was eventually phased out of use. In searching for reasons why a problem-oriented group would voluntarily choose mediocrity over a more successful method, Thamis and Woods discovered that the managers using synectics did not like what they deemed its lack of consequence and logic. In a sense, their linear, left-brain attitudes and habits found the creative excursions into nonlinear thinking too uncomfortable, and they opted for the more traditional but less effective approach.

Who Should Decide—The Leader or the Group?

The bulk of this chapter has been involved with how groups and individuals can become more effective problem solvers. Problem solving is nothing more than the process used for developing alternative forms of action that resolve a source of tension, an uncertainty, or a difficulty. Without giving some thought to *how* we solve problems, we have seen our inclination to fool ourselves, narrow our vision, not look at relevant consequences, and sabotage ourselves without even knowing it. Although we have alluded to the actual selection of various choices after certain creative deliberations, we have not talked about the implications of decision making itself.

THE LEADER'S ROLE

As suggested before, many decisions result naturally from a thorough problem analysis in which clear goals have been established, alternatives developed and systematically weighed, and potential consequences measured. Yet there is a way of thinking about decision making that is essential for both the leader and the participant. The critical questions that forever play on the mind of the leader is "Should I make this decision? Can I risk leaving it to the group?" Leaders get themselves into trouble when they are not willing to define the boundaries of their power—when they refuse to let their constituencies know the limits of their influence. By not defining their range of authority, they are capable of arbitrarily making any decision they wish, or they can benevolently turn authority over to the group if so inclined. Their failure to give real definition to how decisions will be made creates a climate of uncertainty, suspicion, and dependency. Many leaders are fearful that by defining their real areas of decision-making power they will leave themselves vulnerable to the irrationality and perhaps irresponsibility of the group, for which they will ultimately be accountable. They don't realize that groups tend to be thoughtful and rational (often too much so) and, if provided with the necessary time and effective problem-solving procedures, will often contribute significantly and make the best decision.

Effective leaders, then, are willing to look carefully at their areas of influence and let their subordinates know categorically what decisions they themselves will always make and what decisions other groups or individuals will be responsible for. At the beginning of any problem-solving activity, the group should reach an understanding about how any decision will be made. If a group's ideas are advisory, the group's advisory status and the reason for it should be made very clear. If a decision for eventual action is to be in the hands of the group, then the particular decision-making method should be understood and discussed. All too often, the dominant players in a group focus on the norms that yield the greatest advantage to themselves (Murnighan, 1985). Leaders should take care when possible to legitimize *all* members by establishing a decision-making process in which everyone participates.

This decision on making a decision occurs prior to the problem solving, because people often lose their rationality when vested interests are threatened. Thus, people naturally protect themselves regardless of their goodwill toward the group. A group is usually more willing to commit itself to a fair decision-making method (such as a two-thirds majority) prior to problem solving, before they experience the fear that they may actually have to give up their own idea and go along with one that is less acceptable to them. The integrity of problem solving is often salvaged by applying this insight and laying the ground rules early. Let's briefly discuss a few simple approaches to making decisions.

SIMPLE MAJORITY RULE

A group should be willing to accept this approach only when the decision is of relatively little consequence and they need a rather quick response. We all know that there are many ways to block a decision so that implementation never occurs. In theory, decisions are made to be implemented. But if 45 percent of a group disagrees with a decision that has significance for them and the life of the group or organization, then the quick-and-dirty majority rule will be perceived as a means of control and manipulation by the majority. Even if the decision is implemented, the large minority may spend its time deviously attempting to disrupt the decision or seeking the means to overthrow it. Finally, invoking majority rule is an easy way of shutting off discussion and the thoughtful views of the minority. This can leave the group wounded and result in future insensitivity and psychological "paybacks." Thus, the consequences of how a decision is made may have important repercussions later. However, Falk and Falk (1981) found that majority rule reduces power inequalities in groups that have members who vary widely in status and power. Campbell (1981) found that a rule by majority can be more useful than that of a plurality because the subgroup coalitions that form can respond to and reflect individual preferences.

TWO-THIRDS MAJORITY RULE

This approach, also called *plurality rule,* should be used for decisions of greater consequence. If individuals have had the opportunity to discuss various alternatives thoroughly and agree prior to the discussion that a two-thirds vote is "fair," members find it easier to accept the eventual decision. Somehow, the feelings of manipulation that often accompany simple majority rule occur less frequently when members know that it takes 67 percent of the group to influence the total group.

CONSENSUS

This is a terribly misused and abused approach to problem solving and decision making. When using it, a number of conditions must exist, but these are rarely seen in working groups.

- A level of trust exists in the group that allows honesty, directness, and candor.
- The group is aware of its own process and can deal with its own behavior openly so that individuals cannot dominate or manipulate the group, so that ideas are actively solicited, and so that members listen and support each other as individuals even when disagreeing with each other's ideas.
- The group is not leader-dominated.
- There is time available to consider opinions, alternatives, and consequences so that time itself does not become a coercive element in the process.

- Members of the group are privy to all necessary information prior to the meeting so that they are familiar with critical issues and can respond intelligently.

Groups that do enter a decision-making situation under these conditions find consensus an invigorating and often efficient approach. Those that do not will often find the process painful, aggravating, and nonproductive. The major reason why consensus fails is that people do not understand it. It is not a method that demands *agreement* by the total group. It simply requires that individuals be willing to *go along* with the group's predominant view and carry out the implications of the decision in good faith. People may disagree with the view of the great majority. In fact, they are encouraged to hold onto their position until they are willing to live with the decision being recommended. It takes trust to argue for a position in the face of group pressure, and just as much trust to let go of a position and go with the group.

A group that wants to use a consensual approach to decision making must be willing to develop the skills and discipline and take the time necessary to make it work. Without these, the group becomes highly vulnerable to domination or intimidation by a few and to psychological game playing by individuals unwilling to "let go" as the group moves toward a well-conceived decision—and toward inefficiency. Most people are not well trained in the consensus process, so under normal conditions groups are likely to find it neither efficient nor pleasurable. This is because good consensus building induces the need to acknowledge and resolve conflict, which is minimized in the nominal group method. Furthermore, because people are rarely trained in conflict resolution, the consensus process, with its emphasis on grappling with conflict, can alienate members of the group who do not perceive it as a legitimate or welcome part of the problem-solving process.

But even when groups are not particularly well trained in the consensus-building process, once agreement is reached, group satisfaction and the willingness to support a decision are usually high. Furthermore, group members who complete a consensus process tend to be positive about their participation in the group (Schweiger et al., 1986; Tjosvold and Field, 1983). One study (DeStephen, 1983) showed that the more feedback and discussion were encouraged during the decision-making process, the higher was the group's satisfaction with the decision, and this was consistently the case in groups rated high in consensus.

Thus, if people are willing to pay the price in time and training, to see conflict as a natural and healthy part of decision making, and to let go of their personal agendas in favor of what appears to be good for the group, then consensus may work and will certainly provide many benefits. Satisfaction and commitment to the eventual decision will be the primary outcomes. And because successful consensus building requires effective listening and analysis, the result is often a more skilled and cohesive group prepared to solve problems and make decisions even more effectively in the future.

DELEGATED DECISIONS

The more decisions can be delegated to representative bodies or even to individuals, the more efficient most groups will be, especially those composed of more than seven or eight individuals. Delegated decisions hinge on parties being willing to "take the pulse" of a group, testing ideas thoroughly, before moving ahead with a particular one. Again, this depends on the members trusting that decisions made for the group are not based on the vested interests of individuals. Clearly, decisions of a controversial nature should be accorded a problem-solving forum that allows maximum participation. Essential to delegated decisions are procedures for critical review and accountability so that members of any delegated task force realize how the effectiveness of their efforts is to be measured.

DOUBLE VOTE

Many organizations would like to involve relatively large numbers of people in decision making on a wide range of issues that influence their lives. This rarely occurs, however, because leaders believe that these people will not be as rational as they themselves would be or because they fear that an emotional speech or bandwagon effect might influence the outcome in some irrational and undesirable manner. The following method, although imperfect, has proved highly successful in minimizing these legitimate concerns.

Let's imagine that as a result of a thoughtful problem-solving process, a large number of alternatives are being considered for a department of 100 people. The ideas have been drawn from committee and task-force recommendations that have involved a large number of the people at one time or another. Being considered are ideas ranging from alternatives for using the parking lot to methods for participative management, and recommendations, some of which require choosing between two alternatives. Management has agreed that all the ideas are acceptable if the group desires them. Ideas not selected may be explored further at a later date, but present policy will continue if a new idea is not selected. The method for decision making is as follows:

1. Each alternative that is proposed is written as a brief paragraph stating as specifically as possible what changes will occur, when and how they are to be accomplished, and how they will be monitored.

2. The task force or committee responsible for the recommendation is noted so that clarification and discussion can continue during the coming week.
3. The following week a ballot is distributed. Ideally, this would occur at a large meeting where time would be provided for further clarification but not debate, because it is assumed that controversial issues have been discussed at length during the preceding week. Because the voting process is based on 100 percent of the distributed ballots, a meeting at which those who are present vote is often preferred.
4. Individuals are requested to vote for each alternative they find acceptable.
5. Any alternative that receives a two-thirds vote is placed on a second ballot. A report containing all of the results is distributed the next day. The following week, members are encouraged to lobby and discuss their views prior to a second vote. The first vote serves as a reality test and energizes participants to new levels of interest.
6. The second vote, held a week after the first, relates only to those items that received at least two-thirds of the vote on the first ballot. Those alternatives receiving a two-thirds vote on the second ballot are then accepted to be implemented. A representative group is selected from the total population to help in the implementation phase and to monitor the progress of each recommendation for several months.

The benefits of such a complex and time-consuming process are many. First, participation, discussion, and influence on the system are being exercised by individuals who must live with their own decisions. Second, knowing that ideas not accepted in the voting can be raised at a later date encourages members of the organization to seek constructive change and support for their ideas. As a result, they feel potent and interested in the life of the organization. The major drawback is that the leader of such an organization must have a clear view of which areas of influence are shared, and this must be communicated specifically so that false expectations are not raised. Finally, the leader must be willing to accept the group's recommendations even though he or she does not necessarily agree totally with them. Limits on policy issues and on the expenditure of funds can be explored before alternatives reach the ballot.

In many ways, effective decision making requires as much creativity and judgment as the formal problem-solving process. There is no question that decision making should not be taken for granted and that it can be designed in a variety of ways, depending on the realities of each situation and the goals of the leader. Issues of participation, acceptance, and overall morale are all influenced by how a leader decides to decide. For participants, it is important always to understand what is happening, and why, and whether the process seems equitable. Often, leaders have never considered the implications of their own decision-making behavior and would be open to alternatives once educated to the consequences of their actions.

FREQUENTLY ASKED QUESTIONS

The following questions are frequently asked in relation to the use of groups in problem solving and decision making:

ARE GROUPS MORE EFFECTIVE IN PROBLEM SOLVING THAN INDIVIDUALS, ESPECIALLY CONSIDERING THE NUMBER OF HOURS INVESTED? Over the past twenty years there has been little evidence to refute the idea that there are good reasons for using groups in some problem-solving endeavors. However, a few of these reasons involve efficiency. Increasingly, research suggests that individuals and nominal groups are equal to or more effective than "natural groups" (assuming no training) when undertaking problem-solving activities (Campbell, 1968; Rotter and Portergal, 1969; Principle and Neeley, 1983). (A nominal group, as defined earlier, is one in which ideas are generated by members working independently and then pooled; a *natural group* is one in which members work cooperatively at the same task.) Some working groups are slowed down and reduced to a level of performance equal to the slowest member (McCurdy and Lambert, 1952); others become polarized as a result of their group discussions (Moscovici and Zavalloni, 1969). Furthermore, even in groups designed to facilitate the open sharing of ideas, differences in status and perceived authority can inhibit productivity (Collaros and Anderson, 1969; Voytas, 1967; Vroom, Grant, and Cotton, 1969). Yet it is true that in a number of specific instances, a group effort can be justified over that of nominal groups or individuals. For example, when a task involves integrating a number of perceptual and intellectual skills, it has been found that group members tend to supplement one another as resources (Napier, 1967). Also, when a major goal of the group is to create commitment to certain goals or to influence opinions, the involvement of individuals appears essential (Kelley and Thibaut, 1969; Lewin, 1948).

DOES TRAINING ENHANCE THE PROBLEM-SOLVING CAPABILITIES OF A GROUP? There is still little research comparing the quantitative and qualitative products of trained and well-practiced groups with those of individuals or nominal groups. However, the early evidence that laboratory training sessions, in which individuals are given the opportunity to learn group skills through the systematic observation of their own performance on a variety of tasks, have impressive transfer value to other group situations (Hall and Williams, 1970; Stuls, 1969; Tolela, 1967) still holds today.

In one interesting experiment, requiring the solution of a specific task-oriented problem, groups were involved in an interdependent, multistage problem-solving process. Trained groups revealed greater improvement, had higher-quality products, and used the knowledge of members more effectively than untrained groups. In fact, it was shown that trained groups of institutionalized, neuropsychiatric patients scored significantly better than untrained managerial groups, which had been assumed to have greater knowledge of procedures and problem-solving operations (Hall and Williams, 1970). Although such research is limited because of the type of training undertaken and the problems involved, the implications are clear. Effective training can maximize the benefits possible within the framework of problem-solving groups. It is important to remember, however, that a general decision-making model does not *always* apply to all groups (Poole, 1981). A group's membership structure, task, and stage of development all affect how it makes decisions.

WHAT ARE THE STRENGTHS AND LIMITATIONS OF THE DEMOCRATIC APPROACH TO DECISION MAKING IN GROUPS? For most working groups, it seems that the key to decision making is a rather loose concept of the democratic process and the rule of the majority. They provide governing "by the people," reduce the threat of tyranny from within the group, and ensure that at least half the members will support a particular issue. Nevertheless, this approach to decision making has a number of severe limitations for a group that must live by its own decisions. For example:

1. Under pressure of a vote, individual decisions are often made for the wrong reasons. This is partly the result of different levels of knowledge and understanding present in the group and partly because of extraneous pressures (friendships, propaganda, payment of past favors, and so forth). Thus, the group often loses sight of issues in favor of other variables, such as voting "for the person."
2. During discussions leading to a vote, it is assumed that people will have an opportunity to express their opinions and to influence the group, but this is seldom the case. Many individuals simply do not have the skills to influence their own destinies in groups. It is a rare group in which silence is not taken as consent, the shy person is drawn into the discussion, and everyone's intent is to consider all ideas, not just to project their own. Therefore, the basis on which a vote is taken is often faulty or at least premature.
3. The will of the majority can be used effectively as a means of reducing tension (strong differences of opinion) and the time needed to discuss a problem. A vote can be a means of getting on to other business. This, of course, fails to take into consideration whether support for the decision is enough to ensure effective implementation.

4. Power and despotism are problems in a democratically run group. How often is a dissenting minority perceived as a disrupting influence? How often is minority opinion seen as a threat to the cohesion of the group? And how often are such pressures used to coerce dissenters back into line? If a vote is used to override the opinion of a minority faction, the vote itself stands to further polarize the group and magnify the divisive lines upon which the vote is taken.
5. Similarly, rather than providing a solution, a vote may actually create more problems. Instead of resolving differences, a minority may spend its time proving the vote wrong and reasserting itself in the eyes of the group. Or, labeled as radicals or malcontents, it may try to live up to its image and actually become a disruptive force.
6. By encouraging a move toward quick decisions, the democratic approach may foster a tendency to simplify problems in terms of either–or dichotomies, and failure to explore all the issues influencing a problem may result. A quick vote based on an inadequate exploration of issues will inevitably create difficulties. Members may have second thoughts and fail to support the vote or rationalize their vote and become intransigent.

Given that these kinds of problems are often linked with a simplistic notion of the democratic process, it might seem worthwhile to study other alternatives. The fact is that the operation of a truly democratic group requires enormous patience, understanding, and cooperation. It also is very time-consuming. Few groups are willing to face these realities, so they reduce the process to one of convenience rather than effectiveness. Gaenslen (1980) concluded that a group decision-making process that combines trust, the desire for unanimity, and advocacy may yield both efficiency and a sense of democracy.

HOW USEFUL IS *ROBERTS RULES OF ORDER* AS A PROCEDURE WITHIN WHICH TO MAKE DECISIONS? *Robert's Rules of Order* is based on the notion of debate (Robert, 1943). It is a complicated procedural method keyed to the majority vote and the democratic process. It can probably be stated fairly that nearly everyone who has worked in groups has at one time or another been frustrated by the limitations of this system. Those who understand the complexities of the process can easily control the meeting, but few people know the rules of a quorum, tabling a motion, adjourning, or even amending a motion.

Another problem is that because the system is based on debate, there is a constant tendency toward polarization. Furthermore, it is relatively easy for the majority to stifle discussion by pushing for an early vote or using some other defensive measure to shift the focus of discussion. Finally, because the system is not based on a cooperative and interdependent approach to problem solving, there tends to be a great deal of politicking, bargaining, and bidding for power outside the meeting itself. In relatively small groups (under twenty-five or thirty), the method reduces open communication and amount of participation. In larger groups, if participants understand the system, it can prove useful in organizing discussion and stabilizing work procedures. Again, large numbers of participants present a limiting factor in the decision-making process, so accepting *Robert's Rules* entails gaining order at the expense of interdependence and, to some degree, cooperation.

IS DECISION BY CONSENSUS A VIABLE METHOD FOR SMALL-GROUP DECISION MAKING? Reaching a decision through consensus represents the ideal in terms of full group participation, but it is by no means the most efficient or least tension-producing approach to decision making. It assumes that a decision will not be made without the approval of every member, but that does not mean each member must agree totally with what is going to happen. It simply indicates that each member is willing to go along with the decision, at least for the time being. The process relies on a willingness to compromise.

Immature groups that lack skill in processing their own interpersonal behavior may find this a painful approach to problem solving. Unlike a system based on majority vote (basically a tension-reducing system), decision by consensus seeks out alternative viewpoints and then struggles to find a solution at the expense of no particular group or person. The value in using this sometimes slow and belabored process is that by the time a decision is reached, it does represent a group decision, and therein lies an important component of support. Schweiger, Sandberg, and Ragan (1986) found that satisfaction with groups, acceptance of group decisions, and willingness to continue working with decisions were all higher with the consensus approach to decision making than with other approaches tested.

At times, a provisional straw vote is used to test sources of differing opinion so that the full dimension of a problem can be explored. If it becomes coercive, the process breaks down. Usually it requires time, familiarity within the group, and trust in the process before consensus becomes effective. Once this occurs, however, decisions can be made rapidly, because there is a willingness to get to the core of the issue quickly, analyze the alternatives, and then compromise in finding the solution.

WHY DO INSTITUTIONAL COMMITTEES BECOME SO INEFFECTIVE? In many organizations, ongoing committees are used in an effort to help get the business of the organization done and allow some participation of the members in areas of importance to them. There are membership committees, finance committees, disciplinary committees, and so on. The problem is that most committees themselves become part of an inefficient hierarchical system that has developed over time and have little built-in flexibility for change. Procedures become routine and more complex, and the interest of those participating wanes. Within the committees themselves, there are other barriers—for example:

1. Decision-making procedures are usually imposed and based on tradition rather than on what is most useful.
2. People are often appointed to committees, and even if they volunteer, they may be there for a variety of reasons (from interest in meeting important people to helping out a friend who is chairperson).
3. Often committees lack the power to implement the decisions they make; thus, they feel their own impotence.
4. Committees seldom see processing their own interpersonal behaviors as part of the job, especially if the group meets only once every three or four weeks.
5. Committees are not necessarily composed of the people best equipped to discuss the issues confronting the group.

ARE THERE USEFUL ALTERNATIVES TO THE COMMITTEE SYSTEM? One possible alternative is the use of a task force. Ideally, when a special problem arises within an organization, instead of pushing it off to an already overburdened committee, management appoints or elects a task force. This group is composed of representative individuals (or, in some cases, individuals with special skills) who are given the job of solving the problem. It is assumed that their recommendations will be taken most seriously, and, in essence, they are given the power of the large group. Task forces are unlike committees in several ways.

- They often have more power.
- Appointments are for a short term.
- A definite, measurable outcome will be the result.
- The members may develop working procedures that best fit the nature of the task and are not limited by tradition or precedent groups.
- They must work through all phases of the problem-solving process, including the diagnosis, actual implementation, and follow-up.
- Because of the immediacy of the problem, there should be high motivation and involvement, especially because the product will be its own reward.

One potential problem with a task force is that, given support and some feeling of potency, these groups generate recommendations that are much less conservative than might be expected and that are much more thoroughly documented than usual. Unhappy is the executive who turns an issue over to a task force and then, instead of the problem losing importance and momentum—which often happens when problems are referred to committees—the task force provides the organization with clear methods for altering the situation. These methods may unveil other problems.

It is often true that task forces are also used for political purposes. The aim is to look as though something is being done, but the real objective is to mark time. An example of this situation occurs when prestigious people are appointed to a task force but, because of other commitments, find it impossible to do the kind of job necessary. The final product is a watered-down and poorly conceived attempt to look competent with a minimum commitment to action.

WHAT INFLUENCE DOES SOMEONE WHO TALKS EXCESSIVELY OR IN A DOMINATING MANNER TEND TO HAVE ON A GROUP? There are most certainly talkers who are not heard and who wield little influence on the life of a group. But for the most part, socially verbal talkers tend to have a high degree of influence over other members regardless of the chatterers' knowledge or ability (Hoffman, 1979). The simple fact of talking more than others may be all that is necessary to increase someone's impact on the group. It has even been shown that known talkers, when not dominating a conversation, often influence the problem-solving effort through their support of someone else's ideas. Thus, regardless of the intent of the talker (whether out of deviousness, personal need, or interest), talking garners influence. This is a major reason why many problem-solving designs have built-in mechanisms for ensuring greater freedom of participation and access of other members to the ideas of more retiring members. Brainstorming techniques and synectics excursions are but two approaches that address this problem.

Some time ago, Bottger (1984) resolved the conflict in the small-group literature regarding the hypothesis that member influence is determined by the quantity rather than the quality of someone's contribution. In a study of 33 problem-solving groups, Bottger did find that members attributed influence to leaders who commanded the most time. However, the actual *movement* in the group resulted more often from those who were perceived as having the most *expertise*.

It is interesting to note that groups in high-pressure conditions shared time less equitably than did groups not under pressure (Isenberg, 1981). In other words, group members experiencing more stress did a poorer job of sharing the opportunity to speak in the group. It helps to remember that individuals and groups work in settings that place a variety of demands on them.

DO WOMEN AS LEADERS IN SMALL GROUPS GARNER THE SAME RESPECT AND INFLUENCE AS MEN? Research suggests that the gender of a group's leader clearly influences the group. Even though male and female leaders may act the same, there is a tendency for women to be perceived more negatively or to have to act differently to gain leadership.

FOCUS ON DIVERSITY

Culture also affects who should make decisions. Some cultures encourage all members to defer to group leaders. Some expect women to defer to authority.

Also, groups composed primarily of men who have had little experience with a woman as leader show a degree of confusion. The confusion is related to how the men should relate to a woman who is not acting in a supportive (often secretarial) position. It is also confusing to the woman, who may have had little experience leading a primarily male group. In such a group, power and leadership issues remain unresolved longer. These results reflect more on the gender issue itself than on the actual behavior of the leader (Israeli, 1984; Owen, 1986; Staley, 1984). Thus, competent female leaders are often handicapped by unresolved gender issues or negative attitudes of those they are attempting to lead.

If a group is interested in exploring issues of gender, a good way to stimulate such learning is to create a group with a woman leader and allow ample time to "process" the issues that inevitably rise to the surface. No clever initiatives, games, or simulations need be developed. All that is necessary is a "real" task group with a real purpose and one real female leader. Issues of role, membership, expectations, influence, and authority will appear automatically (Reed, 1983).

Summary

Strange as it may seem in light of the many studies discussed in this chapter, group dynamics is still a novel idea in problem-solving theory. Nevertheless, research continues to point in the direction of common sense, confirming the importance of knowledge about groups in problem-solving and decision-making situations. The following statements summarize many points in this chapter and stand as generally accepted principles:

- Leaders must be trained in the way groups work so they can exploit the group process to advantage, not simply react to unanticipated consequences (Hunsaker, 1983).
- Attention to the development of trust and openness is necessary to successful problem solving and must be encouraged and rewarded in a group. Without these qualities, the group can be seduced into groupthink, which will lead to compliance, dependency, and ineffective results (Brightman and Verhoeven, 1986).
- An effective group creates a natural synergy, or the situation in which people working alone are not capable of achieving what the group can accomplish together. Over time, this will increase members' appreciation of the group, which in turn will increase their listening skills, willingness to take risks, abil-

ity to deal with conflict, and openness to new ideas—all essential in effective problem solving (Berry, 1983).

- A smoothly functioning problem-solving group has the ability and desire to deal with its own process so that it does not become blocked by, for example, violation of its own procedural norms, the wielding of undue influence by dominant members, the majority's insensitivity to the needs or ideas of the few, or the tendency to deal from bias and stereotypes rather than objective information (Fox, 1987; Phillips, Wood, and Pedersen, 1986).
- Successful problem-solving groups tend to develop a systematic problem-solving procedure that helps them analyze a problem in a step-wise fashion and reduces the tendency to leap to premature solutions (Hirokawa, 1980, 1983).
- The quality of problem solutions is often linked to a group's ability to generate diverse solutions, then to discuss them, and finally to choose from them the best possible alternative. Implicit in this process is a participant diversity that maximizes the potential of the ideation process (Wanous and Youtz, 1986).
- There is increasing evidence that the quality of a group's performance in problem-solving tasks is related to its cohesion. In a cost-conscious world, this suggests that we ought to invest in problem solving by directing resources toward increased training and team-building activities (Missing and Preble, 1985).
- The dominance of the problem-solving process by a few zealous people can be minimized by use of effective strategies (computer groups, nominal groups, round-robin groups, and the like) determined by the nature of the task (Brightman and Verhoeven, 1986).
- Whenever possible, those affected by the eventual solution should be represented in the problem-solving process.

EXERCISE 1 Brainstorming: Useful in Conducting an Effective Large-Group Needs Assessment

ACTION

Brainstorming can be used as a central activity in a design for assessing the needs of a group where active participation is desired on the part of the group members. The directions below are to be given to a group of 24 participants. (Many alternative formats could easily be designed, but the following one has proved successful.)

After a problem—an issue of relevance and concern to members—has been stated clearly, three large sheets of newsprint are placed next to each other in front of the group. Three participants are chosen as recorders, given markers, and asked to stand in front of one of the newsprints. The group is instructed that it will have between 3 and 5 minutes to list all the possible causes for this particular problem (on another occasion they might brainstorm solutions). The first recorder posts the first response, the second recorder the second, and so on. After approximately 3 minutes, the result should be 3 sheets with an equal number of responses.

The large group of 24 is then broken down into three groups of 8, each taking a sheet with causes for the problem. Their task, to be completed in about 30 minutes, is

1. to clarify and expand any of the statements.
2. to integrate similar statements and delete any that are irrelevant.
3. to develop from the items a list of causes that are most important to deal with immediately and that are within the power of the group (basic priorities).
4. to present this high-priority list of perhaps three causes to the total group of 24. In all, nine high-priority causal factors will have been identified. Some of these will be very nearly the same, so the final list will contain about five items.

If the group agrees that something must be done with these five causal factors, it may prove useful to halve the groups of eight and have each group of four design specific action solutions to two of the problems. Within 45 minutes or an hour the groups of four are to reconvene within their original group of eight and present their ideas to each other for a critique. This will take another 20 to 30 minutes. If integrating the ideas (solutions) is possible, it should be done.

Finally, the crystallized ideas of the three groups are presented to the entire group. There should be about nine separate ideas presented. It is very important that the facilitator stress the need to restrict the time of the various presentations to no more than 5 minutes. The main purpose of this session is to give visibility to the various ideas and bring some closure to the problem-solving process. Because the total time for this session will be between 2.5 and 3 hours, it is an exhausting process and may not result in final decisions. What often helps is to have a representative of each of the groups of four act as a steering committee and, at a later time, report on specific recommendations that incorporate the various solutions offered.

DISCUSSION

A number of practices in this exercise could be used under a variety of circumstances and with different kinds of problems as long as the following guidelines are met:

1. It is important that the ideas being explored are the result of the group's effort. This is the first step in building accountability for the eventual solutions.
2. If the ideas are developed in a nonevaluative atmosphere, there will be less of the vested interests that tend to be present in groups and that surround any important problem.
3. The process forces a look at a variety of alternative approaches *after* important causal factors have been isolated. This builds a norm into the group for exploring new ideas and stimulates interest and involvement in the process itself.
4. The participants must honor strict time limits during their various work sessions. Their being held accountable to other groups at the end of the brief work periods ensures a continuous flow of ideas, and withdrawal because of boredom is almost impossible. It seems to be very true that people will use the time available to them.
5. Each product is the result of a number of people's ideas, and this reduces the possibility of one or two vociferous people taking over the group. Even in the presentation, it is important that the presenting groups not try to sell their ideas, but simply reveal them.
6. Having a representative body make recommendations to the entire group based on *all* the members' efforts makes consensus much easier to use as a final decision-making device. By this time, the group should be ready to stand accountable for its own product. And, of course, the decision is only as good as the group's willingness to implement it.

EXERCISE 2 Phillips 66: Discussion and Decisions in a Large Group

OBJECTIVES

- To involve large numbers of people in discussion of topics relevant to them
- To maximize the use of time as a factor in reducing argument

- To ensure greater accountability in large groups, which tend to be impersonal

GENERAL DESCRIPTION

D. J. Phillips (1948) at first saw this method as a means of involving large numbers of people in the discussion of a particular issue. For example, after a presentation, debate, or panel, he would have the large group break into groups of six and develop, in about 6 minutes, a question that the group could agree was important to them. The relatively small groups would have their interest focused, many people would have an opportunity to interact, and they could have some impact on the total group's discussion. It was impossible for a few people to dominate the discussion, and the technique guaranteed a high rate of interest.

More recently, the method has been adapted to meet the needs of many groups. Members are given 6 minutes (it could just as easily be 10 or 15) to develop an agenda for the meeting. With all groups reporting, certain items are immediately perceived as having interest to many in the group. Or, in other sessions, members are asked to offer a solution for a particular issue. Usually 6 minutes is long enough to define and clarify the issue, and it has been shown that an enormous number of good ideas can be generated in a relatively short period of time and then refined later. Brief reports on these findings can be an important stimulating factor in the large group.

Others, including Maier (1963), have used adaptations of this method for groups with as many as 200 or 300 people. Groups of six are given a problem to solve or an issue to discuss, and then these groups are polled by the facilitator in terms of certain logical categories. Immediately the group gains a picture of how others feel and the range of ideas that exist in the group.

Of great importance in using this method is to make sure that the topics chosen are specific enough to allow an almost immediate discussion to get under way. Questions that are moralistic in tone only frustrate people because there is no hope for any kind of resolution in a limited period of time. Similarly, when looking at a particular problem, the participants should not be limited to an either-or type of response. Enjoyment lies in the opportunity to be creative and to look beyond the commonplace response. The great value of having many people together doing the same thing is that they are assured of wide-ranging responses that may not develop in a more traditional committee work group, which is partly controlled by past experience and behavior.

EXERCISE 3 The Acid Floor Test

OBJECTIVES

- To analyze decision making and problem solving under extreme time pressure
- To develop supportive roles within a group
- To observe individual behavior under stress—both facilitative and inhibiting

SETTING

This task is more effective when it is done competitively. If there are enough materials available, as many as three or four teams of from six to ten players can participate at the same time. If materials are limited, competitiveness can be achieved by placing a time restriction on the exercise (each team works in isolation). For each group that participates, it is necessary to have available eight empty number-10 cans. It is also helpful to have observers assigned to each group to watch carefully the nature of the problem solving that takes place, how resources in the group are maximized, and how leadership develops within the context of the activity.

ACTION

The facilitator gives the following directions to the team(s):

> You are members of a gang that has taken a short-cut across another gang's territory. You have been spotted by one of their lookouts and are aware that they are mobilizing a group of some thirty kids to come after your small group. You have decided to cut through an alley that leads to your own territory. Halfway down the alley you see that the other gang has spread acid across the alley, which stretches at least 30 feet or more ahead of you. You realize that it is too late to go back the way you came. Near the point where the acid begins, the group sees a number of large cans that might offer a way over the acid. But how? Can you figure out how to get all of your gang over the acid before the other gang arrives?

There are some specific rules. No part of a person's body may touch the acid on the pavement. If it does, he or she must return to the starting point and bring his or her cans with him or her. No person may sacrifice himself or herself and run through the acid setting up cans. When the last person crosses, he or she must bring the cans to the far side so that the pursuing gang cannot follow over the acid.

This event is timed.

DISCUSSION

By teams, the observers describe how they saw the decision-making process develop. The group may be asked to comment on these observations and discuss what might have been done better. Why were (or why were not) other alternatives developed? Was there dependence in the group on one or two people? Why? Was there consideration for all the members of the team? Was their performance (going across on the cans) ridiculed, or was there a supportive, all-for-one attitude?

EXERCISE 4 Post-Session Feedback

RATIONALE

Most task groups hardly have time to complete their business commitments, let alone spend much time exploring the process of the group. The comment is often heard, "if we get into that subject, we'll be here all night." This fear of personal overinvolvement outside the actual working agenda can shut down all efforts to develop more effective working relationships. It is not necessary for a group to spend an inordinate amount of time in its process efforts, nor need members become overly personal. However, time must be allowed for a group to improve its own working relationship, or tensions and problems will subtly build up and eventually reduce the group's effectiveness. Following are two simple suggestions for helping to keep the process level of group work legitimized:

1. After a working session, 10 minutes are set aside for a discussion, in pairs, of this question: "What are one or two ways in which this group could improve its working procedures or relationships the next time it meets?" It is important that the participants focus on specific, constructive suggestions. If, for example, one member dominated the discussion and created hostility among many of the other participants, it might be helpful to establish a temporary mechanism for ensuring that more individuals have an opportunity to share their views and also to help move the group past individual roadblocks. In a group with a high level of trust and acceptance, it would not be inappropriate to share with an individual the problems created by his or her particular behavior. But as suggested previously, the climate must be such that the individual desires the information and those giving it are skillful enough not to appear punitive or judgmental.

The group may also find the postmeeting session an avenue for suggesting a change in the structural format of the meeting—for example, the role of the chairperson. Similarly, the way the agenda is formed may influence the feeling of individuals about participating, and a change in how this is accomplished may affect other aspects of a meeting.

The issues raised by the individuals in the paired groups are then shared briefly with the total group. They are first shared without discussion in order to establish how much agreement there is among the members. Then suggestions are taken to remedy the situation in time for the next meeting. The total process should take no more than 20 or 30 minutes. After the group has developed acceptance of the feedback idea, the first step of breaking into twos or threes will be unnecessary, and observations can be shared by the whole group. This would cut the process time down to 10 or 15 minutes, although as groups become more open and communicative, there is a tendency to broaden the scope of the feedback process. It is possible that this can become a problem because many members may find sharing feedback a fascinating and personally satisfying experience. Groups have been known to spend more time discussing their process than the task. Obviously, it is a sign of a mature group if it is able to use feedback in a constructive fashion rather than a means of meeting individual emotional needs that extend far beyond the purpose of the group.

2. If certain members of the work group are involved in establishing the format of a particular meeting (often this is a rotating responsibility in which developing agendas and building procedures for a meeting change hands regularly), the following feedback procedure may prove useful. At the end of a meeting, a reaction sheet is passed out to participants, who answer explicit questions on the operation of the meeting and possible improvements. The group responsible for the next meeting analyzes these responses (thus, it takes only about 5 minutes of the group's time), and they make plans to incorporate various changes in the format of the next meeting that they feel respond to the concerns and suggestions given. These new procedures or innovations are then evaluated in the reaction sheet developed for that meeting. In this way, there is a constant willingness to look at how the group is working together and an opportunity to develop new ideas. Theoretically, each person eventually has a chance to improve the meeting. It may be that a certain format develops that is basically satisfactory to the members; this too will be found through the regular use of reaction sheets.

For Further Information

Kao, J. *Jamming.* New York: Harper Business, 1996.

This is an exploration of why creativity is shut down in the world of business and how to resuscitate it. The book is rich with stories of breaking the mold and of organizations reinventing themselves. The author's tips for thinking and acting have great application in groups or whole organizations.

Morris, K. T., and K. M. Cinnamon. *A Handbook of Verbal Group Exercises.* Springfield, Ill.: Charles Thomas, 1974.

This is a classic that will probably only be found in libraries. The authors focus on some of the critical issues that block effective problem solving, ranging from lack of feedback, to consensus building, and from listening to self-disclosure. Much of what they point out provides the foundation for trust building in any group—the first step toward effective problem solving.

Napier, R., and M. Gershenfeld. *Advanced Games That Trainers Play.* New York: McGraw-Hill, 1998.

Those interested in the concept of "design," discussed at some length in Chapter 8, and the use of creative strategies for moving a group forward will want to explore the forty designs in this book. Consists of rather sophisticated activities for challenging groups to move beyond their normal ways of dealing with a wide range of problems. Can pay huge dividends for the facilitator who is not faint of heart and is willing to help a team or group become unstuck.

Senge, P. M.; A. Kleiner; C. Roberts; and B. J. Smith. *The Fifth Discipline Fieldbook.* New York: Doubleday, 1994.

This is a rich compilation of stories and incidents by people who have successfully solved problems in their organizations by behaving differently. Specific, prescriptive strategies are outlined to fit a wide range of potential problems. The ideas range from simple checklists to more complex computer models, all explained with simple elegance.

von Oech, R. *A Whack on the Side of the Head.* Rev. ed. New York: Warner Books, 1990.

This is von Oech's contribution to thinking "out of the box." A simple, fun approach with quirky drawings and imaginative stories to support different ways of stimulating new ways of thinking in an individual or group.

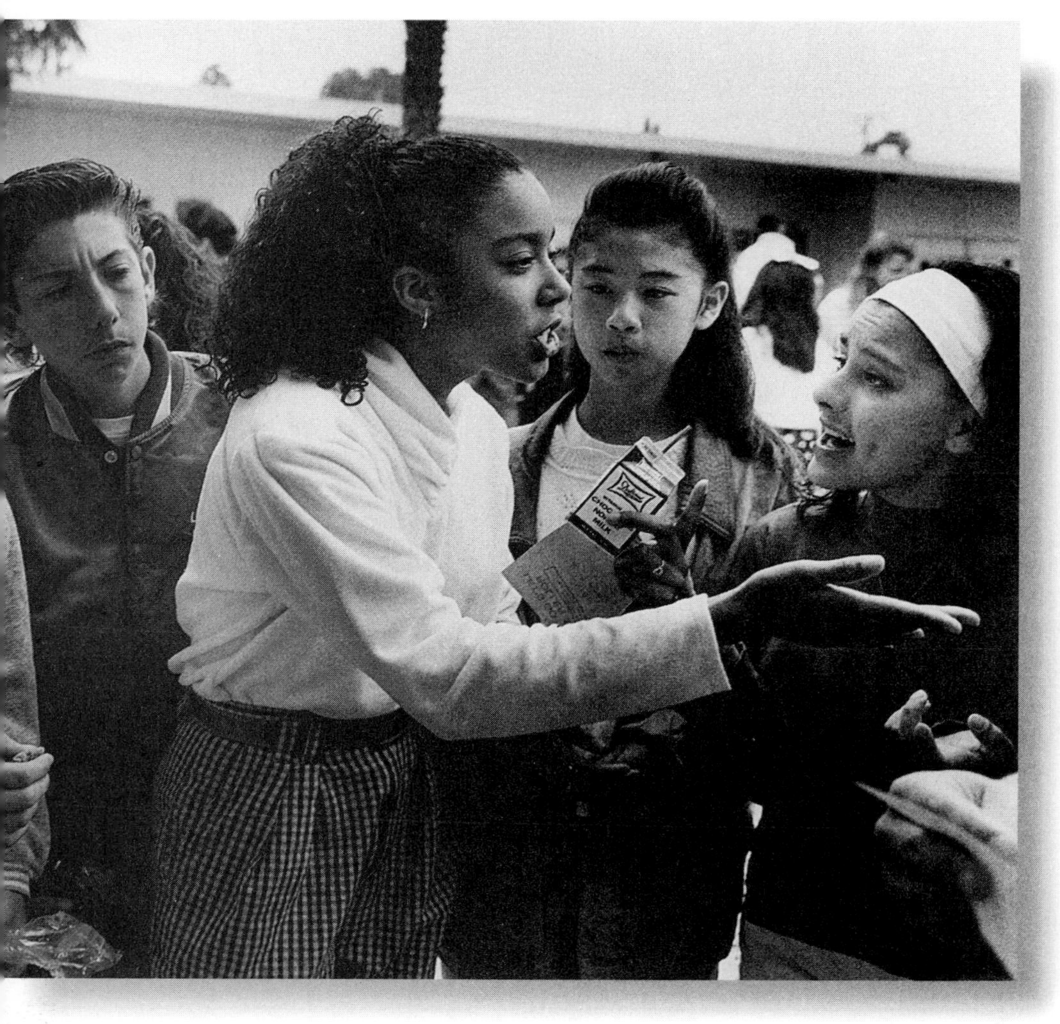

8 The Nature of Group Conflict

The Ubiquitous Nature of Conflict

Conflict is with us every day we live, everywhere we go and in everything we do. At its most extreme, conflict represents open fighting, even warfare. In a less aggressive and hostile form, it may reflect disagreement, tension over styles, opposing values, goals, or even personal choices. Although it is everywhere, conflict is something most of us would like to avoid. Even the common synonyms for conflict, such as *altercation, fight, combat, struggle, strife, friction* or *opposition,* connote conditions we most likely find unappealing.

Whether conflicts affect individuals, families, groups, or organizations, we are inclined to avoid rather than confront them. Being conflict-averse is an expected and pervasive part of most of our lives. Unless there are compelling reasons for dealing with a conflict at hand, our tendency is to avoid taking action until the consequences are severe enough to push us into a response. Scott Peck suggested, in *The Road Less Traveled* (1978), that by far the greatest source of mental illness is derived from our unwillingness to deal with conflicts as they arise. We put them off until the stress surrounding such unfinished business begins to influence our ability to cope and the very quality of our lives. The same is true of the groups in which we are involved. It is the avoided tasks, the unfinished business, or the hostile relations that constantly detract from the group's ability to function as well as it might.

We dislike conflict for many reasons: because it is difficult, because we are poorly trained to deal with it, and because our role models most likely have not been skilled at conflict management either. To make matters worse, media depictions of conflict resolution more often than not suggest violence, coercion, indirectness, or, at best, struggling arbitrations with one group or individual attempting to gain an advantage over the other. So we are left to fend for ourselves in a combative and conflict-prone world without the tools or understanding to cope with something that is virtually ever-present. Is it any wonder that we are such a conflict-averse society? The result of this reality is that conflict is forever going underground, only to reappear in unlikely places with much greater ferocity than had we been willing to deal with it earlier.

In groups, the possibility of conflict seems to both multiply and accelerate. This is because greater numbers of people create more needs and more differences with which to deal or—just as likely—to avoid. Thus, it makes sense for us, as individuals and as members of many groups, to ground ourselves in a clear understanding of how conflict arises and what we can do to minimize its potential negative impact. By understanding its origins and some basic strategies for dealing with it more effectively, it is even possible to turn conflict into more of a friend than an enemy. If we begin to believe that conflict is necessary for constructive change to occur and that dealing with inevitable differences is the best way to more forward, then conflict resolution becomes integral to virtually any problem-solving effort.

The Very Personal Nature of Conflict

To understand the nature of conflict, the place to begin is with a better understanding of ourselves and how we each deal with this challenging part of our lives.

Angeles Arrien (1993) in her study of indigenous peoples, found that many cultures focus on self-knowledge as a crucial element of wisdom and understanding others. If we likewise continue to gain self-knowledge until we are sixty or seventy, we can begin to understand why elders in many traditional societies are considered to have wisdom.

To be successful, part of the search for self-awareness must focus on understanding our own responses to conflict. We must become our own laboratories. Such exploration can be stimulating and challenging, and it can provide clues to the improvement of our own leadership.

Reader Activity

Consider the three or four most influential people in your life. These should be individuals who have helped shape your values, personal goals, and education. Place the name of each at the head of a separate column at the top of a page. Now, under each individual's name, indicate specific things you can remember them doing when faced with a conflict, whether within themselves (as in making a choice between two difficult alternatives) or in response to a conflict with another person or at work. Note what about their approach to conflict management tends to work for them (listening carefully) and not work (losing their temper, becoming stubborn) for them.

Now turn the page over and place your name at the top. Write down the characteristics of your own approach to conflict management that tend to be effective and those that do not. Imagine how others might describe you in this regard. Which of your three significant others most influenced you? Since we are never formally taught skills in this important area, this bit of informal analysis should help you considerably in understanding your own conflict-response patterns and capabilities. Equally important, this brief investigation should reveal where you learned the attitudes that you carry into conflict situations. As you continue reading this chapter, keep the analysis handy; it can be a source of ongoing understanding and personal insight.

A HISTORICAL PERSPECTIVE

Edward deBono (1985) provided a valuable means of understanding some of the powerful historical antecedents that have helped to forge our attitudes about conflict. According to deBono, our current approach to conflict resolution arose from our Western appreciation of logic and the value of argument as a rational means of dealing with differences. The Socratic dialogue and the dialectic of Aristotle are at their roots. Among the ancient Greeks, winners of debates were those who proved to be most skilled in sharply defining their argument and rationally defending a position while destroying that of the opposition. The paradox was that the way to resolve a conflict of ideas was to create conflict in the audience and convince them of the speaker's way of thinking. This tradition had a great influence on the early Roman Catholic church, which used the dialectic to argue everything from one god to the concepts of perfection and justice. The goal became to win the argument regardless of what was ultimately true. Since the church held a virtual lock on formal education up until the Renaissance, the Greco-Roman tradition of argument became the dominant way of approaching conflict.

By its nature, such a process is adversarial, based on the desire to present an antithesis for any thesis presented. This is the seedbed for our present win-lose approach to conflict. The assumption is that if we are able to obliterate the opposition through the force of our argument, we win and they lose. In such a circumstance, those defeated seldom walk away satisfied. Instead, all too often the loser begins almost immediately to discover ways of undermining the winner's position. The end result is that long after the debate is officially over, people will spend huge amounts of energy justifying their own positions. Creative ideas spawned from the best of both positions may well be lost, and time that could be used for looking beyond any single position dissipates into defensiveness and discrediting the other side.

FOCUS ON DIVERSITY

The Japanese approach to conflict reflects an overall collective cultural orientation. The value of collaboration is taking hold in the United States as well (see chapter 5, Transformational Leadership).

Since most problems are complex and allow room for a variety of solutions, a better situation would be to keep thinking with openness and flexibility while considering even better alternatives. Unlike the Western approach, which is based on conflict and self-justification, the Japanese view of differences is built on a premise that a central goal in any problem-solving process is to find something constructive or useful in all the ideas presented. The aim is not to knock down the idea of any individual, but rather to extract what is potentially beneficial from each person's way of thinking. Such a process of building cooperatively creates a stronger outcome and a greater commitment among those who must eventually implement the ideas. Because winning means discovering the best idea or method, and is considerably less ego-driven, the result is a predictably higher degree of "buy-in" at the application stage. Elements of the Japanese approach are incorporated later in this chapter in exploration of the best ways to generate the most creative choices during any group problem-solving effort.

A DOZEN LAND MINES IN A MINEFIELD OF CONFLICT FOUND IN MOST GROUPS

For any of us wishing to understand the root causes of most conflicts, the following should prove helpful. The hard question for each of us is, which of the potential trigger points below tends to set us off? Which creates a reaction in us that, in itself, may jeopardize our ability to be dispassionate and creative as we attempt to resolve an impasse confronting us?

1. *Perceptions—Do We Really Want to See and Hear the Truth?* We are all "owners" of different backgrounds and experiences, which in turn flavor virtually everything we see or hear. Two different perceptions of the same reality will, by definition, result in some level of conflict. The problem is not that such differences in perception exist, but that most of us are not especially open to believing that the perceptions of another individual or group are just as real as our own. If we could step back and attempt to reframe the situation in order to understand the perception of the other, less defensiveness would result. But if we attempt to "argue" or convince another party out of his or her perception, then we immediately strike out. After all, if there is one thing we are entitled to, it is our own point of view.
2. *Stereotypes, Prejudice, and Bias.* We live in a society of religious, racial, ethnic, gender, and a multitude of other differences. The question is not whether we are prejudiced, but whether we are willing to search ourselves continually for clues to our own biases in the effort to understand how they are influencing us. Any group brings together diverse individuals who are bound to stimulate a wide range of responses, some of which will be judgments based on stereotypes. When we attempt to understand conflict it is important to ask ourselves, when do I feel uncomfortable or fearful in the presence of others different from myself? What in my personal history has biased my ability to be objective in my estimation of another person or group of people? It is a constant challenge for group members to deal with issues, and with each other, based on what we experience in the moment rather than what we bring from home or other groups. In many ways, this struggle becomes one of the central but seldom verbalized issues determining whether a group can ever become trusting and develop a true sense of team.

When have other people's stereotypes about you affected your behavior in a group? Was your role improved or diminished?

READER ACTIVITY

Think of three friends or acquaintances who differ significantly from you. One should differ on religious grounds, another ethnically, and the third racially.[1] Think of the first time you met them. What was the strongest feeling you experienced at that moment? From where did the feeling arise? Was tension or discomfort involved? If so, why? Now that you know each of these people better, how does what you have learned about them argue against any stereotypes you carried into the early period of the relationship?

Without giving names, meet with three *other* individuals in your class and explore what you have learned about yourself based on your analysis. Discuss how any of your original stereotypes did or could have generated conflict between you and your friends or acquaintances. Since you are not to talk about people in your class, you should be quite free to explore these issues with each other. Along the way, share where you were raised (what kind of neighborhood); what attitudes people carried about those who were racially, ethnically, or religiously different from you, and how diverse were the schools you attended as well as your place of worship? What impact did these experiences have on your attitudes and levels of comfort among people who are different?

3. *Values and Beliefs*. A belief is something we think is true, something we can stand behind and support because of the strength of our conviction in it. A value is a type of belief. It is based on a standard or principle we tend to hold dear. Conflict arises when two people have differing values and beliefs that appear to clash at some level. The statement, "I couldn't live with myself if . . ." inevitably precedes an example of a strong belief that at least for the time being, appears to be inviolate. What gives us hope about value conflicts is that there are hundreds of examples of values shifting over time, people becoming educated, experiences changing, exceptions being made followed by giving up one belief to embrace another.

   Another conflict generated by values is the frequent discrepancy between our stated values and our actions. Another rather simple definition of a value is something we say we believe that is actually reflected in our behavior. Thus, if we say we believe in personal accountability in business, but we have no functional management-appraisal process to measure performance, then our true value is that we *don't* value personal accountability. Or if we say that one of our values is listening but score 2.8 out of 7 on a listening test, then our real value is that we *don't* value

1. If you are not able to think of someone with racial, ethnic, or religious differences, then this is a clear suggestion that your own background has been biased. Through no fault of your own, your "developmental education" has been short-changed.

listening. It is the observed discrepancy between what people say but don't do that creates simmering unresolved conflict.

A final example will bring clarity to this more finely developed aspect of a value conflict.

> The headmaster at a well-known prep school recently made a statement about how much he valued diversity in the school. Currently there is only one person of color on the faculty of thirty-two, and only 10 percent of his administrative staff are of color. Of the top five administrative jobs, only one is filled by a woman. What does it do to his credibility as a leader and to the morale of those under his leadership when there is such an obvious glass ceiling for people of color and women?

4. *Power, Authority, and Control.* Over forty years ago, Gibb (1961) noted that one of the sure ways of generating defensiveness in people is to place them in a situation where they feel out of control of their own choices and beholden to others. Almost by definition, this is the situation most of us find ourselves in at work or in the classroom. For most people, the issue is not whether we experience conflict concerning power and control, but whether we become hooked into irrational reactions to them. It is our loss of ability to reason and act in a manner that can improve or resolve the situation that can become one of our greatest challenges.

   In a group situation, individual issues of power arise in relation to competition, alignments among various members, ill-defined authority, and unclear goals. The potential for conflict to escalate is considerable. (We will explore this at greater depth later in this chapter.)

5. *Personality and Behavioral Style.* Who has never said or heard, "You know, he's a nice guy, but his management style drives me crazy!"? How we act toward each other is one of the most common triggers of conflict. We may feel comfortable cloaking this conflict in something we call "personality," but what we are usually reacting to is a specific behavior. There is not much chance of influencing anyone's personality, but there is a good chance that we can influence someone's behavior. Although it may not be easy and people may resist, if we can observe a particular behavior, then we can measure it. If we can measure it, we can determine, over time, whether someone is using more or less of the behavior and perceive it as more or less effective.

   What can make a person's behavior so difficult to deal with includes such things as norms that prohibit personal feedback, the power of one person over another in the hierarchy, or behavior that in itself is intimidating or threatening. For example, the mayor of one of our largest cities is known for his good humor, charm, and charisma. Thus, people want to be liked by him. But he also has a terrible temper, and he can be cutting and mean-spirited. His key aides virtually never offer him feedback or suggestions because it might trigger his notorious temper. In fact, few people are willing to approach him to deal with such disturbing behaviors even though the fallout has real consequences for him personally and for his party. It is these and similar behaviors, present in many groups, that go unaddressed and inevitably result in lower morale, trust, and even productivity.

6. *Goals and Personal Needs.* Whenever our own needs and goals are blocked by circumstance, obligations, or the overriding needs of others, we face a natural conflict. Putting off a present need or desire in hopes of later gratification can be judged as a mature act. It still creates tension, however, when we struggle to decide and then act against an impulse pulling us toward the easier gratification of the moment. Choosing to do homework instead of going for a beer with the gang is a simple example. This can become a severe conflict if we see that we are not only losing out on fun, but that such decisions are beginning to affect our social status and isolate us from meaningful social relationships. Similarly, when two people in a group have incompatible goals, whether overt or covert (hidden agendas), the result can be emotional conflict for both the individuals and the group.
7. *Large and Small Transgressions.* Does a day go by when we are not forced to experience an insensitive act or transgression by someone else? Perhaps somebody cuts you off while driving. Or perhaps somebody interrupts before you feel you have been heard, and the subject changes without even being able to complete your thought. These are some of the conflicts many of us experience every day. Like dealing with prejudices, the important issue here is, how conscious are we of our responses to the large and small transgressions against us?

   One block to real self-awareness is the difficulty to understand or accept that we co-create our own realities. For example, if you scream at the driver who has jeopardized your safety, your reality will be quite different than if you ignore the act, realizing that you can't possibly influence the transgressor. Chances are, whatever response we use is predictable and says as much about how we approach life as anything else. We all know people who would respond in one or the other of these ways. The first personalizes every transgression, is constantly in a reactive mode, looking for trouble and creating more problems by being aggressive, and has an attitude that "nobody is going to kick me around." The other lets go of stress and tension and dwells only on what he or she is capable of controlling.

In either situation, imbalance can hurt the individual. If the cool customer who rarely is bothered fails to stand up for his or her own rights, then he or she will often become a victim of others' whims and self interests. Or, if the reactive individual is constantly in turmoil and alienates friends and foes alike, then they too become a victim, incapable of being as effective as they might.

Thus, conflict management is partly about raising our levels of awareness about how we respond to such stress and the consequences of our own actions. Conflict resolution begins with understanding the degree to which each of us is committed to continuing relatively dysfunctional—perhaps dangerous—responses rather than exploring more effective alternatives. In other words, the difficulties in our ability to manage conflict have as much to do with our own predictable and ineffective responses to situations as to conflict themselves. In the extreme we all know an individual who acts ineffectively in a situation and then carries the consequence of their action the rest of the day. They proceed to tell everyone they meet about how they were the victims of the situation, but fail to disclose how their own response accelerated the problem for them.

Reader Activity

Put together a group of three or four and explore your patterns for handling the transgressions and insensitivities you deal with every day. What are your strengths? What do you tend to do that may get you into trouble or further exacerbate the situation? Relate a recent example that reflects your pattern. Finally, if there is one thing about your responses you would like to work on in order to be more effective, what is it? Have each member of your group spend about five minutes discussing these questions.

8. *Roles, Rewards, and Recognition.* Have you ever worked diligently on a project under great duress and finally accomplished the task, only to have your effort taken for granted? Can you remember the lack of appreciation and rising anger you felt? Or can you remember a situation in which ill-defined roles resulted in someone else's receiving recognition that should have fairly come to you? In many ways, who we are as adults centers around the roles we have at work or in task groups in which we participate. Since money and recognition often define our success organizationally, we can be certain that conflict hovers just beneath the surface along with inequality, favoritism, and lack of recognition. That it may appear self-centered to raise the concern means that many such concerns are harbored in silence, festering over time. As often as not, the resentments that develop are reflected in other attitudes and behaviors which can be more legitimately expressed.

9. *Choices, Choices, Choices.* Being faced with choices—between two cars, two dates, two jobs, or two suits when we can only choose one—sets in motion a nearly constant source of conflict. Choosing to stay late at work rather than being with our family (see below), for example, sets in motion dissonance, stress, and, inevitably, internal conflict. Whenever we are faced with such so-called *high-valence choices*—those that will make a significant difference in how we feel or in other ways substantially influence our lives—we create conflicts within ourselves that increase the stress we carry. This in turn lowers our capacity to be patient and thoughtful both at home and at work.
10. *Involvement in Issues That Affect Our Work Lives.* Fifty years ago the idea of participative management was hardly a glimmer in the corporate or educational firmament. The thought of people having a legitimate right to influence their work lives through meaningful involvement and dialogue was, for the most part, unheard of. Today, with increasing understanding that stakeholder participation ties into productivity, morale, and ultimately profits (Kotter and Heskitt, 1992), there is a two-way street of ongoing conflict. Management needs participation but may resent it. Workers like to be involved but can resent the time and bother it represents. Nevertheless, to be heard is a "right" that is increasingly voiced. And with it the response to discrepancies between promises and realities represents a clear channel of conflict not present four decades ago. The openness to ideas and collaboration experienced in many groups and organizations during the late 1960s and '70s established expectations that were often set aside as organizations rushed into the vortex of downsizing during the 1980s and '90s. Lower profit margins and international competition demanded dramatic surgery, and did not lend themselves to the openness promoted in the previous decades.
11. *The Family-Work Dichotomy.* Another source of conflict, which appears to touch most of us, has to do with the push-pull demands of home and family versus work. With two spouses working in the majority of families today, it is increasingly evident that there is less and less time available for quality family relationships, completing necessary household chores, or maintaining intimacy between two working parents. Added to the conflict created by this scenario is greater competition in a downsizing job market, where security is diminishing and there is less and less support for workers on the job. The elimination of many mid-level management positions simultaneous to increases in performance standards results in many feeling squeezed. The end result is more time spent on the job, less time at home—and added tension all around. There is never enough time for personal life, relaxation, and fun. It is easy to imagine

the difficulties that arise in bedrooms, around dinner tables, and on family vacations as people feel increasingly dissatisfied and stressed.

12. *Communication/Information Sharing.* When some people have information and others don't, there is an immediate differential in terms of power and probably influence. In totalitarian countries, one of the first freedoms removed is freedom of the press followed by freedom of the radio and television airways. In the eyes of dictators, communication is power. One of the first lessons we learn in any hierarchical system is that those with knowledge and information are able to communicate while the others are relegated to listening. But what is good for an opportunistic leader (control over information) is not necessarily good for the health of the organization.

    The implicit conflict between those with information and those without, whether on the horizontal or vertical plane of the organization, is ever-present. Particularly fertile ground are highly competitive systems, where individual performance is valued over cooperation. Within a group context, it is not so much that communication of information is poor but that our experiences in other settings creates sensitivity to the issue, increasing our need for timely, relevant information.

In summary, each of us carries the potential for hundreds of conflicts, some of which are actualized every day. Depending on the attitudes and behaviors we experienced growing up in our family, school, work, and community environments, we each have developed a pattern of rather predictable responses to a wide range of conflicts. Our success as a member of a group will, to some degree, then, depend on our ability to be aware of the factors that create conflict and our skill in dealing with them. Awareness alone is a starting point for being less reactive, more understanding, and more dispassionate as a manager of conflict.

Reader Activity

Let's take one more look at you as a conveyor and receiver of conflict. Below are a dozen conflict triggers that can be brought into groups by members. As a member of many groups, you are to consider each of the categories and answer the following questions:

1. Which three areas tend to hook you the most? That is, which are you most sensitive to and which take most of your energy if they are present in a group in which you are a member?
2. Which three areas pose the least problem for you in that they seldom generate a strong response? These are areas in which you feel in control, able to respond with some equanimity.

3. Which three areas do you believe pose the greatest problem for groups in general, and where failure to deal with them has the greatest and most lasting consequences for groups?

Areas of Group Conflict

Place a 1 next to each of the *three* items that respond to question one, a 2 next to each of the *three* items that respond to question two, and a 3 next to the *three* items that respond to question three.

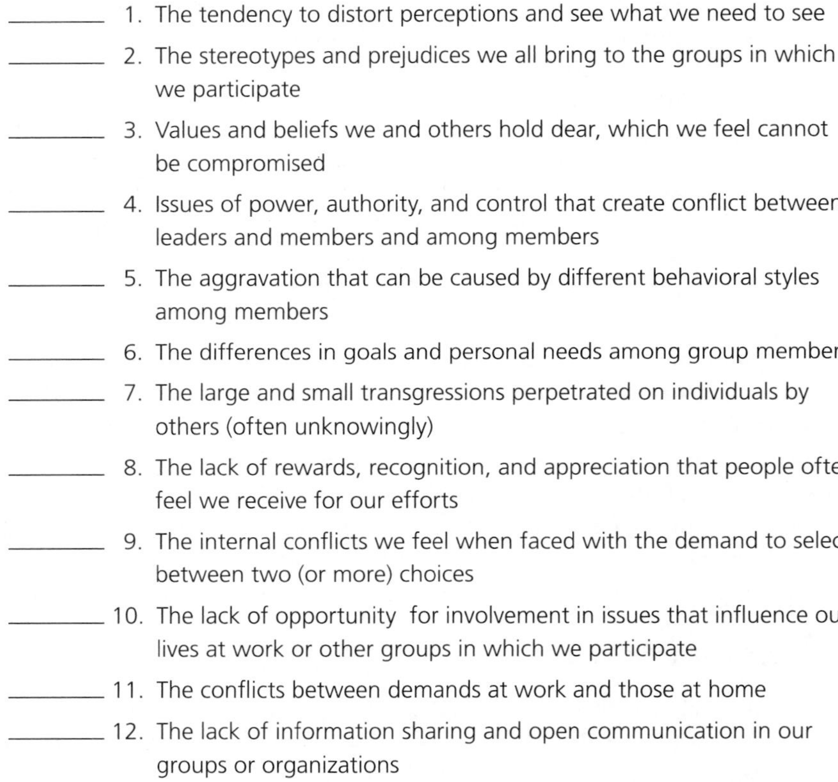

________ 1. The tendency to distort perceptions and see what we need to see

________ 2. The stereotypes and prejudices we all bring to the groups in which we participate

________ 3. Values and beliefs we and others hold dear, which we feel cannot be compromised

________ 4. Issues of power, authority, and control that create conflict between leaders and members and among members

________ 5. The aggravation that can be caused by different behavioral styles among members

________ 6. The differences in goals and personal needs among group members

________ 7. The large and small transgressions perpetrated on individuals by others (often unknowingly)

________ 8. The lack of rewards, recognition, and appreciation that people often feel we receive for our efforts

________ 9. The internal conflicts we feel when faced with the demand to select between two (or more) choices

________ 10. The lack of opportunity for involvement in issues that influence our lives at work or other groups in which we participate

________ 11. The conflicts between demands at work and those at home

________ 12. The lack of information sharing and open communication in our groups or organizations

You can discuss the answers in small groups of members of the class in order to gain a better understanding of each person's sources of vulnerability and sensitivity. In addition, compiling the class responses to question three can make it a useful diagnostic and point of discussion. You could talk about how such conflicts are manifested within groups in which you and your classmates are members, or what could be done to alleviate the problems they cause.

From Individual Sources of Conflict to the Dynamics of Conflict in Groups

Now let's turn to the context of conflict as it presents itself in groups. A useful way to organize our understanding of the potential conflict waiting to burst forth in any group is to revisit the concepts of *goals, membership, norms, and leadership*. As either a member or a leader of a group, if we have the ability to understand what is occurring in these areas at any given time, then we are able to be less reactive and more rational in how we respond.

NORMS: RULES SURROUNDING CONFLICT MANAGEMENT AND THEIR IMPACT ON GROUP LIFE

When was the last time you were in a group and there was an open discussion concerning how people dealt with conflict? Or, for that matter, when have you ever been involved in an open dialogue about how the conflict behavior of certain members shaped the climate of the group? Chances are, your response to both questions is "never." Conflict, though ever-present, is one of those things we seldom discuss; it is like a family secret that's kept in the closet. Yet it flavors almost everything that happens. The fact that it is rarely discussed suggests that, whatever the pattern for dealing with conflict, it rarely changes.

Remember: norms are the unspoken rules that govern the life of a group. If the norm is "don't raise conflict for discussion," there will be little hope for change. But not discussing conflict does not mean there is no conflict. Quite the contrary: conflict may be rampant. Let's look at three examples of "conflict" norms that can shape the climate of a group.

POLITE AND NICE IS THE RULE The group is a department in a large community bank. The bank has a reputation for being friendly and service-directed. The group has established a norm where not only is conflict seen as negative, but any criticism tends to be personalized to the degree that few people ever hear anything but praise.

The department in question consists of seven people, two of whom can't stand each other. These two smile through clenched teeth and continually criticize each other by asking indirect questions, such as, "Well, Helen, I really appreciate your effort, but don't you think it would have made more sense to . . . ?" Helen most likely responds with, "Thanks, Paul. I appreciate your concern, but in my twenty years in this business, I feel that such a response would almost be unethical since the customer would be left with no recourse. Don't you agree?" This kind of attack, dripping with politeness, can continue for months, even years, when such a pervasive norm of conflict aversion exists. When no one dares to confront the situation, the drain on a group's energy and productivity can be enormous.

It is obvious to the other five members that Helen does not feel heard or appreciated by Paul. Furthermore, it is common knowledge that she believes he patronizes her and, for that matter, most women with whom he must deal. For his part, Paul feels Helen is controlling and untouchable because she is so "nice." He resents her holier-than-thou attitude. He also believes that she gets away with murder, but because systems of accountability are loose the quality of her work remains mediocre and over time reflects on the reputation of the bank.

Of the twelve areas of conflict discussed previously, at least five of them are at play here. But because of the norm of conflict aversion, it is predictable that little will be done unless a major problem arises. In the meantime, other norms form to handle the emotional fallout from this situation. For example, since people tend to be indirect, their real feelings go "underground" into the informal system. There, gossip and nastiness find an outlet, and the people who join in feel hypocritical and dishonest. For "nice" people, that can become a burden. The end result is that the group, over time, tends to polarize over the two with the unresolved conflict, and increasing amounts of time are devoted to subterfuge and ineffective behavior.

THE TRUTH IS WHATEVER YOU SAY, BOSS The president of a small, successful, and well-known software firm is extraordinarily likable, gregarious, and intelligent, held in high regard in the industry. She is extremely value-driven and articulate, with the capacity to take ideas and organize them instantly. But she then uses them in devastating arguments, often leaving others beaten in her wake. Although her ability to argue is valued, it also keeps people from expressing their ideas and feelings in her presence. Employees fear that someday they may fall victim to her laserlike rebuke. In spite of her occasional brutal reprimands, people want to be liked and valued by her.

Over the several years of her presidency, a norm has evolved that staff members simply hold their tongue, don't criticize her, and figure that their energy should be saved for battles that can be won. The problem is that the aggressive and punitive behavior modeled by the leader has been well learned by her direct reports, and an intolerance for disagreement has been passed down through the organization. Thus, although the company prides itself on open communication and honesty, the unspoken norm is to hide one's ideas and feelings until you are in a position to win. Kenwyn Smith (1982) explains this as a paradox in which we may resent how those above us treat us, but we will respond by repeating this behavior on those below.

His point is that we model our behaviors after those with whom we most closely associate, in this case the president (Smith, K. K. p. 3).

The president is increasingly frustrated, left wondering why those in her presence are so compliant and passive when she truly believes that she encourages openness and the healthy expression of differences. The result at both the organizational and small-group level is increasing mistrust and unwillingness to risk. In a business that demands quick response and turn-around, such norms surrounding conflict will have to be dealt with—or the all too predictable consequence will be that the company soon begins to lose its competitive edge.

OH, WE'RE ONLY KIDDING The group is an executive team of ten people who pride themselves on being competent and extremely well-functioning. They are all relatively young, highly educated, and as a group tend to keep up with all the latest management trends and fads. If something new is out there, they have either used it or considered it for their organization. In addition, most of them wear designer suits, listen to NPR, and are politically astute. Put plainly, they like to appear "with-it." Because the leader believes that hiring is the most important role of the CEO, he prides himself on hiring the best and brightest and then letting them "do their thing." He is a strong believer in delegation and gives each of his direct reports lots of room in which to maneuver.

One of the norms which undergirds the "team" is to support each other by staying "out of each others' faces" and minding one's own business. This greatly reduces the competitiveness that lies just beneath the surface. But since the boss doesn't believe in much supervision beyond individual goal setting, there is little opportunity to demonstrate one's competence compared to other members of the team. The way they handle the unspoken antagonisms that naturally develop is through penetrating humor and well-placed sarcasm to everyone but the boss. At the end of each devastating comment or put down, comes, "Oh, I was only kidding," or "Hey, can't you take a joke?" Because the norm is to be with-it and such put-down humor is a sign that team members are both with-it and can take it, it would be breaking the rules to say anything to the antagonist telling the joke. This is true even when it is obvious that the humor is being used to put somebody "in his or her place" or take care of some other unfinished business.

A meeting not long ago included two examples of the kind of indirect attacks used to handle unresolved conflict among team members. In one instance, Jim, who had been one of the few not to wear high-priced and trendy clothes, finally got tired of all the barbs about his dress. He had gone out and bought a high-priced and, he thought, stylish suit. But instead of compliments, he was greeted with a spate of negative comments cloaked in humor, including, "Hey, Jim, didn't they tell you discount stores aren't in style this year?" There was lots of laughter—even from Jim. But he did not wear his new suit again. One of his closest competitors in the "noncompetitive" office had spearheaded this effort at humor.

During the same meeting, Dan, whose part of the organization was going through growing pains—some of which were due to Dan's own disorganization—made a comment in response to something Jean had said. It was disconnected, like a non-sequitur, which was not unusual for Dan. Jerry, in a rather loud voice, leaned over as if to share a secret with Barbara and said, "Ain't it a shame when first cousins marry?" As usual, Dan took it with a grin. But the others died a little for him, thanking their lucky stars that it wasn't them who received the shot.

Here, the trouble is not in any one use of hostile humor at someone's expense. Rather, it is the collusion in abuse and indirectness that over time bleed into other areas of communication because individuals hold back.

NORMS AS BUILDING BLOCKS OF ORGANIZATIONAL CULTURE Understanding what one group's norms about conflict are is like having an x-ray of the entire organization. As an institutional subculture, each group most likely replicates what goes on at other levels. In their research, Kotter and Heskitt (1992) revealed that the least successful organizational cultures were indirect, not open to feedback, and often punished people for new and creative ideas. High performing cultures, on the other hand, rewarded new ideas and encouraged people to question the status quo at any level.

In each of three examples above, the norms surrounding conflict suggested that people were failing to be direct or honest. The dishonesty they spawned was beginning to influence each organization's ability to be as successful as it could be. The polarization of the bank department was a clear sign that there was no means of dealing with everyday conflicts and differences, which had begun to tear at the fabric of the team. In this case, the problems of the department were a reflection of similar issues throughout the organization. Similarly, the inability of employees to provide their president with needed feedback was a symptom of other insensitivities and transgressions, which were beginning to spread downward into other levels of the organization. And the norm of using biting humor as a subterfuge for real feelings or a vehicle for misplaced aggression eventually would influence the executive team's ability to do its work. Such perspective might help us to perceive causes of problems in addition to symptoms and thereby lead to a means of dealing with group problems. By reframing our thinking via a normative perspective, many of the other issues take on a different meaning.

MEMBERSHIP: HOW CONFLICT CAN GAIN OR LOSE PARTICIPANT MEMBERSHIP

Remember that certain aspects of membership are not permanent in most groups. That is, members can come and go in response to how relationships, time, and issues are handled. In a group where open conflict is an acceptable way of doing business, those with the courage to fight for their ideas experience greater group membership than those who are less aggressive and less willing to risk. Paradoxically, though, an individual's fear of membership loss might curtail his or her participation. And the unwillingness to act could set in motion a self-fulfilling prophecy and result in his or her actual loss of membership.

In the example of the community bank, the opposite is true. There, avoiding conflict is the norm, and it is directly tied to whether an individual will gain some initial membership. Knowing that something as obvious as being nice, *not* being in conflict, is a key to membership, why would people act differently, especially if they wished to build a future with the bank?

Similarly, the president of the software company appears to wield the wand of membership over her own team. Who would voluntarily risk her wrath and appear incompetent or stupid? With the realization that silence cannot get them into trouble, employees conclude that being passive is clearly the better part of valor. At each level of the organization, the conflict norm to some degree dictates who can provide membership. If it is based on being contrite and dependent, or critical and nonargumentative, is there any question that work will bog down and response time will lengthen?

As for the use of humor as a vehicle for displacing overt conflict and criticism, membership is maintained by "being a good sport," not confronting people about their hostile jokes, and remaining in collusion with the indirect hostility. It is easy to understand how some people would find it painful to come to work. But they can't say anything because it would be seen as complaining and, above all, not being with-it.

THE RECIPROCAL RELATIONSHIP OF NORMS AND MEMBERSHIP To understand groups, we must grasp the compelling relationship between norms and membership. To break a norm is an obvious transgression and thus will lose most people "membership points." Losing membership in a place where "nice is right" is easy to discern. An outburst of anger can result in people being quietly ignored. The disruptive party will be the butt of not-so-nice conversation in the safety of the informal cliques. Continued outbursts will lead to further isolation. This is not to suggest that people in the bank are not genuinely "nice," but it does suggest that one reason the "nice" norm survives is the outlet provided by cliques and subgroups, where people can "let their hair down."

Certain powerful people, however, tend to have "idiosyncrasy credits" and are able to break norms with impunity. The Vice Presidents of the software firm have these, as do certain favored old-timers who have earned their stripes and can raise some criticism without losing their heads. They have also learned "when to shoot" in order to reduce the possibility of being rebuked.

Finally, the negative humor pervading the executive team maintains membership and helps to preserve the desired distance among the competitive groups.

In each of these examples, the norms–membership relationship is essential to maintain the status quo. Constructive change most likely will not occur in the relationships in the three organizations unless there is a rather dramatic intervention that sparks some reshaping of the norms themselves.

GOALS: ADDRESSING INDIVIDUAL AND GROUP GOALS CAN REFRAME THE CONFLICT–MEMBERSHIP RELATIONSHIP

Earlier in this book we explored the different kinds of goals that help influence the life of a group. Most important to the topic of conflict are notions of group goals versus individual goals. A leader's goals may be undermined if either individual or group goals are not in alignment with his or her desired outcomes. Since the ways groups deal with conflict can directly influence both membership and norms, there is probably a clear relationship with goals as well. For example, the group goal at the bank is to maintain appearances of what a community bank is—a bank that offers customer service and is "nice" and personal to a degree that cannot be matched by larger, less personal competitors. A second goal could be expressed as keeping the underground informal system alive and well in order to deal with all of the interpersonal "stuff" which arises in the day-to-day operations and cannot find an outlet in the superficial "niceness" of the bank environment. Were it not for this more authentic aspect of the life at the bank, it would be difficult for many to envision remaining for ten, twenty, or thirty years.

The president of the software firm has an individual and organizational goal of open, honest, and timely communication. However, employees have come to realize that, in relation to the CEO herself, open communication can be dangerous. The group goal has come to be cautiousness about sharing of any information that might contradict the views held by the president or vice presidents. Self-preservation in the eyes of the organization's authority figures is more important than the benefits desired by the CEO for the organization as a whole. And the individual goals driving the group goal are shared by a sufficient number of members to influence organizational norms.

In the case of the executive team, some members feel the need to be perceived as better and brighter than their peers, which is achieved through negative humor or sarcasm at someone else's expense. However, their desire to protect themselves from undue criticism and meddling on the part of others acts as a counterforce. Thus, the individual goal of putting others down in the name of humor works here too. At first glance, the group goal might appear to be "Let's have fun and be with-it as a team." But in reality, the group goal is to use humor to keep real intimacy and closeness from occurring, and at the same time maintain relatively clear boundaries among both individual roles and behavior within the group. Thus, the humor maintains distance among the vice presidents. It also maintains the appearance of conviviality even amidst clear hostilities, while at the same time, ensuring that things don't go too far. This allows individuals to play out their individual transgressions on a tit-for-tat basis.

In these three examples, it becomes relatively easy to observe how the group goals, the norms, and the criteria for membership in the various organizations all feed off each other. It is also possible to begin to understand why change is so difficult; most leaders do not have the ability to observe their total organizations. However, if leaders can begin perceiving these interrelated aspects of group and organizational processes, it is possible to discover the truth about the norms. Usually people are willing to talk—if asked. Most understand at some level the charades and game playing that are occurring and realize that they are destructive to the health of the organization. However, most are also without the slightest clue of what to do without jeopardizing themselves. The result is that they remain silent conspirators in dysfunctional goals and ultimately negative norms.

LEADERSHIP: CONFLICT AVERSION AND SEDUCTION OF THE LEADER

The unstated collusion at work in most organizations maintains a climate that prevails against healthy conflict resolution. At the center of the collusion is the organizational or group leader. For the most part, these are well-intentioned individuals who have worked hard to achieve their positions. Few would admit that their overriding personal goal is anything other than to lead their group to success in achieving it goals. But stated simply, the dilemma they face is that *the older and more skilled they are, and the more influence they have, when they need the most cooperation and truth possible from their employees, this is the very time they are likely to receive half-truths and deception from other people. This is called seduction of the leader.*

There are primarily two forms of seduction. The first has to do with how the individual seduces him- or herself. The second is how people close to the leader collude to seduce him or her. Both forms are much more obvious to others than to the leaders.

For leaders, there is nothing more difficult than standing outside ourselves and witnessing either the impact we are having on others or the impact others are having on us. We are often too close to the situation to maintain any sense of objectivity. Thus, one goal of leaders who want to resolve conflict in their group or organization should be achieving ruthless honesty with themselves. They can accomplish this goal by aggressively seeking anonymous feedback concerning their influence on followers, how well they are achieving their own goals, and the degree to which their own perceptions are similar to or discrepant from those of the people over whom they have influence. If leaders will not take this challenge on themselves, it is the rare subordinate who will even suggest it, let alone initiate it. The result is that many leaders hear what they want to hear—and what others would like them to hear. As long as an authority figure can influence the careers and lives of those who report to him or her, it is naive to assume that most individuals have the courage to be truthful simply because the boss asks them a question. This is especially so in cases where the answer may diminish the employee in the boss's eyes or make the boss look inadequate. Two key questions any leader must continually ask are, "What is the information I need to have in order to lead effectively?" and "How can I protect those around me so they are free to tell me the truth?" Without the truth it will be the murky world of individual goals and negative norms, which will influence critical elements of organizational decision making.

SELF-SEDUCTION This form of seduction stems from the phenomenon of leader infallibility. Leaders are often victims of a belief that they need to know everything, need to be in charge, and above all must act the role—whatever that means to them. Needing to appear nearly perfect at all times means that leaders can't make mistakes or appear weak or out of control. That is a huge and unfair burden on any leader. First, it keeps many competent individuals from being able to relinquish control and delegate effectively. It can also reduce the leader's willingness to take chances, to risk the possibility of failure. The catch is that if we need to look perfect we will be less inclined to seek the kind of feedback that might reveal that we are less than perfect. But not receiving feedback in a timely way can result in our inability to respond. Worse yet, if employees see us as needing to be perfect, they receive the message loud and clear that they, too, must be mistake-free. Thus, the leader prevents them from being as truthful as they can and creates an increasing need for employees to hide their problems and mistakes. Over time, this type of seduction helps create a climate of dishonesty and mistrust. Such deception, half-truths, and withholding of important information can have serious consequences. In the case of the software company president, for example, her need to appear competent and right sowed the seeds of the dishonesty she truly wanted to avoid. It was her intolerance of her own imperfection, translated into criticism of others, that drove the employees into retreat. In turn, it provided them permission to initiate their own brand of control over and judgments of those reporting to them, exacerbating the atmosphere of zero tolerance for mistakes.

SEDUCTION BY OTHERS In addition to being seduced by the biases, personal histories, and educations that shape our unique styles as leaders, we are inevitably seduced as a result of the needs of others. As a "best-case" scenario, imagine a leader who is open, honest, and liked by those around him. You would expect that he could expect to receive a high degree of honesty in return, and to some degree that will be true. But, just as likely, others will want to protect this good boss. After all, he is such a good guy, so well-intentioned, and tries so hard, he doesn't need any more aggravation, does he? And worse yet, the more likable he is and the more we wish to be liked and appreciated by him, the more we may feel inadequate and wish to hide our own mistakes and limitations.

At the other end of the continuum, imagine a boss, parent, or teacher who is a tyrant, a critical and abusive character (Cloven and Roloff, 1993). What hope would there be for him or her receiving the kind of information required to improve morale, productivity, or interpersonal relationships? If the problem is the boss him- or herself, what then? By definition, this is seduction as well; it is also one of the most pervasive sources of conflict.

Diagnosis: The First and Most Critical Step in Conflict Resolution

To this point we have explored a variety of ways for understanding how conflict occurs. Without this preliminary information it is difficult to diagnose a conflict situation adequately. That is, without an effective diagnosis it will be impossible to "design" an effective means of resolution. The twelve individual conflict areas, discussed above, raised our awareness of the conflict sources each of us may bring to the groups with whom we are engaged. Then, revisiting norms, membership, goals, and leadership has allowed us to reframe individual conflict into a group and system perspective. Finally, the notion of seduction has shed some light on why so much conflict stays underground, rarely surfacing to be dealt with even when there are good intentions to do so.

It should be apparent that without a good diagnosis of what is actually causing a conflict, it is unlikely that an effective solution will be found. Thus, the apparent friendliness of the community bank hides a labyrinth of unresolved conflicts that influence the employees' productivity and morale. The formal system denies people open acknowledgment of any conflict, so the informal system is a beehive of gossip and misplaced energy.

In the case of the brilliant president, she could easily deem the problem to be passivity and lack of risk taking on the part of her employees. By understanding the situation from several perspectives, however, we can discover that passivity is merely a symptom. The real problem resides in the leadership style being modeled by the president herself, and the inability of those around her to let her know.

In the situation of the executives who use humor at each other's expense, it would be of little value to clean up the humor without looking at the deeper and more pervasive norms that exist in the group. These act to protect the young, competitive executives from being destructively competitive by maintaining distance among them so they do not become overly critical of each other. Again, humor is merely a symptom of the deeper conflicts that affect productivity and relationships among the critical players.

If we are able to identify the real conflict, then we will be able to design an appropriate response with which to intervene.

Reader Activity

Consider a group with whom you meet regularly. What are the signs of conflict that seem apparent and remain unresolved within the group? From your perspective, what keeps the group from resolving these issues? Are there norms that work against the group dealing with its conflict? How do individual goals and membership issues play out in your assessment of the group? Is "seduction" alive and well? Once you have completed your assessment, join a four-person group. Allow each person 5 minutes to summarize his or her diagnosis of the particular group they have chosen to explore. The three listeners are then given another 5 minutes to ask questions about the diagnosis in an effort to help shed additional light on the situation. These might include, "It sounds as though your group is quite dependent on the leader. Is that true?" or "What are the consequences on membership?" or "Are the group goals in alignment with those of the leader?"

FEAR AND CONFORMITY IN THE TRENCHES—THE CONSEQUENCES OF UNRESOLVED CONFLICT

The following case represents a true story of how ineffective leadership can spawn a wide range of conflicts. In it you will be able to pick out powerful examples of many of the reasons mistrust, seduction, and groupthink are the consequences of what appear to be obviously destructive behaviors.

He was to be a breath of fresh air. He had been hand-picked to help raise the bar for his organization, as his Communications Division touched every part of the sprawling midwest utility. He had inherited a leadership team that was composed of ten good and talented people who cared about their organization. They did their work with a certain mindless competence, which was one of the prices they paid for working in a noncompetitive industry. In fact, the security of holding a local monopoly had swooned more than a few of the team members into a state of understandable complacency. After all, there were few real threats. Virtually no conflict and only an occasional challenge ever crossed their work horizon. In fact, workers at this particular utility prided themselves on being part of a 12,000 person family, where if differences couldn't be resolved with a smile, "you'd better go home and think about it."

The threat of deregulation had been around for years, but nothing really changed. It was difficult to crank up enthusiasm among the troops when customer demands still filled their days. After all, the team did not sign on as entrepreneurs and found it difficult to even think about how things would be different once deregulation set in. At least that was the way it was before George Metz, the new Vice President for Communications, arrived on the scene. Then all hell broke loose.

For the team, the trauma wasn't deregulation, it was George. Blonde, with a golden tan, he had steel-blue eyes that took in the whole room, along with your soul, in a single glance. He was also physically intimidating at 6′4″ and 250 pounds, and looked more like a pulling guard for an NFL team than an executive who had been stolen from one of the great industrial manufacturing giants of the world. His booming laugh could be heard halfway across the building, and he laughed often. If he wasn't laughing he was just as loud in his exclamations of disbelief or his rebukes. He could fill a room more than anyone the team had ever met, whether by his physical size or his gigantic ego and personal charisma. Most of those who had to deal with him on a day-to-day basis—both peers or subordinates—were caught on the horns of an emotional dilemma. What were they to do with someone who could charm your socks off one minute and terrify you the next? He could pull you in with charm and then slam you down with his mercurial anger. He had the careers of his team in his hands, and he and they knew it. Some wanted to hate him and the power and confidence he exuded, yet at the same time, it was difficult not to like him and want to be liked by him. Needless to say, the team walked around on eggshells. There were two modes of operating with George on the scene. One was to stay out of sight, just do your job and remain as invisible as possible. The other, just as flawed, was to try to befriend him and gain his confidence by pleasing him.

To make matters even more difficult, he spent most of his time—twelve- to fourteen-hour days— with large customers who loved the attention they received from this irrepressible force. He knew it was these customers who could make the difference between success and failure in the change to free competition. The result was that he had little time for his team, other than a four-hour weekly meeting when they and perhaps a dozen others sat around a large table and listened to his high-energy pontifications and warnings of catastrophe if things didn't turn around. Every week he would find a new way to say how he expected them to step up to the plate and meet the challenges. Yet, he had no time to help them establish their goals, measure outcomes, or understand the threats he talked about. Those used to hiding would hunker down in their seats and attempt to avoid his gaze once the thirty-minute show-and-tell part of the meeting started. During that thirty minutes, everyone attempted to impress him and others with how much they were accomplishing. But not knowing what success looked like or what would please him often resulted in a certain amount of flailing around. It was a bit like children attempting to be noticed by parents who would normally pay them no mind, realizing all the while that what they were saying might easily backfire and annoy them. In fact, most of those on the team regressed into dependent and childlike behavior in George's presence.

CONFLICT, CONFLICT EVERYWHERE The reason this example is particularly useful is because it allows us to witness the impact of unresolved conflict in a small group which, by most accounts, had been fairly normal and successful in the past. It was clear that the reason George was hired was to wake the team up and ready its members for the new day of deregulation. The result, however, was that after nearly two years George had not figured out why the group did not act like a team, and performance had, if anything, deteriorated. A brief interview by an outside consultant with each member revealed the profound impact George had had on the team and each player individually. And George had apparently become sufficiently frustrated that he was willing to look at the resulting data, including information concerning his own role. The data suggested that a wide range of real and potential conflicts were occurring within the group.

1. Membership in the group had historically been based on informal support and the respect that stemmed from shared status rather than any real interdependency. With George's arrival, membership was strictly dependent on the degree to which employees were able to gain favor with George. The result was that the team members often flailed around in their attempts to impress him. Their behaviors were often inappropriate, sometimes competitive, or appeared to be at the expense of other team members.

   Anytime comfortable, predictable membership is altered and becomes out of our control, conflict will be the result.

2. The group goal shifted: appearing competent and remaining invulnerable in the face of the challenges and criticisms of George took precedent over the casual, more socially-directed goal of the past. This was accomplished by individuals' avoiding the risk of failure or embarrassment in the group and agreeing with virtually anything George said. Even when he encouraged debate or sharing of ideas, the game was to find out exactly what George believed and then to accommodate that belief through agreement or no response at all.

   The danger of being criticized and losing credibility in George's eyes kept the group in a constant state of conflict.

3. Individual goals varied from not participating, in order to avoid mistakes, to active responses to virtually anything George said, in order to appear alert and interested. For some individuals, the hope was to deflect his attention to other, non-active members. *Conflict resulted from the tension of implicit competition for George's favor, which became increasingly obvious and was exacerbated when he did show favoritism, for whatever reason, to an individual.* The sense was that there was only so much favor available and, since standards for individual success were not clearly defined by George, his responses appeared to be whimsical and arbitrary.

4. Under the previous leadership, the norm of team support was easy to maintain, especially since roles were clearly defined, as were standards of performance. Under George, favored individuals were asked to undertake tasks that blurred these once-clear boundaries, and now various individuals on the team found their *lack of role clarity a source of nearly daily conflict.* The group deteriorated from being a group of polite, supportive, and somewhat cooperative individuals to being increasingly suspicious, isolated, and competitive. Informal pairs developed out of sympathy among individuals whose roles were totally unrelated.

5. In the area of leadership, George's behaviors, which according to him had been successful in the highly-charged and competitive world of his previous job, were disastrous. Instead of creating a sense of team, openness, and cooperation, the opposite occurred. The more he felt the team disintegrate, the more he cajoled, threatened, played favorites, and outwardly showed disappointment. The consequence was that the group felt increasingly vulnerable, insecure, and unappreciated.

Here is a highly-paid, esteemed, and previously successful leader who, in relation to the twelve sources of conflict explored earlier, has

- helped generate a variety of distorted perceptions.
- brought into conflict values and beliefs about the group, the work, leadership, and management practices.
- poorly-defined authority, creating insecurity and dependency.
- demonstrated a behavioral style in sharp contrast to the work culture.
- been insensitive to the personal needs and individual goals of those in his work group.
- perpetrated transgressions on many of the team's members, such as humiliating them in public or not responding to voice- or E-mail.
- failed to provide a sense of encouragement through recognizing and appreciating the efforts of various team members.
- created endless conflicts of choice for individuals, such as needing to choose whether to be honest about their boss's request for information when they realize honesty will very likely lead to abuse.

What to Do with Conflict: Creating a Design

Conflict, by nature, is something that usually is not sought. More often than not, it appears on the scene rather unexpectedly. The result is that its presence tends to be either reactive (the classic fight response), or to avoid it altogether (the flight response). Being planful and proactive when our "conflict juices" are flowing is not the strong suit of most people. Being reactive in the face of conflict often brings out the very worst in us. Being adversarial, aggressive, or even hostile when fueled by anger can be a natural response, but it is a recipe for disaster.

However, for those able to put their feelings and immediate reactions on hold, the chances for a positive resolution immediately rise. Willingness to consider all the possibilities, explore the consequences of any action taken, and delve into the most creative solutions possible can pay substantial dividends over more immediate reactions.

The key to effective conflict resolution is to establish a dispassionate approach to the situation, as someone would for any problem he or she would like to solve. The only difference between a "conflict" and the hundreds of problems we solve every day is degree. Somehow, the emotional energy generated makes us vulnerable. One of our colleagues likes to say that when she becomes emotional in a conflict situation, she immediately loses fifty IQ points. In her words, she becomes "conflict stupid," and she realizes the result can be disastrous. If we multiply this by the number of people in a group, it is easy to see how necessary it is to take special care when we begin to deal with a conflict within our own group or between two groups.

A DESIGN MENTALITY In theory, everything we do as a teacher, boss, facilitator—as a leader of any kind—should be intentional. We would instantly consider the consequences of each action, and whether it would have the impact we desire. We would "design" our response to a situation so that we could help to ensure the best outcome possible. The less thoughtful we are, the more reactive and less skillful in our diagnosis of the situation, the more vulnerable we are to outcomes not beneficial to us or the group. Of course, it's impossible to anticipate all the hundreds of variables that can influence our chosen behavior or action. Nevertheless, the most effective leaders are those who can anticipate the best and, at the same time, are the most creative and adaptable in what they choose to do.

Design is exactly like what occurs in a good chess match. The players are constantly faced with multiple choices and must respond, hoping that they have been able to anticipate the move of their opponent. If they are particularly skilled, they will be able to think several moves ahead, planning a strategy so that the ultimate goal, winning the game, can be achieved. Not paying attention, for even a minute, can lose them the game. In a conflict situation, asking a number of "tough" questions can prepare us to develop a "design strategy" that may prove successful. The less willing we are to discipline ourselves to ask such questions, the more vulnerable we become. The answer to questions such as the following can determine roles and eventual effectiveness of both leaders and group members:

- What are the unresolved issues (unfinished business) of the group?
- Which members are "in" and which appear "out"? What impact does each group member have on the climate of the group?
- Is the physical setting (for example, large table, same seats, predictable roles and behaviors of the participants) conducive to undertaking the work of the group? Would a change in the physical design be helpful?
- Is the task goal of the group clear? How does it relate to the evolving group goal(s)?

- Have certain norms evolved that are inhibiting the progress of the group and that need to be altered?
- Are the leader's behaviors facilitating or blocking the group's ability to do its work?
- Are the members able to express both feelings and ideas freely?
- What is the time of day? Does the group need a change of pace to help energize it?
- Are there personal issues blocking the group's productivity that need to be dealt with?
- Given this information, what type of intervention must occur to move the group forward in its ability to achieve its goal(s)?

Design is a strategic term. It involves planning a number of development activities that should move the group toward its goals. Since most people who meet in groups are engaged in some sort of "meeting" with an agenda, the leaders should think about where the group is now, where is has been, who is present, what the unfinished business is, and how time can be best utilized to maximize the energy and brain power in the group. Failure to ask such hard-nosed questions tends to make most meetings unproductive, boring, and uncreative. When we add to the mix the natural (or unnatural) conflicts that arise, we can begin to see how important "designing" can be and how important such diagnostic questions as these are.

Thus, designing various interventions for a group by the leader or members can have a great impact on the quality of work accomplished and on how conflict is resolved. Conflict will not usually go away by itself. For this reason, it is crucial that leaders think with a design mentality. Although not all design interventions will be successful, a thoughtful response to a conflict situation will result in a greater opportunity for success than might otherwise be expected (Amason, 1996; van de Vliert, Euwema, and Huismans, 1995; Amason et al., 1995; Mondros, Woodrow, and Weinstein, 1992).

TURNING A LIABILITY INTO AN ASSET

What makes most conflicts so difficult to resolve often has more to do with overcoming impediments than with the actual differences that exist. Dealing with rational, cognitive differences usually leads to a better situation in the future. But it is the getting there, the "process" of dealing with the tensions, the various personalities, and the potential of loss that results in groups and individuals becoming "stuck." The pertinent question is, what do we know about design that can help us deal with conflict in a group context more effectively? There is certainly no single set of answers, and authors have devoted whole books to the subject (Weeks, 1994; Folger, Poole, and Stutman, 1997). But the following ideas should act as a guide as we think about some of the elements useful in conflict resolution with groups. One thing is for certain: conflict resolution should be perceived as a process rather than as a definitive set of prescriptions.

1. *Groups respond favorably to training in problem solving, conflict resolution, and decision making.* An ultimately constructive means of helping groups become more effective in conflict situations is to increase their competence in conflict management itself. Something as simple as providing a common language with which to discuss conflict can provide an essential framework for efforts at resolution. By raising the level of group consciousness about the value of particular roles, the use of design interventions, and norms that help to define acceptable behavior of members, a great deal of progress can be made early in the life of a developing team, committee, or task force (van de Vliert, Euwema, and Huismans, 1995; Drinka, 1994; Jehn, 1995).

   For example, one study (Johnson et al., 1995) revealed that, by training an entire class of third-, fourth-, and fifth-grade students in conflict mediation skills, individuals were able to use their learnings successfully in actual conflict situations. The trained group also was able to maintain these skills throughout the school year, and they significantly outperformed the control group. If training can have a measurable impact on such young and naive groups, imagine the possibilities for more mature ones.

   A wide range of other studies have shown how training improved relations and enhanced conflict resolution in groups as diverse as white Anglo-Canadians and Chinese immigrants (Wong, Tjosvold, and Lee, 1992), adolescents and their parents (Openshaw et al., 1992; Wood and Davidson, 1993), elderly people (Drinka, 1994), and workers and managers in an industrial setting (Analoui, 1992). These findings fly in the face of the assumption that, somehow, by using common sense, we should be able to handle conflict in groups. Perhaps because of this popular notion, it appears to be extraordinarily difficult for management in most organizations to commit to the training and development of its workers in basic conflict-management skill areas. Lee (1993), for example, concluded from a study of fifty discussion groups that even minimal training can measurably reduce conflict. By merely teaching participants the importance of focusing on specific areas of agreement before arguing a particular point, it became easier to create a "common ground" on which to build. All too often

FOCUS ON DIVERSITY

Even vastly different groups experience some similar sources of conflict. What factors, in your experience, engender conflict in almost any group?

the phrase, "Yes, I agree but . . ." is used as a way of supposedly agreeing that is followed by a salvo of criticism on a particular point. Before long, the entire set of ideas has gone down in flames. The group is suddenly thrown out of sync and loses focus and energy as the area of disagreement overrides many areas of potential agreement.

2. *Because conflict brings out such emotions as insecurity, fear, and hostility, establishing a positive climate is crucial.* If anyone has ever been present when two bargaining units come together, they have had the privilege of witnessing why conflict resolution is so difficult. Instead of searching for areas of possible agreement, both sides begin in the first minutes to polarize the situation by making outrageous claims of their own and tearing down any position of the other party. The predictable result is that people feel misunderstood and rarely heard. Not only this, but the vitriolic language that accompanies such extreme positions is bound to make both parties feel demeaned and angry. The climate for war is established, rather than one for reconciliation. The remainder of the negotiation is spent either attacking the enemy's position or defending one's own. Polarization is inevitable and trust deteriorates rapidly. Even worse, after this conflicted beginning, it is nearly impossible for either party to walk away from the final agreement feeling good about themselves or, for that matter, the other party.

   Climate—the "weather" in a group—is the result of many variables. Simplistically, group members can talk about the atmosphere being stormy or calm, hot or cool, heavy or light, gloomy or bright. It's impossible, though, to explain the climate of a group based on any one or two variables. Some researchers (Folger, Poole, and Stutman, 1997) contend that climate is something that is maintained over some time, although like any weather system it can be influenced fairly dramatically at any moment. When walking into the negotiations discussed above, the climate might be described as suspicious, hostile, pessimistic, difficult, or even shaky. In weather terms, it might be stormy, with hurricane warnings and all communication lines down.

   The climate in a group has a lot to do with feelings and attitudes, emotions, and the behaviors that determine each. Sometimes we can walk into a room and the climate seems to leap out at us. The prevailing climate in George's group, above, included words like *fear, intimidation, competition,* and *favoritism.* It was easy to feel. People talked in whispers, acted secretively, and seldom laughed out loud. The prevailing climate in a group, like the prevailing wind in a weather system, is also determined by the goals, norms, membership, and the leadership being demonstrated at any one time.

Let's look at the facts in our example that caused a climate of mistrust, fear, and suspicion.

A. George said loudly and clearly that one of his goals was to have a team. The problem was the individuals were rewarded, not for collaborating with each other, but for competing for his attention and favor—often at the expense of others. Thus, membership was tenuous at best and totally dependent on George's favor.
B. Norms were established to not risk, not speak the truth, and never place oneself in the position of being vulnerable. Thus, speaking a minimal amount, about superficial things, was accepted. People would not raise issues that could be criticized. People would not criticize each other either. The silent agreement was, "If you don't attack me, I won't attack you." This left most of the criticism in the hands of George, which increased his power and danger to the group. It also increased the group's dependency.
C. Because George did not define his own boundaries of authority, individuals never knew if they had real authority to make decisions even if the authority was in their job description. If George got wind of anything he didn't like, there was no question which way the decision would go. The consequence was that members lost their confidence, their desire to risk, and their willingness to take initiative unless George had given his blessing. In this way too, George fostered a climate of dependency in spite of his desire for staff members to think and act independently.
D. In an organizational culture where norms of niceness, being indirect, and being nonconfrontational had predominated, George's leadership behavior proved disorienting; he could be direct, abusive, and confronting. This left people unsure, insecure, and confused at a time when George himself demanded greater certainty, confidence, and clarity from his direct reports.

In weather terms, George represented a hurricane, and all hands battened down the hatches. To survive, people watched the direction of the storm and its intensity before risking anything. The one slight benefit was that a certain sympathy for each other's plight developed among the team members. That is, even though the team didn't trust each other, and wondered who would be George's favorite of the month, they hunkered down together and became more cohesive because of the similar threat they all faced. Strange as it may seem, cohesion was rising as trust and security continued to plummet.

If a member or leader has the capacity to understand the predominant norms, he or she will be able to determine how open, intimate, dependent, or committed a group is. The norms are like boulders on a path, which indicate not only the direction of the group but also how much of a struggle it will have along the way toward achieving its goals. Similarly, an observant person will be able to determine how cohesive a group is, and how membership is gained or lost. The nature of individual and group goals will also influence climate.

It's interesting to note that just as a culture cannot be shaped or determined by a single person, neither can a climate (Fink and Chen, 1995). It is, for example, the interaction of George with the others on the team that synergistically creates the climate of that particular organization. Even though George is a huge negative influence on the group and the climate is clearly negative—even hostile—he personally would deny that the climate is negative. Worse yet, many in the group would overtly agree with him since to admit that there are problems would place them in jeopardy. They would have to defend their view with specific examples, which would mean identifying George as a problem. This would not happen in the climate of mistrust and fear.

Recently one of the authors worked with an organization of 1,200 people that had spent years struggling to build a trusting and highly productive workforce. They had decided on four core values that were to be the pillars of how they operated. These were: *speaking the truth, showing respect, working as a team, and doing excellent work.* These four values were meant to drive the organization toward a climate fostering greater competence and trust.

The organization's members scored high on excellence and teamwork but fell short on showing each other the respect they desired. Furthermore, the openness and truth telling many desired was undermined by gossip. Conversations the bosses needed to hear were seldom held openly.

Rather than being satisfied with "do good" slogans, the leaders, along with selected staff, took a hard look at the factors that inhibited people from telling the truth and being as open as they would like. They found that the source of most of the grumbling going on behind the scenes stemmed from a perceived lack of accountability. Apparently, some people's ineffective behavior was actually being rewarded because leaders didn't wish to rock the boat. Frustrated, individuals and small groups talked up a storm, griping and complaining among themselves. However, they never confronted the admired boss, whose one Achilles' heel was difficulty in holding some poor-performing, high-level employees to the standards he espoused. The gossiping and backbiting, which were symptoms of larger system dysfunction, had begun to eat away at the organizational climate and had undermined the spoken values of the organization. By addressing the functional issue of accountability and establishing measurable standards, the values of truth and respect were fostered and the climate became more positive.

3. *By providing clear structure, guidelines, and ground rules for task or cognitive conflicts (versus affective or relationship conflicts), conflict resolution can be significantly enhanced.* Many studies confirm that when groups are provided guidelines for operating in the face of conflict, the amount of conflict diminishes significantly. In one study of nearly 200 nurses, those who simply took time to gain perspective and avoid being reactive in conflict situations were able to reduce significantly the amount and type of responses they made to task conflicts (Sessa, 1996). Similarly, in a group of 150 business students, the use of a structured process of inquiry that actually encouraged conflict was paradoxically shown to enhance the quality of decision making. And people who were encouraged to be open about their conflict had greater satisfaction in their groups than did control groups in which conflict was not overtly supported (Prien, Harrison, and Muir, 1995).

George deBono is best known for his insights into how to release creativity in problem-solving groups. According to him, the notion that creativity is gained by reducing all social and emotional constraints and encouraging free-wheeling and spontaneous interaction is simplistic and often counterproductive. Recent research, for example, has revealed that brainstorming does not necessarily create a spontaneous and free environment. The degree to which individuals participate depends on existing norms and trust. People will be free to participate in a brainstorming exercise only if they are free to participate in the group in general. If they fear criticism, this is likely to inhibit their willingness to participate. And without effort to dissipate extraneous stimuli, thinking remains at a superficial level.

However, deBono (1992) believes that, by designing structure and discipline into group problem solving, participants are provided both freedom and safety. DeBono's so-called *lateral-thinking approach* creates focus, uses time as a prod, and generates provocations for a group. This approach frees participants from competition with others and lets them focus their attention. DeBono has shown that such discipline and structure can foster deep and rich thinking, which propels individuals into a safe and productive environment, and that this process is self-reinforcing.

DeBono believes the same considerations are true in the area of conflict resolution (deBono, 1985). Controlling the climate of a group through carefully designed structures allows members to focus on the task rather than concerns about trust or personal safety in what might be a hostile environment. He minimizes the need to compete by reducing criticism, which at the same time increases the ability to contribute. This is accomplished by establishing simple guidelines and structured activities. The activities let participants help generate alternatives, explore areas of agreement, and reframe issues. Adversaries are provided with new choices, and craft solutions together. Depending on the nature of the conflict, deBono's activities allow differences to be explored with objectivity. Without such structure, most conflict deteriorates into "I-said-you-said" debates of justification, without moving the group into the arena of solution.

Another study (Amason et al., 1995) revealed how valuable even a little structure can be. In this case, groups which could focus on substantive issues reported that their disagreements were more creative, they had more open communication, and they were better able to integrate information than groups that became embroiled in personal or emotional issues. Thus, those wishing to diminish conflict and improve team relations should

- provide structured tasks.
- ground the group or team in a clear philosophy.
- agree on specific behavioral strategies for meetings.
- provide good, proactive facilitation.

It is containment of emotions and focus on workable problems that provide safety. Such structuring of conflict situations also equalizes contributions so that the more powerful people cannot dominate an already tense situation. (A good example of proactive facilitation is the Future Search Design, below, which can easily be used in a situation of conflict between two groups or where differences among members of a team occur.)

UTILIZING A STRUCTURED DESIGN TO REDUCE CONFLICT IN A GROUP

Groups, like individuals, can lose sight of their objectives, become frustrated, and be ineffective when conflict becomes emotional and enmeshed in personality differences. But appropriate structures designed for a potentially divisive situation can help maintain focus, provide safety, generate humor, and increase levels of objectivity and rationality in the group. A concrete example of how this can occur follows. It is a design used to reduce conflict among a work team in which interpersonal issues had kept members from working effectively together. The group could no longer afford to be blocked by their typical dysfunctional behavior.

The team was comprised of twelve people. Over the course of a year, the group had degenerated from a positive and rather cohesive unit to one that seemed divisive, adversarial, and noncommunicative. The problems appeared to stem from the beliefs of some members that not everyone on the team was sharing equally in the work load. Some felt that there were great differences in levels of both productivity and work quality. Sharp words and negative judgments had turned into screaming matches, blaming, and defensiveness. It was clear that something had to be done but that conversation would be very difficult. A two-day retreat was planned to get the team back on track by dealing with the issues of productivity, fairness, and trust. Needless to say, however, the idea of the meeting was greeted with considerable trepidation.

GOALS OF THE RETREAT Identifying specific goals is an essential aspect of designing an effective intervention. The team leader and two individuals representing different perspectives were given the task of designing activities to satisfy the following goals:

1. To ensure an open discussion of issues, without fear of intimidation or abuse
2. To raise the level of trust
3. To provide problem-solving strategies that resulted in agreed-upon action steps to move the group forward
4. To have some fun as a team

As a means of identifying the underlying issues, the three members of the planning group asked each of the other members to name the "hardest" questions that each thought needed to be answered during the retreat. The planning group hoped that these questions could provide the foundation for a diagnostic design that would generate the critical issues without polarizing the group. The three planners believed that if the team could experience meaningful communication during the first morning of the two days, their chances of success would greatly improve. Thus, the intervention of the first morning would be critical. The intentions were to help group members feel heard, to recognize that they could begin to deal with difficult issues in a safe manner, and to allow each person the opportunity to express himself or herself in an honest open manner.

THE FUTURE SEARCH The planners believed that the design strategy below would fulfill the group's initial needs and provide a necessary foundation for meeting the goals of the two days.

First, the planners culled the following six "tough" questions from the list developed from the initial interviews of the twelve team members:

1. What ground rules can we establish during our meetings to ensure that we treat each other with the respect each member of this team deserves? Please be specific.

2. What are the values we say we believe as a group but somehow fail to live (areas of value where we don't "walk" our "talk")?
3. What are the qualities we have in our team that, before our recent struggles, made us unique and quite effective?
4. Without changing the composition of the team, if you were the leader, what three things would you do to get us back on track, raise morale, and improve our productivity?
5. It is clear that we have issues surrounding the distribution of work and expectations. What do you and others believe we could do to improve the current situation in this area?
6. What are the behaviors or factors that you believe cause the most tensions for us in our team?

Once the planners had chosen the questions they believed had to be addressed, the issue became, How do we raise such difficult questions in a manner that will allow people to be as honest as possible without becoming defensive? It was clear that any blaming and finger pointing could further polarize the already-divided group. Furthermore, it could be anticipated that members would arrive at the session feeling vulnerable and mistrusting each other. For that reason, the planning committee decided not to work with the whole group initially; working individually and in pairs on specific tasks would be much safer and more productive.

The specific exercise the planners chose was the Future Search. The Future Search is useful because it

- requires people to listen.
- enables people to feel heard.
- allows tough issues to be addressed in a safe, structured environment.
- is active and engaging.
- keeps individuals from having to justify or defend their beliefs.
- establishes a climate where objectivity and clear thinking is valued.
- provides opportunity for having fun while tackling serious issues.
- tends to raise trust levels among participants.

After a brief orientation to the two days, the twelve team members were divided into two rows of six, each member facing another directly across from him or her.

Row <u>A</u>	X	X	X	X	X	X	Stationary Row
	Q1	Q2	Q3	Q4	Q5	Q6	
Row <u>B</u>	O	O	O	O	O	O	Moving Row
	Q3	Q6	Q5	Q1	Q2	Q4	

Each person sitting in **Row A** (the **X row**) was provided a question numbered 1 through 6, as shown in the diagram. Likewise, each person in **Row B** (the **O row**) also received a question numbered from 1 through 6. Each row had the same six questions, but no one was sitting across from anyone with the same question.

The activity began with each person in the X row asking the person in front his or her question. Three minutes were allowed for interviewing responders, and questioners were to probe, ask for clarification, seek examples and generally gather as much information as the other person was willing to share. The interviews themselves were confidential; any information drawn from them would become part of a total "picture" of information based on six interviews, and individual contributors would not be identified.

At the end of three minutes, the person in the O row had the opportunity to ask his or her question of the person sitting opposite.

In the next step, the people in Row A (the X row) remained seated while those in Row B (the O row) shifted one seat to their left, with the person at the left end taking the empty chair at the right end. Now each member was faced with a new person to interview, and the process took place as before.

The activity continued until each person in Row A interviewed everyone in Row B and was in turn interviewed by everyone in Row B. Thus, at some point in the rotation, each interviewer has the opportunity to respond to his or her own question.

WHY AN UNREMARKABLE DESIGN HAS REMARKABLE RESULTS What appears to be a rather simple design has proven successful in dozens of difficult conflict situations. Over years, the following reasons have been identified (Napier, Sidle, and Sanaghan, 1998):

1. The *physical structure of the activity,* as well as its specific and boundaried directions, add to the safety of participants. People are fearful that unresolved feelings and resentments will explode into hostile and reactive behaviors, but it is extremely difficult for this to happen when they are given specific responsibilities and accountability is so visible.
2. *Clear time boundaries* accompanying specific tasks hold the attention of members on what they are doing rather than on old feelings of fear or anger.
3. The intentional *physical proximity* of the participants—next to each other and directly across from each other—allows them to move close and listen carefully so that the interview is successful. Participants report that a sense of secrecy and intimacy develop as a result of the physical setting imposed.

4. The *structure of the interview* itself does not allow for heated debate. Instead, individuals are placed in the unusual position of having to listen dispassionately. Simultaneously, listeners have the rare experience of feeling heard, in some cases by people with whom they often disagree or for whom they have leftover feelings or unfinished business.
5. The *provocative nature of the questions* tends to get the critical issues "on the table" and to legitimize talking about ideas that are usually discussed secretly or only within informal groups.
6. *Participants have control over how much they say.* Part of the integrity of the process is that individuals feel they have a real choice in how much they choose to reveal. Nevertheless, witnessing the intense interviewing going on around them, people have a tendency to speak the truth.
7. *The shared-risk* nature of the experience apparently raises the stakes for participants, and creates a sense of exhilaration after the group has walked on eggshells for so long. People are ready to talk, and the risky nature of the talk feels good, as does the catharsis that occurs.
8. The opportunity to be *fully involved* in influencing the outcome of the process is perceived as positive by most participants.

This is a good example of a design, then, in which participants have considerable freedom to control what and how much they say. Yet the control and structure of the activity itself provides the safety critical to success. One of the truisms of conflict resolution is that everything a leader or facilitator does should be intentional, and all consequences should be anticipated. This wisdom is demonstrated by the Future Search design, the outcomes of which include more safety, trust, and optimism than existed previously. People in conflict need a sense of hope if they are to move such treacherous waters, followed by growing certainty and greater willingness to risk.

PROCESSING THE INFORMATION OF THE FUTURE SEARCH Following the interviews, each person was asked to take fifteen minutes to organize his or her data into truths or facts, trends, or unique ideas. By organizing the data in this manner, participants had the opportunity to objectify information that may have contained the potential for considerable tension. A truth represents an idea that four, five, or six people mentioned; it is an idea or feeling that stands out or "jumps off the page." A trend represents an idea or theme that arises two, three, or perhaps four times and therefore warrants being raised. Because most facts started as trends, group members who wish to head off conflicts before they become crises need to pay attention to such concerns. Finally, unique ideas represent the few gems that arise in the interviews. These may be a creative idea or insight of a single individual that the interviewer believes warrants further consideration by the group. Unique ideas represent a rare and valuable point of view that might otherwise be lost.

Together, the two individuals who have interviewed using the same question hold information representing 100 percent of those present. So as the next step, once everyone organized their information, these pairs got together. They negotiated a presentation to the whole group of their agreed-upon truths, trends, and unique ideas. It was their job to educate the group to the information they had gathered.

Finally, they were asked to develop a skit or vignette depicting one of their salient *truths,* which they hoped the groups would never forget.

Although people often resist doing skits, they inevitably prove to be a huge source of insight—and hilarious fun. The tendency to exaggerate, and the fact that the truth being portrayed can't be denied, gives the group the much-needed opportunity to lighten up and laugh at itself. Once a group can begin to see the humor in its own plight, it becomes much easier for individuals to "own" their part of an issue. The truths and trends provide the opportunity to step back and become more dispassionate, and less blaming and angry. The humor allows play to creep into the often deadly black-and-white, win-lose nature of most arguments. Finally, the unique ideas provide some creative, outside-the-box thinking, which is in short supply as differences accelerate and positions solidify.

The Future Search can be both diagnostic—identifying the underlying issues that exist and must be addressed—and solution-directed. In our example, question 1 had a solution focus and would provide ground rules for working together in spite of differences. Question 2, concerning values "talked but not walked," was diagnostic, as was question 3, relating to strengths of the group. This type of question is especially important to include, since so much time in conflict situations focuses on criticism and blame and the considerable strengths of a team are often forgotten. Question 4 was solution-directed, generating alternatives for helping get the group's process back on track. And Question 5 focused directly on the tough issue of the unequal distribution of work that had to be addressed. In no case, however, was the information seen as an end point even if lots of good ideas were generated.

PROBLEM SOLVING, NEGOTIATING, AND DECIDING Once anger has been diffused, tension reduced, and people are once again talking and listening to each other, then it is possible to design even more formalized problem-solving activities (see Chapter 7). In this case, the Future Search was followed by a problem-solving activity after lunch, which was chosen by the design team based on the successes of the morning session. With acrimony on the run and optimism up, two groups engaged in an extensive problem-solving activity addressing norms surrounding accountability, which was seen as the most crucial factor uncovered in the morning session. The two groups then discussed the strengths and limitations of each set of proposed strategies. Finally, they developed an experimental plan to be evaluated by the whole group in a follow-up session after six months.

Summary Considerations for Managing Conflict in a Group Setting

Dealing with conflict is perceived as difficult and often dangerous. Many liken it to a minefield, where we can see the desired goal, but any direction we go could lead to mayhem or death. The rule is to proceed, but very carefully.

True, there is always risk. But to stay where we are, not to move, not to intervene, will almost never improve the situation. The idea of carefully *designing* a strategy for intervening, and giving attention to the consequences of each action, is essential. Following is a list of the tough-minded questions that can provide perspective for a member, leader, or facilitator seeking to normalize conflict in a group setting. The questions summarize the critical aspects of this chapter.

1. What individual needs do the various participants have that might influence their ability to deal with an identified conflict in an open and positive manner?
2. Has some effort been made to educate those involved in the conflict in the principles and terminology of conflict resolution?
3. Has an effort been made to understand, and improve, the current climate within the group in order to increase trust among those involved in the conflict-resolution process?
4. Is the identified conflict a symptom of other, less visible and perhaps more systemic issues that must be addressed by the group?
5. Has the information which needs to surface been gathered in a manner that ensures the safety of those involved?
6. Has the identified conflict been related to issues of membership, communication, goals, norms, and leadership, especially as to how any one characteristic affects the others?
7. Have the parties in conflict been provided the necessary safety through the security of structure and well-designed activities that deal with the physical setting and the emotional needs of those participating?

For Further Information

Folger, J. P.; M. S. Poole; and R. K. Stutman. *Strategies for Relationships, Groups, and Organizations.* New York: Longman, 1997.

Deutsch, M. *The Resolution of Conflict.* New Haven, Conn.: Yale University Press, 1973.

This highly readable book ties theory and research over a fifty-year period into logical and applied conclusions. Focuses more than other books on the research roots of a particular approach. The attempt is to bring clarity to what readers can actually do when faced with a conflict. Provides some examples that may be useful.

Game theory, problem solving, and choices were of interest to early conflict theorists. The following books provide solid foundations in game theory and for later discussions of conflict resolution:

In many respects, Martin Deutsch is recognized as the father of modern conflict theory and research. Using laboratory techniques in the fledgling field of social science research and group dynamics, he influenced the thinking of three decades of research and applied thinking.

Shubik, M. *Game Theory in the Social Sciences: Concepts and Solutions.* Cambridge, Mass.: MIT Press, 1985.

Von Neumann, J., and O. Morganstern. *Theory of Games and Economic Behavior.* Princeton, N. J.: Princeton University Press, 1947.

Hendrix, H. *Getting the Lover You Want: A Guide for Couples.* New York: Harper & Row, 1988.

Few would deny that if we bring two people together, there is likely to be some conflict based on differences in values, opinions, or style. Thus, one of the fertile grounds for understanding the nature of conflict has to do with couples. The two books above can help those who would like to be more effective in relationships with others, especially in conflict situations.

Hendrix is a master teacher who builds theory into practical activities for helping couples learn skills and tools for handling their differences. He concludes that such differences usually result from deeply ingrained patterns stemming from unsatisfactory relationships with parents. His approach to active listening is among the most useful the authors have experienced. He is at his best in the activities to unblock ineffective communication and at the same time resolve or heal differences.

Lerner, H. G. *The Dance of Anger.* New York: Harper & Row, 1986.

Gordon, T. *Parent Effectiveness Training.* New York: New American Library, 1975.

Issues surrounding how children are to be raised and disciplined can be among the most challenging when the parents have been raised under different values and parenting behaviors. More than two decades ago, Gordon provided many of the insights and much of the language on effective conflict resolution when he introduced this now-famous book. Many of his ideas still remain in vogue.

Bush, R. B., and J. P. Folger. *The Process of Mediation: Responding to Conflict Through Empowerment and Recognition.* San Francisco: Jossey-Bass, 1994.

During the past decade, conflict management has placed much more emphasis on such notions as negotiations, common ground, and mediation. The five following books successfully portray this approach:

Fisher, R., and S. Brown. *Getting to Yes.* Boston: Houghton Mifflin, 1981.

Fisher, R., and S. Brown. *Getting Together.* New York: Penguin, 1988.

Fisher and Brown (1981) take a tactical or transactional approach to getting what it is desired in a negotiation. Their second book reflects on their further work on the Harvard Negotiation Project and focuses much more on the need to build solid and trusting relationships so as to continue resolving differences in the future.

Moore, C. W. *The Mediation Process.* San Francisco: Jossey-Bass, 1986.

Putnam, L., and M. E. Roloff. *Communication and Negotiation.* Newbury Park, Calif.: Sage, 1992.

Weisinger, H. *Anger at Work.* New York: William Morrow, 1995.

Since most of us work now or will work in the future, readers may be interested in the nature of conflict in work situations. Even more important is to develop some understanding of how to deal with conflict, and the anger that usually accompanies it. This book deals with these issues in a straightforward and helpful manner:

The following two books take a very personal approach to conflict. Both assume, at some level, that if we pay close attention to how we feel, the messages we send, and our own behavior in a conflict situation, the likelihood is great that we will be able to reduce our levels of conflict.

Weeks, D. *The Eight Essential Steps to Conflict Resolution.* New York: Putnam, 1992.

This book is a very practical guide for handling a wide variety of interpersonal conflicts. Explores the source of a particular type of conflict and then how to handle it, from both emotional and strategic points of view.

Crum, T. F. *The Magic of Conflict.* New York: Touchstone, 1988.

This book is also strategic, but the author's approach has much more to do with the way we live. He can help readers become more conscious, open, and aware of their possibilities. Using Aikido[1] as a metaphor, he advocates knowing ourselves and eliminating judgments so that we are able to truly see "what is"; only then is it possible to be truly flexible and capable of changing in a way that helps in conflict situations.

1. A Japanese art of self-defense employing locks and holds and utilizing the principle of nonresistance to cause an opponent's own momentum to work against him.

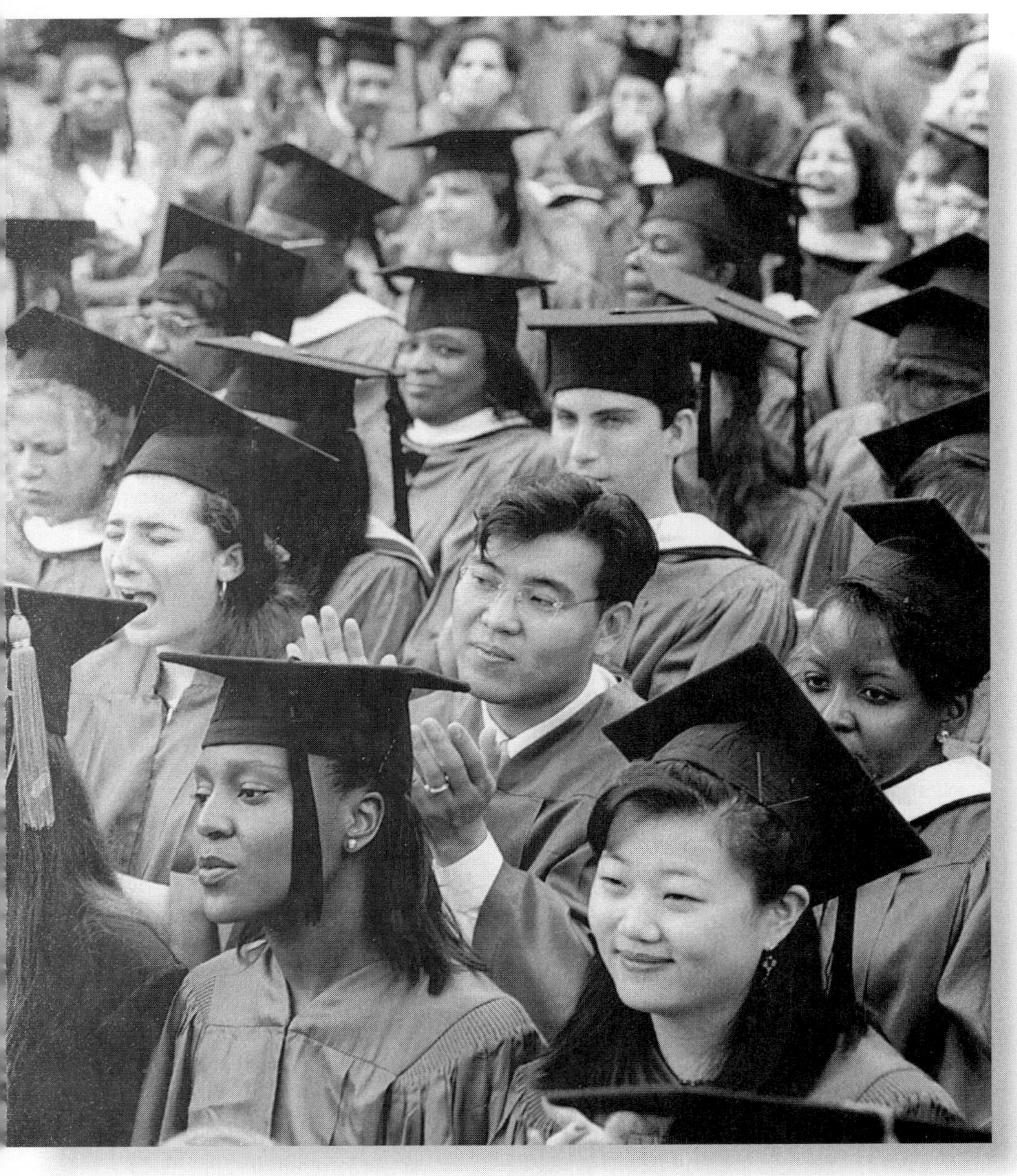

9 The Evolution of Groups

The young assistant professor, not yet used to the letters *Ph.D.* following his name, had been hired by the large, urban university to teach courses in the behavioral sciences. He arrived on campus both excited about sharing his new wisdom and terrified that he was ill-equipped to deal with his students.

Before classes began, one of his colleagues asked if he had ever had a course in group dynamics. Nonchalantly, he told her he had had several experiences with it, though in truth he had no idea what she was talking about. She invited him to join her group dynamics class as a student to help orient him, and out of courtesy he accepted, wondering how much more there was to learn after nearly seven years of graduate school in psychology.

The course was like nothing he had ever experienced. The group members sat around in a circle attempting to learn about group behavior simply by becoming a group. There was no other agenda, no text on which to lean, no rules, no predetermined roles or goals. The instructor sat quietly, observing the students as they struggled to define their goals and determine whether they were succeeding or failing. The void filled with the students' identity, influence, purpose, and control. Occasionally the professor made an observation on the group's process, but she kept her contributions to a minimum. The lack of structure resulted in an explosion of feelings.

The young man was amazed at what he saw. In the fertile ambiguity of this unstructured environment, every kind of behavior he had ever studied began to surface; the group became a true laboratory of human behavior. Three-hour meetings took place once a week for thirteen weeks, and at every one the group faced a new crisis as it came to grips with issues of identity, trust, frustration, and power.

What amazed him most of all was his colleague's behavior. Each week, she calmly threw out one or two brilliant, pointed observations that propelled the group to new levels of understanding. He was both grateful for her wisdom and angered by his own inability to see and understand what seemed obvious to her. She seemed to see deeply not only into the present but also into future events, while he floundered along with everyone else, struggling with whatever was blocking the group's purpose at any given moment. Long after the course ended, he confided to her that at times he had seen her as a cross between a witch and a magician—serene, all powerful, and one who somehow knew what would happen in the group, perhaps in all groups, before it even occurred.

This woman's power and the source of her influence on the group was her ability to understand the predictable developmental patterns of virtually any group—but particularly one so ill defined as this one. Her "crystal ball" consisted of her experience with the issues all groups face and the predictable consequences of dealing with, or failing to deal with, them. This chapter probes the phenomenon of group development and explores those identifiable stages.

The Task and Emotional Aspects of Groups

Society, institutions, and small groups are often established with the goal of being democratic and egalitarian and maintaining lines of communication, yet contradictory forces create tensions. The forces are real, and we must grasp their nature if we are to understand the sources of many stresses that derive from human interaction. An example will help describe the nature of these forces (Cooley, 1909; Parsons, 1951).

> The young religious novice enters the convent in an order that specializes in medical services. Her goal is to be a missionary and to work as a hospital administrator in one of the developing countries. Her personal training focuses on two areas: the technicalities of hospital administration (accounting, deployment of services, supervision) and her own personal growth as a sister dedicated to such virtues as love, charity, and faith. Her relationships with the other novices and sisters are warm and affectionate, and she finds it difficult to leave for her first assignment in a small Ghanaian hospital. The transition proves to be overwhelming. From the nurturing atmosphere of the convent, where acceptance was immediate and unqualified, where gentleness and consideration for others were rewarded, she enters her new environment. Here, there is never enough time, every day is a new crisis, and decisions are immediate and based less on human feelings than on expediency and efficiency. Her value to the hospital has little to do with Christian virtues. It depends on how effectively she can keep the hospital out of the red, how efficiently she can keep the illiterate workers working, and how well she is able to marshal the limited resources available. Failure means transfer, perhaps into an even less desirable situation or into another area of work.

In this example, there was a large discrepancy between expectations and reality, between what was desirable and conditions that prevailed. What stands out is the constant struggle between work efficiency and personal needs, between success measured in terms of task roles and success in terms of emotions. The dichotomy, of course, is less apparent in the absence of such a dual set of expectations. In the army, the rules, regulations, and codes of behavior are clearly detailed. A career soldier is fully cognizant of these and can accept the depersonalized nature of many of the relationships that exist. Similarly, a young person applying for a job with a Wall Street bank finds a complex set of rules (both explicit and implicit) that governs his or her behavior, clothes, hair style, language, accepted level of feelings to be displayed, and relations with other workers in the bank. When individuals accept these rules and know full well what is expected of them, they usually experience little tension, because the personal-emotional factor has been largely screened from their work involvement.

In most groups and organizations, however, no such clear distinction exists, and this is exactly where stress often originates. For example, in some groups, people wish to be accepted for themselves and not because of academic degrees, superficial knowledge, or other artificial standards; but some groups tend to define success in terms of some visible achievement. Material wealth (how much do you earn?), status (executive assistant to whom?), power (how many people under you?), or tenure (you have twenty-five years with this department?) are much easier to grasp than the hazy variables that form the basis of most personal relationships. Thus, most groups and organizations are established in such a manner that personal acceptance is conditional and based on some implicit or explicit achievement criteria.

Work-oriented task groups tend to be high in control, depend on material rewards for motivation, stress accuracy, organize their use of time, and minimize the range of free expression and autonomy allowed. Similarly, such conditions encourage individual competition rather than interdependence, conformity rather than individuality. Management becomes uncomfortable when informality creeps in, when personal relations begin to get in the way of efficiency, and when regulations are altered to meet the peculiar needs of particular individuals. The fabric of army life would break down if exceptions were made to the rule. The same could be said for big business, the organized church, and large school systems.

For example, it is difficult to imagine the following situations occurring:

On the day of a major battle, a young private remarks to his field sergeant, "I hope you won't mind, but I probably won't be going to the front today. This headache is killing me." The sergeant looks on with great sympathy and says, "That's all right, Joe, we all have days like that. Why don't you just rest and take it easy today and save yourself for tomorrow?"

"Miss Jones, you mean you didn't get that rush report out that I asked you to do?" "No, I'm sorry," she replied, "but Johnny surprised me last night, and we went out for the most heavenly Lobster Thermidor you can imagine." "Well," he said, "I know how you feel about John, and there will be other contracts. After all, we're only young once."

"Well, Mr. Gibbs, how are you today, and did you like my sermon?" The minister waited expectantly for the usual monitored reply. "To tell the truth, I really felt you were talking down to us, and if there is one thing I don't appreciate, it's being lectured to in a condescending fashion. Also, you tended to stray from the point by bringing in humorous asides which, although interesting, tended to distract me from the issue."

Sympathy from a field sergeant, acceptance of gross inefficiency from one's boss, and criticism of a minister are difficult to imagine within the context of expected role behaviors and institutional demands. Multiplied a thousand times, these expectations condition our behavior in nearly all groups in which people are involved. They are tied to a Puritan ethic and years of involvement in schools, businesses, and churches, where acceptance is linked to our output, dependability, efficiency, and conformity.

IMPLICATIONS FOR SMALL GROUPS

When entering a group, we look for familiar hooks on which to hang our hats, signs that make the unpredictable predictable, sure ways of being accepted. Even in a social group, we often begin by sharing credentials, strengths, or skills in order to establish a tone of respectability. When working on a task, meeting a deadline, or in some way remaining highly task-oriented, there tends to be an order and safety in working relations. But if the curtain of formality is drawn away, we can almost feel the strain of another set of forces pushing for greater intimacy and the personalizing of behavior, as well as greater authenticity. Informality implies increasing our vulnerability and willingness to take risks in a group in which trust is typically built around performance. Indeed, it is the rare group that can effectively combine social–emotional interests with those necessary for getting the job done. It is not so much that they cannot be combined, but that the combination necessarily increases the complexity of the existing relationships and the risks for the participants. It simply may not be worth the trouble, and, in fact, efficiency may decline and overall problems increase.

Reader Activity

We seldom take the time to sit back and consider the subtle, rarely discussed sources of stress and tension that we experience within an organization simply because its values and priorities differ from our personal needs, self-interests, and values. These differences are natural and, to some degree, we must accommodate them. Take a moment and respond to the following questions in relation to an organization (and group) in which you are a participant. This could be a church, social or professional club, school, place of work, or even your family.

1. What gives members status? Are there certain attitudes, behaviors, or accomplishments that are particularly important to the group that seem much less important to you as an individual?
2. If a new person were to join your group, what would he or she have to do to gain the most immediate acceptance? How do you feel about this? Are there behaviors that you believe are important but that are given almost no weight by the group or the organization of which it is a part?
3. In a typical day, what are the kinds of emotions people tend to show? Are there emotions or feelings you wish would be acceptable but are not?
4. Are there certain rules (stated or unstated) within the group or organization that are absolutes, that you feel are too inflexible, or that tend to dehumanize its members? In what areas is there no room for individual differences where there should be?

In many cases, the nature of a group or organization simply will not allow the legitimate expression of basic social–emotional needs. If the resulting pressures and frustrations do not find release outside the group, or if informal avenues are not created within, it is likely that tensions will be released indirectly. Usually this occurs by creating interpersonal conflicts around the task at hand. Thus, the task itself becomes the avenue for non-task-related expression of tension. Strange as it may seem, the very presence of restrictions designed to prevent extraneous issues from undermining a group's work creates new areas of stress that may be even more insidious and difficult to deal with. A group goes through predictable stages in development that affect how these interpersonal forces influence it.

The Stages of Group Development

Groups, like individuals, develop through predictable stages of growth over time. In work groups, social or political groups, sports teams, and classroom groups, a predictable pattern of group evolution emerges in which each stage has certain definite characteristics. The following description of the events that may occur as a group develops, and the accompanying driving forces, is a composite of many views.[1] It is presented not as a model for all groups but as an example of events that may take place and needs that may exist. The case that follows assumes an ongoing group with a reason for being, wherein members have relatively little personal information about fellow members, differing perceptions of the task, and different methods in mind for reaching the goals. Finally, it assumes a group that is starting out, although much that is suggested is relevant to groups at various stages of development.

THE BEGINNING

People have expectations of what will occur in a group even before they attend. We flavor our first perceptions with these expectations and our personal needs. We bring with us our individual histories and experiences in previous groups. It is these factors that provide the lenses through which the group is perceived. First, it is necessary to become included in the group, and then to attempt to be relatively secure in an unknown situation. For most, it appears to be a time for waiting, anticipating what lies ahead, sorting out potential dangers, and acting with discretion. Thus,

1. The composite was drawn from the views of many people working with a wide range of experiences and types of groups. They include W. Bennis, W. Bion, R. B. Cattell, V. Cernius, A. M. Cohen, E. Erikson, J. Gibb, R. Handfinger, G. C. Homans, B. C. Kuypers (et al.), R. Lacoursiere, D. C. Lundgran, E. A. Mabry, R. D. Mann, T. Mills, F. Redl, W. Schutz, H. Thelen, C. Theodorsen, B. W. Tuckman, and J. P. Wanous (et al.).

there is a period of gathering data and processing them through the filter of our own previous experiences, biases, and stereotypes. We tend to

keep our feelings to ourselves until we know the situation.

look more secure in our surroundings than we might feel.

be watchful.

lack a feeling of potency or sense of control over our environment.

act superficially and reveal only what is appropriate.

scan the environment for clues to what is proper: clothes, tone of voice, vocabulary, who speaks to whom.

be nice, certainly not hostile.

try to place other participants in pigeonholes so that we can feel comfortable with them.

be confused about what is expected of us.

desire structure and order to reduce our own pressure to perform.

wonder what price we must pay to be "in" and whether the rewards are worth the effort.

find our own immediate needs to be of primary importance.

wait for the leader to establish goals, roles, and who has responsibility (even if we resent its being done).

Our needs to be liked and accepted tend to light the way, and though we are seldom satisfied, there usually are indications of better things to come. On either side of this position there are, of course, the groups that from the first minute are so tightly controlled that our very individuality is lost, and those equally rare groups in which a sense of openness and security prevails immediately. However, most groups are a mix of hope and trepidation, in which our own needs and the views of others provide the ingredients for an initial climate of doubt and hesitation.

MOVEMENT TOWARD CONFRONTATION

It is not until the initial probing into the boundaries of appropriate behaviors has taken place that façades are dropped and individuals establish personal roles and reveal more characteristic behaviors. Much of the new movement in the group relates to the patterns of power and leadership that are being established. How to be liked and accepted by those with influence becomes of central importance to some, and others begin to seek personal recognition and their own spheres of influence. Suddenly the leader becomes not only a source of dependency and admiration but also an object of criticism whose inadequacies become a regular topic of discussion. How things are to be done, how decisions are made and by whom, and issues of freedom and control all become preeminent. Whether there is a leader focus or a member focus, influence and so-called *territoriality* among the participants become central. It is the assertive seeking of our place in the group that promotes behavior formerly hidden, and thus it is a period of new behavioral dimensions for various members and a period in which stereotypes are often revealed as invalid. This springing forth of new behaviors creates suspicion and mistrust in some, and forms the basis for new alliances within the group. It is bound to cause tensions and conflict. Not uncommon are such statements as, "I wouldn't have suspected that of John"; "I knew there was more to her than that soft voice and smile"; and "I didn't know he was capable of being so angry."

Within this more assertive environment, members begin to take more definite stands, and issues become polarized. Instead of an argument being looked at in terms of data and facts, it also becomes a testing ground for personal influence and prestige. Tenacity may be as important as rationality in winning, and for some it is winning or losing, not the issue itself, that is important. The tentativeness is gone, hostility is legitimized, and in many ways the group is much more real than it was in the beginning. Alliances within the group are redrawn more on the basis of experience and behavior than expectations and wishful thinking. Along with the increased amounts of anger being shown, there is probably more laughter and a generally wider range of affective behaviors.

In this phase, we as group members may feel dissatisfied, angry, frustrated, and sad because we perceive the discrepancy between our initial hopes and expectations and the reality of group life, between the task and our ability to accomplish the task. Amid increased signs of rigidity among the participants and an unwillingness to compromise, less assertive members tend to withdraw as others in the group now bring personality issues into what previously had been content or task issues. If the group is able to face its own natural destructive tendencies, there is very likely to be a confrontation followed by resolution and an effort to get people together and back on the track.

COMPROMISE AND HARMONY

A confrontation over work and personal issues will usually occur when individuals who are more willing to compromise recognize how self-defeating the present course of events seems to be. Acting as intermediaries, they reopen issues and help to get individuals talking again. Such a confrontation may also result when some of the more aggressive members realize that their own personal aims are not being met as a result of the present course of action. They begin to see a more amicable climate as essential to any further movement or growth on the part of the group.

The result is a countermovement to shut off the growing hostility, reopen communication, and draw the group together into a more smoothly working body. This effort often ushers in a period of good will and harmony during which there is a reassessment of how people have or have not been working together and how conditions for work might be facilitated. Dissensions ease, deviations in member behaviors appear to be more readily accepted, and self-expression is encouraged. Collaboration is more readily sought, and competitiveness is played down, if not rejected, by the members. The group tends to exude a new confidence and begins actually to see itself as an integrated unit that can be facilitative when it wishes to be. There is a genuine effort to look at issues, discover appropriate resources, and avoid the personalizing of issues that occurred earlier.

After the nearly destructive series of events and the mistrust previously generated, members are careful not to step on one another's toes, to avoid signs of hostility, and to make sure everyone is heard. Real honesty and openness are encouraged, on the one hand, but on the other hand, there is a subtle pressure not to raise any problems that might break down the harmony that has been so difficult to obtain. The denial of personal issues tends to increase tensions that remain unexpressed. With this submergence of issues there is less participant involvement, stimulation, and overall interest.

Thus, although fences have been repaired and wounds covered, it has been done at a cost of some of the group's integrity and efficiency. Resistance appears to be more covert. Instead of leading to greater productivity, this harmony often spells even less efficiency. Eventually the realization dawns that the behaviors within the group are actually inhibiting authenticity and directness. One reason it takes so long to reach decisions is that covert resistance and passivity block progress. The initial elation shared during the beginning of the period gives way to disillusionment and increasing tension. The group's efforts toward harmony simply have not succeeded.

REASSESSMENT

Having worked under a period of relative structure and under conditions of less control, with neither resulting in a satisfactory climate for work, the group seeks a new alternative. One obvious solution is to impose greater operational restrictions to ensure a more rational approach to decision making. Such a thrust would streamline work procedures and redirect the group toward the task with greater efficiency. It would not, however, confront the source of many of the problems created within the group. As with many life problems, this approach only attacks the symptoms and eases the pain of the current situation, but it may be enough to ensure a smoother decision-making process.

If, however, the group decides to delve more deeply into the problems at hand—into causal factors—then considerably more time, energy, and involvement will be the cost. It requires a sizable risk on the part of the members because many issues that have long been submerged will be forced to the surface. Member roles, decision-making procedures, and leadership and communication patterns are likely to come under close scrutiny, as are the personal behaviors that facilitated or inhibited the group. Thus, this becomes a period of reflection on goals and performance, means and ends. There is usually a recognition of how vulnerable the group is to the personal needs, suspicions, and fears that can determine how successful the group is in reaching these goals.

If a group chooses this latter course of action, it must build a mechanism that allows it to appraise its own ongoing operations and to alter its pattern of working behaviors when it is obvious that current methods are not proving effective. The group must face the question of how honest it can be and just what level of personal intimacy must be reached before it can accomplish its goals in the most effective manner.

Often there is a simultaneous realization that, as the functions of the group become increasingly complex and there is a need for more resources, greater interdependence is necessary. Greater participation through division of labor becomes essential, and with it accountability and personal responsibility are spread throughout the group. With greater freedom to communicate and methods of feedback built into the group's operations, necessary tasks are increasingly undertaken by those with particular skills and interests, leadership is shared, and participant involvement generally increases. The notion of accountability is crucial here, and it suggests that individuals know what is expected of them, that their expectations are shared by the group, and that their progress toward meeting these expectations is to some degree measurable.

There is, of course, the possibility that a temporary period of intense conflict will result as tensions and stresses previously withheld are brought out. If a group can overcome the fear of such conflict and realize that conflict can be put to effective use without being destructive to individuals (see Chapter 8), then there will be less reluctance to deal more openly with such issues in the future.

RESOLUTION AND RECYCLING

Effective working groups are not necessarily harmonious and free of tensions and conflict. There seem to be periods of conflict resolution and harmony, and even times when groups tend to regress into a pattern of indecisiveness and floundering. As a group matures, it should find itself resolving conflicts more quickly and with a minimal expenditure of energy. The group at this stage is quite productive, and positive feelings are often generated by succeeding in the task and being part of the group. And, like any mature person, the group should be increasingly able to recognize its own limitations and strengths and build effectively around them. It has been found, however, that if a group is suddenly faced with a crisis, a series of critical deadlines, a number of new participants, or even a controversial new idea, that event may usher in a period of readjustment and a reappearance of old and not necessarily helpful behaviors.

Let's take the example of the South Pointe School in Miami Beach, Florida. As in most schools, the teachers and the principal had worked together for a long time, some even decades. They all knew how the principal "operated" the school and how teachers related to him.

Suddenly, there was a major change. In response to complaints that children were neither learning nor being stimulated, South Pointe was selected as the first public school in the country to be managed by a private company. South Pointe became a very public trial of educational reform. How would the teachers and principal fare in a very different form of education?

The behavior of teachers suddenly being held to a different standard may range from rising to the challenge to becoming repressed, angry, and dogmatic. There may be frequent conflict about how much their school should change and how much they will be influenced by the pilot school.

Confronted with a controversial new idea, any group can enter a period when lines of communication break down, feelings and emotions are denied, and tensions build. Such tensions quite often are released through hostility directed toward other members, thus creating further points of stress.

It is not a sign of group immaturity that such tensions develop, but the degree of maturity is revealed in how effectively the group is able to cope with these very natural problems. A mature group will stop the deteriorating cycle of events by openly exploring the possible causal factors and then providing at least temporary solutions during the period of adjustment. Confronting the issues that tend to debilitate the group reinforces a norm of positive and constructive problem solving, and this will reduce the length and intensity of the regressive cycle.

But groups, like people, can instead become immobilized at certain levels or stages of their development. Some groups never develop the feedback channels or problem-solving mechanisms that allow them to mature and function smoothly. Such groups remain predictably volatile or passive, trapped in a nonproductive pattern without the tools to extricate themselves. In most such groups, members realize that

FOCUS ON DIVERSITY

Do feedback and collaboration occur when an organization's population is diverse? With what results?

things are not "right" but may be unable to ask the tough questions necessary to gain perspective. Where this is the case, groups simply muddle along in their daily routines with little hope for growth or significant improvement.

The concept of *situational leadership* (see Chapter 5) has particular relevance in such circumstances. A situational leader might, for instance, identify the factors impeding a "stuck" group and intervene in its process to enable growth and development to occur. Maturity evolves from the group's skill development, practice, and ability to provide itself with the support and experience required at the time. If the leader fails to view the group developmentally and situationally, the group may lose the opportunity to mature by these means (Carew, Eunice, and Blanchard, 1986).

TERMINATION (ADJOURNMENT)

Group termination or adjournment is the final stage in many theories of group development. It is a critical stage, but one that is often neglected both by researchers and group members. Although the literature on groups and organizations has focused on the development and maintenance of groups, the same groups' closure has been excluded from research agendas.

In addition, the termination or adjournment stage is difficult to study because the groups under scrutiny are usually temporary, one-time, laboratory groups without a larger organizational context.

In some group situations, the final stage represents an end to both the task and relationships that were formed during the task functions. But for many groups, members move back into a larger organizational context to work with similar and different coworkers in other ventures. "Relationships do not cease after the face-to-face events (conversations) engaged in by comembers are terminated" (Sigman, 1991, p. 108). The work that was accomplished in the work group and the way it was accomplished impacts each member and will have implications for future assignments. Shea and Guzzo (1987) perceive groups as a vital human resource and argue that "organizational members will need to know how to start up, maintain, and shut down groups as well as how to handle their individual jobs" (p. 327).

Many work groups end their task work in a frantic, pressurized fashion, leaving little time for interaction or reflection. Yet the termination stage, when approached in a planful way, can provide a rich opportunity for evaluation, reflection, closure. It gives members a chance to collectively assess what was learned and accomplished during their time together. It provides opportunity to honor both effort and achievement. There are both task and relationship issues to consider in this context. Knapp and colleagues (1973) identify accessibility, supportiveness, and summarizing as three valuable behaviors to foster during the adjournment phase. When conducted in a conscious and planned manner, the final stage of a group can add to the personal and professional growth of the members. The experience will feed into the larger organizational memory, for better and worse. The goodbyes allow participants to achieve a cooperative parting. "To not say goodbye is to virtually not recognize having been together, in some concrete and significant sense" (Adato, 1975, p. 257). It can be difficult to terminate a relationship. But whether the relationship was a positive or negative one, the group benefits from the opportunity to reach a level of closure and learning that will strengthen members' ability to work in group settings in the future.

Keyton (1993), seeking to build a model of work group termination, reviewed literature from communication, organizational behavior, sociology, and psychotherapy for assistance. According to this model, after notification of group termination, the members must be involved in termination decisions. In regard to substantive (task) decisions they must

1. review what was completed.
2. assess output compared to objectives.
3. assess the group's ability to meet the evaluation criteria of those who view the group output.
4. prepare the group output for final disposition.
5. decide who will be responsible for future inquiries about the group's work.

At the same time, concerning symbolic (maintenance) function, group members should

1. review the process and procedures used.
2. facilitate the ending of group relationships.
3. celebrate group accomplishments.

Other Views of Group Development

FORMING, STORMING, NORMING, PERFORMING, AND ADJOURNING

On the basis of a twenty-year review of the literature related to group development in therapy, natural, self-study, and laboratory groups, Tuckman and Jensen (1977;

see also Tuckman, 1965) concluded that task groups, like all others, go through five basic stages of development that are rather predictable.

The first stage, *forming,* incorporates all the discomfort found in any new situation in which someone's ego is involved in new relationships. This initial period of caution is followed by a period of predictable *storming,* as members react to the demands of what has to be done, question authority, and feel increasingly comfortable being themselves. The third stage is defined as *norming,* in which the rules of behavior appropriate and necessary for the group to accomplish its task are spelled out, both explicitly and implicitly, and a greater degree of order begins to prevail. Next comes a period of *performing,* in which people are able to focus their energies on the task, having worked through issues of membership, orientation, leadership, and roles. The group is now free to develop working alternatives to the problems confronting it, and a climate of support tends to remain from the norming stage. Finally, with the task nearing completion, the group moves into what is called the *adjourning* period, in which closure to the task and a change in relationships is anticipated.

Although some believe it is most difficult to consider the development of a group without stressing the interdependency of task and maintenance or process functions, Tuckman found it helpful to view each of the stages from two points of view. The first is that of interpersonal relationships. Thus, a group moves through predictable stages of testing and dependency (forming), tension and conflict (storming), building cohesion (norming), and, finally, establishing functional role relationships (performing) before it adjourns. Each of these substages focuses on the problems inherent in developing relationships among members.

At the same time, a group is struggling with the problems of the task. In light of this, the initial stage focuses on task definition, boundaries, and the exchange of functional information (forming), followed by a natural emotional response to the task (storming), a period of sharing interpretations and perspectives (norming) before reaching a stage of emergent solutions (performing).

A TASK VIEW OF GROUP DEVELOPMENT

Paul Hare and David Naveh (1984) spent years researching crucial and predictable stages in the development of small groups. According to them, in every problem-solving group there are four identifiable stages. The first phase, called *L,* stands for *latent* pattern maintenance and tension reduction. It is marked by a group's natural need to reach agreement as to its purposes, work methods, expectations, and participant obligations. This agreement reduces the inevitable tensions surrounding the group's direction, priorities, and maintenance in the problem-solving process.

The second phase, *A,* involves what they refer to as *adaptation.* During this phase, a group generates critical information necessary to solving the problem at hand. It lays out facts and identifies the necessary skills and resources required for eventual solution. Also, participants identify and take on essential roles that are key to the problem-solving effort.

Integration (*I*) is the focus of the third phase. This phase requires flexibility, reassessment, and innovation on the part of members and leaders alike as they struggle to compromise and create the alternatives necessary to move the group into the final phase—*goal* attainment (G).

The whole process—LAIG—is the pattern of expected development in a successful problem-solving group. In describing this pattern, Hare and Naveh noted that the phases are not necessarily linear but rather may recur at different points and may also incorporate significant subphases.

Leaders who understand the theory of group development, especially in task groups, can visualize the process as predictable and "normal" and respond to resistance by developing new alternatives rather than meeting it with ignorance and defeatism. Fisher and Stutman (1987), identified critical "break points" and a process for moving a group through natural points of resistance.

FIRO: A THEORY OF INTERPERSONAL BEHAVIOR

William Schutz (1966) developed a theory of interpersonal behavior derived from a psychoanalytic orientation. The theory is called *Fundamental Interpersonal Relations Orientation* or FIRO. As the name indicates, the theory attempts to explain interpersonal behavior in terms of orientation toward others.

According to Schutz, a group develops in phases that reflect patterns of fundamental individual needs. In the first phase, *inclusion,* the question is how involved individuals will be, how prominent. What will the relationship with the leader be? How dependent? What are the group boundaries? Who's "in" and who's "out"?

The next phase is about *control* (power and influence). Now the group encounters a stage of conflict as it deals with issues of interpersonal dominance. Issues that come to the fore involve leadership, competition, and amount of structure. How will decisions be made? If in phase 1 the issues can be thought of as "in or out," in phase 2 the issues center on "top or bottom."

In the third phase, *affection,* the group becomes increasingly concerned with intermember harmony, while intermember differences recede in the service of group cohesiveness. In this phase, there are expressions of positive feelings, emotional support, extensions of friendship, and close personal attachment. For some, this is smothering. Within the group each person looks for a comfortable position in terms of the extent of giving and receiving affection. The third phase is characterized by concern about "near or far." The primary anxieties have to do with being liked, with being close enough to people or being too close.

Much later, the mature group emerges. It exhibits great cohesiveness, considerable interpersonal investigation, and a full commitment to the primary task of the group and to each of its members (Yalom, 1985).

The phases are not distinct, however. Schutz uses the metaphor of replacing a wheel on a car: Someone tightens the bolts one after another, just enough so that the wheel is in place. Then the process is repeated, each bolt being tightened in turn, until the wheel is entirely secure. In a similar way, phases of a group emerge, come to the fore, and then recede only to have the group return later to deal with these same issues again at greater depth.

Schutz says that at termination of a group, the phase process recurs but in reverse. There is less involvement with closeness and intimacy, then a reduction in concerns of control and dominance, and finally diffusion of boundaries and cessation.

This model is frequently used in therapy groups.

PHASE MOVEMENT OF GROUPS

There are essentially two approaches to how groups change over time. One approach, which might be called a *sequential-stage* theory, specifies the typical order of phases. The Tuckman and Hare theories are such theories. The other approach is that of *recurring phases*. Such theories specify issues that dominate group interaction and recur again and again.

Problem-solving groups (groups with a purpose, goal, or task) are continually faced with two related but distinct concerns: task-oriented concerns, associated with the effort to accomplish the group task; and socio-emotional concerns, related to the relationships among members. Both of these areas of concern operate continually. The group's devoting attention and effort to one of these may produce strain on the other. Spending time on member relationships takes time away from the task. Time invested in the task takes time away from members' interpersonal "work."

Robert Bales (1950, p. 195; Borgatta and Bales, 1953) suggests that there is an orderly series of phases involved in the task-oriented activities of problem-solving groups, and a parallel cycle of phases characterizes groups' socio-emotional behavior.

There are three problem-solving steps: orientation (gathering information and clarifying what the task is), evaluation (assessing that information), and control (deciding what to do). As a group moves through its task efforts, it follows a predictable pattern. Orientation is highest at the beginning and declines as the session progresses. Evaluation (opinions, thoughts, wishes) rises from the beginning to the middle of the session, then declines. Control (decision making) is low at the beginning and rises to its highest at the end of the session.

At the same time, in the continuing task/socio-emotional equilibrium process, there is a phase process in the socio-emotional level. There is less emotion on the orientation level, it increases during the evaluation stage, and it is most dominant, with the greatest tension, when a group is in the control phase. This increased strain is reflected in an increase in negative reactions. Efforts to deal with this strain bring an increase in positive reactions through the course of the session.

As a consequence, both positive and negative reactions increase from beginning to end, though they still account for a smaller proportion than task-related acts. Both positive and negative reactions reach their highest level in the last phase, but positive reactions in the form of tension release and expressions of solidarity predominate at the very end in successful problem-solving groups.

The Bales system has been especially illuminating because the theory can be confirmed by observing a group over a session and over time, and by analyzing the group in terms of its phase movement and its problem-solving success.

WORCHEL THEORY OF STAGES OF GROUP DEVELOPMENT

Stephen Worchel and colleagues (1992) found that groups progress through cycles that are repeated throughout its life rather than, or in addition to, the linear model presented by some of the previous investigators. It is therefore possible to observe and study developmental stages during segments of a group's life as well as its entire life span.

The following is a summary of their model for group development:

Stage 1: Discontent. This stage is characterized by feelings of alienation. Members feel helpless to influence the group. Participation is low. The group is dominated by a few individuals. The group at this point is not a major part of the individuals' identities.

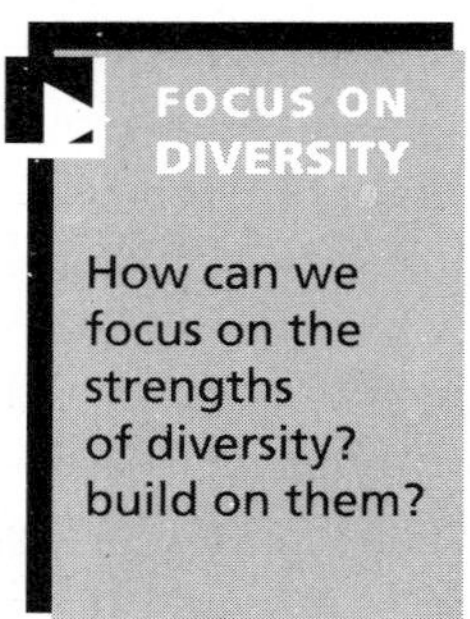

FOCUS ON
DIVERSITY
How can we
focus on the
strengths
of diversity?
build on them?

Stage 2: Precipitating Event. Some precipitating event occurs which allows the group to move to a more positive, productive place in terms of group dynamics and productivity. The precipitating event could be a minor incident (an emotional outburst; rumors of mistreatment), or something more dramatic. It can be unplanned or staged. Any event which represents dissatisfaction with the group will enable members to identify common ground for disaffected members. This in turn initiates contact among members and leads to action.

Stage 3: Group Identification. In this stage, members focus on defining the group and determining its membership. Conformity is high, and there is a reluctance to draw distinctions among members. Leadership is centralized and strong. The group establishes high group identity and uniformity. Conflict with outside groups may develop. Members tend to view the group as homogeneous at this point.

Stage 4: Group Productivity. As its identity becomes clearer, the group turns its attention to group productivity. It identifies goals and develops plans to achieve these goals. Leadership is task-oriented. In Tuckman's terms, the group engages in norming and performing stages at this point. Members of the group become less antagonistic toward outside groups.

Stage 5: Individuation. As the group achieves goals, members turn attention to their individual needs. They demand recognition for their contributions. Members may magnify differences between themselves and other group members at this point in the group's development. The group views itself as more heterogeneous. More personal freedom is requested. Solutions may become individually-based and less group-oriented. The group takes a more cooperative stance toward outside groups. Members begin to explore opportunities outside the group. The threat of defection becomes a bargaining tool. The group remains the focal point, but the individual's relationship with the group becomes increasingly important.

Stage 6: Decay. As members become more interested in meeting their own needs, conflict and competition within the group increase. Failures are blamed on the group and one another. There is a turnover in leadership as the group insists that leaders have less power. Individuals hoard resources. Some members may leave and join other groups. Discontent abounds (Worchel, 1994; Worchel, Coutant-Sassic, and Grossman, 1992; Worchel, Coutant-Sassic, and Wong, 1993).

This model suggests that the cycle of development can be interrupted and that a group can return to an earlier stage at any point. For example, a threat to the group may force it back into the identification stage, which would in turn motivate the members to protect the independence of the group and reestablish its identity (Worchel, 1994).

IMPACT OF GROUP SIZE ON GROUP DEVELOPMENT

Wheelan and McKeage (1993) conducted a study that explored the effect of group size on group development. The researchers studied a group of adults who were assembled, not for the purpose of research, but as participants at a group relations conference held in 1988. Participation was voluntary. The researchers audiotaped a series of small- and large-group sessions. They reviewed statements made by participants and categorized them according to types of verbal statement associated with the various stages of group development outlined in research literature. The categories were dependency statements, counterdependency statements, fight statements, flight statements, pairing statements, counterpairing statements, and work statements. The results suggest that there are both similarities and differences in the developmental patterns of small and large groups. The quantity and sequencing of most statements in the two group types were similar. But the small group generated significantly more pairing statements, and the large group produced significantly more fight statements. The sequencing of flight statements remained fairly constant in the small groups but steadily increased in the large group. Work statements remained constant in the small group until the end, when the number decreased. The production of work statements was highest early in the large group and declined thereafter. Wheelan and McKeage concluded that the sequencing of five of the seven categories, in both group types, is consistent with previous research and lends added support to the theory of group developmental patterns.

There were, however, some important differences. The study supported research suggesting that larger groups are less cohesive than smaller ones (Bogart and Lundgren 1974; Seashore, 1954; Berkowitz, 1956; Galvanovskis and Nemov, 1982; Slater, 1958), which may be related to the restraining effect of large groups on participation (Callahan, Owen and Renzulli, 1974; Gentry, 1980).

Their study also supports the view that increased group size negatively affects productivity (Gist, Locke, and Taylor, 1987).

INTEGRATIVE MODEL OF GROUP DEVELOPMENT

Wheelan and Hochberger developed a model for group development referred to as an *integrative model of group development* (Wheelan and Hochberger, 1996). (Note that there seems to be agreement between Wheelan and Tuckman. The stages of development in their theories are similar, but with different names.) The stages of the integrative model are these:

> *Stage 1: Dependency and Inclusion.* In this stage there is a great deal of dependency on the designated leader. Group members look to him or her to clarify roles and responsibilities and provide safety. There is a tendency to be polite and tentative. Members want to get to know each other. They need to fit in and be accepted. Conflict is often avoided at this point. Groups during this early stage are eager to please the authority figure.

Stage 2: Counterdependency and Flight. This stage is marked by conflict among and between members and leaders. It also includes flight from tasks and avoidance of tensions. The group struggles with how it will operate and what roles the various members will play. Members are not as concerned about fitting in as they are about expressing opinions. There is a tendency for subgroups or cliques to emerge at this point.

Stage 3: Trust and Structure. If Stage 2 is successfully navigated, group members will emerge feeling more secure and trusting of one another. It is as if the conflict and struggle they experienced supports their ability to work in productive ways with one another. Now the group can begin a more mature planning process about group goals, organizational structure, procedures, roles, and division of labor. Communication is more open and task-oriented. Power struggles that were important during Stage 2 lessen in intensity. Information is shared for the group good, not as a way to gain status and power.

Stage 4: Work. Although work is occurring at each stage of development, once goals, structure, and norms are established, the group can work more in more effective and efficient ways. Members of the group continue, in this stage, to communicate in constructive ways. There is a higher degree of collaboration, creativity, and productivity.

Stage 5: Termination. This is the point when a group comes to an end. Even in continuous groups, there are endings. Work colleagues retire or are reassigned, family members may leave home or tasks get completed. At each ending point groups have an opportunity to evaluate and reflect on the work or relationships. They have a chance to share feelings and thoughts, give feedback, celebrate effort and achievement, and reflect on learnings.

This integrative model of group development assumes that there is an order to these stages, but at the same time, that events can cause a group to return to a previous stage at any point. For example, the addition of new members, a change in structure, or new sets of demands upon a Stage-2 group may well return that group to Stage 1. A group that has not successfully navigated conflict may stay stuck in Stage 2 and not progress, or even regress to Stage 1. Groups, like individuals, are affected by a wide range of forces at any given time.

Validation studies of this model have been undertaken with a number of groups (Abraham and Wheelan, 1993; Verdi and Wheelan, 1992; Wheelan and Krasick, 1993; Wheelan and McKeage, 1993). From this model, for example, Wheelan developed the Group Development Questionnaire, which consists of four scales corresponding to the first four stages of group development. The questionnaire seems to accurately measure group development at a given time (Wheelan and Hochberger, 1996). Recent work by Jacob and his associates (1995) has also developed an observational coding system for understanding small groups. Their system observes behavior at the dinner table to understand the development of families as small groups.

Reader Activity

Like individuals, whose lifestyles become routinized, groups too can become predictable. Instead of moving through certain developmental stages, members of a group will find themselves caught in one stage, unable to move beyond it.

Can you think of a group of which you are a member that is stuck in a particular developmental phase and for some reason is not able to move ahead? What is the cost to the group of being immobilized?

In contrast, are you aware of a group that is not stuck—that is active and evolving? What makes it different from the first group? What are the factors that allow it to grow and develop? Is there any chance that it may become blocked like the first?

What are you doing as a member of the first group to help sustain its inertia? What can you and others do to move it to a more productive level of activity?

Facilitating Group Success

Whether you are a member of a group or are in a position of leadership, it is your responsibility to help the group function effectively and accomplish its goal. Being aware of factors that influence the successful development of a group will put you in a better position to make an effective contribution. Each of the methods for viewing the development of a task group can arm you with the questions to ask in order to understand what is happening, what is needed, and how to help the group. Thus, it is essential to be aware of how the group is developing, know where deviations are occurring, realize what tensions can be expected, and understand what might facilitate the group's passage through a particular stage.

Similarly, it is important to consider the implications of critical incidents that may influence the development of the group. This information, as well as insight into essential group needs, will provide anyone with the essential tools for understanding. It will provoke useful questions for gathering data and testing personal hypotheses. At this point, as a member and/or leader, you will be aware of alternatives and begin to sense your own ability to influence the group. Individuals who feel impotent or victimized as members of a small group seldom have a framework for looking at and conceptualizing the group as a developing entity. Obviously, it requires some skill to translate theory into constructive action, but understanding the theory is the first critical step (Gist, Locke, and Taylor, 1987).

READER ACTIVITY

Pick a group in which you participate and pay attention to the process of one meeting during which the whole group is present. How do people talk? Who talks? What is the emotional tone of the conversation? From the way group members interact, can you determine what theme—anxiety, power, norms, interpersonal relationships, personal growth—is in the foreground? Can you determine what stage—forming, storming, norming, performing, adjourning—the group appears to be in? What in the process of the group leads you to your conclusions? Do these interpersonal issues appear to be inhibiting the group's effort to accomplish its goals? If so, what do you think the group should do to manage these issues productively?

SEEKING THE IDEAL

When people come together for an extended time, they have expectations of how the group experience will go. The community-building retreat described earlier is a good example. One of the first tasks each group on retreat tackles is defining the elements of an ideal community. Among the 24 members of the most recent group were a bank president, a student from China, an actress, an environmental educator, an author, a secondary school teacher, an athletic director, a doctor, a therapist, a carpenter, a homemaker, and a social worker. To their surprise, the participants were able to come to an agreement in a mere 30 minutes. These are the qualities they agreed their ideal community would have:

- Shared leadership
- Open communication of all relevant information
- Channels for listening and being heard
- The soliciting of feelings and ideas
- A sense of equality among all members
- A climate of openness and trust
- Collaborative problem solving, especially involving those having to live with the decisions
- Shared labor in menial tasks
- Respect for nature and the environment
- Opportunities for play and celebration

- Ways of dealing with conflict when it arises and before it builds up
- Willingness to provide personal feedback to members of the community
- Valuing personal growth and development
- Time to be alone

The challenge for the group would lie not in agreeing on the characteristics of an ideal community but in evolving to a state where such ideas could take precedence over personal needs, biases, and vested interests. This community, after all, would be built on individual differences and egos, interpersonal conflict, differing goals and priorities, varying standards and levels of need, and a hundred unanticipated variables that could create system dysfunction. The group found that it needed patience, discipline, and care to resolve problems so that the common ideals could eventually be experienced.

Most work groups and families only glimpse the possibilities outlined by the retreat group. They are either unskilled in creating a functional and responsive group or unwilling to devote the time required to do so. Without the tools (skills) or time to deal with issues that arise, members are unable to stop the inevitable "noise" or entropy (see Chapter 6 on Systems) because the necessary problem solving does not occur. Typical groups collude in not spending the necessary time or not dealing with conflicts that arise (Obert, 1983). Furthermore, they collude not to agree on goals, communicate on issues of membership, or share in problem solving. The result of such agreement *not* to agree is disharmony and eventual dysfunction. Building a functional group does not require expert knowledge or a college degree, but it does require the desire and discipline to look beyond ourselves to analyze events and to follow the basic rules of productive human relations (Allcorn, 1985).

POSITIVE STRUCTURED INTERVENTIONS

An increasing body of research confirms the belief that carefully designed interventions into a working group can alter levels of problem-solving effectiveness, cohesion, risk taking, and productivity (Bednar and Battersby, 1976; Evensen, 1976; Hall and Williams, 1970; Stogdill, 1972). Although much of this work is in the formative stages (Laughlin and Futuron, 1985; Worchel, Cooper, and Goethals, 1988) and there are still more questions than answers, it seems appropriate to explore some of the tentative findings here.

One series of studies, exploring the impact of structure on self-study groups, noted that "empirical evidence supports structure as a robust variable which positively affects interpersonal behavior, group attraction and client improvement" (Evensen, 1976, p. 152). Thus, in groups whose purpose was to explore the nature of group behavior and interpersonal relationships, effectively placed structural interventions by leaders allowed various group goals to be attained more rapidly, even though leaders in such groups traditionally are a focus of group attention, anxiety, and frustration. More specifically, it was found that providing more structure encouraged members to risk more and be more disclosing of feelings and attitudes and, as a result, increased the level of measured cohesion in the group. Apparently, the structure gave members legitimate permission to say what was on their minds. This is particularly promising because individuals measured as low risk takers were consistently nudged toward greater participation and involvement. The lack of structure in groups can be destructive because it activates individual regressive trends, which can result in less productive and less mature behavior (Kernberg, 1980).

There is further corroboration for small group structure being helpful, in this case, in aiding students. Harvard conducted a five-year study on what constitutes effective teaching and learning (*New York Times,* 1991). One of the major findings of the study was that students learned more effectively when they worked in small groups in classes, and that they were more successful at retaining and integrating what they had learned when they studied in small groups.

In addition, there is evidence that groups given specific training in problem solving tend to be more effective. A study by Hall and Williams (1970) implies that groups can translate such learnings directly into their work efforts. Thus, large numbers of working groups performed work of higher quality on new tasks of a similar nature after training in a rational approach to problem solving. This simply supports what many group facilitators have learned from experience. Groups that are provided appropriate structure, models for work, experience in problem solving, and guidelines for maintaining their own process tend to perform with less tension and with greater productivity than groups that do not receive such support (Reddi, 1983).

MAXIMIZING THE GROUP'S POTENTIAL

The effective group leader or member tends to have an awareness of the group, its needs, and its present level of development. Just a few probing questions, a structure for observing, and the willingness to look carefully at what is happening are all that someone needs to contribute to the group's effectiveness. Understanding the stages of development, group needs, and critical events that may occur in any working group increases the possibility of responding in appropriate and constructive ways that may facilitate or unblock a group and help it be more effective. The more fully developed a group is, the greater is the likelihood that member-to-member relationships will strengthen (Berman-Rossi, 1992). The most frustrated members of groups are those who fail to understand what is happening and feel victimized by what may be a predictable course of events. Knowledge of developmental trends allows for a proactive rather than a defensive response and brings some modicum of control back to those privy to such insight.

FOCUS ON DIVERSITY

Conversely consider how nonnative-born white people feel in a group. How can they contribute to discussion or even feel more comfortable?

Few people have ever experienced the ideal working group, with the participative approach outlined earlier in the discussion of the conditions facilitating people's involvement in groups. (A review of Chapter 3 on Norms might be helpful here.) Nevertheless, knowledge of these qualities provides a basis for comparison as well as ideas for improvement. Developing such a working climate is rare indeed, because ignorance rather than awareness of effective group process is the rule, not the exception. It can be likened to being in a foreign country where everything appears to be familiar but it seems next to impossible to communicate effectively. Most of us are used to strong leaders who control rewards, establish the ground rules of a particular task, and provide the necessary push to get the job done. We expect to be directed, motivated, intellectual, impersonal, and rational in our approach to problem solving.

As a result, we tend to see ourselves as alienated from the group, often competing with other members for recognition and responding to authority rather than to member peers. Such a climate is not conducive to establishing free and open communication, role flexibility, and a truly nonpunitive atmosphere. It is this kind of atmosphere that helps predetermine the kind of development possible for a group. We are used to being dependent and, even if we do not like it, often demand behaviors from those in control that ensure our dependence. Even when a work group is responsive to democratic principles, members too often become the victims of the majority vote—the conflict-reducing option that, if used indiscriminately, may polarize a group and erase the vital thread of compromise on which the effective decision-making group must be based.

If a group has never had experience outside the confines of a rigid time schedule, agenda, and parliamentary procedure, it is doubtful that it will ever develop the trust necessary for processing its own behaviors or the interdependence necessary to see issues as other than politically expedient and strategic. Certainly decisions will be made and groups will function, sometimes in an extraordinarily efficient manner. The price paid, however, may be in participant involvement, interest, cooperation, and member accountability. Staw, Sandelands, and Dutton (1981) report "rigidity effects" on small groups in response to an external threat. More specifically, they identify restriction in information processing and constriction of control under this condition. Interpersonal needs for involvement and influence are also downplayed in such incidents. Like growing children, groups respond best to patience, freedom within limits, concerns from others, and a climate that encourages spontaneity and authenticity. It is a mixture that varies from group to group, and intangibles often spell the difference between success and failure. Yet, more and more success can be ensured if the leader-facilitator is able to formulate the necessary questions to help him or her understand the group. This, added to familiarity with diagnostic techniques and a few basic approaches to working with the task and emotional problems that inevitably face any working group, is essential. Much more than the use of gimmicks and techniques, success seems geared to how effectively a group is able to respond to its very human needs in a manner that exploits no one and maximizes its own potential.

The value of positive, structured interventions into the life of a working group to facilitate its development, improve cohesion, open communication, and reduce the threat of participant risk taking while improving the quality of problem solving is becoming increasingly clear. The biggest challenge now is convincing those individuals who are stuck in ineffective patterns of leadership that both they and the group will benefit from the adoption of these new approaches.

EXERCISE 1 Maslow's Hierarchy of Needs[2]

OBJECTIVES

- To help a group begin to understand the kinds of restraints inhibiting individual members
- To focus on the emotional aspects of group process
- To provide a theoretical frame of reference for understanding the group process
- To create open communication and feedback in a group

RATIONALE

According to A. H. Maslow, individuals tend to pass through certain stages of development, and their needs tend to change. How a person acts in a given situation depends partly on the demands and uniqueness of the moment and partly on the general developmental level at which he or she is functioning. It is not that we ever

2. Adapted from Maslow, 1954.

are able to satisfy all of our needs; in fact, even as mature adults many are still unsatisfied. The point is that as we mature developmentally, from childhood through adulthood, the focus of our needs and our ability to see beyond them change.

Thus, the first year or so of a baby's life is dominated by physiological needs. But even though a preoccupation with such things as food, water, and sex are later brought under rational control, there are times when even the most mature individuals feel the overpowering push of some physiological need.

The growing child is often greatly concerned with the safety of his or her environment. Whether he or she is safe from harm or threat can prove to be a dominant theme in his or her developmental system of needs. For the adult, however, familiarity and experience have provided the feeling of safety except in unusual crisis situations.

Actually, it is the higher-order needs such as love and self-esteem that seem most difficult for people to handle. If these needs were met to a satisfactory degree, people would no longer have to expend a great amount of time fulfilling them at a period in their lives when they should be able to accept themselves as they are and concentrate on developing their own potentials.

Included with this exercise is Maslow's well-known hierarchy of needs (see p. 451). Theoretically, people move upward through the hierarchy, satisfying one level of need before tackling the next. It is a rare person, however, who feels fulfilled in the areas of love and self-esteem. How few are the people who are able to give and accept love and feel unconditionally accepted. Even fewer resolve the need to dominate and control, to achieve and be important.

SETTING

In any group there are individuals who are controlled to some degree by their own needs. The person who blatantly says, "Why can't we be open here and just say what we really feel?" is either completely unaware of the forces restricting an individual's ability to be open or is sending up a smoke screen to hide his or her own apprehensions. Personal needs act as an important inhibiting factor in the communication and development of any group. This in itself is neither good nor bad, merely an important reality. When individuals within a group push too rapidly for openness, being personal, and freely giving feedback, it may lead to considerable pain as the group struggles to protect itself from itself. People do not wish to be rejected or to fail in a particular task. Thus, most will play it relatively safe. Some-

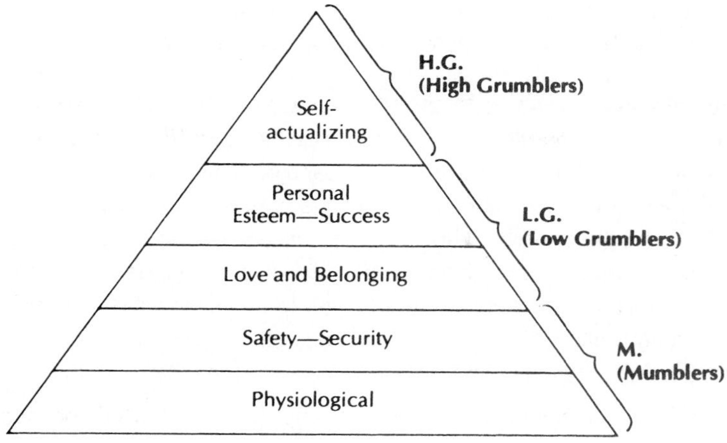

times it is important to help a group gain new respect for the various levels at which people operate. If such is the case, this exercise may provide some insights. This particular activity assumes that the facilitator has some sort of authority role and wields considerable influence. It also assumes that he or she is willing to be open about his or her own role and willing to alter his or her own behavior if it will benefit the functioning of the group.

ACTION

The group is broken into trios to discuss specifically the role of the facilitator, his or her strengths and limitations (with examples), and how he or she might improve his or her role in ways that would facilitate the working of the group. After the initial groan, an unusually loud and animated discussion usually takes place, with nearly everyone participating and sharing ideas. There is no doubt that they are dissecting the facilitator (and probably enjoying it). It is essential to remind them that they need to be specific on all counts. After 10 or 15 minutes, the facilitator stands by the board and asks the group to list the limitations that were discussed with such zest. It is quite possible that no one will volunteer. Those comments that are made will tend to be rather vague and indirect unless the facilitator's rapport with the group is unusually good. Even when the facilitator is asking for good points or ways in which his or her performance could meet the group's goals, the discussion will probably drag, with few individuals participating.

DISCUSSION AND REFERENCE TO MASLOW'S THEORY

It is important to reaffirm the significance of the discussion and the data presented (the facilitator should take notes and expand on them). But it is also clear that the discussion lacked something vital that was present during the discussions in the trios. If possible, the group should develop reasons for the obvious change in spontaneity and involvement. There are many possible reasons: fear of being evaluated by the facilitator or other members, discomfort in making direct criticism (for fear of getting it back), the leader–subordinate relationship that exists, and perhaps the fact that it is easier to be candid with two or three than with the whole group.

At this point it is helpful to give a brief description of Maslow's theory of needs and how it relates to the behaviors people are willing to exhibit. In most groups, when individuals do not like something about how the group is being conducted, sense becomes the better part of valor and a disgruntled "mumble" is the most that rises to the surface. Some individuals will "grumble" to another person or to the group about what is happening, but it is the rare person who will take the bull by the horns and do something about the situation. This condition is particularly obvious in many classrooms, where a teacher may be ineffective or is not meeting the needs of the students, yet nothing is said or done. The same is true with bosses. To say something places the person in jeopardy of losing the boss's goodwill—and his or her own esteem because of being stereotyped as being negative or adversarial with the boss, or not a team player. There may even be a distancing by peers, who now perceive him as someone going "nowhere" in the company.

As a result, people tend to mumble (see M. on the diagram) or grumble (L.G. = Low Grumble), but few are willing to pay the potential price and speak bluntly (H.G. = High Grumble). High grumblers in a group are usually either those who have worked through their own needs and feel accepted and secure (self-actualizing level) or those who are striving for personal recognition (often need for esteem). The two types are easily recognized by the group.

The theory raises an important question: How can a group climate be developed that minimizes the threat to personal needs and helps set the stage for a free expression of opinions and ideas? The facilitator may wish to explore this question in a variety of ways, or he or she may choose to let the implications go for a future discussion.

EXERCISE 2 Tower Building[3]

OBJECTIVES

- To help a group focus on the aspects of helping within the context of a particular task
- To alert a group to the problems that may develop when they are working under severe pressures (in this case, time and competition)
- To deal directly with the inhibiting norms, roles, and leadership practices that can minimize the use of the group's resources

SETTING

This exercise is as close to real life as participants can get and still remain "in the laboratory." It involves all the important aspects of group planning and decision making, such as allocation of human and material resources, working against deadlines, altering strategies in the face of unexpected crises, and seeking the problems inherent in negotiations. It provides an opportunity to view the evolution of conflict and compromise as they exist in many working groups, particularly groups that have not developed skills in group problem solving.

Two and a half to three hours should be allowed for this exercise. It can be undertaken with as few as twelve participants divided into two groups (two observers and two groups of five). However, the activity generates greater excitement and involvement among the participants if there are four or six groups with from seven to nine members and an observer or two in each group. It should be noted that, given space, materials, and an effective communication system, virtually any even number of groups can participate (on one occasion, the authors witnessed 200 students and teachers in 20 groups enthusiastically involved for three and a half hours). As in many of the other exercises that focus on the dimensions of group process, it may prove interesting and enjoyable for groups unsophisticated in group analysis, but many of the potential learnings will pass them by. Participants with at least an understanding of basic group concepts will gain considerably more from the exercise. The following description is based on four groups of seven members each, with an observer in each group. The room should be large enough

3. The idea for this exercise was originally developed by Clark Abt in his simulation activity, "An Education System Planning Game," originally played in 1965 at Lake Arrowhead, Calif.

for each group to meet with some privacy. In most cases heterogeneous groups seem to be especially effective.

ACTION

After the large group has been divided into four groups of equal size (some stratification may be necessary if groups are to be truly heterogeneous), the facilitator says:

You are a group of architects (each group) who have won one of four contracts to build a tower. Although your tower will be built independently of the other three, it is to be judged in competition with the others. There is to be a planning deadline and a construction deadline. The criteria to be used in judging the four towers include height, beauty, strength, and message [symbol or motto and so forth]. A prize will be distributed to each of the three best towers. Independent judges will appraise the towers, and their decisions will be final.

Your groups now have 30 minutes to develop a diagrammatic plan of the tower you are going to build. You should know that you will have to plan in terms of certain materials that will be made accessible to you only during the building phase. The judges will also be asked to consider the completeness of this initial plan in their overall judging. The materials available for building will include the following for each group:

2 rolls of masking tape (1″ wide)

2 rolls of colored streamers

1 pair of large scissors

1 ruler

1 roll of colored toilet paper

150 sheets of medium newsprint (36″)

4 felt-tip markers (different colors)

12 large sheets of construction paper (different colors)

It may be possible to negotiate with other groups for certain additional materials. Also, other personal materials of the participants may be used; however, no artificial bases—for example, from chairs, wastebaskets, and the like—may be used. The lower must stand alone on its own support—it may not be attached to the ceiling.

You may begin your planning. Because this is a competitive situation, no additional directions will be given during the planning period.

After 25 minutes of the planning period, the following announcement is made to the four groups:

We are disappointed to have to announce that because of the existing crisis in government funding, we have not been allocated all of the materials we originally anticipated. As a result, there are only enough materials available for building two towers. We are extremely sorry for this inconvenience. Rather than selecting two groups from the plans developed at this stage, we have decided to allow two groups to merge, decide on one plan, and build a tower together. Thus there will be two towers, each constructed by two teams from a plan on which they both agree. You will have an additional 30 minutes of planning time to integrate your ideas or to come up with a new plan. Remember, both teams must agree on the final plan. (The facilitator will select the teams that are to join forces.)

After 30 minutes, the following announcement is made:

You now have 30 minutes to build your tower. It must be completed by __________, at which time the judging will take place. Remember the criteria of height, beauty, strength, and message. The judges will also circulate among the groups to make certain that all regulations are being followed. Good luck.

OBSERVATION AND DATA COLLECTION

Four major sources of information will be discussed with the participants.

1. Information is gained by the observer during the initial planning phase. He or she will find it most useful to focus on a few salient features of the groups, such as (a) communication pattern (who to whom), (b) leadership styles exhibited, and (c) specific behaviors that seem to inhibit or facilitate the group during the planning.
2. The second planning session provides another distinct period of observation. One of the observers should collect the same type of data gathered during the first observation period, except now on the combined group. The other observer should turn his or her attention to the developmental aspects of the new, combined group. This should be carried through the actual construction period. For example, he or she might ask the following questions while observing the group:
   a. How is the potential leadership conflict either resolved or not resolved?
   b. What norms are developing within this group, and are they different from those that existed in the original, smaller group?

c. Have individuals with certain roles in the first group taken new ones in the larger group, and if so, what is their reaction to this state of affairs?
d. How is the decision-making process developed in this second planning session? Is consensus actually reached, or is one plan forced on the total group? What are the responses of the group members? How is resistance exhibited (actively or passively)?
e. Is there a real attempt to involve members from both groups through the allocation of responsibility during the building phase? How?

3. During the actual building phase, both observers should concentrate on the question in *b* above. Special attention should be given to the quality of participation of the various group members. Is there any difference in the quality of participation among those in leadership (control) roles and those less involved in the planning? Are there signs of withdrawal and resistant behaviors by certain members? Can these behaviors be explained as a result of the historical development of the two groups, that is, the merger? Do the two groups tend to work together as one, or are the original relationships developed before the merger still the basis for most communication and participation during the building stage?
4. The final source of data is collected from a reaction sheet handed to all participants at the time the tower is finally completed. Information from this instrument will be used by the facilitator in a summary of the activity. This may provide a wide range of data. The following questions might be useful for a summary discussion:

1. Please note the letter of the original planning group you joined:

   A B C D

2. My opinions were valued and solicited in the first planning group. (Circle one.)

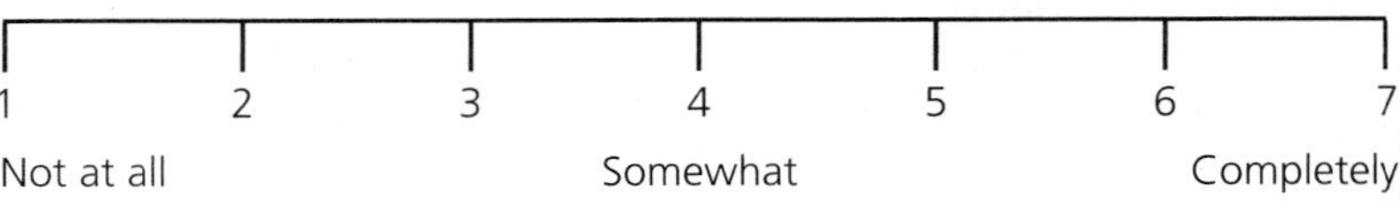

3. My opinions were valued and solicited in the second planning group.

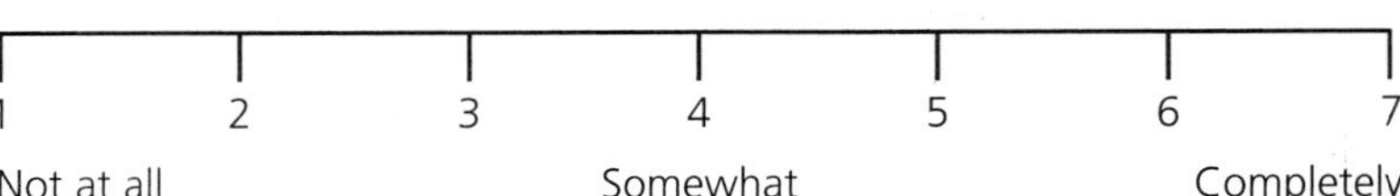

4. If there was a difference in the problem-solving climate that developed in one group, briefly explain why.

5. How satisfied are you with the product of your merged group?

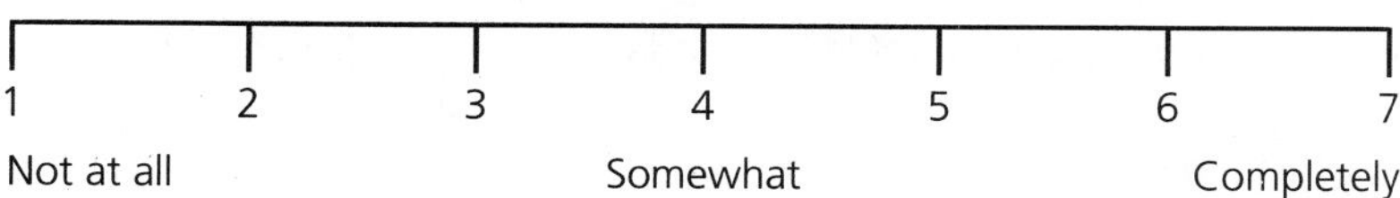

6. What specific behaviors hurt your (merged) group's efforts to work together and be as successful as it might have been?
7. What behaviors were facilitative as the two merged groups attempted to work together?

JUDGING AND DISCUSSION PERIOD

Immediately after the towers have been completed, take a period of about 20 minutes to (a) have participants complete the brief reaction sheet, (b) have about a 10-minute break, and (c) have the judges (a team of three) decide on the winning tower. The winner and prize are not announced until after the discussion period.

JUDGES' EVALUATION SHEET

On a scale of 1 (low) to 7 (high), rate the towers on the following criteria:

	Height	Beauty	Strength	Message	Total
Team 1 (A & B)	______	______	______	______	______
Team 2 (C & D)	______	______	______	______	______

After the break, each merged team (A & B and C & D) meets together to discuss what happened. It is assumed that during the break the two observers compared notes and have agreed on a procedure for processing what occurred during the planning session prior to merging as well as the one after the two teams had to join forces.[4] If the group is helped with stimulating questions about what hap-

4. If time allows, it is usually very helpful for the facilitator to spend as much as 30 minutes prior to the exercise with the observers, giving them the sequence of events and explaining their role in the postsession processing. It is important that they interject their process data as a stimulus for further discussion and underline a point being made in the group. They should not simply report data and await a reaction.

pened as the participants worked together, the discussion should require at least 45 minutes. Special attention should be given to the behaviors or situations that helped or did not help the two groups merge into a working team.

SUMMARY

During this discussion, the facilitator should organize the data from the participant reaction sheets. His or her 10- or 15-minute presentation of these data should underline the learnings being discussed in the two groups. He or she should be free to draw both inter- and intragroup hypotheses from the data and then be willing to ask for confirmation or denial of his or her views. This type of presentation and discussion can help demonstrate the importance of reaction sheets and process periods after a time of problem solving and group involvement.

CONCLUSION

A natural end to the exercise is to report the judges' results. This can be done with humor and zest. If possible, the winning team can be given a prize that is easily divided (soft drinks, for instance) and the losers a booby prize that can also be divided (perhaps a large candy bar). Occasionally, this award period offers new information for discussion.

For Further Information

Agazarian, Y. M. *Systems-Centered Therapy for Groups.* New York: Guilford Press, 1997.

The author, the founder of systems-centered training, believes the smallest part of a group is not an individual but a subgroup. Her training is as both a Freudian psychoanalyst and as a Lewinian group therapist, and she utilizes both orientations. The book identifies three discrete phases in group development—authority, intimacy, and work—and shows how treatment in each phase comprises a sequenced hierarchy in defense modifications, beginning with the simplest and progressing to the most complex. An original theorist! Includes many illustrations, samples of dialogue, and examples of "forks-in-the-road" forced-choices technique for group members.

Bolman, L. G., and T. E. Deal. *Reframing Organizations.* San Francisco: Jossey-Bass, 1991.

A book about organizations, management, and leadership. The most significant focus is on "reframing," or showing how the same situation can be viewed in four different ways: structural, human resource, political, and symbolic. Also includes an effort to provide a comprehensive overview of organization theory using a wide range of examples from business, military, educational, and health care organizations, as well as cases and examples from different nations and cultures. A perspective on organizations and leadership for the future.

Covey, S. R. *The Seven Habits of Highly Effective Families.* New York: Golden Books, 1997.

The family as the ultimate small group. The author applies business principles to families and examines how they can be effective. He offers seven habits that constitute a powerful framework of universal principles allowing family members to communicate about their problems and resolve them. Examples: #2, Developing a Family Mission Statement; #4, Think Win-Win.

Katzenbach, J. J., and D. K. Smith. *The Wisdom of Teams.* New York: HarperCollins, 1993.

A critical review of teams by two expert consultants. Includes sections on understanding teams, becoming a team, the team performance curve, obstacles for teams, and getting teams unstuck.

Massie, R. K. *Loosing the Bounds: The United States and South Africa in the Apartheid Years.* New York: Nan A. Talese/Doubleday, 1997.

A dramatically told story of how America and South Africa became entangled in each other's struggle for justice in the second half of the 20th century. At its heart is the persistent story of race. Based on hundreds of interviews and extensive research recreating the struggles, people, politics, and personalities of the period. The author develops movements over time and the effects in South Africa and the United States.

Nilson, C. *Team Games for Trainers.* New York: McGraw-Hill, 1993.

This book is part of a series of games, or learning activities, for trainers. The games are to be used with groups, especially those working on team development. Offers 100 activities on team development, team maintenance, and team functioning. The wide variety allows facilitator to select the one that will work at any point in an organization's life.

Piercy, F. P., and D. H. Sprenkle. *Family Therapy Sourcebook.* New York: Guilford, 1986.

A guide to where the field of family therapy has been, where it is, and where it is going. Each chapter, on a different form of family therapy, includes a compact introductory section explaining the major methods of that therapy. There are many exercises and examples, a glossary of core terms, and a guide to videotapes on family therapy. A comprehensive overview.

Shank, J. H. *Team-Based Organizations.* Homewood, Ill.: Business One—Irwin, 1997.

This book's approach is to structure and manage an organization that is built around teams, as opposed to putting a team approach into an already-existing organization. The author writes about how to institute a team system and gives lots of tips and techniques that may come in handy in working with teams. He discusses everything about teams, from where they will work and where they won't to how a new organization evolves; from training to leading a team-based organization.

10

Small Group Processes: Three Contemporary Applications

This chapter examines three kinds of small groups: self-help groups, quality circles, and focus groups. It uses the group process concepts covered in previous chapters to investigate how these groups function. The goal of this chapter is to illustrate the application of group processes in small groups.

Self-help groups, quality circles, and focus groups were chosen as examples of small groups because of their increasing prevalence and their ability to address the needs of individuals for identity and empowerment. Since World War II, people in our industrial society have often found their lives fragmented and isolated. People frequently experience the structures associated with large businesses, communities, and governments as dehumanizing or unresponsive to their personal and social needs. This sense of alienation and lack of control over our immediate social environment creates feelings of stress and apathy. As a result of rapid social change and increased social mobility, the traditional supports of the extended family, religion, and the community have diminished. In contemporary society, people seek stability, connection, faith, and a sense of empowerment in small groups.

Self-help groups offer emotional anchors and sources of identity and meaning for many individuals struggling with the ups and downs of daily life. At work, quality circles provide opportunities for employees to influence their environment and develop a greater sense of self-satisfaction. Focus groups help us understand how people view controversial issues. They enable participants to express themselves more personally and idiosyncratically than do surveys and questionnaires. Self-help groups and quality circles empower their members by helping them to cope with emotional stress, to solve problems, and to improve their work environment. Focus groups give people a voice in decisions that affect issues from the mundane to the international. Small groups that provide people with a sense of identity, a way to assert themselves and their values, and a sense of empowerment have become essential to the lives of increasing numbers of people.

Self-Help Groups

A number of chairs stand around a long conference table in an otherwise empty room. Within a few minutes, people begin to walk into the room, serve themselves coffee, find seats, and make themselves comfortable. It is clear that some people know one another; greetings are exchanged and certain people sit together. It also looks as though some individuals are new and awkward in the situation. They pick unobtrusive seats, fidget, and do not meet anyone else's gaze. The room fills quickly; soon all the seats are taken, and latecomers sit on the windowsills or stand against the walls. At the designated time, a young woman stands up and welcomes everyone to the meeting. The woman continues by leading the group in a short prayer and then introduces the speakers for the evening. Each one stands, introduces himself or herself, and tells his or her story of alcoholism—the pain, the depths of despair, and the long road toward sobriety. Every person in attendance is a recovering alcoholic, and the members of this group have joined together in their individual and collective struggle to live as sober, productive members of Alcoholics Anonymous (AA).

This scenario is repeated thousands of times each day. It is estimated that there are more than 500,000 self-help groups and 6 million members in the nation. In fact, there are now as many people who use self-help groups in a year as use psychotherapy (Jacobs and Goodman, 1989). Thus, the self-help movement extends much further than AA meetings. Who joins these groups and for what reasons? How do groups get started, who leads, and who follows? How long have self-help groups been around, and what purpose do they serve?

DEFINITION OF SELF-HELP GROUPS

Self-help groups are voluntary gatherings of peers who share needs or problems that are not being addressed by existing organizations, institutions, or other types of groups. The broad goals of a self-help group are to bring about personal and/or social change for its members and society. All of these groups (and there is an almost overwhelming variety) emphasize face-to-face interaction among members and stress a set of values or ideology that enhances a member's personal sense of identity (Katz and Bender, 1976).

In the example of an AA meeting, members attend the meeting because they think it will be helpful, not because of outside coercion or pressure. The group described has fifty regular members. Although this makes for large meetings of twenty to thirty people, it is within the limit that allows for interpersonal contact. Everyone in AA is there because of a drinking problem; there are no mental health professionals dispensing treatment. In short, AA provides a set of values (one day at a time, the serenity prayer) and a structure that help a group of people help themselves stop drinking.

Generally, self-help groups start from a position of powerlessness, in that their initial resources of money, influence, and status are limited, and their objective is not to amass power. This position and the fact that self-help groups fill a gap in existing services distinguish these groups from other voluntary group experiences. Think about groups in our culture that you consider powerless or disenfranchised. Certainly former mental patients, people of minority ethnic background, families living in poverty, and individuals with a debilitating illness are among those who usually lack access to traditional forms of power. Hence self-help groups differ from traditional service organizations or political parties in their narrow power base and the alienation that group members may feel about their place in the social world. In addition, self-help groups differ from other activity, craft, or social groups because the goal of personal growth carries deep emotional sustenance, something not usually provided in other groups.

ECOLOGICAL NICHES To enhance our understanding of self-help groups, some theorists have likened the meeting place of these groups to the "niche" sometimes located in a kitchen or stairwell, which provides extra space for valued mementos, art objects, or a flower-filled vase. The notion that the space occupied by self-help groups conceptually resembles a niche also evokes ecological niches, or alternative social environments. Members may occupy these niches while responding to their common need (Levine, 1987). The importance of the "niche" simile lies in its implication that a niche is not disconnected from the rest of the environment; it is a solid recess in a wall with an opening to the rest of a kitchen or stairwell. The opening signifies a connection to the rest of (the larger environment of) the house.

The "niche" perspective has influenced the course of research on self-help groups. Instead of studying these groups as separate and independent entities, apart from the total environment in which group members live, work, and play, research has adopted the ecological viewpoint, expanding to include the environment of which members are a part. Applying the concept of ecological niches, Maton et al. (1989) viewed self-help groups as entities housed under the roof of larger entities, such as the community or the health care/human services system. In short, self-help group dynamics extend to a larger environment than the group itself.

HISTORY OF SELF-HELP GROUPS

Self-help or mutual aid groups have a long history. The idea of cooperative groups or societies was traced to prehistoric times by Kropotkin (1955), who found that the most viable groups had rudimentary mutual aid practices, such as food gathering, child rearing, and common defense. Medieval city-states evolved from such cooperative roots. The Freemasons became one of the best-known examples of a self-help group when, after the Black Death decimated much of Europe, the organization provided an essential social anchor during devastating upheaval.

In more recent times, cooperative societies have flourished in both Europe and America to help members with anything from a financial crisis to livestock and grain management. The utopian communities of the 1800s were based on cooperative principles and were formed in response to the ills brought on by the urbanization of the Industrial Revolution. Today, trade unions and worker-organized businesses share a strong commitment to peer-organized structures that address a common need.

Self-help or mutual aid groups have also evolved steadily and flourished in the field of health and human services. With a growth rate of 9 percent a year (Maton, et al.), self-help groups have gained respect and recognition as viable groups. They promote individual feelings of self-satisfaction derived from awareness that individuals are valued, are not powerless or disenfranchised, and are bound by a common need that allays their sense of isolation.

TYPES OF SELF-HELP GROUPS

FOCUS ON DIVERSITY

Note the wide diversity of membership in the three types. Self-help groups are a way to cope with a multitude of issues.

Social scientists have developed a number of ways to categorize types of self-help groups. Because the incredibly rapid growth of self-help groups is in itself a phenomenon worth examining, let's start by looking at how people have classified self-help groups in the context of social movements. Blumer (1951) differentiated three types of social movements. *General* movements refer to groups organized around a large issue such as peace, women's rights, or the environment. The goal is to change members' and the public's values. This type of movement often lacks established leaders, and membership and group structure are flexible and rapidly changing. The second type is a *specific* movement, which has well-defined objectives and a recognized leadership and membership, as well as established rituals, traditions, and a status hierarchy. Groups such as welfare rights organizations, Black Muslims, and the Industrial Workers of the World during World War I are examples of this type. The third type is labeled *expressive,* and includes Alcoholics Anonymous, groups for people with AIDS, the National Mental Health Consumer's Association (for former mental patients), and Compassionate Friends (for parents who have lost a child). The emphasis is on intimate interactions and personal support and change.

Another way to classify self-help groups is to assess whether their goals and activities support the status quo of society or challenge established societal norms (Katz,

1972). Groups such as AA, Parents Without Partners (PWP), Recovery, Inc., and Take Off Pounds Sensibly (TOPS) do not challenge widely held values but rather focus on helping their members develop a comfortable existence within societal norms and values. Other groups, such as gay rights organizations, women's rights groups, and Little People of America are interested in changing existing prejudices.

Sagarin (1969) looked at self-help groups composed of deviants and analyzed the ways the public perceives these groups, as well as the way group members think about themselves in relation to established institutions and cultural expectations. He found that stigmatized people—that is, people who do not conform to accepted norms—join self-help groups for two reasons: either to conform more easily to social norms or to create new standards that will accommodate their "deviant" behavior.

Certain groups come together for both support and information. For example, many divorced women who have young children find self-help groups a means of learning how to be a single parent, how to find acceptance for a family headed solely by a mother, and how to integrate child rearing and career building. Many such women have gained sufficient support from their groups to campaign for more and better child care, tax deductions for child care, and legislation to enforce negligent fathers' payment of child support. There are also divorced men's support groups who are concerned with caring about their children's rearing; members want to be more involved than every other weekend. These groups have taken action to secure greater visitation rights, have more vacation time with children, and generally move toward more equal time.

As you can see, we can organize this diversity in a variety of ways. Many categories overlap, and many groups have similar dynamics despite the fact that they address different problems or needs. In the next section, we will look at what makes self-help groups tick using the group concepts discussed in previous chapters. The emphasis will be on expressive self-help groups, which lend themselves readily to analysis of their dynamics from a small group perspective.

Levy (1979) classified self-help groups in accordance with group composition and purpose. His four categories were (1) behavioral-control or conduct-reorganization groups; (2) stress-coping and support groups; (3) survival-oriented groups; and (4) personal-growth and self-actualization groups.

Behavioral-control groups and conduct-reorganization groups consist of members who are trying to eliminate or control some problematic behavior. This desire is often the only requirement for membership, because the group's sole purpose is to help members control the problem common to them all. Groups in this category include Alcoholics Anonymous, Gamblers Anonymous, and Weight Watchers.

Stress-coping and support groups are composed of members who share a status or predicament that entails some degree of stress. The goal of these groups is to alleviate the stress through mutual support and the sharing of coping strategies and advice. Members' status is accepted, so no attempt is made to change that status. Rather, the goal is to help members carry on with their lives despite their current status. Such support groups as Parents Without Partners and Make Every Day Count (for people with cancer or serious chronic illness) are characteristic of this type.

Survival-oriented groups consist of people labeled by society—and discriminated against—as a result of their life styles, values, sex, sexual orientation, socioeconomic class, or race. The major concern of these groups is to help their members maintain or enhance their self-esteem through mutual support and consciousness-raising activities. These groups attempt to gain societal acceptance for their members through educational and political activities aimed at legitimizing their life styles and eliminating the stigma associated with them. Examples of this type include the National Organization for Women, gay activist groups, and various racial and ethnic activist support groups.

Personal-growth and self-actualization groups are composed of people who share one common goal: enhanced effectiveness in all aspects of their lives, especially those involving their emotionality, sexuality, and capacity to relate to others. The shared belief that together the members can help each other improve the quality of their lives is the primary reason for such a group's existence. Examples include some professional women's groups, Achieving Your Potential groups, and self-esteem groups. In recent years, self-help or mutual aid groups have grown not only quantitatively but, it might be said, qualitatively. They are perceived as providing such benefits that their approach has been enlarged. Three types are illustrative.

The support group movement has been actively supported by religious organizations, which have provided facilities, leaders, and a common culture of caring. Now, many Americans join support groups explicitly to enrich their faith or to grow spiritually, and they feel spiritually nurtured by their groups. However, instead of only studying text together, the group provides a context in which personal stories are told and imbued with spiritual meaning (Wuthnow, 1994). Wuthnow sees the support group movement as being a major force in transforming Americans' views of spirituality.

Another offshoot is the growth of the current reading club. Once reading clubs were places where typically white, educated, middle-aged women discussed literary tomes. They were viewed as esoteric and societally marginal. However, book clubs are an explosive trend.

Since 1996, with the Book Club on the Air on NPR, there has been a "magic moment." The question is, "Why now?" In a report, the answer seems to be that a trend becomes a life style: "More than a neighborhood forum for continuing education, book groups can diffuse pressures of the work place and home life, counteract the isolation of television and cyberspace, and ward off the general malaise of the late twentieth century. They're good for the heart, mind and soul" (*New York Times,* June 22, 1997).

The third expansion, of course, is the computer-based, self-help group. Finn and Lavitt (1994) report on their explorations with computer groups for those recovering from sexual abuse. Potential advantages include providing greater access to support, reducing barriers related to social status cues, encouraging participation of reluctant members, and enhancing communication of those with relational difficulties. The potential disadvantages include destructive interaction, lack of clear and accountable leadership, and the promoting of social isolation.

A pilot study of a support group for women with breast cancer found that some therapeutic factors were at work in their group, but only three of seven factors usually associated with such groups were reported. (Weinberg et al., 1995).

Computer support groups are definitely in their infancy. But various organizations are attempting them where special needs exist and computer groups overcome some of the obstacles. Family Services of Montgomery County in Pennsylvania has developed Parent-to-Parent, an Internet support group for families with children who have developmental, physical, and mental disabilities. Parents from around the state have access to one another through email providing information and support. This group would have special difficulty finding competent sitters, and would be further restricted by the necessity to drive long distances, let alone the consideration of cost-and-time factors. The computer support group may offer the possibility of rendering support that we are only beginning to recognize.

INDIVIDUAL EXPERIMENT

Sit down with a copy of your school or community paper and look in the Announcements section. Count the number of self-help group meetings listed. Use the definition of self-help groups to distinguish between self-help and other kinds of group meetings. Are the self-help groups' focuses similar or widely divergent? If you do not know what a particular group does, give it a call and find out.

ORIGINS AND MEMBERSHIP OF SELF-HELP GROUPS

When we think about the issue of membership in self-help groups, we are concerning ourselves with those people who are considered formal members of the group. They perceive themselves and are seen by others as a bona fide part of the group.

ORIGINS These groups may originate in a variety of ways. Some of the earliest groups (for example, AA) were begun by strong, authoritarian people who recognized the need for such groups. These groups still have strong leaders. Other self-help groups originate, for example, in a hospital's concern for patients with a particular problem. Recognizing that the professional staff can have only limited impact, hospitals have been helpful in organizing and promoting self-help groups and setting aside space for their meetings. For example, Allegheny University Hospital in Philadelphia has established a self-help group for young people with cystic fibrosis. Certain affiliates of the American Diabetic Association sponsor young-adult support groups. And many hospitals sponsor "new-parent support groups." Groups originated by a hospital or other organization may have a coordinator/leader, but members of the group are usually encouraged to take on leadership and develop their own meeting structure and style.

Some self-help groups are founded by individuals searching for people who have the same problem that afflicts them. For example, the Adoption Forum was founded by two adult adoptees who met and discovered they shared a need to explore the adoption experience with other adoptees. They ran ads making themselves known to such adults and began to develop strategies for searching for birth parents.

The potential focuses of self-help groups are so wide ranging, and the stress-reduction benefits so needed, that today groups even exist whose sole purpose is to form self-help groups. For example, the Health and Human Issues Outreach Department at the University of Wisconsin, Madison, has helped form self-help groups for Wisconsin farm families. This organization begins a group with a few members and then encourages the group to continue on its own course, developing according to the interests of those present.

MEMBERSHIP Membership in self-help groups is voluntary. Because all these groups are organized around a need, disabling condition, or problem that their members share, it is important to distinguish between having the "problem" and becoming a member of a self-help group addressing that problem.

For example, Mended Hearts is a self-help group composed of people who have had heart surgery. Along with regular meetings, one of their main activities is going to see other people in the hospital who are awaiting or recovering from surgery. Mended Hearts visitors give support and general information about what the patient can expect, and they serve as models of people who have successfully gone through the same experience.

What reasons do people give for joining a self-help group? There has been an almost endless flood of writing about alienation in the twentieth century and the finger has pointed at the increasing complexity of life brought on by industrialization, urbanization, and bureaucratization. This leaves the individual feeling powerless to effect any change, frustrated, and helpless. This predicament is exacerbated by the deterioration of traditional support systems such as the family, neighborhood, and community. Many have looked to small groups to find support, emotional nurturance, and a sense of identity that is lacking in their lives.

Some self-help groups address the needs of those considered deviant by society: people with physical or psychological disabilities that limit their social acceptance. Multiply the impact of being outside the mainstream of society by the sense of isolation felt by everyone, and we can begin to get a sense of the compelling pull of self-help groups.

People who join self-help groups must define themselves as in need of help from others. They must affirm that they have a problem, need, or disability rather than denying its existence. For example, people who join TOPS or Weight Watchers have admitted that their weight problem is just that, a problem. And it is a problem that they cannot manage by themselves, either. Like other groups, self-help groups serve as reference groups for their members. Groups exert social pressure to influence members to abide by group norms. In weight control groups, for example, individuals are weighed at the beginning of each meeting. Individuals who lose pounds are cheered and applauded, whereas those whose weight is stable or rising are admonished to do better.

By serving as reference groups with which members strongly identify, self-help groups facilitate changes in self-perception, which empowers the individuals. Several social scientists (Kahn, 1985; Wuthnow, 1994) have suggested that people not only empower themselves within the context of self-help groups and then extend this power to their lives but also extend their new power into the community by influencing organizations, institutions, and even society's development. For example, diabetic self-help groups have formed powerful lobbies for insurance coverage for blood glucose monitors and other health needs. MADD (Mothers Against Drunken Driving) started as a self-help group and has been instrumental in the passage of laws punishing drunken drivers in almost every state. Further, Chesney and Chesler (1993) found that membership in a self-help group was a major facilitator of activism for parents of children with cancer and played the most important role in explaining parents' life change in this aspect.

A brief look at research on the effectiveness of self-help groups confirms the assumption that their members gain empowerment. And further research is helping to determine which populations are most likely to be helped by group membership and under what conditions. One study investigated the impact of self-help group participation on people with scoliosis (curvature of the spine) and their families. The 245 participants in the study were divided into three groups: adolescent scoliotics, parents of adolescent scoliotics, and adult scoliotics. On a questionnaire, most members of the three groups reported considerable satisfaction with the self-help groups. However, it is important to note that being a member had no discernible impact on the psychosocial adjustments of the adolescent patients or their parents. It was a different story for the adults and those who had undergone demanding medical treatment. These populations seemed to benefit the most from the self-help groups (Hinrichsen et al., 1985).

A study on the impact of self-help groups on the mental health of widows and widowers found that presence at sessions alone was insufficient to produce positive changes, but that significant positive changes occurred for those who participated actively (Lieberman and Videka-Sherman, 1986). And after examining whether self-help groups meet the needs of the bereaved, Cluck and Cline (1986) reported that such groups seemed more effective than traditional resources, such as family, friends, and professional help givers.

There continues to be research attempting to understand how support groups work and how they can be more effective. Caserta and Lund (1993) studied almost 300 recently bereaved adults. Some had greater personal competencies, some had fewer. The subjects were randomly assigned either to a group which met for eight weekly sessions, another which met for an additional ten monthly sessions, or a control group. They found that the level of competency was a significant factor. Those with lesser competencies reported decreases in depression with greater attendance. This was not true for the more competent who only reported diminished depression and guilt if they attended the post-eight-week sessions.

Heller and Associates (1997) studied participation by families in support groups with mental patients. The families came, and continued to come, when they received emotional support and received information about mental illness. They dropped out when they felt a lack of comfort with other members and felt there was inadequate leadership.

Humphreys and Woods (1993) researched self-help group participation in substance abuse treatment. They argued that self-help group participation should consider racial and cultural segregation. One year after treatment intake they found that different factors predicted attendance for each racial group: for whites, being in a residential setting for a longer time predicted support group participation positively; among African-Americans, length of treatment affected attendance positively, but psychological problems affected participation negatively. They found that for both racial groups, similarity of the individual's race to the predominant race in the area predicted support-group involvement positively.

Still another perspective in understanding the effectiveness of support groups relates to whether groups led by professionals were helpful. More than 800 professionals working in community mental health centers, private psychiatric hospitals, and state hospitals were asked how helpful they perceived groups led by professionals, support groups, and self-help groups. Results indicate that professionals may hold certain attitudes that interfere with collaboration with self-help organizations. The setting in which the professional worked had great impact on how they worked with self-help groups (Salzer, McFadden, and Rappaport, 1994).

Katz and Bender (1976) outlined seven steps that self-help groups help their members to take.

1. Develop and sustain a coherent world view. Members share a rationale and common understanding of their problem.
2. Learn new, more gratifying behavior. Members benefit from learning better ways to manage their dilemmas.
3. Tap unconscious feelings.
4. Fortify self-image and pride. Members receive support and feedback that give them external validation when they change.
5. Achieve mastery by uncovering competence. With group support, members are encouraged to try new skills and discover previously unknown qualities and abilities.
6. Increase coping abilities through participation in group tasks of graduated difficulty. A self-help group is a good place for people to be challenged. Members are given more responsibility within the group as they progress.
7. Advance to new status within the group, then perhaps leave. Self-help groups demand that people give as well as receive help, commensurate with their abilities. Although some groups expect long-term involvement, many encourage leaving once the person is coping better with his or her problem.

In summary, self-help groups provide a cooperative climate for growth, frequent interaction of their members, and the opportunity to see successful senior members. All of these factors serve to support and reassure members and increase the attractiveness of such groups.

SELF-HELP GROUP NORMS

All groups develop norms—rules, policies, and unwritten expectations—to control members' behavior. In self-help groups, many of the norms help members feel better about themselves and learn better ways of coping. In some groups, norms are quite formal, written documents that not only delineate an overall world view but also specify in detail the steps a member is to take in order to change. For example,

AA has twelve steps that point the alcoholic in the right direction, as well as a host of other written material describing the problem of alcoholism.

Other norms may not be in black and white but are explicitly stated and consciously shared by the membership. At Eagleville, a rehabilitative facility in Pennsylvania, and other spin-off self-help groups for drug addicts, there are a variety of sayings that communicate strong normative expectations. "No pain, no gain" and "Remember, when you point your finger at someone else, there are three pointing back at you" both illustrate norms of accepting responsibility for your actions, being honest, and acknowledging that change is a difficult process that can be expected to be uncomfortable and painful.

Two other group norms that serve as basic underpinnings for many self-help groups are mutual aid and activity as means to solve one's problems.

MUTUAL AID Group members are expected to provide support and concern for other members. The idea that assistance is a reciprocal process is congruent with the basic belief that individuals can join together to help themselves without the aid of professionals. This also speaks to the expectation that members will be active participants in their own recovery or rehabilitation, not passive receivers of a service in which there is little expected from them other than "getting better." This type of self-help group provides an arena in which getting better has some specific, behavioral components. New members who are recipients of help become veteran members who are dispensers of help. AA states, "You have to give it away in order to keep it." "It" is personal learning and change for the better. By expecting that he or she will help others in need, the individual can reverse his or her established role from receiver to giver and then can feel more competent and receive approval from others.

Another dynamic that is set up is that more senior members become role models and referents for newer members. Every formerly obese person who gets up in an Overeaters Anonymous meeting to tell his or her story not only is telling a tale of struggle but is also a living affirmation that it works!

ACTIVITY Self-help groups support members, sharing their feelings and emotions, but there is a strong emphasis on activity. People are urged, supported, and advised to cope with their disabilities, problems, or needs and continue to function. In Recovery, Inc., members advise one another to act as though they are "normal," even when they hear voices or suffer from delusions. AA exhorts members to take it "one day at a time." Groups for bereaved parents, children, or spouses encourage their members to mourn, but they also share how people have resumed regular social engagements. Patients who have undergone mastectomy, colostomy, amputation, or other surgeries also have self-help groups that share information, resources, and personal experience about how to adjust to one's body and its demands. Constructive action toward shared goals is the hallmark of self-help groups.

NEGATIVE AND POSITIVE GROUP NORMS Interestingly, emerging data indicate that self-help groups in which negative norms evolve do not help members. For example, in some self-help groups for women on welfare, the longer people remained members, the more depressed they became. When women joined, they hoped to build contacts that might help them get jobs or gain tips on child rearing in neighborhoods with heavy drug use. But after listening to other members' stories about their difficulties in getting or keeping jobs and influencing their children to stay in school and remain drug-free, initially hopeful joiners came increasingly to feel that their own situations were hopeless. In another example, a professional woman who had been raped reported her experience in joining a self-help group for survivors of sexual assault. For her, the self-help group was a negative experience, because it caused her to relive the horror continually rather than integrating the experience into her life and getting on with daily living. Each new member recounted another horrible experience, reigniting her own memories. This particular woman found it more helpful to call a "hotline" counselor at moments when she was overwhelmed by negative feelings. Finally, a successful accountant who was confined to a wheelchair as a result of polio reported joining a support group to hear how others coped with continuing physical disability. However, he found the norms of the group he entered to be doom, gloom, passivity, and depression. Two sessions convinced him that the group was not for him.

In many cases, then, when their norms are positive, problem-solving, and encouraging, self-help groups can offer powerful and positive experiences. But as with any other group, when the norms are negative and an atmosphere of defeat and futility prevails, self-help groups might actually be detrimental.

Some data suggest that the benefits of groups to members can be questionable even where norms are positive. For example, Peele (1984), in examining AA, identified a powerful group-socialization process—a kind of brainwashing. And Scheffler (1983), in her experience with members of Overeaters Anonymous, became concerned about the possible damaging effects of matching new members with sponsors, experienced members who serve as guides. She stated that the counseling from a sponsor can be a negative influence in some people's lives.

Similarly, some social scientists express concern about how self-help groups create change. Lieberman (1986) stressed that "to generalize that all self-help groups work because of social support would be utter nonsense." In a series of studies, Lieberman and Borman (1979) found that those who had established "give-and-take" relationships with other members benefited from being in a self-help group more than those who had not done so. But in another study, involving bereaved parents, they found that the give-and-take relationship produced no added benefits. In still other groups, they found that members showed no psychological improvement whatsoever. Lieberman noted that although studies with self-help groups are encouraging, it has not been determined how, why, and for whom such groups work. These questions are currently provoking much research and study.

Still, it is generally acknowledged that a way to increase the effectiveness of self-help groups is for members to be trained in leading groups, facilitating communication, understanding group norms, and helping groups create positive norms. Simultaneously, group members need training in dealing with typical group problems, such as people who monopolize sessions or insist on their solutions to problems as the only ones worth considering. Small group training of this sort has been found to increase member participation and group longevity.

Self-help groups provide a small group experience that can support and enrich their members. This is one of the major trends in group development, in coping with social problems, and in small group research at this time.

GROUP STRUCTURE AND NORMS In order to establish and maintain positive norms, groups need structure so that mutual aid and cooperative support can continue throughout meetings. Basic to the structure is the norm that each member is valued. To establish this norm, facilitators should encourage each person to introduce himself or herself and relate personal reasons for joining the group. Furthermore, he or she should encourage each member to participate in every discussion, and foster an atmosphere of receptivity and empathy. Members need to know that they can safely express their true feelings and that their honesty will be acknowledged and welcomed. Acceptance and a shared understanding of a previously hidden problem are central to the effectiveness of self-help groups in meeting members' needs.

Another positive norm is the free flow of information among members, especially information derived from personal disclosure. Fawcett and his colleagues (1988) listened to tapes to get a sense of the "anatomy of self-help groups" and were surprised to find that the predominant activity seemed to be information giving.

Leadership may be rotated throughout the membership, which reinforces personal involvement and responsibility. Authority is shared by peers; there are no designated leaders or healers or people with special expertise that sets them apart from others. Status is earned by furthering the interests of the group. Within a self-help group, it is possible to enter as a new member who has hit rock bottom and rise through the ranks to a position of authority and responsibility—something that would not be possible in more traditional groups. In group psychotherapy, no matter how good a client someone is, he or she will never become the therapist.

Decisions in a self-help group are made by the group as a whole, usually through consensus, with much discussion and sharing of thoughts and feelings. Although not everyone may agree with a decision, the process of reaching a decision is built on the group's commitment to give everyone an opportunity to be heard.

Reader Activity

Think back to the last time you sat down with a group of people from school or colleagues from work. Identify the common experiences all of you share. You may never have talked about them with each other, but they still exist. Think about what the group did talk about. Were there shared problems or concerns that surfaced? Did people offer empathic support or advice to one another, or was there confrontation and conflict? How did you feel afterward?

SELF-HELP GROUP GOALS

Individuals come to self-help groups with personal goals—perhaps to seek relief from an addiction, to regain a better body image, or to attain self-confidence despite a stutter. In order for a group to continue to function successfully, it must address each individual's needs. There is also a process of self-selection that takes place in self-help groups. Some people may initially be drawn to a particular group and then find that it does not suit them.

One of the goals of any self-help group is to assist its members. However, groups have many other goals too, which work in the service of the larger goal of filling a need. A self-help group has goals that focus on its own survival: Will members be committed and keep coming? How will we let other people know we exist so they can benefit? How will we manage when we have too many members for just one group? What will our relationship be with professionals who work with people having similar problems? Can they be a source of referrals or do we disagree with their methods and want them out of our hair? In order for a group to flourish, its members have to identify with the group's goals and be willing to commit themselves to seeing that the goals are accomplished.

Goals vary in duration and breadth. For example, neighborhood self-help groups that develop to meet some terrible adversity such as a tornado or flood tend to focus on a narrow concern or problem. When the crisis is over, people go back to their normal routines and the group disbands. At the other end of the continuum is a self-help group such as AA. It is common for AA members to remain involved and active in the organization for a number of years after their initial decision to remain sober (Bear, 1975).

A TYPICAL SELF-HELP MEETING

Although self-help groups such as AA have a particular belief system that is actually written out and expressed in various prescribed activities (for a complete review, see Johnson and Phelps, 1991), many others have no such ideology. Others, such as the Adoption Forum, widow and widower groups, young-adult diabetic groups, and Compassionate Friends, achieve their results through a relatively simple cluster of social psychological processes: mutual identification, confession, catharsis, the elimination of stigmatizing feelings, and mutual support in problem solving. In this process, the "I" feeling is replaced with a "we" feeling, the individual gains a sense of belonging, and together members redefine certain norms of behavior.

A typical self-help meeting is usually set for a certain day of the week. Often, meeting times are listed in the local paper. The meetings usually last an hour or two, and sometimes juice or coffee is served before or after the meeting. In some meetings, no refreshments are served and members may go out together to socialize.

Meetings start fairly promptly. Members enter and sit in a circle. The person who is the leader (almost always a volunteer) begins by asking those present to introduce themselves and briefly describe their situations. For example, at a meeting of Compassionate Friends, a self-help organization for bereaved parents, members state their names, give the names and ages of the children who died, and briefly recount how the deaths occurred. Usually, new members speak first and then the older members recount their experiences. Members listen attentively, ask questions, and give affirmations of support. After both new and old members have spoken, the meeting may go in one of two directions. An expert guest speaker—a psychologist, physician, or social worker, for example—might open the discussion, addressing a particular aspect of the grieving process. The speaker delivers prepared remarks and then invites members to express their feelings or share their particular methods of dealing with the phase under discussion. The other option is to hold a general discussion on a particular topic. For example, in the Compassionate Friends meeting, the discussion of the evening might center on the topic of guilt. Members speak of their own feelings and experiences, and the leader brings the discussion to a close perhaps 15 to 20 minutes before the end of the session. There might then be a "go-around," in which each member responds to a question posed by the leader, for example, "What was most helpful to you in tonight's meeting?"

The last few minutes might be taken up with business, such as setting up the next meeting and selecting the next volunteer leader. There might also be announcements of an upcoming lecture or other event of particular relevance to the members. Often, once the meeting is adjourned, members stay on to talk with each other about issues raised during the evening. Also at this time, newcomers might be asked to sign the mailing list, dues or contributions might be collected, and literature might be circulated or laid out for the perusal of members.

The norms at a typical meeting support open communication. Members are encouraged to speak up about their own experiences. The others are encouraged to listen and support those who tell their stories. Those who have been in the group for a time encourage and affirm new participants in their self-revelations and, at the end of a meeting, make a point of personally welcoming them, thanking them for coming and sharing their experiences, and asking them to return. Tears, sadness, and anger are all acceptable within the groups. Members are encouraged to explain how they coped with difficult situations and to recount both successes and failures. The prevailing climate might be summed up this way: "We've all been there. *We* especially understand the problems, and therefore we can help each other."

STAGES OF DEVELOPMENT OF SELF-HELP GROUPS

Groups, like people, have different needs at different times in their life cycle. Growth always involves change and a certain amount of tension between past experience and goals for the future. Even healthy, functional change incurs stress and conflicts, so it is no surprise that self-help groups struggle with certain dilemmas as they grow and mature. Each group is unique, but it is possible to outline a normative path of growth that can serve as a map for self-help groups.

Katz (1970) has outlined a developmental model for self-help groups.

1. *Origin.* The hallmark of this beginning stage is the presence of a founder—someone who assumes responsibility for getting people together. In many groups, this person is a professionally trained individual, such as a psychologist, minister, or physician. He or she may be in disagreement with the accepted treatment or service for a problem, seeing the gaps that are unaddressed or being aware of groups of people who lack adequate service. Typically, this perspective leads the professional to a different vision of how the problem can be rectified. In the case of Recovery, Inc., Abraham Low, a psychiatrist, saw a need for some sort of continued support for people leaving a mental hospital (Low, 1950). A cardiologist and founder of Mended Hearts, Dwight Harken, saw the potential benefits that peer support could offer heart patients (Harken et al., 1979). Founders, whether lay or professional, share one characteristic: they all have a charismatic presence that allows them to effectively organize a group of people burdened with a common concern or problem. Their personal energy and drive help mobilize potential members to begin to meet, and they provide a vision of how to help, as well as initial guidelines.

2. *Informal organizational stage.* Few hard-and-fast rules govern a group as it continues to meet. People join and continue membership because they get emotional sustenance and a sense of identity. People informally share the responsibility for running and organizing activities of the group; its small size and lack of complexity readily allow this to happen. Also, the role of the founder typically decreases, as does his or her responsibility.
3. *Emergence of leadership.* As a beginning group develops cohesion and new members are added, new leadership emerges from within the group. The self-help group's norm of mutual aid and personal responsibility propels individuals into leadership roles. As the group continues to flourish and increase in size, there is a need to establish rules and structures so that the group can still function. At this point, natural leaders provide direction and help clarify the group's needs.

   Most social scientists would agree that the first three stages characterize most self-help groups (Caplan and Killilea, 1976; Lieberman and Borman, 1979). After leaders emerge from the membership, there are a number of different paths for self-help groups to take. Some continue through the next two steps that Katz presented. Others maintain their growth and continue at the same level; and still others become affiliated with more traditional institutions while retaining their independence. Katz's model follows the theory that organizations become more bureaucratic the longer they exist.
4. *Beginnings of formal organization.* Often, when a group continues to grow in size, it also grows in complexity. Not only does it start to serve as a self-help group, but it also must consider how it recruits new members, supports itself financially, locates space for meetings, charters new chapters, and expands its audience to include people with different yet related problems. In organizational terms this is called *specialization:* one part of the group attends to one piece of business, and others do other tasks. The organization becomes more defined and rigid in order to get the jobs done.
5. *Beginnings of professionalism.* In this last stage, professional fundraisers, accountants, managers, and others are hired to do the work of the organization. The self-help group has expanded to many, many chapters with a multitude of concerns, only one of which is the original face-to-face interaction of its members in small supportive groups. Obviously, the norms of the organization must shift to accommodate a nonvolunteer staff before any group can successfully negotiate this final stage. The National Association for Retarded Citizens is one such group, which began as a self-help group for parents of retarded children. It has since grown into

a national organization serving as a source of education and information for parents, as well as engaging in many other activities that advance retarded people's status and mobility in society.

One way to increase the effectiveness of self-help groups is for members to receive instruction in group leadership and communication, creating and understanding positive group norms, and dealing with group issues such as sharing session time and realizing that problems often have more than one possible solution. Training in working with small groups has been found to increase member participation and the likelihood of group continuance (Miller and Katz, 1992).

EVOLVING UNDERSTANDING OF SELF-HELP GROUPS

In the last decade or so, further developments have lent promise to increasing awareness of self-help groups as significant contributors to physical and mental health and a humane quality of life. With this in mind, former Surgeon General C. Everett Koop sponsored a workshop entitled Self-Help and Public Health in 1987. The workshop resulted in a voluntary association to promote linkages among self-help groups and formal systems to increase their visibility and credibility. Four principles, regarded as central, came out of this endeavor.

1. Self-help groups (that is, member-governed voluntary associations) exist in areas of prime concern to members.
2. Egalitarian, respectful relationships, not superordinate–subordinate relationships, among self-help groups and the formal system should be developed.
3. An emphasis on increasing ethnic and minority participation in self-help groups is a high priority.
4. Self-help groups should not be viewed as substitutes for health and human services for which the government is responsible.

Following the workshop, the Surgeon General's Office sponsored the formation of the National Council on Self-Help and Public Health, in 1988, to implement these recommendations (Borkman, 1990).

Self-help groups provide a small group experience that supports and enriches their members. The next section focuses on a small group application in the workplace: total quality management, or TQM. This type of management technique utilizes small groups in the form of "teams" that share some characteristics with self-help groups yet also differ greatly in function.

Total Quality Management (TQM)

Since the first edition of this text was published in the late 1970s the use of groups as working units has increased tenfold. Then, it would have been unheard of to incorporate any kind of cooperative system into the workplace. Today, we find many different kinds of small group applications in this very area, from the problem-solving strategies of quality circles to self-managing work teams responsible for the production of a whole product (Lawler, 1990). The use of teams to improve the quality of a business or institution has been part of a growing trend toward participative management and improvement in quality. One reason for this trend may be that extreme competitiveness, which was once thought to lead to higher performance and achievement, is now often thought to interfere with achievement (McGarvey, 1992). Perhaps the most talked-about method of using small groups in the workplace this decade is TQM: total quality management. This portion of the chapter will briefly trace the history of the TQM process, show how it fits in with the scheme of small group processes, and suggest some of its practical applications and potential pitfalls.

HISTORY OF TQM

JAPANESE INFLUENCE Total quality management began as an offshoot of total quality control, a management policy developed in Japan after World War II. At that time, Japan was in the process of rebuilding its industry and trying to establish itself in the world market. The Japanese Union of Scientists and Engineers, in an effort to improve the quality of Japanese products, sponsored lectures by several U.S. industrial specialists, including W. Edwards Deming. Deming presented a statistical method for controlling quality that had received little attention in the United States but was enthusiastically embraced by Japanese industry and government. By the early 1960s, Japan had implemented these ideas in the form of quality control circles. The circles were composed of five to ten workers from the same work area who, using statistical control methods, identified and developed solutions for a variety of problems that negatively affected the quality of industrial products. The quality control circle was one manifestation of an overall quality improvement effort.

FOCUS ON DIVERSITY

Japan had a critical need for manufacturing improvement then. How is that like the situation now in the U.S., with an all-time low unemployment rate?

Several factors existed in Japan at the time TQM was developed that made it particularly suitable. Japan was notorious for producing cheap, poorly made industrial products, and in order for it to compete internationally, quality and productivity had to be dramatically improved. Japan was reliant on its people as critical resources, because there was both a labor shortage after the war and a shortage of technology and industrial resources.

Japan also had an industrial policy that focused on "people building," which included an emphasis on lifetime employment, training and educational programs, and expenses for housing, medical, and recreational needs. The Japanese company was viewed as an extended family, in which employees remained for long periods of time—sometimes their entire careers—and developed close personal relationships with coworkers and superiors. All these factors made Japan fertile ground for the emergence of a team-oriented quality control effort such as TQM (Watanabe, 1991; Dumas et al., 1989; Axline, 1991; Hatvang and Pucik, 1981).

QUALITY CIRCLES IN THE UNITED STATES Quality circles were introduced in the United States in 1974, at the Lockheed Missile Corporation. There conditions were favorable for quality circles because the labor force was highly skilled and success was highly dependent on quality. Lockheed reported saving $3 million by introducing quality circles. The types of projects that quality circles took on included developing a plastic mold assembly that required fewer operations, improving the defect rate in producing circuit boards, and testing and choosing a more effective method for identification of parts. Several managers involved in introducing quality circles at Lockheed left the corporation and began a consulting firm for establishing quality circles in other companies. In 1974, Honeywell Corporation also introduced quality circles and reported considerable savings. Since then quality circles have blossomed in many diverse companies.

THREE COMPONENTS OF TQM: PARTICIPATIVE MANAGEMENT, CONTINUOUS PROCESS IMPROVEMENT, AND USE OF TEAMS

According to Joseph R. Jablonski, writing in *Implementing Total Quality Management: An Overview,* TQM is "a cooperative form of doing business that relies on the talents and capabilities of both labor and management to continually improve quality and productivity using teams" (Jablonski, 1991). Implicit in this definition are three ingredients that are essential for the TQM process to take place: participative management, continuous process improvement, and use of teams. The second element follows directly from the idea that TQM is indeed a process, a continual transformation of the way management or an administration utilizes the knowledge and abilities of its employees (Walton, 1990). It is the last element that makes TQM an interesting contemporary application of small group processes. In the following pages, each of these elements is discussed in more detail.

PARTICIPATIVE MANAGEMENT TQM in the United States has become part of a trend toward increased employee involvement in a variety of work decisions and concerns that traditionally have been the domain of management. *Participative management* is a generic term for a broad range of innovations of this type (Jenkins, 1981; Likert, 1961, 1967; McGregor, 1960). It has developed as a result of several factors, including the voice of the labor force expressed through unions; theories about human nature, motivation, and work; and many other changes that have evolved in the workplace over the last forty years.

Over the years, a rising level of employee dissatisfaction and a decline in worker productivity have given additional impetus to acceptance of a participative management philosophy. According to social scientists, worker dissatisfaction, apathy, and alienation have been associated with increased task specialization of work and increased bureaucratization of organizations. Employees are segregated and have specialized work tasks that isolate them from peers and from completion of the products they work on. Jobs have become dull and routinized to the point where workers, despite higher pay and better work conditions (even ability to work from home), lack motivation and job satisfaction with concern about permanence, and part-time work with lack of benefits. They have limited contact with authority and little ability to affect their immediate work environment (Sashkin, 1984).

According to Johnson et al. (1991), behavior analysts have often suggested that "participation by the consumers of behavioral intervention will enhance cooperation and maintenance." If this is true, taking part in decision-making processes will boost employee interest in work-related tasks. Several social scientists have also proposed theories concerning individual behavior at work that support participative management. Maslow (1954) developed a theory of motivation that emphasized the human desire to work and function to our capacity and potential. Hackman (1975; Hackman and Suttle, 1977) demonstrated that employee motivation and satisfaction result from the job itself as well as from the work environment. He suggested that employees would be motivated by a job in which they had some degree of autonomy, were able to perceive results of their work, and obtained feedback about their job performance.

Work experiments in various countries have further shaped the trend toward increased employee participation. For example, Volvo, in Sweden, organizes work to be completed by teams rather than the traditional assembly lines. Autonomous work groups have been formed in a number of British coal mines (Ellerman, 1984; Kelly and Khozan, 1980; Trist, 1981). In the United States, General Motors Corporation and Donnelly Mirror Company, among others, have developed similar innovations ("Participative Management at Work," 1977; Walton, 1979). These experiments expand the influence and responsibility of rank-and-file employees and attempt to incorporate consideration of human social needs into the organization of work (Bernstein, 1982; Burck, 1981; Main, 1981).

Total quality management represents a workplace experiment that emphasizes employee involvement through the use of teams designed to analyze the process in which a systemic problem is occurring and then to solve the problem. Before describing in more detail the functioning of such teams, let's further explore the concept of continuous process improvement, the second essential element of TQM.

FOCUS ON DIVERSITY

How has this process affected integration, racial or ethnic, in the U.S.?

CONTINUOUS PROCESS IMPROVEMENT According to Ellen Earle Chaffee of North Dakota University, "quality is a verb, not a noun" (Sherr and Teeter, 1991). It follows that TQM is something that an organization actively engages in, and it is anything but random. Many people have tried to explain exactly what continuous process improvement entails, but probably the simplest yet most revealing definition comes from the Japanese in the form of one word: *kaizen*. *Kaizen* means "constant improvement and incremental growth from taking very small risks each day" (Lagana, 1989). *Kaizen* is associated with quality control that is not concerned simply with "product quality or productivity improvements" but with improvements in general organizational activities. In other words, the entire system needs constant reevaluation (Watanabe, 1991).

If an organization can control its processes—the way it does business or conducts itself generally on a daily basis—it is well on the road to quality improvement. Many companies have reported that "up to 80 percent of low-quality and organizational performance problems are traceable to processes, not employees" (Axline, 1991). In fact, a direct link has been found between quality and productivity. For example, when Bell of Canada began monitoring the speed of its operators as a group rather than individually, not only did productivity stay up but the operators themselves also claimed both that their services improved and that they liked their job more (Bernstein, 1991). All of which leads directly to the next element: how the continuous process of improvement gets implemented. The vehicle for change in the previous example, as with the entire TQM process, is the work team.

THE USE OF TEAMS The use of teams, or small groups, to solve problems in the workplace is another aspect of total quality control. It is estimated that problem-solving teams are used by more than half of all large corporations. On the other side of the coin is the use of self-managing work teams that are responsible for producing a whole product or providing a complete service within a large work environment. All team members are expected to know, thoroughly, all aspects of each of their teammates' jobs as well as their own. But although this type of team has gained popularity, less than 10 percent of the work force utilizes it (Lawler, 1990). Each of these kinds of teams represents an extreme, as we shall see.

The purpose of using teams in the TQM process is so that the best cross section of individuals who work within a given process are brought together to change and improve that process. The process could be the regular functioning of a university staff or the production of automobiles. In the former case, the teams might include administrators, professors, office personnel—whoever is deeply enough involved in the process to recognize opportunities for improvement (Jablonski, 1991). In the latter case, the teams might include everyone on a given production line, as well as the engineers and upper management—again, anyone who would recognize, at any level, an opportunity for improvement. Because so many problems in an organization are interdepartmental, they are often difficult to solve. What the TQM process suggests is that an organization becomes "seamless" by dissolving interdepartmental divisions so that problems can be addressed without the barriers that often prevent an organization from moving forward (Leebov and Scott, 1990). The teams must therefore be composed of employees from all levels of management as well as the "frontline" workers. Membership depends not on status or placement but on proximity to the process or problem under consideration.

Quality circles were initially viewed as a major step to increased worker involvement. By using this method, groups of workers could examine problems of their department (or assigned problems), and as a group, recommend solutions based on their intimate knowledge of the work organization. The group was free to analyze problems as it wanted; it was not directed to reach specific, desired solutions by management. The reports on quality circles were very positive at first. However, after greater experience with the method, the outcomes raise many questions about why some have greater success than others.

WHY SOME QUALITY CIRCLES SUCCEED AND OTHERS FAIL

The functioning of a quality circle, just like that of any small group, depends on a variety of internal factors that the circle leader and members must manage. The circle is more likely to be successful if members participate voluntarily (Geehr, Burke, and Sulzer, 1995). The circle must have a task and goal for which members have sufficient skill and access to resources to succeed. The membership of the circle must be relevant to the task, and vice versa. The group must be able to translate circle values into norms that successfully guide group behavior (Procopio and Fairfield-Sonn, 1996). The leader must establish procedures for decision making and conflict resolution that enable the group to reach its goals and manage its interpersonal and emotional needs. And in addition to the group process issues, the "fit" of the circle into the larger organization is a critical factor in determining its success or failure.

Supporters claim that quality circles have the potential to do anything, that they give workers opportunities to identify and solve real problems of any type. They consider circles' solutions superior to those reached by other means, and argue that because workers participated in finding those solutions, workers in general are highly committed to their implementation. But others consider quality circles a fad, an easy-to-implement package that calls for little administrative commitment. These critics point out that more than 60 percent of the quality circles in American organizations have failed (Marks, 1986; Pascarella, 1982).

Two studies shed some light on the debate over the value of quality circles. Marks and his colleagues (1985) and later Marks alone (1986) examined the claims that quality circles improve the quality of work life and job performance of participants. These researchers worked in a manufacturing department and collected data over a thirty-month period beginning six months before a quality circle program began. They found that participation in the quality circle did indeed have a strong impact on areas of participants' lives that were directly related to quality circle activity—for example, decision making, group communications, and job advancement. But participants themselves did not change in their attitudes about the organization or in their feelings about organizationwide communication, job challenge, personal responsibility for getting work done, an overall job satisfaction. Among machine operators, participation in quality circles raised productivity and reduced absenteeism but did not increase satisfaction with the work.

In another study, Lawler and Ledford (1986) examined nine separate units of a large conglomerate that varied greatly in employment criteria and amount of training provided. The researchers found that certain quality circles did succeed in changing the organization and that these shared several characteristics.

1. Sufficient training of members, including efforts to improve members' understanding of group dynamics and ways to work effectively in groups
2. Both inside and outside the circles, good access to useful information
3. Accurate record keeping, including the establishment of measurable goals for the quality circles
4. The creation of the circles themselves from intact work teams

These researchers found little evidence, however, that quality circles change corporate culture or improve individual work satisfaction and productivity. The general conclusion was that the quality circle technique was not strong enough to promote real organizational change.

Since quality circles were introduced in the United States in 1974, their goals have been to increase productivity and improve the quality of work life. Although quality circles have been successful in Japan, in the United States they have yielded mixed results. Current research on U.S. quality circles has uncovered some of the factors responsible for the failure of quality circles to fully meet their goals. Gmelch and Misking (1986) identified one of these factors as the inability of American companies to recognize and react to circle members' need to coordinate their efforts. The basis for this inability seems to be a conflict between widely held ideas and the basic notions on which quality circles are founded. Ferris and Wagner (1985) identified three notions that support quality circles.

1. Group performance is superior to individual performance.
2. Workers desire participation.
3. Participation improves productivity.

However, these researchers' analysis of the differences between workers' perspectives on work in the United States and in Japan suggest that workers in most U.S. companies do not subscribe to these ideas. U.S. workers have an individualistic orientation toward work, whereas Japanese workers have a collectivistic orientation. The concepts that Ferris and Wagner identified conflict sharply with the embedded U.S. ideology. Thus, for the typical U.S. worker, quality circles themselves go against the grain.

Another factor responsible for the failure of quality circles in the United States is the relative lack of problem-solving skills among U.S. workers and of team-building skills among U.S. leaders (Gmelch and Misking, 1986). Two other factors are a lack of receptiveness to circle members' ideas and a failure of commitment to the basic idea of the circles among managers (Werther, 1983). The success and longevity of quality circles depend on management's receptivity to solutions proposed by the circles and a willingness to implement them. When their solutions languish, circle members lose interest and energy.

Nevertheless, in studies by Mohrman and Novelli (1985), Lawler and Ledford (1986) and Lawler and Mohrman (1985), the researchers concluded that quality circles can succeed at three kinds of tasks. First, quality circles can operate to suggest ways of improving work group communications and increasing awareness about quality and employee productivity. Second, quality circles can be useful in special short-term situations—for example, introducing a new technology or solving a major quality problem. Finally, quality circles can perform a bridging function when a company changes over from a traditional hierarchical organization to a more participative one.

The culture and management style of the organization must allow and actively support the participative approach of quality circles. A parochial, unyielding, autocratic management style will not respond to the participative input of a circle (Bruning and Liverpool, 1993). Often circles fail because management did not assess the readiness and preparation of the organization before instituting the new program. Organizations underestimate the attitudinal and organizational changes that occur when a participatory program such as quality circles is implemented.

A successful quality circle program necessitates visible support from both top and middle management. Where they are present, unions must also be involved in the planning and implementation stage to ensure their support. In a study to determine why quality circles failed in five U.S. companies, results suggested that the success of quality circles ultimately depended on continuing support from trade unions (Dale and Hayward, 1984).

Management must fully understand the circle program and its values, and be prepared to respond positively to the input from the circles. Not only must the changes suggested by quality circles be compatible with the organization (Steel and Shane, 1986), but managers, supervisors, and workers must truly subscribe to the basic notion of voluntarism upon which quality circles rest (Meyer and Stott, 1985).

Middle managers, to whom quality circles' solutions are usually presented, often resist these solutions, probably because (1) they are reluctant to accept ideas from subordinates, and (2) they are uncomfortable with the problem-solving process characteristic of quality circles. Moreover, middle managers have no direct involvement until they are called on to approve or implement a quality circle suggestion, which increases their distance from a solution.

This resistance to quality circles on the part of middle managers has been a major concern to those who would expand their use. One suggested means of overcoming resistance (Bushe, 1987) was to involve middle managers in problem-solving groups of their own, on the assumption that such involvement would produce attitude differences in them. In a study of 415 middle managers in the U.S. automobile industry, managers in permanent quality circles had the most positive attitude toward them. Those in temporary groups, however, had the most negative attitudes toward the circles—even more negative than managers with no group experience at all. It would seem, then, that a commitment to a quality circle grows over time.

Training is often a key element in the success of circles. The entire organization, not only those who volunteer to be in circles, needs training in the basic principles and functioning of quality circles. The circle leaders and members need sufficient training to develop the skills necessary for team problem solving.

There is increasing emphasis on the training of quality circle leaders and participants in communication, group dynamics, and team decision making. Certain monographs, such as that of Blaker (1982), present detailed information on quality circle training. Still, companies that hope to use quality circles as quick-fix solutions will find the effects similar to those of aspirin—they treat symptoms and provide some immediate relief but don't touch underlying issues, such as management–employee tension and underutilization of workers, that caused problems in the first place. Companies that try to cut corners by limiting the planning and training stages inevitably run into difficulties down the road.

In some organizations, circles are inadequately implemented because management is not truly interested in or prepared for employee participation or is not committed to the "people-building" attitude necessary for successful circles. Management can sabotage circles in endless ways, including overcontrolling them, not providing adequate budgets, not allowing access to necessary information or resources, setting restrictive deadlines, focusing too narrowly on the financial return, acting in an autocratic leadership style disguised as participative, repeatedly rejecting circle recommendations, and not building in avenues of recognition for circles' accomplishments. Setting unreasonably high expectations for a circle program can also set it up for failure and disillusionment. Many people, especially organized labor, distrust the labor–management cooperation inherent in a quality circle program. They fear that circles will be used as another guise for production speed-ups and believe that workers should get a financial share of any profits generated by them.

It has become increasingly evident that the quality circle is not a panacea for all the problems associated with productivity, quality, and employee dissatisfaction (Adam, 1991). If a company institutes a circle program to resolve a poor labor–management relationship, the circle is destined to fail. If a company has been mismanaged, lacks sufficient critical resources, or has an ineffectual administrative structure, a quality circle program will not make up for these failures. But quality circles can succeed in an organizational environment in which upper and middle management attend (Tang et al., 1991), participation is encouraged, employees can have an impact in areas of quality and productivity problems, and the company perceives its employees as a valuable resource.

SOME CURRENT EXAMPLES OF TQM

In the next few pages are some real world examples of the TQM process in action. Although the organizations involved are quite different, the theory behind all these applications of TQM is the same, and the problems that arise in its implementation are strikingly similar as well.

TQM IN THE PUBLIC SECTOR The issue of quality in the public sector is especially problematic because it often must be achieved in an environment of increasingly scarce public resources. Like many troubled organizations, government offices must continuously evolve and implement new management policies if improvement in the quality of their services is to occur (Milakovich, 1991).

When Joseph Sensenbrenner became mayor of Madison, Wisconsin, in 1983, he decided that his organization, the city government, would have to create a "culture of quality" rather than allow the "we'll fix it downstream" mentality, which is so pervasive in our culture, to continue to gnaw away at the city's infrastructure. Sensenbrenner knew this would be a difficult task, given that "government invented the status quo."

What Sensenbrenner found to be one of the most difficult things to accomplish—and indeed what Deming himself presented as one of the most important points in achieving the TQM transformation—is the process of driving the fear out of an organization. What Michael Milakovich, associate professor of political science at the University of Miami, says is that there is such a fear of change in the public sector that great productivity losses may occur merely as a result of "chronic anxiety." These feelings are often not unfounded; the old school of management has always held that the use of fear is the only way to ensure employee loyalty and increase job performance (Milakovich, 1991). For TQM to be successful, managers must relinquish power and loosen the stranglehold of fear on their workers.

Another thing Sensenbrenner found was that his departments were "too self-contained to be useful to one another" and that the very concept of being helpful was something completely out of his workers' realm of experience. What the city needed, and ultimately got, was a "quality army" comprising managers and frontline employees who would lead the way in taking "responsibility for risk as well as sharing credit for success" within his organization. He found that consulting and enlisting frontline employees in the team problem-solving and improvement processes enormously improved both morale and productivity (Sensenbrenner, 1991).

A similar story is that of the Parkview Episcopal Medical Center in Pueblo, Colorado. Another publicly funded institution, Parkview had to be very careful not to increase quality at the expense of its clientele. And, like the city of Madison, it found one of the major barriers to success to be managers who were afraid to stand up and say what they thought instead of trying to figure out what the boss wanted them to think. Once Parkview's employees overcame their fear, teams made up of surgeons, technicians, nurses, and scheduling managers were able to examine more easily the problems they faced and identify places where improvement could be achieved (Koska, 1990). Although garnering the support of all levels of the staff is often a lengthy process, no less is required for the TQM process to work. As we shall see, these are problems and solutions that are not unique to the public sector.

SCHOOL-BASED MANAGEMENT: TQM IN EDUCATION One very controversial application of the TQM process is that of school-based management, an obvious descendent of the participative policy of management. Just as in the public sector, years of top-down management have created deep wells of mistrust and suspicion. Thus, what should be an ultimately collaborative process whereby teachers become involved in the process of managing their own school is often perceived by teachers as another demand by an insensitive administration that hasn't done its own job. The training required to learn the skills and tools associated with turning the responsibility—and ultimately the rewards—over to teachers and administrators as a working team is not to be taken lightly. It is very easy for middle managers, or their equivalents, in an attempt to regain control and consolidate authority, to abandon collaborative principles early. This, of course, is recognized by the faculty as exactly what they expected, and it generates predictable resistance.

School-based management can be viewed as a partial remedy to the deteriorating performance, bankruptcy, and despair so frequently found throughout our public schools today. In implementing the process, however, administrators must take care not to sacrifice training to save money and, even more important, not to undermine the level of risk taking required for such a system to work (Lagana, 1989). In the end, once again, involving individuals in the decision making makes those decisions more durable and acceptable—an important outcome for an education system whose participants are growing ever more alienated and isolated (Hansen, 1990; Friedler, Cherniss, and Fishman, 1992).

TQM IN THE PRIVATE SECTOR: WHERE IT ALL BEGAN Deming designed TQM to take advantage of the excellence within a company by putting the responsibility for quality into the hands of all who can potentially control it. It has worked for the Japanese, but businesses in the United States seem to have had more of a struggle. For many of the same reasons cited when we discussed its applications in the private and educational sectors, TQM may fail in the business arena.

One important factor that often spells failure when private industries try to implement the TQM process is the high level of competitiveness that exists not only between companies but also among workers within a company. According to Harvard Business School professor Rosabeth Moss Kanter, "A sure sign of competitiveness gone awry is when the players pay more attention to beating their rivals than to performing the task well" (McGarvey, 1992). If TQM depends on the use of teams, how do we engender a team attitude in a market characterized by competition? How do cooperative attitudes become a part of a business world where quality has rarely been made a priority? The answer is that it must become a priority. American businesses are slowly learning that it pays off in the end. The Ford Taurus is an excellent example of how some of the ideas in TQM theory become a success story. Not only did Ford create a vehicle that was built well but its features were determined by teams of researchers and employees who ultimately had the greatest familiarity with both the process and the product.

In another success story, Federal Express learned that because it began by putting quality ahead of quantity or profitability, in time both quantity and profitability followed. Just as in the public sector, however, none of this can be achieved without careful consideration of and protection against the problems inherent in the TQM strategy. One employee in a midwestern factory likened his situation to being afraid of "pushing the button" and stopping production in order to allow "impromptu work teams to whirl into troubleshooting activities." The problem is that he then must take responsibility for the lost time, even if, in the long run, more problems are avoided through his conscientiousness (Dumas et al., 1989). In short, the temptation to maintain the status quo is pervasive throughout our society, and one of the greatest inhibitors of the success of TQM, whether applied in business, government, health care, or education. The last section in this part of the chapter deals with this and other common problems encountered by organizations attempting to implement TQM, as well as some suggestions for overcoming them.

TOTAL QUALITY MANAGEMENT: THE ULTIMATE CHALLENGE

We have seen that the process of total quality management is one that might be profitably applied to many different sectors of our society. In fact, one of the greatest barriers to innovation using the TQM process is social rather than organizational. If businesses, institutions, or organizations of any kind continue to ignore whole categories of people as sources of ideas, they will certainly stifle innovation. Many organizations that have "jumped on the quality bandwagon" in the last few years have found that their shortcomings exist not "within existing organizational lines" but at the boundaries between work teams (Kanter, 1982). Problems arise as a result of a dilemma faced by middle managers, who must juggle the demands of subordinates who are dealing with their own increased responsibilities and those of top managers who are pushing for results (Schlesinger and Oshrey, 1984).

The solutions are not simple. From the top down, upper managers must learn to engender a high level of trust among all organizational members. As a result, middle managers will be able to focus on giving the necessary support and attention to the frontline workers. This will afford all those who have access to the process an area in which they can "dare to look for improvement." According to Susan

Leddick, "managers need definition to help them behave . . . supportively toward their subordinates [who are] working on quality improvement" (Leddick, 1990).

In many ways, the ability of managers to relinquish their traditional source of power and authority can be considered the "foundation for the future success or failure of a new work system" such as total quality management (Manz et al. 1990). The new management role, as "facilitator" of work processes, requires extra training and consideration. Here team leaders coach rather than control (Milakovich, 1991). Another essential factor is that teams must be trained as teams. Many team managers think they can train team members individually, then send them to Outward Bound–type programs to learn generic team skills. Team training is different from team building. With team building people get to know each other at a personal level. Team training is more specific: people learn each other's competencies and the requirements of their team's task. Such training must continue throughout the life of a team as tasks change and members come and go (Azar, 1997).

TQM, then, requires three essential elements to survive: trust, support, and training. There's a world of potential for implementing the TQM process, but the process is doomed to fail unless some of the same qualities inherent in any successful group are exaggerated in work teams using TQM.

Focus Groups

Suppose you have just come home from the mall, where you happily found and purchased a battery-operated mobile for your sister's first child. Anxiously, you look at the clock: 3:55 P.M. Still in your coat, you flick on the television, press the Channel 6 button, and sink into the couch cushions while taking your coat off. The theme music of your favorite program seeps into your consciousness. Then you see her: Oprah Winfrey. You know the topic of her show—unusual sexual and behavioral habits—because you saw it advertised the day before.

As you watch, your curiosity peaks, but the telephone rings. Reluctantly, you answer it. A man asks whether you have watched the Oprah Winfrey program and how often. You tell him that you have seen it at least three or four times a week for the last two years and that you tape the shows you have to miss. Because you meet the criterion of watching Oprah daily, the man (a representative of a research company) selects you to participate in a study of the pros and cons of revealing intimate behaviors and thoughts via the mass media. After the caller answers your questions and satisfies you that the research is legitimate, he invites you to a one-time meeting to discuss intimate disclosures in public. A free trip and ticket to the Oprah Winfrey show are offered for your effort. Excited and flattered, you agree to attend the meeting. You are about to experience a focus group.

The rationale for creating such a group is that people will tell more about what they think or feel about a specific topic. Social scientists have always been curious about exactly what type of behavior or event evokes negative or positive responses to a given social situation, and why. As they studied the audience responses to radio programs, films, advertisements, and government decisions (both domestic and foreign), the method they used to extract information during the in-depth interviews became known as group depth interviews, or focus groups.

THE FOCUS GROUP DEFINED

Focus groups are distinguished from others (therapy, advisory, assertiveness, training, self-help groups, and quality circles) by the following characteristics (Krueger and Patton, 1988):

1. Seven to ten voluntary members participate in one meeting that lasts 1 to 1½ hours under the direction of a moderator. Members do not know each other.
2. Group members share a commonality, such as watching Oprah! in our hypothetical case.
3. Group members generate data that are recorded and/or observed unobtrusively, through a two-way mirror.
4. The data generated are qualitative—that is, they proceed from in-depth, spontaneous, natural responses. The data are expressed in the respondents' own words and in the context of the question asked.
5. The in-depth discussion is focused in terms of the research interests of the sponsor of the study by the interviewer (who is referred to as the *moderator* in focus-groups literature). The moderator steers the discussion, probes selectively, and maintains the focus of the discussion.

Besides defining and setting focus groups apart, these features offer social scientists guidelines for conducting studies. Thus, although some variation may occur when the technique of focus-group interviews is applied to research, the basic characteristics are upheld and followed.

HISTORY OF FOCUS GROUPS

Originally, the focus-group-interview technique, or the focus group, grew out of Lazarsfeld and Merton's efforts to glean an understanding of how radio audiences evaluate radio programs and the reasons for their judgments (Stewart and Shamdasani, 1990). Shortly after the outbreak of World War II, their research subjects consisted of studio audience members who, while listening to a radio program, were asked to push a red button when they heard anything that provoked anger, boredom, or disbelief. They were asked to push a green button whenever their responses were pleasant, amusing, or thought-provoking. After recording their responses, members of the audience were invited (on a voluntary basis) to discuss and explain their responses. These spontaneously recorded reactions functioned as guidelines by giving the discussion a firm and structured focus while it delved into discourse geared to unearth the emotional/logical underpinnings of the choices. The focus group, as a research tool, took on the dimension of gathering information not via surveys, questionnaires, or individual interviews that distance the respondents from the researcher, but via a person's repertoire of perceptions, ideas, assumptions, opinions, and beliefs expressed in the presence of the researcher.

During World War II, the focus-group-interview technique was also applied to populations other than radio audiences. For the research branch of the United States Army Information and Education Division, Merton and colleagues applied the technique to the study of army personnel who had watched training and morale-booster films (Merton, Fiske, and Kendall, 1956). Their research findings, gathered during the war and later at Columbia University, laid the groundwork for *Mass Persuasion,* which focused on the persuasive impact of mass media (Merton, Fiske, and Kendall, 1946). Soon the focus-group interviews, known as focus groups, developed and expanded into such fields as marketing, advertising, program evaluation, communications, and public policy.

Like any type of research on humans, focus-group research has its limitations: each focus group represents data derived from group members as they respond to the group. In other words, each group member is affected and influenced by the others and by the interviewer's questions, probings, reactions, and over-all demeanor. Still, the information that social scientists have gathered by applying the focus-group technique has contributed to our knowledge about how people think, form ideas, beliefs, opinions, and judgments; and how they explain them.

USES OF FOCUS GROUPS

Just as self-help groups and quality circles are not cures for all problems represented by, and reflected in, the purposes and goals of these groups, neither are focus groups. However, focus groups are a useful research tool with which to extract information from people who otherwise would have to report their thoughts, ideas, opinions, and judgments by either making a check mark or circling a number in a questionnaire. The exciting part about focus groups is that people, sitting together in a small group with a moderator, have a chance to explore their thinking about specific topics and thus contribute to the growing pool of knowledge about human behavior. Focus groups are being utilized in an amazing range of research with a variety of participants. For example, groups have been composed of physically disabled elderly (Quine and Cameron, 1995); care givers for family members with Alzheimer's disease (Gray-Vickery, 1993), family physicians, teachers, and even children. The list of issues using focus groups is equally wide-ranging, including federal policy and program evaluation studies (Straw and Smith, 1995), physicians' experiences in the identification and treatment of abused women (Brown and Sas, 1994); children's knowledge and beliefs about HIV and AIDS (Hoppe et al., 1995); and in Spain, teachers' perceptions of recently introduced educational reforms (Flores and Alonso, 1995).

Hughes and DuMont (1993) describe how focus groups facilitate culturally sensitive research. In their research program, which examines work and parenting issues in African American dual-earner families, they find that focus groups enhance understanding of particular phenomena and provide raw material to aid in development of appropriate instruments for specific populations. This is accomplished by personal perspectives and experiences of the topic. Focus group methodology has been carried further in an anonymous, telephone-based focus group. In these studies, researchers examined family physicians' attitudes to social and sexual contact between family physicians and their patients. The method adapted the traditional focus group approach as a means of exploring a sensitive family-practice topic while concealing participants' identities. Using this method, a safe environment could be created in which participants freely discussed the issues. Afterwards, participants expressed positive comments about the experience (White and Thomson, 1995).

FOCUS ON DIVERSITY

Is this research a possible way of understanding Mexican or Asian families? other cultural or religious groups in America?

Participating in focus groups seems to be invigorating; people report gaining enthusiasm and satisfaction from the experience. Focus groups instill in members a sense of being important. What they have to say matters. This is especially appealing in a world where a common complaint—between bosses and employees, wives and husbands, parents and children, students and teachers, government leaders and their constituents—is "You're not listening to me."

Some New Directions for Small Groups

In their most current applications, quality circles and focus groups are both being used at universities. Universities are confronted with a shrinking pool of students and less financial support. They are realizing that their staff theoreticians and professors/consultants do not have a magic formula for attracting and retaining "customers." As a result, universities are now turning to industry to learn about quality, customer service, and focus groups.

University administrators are setting up total quality management programs. These programs are as much mindset as method. They require each department to define its customers, enhance activities linked to servicing these customers, and eliminate almost everything else.

TQM is a leadership philosophy that looks at each product and service from everyone's point of view. In 1990 more than 500 academics came to hear industry speakers at the first TQM symposium, hosted by the University of West Virginia. But the lessons of TQM are not easy to learn. TQM is not political, and academia is a political minefield. TQM is a team approach, and universities are not known to work well in teams. Universities deal with multiple customer groups: students who pay tuition, the companies who will hire the students, people who approve research grants, and the people who use the research. Universities are very bureaucratic. Many diverse types of people are involved in the "simple" process of collecting money for grant programs. There are faculty members, department chiefs, the head of the school, the office of research negotiation, and so on. There are hundreds of ways to make mistakes.

TQM breaks such problems into manageable tasks. The University of Pennsylvania carved a team out of each group in the process and charged it with reducing errors and lowering deficits. It designed new invoices, set out negotiation guidelines, and simplified communications and accounting.

Most universities are now trying this approach. TQM teams interview students, faculty members, recruiters—all sorts of "customers"—to see what they want done differently and how to do it. There is also talk of using TQM principles with the faculty. Suggestions include distributing a clear syllabus on day 1, having accessible office hours, and giving advance notice of when final exams will be.

After conducting focus groups with students, the University of Tennessee's College of Business Administration changed an arbitrary system of scheduled 15-minute sessions with counselors in favor of one that allots time in accordance with the complexity of the problem. On the request of participants in the advanced management program, it arranges follow-up visits by faculty members to company premises months after the course's end. To please other departments, the financial affairs office provides simplified accounting statements for department heads and more detailed ones for donors who want to see where their money goes.

Universities, then, are establishing and using adaptations of what were corporate quality circles and reaping the benefits of focus groups. It is not in business and industry alone that the effectiveness of small groups is being put to the test.

EXERCISE 1 Speaking Clearly in a Quality Circle

OBJECTIVES

- To experience some of the training given to quality circle members
- To distinguish between observation and inference
- To build observation and inference skills

RATIONALE

Building team leadership in a quality circle requires members to speak clearly and concretely. One common communication error is to present inferences as though they were facts. Inferences are actually interpretations, whereas facts are established by observing, hearing, touching, and smelling. For example, a person may say, "You are tired," presenting the observation as though it were a fact. The other may become angry at the speaker's audacity, while the speaker, unaware of his or her error, decides that the other is oversensitive. This problem in communication would have been avoided if the speaker had understood the difference between observation and inference.

MATERIALS One copy of the Observation-Inference Sheet

OBSERVATION-INFERENCE SHEET[1]

The statements that follow are either observation (left column) or inference (right column). Where there is an observation, you furnish an inference. Where there is an inference, you furnish the kind of data that might lead to that inference. Don't be concerned about "right" answers; the point of the exercise is simply to help you distinguish between data and interpretation.

Observation	Inference
1. I see my dog scratching.	
	2. Today must be a federal holiday.
3. My utility bill is 30 percent higher this month than last month.	

1. "Observation-Inference Sheet" from *Facilitation Skills in Quality Circles* by K. E. Blaker (1982).

4. My friend was out late last night.
5. My lover/spouse is in an amorous mood.
6. I see the hood of a car raised and someone has his head under the hood.
7. My child received 1 C, 2 Ds, and an F on her grade report.
8. My companion enjoys Mexican food.
9. I see people around me looking up into the sky.
10. I've been waiting 40 minutes for a subway that runs on a 15-minute schedule.
11. You don't love me anymore.
12. It is going to rain.

QUESTIONS FOR DISCUSSION

1. How did you respond to each question? Compare your responses with those of the other participants.
2. What was your reasoning in coming to these decisions?
3. What is the difference between observation and inference?
4. How can presenting inferences as fact cause difficulties in a group?
5. How would training like this be helpful for participants in quality circles?
6. How important do you think training would be?

ACTION

Members assemble in groups of three to four. The facilitator distributes the sheets, announcing, "Before proceeding with this task, please read the introductory statement and follow the instructions there." Participants then fill in the sheets individually.

For Further Information

READING

Capezio, Peter, and D. Morehouse. *Taking the Mystery Out of TQM: A Practical Guide to Total Quality Management.* 2nd ed. Franklin Lakes, N.J.: Career Press, 3 Tica Road, 07417, 1995.

This easy-to-follow guide begins by explaining TQM, then moves on to TQM companies, how to get ready for TQM implementation, leadership, training, team development, evaluation, and TQM in the future. The current state of TQM.

Giddan, Norman, and M. Austin, eds. *Peer Counseling and Self-Help Groups on Campus.* Springfield, Ill.: Charles Thomas, 1982.

This book is a classic. The range is extensive, from organizing and leading women's self-help discussion groups to an academic advising service of students helping students.

Latzko, William J., and D. M. Saunders. *Four Days with Dr. Deming: A Strategy for Modern Methods of Management.* Reading, Mass.: Addison-Wesley Longman, 1995.

Deming is the founder of Total Quality Management. After attending his seminars the authors wrote this book to convey Deming's theories. Written in an easy, entertaining style. An outstanding introduction to Deming.

Mallory, Lucretia. *Leading Self-Help Groups.* New York: Family Service of America, 44 E. 23rd Street, 10010, 1984.

This is a short, step-by-step book on how to lead a self-help group. Appropriate for people of varied backgrounds and education.

Ouchi, William. *Theory Z: How American Business Can Meet the Japanese Challenge.* Reading, Mass.: Addison-Wesley, 1981.

In this book, the author takes the TQM principles of Deming in Japan and adapts them to the unique corporate environment of the United States. A best seller in 1981, as everyone concerned with management and leadership sought to understand the Japanese management/productivity phenomenon. Ouchi added Theory Z to the management language. A classic!

Quantitative Health Research 5, 4 (Nov. 1995). Special issue entitled "Issues and Applications of Focus Groups."

This comprehensive collection of articles on focus groups includes coverage of when focus groups are the appropriate strategy, recruiting participants, preparing for a meeting, and analyzing data.

Silverman, Phyllis R. *Mutual Help Groups: Organization and Development.* Sage Human Services Guide Vol. 16. Beverly Hills, Calif: Sage Publications, 275 S. Beverly Drive, 1980.

This simply written book covers the basic aspects of support groups in the community. Includes chapters on relationships with the professional community, making helping work, initial meetings, and problems groups develop. Another classic.

Wuthnow, Robert. *Sharing the Journey: Support Groups and America's New Quest for Community.* New York: Free Press, 1994.

Using a representative sample of the U.S. public that includes more than 1,000 small group members, the author provides the first national analysis of group membership, varied types of groups, motives people have for joining groups, and group dynamics. His interpretation of the support group movement in terms of religious and communal dimensions is both complex and provocative. A compelling social analysis of a significant facet of U.S. life.

THE INTERNET

To tap into the world of reading groups/support groups consider the *Vintage Reading Group* on-line. You can jump into a lively discussion, listen to a taped interview and reading by an author, and get information on group meetings.

http://www.random house.com/vintage/read

References

Abele, A., and P. Petzold. "Asymmetrical evaluation of ingroup versus outgroup members: A look from an information integration perspective." *European Journal of Social Psychology,* 26, 2 (1996), 219–231.

Abraham, A. "Le Groupe en images. Le test: 'Dessinez un Group'" (The group in pictures: The Draw-a-Group (DAG) Test). *Bulletin de Psychologie,* 37, 1–5 (1983–84), 177–191.

Abraham, M., and S. Wheelan. "The concept of intergroup mirroring: Reality or illusion?" *Human Relations,* 46, 7 (1993), 803–826.

Abrahamson, M., and J. Smith. "Norms, deviance, and spatial location." *Journal of Social Psychology,* 80, 1 (1970), 95–10l.

Ackerman, N. W. *The Psychodynamics of Family Life.* New York: Basic Books, 1958.

Ackerman, N. W., ed. *Family Therapy in Transition.* Boston: Little, Brown, 1970.

Adam, E. E. "Quality circle performance." *Journal of Management,* 17, 1 (1991), 25–39.

Adato, A. "Leave-taking: A study of common sense, knowledge of social structure." *Anthropological Quarterly,* 48, 4 (1975), 255–271.

Agazarian, Y., and R. Peters. *The Visible and Invisible Group.* Boston: Routledge & Kegan Paul, 1981.

Agyris, C. *Reasoning, Learning, and Action.* San Francisco: Jossey-Bass, 1982.

Agyris, C. *Strategy and Business,* 1st quarter, 10 (1998), 96.

Aiken, M. W., and M. Riggs. "Using a group support system for creativity." *Journal of Creative Behavior,* 27, 1 (1993), 28–35.

Aldag, R. J., and S. R. Fuller. "Beyond fiasco: A reappraisal of the groupthink phenomenon and a new model of group decision processes." *Psychological Bulletin,* 113, 3 (1993), 533–552.

Alderfer, C. P. "An intergroup perspective on group dynamics." In *Handbook of Organizational Behavior.* Ed. J. Lorsch. Englewood Cliffs, N. J.: Prentice-Hall, 1986.

Allcorn, S. "What makes groups tick?" *Personnel,* 62, 9 (1985), 52–58.

Allison, S. T., and D. M. Messick. "The attribution of attitudes to groups." Paper presented at the 65th Annual Meeting of the Western Psychological Association, San Jose, Calif., Apr. 18–21, 1985.

Allport, F. *Social Psychology.* Boston: Houghton Mifflin, 1924.

Amason, A. C. "Distinguishing the effects of functional and dysfunctional conflict on strategic decision making: Resolving a paradox for top management teams." *Academy of Management Journal,* 39, 1 (1996), 123–148.

Amason, A. C., et al. "An important dimension in successful management teams." *Organizational Dynamics,* 24, 2 (1995), 20–35.

American Heritage Dictionary of the English Language. Ed. W. Morris. New York: American Heritage Publishing Co. and Houghton Mifflin, 1969, p. 600.

Amir, Y. "The effectiveness of the kibbutz-born soldier in the Israeli defense forces." *Human Relations,* 22, 4 (1969), 333–344.

Analoui, R. "Industrial conflict and its expression." *Leadership and Organizational Development Journal,* 13, 7 (1992), 23–25.

Anderson, L. E., and W. K. Balzer. "The effects of timing of leaders' opinions on problem-solving groups: A field experiment." *Groups and Organization Studies,* 16, 1 (1991), 86–101.

Archer, D. "Power in groups: Self-concept changes of powerful and powerless group members." *Journal of Applied Behavioral Science,* 10 (1974), 208–220.

Aronson, E. "Who likes whom and why." *Psychology Today* 4, 3 (1970), 48–50, 74.

Aronson, E., and D. Linder. "Gain and loss of esteem as determinants of interpersonal attractiveness." *Journal of Experimental and Social Psychology,* 1, 2 (1965), 156–171.

Aronson, E., and J. Mills. "The effect of severity of initiation on liking for a group." *Journal of Abnormal and Social Psychology,* 59 (1959), 177–181.

Aronson, M. L. "A group therapist's perspectives on the use of supervisory groups in the training of psychotherapists." Special issue on the supervision of the psychoanalytic process. *Psychoanalysis and Psychotherapy,* 8, 1 (1990), 88–94.

Arrien, A. *The Four-Fold Way.* San Francisco: HarperSan Francisco, 1993, 109–126.

Asch, S. E. "Effects of group pressure upon the modification and distortion of judgments." In *Groups, Leadership, and Men.* Ed. H. Guetzkow. Pittsburgh, Pa.: Carnegie Press, 1951, 177–190; 2nd ed. Ed D. Cartwright and A. Zander. Evanston, Ill.: Row Peterson, 1960, 189–200.

Asch, S. E. "Opinions and social pressure." *Scientific American,* 193, 5 (1955), 31–35.

Asch, S. E. "Studies of independence and conformity: I. A minority of one against a unanimous majority." *Psychological Monographs,* 70, 9, Whole No. 416 (1956).

Atkinson, J. W., and N. Feather. *A Theory of Achievement Motivation.* New York: Wiley, 1966.

Austin, J. T., and J. B. Vancouver. "Goal constructs in psychology." *Psychological Bulletin,* 120, 3 (1996) 338–375.

Avolio, B. J., and B. M. Bass. *The Full Range of Leadership Development: Basic/Advanced Manuals.* Binghamton, N.Y.: Bass/Avolio Associates, 1990.

Axline, L. L. "TQM: A look in the mirror." *Management Review,* 80 (1991), 64.

Azar, B. "Team building isn't enough: Workers need training, too." *APA Monitor,* (Jul. 1997), 14–15.

Azar, B."Influences from the mind's inner layers." *APA Monitor,* 27, 2 (1996), 1, 25.

Back, K. "Influence through social communication." *Journal of Abnormal and Social Psychology,* 46 (1951), 9–23.

Bader, G. "Pareto analysis and diagram." Bader Group, San Diego.

Bailey, G. D., and W. F. Adams. "Leadership strategies for nonbureaucratic leadership." *NASSP Bulletin,* (Mar. 1990), 21–28.

Baird, J. "Conservation of the commons: Effects of group cohesiveness and prior sharing." *Journal of Community Psychology,* 10 (1982), 210–215.

Bales, R. *Interaction Process Analysis.* Reading, Mass.: Addison-Wesley, 1950.

Bales, R. *Personality and Interpersonal Behavior.* New York: Holt, Rinehart and Winston, 1970.

Bandler, R., and J. Grinder. *Frogs into Princes: Neurolinguistics Programming.* Moab, Ut.: Real People Press, 1979.

Bandura, A. *Social Learning Theory.* Englewood Cliffs, N. J.: Prentice-Hall, 1977.

Bantel, K. A. "Comprehensiveness of strategic planning: The importance of heterogeneity of a top team." *Psychological Reports,* 73, 1 (1993), 35–49.

Bantz, C. R. "Cultural diversity and group cross-cultural team research." *Journal of Applied Communication Research,* 21, 1 (1993), 1–20.

Barlow, S.; W. Hansen; A. Fuhriman; and R. Finley. "Leader communication style: Effects on members of small groups." *Small Group Behavior,* 13 (1982), 518–531.

Barnard, C. I. *The Functions of the Executive.* Cambridge, Mass.: Harvard University Press, 1938.

Barnard, R. A.; C. Baird; M. Greenwalt; and R. Karl. "Intragroup cohesiveness and reciprocal social influence in male and female discussion groups." *Journal of Social Psychology,* 32, 2 (1992), 179–188.

Baron, R. A. "The foot-in-the-door phenomenon: Mediating effects of size of the first request and sex of requester." *Bulletin of the Psychonomic Society,* 29 (1973), 113–114.

Baron, R. S.; G. Roper; and P. H. Baron. "Group discussion and the stingy shift." *Journal of Personality and Social Psychology,* 39 (1974), 538–545.

Barret, R. A. *Culture and Conduct.* Belmont, Calif.: Wadsworth, 1984.

Bass, B. M. *Leadership and Performance Beyond Expectation,* New York: Free Press, 1985.

Bass, B. M. "Does the transactional-transformational leadership paradigm transcend organizational and national boundaries?" *American Psychologist,* 52, 2 (1997), 130–139.

Bass, B. M. *Organizational Psychology.* Boston: Allyn and Bacon, 1965.

Bass, B. M., and B. J. Avolio. "Potential bias in leadership measures: How prototypes, lenience, and general satisfaction relate to rating and rankings of transformational and transactional leadership constructs." *Educational and Psychological Measurement,* 49 (1989), 509–527.

Bass, B. M., and B. J. Avolio. "Transformational leadership and organizational structure." *International Journal of Public Administration Quarterly,* 17 (1993), 112–117.

Bavelas, A. "Communication patterns in task-oriented groups." *Journal of the Acoustical Society of America,* 22, 725 (1950).

Beavers, W. R. *Psychotherapy and Growth: Family Systems Perspective.* New York: Brunner/Mazel, 1977.

Bechler, C., and S. D. Johnson. "Leadership and listening: A study of member perceptions." *Small Group Research,* 26, 1 (1995), 77–85.

Bednar, R. L., and Bauersby. "The effects of specific cognitive structure on early group development." *Journal of Applied Behavioral Science,* 12 (1976), 513–522.

Bell, J. E. *Family Therapy.* New York: Jason Aronson, 1978.

Benjamin, G. R. *A Year in a Japanese School Through the Eyes of an American Anthropologist and Her Children.* New York: New York University Press, 1997.

Benne, K. D., and P. Sheats. "Functional roles of group members." *Journal of Social Issues,* 1, 2 (1948), 42–47.

Bennett, E. "Discussion, decision, commitment and consensus in 'group decision'." *Human Relations,* 21 (1955), 251–273.

Bennis, W., and B. Nanus. *Leaders: The Strategies for Taking Charge.* New York: Harper & Row, 1985; audiocassette study guide (nos. 1 and 2), *Sybervision.* Newark, Calif.: CML Co., 1985.

Bennis, W. G., and H. A. Shepard. "A theory of group development." In *Analysis of Groups.* Ed. G. S. Gibbard, J. J. Hartman, and R. D. Mann. San Francisco: Jossey-Bass, 1987.

Bennis, W., and H. Shepherd. "A theory of group development." *Human Relations,* 9 (1956), 418–419.

Berdahl, J. L. "Gender and leadership in work groups: Six alternative models," *Leadership Quarterly,* 7, 1 (1996), 21–40.

Berelson, B., and C. A. Steiner. *Human Behavior.* Short ed. New York: Harcourt, Brace and World, 1964.

Berger, J.; M. H. Fiske; S. J. Rosenholtz; and M. Zelditch, Jr. "Status organizing processes." *Annual Review of Sociology,* 6 (1980), 479–508.

Berger, J.; M. H. Fiske; R. Z. Norman; and M. Zelditch, Jr. *Status Characteristics and Social Interaction: An Expectation States Approach.* New York: Elsevier, 1977.

Berkowitz, L. "Group standards, cohesiveness, and productivity." *Human Relations,* 7 (1954), 509–519.

Berkowitz, W., and H. Shepard. "A experimental study of the relationship between group size and social organization." Doctoral dissertation. New Haven, Conn.: Yale University, 1956.

Berman-Rossi, T. "Empowering groups through understanding stages of group development." Special Issue: Group work reaching out: People, places and power. *Social Work with Groups,* 15, 2–3 (1992), 239–255.

Berne, E. *Beyond Games and Scripts.* New York: Grove Press, 1976, 44–45, 123–135.

Berne, E. *The Structure and Dynamics of Organizations and Groups.* New York: Grove Press, 1963.

Bernstein, M. D. "Autocratic and democratic leadership in an experimental group setting: A modified replication of the experiments of Lewin, Lippitt, and White, with systematic observer variation." *Dissertation Abstracts International,* 31, 12A (1971), 6712.

Bernstein, P. "Necessary elements for effective worker participation in decision making." In *Workplace Democracy and Social Change.* Ed. F. Lindenfeld and J. Kothschild-Whitt. Boston: Porter, Sargent, 1982.

Berry, W. "Group problem solving: How to be an effective participant." *Supervisory Management,* 28, 26 (1993), 13–19.

Bettenhausen, K., and J. K. Murnighan. "The emergence of norms in competitive decision-making groups." *Administrative Science Quarterly,* 30 (1985), 350–372.

Bettenhausen, R. L., and J. R. Murnighan. "The development of an intragroup norm and the effects of interpersonal and structural challenges." *Administrative Science Quarterly,* 36, 1 (1991), 20–35.

Bilimoria, D., and S. K. Piderit. "Board committee membership: Effects of sex-based bias." *Academy of Management Journal,* 37, 6 (1994), 1453–1477.

Bion, W. R. *Experiences in Groups.* New York: Basic Books, 1961.

Bird, C. *Social Psychology.* New York: Appleton-Century, 1940.

Blake, R. R., and J. S. Mouton. "Don't let group norms stifle creativity." *Personnel,* 62, 8 (1985), 33.

Blake, R., and J. S. Mouton. *Building a Dynamic Corporation Through Grid Organization Development.* Reading, Mass.: Addison-Wesley, 1969.

Blaker, K. E. "Facilitation skills in quality circles." Redwood City, Calif.: Educational Quality Circles Consortium, San Mateo County Office of Education, 1982.

Bloomberg, M. *Bloomberg by Bloomberg.* New York: Wiley, 1997.

Blumer, H. *New Outline of the Principles of Sociology.* Ed. A. Lee. New York: Barnes and Noble, 1951, 199–220.

Bodin, A. M. "Family therapy training literature: A brief guide." *Family Press,* 8 (1969), 729–779.

Bogart, D., and D. Lundgren. "Group size, member dissatisfaction, and group radicalism." *Human Relations,* 27, 4 (1974), 339–355.

Bonacich, P. "Norms and cohesion as adaptive responses to potential conflict: An experimental study." *Sociometry,* 35, 3 (1972), 357–375.

Borgatta, E. F., and R. F. Bales. "Interaction of individuals in reconstituted groups." *Sociometry,* 16 (1953), 302–320.

Borkman, T. "Self-help groups at the turning point: Emerging egalitarian alliance with the formal health system." *American Journal of Community Psychology,* 18, 2 (1990), 321–332.

Boszormenyi-Nagy, I., and G. M. Spark. *Invisible Loyalties: Reciprocity in Intergenerational Family Therapy.* New York: Harper & Row, 1973.

Bottger, P. C. "Expertise and air time as bases of actual and perceived influence in problem-solving groups." *Journal of Applied Psychology,* 69, 2 (1984), 214–221.

Boulton, M. J., and P. K. Smith. "Affective bias in children's perceptions of dominance relationships." *Child Development,* 61 (Feb. 1990), 221–229.

Bower, G. S. "Mood and memory." *American Psychologist,* 36 , 2 (1981), 129–148.

Bradford, L. "Hidden agenda." In *Group Development.* Ed. L. Bradford. Washington, D. C.: National Training Laboratories, 1961, 60–72.

Branwyn, G. "Jargon watch." *Wired;* cited in *Modern Maturity,* (Sept.-Oct. 1997), 26.

Brawley, L. R.; A. V. Carron; and W. N. Widmeyer. "The influence of the group and its cohesiveness on perceptions of group goal-related variables. *Journal of Sport and Exercise Psychology,* 15, 3 (1993), 245–260.

Brawley, L.R.; A. V. Carron; and W. N. Widmeyer. "The nature of group goals in sport teams: A phenomenological analysis. *Sport Psychologist,* 6, 4 (1992), 323–333.

Brehm, J. "Postdecision changes in desirability of alternatives." *Journal of Abnormal and Social Psychology,* 52 (1956), 384–389.

Brightman, H. J., and P. Verhoeven. "Running successful problem-solving groups." Pt. 2. *Business* 36, 2 (1986), 15–23.

Brill, A. A. *Freud's Contribution to Psychiatry.* Gloucester, Mass.: Peter Sanith Publishing, 1972.

Brinthaupt, T. M.; R. L. Moreland; and J. M. Levine. "Sources of optimism among prospective group members." *Personality and Social Psychology Bulletin,* 17, 1 (1991), 36–43.

Briton, N. J., and J. A. Hall. "Beliefs about female and male nonverbal communication." *Sex Roles,* 32, 1–2, 79–90.

Brothen, T., and T. Showalt. "Social comparison theory and the universality of experience." *Psychological Reports,* 48 (1981), 114.

Brown, J. B., and G. Sas. "Focus groups in family practice research: An example study of family physicians' approach to wife abuse." *Family Practice Research Journal,* 14, 1 (1994), 19–28.

Brown, L. H. *Organization Studies,* 6, 4 (1985), 313–334.

Bruning, N. S., and P. R. Liverpool. "Membership in quality circles and participation in decision making." *Journal of Applied Behavioral Science,* 29, 1 (1993), 76–95.

Buchwald, A. "The grown-up problem." In *Son of the Great Society*. New York: Putnam, 1966.

Buck, R. W., and R. D. Parke. "Behavioral and physiological reponse to the presence of a friendly or neutral person in two types of stressful situations." *Journal of Personality and Social Psychology,* 24, 2 (1972), 143–153.

Burck, C. "Working smarter." *Fortune* (June 15, 1981), 68–73.

Burnette, E. "'Father of Ebonics' continues his crusade." *APA Monitor,* 28, (1997), 12.

Burns, J. M. *Leadership*. New York: Harper & Row, 1978.

Bushe, G. R. "Temporary or permanent middle-management groups? Correlates with attitudes in QWL change projects." *Group and Organization Studies,* 12, 1 (1987), 23–37.

Butler, L. "Anatomy of collusive behavior." *NTL Connections,* 4, 1 (1987), 1–2.

Calabrese, R. L., and J. Noboa. "The choice for gang membership by Mexican-American adolescents." *High School Journal,* 78, 4 (1995), 226–235.

Calabrese, R. L. "Ethical leadership: A prerequisite for effective schools." *NASSP Bulletin* (Dec. 1988), 1–4.

Callahan, C.; S. Owen; and J. Renzulli "Fluency, flexibility and originality as a function of group size." *Journal of Creative Behavior,* 8, 2 (1974), 107–113.

Camacho, L. M., and P. B. Paulus. "The role of social anxiousness in group brainstorming." *Journal of Personality and Social Psychology,* 68, 6 (1995), 1071–1080.

Campbell, D. "Some strategic properties of plurality and majority voting." *Theory and Decision,* 13 (1981), 93–107.

Campbell, H. P., and M. D. Dunnette. "Effectiveness of T-group experiences in managerial training and development." *Psychological Bulletin,* 70 (1968), 73–104.

Campbell, J. D., and P. J. Fairey. "Informational and normative routes to conformity: The effect of faction size as a function of norm extremity and attention to stimulus." *Journal of Personality and Social Psychology,* 57, 3 (1989), 457–468.

Campbell, J. D.; A. Tesser; and P. J. Fairey. "Conformity and attention to the stimulus: Some temporal and contextual dynamics." *Journal of Personality and Social Psychology,* 51, 2 (1986), 315–324.

Campbell, J. P. "Individual versus group problem solving in an industrial sample." *Journal of Applied Psychology,* 52 (1968), 205–210.

Caplan, G., and M. Killilea, eds. *Support Systems and Mutual Help: Multidisciplinary Explorations*. New York: Grune & Stratton, 1976.

Carew, D. K.; P. C. Eunice; and K. H. Blanchard. "Group development and situational leadership: A model for managing groups." *Training and Development Journal,* 40, 6 (1986), 46–50.

Carnevale, A. R.; L. J. Gainer; and J. Villet. *Training in America*. San Francisco: Jossey-Bass, 1990, 159–163.

Carpenter, W., and E. Hollander. "Overcoming hurdles to independence in groups." *Journal of Social Psychology,* 117 (1982), 237–241.

Carr, D. F. "A comparative study of nominal interacting and brainstorming groups and pooled individual work in ideation phases of the reflective thinking process." Unpublished Masters thesis, Auburn University, 1975.

Cattell, R. B.; D. R. Sanders; and G. F. Stice. "The dimensions of syntality in small groups." *Human Relations,* 6 (1953), 331–336.

Charier, M. R. "Clarity of expression in interpersonal communication." *The 1976 Annual Handbook for Group Facilitators.* La Jolla, Calif.: University Associates, 1976, 149–156.

Chatman, J. A., and S. G. Barsade. "Personality, organizational culture, and cooperation: Evidence from a business simulation." *Administrative Science Quarterly,* 40, 3 (1995), 423–443.

Christian, R. "Probability vs. precedence: The social psychology of jury selection." In *Psychology and Law.* Ed. G. Bermant. Springfield, Mass.: Thomas, 1978.

Chung, K. H., and M. J. Ferris. "An inquiry of the nominal group process." *Academy of Management Journal,* 14 (1971), 520–524.

Clemens, J. K, and D. F. Mayer. *The Classic Touch: Lessons in Leadership from Homer to Hemingway.* Homewood, Ill.: Dow Jones-Irwin, 1987.

Cline, R. J. "Small group dynamics and the Watergate coverup: A case study of groupthink." Paper presented at the annual meeting of the Communication Association, Ocean City, Md., Apr. 1983, 27–30.

Cloven, D. H., and M. E. Roloff. "The chilling effect of aggressive potential on the expression of complaints in intimate relationships." *Communications Monographs,* 60, 3 (1993), 199–219.

Cluck, G. G., and R J. Cline. "The circle of others: Self-help groups for the bereaved." *Communication Quarterly,* 34, 3 (1986), 306–325.

Coan, R. W. "Dimensions of psychological theory." *American Psychologist,* 23 (1968), 715–722.

Coffman, I. "Choosing the veil." *Mother Jones* (Nov.-Dec. 1991), 23–24.

Cohen, A. M., and R. D. Smith. *Critical Incidents in Growth Groups: Theory and Techniques.* La Jolla, Calif.: University Associates, 1976.

Collaros, R. A., and L. Anderson. "Effects of perceived expertness upon creativity of members of brainstorming groups." Pt. 1. *Journal of Applied Psychology,* 53, 2 (1969).

Compas, B. "Psychological sense of community among treatment analogue group members." *Journal of Applied Social Psychology,* 11 (1981), 151–165.

Constanzo, P. R. "Conformity development as a function of self-blame." *Journal of Personality and Social Psychology,* 14 (1970), 366–374.

Cooley, C. H. *Social Organization.* New York: Charles Scribner's Sons, 1909.

Cooper, H. M. "Statistically combing independent studies: A meta-analysis of sex differences in conformity research." *Journal of Personality and Social Psychology,* 37 (1979), 131–146.

Cooper, L., and J. Gustafson. "Family-group development: Planning in organizations." *Human Relations,* 34 (1981), 705–730.

Covey, S. R. *Seven Habits of Highly Effective People.* New York: Simon & Schuster, 1990.

Crandall, C. S. "Social contagion of binge eating." *Journal of Personality and Social Psychology,* 55, 4 (1988), 588–598.

Crawford, M. "Classroom climate at Westchester University: A report on the university community." Unpublished report by the Women's Consortium of SSHE, West Chester, Pa., 1986.

Crook, R. "Communication and group structure." *Journal of Communication,* 11 (1961), 136.

Crosby, F., and S. D. Clayton. "Introduction: The search for connections." *Journal of Social Issues,* 42, 2 (1986), 1–9.

Crown, D. F., and J. G. Rosse. "Yours, mine, and ours: Facilitating group productivity through the integration of individual and group goals." *Organizational Behavior & Human Decision Processes,* 64, 2 (1995), 138–150.

Dale, B. G., and S. G. Hayward. "Some reasons for quality circle failure: Part 3." *Leadership and Organization Development Journal,* 5, 4 (1984), 27–32.

Davies, D., and B. C. Kuypers. "Group development and interpersonal feedback." *Group and Organizational Studies,* 10, 2 (1985), 184–205.

Davis, J. M. *Social Behavior and Personality,* 12, 1 (1984), 1–5.

deBono, E. *Conflicts: A Better Way to Resolve Them.* London: Penguin Books, 1985, 1–19.

deBono, E. *Serious Creativity.* New York: HarperCollins, 1992.

Delbecq, A. L.; A. H. Van de Ven; and D. H. Gustatson. *Group Techniques for Program Planning.* Glenview, Ill.: Scott, Foresman, 1975.

Denisi, A.; W. Randolph; and A. Blencoe. "Potential problems with peer ratings." *Academy of Management Journal,* 26 (1983), 457–464.

Dennis, A. R., and J. S. Valacich. "Group, sub-group, and nominal group idea-generation: new rules for a new media?" *Journal of Management,* 20, 4 (1994), 723–736.

DeShon, R. P., and R. A. DeShon. "Goal setting effects on implicit and explicit learning of complex tasks." *Organizational Behavior and Human Decision Processes,* 65, l(1996), 1836.

DeStephen, R. S. "High- and low-consensus groups: A content and relational interaction analysis." *Small Group Behavior,* 14, 2 (1983), 143–162.

Deutsch, M. "An experimental study of the effects of cooperation and competition upon group process." *Human Relations,* 2 (1949), 129–152, 199–231. Reprinted in *Group Dynamics,* 2nd ed. Ed. E. Cartwright and A. Zander. New York: Harper & Row, 1960, 348–352.

Deutsch, M. "Some factors affecting membership motivation and achievement motivation." *Human Relations,* 12 (1959), 81–85.

Deutsch, M.; Y. Epstein; D. Canavan; and P. Gumpert. "Strategies of inducing cooperation: An experimental study." *Journal of Conflict Resolution,* 11, 3 (1967), 345–360.

Dion, K.; N. Miller; and M. Magnan. "Cohesiveness and social responsibility as determinants of group risk taking." *Proceedings of the Annual Convention, American Psychological Association,* 5, Pt. 1 (1970), 335–336.

DiStefano, J. J., and M. L. Mazuevaki. "Managing diversity for competitve advantage." Unpublished manuscript (1996), London, Canada. University of Western Ontario, Western Business School.

Dolcini, M. M., and N. E. Adler. "Perceived competencies, peer group affiliation, and risk behavior among early adolescents." *Health Psychology,* 13, 6 (1994), 496–506.

Drinka, T. J. K. "Interdisciplinary geriatric teams: Approaches to conflict as indicators of potential to model teamwork." *Educational Gerontology,* 20, 1 (1994), 87–103.

Drory, A., and U. Gluskinos. "Machiavellianism and leadership." *Journal of Applied Psychology,* 65 (1980), 81–86.

Dumas, R. N.; Cushing; and C. Laughline Zenger-Miller, Inc. Foundations for Company-Wide Quality Programs. Zenger Miller, M0066 (Jan. 1989).

Dunnette, M. D.; J. P. Campbell; and K. Jasstad. "The effect of group participation on brainstorming effectiveness for two industrial samples." *Journal of Applied Psychology,* 47 (1963), 30–37.

Dutton, D. G., and A. P. Aron. "Some evidence of heightened sexual attraction under conditions of high anxiety." *Journal of Personality and Social Psychology,* 30, 4 (1974), 510–517.

Eagly, A. H. "Sex differences in influenceability." *Psychological Bulletin,* 85 (1978), 86–116.

Eagly, A. H., and C. Chrvala. "Sex differences in conformity: Status and gender role interpretations." *Psychology of Women Quarterly,* 10 (1986), 203–220.

Eagly, A. H., and L. L. Carli. "Sex of researchers and sex-typed communications as determinants of sex differences in influenceability: A meta-analysis of social influence studies." *Psychological Bulletin,* 90 (1981), 1–20.

Eakins, B. W., and R. G. Eakins. *Sex Differences in Communication.* Boston: Houghton Mifflin, 1978.

Easton, A. *Decision Making: A Short Course in Problem Solving.* New York: Wiley, 1976.

Eden, D. "Leadership and expectations: Pygmalion effects and other self-fulfilling prophecies." *Leadership Quarterly,* 3, 4 (1992), 271–305.

Ehrlich, H. J. "Affective style as a variable in person perception." *Journal of Personality,* 37 (1969), 522–539.

Elias, F. G.; M. E. Johnson; and J. B. Fortman. "Task-focused self-disclosure: Effects on group cohesiveness, commitment to task, and productivity." *Small Group Behavior,* 20, 1 (1989), 87–96.

Ellerman, D. "What is a workers' cooperative?" Reprint. Somerville, Mass.: Industrial Cooperative Association, 1984.

Elliot, A. J., and J. M. Harackiewicz. "Approach and avoidance achievement goals and intrinsic motivation: A mediational analysis. *Journal of Personality and Social Psychology,* 70, 3 (1996), 461–475.

Endler, N. S. "Conformity as a function of different reinforcement schedules." *Journal of Personality and Social Psychology,* 4 (1966), 175–180.

Epstein, R. S., and N. Liebman. "Biz speak: A dictionary of business terms, slang, and jargon." *Time,* 128, 18 (Nov. 3, 1986), 31.

Erez, M.; R. C. Earley; and C. L. Hulin. "The impact of participation on goal acceptance and performance: A two-step model." *Academy of Management Journal,* 28, 1 (1985), 50–66.

Erikson, E. *Childhood and Society.* New York: Norton, 1950.

Evensen, P. E. *Effects of Specific Cognitive and Behavioral Structures on Early Group Interactions.* Louisville, Ky.: University of Kentucky Press, No. 76–20 (1976), 152.

Fairhurst, G. T., and T. A. Chandler. "Social structure in leader–member interaction." *Communication Monographs,* 56 (Sept. 1989).

Falk, G. "An empirical study measuring conflict in problem-solving groups which are assigned different decision rules." *Human Relations,* 35 (1982), 1123–1138.

Falk, G., and S. Falk. "The impact of decision rules on the distribution of power in problem-solving teams with unequal power." *Group and Organizational Studies,* 6 (1981), 211–223.

Fawcett, S. B. In "Getting help from helping," by D. Hurley. *Psychology Today,* 22, 1 (Jan. 1988), 63–67.

Feldman, D. C. "The development and enforcement of group norms." *Academy of Management Review,* 9, 1 (1984), 47–53.

Fennell, M. L., and G. D. Sandefur. "Structural clarity of interdisciplinary teams: A research note." *Journal of Applied Behavioral Science,* 19, 2 (1983), 193–202.

Fensterheim, H., and J. Baer. *Don't Say Yes When You Want to Say No.* New York: Dell, 1975.

Ferreira, A. J. "Family myth and homeostasis." *Archives of General Psychiatry,* 9 (1963), 457–463.

Ferris, ed. *Research in Personal and Human Resource Management.* Greenwich, Conn.: JAI, 1987.

Ferris, G. R., and J. A. Wagner III. "Quality circles in the United States: A conceptual re-evaluation." *Journal of Applied Behavioral Science,* 21, 2 (1985), 155–167.

Ferris, T., et al. "De-programming Heaven's Gate." *The New Yorker,* 23, 8 (1997), 31.

Festinger, L. *A Theory of Cognitive Dissonance.* Evanston, Ill.: Row, Peterson, 1957.

Festinger, L. "A theory of social comparison processes." *Human Relations,* 7 (1954), 117–140.

Festinger, L. "Informal social communication." *Psychological Review,* 57 (1950), 271–282.

Festinger, L., and E. Aronson. "Arousal and reduction of dissonance in a social context." In *Group Dynamics Research and Theory.* Ed. D. Cartwright and A. Zander. New York: Harper & Row, 1968, 125.

Festinger, L., and J. Carlsmith. "Cognitive consequences of forced choice alternatives as a function of their number and qualitative similarity." *Journal of Abnormal and Social Psychology,* 58 (1959), 203–210.

Festinger, L., and J. Thibaut. "Interpersonal communication in small groups." *Journal of Abnormal and Social Psychology,* 16 (1951), 92–99.

Fiedler, F. E. *A Theory of Leadership Effectiveness.* New York: McGraw-Hill, 1967.

Fink, E. L., and Chen, S. "A galileo analysis of organizational climate." *Human Communications Research,* 21, 4 (1995), 494–522.

Fink, L. "Ad agency is target of angry women's groups." *City Business* (Dec. 28, 1987), 1, 17.

Fisher, B. A., and R. K. Stutman. "An assessment of group trajectories: Analyzing developmental breakpoints." *Communication Quarterly,* 35, 2 (1987), 105–124.

Fisher, J. D. "Possible effects of reference group–based social influence on AIDS-risk behavior and AIDS prevention." *American Psychologist* (Nov. 1988), 914–920.

Flores, J. G., and C. G. Alonso. "Using focus groups in research: Exploring teachers' perspectives on educational change." *Evaluation Review,* 19, 1 (1995), 84–101.

Foley, V. D. *An Introduction to Family Therapy.* New York: Grune & Stratton, 1974.

Folger, J. P.; M. S. Poole; and R. K. Stutman. *Working Through Conflict.* Reading, Mass.: Addison-Wesley Longman, 1997, 153–181.

Ford, D. L.; P. M. Nemiroff; and W. A. Pasmore. "Group decision-making performance as influenced by group tradition." *Small Group Behavior,* 8, 2 (1977).

Fouriezos, N. T.; M. L. Hutt; and H. Guetzkow. "Measurement of self-oriented needs in discussion groups." *Journal of Abnormal and Social Psychology,* 45 (1950), 682–690.

Fouriezos, N.; M. Hutt; and H. Geutzlow. "Measurement of self-oriented needs in discussion groups." *Journal of Abnormal and Social Psychology,* 52 (1950), 296–300.

Fox, W. M. "The improved nominal group technique (INGT)." *Journal of Management Development,* 8 (1989), 20–27.

Fox, W. M. *Effective Problem Solving.* San Francisco: Jossey-Bass, 1987, 3–6.

Frederick, L. F. "A comparison of performance, personality characteristics, and perceived satisfaction in nominal and interacting groups in the problem-analysis stage of the problem-solving process." *Dissertation Abstracts International,* 37, 1468B (1976), 756.

Freedman, J. L., and S. C. Fraser. "Compliance without pressure: The foot-in-the-door technique." *Journal of Personality and Social Psychology,* 4 (1966), 95–102.

Freedman, J. L.; S. Klevansky; and P. R. Ehrich. "The effect of crowding on human task performance." *Journal of Applied Social Psychology,* 1, 1 (1971), 7–25.

Freeman, M. "A conversation with Margaret Singer." *APA Monitor* (Jul.-Aug. 1979), 6–7.

French, J. R. P., Jr., and B. Raven. "The bases of social power." In *Group Dynamics,* 2nd ed. Ed. D. Cartwright and A. Zander. Evanston, Ill.: Row, Peterson, 1960, 607–623.

Friedler, M. E.; C. Cherniss; and D. B. Fishman. "Quality circles and classroom teachers." *Special Services in the School,* 6, 3–4 (1992), 155–178.

Friesen, J. D. *Structural-Strategic Marriage and Family Therapy.* New York: Gardner Press, 1985, 3, 5.

Frueh, B. C., and J. A. Becker. "The effects of gender role appropriate language on listener attributions." *Journal of Pragmatics,* 18, 5 (1992), 505–506.

Gaenslen, F. "Democracy vs. efficiency: Some arguments from the small group." *Political Psychology,* 2 (1980), 15–29.

Galam, S., and S. Moscovisi. "Towards a theory of collective phenomena: II. Conformity and power." *European Journal of Social Psychology,* 24, 4 (1994), 481–495.

Galbraith, J. K. *Time* (Mar. 30, 1970), 88.

Galenter, M. "Charismatic religious experience and large-group psychology." *American Journal of Psychiatry,* 12 (198), 1550–1552.

Galvanovskis, A., and R. Nemov. "Level of development as a group factor determining the functional correlation between the efficiency of a group and its size." *Voprosy-Psikhologlii,* 2 (1982), 103–108.

Gardner, J. W. "The moral aspects of leadership." *NASSP Bulletin* (Jan. 1989), 43.

Gebhardt, L. J., and R. A. Meyers. "Subgroup influence in decision-making groups: Examining consistency from a communication perspective." *Small Group Research,* 26, 2 (1995), 147–168.

Geehr, J. L.; M. J. Burke; and J. L. Sulzer. "Quality circles: The effects of voluntary participation on employee attitudes and program efficacy." *Educational and Psychological Measurement,* 55, 1 (1995), 124–134.

Geertz, C. *Local Knowledge.* New York: Basic Books, 1983.

Geller, D.; L. Goodstein; M. Silver; and W. Sternberg. "On being ignored: The effects of the violation of the implicit rules of social interaction." *Sociometry,* 37 (1974), 541–556.

Gentry, G. "Group size and attitudes toward the simulation experience and simulation games." *Simulation and Games,* 11, 4 (1980), 451–460.

Gerard, H. B.; R. A. Wilhemy; and E. S. Conolley. "Conformity and group size." *Journal of Personality and Social Psychology,* 8 (1968), 79–82.

Gershenfeld, M. K. "A project to improve classroom climate at Westchester University: An intervention." Paper presented at the Fourth International Kurt Lewin Conference , 1990.

Gershenfeld, M. K. "Leadership on community boards." Report for the Federation of Jewish Agencies, Phila., Pa., 1964.

Gibb, C. A. "Leadership." *Handbook of Social Psychology,* 2 (1954), 877–920.

Gibb, J. "Defensive communications." *Journal of Communication* 11 (Sept. 1961), 141–148.

Gibb, J. R. "The effect of group size and threat reduction on creativity in a problem solving situation." *American Psychologist,* 6 (1951), 324.

Gilbert, L. A.; R. W. Holt; and K. M. Long. "Teaching gender-related material: The effect of group sex composition on perceptions of a female instructor." *Sex Roles,* 19, 3–4 (198), 241–254.

Gist, M. E.; E. A. Locke; and S. M. Taylor. "Organizational behavior: Group structure, powers and effectiveness." *Journal of Management,* 13, 2 (1987), 237–257.

Glazer, M., and R. Glazer. "Techniques for the study of group structure and behavior: Empirical studies of the effects of structure in small groups." *Psychological Bulletin,* 58 (1961).

Gmelch, W. H., and V. D. Misking. "The lost art of high productivity." *Personnel,* 63, 4 (1986), 34–38.

Goddard, R. W. "The healthy side of conflict." *Management World,* 15, 5 (1986), 8–12.

Goffman, E. *Behavior in Public Places.* Glencoe, Ill.: Free Press, 1963.

Goffman, E. *The Presentation of Self in Everyday Life.* Garden City, N. Y.: Doubleday, 1959.

Goldenberg, I., and H. Goldenberg. *Family Therapy: An Overview.* Belmont, Calif.: Wadsworth, 1980.

Goldman, M., and L. A. Fraas. "The effects of leader selection on group performance." *Sociometry,* 28, 1 (1965), 82–88.

Good, L. R. "Effects of intergroup and intragroup attitude similarity on perceived group attractiveness and cohesiveness." *Dissertation Abstracts* (1970) 60–3, 3618-B.

Gordon, R. "An investigation of the giving and receiving of interpersonal feedback within the human relations group." Paper presented at the Annual Conference of the Communication Association of Pacific America, Honolulu, Aug., 1983.

Gordon, W. J. *Synectics.* New York: Collier, 1961.

Gould, L. J. "The two faces of alienation." *Journal of Social Issues,* 25, 2 (1969), 39–63.

Gouran, D. S. *Discussions: The Process of Group Decision Making.* New York: Harper & Row, 1972.

Grace, H. "Confidence, redundancy and the purpose of communication." *Journal of Communication,* 6 (1956), 16.

Gray, L. N.; J. T. Richardson; and R. H. Mayhew, Jr. "Influence attempts and effective power: A reexamination of an unsubstantiated hypothesis." *Sociometry,* 31, 1 (1968), 245–258.

Gray-Vickery, P. "Gerontological research: Use and application of focus groups." *Journal of Gerontological Nursing,* 19, 5 (1993), 21–57.

Green, 1991.

Greenspoon, L. "The reinforcing effect of two spoken sounds on the frequency of two responses." *American Journal of Psychology,* 68 (1955), 409–416.

Griffitt, W. B. "Environmental effects on interpersonal affective behavior: Ambient effective temperature and attraction." *Journal of Personality and Social Psychology,* 15, 3 (1970), 240–244.

Griffitt, W. J., and R. Veitch. "Hot and

crowded: Influence of population density and temperature on interpersonal affective behavior." *Journal of Personality and Social Psychology,* 17, 1 (1971), 92–98.

Gruenfeld, D. H., et al. "Group composition and decision-making: How member familiarity and information distribution affect process and performance." *Organizational Behavior and Human Decision Processes,* 67, 1 (1996), 1–15.

Guastello, S. J. "Facultative style, innovation and emergent leadership in problem solving groups." *Journal of Creative Behavior,* 1, 4 (1995).

Gurnee, H. "Group learning." *Psychological Monographs,* 76, 13 (1962).

Gustafson, D. H.; R. K. Skukla; A. L. Delbecq; and G. W. Walsler. "A comparative study of differences in subjective liking: Estimates made by individuals, interacting groups, delphi groups, and nominal groups." *Organizational Behavior and Human Performance,* 9 (1973), 280–291.

Guyer, B. P. "The relationship among selected variables and the effectiveness of discussion leaders." *Dissertation Abstracts International,* 39, 2A (1978), 697–698.

Haberman, C. "Straight talk brings down Japan house." *New York Times* (Feb. 14, 1988), 6.

Hackman, J. *Improving the Quality of Work Life: Work Design.* Washington, D. C.: Office of Research, ASPER, U. S. Department of Labor, 1975.

Hackman, J. R., and N. Vidmar. "Effects of size and task characteristics on group performance and member reactions." *Sociometry,* 33, 1 (1970), 37–54.

Hackman, J., and J. Suttle. *Improving Life at Work: Behavioral Science Approaches to Social Change.* Santa Monica, Calif.: Goodyear, 1977.

Hackney, S. Interview on "Morning Edition." Public Radio International, Jan. 2, 1998.

Haley, J. *Problem Solving Therapy.* San Francisco: Jossey-Bass, 1976.

Hall, J., and M. S. Williams. "Group dynamics training and improved decision making." *Journal of Applied Behavioral Science,* 6 (1970), 39–68.

Hall, R. M., and B. R. Sandler. "The classroom climate: A chilly one for women?" Washington, D. C.: Project on the Status and Education of Women, Association of American Colleges, 1982.

Hall. J. "Decisions, decisions, decisions." *Psychology Today,* 5, 6 (1971), 51–54, 86–88.

Hallam, G. L., and D. P. Campbell. "Selecting team members? Start with a theory of team effectiveness." Paper presented at the 7th Annual Meeting of the Society of Industrial and Organizational Psychology, Montreal, Can., May 1992.

Hammond, L., and M. Goldman. "Competition and noncompetition and its relationship to individuals' non-productivity." *Sociometry,* 24 (1961), 46–60.

Handbook of Social Psychology, Vol. 11. Ed. G. Lindzey. Reading, Mass.: Addison-Wesley, 1954, 810.

Handfinger, R. "A theoretical tool for practitioners in the behavioral sciences." *Small Group Behavior,* 15, 3 (1984), 375–386.

Hanke, J. J., and B. O. Saxburg. "Isolates and deviants in the United States and Japan: Productive nonconformists or costly troublemakers?" *Comparative Social Research,* 8 (1985), 219–243.

Hansen, J. M. "Site-based management and quality circles: A natural combination." *NASSP Bulletin,* 74, 528 (1990), 100–103.

Hare, A. P. *Handbook of Small Group Research.* 2nd ed. New York: Free Press, 1976, 19–59, 207, 214.

Hare, P. *Creativity in Small Groups.* Beverly Hills, Calif.: Sage, 1982, 241.

Hare, P., and D. Naveh. "Group development at the Camp David Summit." *Small Group Behavior,* 15, 3 (1984), 299–318.

Harken, D.; G. Bond; L. Borman; E. Bankoff; S. Daiter; M. Lieberman; and L. Videka. "Growth of a medical self-help group." In *Self-Help Groups for Coping with Crisis.* Ed. M. Lieberman and L. Borman. San Francisco: Jossey-Bass, 1979, 43–66.

Harlow, K. C. *Psychology Reports,* 65, 3, Pt. 1 (Dec. 1989), 861–862.

Harragan, B. L. "The $10 million blunder." *Working Women,* (May 1988), 94–98.

Harrison, A. A. *Individuals and Groups.* Monterey, Calif.: Brooks/Cole, 1976, 100–107.

Hattrup, K., and J. K. Ford. "The roles of information characteristics and accountability in moderating stereotype-driven processes during social decision making" *Organizational Behavior and Human Decision Processes,* 63, 1 (1995), 73–86.

Hearn, G. "Leadership and the spatial factor in small groups." *Journal of Abnormal and Social Psychology,* 54 (1957), 219–272.

Heckel, R. V., and H. C. Salzberg. *Group Psychotherapy: A Behavioral Approach.* Columbia: University of South Carolina Press, 1976.

Hellervik, L. W.; J. F. Hazucha; and R. J. Schneider. "Behavior change: Models, methods and reviews of the evidence." In M. D. Dunnette and L. M. Hough, eds., *Handbook of Industrial and Organizational Psychology.* Vol 3. 2nd ed. Palo Alto, Calif.: Consulting Psychologists Press, 1992.

Herndon, E. J., and W. L. Mikulas. "Using reinforcement-based methods to enhance membership recruitment in a volunteer organization." *Journal of Applied Behavior Analysis,* 29, 4 (1990), 577–580.

Hersey, P., and K. H. Blanchard. "Life-cycle theory of leadership." *Training and Development Journal,* 23, 5 (1969), 26–34.

Hersey, P., and K. H. Blanchard. "A situational framework for determining appropriate leader behavior." In *Leadership Development: Theory and Practice.* Ed. R. N. Cassel and R. L. Heichberger. North Quincy, Mass.: Christopher Publishing, 1975, 126–155.

Hersey, P., and K. H. Blanchard. *Management of Organizational Behavior: Utilizing Human Resources.* Englewood Cliffs, N. J.: Prentice-Hall, 1977, 106–107, 162–183, 307–324.

Hewitt, J. P. *Dilemmas of the American Self.* Philadelphia: Temple University Press, 1989.

Hill, G. W. "Group versus individual performance: Are N + 1 heads better than one?" *Psychological Bulletin,* 91, 3 (1982), 517–539.

Hilts, P. J. *New York Times* (Jul. 17, 1990).

Hinrichsen, G. A.; T. A. Revenson; A. Tracey; and M. Shinn. "Does self-help help? An empirical investigation of scoliosis peer support groups." *Journal of Social Issues,* 41, 1 (1985), 65–87.

Hinsz, V. B. "Individual versus group decision making: Social comparison in goals for individual task performance." *Journal of Applied Social Psychology,* 21, 12 (1991), 987–1003.

Hinsz, V. B. "Goal setting by groups performing an additive task: A comparison with individual goal setting." *Journal of Applied Social Psychology,* 25, 11 (1995), 965–990.

Hirokawa, R. "A comparative analysis of communication patterns within effective and ineffective decision-making groups." *Communication Monographs,* 47 (1980), 312–321.

Hirokawa, R. Y. "Group communication and problem-solving effectiveness. 1: An investigation of group phases." *Human Communication Research,* 9, 4 (1983), 291–305.

Hirokawa, R. Y. "Group communication and problem-solving effectiveness. 2: An exploratory investigation of procedural functions." *Western Journal of Speech Communication,* 47, 1 (1983), 59–74.

Hirsch, E. D., Jr. *Cultural Literacy.* Boston: Houghton Mifflin, 1987.

Hoffman, L. R. "Applying experimental research on group problem solving to organizations." *Journal of Applied Behavioral Science,* 1593 (1979), 375–391.

Hoffman, L. R.; R. J. Burke; and N. R. E. Maier. "Participation, influence, and satisfaction among members of problem-solving groups." *Psychological Reports,* 16 (1965), 661–667.

Hogan, R. C.; G. J. Curphy; and J. Hogan. "What we know about leadership effectiveness and personality." *American Psychologist,* 49, 6 (1994), 493–504.

Hollander, E. P. "Competence and conformity in the acceptance of influence." *Journal of Abnormal and Social Psychology,* 61 (1960), 365–370.

Hollander, E. P. "Conformity, status, and idiosyncracy credit." *Psychological Review* 65 (1958), 117–127.

Hollander, E. P. *Leaders, Groups, and Influence.* New York: Oxford University Press, 1964.

Holloman, C. R. "Leadership and headship: There is a difference." *Personnel Administration,* 31, 4 (1968), 38–44.

Holtgraves, T. "Interpreting questions and replies: Effects of face-threat, question form, and gender." *Social Psychology Quarterly,* 54, 1 (1991), 15–24.

Homans, G. C. *The Nature of Social Science.* New York: Harcourt, 1967.

Homans, G. *The Human Group.* New York: Harcourt, Brace, 1950.

Hoppe, M. J.; E. A. Wella; D. M. Morrison; M. R. Gillmore; et al. "Using focus groups to discuss sensitive topics with children." *Evaluation Review,* 19, 1 (1995), 102–114.

Horowitz, M.; R. Exline; M. Goldman; and R. Lee. "Motivation effects of alternative decision making process in groups." ONR technical report. Urbana: University of Illinois, Bureau of Educational Research.

Horwitz, M. "The recall of interrupted group tasks: An experimental study of individual motivation in relation to social groups." *Human Relations,* 7 (1954), 3–38.

Howell, J. M., and C. A. Higgins. "Champions of technological innovation." *Administrative Science Quarterly,* 35 (1990), 317–341.

Huberman, S. "Making Jewish leaders." *Journal of Jewish Communal Service,* 64, 1 (1987), 32–41.

Hughes, D., and K. DuMont. "Using focus groups to facilitate culturally anchored research." Special issue: Culturally anchored methodology. *American Journal of Community Psychology,* 21, 6 (1993), 775–806.

Hunsaker, P. L. "Using group dynamics to improve decision-making meetings." *Industrial Management,* 25, 4 (1983), 19–23.

Hurwitz, J.; A. Zander; and B. Hymovitch. "Some effects of power on the relations among group members." In *Group Dynamics.* 3rd. ed. Eds. D. Cartwright and A. Zander. New York: Harper & Row, 1968, 29–297.

Ingram, L. C. "In the crawlspace of the organization." *Human Relations,* 39, 5 (1986), 467–468.

Isenberg, D. "Some effects of time-pressure on vertical structure and decision-making accuracy in small groups." *Organizational Behavior and Human Performance,* 27 (1981), 119–135.

Israeli, D. N. "The attitudinal effects of gender mix in union committees." *Industrial and Labor Relations Review,* 37, 2 (1984), 212–221.

Jablonski, J. R. *Implementing Total Quality Management: An Overview.* San Diego, Calif.: Pfeiffer, 1991, 4.

Jacob, T.; D. Tennenbaum; K. Bargiel; and R. A. Seiljamer. "Family interaction in the home: Development of a new coding system." *Behavior Modification,* 19, 2 (1995), 147–169.

Jacobs, M., and G. Goodman. "Psychology and self-help groups: Predictions on a partnership." *American Psychologist,* 44 (1989), 1–10.

Jacobs, M.; A. Jacobs; G. Feldman; and N. Cavior. "Feedback II—the credibility gap: Delivery of positive and negative and emotional and behavioral feedback in groups." *Journal of Consulting and Clinical Psychology,* 41, 2 (1973), 215–223.

Jacobs, S. "Managing departments in conflict." *Computerworld,* 17, 10 (1983), 25–33.

Jaffe, J. M. "Of different minds." *Association Management,* 37, 10 (1985), 120–124.

Jahoda, M. "Psychological issues in civil liberties." *American Psychologist,* 11 (1956), 234–240.

Janis, I. L. "Groupthink and group dynamics: A social psychological analysis of defective policy decisions." *Policy Studies Journal,* 2, 1 (1973), 19–25.

Janis, I. L. "Groupthink." *Psychology Today,* 5, 6 (1971), 43–46, 74–76.

Janis, I. L. *Groupthink: Psychological Study of Policy Decisions and Fiascos.* 2nd ed. Boston: Houghton Mifflin, 1982.

Janis, I. L. *The Anatomy of Power.* Boston: Houghton Mifflin, 1982.

Janis, I. L., and L. Mann. *Decision Making: A Psychological Analysis of Conflict, Choice, and Commitment.* New York: Free Press, 1977.

Janssens, L., and J. R. Nuttin. "Frequency perception of individual and group successes as a function of competition, coaction, and isolation." *Journal of Personality and Social Psychology,* 34 (1976), 830–836.

Jehn, K. A. "A multimethod examination of the benefits and detriments of intragroup conflict." *Administrative Science Quarterly,* 40, 2 (1995), 256–282.

Joe, K. A., and M. Chesney-Lind. "Just every mother's angel: An analysis of gender and ethnic variations in young gang membership." *Gender and Society,* 9, 4 (1995), 408–431.

Johnson, D. "Effects of cooperative, competitive, and individualistic goal structures on achievement: A meta-analysis." *Psychological Bulletin,* 89 (1981), 47–62.

Johnson, D. W., and F. Johnson. *Joining Together.* 4th ed. Englewood Cliffs, N. J.: Prentice-Hall, 1991, 89–93, 111–112.

Johnson, D. W., and R. T. Johnson. "Relationships between black and white students in intergroup cooperation and competition." *Journal of Social Psychology,* 125, 4 (1985), 421–428.

Johnson, D. W.; R. T. Johnson; and M. B. Stanne. "Impact of goal and resource interdependence on problem-solving success." *Journal of Social Psychology,* 129 (Oct. 1989), 621–629.

Johnson, D. W., et al. "Training elementary students to manage conflict." 135, 6 (1995), 673–686.

Johnson, M. P., and W. L. Ewens. "Power relations and affective style as determinants of confidence in impression formation in a game situation." *Journal of Experimental Social Psychology,* 78, 1 (1971), 98–110.

Johnson, N. P., and G. L. Phelps. "Effectiveness in self-help groups: Alcoholics Anonymous as a prototype." *Family and Community Health,* 14, 1 (1991), 22–27.

Johnson, S. R.; T. M. Welsh; L. K. Miller; and D. E. Altus. "Participatory management: Maintaining staff performance in a university housing cooperative." *Journal of Applied Behavior Analysis,* 24, 1 (1991), 119–127.

Johnson, W., and A. Packer. *Workforce 2000: Work and Workers for the 21st Century.* Indianapolis, Ind.: Hudson Institute, 1987.

Johnson, D. W., and R. Johnson. *Leading the Cooperative School.* Edina, Minn.: Interaction Book, 1989.

Jones, E. E. *Ingratiation: A Social Psychological Analysis.* New York: Appleton-Century-Crofts, 1964.

Jorgenson, D., and A. Papciak. "The effects of communication, resource feedback, and identifiability on behavior in a simulated commons." *Journal of Experimental and Social Psychology,* 17 (1981), 373–385.

Jose, P. E., and W. J. McCarthy. "Perceived agentic and communal behavior in mixed-sex group interactions." *Personality and Social Psychology Bulletin,* 14, 1 (1988), 57–67.

Joseph, J. J., S. B. Montgomery, C. Emmons, et al. "Magnitude and determinants of behavioral risk reductions: Longitudinal analysis of a cohort at risk for AIDS." *Psychological Health,* 1, 1 (1987), 73–95.

Julian J. W.; E. P. Hollander; and C. R. Regula. "Endorsement of the group spokesman as a function of his source of authority, competence, and success." *Journal of Personality and Social Psychology,* 11, 1 (1969), 42–49.

Jung, D. I.; B. M. Bass; and J. Sosik. "Collectivism and transformational leadership." *Journal of Management Inquiry,* 2 (1995), 3–18.

Kahn, A., and E. I. Bender. "Self-help groups as a crucible for people empowerment in the context of social development." *Social Development Issues,* 9, 2 (1985), 4–13.

Kahn, A.; R. Nelson; W. Gaeddert; and J. Hearn. "The justice process: Deciding upon equity or equality." *Social Psychology Quarterly,* 45 (1982), 308.

Kameda, T., and S. Sugimori. "Psychological entrapment in group decision making: An assigned decision rule and a groupthink phenomenon." *Journal of Personality and Social Psychology,* 65, 2 (1993), 282–292.

Kanter, R. M. "Dilemmas of managing participation," *Organizational Dynamics,* 11 (1982), 5–27.

Kashyap, A. "Differential efficacy of power base in opinion change in group discussion." *Journal of Psychological Researches,* 26 (1982), 9–12.

Katz, A. "Self-help groups." *Social Work,* 17 (1972), 120–121.

Katz, A. "Self-help organizations and volunteer participation in social welfare." *Social Work,* 15 (1970), 51–60.

Katz, A., and E. Bender. *The Strength in Us: Self-Help Groups in the Modern World.* New York: New Viewpoints, 1976.

Katz, D., and R. L. Kahn. *The Social Psychology of Organizations.* New York: Wiley, 1966.

Keating, J. P., and T. C. Brock. "Acceptance of persuasion and the inhibition of counterargumentation under various distraction tasks." *Journal of Experimental Social Psychology,* 10, 4 (1974), 301–309.

Keeley, H. "Communication in experimentally created hierarchies." *Human Relations,* 4 (1951), 39.

Kegan, R. *The Evolving Self.* Cambridge, Mass.: Harvard University Press, 1982.

Kelley, H. H. "Communication in experimentally created hierarchies." *Human Relations,* 4 (1951), 39–56.

Kelley, H. H., and J. Thibaut. "Group problem solving." In *The Handbook of Social Psychology.* 2nd ed. Vol. 4: *Group Psychology and Phenomena of Interaction.* Ed. G. Lindzey and E. Aronson. Reading, Mass.: Addison-Wesley, 1969, 1.

Kelley, H., and J. Thibaut. "Experimental studies of group problem solving and process." In *Handbook of Social Psychology,* Vol. 11. Ed. G. Undzey. Reading, Mass.: Addison-Wesley, 1954, 735–785.

Kelly, J., and K. Khozan. "Participative management: Can it work?" *Business Horizons,* (Aug. 1980), 74–79.

Kelman, H. C. "Compliance, identification, and internalization: Three processes of attitude change." *Journal of Conflict Resolution,* 2 (1958), 51–60.

Kenny, D.; A. L. Zaccaro; and J. Stephen. "An estimate of variance due to traits in leadership." *Journal of Applied Psychology,* 68, 4 (Nov. 1983), 678–685.

Kephart, W. M. "A quantitative analysis of intragroup relations." *American Journal of Sociology,* 60 (1950), 544–549.

Kepner, H., and B. Tregoe. *The Rational Manager.* New York: McGraw-Hill, 1968.

Kernberg, O. "Regression in groups: Some clinical findings and theoretical implications." *Journal of Personality and Social Systems,* 2 (1980), 51–75.

Kerr, N., and S. Bruun. "Ringelmann revisited: Alternative explanations for the social loafing effect." *Personality and Social Psychology Bulletin,* 7 (1981), 224–231.

Key, N. "Abating risk and accidents through communication." *Professional Safety,* 31, 11 (1986), 25–28.

Keyton, J. "Group termination: Completing the study of group development." *Small Group Research,* 24, 1 (1993), 84–100.

Keyton, J. "Is group self-selection an important organizational variable?" Paper presented at the Annual Meeting of the Southern States Speech Association, Memphis, Tenn., Apr. 1988.

Keyton, J., and J. Springston. "Redefining group cohesiveness and effectiveness: Replicating and extending within new perspectives." Paper presented at the Annual Meeting of the Speech Communication Association, San Francisco, Nov. 1989.

Khoury, R. M. "Norm formation, social conformity, and the confederating function of humor." *Social Behavior and Personality,* 13, 2 (1985), 159–165.

Kiesler, C. A. "Attraction to the group and conformity to group norms." *Journal of Personality,* 31 (1963), 559–569.

King, A. S. "Self-fulfilling prophecies in training the hard-core: Supervisor's expectations and the underprivileged workers' performance." *Social Science Quarterly,* 52 (1971), 369–378.

Kinney, E. E. "A study of peer group social accountability at the fifth-grade level in a public school." *Journal of Educational Research,* 47 (1953), 57–64.

Kipnis, I. "Does power corrupt?" *Journal of Personality and Social Psychology,* 24 (1972), 33–41.

Klein, D. C. *Community Dynamics and Mental Health.* New York: Wiley, 1968, 47–56.

Klein, J. *The Study of Groups.* London: Routledge, 1956.

Kluckhohn, F. R., and F. L. Strodtbeck. *Variations in Value Orientations.* Evanston, Ill.: Row, Peterson, 1961.

Knapp, M. L.; P. R. Hart; G. W. Friedrich; and G. M. Shulman. "The rhetoric of goodbye: Verbal and nonverbal correlates of human leave taking" *Speech Monographs,* 40 (1973), 182–198.

Koberg, D., and J. Bagnall. *The Universal Traveler.* Los Altos, Calif.: Kaufman, 1981, 21.

Koch, J. L. "Managerial succession in a factory and changes in supervisory leadership patterns: A field study." *Human Relations,* 31 (1978), 49–58.

Koch, J. W. "Is group membership a prerequisite for group identification?" *Political Behavior,* 15, 1 (1993), 49–60.

Kohlberg, L., and C. Gilligan. "The adolescent as a philosopher." In *Twelve to Sixteen: Early Adolescence.* Ed. J. Kagan and R. Coles. New York: Norton, 1972.

Kohler, W. *Gestalt Psychology.* New York: New American Library, 1947.

Konigsweiger, R., and J. Pelikan. "Anders—gleich—beides zugleich: Unterschiede und Gemeinsamkeiten in Gruppendynamik und Systemansatz ("Different, the same, or both? Differences and similarities in group-dynamic and systems approaches"). *Gruppendynamik,* 21 (Feb. 1990), 69–94.

Koomen, W. "The relationship between participation rate and liking ratings in groups." *British Journal of Social Psychology,* 27, 2 (1988), 127–132.

Korman, A. K. "Consideration," "Initiating structure," and "Organizational criteria—A review." *Personnel Psychology,* No. 4 (Winter 1966), 349–361.

Korten, D. C. "Situational determinants of leadership structure." *Journal of Conflict Resolution,* 6 (1962), 222–235.

Koska, M. T. "Adapting Deming's quality improvement ideas: A case study." *Hospitals,* (Jul. 5, 1990).

Kotter, J. P., and J. L. Heskett. *Corporate Culture and Performance.* New York: Free Press, 1992.

Kouhara, S. "An experimental study on deviation behavior which promotes group outcome." *Japanese Journal of Experimental Social Psychology,* 30, 1 (1990), 53–61.

Kramer, R. M.; C. G. McClintock; and D. M. Messick. "Social values and cooperative response to a simulated resource conservation crisis." *Journal of Personality,* 54, 3 (1986), 576–592.

Kraus, G., and G. Gemmill. "Idiosyncratic effects of implicit theories of leadership." *Psychological Reports,* 66 (1990), 247–257.

Krech, D., and R. S. Crutchfield. *Theory and Problems of Social Psychology.* New York: McGraw-Hill, 1948.

Kropotkin, P. *Mutual Aid: A Factor in Evolution.* Boston: Extending Horizons, 1955.

Krueger, R. A., and M. Q. Patton. *Focus Groups: A Practical Guide for Applied Research.* Newbury Park, Calif.: Sage, 1988.

Kuypers, B. C.; D. Davies; and A. Hazewinkel. "Developmental patterns in self-analytic groups." *Human Relations,* 39, 9 (1986), 793–815.

Lacoursiere, R. *The Life Cycle of Groups.* New York: Human Sciences Press, 1980.

Lagana, J. F. "Managing change and school improvement effectively." *NASSP Bulletin,* 73, 518 (1989), 52–55.

Laing, R. D. *The Politics of the Family and Other Essays.* New York: Vintage Books, 1972.

Lamb, T. A., and M. Alsikafi. "Conformity in the Asch experiment: Inner-other directedness and the 'defiant subject.'" *Social Behavior and Personality,* 8 (1980), 13–16.

Landers, D. M., and T. F. Crum. "The effects of team success and formal structure on interpersonal relations and spirit of baseball teams." *International Journal of Sport Psychology,* 2, 2 (1971), 88–96.

Lane, I. "Making the goals of acceptance and quality explicit: Effects on group decisions." *Small Group Behavior,* 13 (1982), 542–554.

Lang, P. A. "Task group structuring, a technique: Comparison of the performance of groups led by trained versus nontrained facilitators." *Dissertation Abstracts* (1977), 38 (6-A), 3186–3187.

Latane, B., and N. Nida. "Ten years of research on group size and helping." *Psychological Bulletin,* 89 (1981), 308–324.

Lawler, E. E., III, and G. E. Ledford, Jr. In Marks, M. L. "The question of quality circles." *Psychology Today,* 20, 3 (1986), 36–46.

Lawler, E. E., III. "The new plant revolution revisited." *Organizational Dynamics,* 19, 2 (1990), 5–14

Lawler, E. E., III, and S. A. Mohrman. "Quality circles after the fad." *Harvard Business Review,* 63 (Jan./Feb. 1985), 65–71.

Leddick, S. "Teaching managers to support quality-improvement efforts." *National Productivity Review,* (Winter 1990/91), 69–74.

Lee, C. "Followship—The essence of leadership." *Training* (Jan. 1991), 27–35.

Lee, C. "The relationship between goal setting, self-efficacy, and female field hockey team performance." *International Journal of Sport Psychology,* 20, 2 (1989), 147–161.

Lee, I. J. "Why discussions go astray." *Etc.,* 50, 1 (1993), 41–53.

Lee, Y. T., and V. Ottati. "Perceived ingroup homogeneity as a function of group membership salience and stereotype threat." *Personality and Social Psychology Bulletin,* 21, 6 (1995), 610–619.

Leebov, W., and G. Scott. *Health Care Managers in Transition.* San Francisco: Jossey-Bass, 1990, 136–137.

Levine, M. "An analysis of mutual assistance." Presentation at the annual meeting of the American Psychological Association, New York, Aug. 1987.

Levy, L. H. "Processes and activities in groups." In *Self-Help Groups for Coping with Stress.* Ed. M. A. Lieberman, L. D. Borman, et al. San Francisco: Jossey-Bass, 1979, 241–256.

Lewin, K.; R. Lippin; and R. K. White. "Patterns of aggressive behavior in experimentally created social climates." *Journal of Social Psychology,* 10 (1939), 271–299.

Lewin, K. *Field Theory in the Social Sciences.* New York: Harper & Row, 1951.

Lewin, K. "Field theory and experiment in social psychology: Concepts and methods." *American Journal of Sociology,* 44 (1939), 868–897.

Lewin, K. "Frontiers in group dynamics." *Human Relations,* 1 (1947), 5–42.

Lewin, K. *Resolving Social Conflicts.* New York: Harper & Row, 1948.

Lewis, J. M.; W. R. Beavers; J. T. Gossett; and V. A. Phillips. *No Single Thread: Psychological Health in Family Systems.* New York: Brunner/Mazel, 1976.

Leyens, J. P., and V. Y. Yzerbyt. "The ingroup overexclusion effect: Impact of valence and confirmation on stereotypical information search." Special issue on positive-negative asymmetry in affect and evaluations. *European Journal of Social Psychology,* 22, 6 (1992), 549–569.

Liberman, R. "A behavioral approach to group dynamics: I. Reinforcement and prompting of cohesiveness in group therapy." *Behavior Therapy,* 1 (1970), 141–175; "II. Reinforcing and prompting hostility-to-the-therapist in group therapy." *Behavior Therapy,* 1 (1970), 312–327.

Lichman, R. J., and I. M. Lane. "Effects of group norms and goal setting on productivity." *Group and Organization Studies,* 8, 4 (1983), 406–420.

Lieberman, M. A., and L. Videka-Sherman. "The impact of self-help groups on the mental health of widows and widowers." *American Journal of Orthopsychiatry,* 56, 3 (1986), 435–449.

Lieberman, M., and L. Borman, eds. *Self-Help Groups for Coping with Stress.* San Francisco: Jossey-Bass, 1979.

Likert, R. *New Patterns of Management.* New York: McGraw Hill, 1961.

Lindeman, M., and P. Koskela. "Group size, controllability of group membership, and comparative dimension as determinants of intergroup discrimination." *European Journal of Social Psychology,* 24, 2 (1994), 267–278.

Lippitt, G. "How to get results from a group." In *Group Development.* Ed. L. Bradford. Washington, D. C.: National Training Laboratories, 1961, 34.

Lippitt, R.; J. Watson; and B. Westley. *The Dynamics of Planned Change: A Comparative Study of Principles and Techniques.* New York: Harcourt, 1958.

Livesley, W. J., and D. B. Bromley. *Person Perception in Childhood and Adolescence.* New York: Wiley, 1973.

Livingston, J. S. "Retrospective commentary." *Harvard Business Review* (Sept.-Oct. 1998), 125.

Locke, E. A. "Motivation through conscious goal setting." *Applied & Preventive Psychology,* 5, 2 (1996), 117–124.

Locksley, A.; V. Ortiz; and C. Hepburn. "Social categorization and discriminatory behavior: Extinguishing the minimal intergroup discrimination effect." *Journal of Personality and Social Psychology,* 39 (1980), 773–783.

Lombardo, M. M.; M. N. Ruderman; and C. D. McCauley. "Explanations of success and derailment in upper level management positions." *Journal of Business and Psychology,* 2 (1998), 199–216.

Loomis, J. "Communication, the development of trust and cooperative behavior." *Human Relations,* 12 (1959), 305.

Louis, K. S.; D. Blumenthal; M. E. Gluck; and M. A. Stoto. "Entrepreneurs in academe: An exploration of behaviors among life scientists." *Administrative Science Quarterly,* 34 (1989), 110–131.

Low, A. A. *Mental Health Through Will-Training.* Boston: Christopher Publishing, 1950.

Luchins, A. S. "Focusing on the object of judgment in the social situation." *Journal of Social Psychology,* 60 (Aug. 1963), 231–249.

Luft, J. *Of Human Interaction.* Palo Alto, Calif.: Mayfield, 1969.

Luke, R. A. "The internal normative structure of sensitivity training groups." *Journal of Applied Behavioral Science,* 8, 4 (1972), 421–427.

Lundgran, D. C. "Developmental trends in the emergence of interpersonal issues in T-groups." *Small Group Behavior,* 8, 2 (1977), 179–200.

Mabry, E. A. "Exploratory analysis of a developmental model for task-oriented small groups." *Human Communications,* 2, 1 (1975), 66–74.

Maccoby, E. E., and C. N. Jacklin. *The Psychology of Sex Differences*. Palo Alto, Calif.: Stanford University Press, 1974.

Maginn, B., and R. Harris. "Effects of anticipated evaluation on individual brainstorming performance." *Journal of Applied Psychology,* 65 (1980), 219–225.

Magnan, K. S. "Academic psychologists are dropping out of association in discord with practitioners." *Chronicle of Higher Education,* 33, 33 (1987), 12–14.

Maier, N. R. F. *Problem-Solving Discussions and Conferences*. New York: McGraw-Hill, 1963, 193–195.

Maier, N. R. F., and L. Hoffman. "Group decision in England and the United States." *Personnel Psychology,* 15 (1962), 75–87.

Main, J. "Westinghouse's cultural revolution." *Fortune* (June 15, 1981), 74–93.

Maltz, D. N., and R. A. Borker. "A cultural approach to male–female miscommunication." In *Language and Social Identity.* Ed. J. J. Gumperz. Cambridge: Cambridge University Press, 1982, 196–216.

Mamali, C., and G. Paun. "Group size and the genesis of subgroups: Objective restrictions." *Revue Roumaine des Sciences Sociales—Serie de Psychologie,* 26 (1982), 139–148.

Mann, M. R. "An analysis of faculty goals: Personal, disciplinary, and career development decisions." Presentation at Annual Meeting of the American Educational Research Association, San Francisco Mar. 27–31, 1989.

Mann, R. D. "A review of the relationships between personality and performance in small groups." *Psychological Bulletin,* 56 (1959), 241–270.

Mann, R. D. *Interpersonal Styles and Group Development.* New York: Wiley, 1967.

Manz, C. C.; D. E. Keating; and A. Donnellon. "Preparing for an organizational change to employee self-management: The managerial transition." *Organizational Dynamics,* 19, 2 (1990), 15–26.

Markowitz, L. "The context of intimacy." *Networker* (Sept.-Oct. 1997), 50–58.

Marks, M. L. "The question of quality circles." *Psychology Today,* 20, 3 (1986), 36–46.

Marks, M. L.; P. H. Mirvis; F. Grady; and E. J. Hackett. "Employee participation in a quality circle program: Impact on quality of work life, productivity, and absenteeism." *Journal of Applied Psychology,* 71 (1985), 61–69.

Martin, B. A., and J. D. Manning. "Combined effects of normative information and task difficulty on the goal commitment performance relationship." *Journal of Management,* 21, 1 (1995), 65–80.

Martin, J. D.; J. S. Williams; and L. N. Gray. "Norm formation and subsequent divergence: Prediction and variation." *Journal of Social Psychology,* 93, 2 (1974), 261–269.

Martin, P. Y., and R. A. Hummer. "Fraternities and rape on campus." *Gender and Society,* 3, 4 (1989), 457–473.

Martin, R. "The effects of ingroup–outgroup membership on minority influence when group membership is determined by a trivial categorization." *Social Behavior and Personality,* 20, 3 (1992), 131–141.

Martin, R., and D. Lauridsen. *Developing Student Discipline and Motivation: A Series for Teacher Inservice Training*. Champaign, Ill.: Research Press, 1974.

Maslow, A. H. *Motivation and Personality.* New York: Harper & Row, 1954.

Maton, K. I.; G. S. Leventhal; E. J. Madara; and M. Julien. "Factors affecting the birth and death of mutual health groups: The role of national affiliation, professional involvement, and member focal problem."

American Journal of Community Psychology, 17 (1989), 643–671.

Maznevski, M. L., and J. J. DiStefano. "Measuring culture in international management: The cultural perspectives questionnaire." (Working paper 95–139). London, Can.: University of Western Ontario, Western Business School, 1995.

Maznevski, M., and M. F. Peterson. *Societal Values, Social Interpretation, and Multinational Teams in Cross-Cultural Work Groups.* Ed. C. Granrose, S. R. Romme, and S. Oskamp (1997), 61–89.

McCauley, C. D.; M. M. Lombardo; and Morrison. *The Lessons of Experience.* 1988.

McCauley, C. D.; M. M. Lombardo; and C. J. Usher. "Diagnosing management development needs: An instrument based on how managers develop." *Journal of Management,* 15, 3 (1989), 389–401.

McCurdy, H. G., and W. E. Lambert. "The efficiency of small human groups in the solution of problems requiring genuine cooperation." *Journal of Personality,* 20 (1952), 478–494.

McDavid, J. W., and H. Harari. *Social Psychology.* New York: Harper & Row, 1968.

McGarty, C.; S. A. Haslam; K. J. Hutchinson; and J. C. Turner. "The effects of salient group memberships on persuasion." *Small Group Research,* 25, 2 (1994), 267–293.

McGarvey, R. "The competitive edge." *US Air Magazine* (Feb. 1992).

McGowan, W. "A sense of belonging." *New York Times Magazine* (Aug. 23, 1987), 46–48.

McGrath, J. E. *Groups, Interaction, and Performance.* Englewood Cliffs, N. J.: Prentice-Hall, 1984, 128.

McGregor, D. *The Human Side of Enterprise.* New York: McGraw-Hill. 1960.

McGregor, D. *The Professional Manager.* New York: McGraw-Hill, 1967.

Meir, E. I.; G. Kleinen; and Z. Segal. "Group importance as a mediator between personality-environment congruence and satisfaction." *Journal of Vocational Behavior,* 28, 1 (1986), 60–69.

Merton, R K.; M. Fiske; and P. L. Kendall. *Mass Persuasion.* New York: Harper & Row, 1946.

Merton, R. K. "The self-fulfilling prophecy." *Antioch Review,* 8 (1948), 210.

Merton, R. K.; M. Fiske; and P. L. Kendall. *The Focused Interview.* New York: Free Press, 1956.

Meyer, G. W., and R. G. Stott. "Quality circles: Panacea or Pandora's box?" *Organizational Dynamics,* 13, 4 (1985), 34–50.

Milakovich, M. E. "Total quality management in the public sector." *National Productivity Review,* (Spring 1991), 195–205.

Milgram, S. "Behavior study of obedience." *Journal of Abnormal and Social Psychology,* 67 (1963), 371–378.

Milgram, S. "Group pressure and action against a person." *Journal of Abnormal and Social Psychology,* 69 (1964), 137–143.

Milgram, S. "Liberating effects of group pressure." *Journal of Personality and Social Psychology,* 1 (1965), 127–134.

Miller, A. "A donnybrook in the ad world." *Newsweek,* 111 (Jan. 18, 1988), 55.

Miller, D. T., and W. Turnbull. "Expectancies and interpersonal processes." *Annual Review of Psychology,* 37 (1986) 233–256.

Miller, E. J., and A. K. Rice. "Systems of organizations." In *Group Relations Reader.* Ed. A. D. Coleman and W. H. Bexton. Washington, D. C.: Rice Institute, 1975.

Miller, S., and G. Katz. "The educational needs of mental health self-help groups."

Psychosocial Rehabilitation Journal, 16, 1 (1992), 160–163.

Mills, T. M. *The Sociology of Small Groups.* Englewood Cliffs, N. J.: Prentice-Hall, 1967, 81–82.

Minnchin, S. *Families and Family Therapy.* Cambridge, Mass.: Harvard University Press, 1974.

Mintzberg, H. "Crafting strategy." In *On Management.* Cambridge, Mass.: Harvard Business School, 1976a, 25–42.

Mintzberg, H. "Planning on the left side and managing on the right." *Harvard Business Review* (Jul.-Aug. 1976b), 49–58.

Missing, P., and J. F. Preble. "Group processes and performance in a complex business simulation." *Small Group Behavior,* 16, 3 (1985), 325–338.

Misumi, J. "The development in Japan of the performance maintenance (PM) theory of leadership." *Journal of Social Issues,* 51, 1 (1995), 213–228.

Mohrman, S. A., and L. Novelli. "Beyond testimonials: Learning from a quality circles programme." *Journal of Occupational Behaviour,* 6, 2 (1985), 93–110.

Mondros, J. B.; R. Woodrow; and L. Weinstein. "The use of groups to manage conflict." *Social Work with Groups,* 15, 4 (1992), 43–57.

Mone, M. A., and C. E. Shalley. "Effects of task complexity and goal specificity on change in strategy and performance over time." *Human Performance,* 8, 4 (1995), 243–262.

Moorman, R. H., and G. L. Blakely. *Journal of Organizational Behavior,* 6, 2 (1995), 127–142.

Morris, W. N. "Collective coping with stress: Group reactions to fear, anxiety, and ambiguity." *Journal of Personality and Social Psychology,* 33, 6 (1976), 674–679.

Morrison, T. L., and D. D. Stein. "Member reaction to male and female leaders in two types of group experience." *Journal of Social Psychology,* 125, 1 (1985), 7–16.

Moscovici, S., and M. Zavalloni. "The group as a polarizer of attitudes." *Journal of Abnormal and Social Psychology,* 12 (1969), 125–135.

Mugny, G. "Compliance, conversion and the Asch paradigm." *European Journal of Social Psychology,* 14, 4 (1984), 353–368.

Mulder, M. "Power equalization through participation." *Administrative Science Quarterly,* 16 (1971), 31–38.

Mullen, B., et al. "Boundaries around group interaction: A meta-analytical integration of the effects of group size." *Journal of Social Psychology,* 131, 2 (1991), 271–283.

Mullen, B., and C. Copper. "The relation between group cohesiveness and performance: An integration." *Psychological Bulletin,* 115, 2 (1994), 210–217.

Mullen, B.; J. Chapman; and E. Salas. "Efectos do las composicion del grupo: 'Perdido en la multitude,' o 'centro de atencion.'" (Effects of group composition: "Lost in the crowd," or "center of attention.") *Revista Latinoamericana de Psycologia,* 21, 1 (1989), 43–55.

Murnighan, J. K. "Coalitions in decision-making groups: Organizational analogs." *Organizational Behavior and Human Decision Process,* 35, 1 (1985), 1–26.

Myers, M. R.; M. J. Slavin; and W. T. Southern. "Emergence and maintenance of leadership among gifted students in group problem solving." *Roeper Review,* 12, 4 (1990), 256–260.

Napier, H. "Individual versus group learning: Note on task variables." *Psychological Reports,* 23 (1967), 757–758.

Napier, R., and M. Gershenfeld. *Making Groups Work*. Boston: Houghton Mifflin, 1982.

Napier, R.; C. Sidle; and D. Sanaghan. *High Impact Tools and Activities for Strategic Planning*. New York: McGraw-Hill, 1998, 156–163.

Nelson, E. S., and M. A. Harris. "The relationship between birth order and need affiliation and group orientation." *Journal of Adlerian Theory, Research and Practice,* 51, 3 (1995), 282–292.

Nemiroff, P. M.; W. A. Pasmore; and D. L. Ford. "The effects of two normative structural interventions on established ad hoc groups: Implications for improving decision-making effectiveness. *Decision Sciences,* 7 (1976), 841–855.

New York Times (Nov. 6, 1991), B–9.

New York Times (Dec. 8, 1991), E–5.

Nidorf, L. J. "Information seeking strategies in person perception." *Perceptual and Motor Skills,* 26, 2 (1968), 355–365.

Nidorf, L. J., and W. H. Crockett. "Some factors affecting the amount of information sought by others." *Journal of Abnormal and Social Psychology,* 69, 1 (1964), 98–101.

Nisbett, R. E., and T. D. Wilson. *Institute of Social Research Newsletter,* 4 (1978), University of Michigan.

Norris, D., and R. Niebuhr. "Group variables and gaming success." *Simulation and Games,* 11 (1980), 301–312.

O'Brien, G., and W. Gross. "Structural indices for potential participation in groups." *Austrian Journal of Psychology,* 33 (1981), 135–148.

O'Leary-Kelly, A. M.; J. J. Martocchio; and D. D. Frink. "A review of the influence of group goals on group performance. *Academy of Mangement Journal,* 37, 5 (1994), 1285–1301.

Obert, S. L. "Developmental patterns of organizational task groups: A preliminary study." *Human Relations,* 36, 1 (1983), 37–52.

Openshaw, D. K., et al. "Conflict resolution in parent–adolescent dyads: The influence of social skills training." *Journal of Adolescent Research,* 7, 4 (1992), 457–468.

Opp, K. D. "The evolutionary emergence of norms." *British Journal of Social Psychology,* 21 (1982), 139–149.

Ornstein, R. *The Psychology of Consciousness*. San Francisco: Freeman, 1975.

Osborn, A. F. *Applied Imagination*. New York: Charles Schribner's Sons, 1953.

Ouchi, W. *Theory Z*. Reading, Mass.: Addison-Wesley, 1981.

Owen, W. F. "Rhetorical themes of emergent women leaders." *Small Group Behavior,* 17, 4 (1986), 475–486.

Palich, L. and Hom, P. W. "The impact of leader power and behavior on leadership perceptions." *Group and Organizational Management,* 17, 3 (1992), 279–296.

Pantin, H., and C. Carver. "Induced competence and the bystander effect." *Journal of Applied Social Psychology,* 12 (1982), 100–101.

Parsons, T. *The Social System*. Glencoe, Ill.: Free Press, 1951.

Parsons, T., and E. A. Shils, eds. *Toward a General Theory of Action*. Cambridge, Mass.: Harvard University Press, 1951.

"Participative management at work: An interview with John F. Donnelly." *Harvard Business Review,* 55 (1977), 117–127.

Paulus, P. B.; M. T. Dzindolet; G. Poletes; and L. M. Camacho. "Perception of performance in group brainstorming: The illusion of group productivity." *Personality and Social Psychology Bulletin,* 19, 1 (1993), 78–89.

Pearce, J. A. II, and R B. Robinson, Jr. *Strategic Management: Strategic Formulation and Implementation.* 2nd ed. Homewood, Ill: Irwin, 1985, 15.

Pearson, J. "The effects of setting and gender on self-disclosure." *Group and Organization Studies,* 6 (1981), 334–340.

Peck, S. *The Road Less Traveled.* New York: Simon & Schuster, 1978, 17.

Peele, S. *The Meaning of Addiction: Compulsive Experience and Its Interpretation.* Lexington, Mass.: Lexington Books, 1984.

Petzel, T. P.; J. E. Johnson; and L. Bresolin. "Peer nominations of leadership and likability in problem-solving groups as a function of gender and task." *Journal of Social Psychology,* 130, 5 (1990), 641–648.

Phillips, D. J. "Report on discussion 66." *Adult Education Journal,* 7 (1948), 81.

Phillips, G.; J. T. Wood; and D. T. Pedersen. *Group Discussion: A Practical Guide to Participation and Leadership.* New York: Harper & Row, 1986.

Piaget, J. *The Construction of Reality in the Child.* New York: Basic Books, 1954.

Piaget, J. *The Origins of Intelligence in Children.* New York: International Universities Press, 1952.

Piers, Lyndon. "The Leader and the Scapegoat: A Dependency Group Study." *Group Analysis,* 27, 1 (1994), 95–104.

Piper, W. "Cohesion as a basic bond in groups." *Human Relations,* 36 (1983), 93–108.

Pool, F. E. "The psychic infection of Heaven's Gate." *The Humanist,* 52, 4 (1997), 4.

Poole, M. "Decision development in small groups: A comparison of two models." *Communication Monographs,* 48 (1981), 1–24.

Price, V. "Social identification and public opinion: Effects of communicating group conflict." *Public Opinion Quarterly,* 53 (1989), 197–222.

Prien, R. L.; D. A. Harrison; and N. K. Muir. "Structured conflict and consensus outcomes in group decision making." *Journal of Management,* 21, 4 (1995), 691–710.

Prince, G. *The Practice of Creativity.* New York: Collier Books, 1970.

Principle, C. D., and S. E. Neeley. "Nominal versus interactive groups: Further evidence." *Mid-Atlantic Journal of Business,* 21, 2 (1983), 25–34.

Prochaska, J. O. *Systems of Psychotherapy.* Homewood, Ill.: Dorsey Press, 1984.

Procopio, A. J., and J. W. Fairfield-Sonn. "Changing attitudes toward quality: An exploratory study." *Group and Organizational Management,* 21, 2 (1996), 133–145.

Puckett, S. B. "When a worker gets AIDS." *Psychology Today,* 22, 1 (1988), 26–27.

Quattrone, G., and E. Jones. "The perception of variability within in-groups and outgroups: Implications for the law of small numbers." *Journal of Personality and Social Psychology,* 38 (1980), 141–152.

Quey, R. L. "Functions and dynamics of work groups." *American Psychologist,* 26, 10 (1971), 1077–1082.

Quine, S., and I. Cameron. "The use of focus groups with the disabled elderly." Special issue: Issues and Applications of Focus Groups. *Qualitative Health Research,* 5, 4 (1995), 454–462.

Rao, V. S. "Effects of teleconferencing technologies: An exploration of comprehension, feedback, satisfaction and role-related differences." Special issue on distributed communication systems. *Group Decision and Negotiation,* 4, 3 (1995), 251–272.

Reddi, M. "Team development: A review." *ASCI Journal of Management* (India), 13, 1 (1983), 57–75.

Reddin, W. *Managerial Effectiveness*. New York: McGraw-Hill, 1970.

Reddy, D.; A. Baum; R. Fleming; and J. Aiello. "Mediation of social density by coalition formation." *Journal of Applied Social Psychology,* 11 (1981), 529–537.

Reddy, W. B., and A. Byrnes. "Effects of interpersonal group composition on the problem-solving behavior of middle managers." *Journal of Applied Psychology,* 56, 6 (1972), 516–517.

Redl, F. *When We Deal with Children*. New York: Free Press, 1966.

Reed, B. G. "Women leaders in small groups: Social psychological strategies and perspectives." *Social Work with Groups,* 6, 3 and 4 (1983), 35–42.

Regan, D. T. "Effects of a favor and liking on compliance."*Journal of Experimental Social Psychology,* 7 (1971), 627–639.

Reid, D. W., and E. E. Ware. "Affective style and impression formation: Reliability, validity, and some inconsistencies." *Journal of Personality,* 40, 3 (1972), 436–450.

Rickards, T. *Problem Solving Through Creative Analysis*. London: Halsted Press, 1974, 10.

Rieken, H. W., and G. C. Homans. "Psychological aspects of social structure. In *Handbook of Social Psychology.* Vol. 2. Ed. G. Lindzey. Reading, Mass.: Addison-Wesley. 1954, 786–832.

Rioch, M. "The work of Wilfred Bion on groups." In *Analysis of Groups*. Ed. G. S. Gibbard, J. J. Hartman, and R. D. Mann. San Francisco: Jossey-Bass, 1978.

Robert, H. M. *Robert's Rules of Order.* Chicago: Scott, Foresman, 1943.

Roberts, J. "Observing and Gender." Presentation at the National Council on Family Relations Annual Conference, Atlanta, 1987.

Roethlisberger, E. J., and W. J. Dickson. *Management and the Worker: Technical vs. Social Organization in an Industrial Plan.* Cambridge, Mass.: Harvard University Press, 1939.

Rogelburg, S. G.; J. L. Barnes-Farrell; and C. A. Love. "The stepladder technique: An alternative group structure facilitating effective group decision making." *Journal of Applied Psychology,* 77, 5 (1992), 730–737.

Rogers, C., and F. J. Roethlisberger. "Barriers and gateways to communication." *Harvard Business Review,* 30, 4 (1952), 46.

Roggenbuck, J.; D. R. Williams; S. P. Bange; and D. J. Dean. "River float-trip encounter norms: Questioning the use of the social norms concept." *Journal of Leisure Research,* 23, 2 (1991), 133–153.

Rohde, R. I., and R. Stockton. "The effect of structured feedback on goal attainment, attraction to the group, and satisfaction with the group in small group counseling." *Journal of Group Psychotherapy, Psychodrama & Sociometry,* 44, 4 (1992), 172–180.

Rokeach, M. "Long-range experimental modification of values, attitudes, and behavior." *American Psychologist,* 26, 5 (1971), 453–459.

Rose, S. D. *Group Therapy: A Behavioral Approach*. Englewood Cliffs, N. J. Prentice-Hall, 1977.

Rosenfeld, D.; W. Stephan; and G. Lucker. "Attraction to competent and incompetent members of cooperative and competitive groups." *Journal of Applied Social Psychology,* 11 (1981), 416–433.

Rosenor, J. B. "Ways women lead." *Harvard Business Review* (Nov.-Dec. 1990).

Ross, L.; G. Bierbrauer; and S. Hoffman. "The role of attribution processes in conformity and dissent: Revisiting the Asch situation." *American Psychologist* (Feb. 1976), 148–157.

Rotter, G. S., and S. M. Portergal. "Group and individual effects in problem solving." *Journal of Applied Psychology,* 53 (1969), 338–342.

Rouche, J. E.; G. A. Baker III; and R. R. Rose. *Shared Vision (Transformational Leadership in American Community Colleges).* Washington, D. C.: Community College Press, 1989.

Royal, E., and S. Golden. "Attitude similarity and attraction to an employee group." *Psychological Reports,* 48 (1981), 251–254.

Rubin, J. Z., and R. J. Lewicki. "A three-factor experimental analysis of promises and threats." *Journal of Applied Social Psychology,* 3 (1973), 240–257.

Rubin, J. Z.; C. T. Mowbray, L. Collette; and R. J. Lewicki. "Perception of attempts at interpersonal influence." *Proceedings of the 79th Annual Convention of the AOA,* 6 (1971), 391–392.

Sagarin, E. *Odd Man In: Societies of Deviants in America.* New York: Quadrangle Books, 1969.

Sagie, A. "Effects of leader's communication style and participative goal setting on performance and attitudes." *Human Performance,* 9, 1 (1996), 51–64.

Sanders, G., and F. Malkis. "Type A behavior, need for control, and reactions to group participation." *Organizational Behavior and Human Performance,* 30 (1982), 71–86.

Sargent, J. F., and G. R. Miller. "Some differences in certain communication behaviors of autocratic and democratic group leaders." *Journal of Communication,* 21 (1971), 233–252.

Sashkin, M. "Participative management is an ethical imperative." *Organizational Dynamics* (Spring 1984), 5–21.

Satir, V. *Conjoint Family Therapy.* Palo Alto, Calif.: Science and Behavior Books, 1967.

Savell, J. M. "Prior agreement and conformity: An extension of the generalization phenomenon." *Psychonomic Science,* 25 (1971), 327–328.

Schachter, S. *The Psychology of Affiliation.* Palo Alto, Calif.: Stanford University Press, 1959.

Scheffler, L. *Help Thy Neighbor: How Counseling Works and When It Doesn't.* New York: Grove Press, 1983.

Schein, E. H. *Organizational Psychology.* Englewood Cliffs, N. J.: Prentice-Hall, 1965.

Schein, E. H. *Process Consultation.* Reading, Mass.: Addison-Wesley, 1969.

Schellenberg, J. A. "Group size as a factor in success of academic discussion groups." *Journal of Educational Psychology,* 33 (1959), 73–79.

Schleicher, W. "Quality control circles save Lockheed nearly $3 million in two years." *Quality* (May 1977), 14–17.

Schlesinger, L. A., and B. Oshry. "Quality of work life and the manager: Muddle in the middle." *Organizational Dynamics,* 13, 1 (1984), 5–19.

Schriesheim, J. "The social context of leader–subordinate relations: An investigation of the effects of group cohesiveness." *Journal of Applied Psychology,* 65 (1980), 183–194.

Schultz, B. "Communicative correlates of perceived leaders in small groups." *Small Group Behavior,* 17, 1 (1986), 51–65.

Schutz, W. C. *FIRO: A Three-Dimensional Theory of Interpersonal Behavior.* New York: Holt, Rinehart and Winston, 1958.

Schutz, W. *The Interpersonal Underworld.* Palo Alto, Calif.: Science and Behavior Books, 1966.

Schwartz, T. M.; R. A. Eberle; and D. R. Moscato. "Effects of awareness of individual group membership on group problem solving under constrained communication." *Psychological Reports,* 33, 3 (1973), 823–827.

Schweiger, P. M.; W. R. Sandberg; and J. W. Ragan. "Group approaches for improving strategic decision making: A comparative analysis of dialectical inquiry, devil's advocacy, and consensus." *Academy of Management Journal,* 29 (1986), 51–71.

Sciolino, E. "The British carried umbrellas to Waterloo." *New York Times* (Aug. 3, 1997), 4-2.

Scontrino, M. R. "The effects of fulfilling and violating group members' expectations about leadership style." *Organizational Behavior and Human Perfomance,* 8 (1972), 118–138.

Scott, M. M. "Recent changes in family structure in the United States: A developmental-systems perspective." *Journal of Applied Developmental Psychology,* 14, 2 (1993), 213–230.

Scott, C. R., and A. C. Easton. "Examining equality of influence in group decision support system interaction." *Small Group Research,* 27, 3 (1996), 360–382.

Seaman, D. F. *Working Effectively with Task-oriented Groups.* New York: McGraw-Hill, 1981, 43–44.

Seashore, S. E. "Group cohesiveness in the industrial work group." Ann Arbor, Mich.: Institute for Social Research, University of Michigan, 1954.

Selekman, M. "The solution-oriented parenting group: A treatment alternative that works." *Journal of Strategic and Systemic Therapies,* 10, 1 (Spring 1991), 36–49.

Selman, R. *The Growth of Interpersonal Understanding: Developmental and Clinical Analyses.* New York: Academic Press, 1980.

Senge, P. M. *The Fifth Discipline: Tbe Art and Practice of the Learning Organization.* Garden City, N. Y.: Doubleday, 1990.

Senge, P. M. "The leader's new work: Building learning organizations." *Sloan Management Review* (Fall 1990), 7–23.

Sensenbrenner, J. "Quality comes to city hall." *Harvard Business Review* (Mar.-Apr. 1991), 64–69.

Sessa, V. I. "Using perspective taking to manage conflict and affect in teams." *Journal of Applied Behavioral Science,* 32, 1 (1996), 101–115.

Shaw, J. S., and K. A. McClure. *Law and Human Behavior,* 20, 6 (1996), 629–653.

Shaw, M. *Group Dynamics: The Psychology of Small Group Behavior.* 3rd ed. New York: McGraw-Hill, 1981, 134–135.

Shaw, M. "Communication networks." In *Advances in Experimental Social Psychology.* Vol. 1. Ed. L. Berkowitz. New York: Academic Press, 1964.

Shaw, M. E. *Group Dynamics, The Psychology of Small Group Behavior.* New York: McGraw-Hill, 1981.

Shaw, M. E., and G. R. Breed. "Effects of attribution of responsibility for negative events on behavior in small groups." *Sociometry,* 33, 4 (1970), 382–393.

Shea, G. P., and R. A. Guzzo. "Groups as human resources." In *Research in Personnel and Human Resource Management.* Ed. K. M. Rowland, and G. R. Ferris. Greenwich, Conn.: JAI, 1987.

Sherif, M. *The Psychology of Social Norms.* New York: Harper, 1936.

Sherif, M. "A study of some social factors in perception." *Archives of Psychology,* 27, 187 (1935).

Sherif, M. "Conformity-deviation, norms, and group relations." In *Conformity and Deviation.* Ed. I. A. Berg, and B. M. Bass. New York: Harper, 1961, 159–181.

Sherr, L. A., and D. J. Teeter. *Total Quality Management in Higher Education.* San Francisco: Jossey-Bass, 1991, 3–10.

Sigman, S. J. "Handling the discontinuous aspects of social relationships: Toward research on the persistence of social forms." *Communication Theory,* 1, 2 (1991), 106–127.

Sime, J. D. "Affiliative behavior during escape to building exits." *Journal of Environmental Psychology,* 3, 1 (1983), 21–41.

Singleton, R. "Another look at the conformity explanation of group-induced shifts in choice." *Human Relations,* 32, 1 (1979), 37–56.

Skinner, W. E., and A. M. Cattarello. "Understanding the relationships among attitudes, group norms, and behavior using behavioral commitment: A structural equation analysis of marijuana use." *Journal of Applied Social Psychology,* 19 (1989), 1268–1291.

Slater, P. "Role differentiation in small groups." *American Sociological Review,* 20 (1955), 300–310.

Smith, B. L. "Interpersonal behaviors that damage the productivity of creative problem-solving groups." *Journal of Creative Behavior,* 27, 3 (1993), 171–187.

Smith, G. B., and A. I. Schwebel. "Using a cognitive-behavioral family model in conjunction with systems and behavioral family therapy models." *American Journal of Family Therapy,* 23, 3 (Fall 1995), 203–212.

Smith, K. K. *Groups in Conflict.* Dubuque, Ia.: Kendall/Hunt, 1982, 3.

Smith, M.; R. Reinheimer; and A. Gabbard. "Crowding, task performance, and communicative interaction in youth and old age." *Human Communication Research,* 7 (1981), 259–272.

Smith, R. D., and R. H. Culhan. "MS/OR Academic and practitioner interactions: A promising new approach." *Interfaces,* 16, 5 (Sept./Oct. 1986), 27–33.

Smith, R. J., and R. E. Cook. "Leadership dyadic groups as a function of dominance and incentives." *Sociometry,* 36, 4 (1973).

Smith, R. R.; L. Smythe; and D. Lien. "Inhibition of helping behavior by a similar or dissimilar nonreactive fellow bystander." *Journal of Personality and Social Psychology,* 23, 3 (1972), 414–419.

Snyder, C., and C. Newburg. "The Barnum effect in a group setting." *Journal of Personality Assessment,* 45 (1981), 622–629.

Snyder, M.; E. D. Tanke; and E. Berscheid. "Social perception and interpersonal behavior: On the self-fulfilling nature of social stereotypes." *Journal of Personality and Social Psychology,* 35 (1977), 656–666.

Sorenson, G., and J. C. McCroskey, "The prediction of interaction behavior in small groups: Zero history vs. intact groups." *Monographs,* 44, 1 (1977), 73–80.

Sorrels, J. P., and J. Kelley. "Conformity by omission." *Personality and Social Psychology Bulletin,* 10 (1984) 302–305.

Sorrentino, R. M. "An extension of achievement motivation theory to the study of emergent leadership." *Journal of Personality and Social Psychology,* 26 (June 1973), 356–368.

Spears, R.; M. Lea; and S. Lee. "Deindividuation and group polarization in computer-mediated communication." *British Journal of Social Psychology,* 29, 2 (1990), 121–134.

Spillane, R. "Authority in small groups: A laboratory test of a Machiavellian observation." *British Journal of Social Psychology,* 22 (1983), 51–59.

Spradley, J. P., and D. W. McCurdy. *Conformity and Conflict.* Glenview, Ill.: Scott, Foresman, 1990.

Staley, C. C. "Managerial women in mixed groups: Implications of recent research." *Group and Organizational Studies,* 9, 3 (1984), 316–332.

Stang, D. J. "Conformity, ability, and self-esteem." *Representative Research in Social Psychology,* 3 (1972), 97–103.

Stang, D. J. "The effect of interaction rate on ratings of leadership and liking." *Journal of Personality and Social Psychology,* 27 (1973), 405–408.

Stasson, M. F., and R. G. Hawkes. "Effect of group performance on subsequent individual performance: Does influence generalize beyond the issues discussed by the group?" *Psychological Science,* 6, 5 (1995), 305–307.

Staw, B.; L. Sandelands; and J. Dutton. "Threat-rigidity effects in organizational behavior: A multilevel analysis." *Administrative Science Quarterly,* 26 (1981), 501–524.

Steel, R. P., and G. S. Shane. "Evaluation research on quality circles: Technical and analytical implications." *Human Relations,* 39, 5 (1986), 449–466.

Stewart, D. W., and P. N. Shamdasani. *Focus Groups—Theory and Practice.* Newbury Park, Calif.: Sage, 1990.

Stiles, D. B. "The significant other as a determinant of positive perceptions of group process experience." *Dissertations in Education, Guidance, and Counseling* (1973), 51.

Stinnett, N., and J. Defrain. *Secrets of Strong Families.* New York: Berkley, 1986.

Stogdill, R. M. *Handbook of Leadership: A Survey of Theory and Research.* New York: Free Press, 1974.

Stogdill, R. M. "Group productivity, drive, and cohesiveness." *Organizational Behavior and Human Performance,* 8 (1972), 26–43.

Strauss, S. G. "Getting a clue: The effects of communication media and information distribution on participation and performance in computer-mediated and face-to-face groups." *Small Group Process,* 27, 1 (1996), 115–142.

Straw, R. B., and M. W. Smith. "Potential uses of focus groups in federal policy and program evaluation studies." Special issue: Issues and Applications of Focus Groups. *Qualitative Health Research,* 5, 4 (1995), 412–427.

Stroebe, W.; M. Diehl; and G. Abakounkin. "The illusion of group effectivity." *Personality and Social Psychology Bulletin,* 18, 5 (1992), 643–650.

Stroebe, W., and M. Diehl. "You can't beat good experiments with correctional evidence: Muller, Johnson, and Salas's meta-analytic misinterpretations." *Basic and Applied Social Psychology,* 12, 1 (1991), 25–32.

Stuls, M. H. "Experience and prior probability in a complex decision task." Pt. 1. *Journal of Applied Psychology,* 53 (1969), 112–118.

Sudolsky, M., and R. Nathan. "A replication in questionnaire form of an experiment by Lippitt, Lewin, and White concerning conditions of leadership and social climates in groups." *Cornell Journal of Social Relations,* 6 (1971), 188–196.

Swidler, A. "The ideal society." *American Behavioral Scientist,* 34, 5 (1991), 563–580.

Tajfel, H. *Social Identity and Intergroup Relations.* Cambridge: Cambridge University Press, 1982.

Tang, T.; P. S. Tollison; and H. Whiteside. "Managers and effectiveness in small groups: The case of quality circles." *Journal of Social Psychology,* 131, 3 (1991), 335–344.

Tannen, D. *You Just Don't Understand: Women and Men in Conversation.* New York: Ballantine, 1990.

Tarnow, E. "Like water and vapor: Conformity and independence in the large group." *Behavioral Science,* 41, 2 (1996), 136–150.

Taylor, D. W.; P. C. Berry; and C. H. Block. "Does group participation when using brainstorming facilitate or inhibit creative thinking?" *Administrative Science Quarterly,* 3 (1958), 23–47.

Taylor, D.; J. Doria; and J. Tyler. "Group performance and cohesiveness: An attribution analysis." *Journal of Social Psychology,* 119 (1983), 187–198.

Taylor, W. C. "How to succeed in the business news business." *New York Times* (Jul. 27, 1997).

Terry, D. J., and M. A. Hogg. "Group norms and the attitude–behavior relationship: A role for group identification." *Personality and Social Psychology Bulletin,* 22, 8 (1996), 776–793.

Terry, R. "The leading edge." *Minnesota,* (Jan.-Feb. 1987), 17–22.

Thamis, S., and M. Woods. "A systematic small group approach to creativity and innovation: A case study." *Research and Development Management,* 14, 1 (1984), 25–35.

Thelen, H. *Dynamics of Groups at Work.* Chicago: University of Chicago Press, 1954.

Theodorsen, G. A. "Elements in the progressive development of small groups." *Social Forces,* 31 (1953), 311–320.

Tjosvold, D. "Implications of controversy research for management." *Journal of Management,* 11, 3 (1985), 21–37.

Tjosvold, D., and R. Field, "Effects of social context on consensus and majority vote decision making." *Academy of Management Journal,* 26, 3 (1983), 500–506.

Tjosvold, D.; D. Johnson; and J. Lerner. "Effects of affirmation and acceptance on incorporation of opposing information in problem solving." *Journal of Social Psychology,* 114 (1981), 103–110.

Tolela, M. "Effects of T-group training and cognitive learning on small group effectiveness." Unpublished doctoral dissertation. University of Denver, 1967.

Torrance, E. "Some consequences of power differences on decision making in permanent and temporary three-man groups." In *Small Groups.* Ed. A. Hare, E. Borgatta, and R. Bales. New York: Knopf, 1955.

Trist, E. *The Evolution of Sociotechnical Systems.* Toronto: Ontario Quality of Working Life Centre, 1981.

Tschan, F., and Fanziska. "Communication enhances small group performance if it conforms to task requirements: The concept of ideal communication cycles." *Basic and Applied Social Psychology,* 17, 3 (1995), 371–393.

Tsouderos, J. "Organizational change in terms of a series of selected variables." *American Sociological Review,* 20 (1955), 207–210.

Tuckman, B. W. "Developmental sequence in small groups." *Psychological Bulletin,* 6396 (1965), 384–399.

Tuckman, B. W. "Group composition and group performance of structured and unstructured tasks." *Journal of Experimental Social Psychology,* 3 (Jan. 1967), 25–40.

Tuckman, B. W., and M. A. C. Jensen. "Stages of small-group development revisited." *Group and Organizational Studies,* 2, 4 (1977), 419–427.

Tuckman, J., and I. Lorge. "Individual ability as a determinant of group superiority." *Human Relations,* 15 (1962), 45–52.

Turner, J. "Towards a cognitive redefinition of the social group." *Cahiers de Psychologie Cognitive,* 1 (1981), 93–118.

Turney, J. R. "The cognitive complexity of group members, group structure, and group effectiveness." *Cornell Journal of Social Relations,* 5, 2 (1970), 152–165.

Turquet, P. M. "Leadership: The individual and the group." In *Analysis of Groups.* Ed. G. S. Gibbard, J. J. Hartman, and R. D. Mann. San Francisco: Jossey-Bass, 1978.

Ulman, R. B., and D. W. Abse. "The group psychology of mass madness: Jonestown." *Political Psychology,* 4, 4 (1983), 637–661.

Van de Ven, A. H., and A. L. Delbecq. "Nominal vs. interacting group processes for committee decision-making effectiveness." *Academy of Management Journal,* 14, 2 (1971), 203–212.

Van de ven, A. H., and A. L. Delbecq. "The effectiveness of nominal, delphi, and interacting group decision-making processes." *Academy of Management Journal,* 17 (1974), 605–621.

van de Vliert, E.; M. C. Euwema.; and S. E. Huismans. "Managing conflict with a subordinate or a superior: Effectivenss of conglomerated behavior." *Journal of Applied Psychology,* 80, 2 (1995), 271–281.

VanGundy, A. B. *Managing Group Creativity.* New York: American Management Association, 1984, 16–23.

Verdi, A. F., and S. A. Wheelan. "Developmental patterns in same-sex and mixed-sex groups." *Small Group Research,* 23, 3 (1992), 356–378.

Verplank, W. "The control of the content of conversation." *Journal of Abnormal and Social Psychology,* 51 (1955), 668–675.

Vleeming, R. "Intergroup relations in a simluated society." *Journal of Psychology,* 113 (1983), 81–87.

von Bertalanffy, L. *General Systems Theory.* New York: George Braziller, 1968, 16, 36, 37.

von Bertalanffy, L. *Perspectives on General System Theory.* New York: George Braziller, 1975.

Voytas, R. M. *Some Effects of Various Combinations of Group and Individual Participation in Creative Productivity.* Unpublished doctoral dissertation. University of Maryland, 1967.

Vroom, V. H.; L. D. Grant; and T. S. Cotton. "The consequences of social interaction in group problem solving." *Journal of Organizational Behavior and Human Performance,* 4 (1969), 79–95.

Wagner, H. L.; R. Buck; and M. Winterbotham. "Communication of specific emotions: Gender differences in sending accuracy and communication measures." *Journal of Nonverbal Behavior,* 17, 1 (1993), 29–53.

Waldman, P. "Motivate or alienate? Firms hire gurus to change their 'cultures.'" *Wall Street Journal* (Jul. 24, 1987), 2-19.

Wall, J., and R. R. Callister. "Conflict and its management." *Journal of Management,* 21, 3 (1995), 15–23.

Wall, V. D., and L. L. Nolan. "Perceptions of inequity, satisfaction, and conflict in task-oriented groups." *Human Relations,* 39, 11 (1986), 1033–1051.

Walton, M. "Deming management at work." *Soundview Executive Book Summaries,* 13, 2, Pt. 1 (1990).

Walton, R. "Work innovation in the United States." *Harvard Business Review,* 57 (1979), 88–98.

Wann, D. L.; K. A. Weaver; and S. F. Davis. "The effects of disposition, situation, and setting on ingroup favoritism." *Bulletin of the Psychonomic Society,* 30, 4 (1992), 268–270.

Wanous, J. P., and M. A. Youtz. "Solution diversity and the quality of group decision." *Academy of Management Journal,* 29, 1 (1986), 149–159.

Wanous, J. P.; A. E. Reicheri; and S. D. Malik. "Organizational socialization and group development: Toward an integrative perspective." *Academy of Management Review,* 9, 4 (1984), 670–683.

Ward, L., and J. Wilson. "Motivation and moral development as determinants of behavioral acquiescence and moral action." *Journal of Social Psychology,* 112 (1980), 271–286.

Watanabe, S. "The Japanese quality control circle: Why it works." *International Labour Review,* 130, 1 (1991).

Watson, W. E., and K. Kumar. "Differences in decision making regarding risk-taking: A comparison of culturally diverse and culturally homogeneous task groups." *International Journal of Intercultural Relations,* 16, 1, 53–65.

Watson, C. "Motivational effects of feedback and goal setting on group performance." Paper presented at the 91st annual convention of the American Psychological Association, Anaheim, Calif., Aug. 1983.

Watson, R. I. "Psychology: A prescriptive science." *American Psychologist,* 22 (1967), 435–443.

Watzlawick, P. *How Real Is Real? Confusion, Disinformation, Communication: An Anecdotal Introduction to Communications Theory.* New York: Vintage Books, 1977.

Watzlawick, P. *The Language of Change.* New York: Basic Books, 1978, 117.

Watzlawick, P.; J. H. Beavin; and D. D. Jackson. *Pragmatics of Human Communication: A Study of Interpersonal Patterns, Pathologies, and Paradoxes.* New York: Norton, 1967.

Waung, M.; M. MacNeil; and R. J. Vance. "Reactions to feedback in goal choice and goal change processes." *Journal of Applied Social Psychology,* 25, 15 (1995), 1360–1390.

Weeks, D. *Eight Essential Steps to Conflict Resolution.* New York: Putnam, 1994.

Weingart, L. R., and E. Weldon, "Processes that mediate the relationship between a group goal and group member performance." *Human Performance,* 4, 1 (1991), 33–54.

Weinstein, A. G., and R. L. Holzbach. "Effects of financial inducement on performance under two task structures." *Proceedings of the 80th Annual Convention of the American Psychological Association,* Pt. 1, 7 (1972), 217–218.

Weldon, E., and L. R. Weingart. "Group goals and group performance." *British Journal of Social Psychology,* 32, 4 (1993), 307–334.

Werther, W. B., Jr. "Going in circles with quality circles? Management development implications." *Journal of Management Development,* 2 (1983), 3–18.

Wheelan, S. A., and J. M. Hochberger. "Validation studies of the group development questionnaire." *Small Group Research,* 27, 1 (1996), 143–170.

Wheelan, S. A., and McKeage. "Developmental patterns in small and large groups." *Small Group Research* (Feb. 1993), 60–83.

Wheelan, S., and C. Krasick. "The emergence, transmission, and acceptance of themes in a temporary organization." *Group and Organization Management,* 18, 2 (1993), 237–260.

Wheelan, T. L., and J. D. Unger. *Strategic Management and Business Policy.* 2nd ed. Reading, Mass.: Addison-Wesley, 1986, 4–5.

Wheeless, L., V. Wheeless, and E. Dickson-Markman. "A research note: The relations among social and task perceptions in small groups." *Small Group Behavior,* 13 (1982), 373–384.

White, D. D.; S. E. Blythe; and D. R. Corrigan. "A comparative analysis of three group decision-making techniques applied to organizations in varying phases of physical expansion." In *Management in an Age of Complexity and Change.* Ed. D. Ray, and T. Green. Southern Management Association, Mississippi State University, 1977, 90–95.

White, G. E., and A. N. Thomson. "Anonymized focus groups as a research tool for health professionals." *Qualitative Health Research,* 5, 2 (1995), 256–261.

White, R., and R. Lippitt. "Leader behavior and member reaction in three social climates." In *Group Dynamics.* 3rd ed. Ed. D. Cartwright and A. Zandler. New York: Harper & Row, 1968.

Whitney, K. "Improving task performance: The role of group goals and group efficacy." *Human Performance,* 7, 1 (1994), 55–78.

Wicker, A. W. "Size of church membership and members' support of church behavior settings." *Journal of Personality and Social Psychology,* 13, 3 (1969), 278–288.

Wilden, A. *Systems and Structure: Essays in Communication and Exchange.* 2nd ed. London: Tavistock, 1980.

Wilmer, S., and V. Derlega. "A test of Kelly's ANOVA model." *Small Group Behavior,* 14 (1983), 50–62.

Winthrop, H. "Focus on the human condition: Interpersonal and interactional processes as extinguishers of structured communication." *Journal of Human Relations,* 19, 3 (1971), 418–438.

Wong, C. L.; D. Tjosvold; and F. Lee. "Managing conflict in a diverse work force: A Chinese perspective in North America." *Small Group Research,* 23, 3 (1992), 302–321.

Wood, C., and J. Davidson. "Conflict resolution in the family: A PET evalution study." *Australian Psychologist,* 28, 2 (1993), 100–104.

Woollams, S., and M. Brown. *Transactional Analysis.* Dexter, Mich.: Huron Valley Institute Press, 1978, 118–120.

Worchel, S. "You can go home again: Returning group research to the group context with an eye on developmental issues." Special Issue: Social cognition in small groups. *Small Group Research,* 25, 2 (1994), 205–223.

Worchel, S.; D. Couctant-Sassic; and F. Wong. "Toward a more balanced view of conflict: There is a positive side." In *Conflict Between People and Groups.* Ed. S. Worchel and J. Simpson. Chicago: Nelson-Hall, 1993.

Worchel, S.; D. Countant-Sassic; and M. Grossman. "A developmental approach to group dynamics: A model and illustrative research." In *Group Process and Productivity.* Ed. S. Worchel, W. Wood, and J. Simpson. Newbury Park, Calif.: Sage, 1992.

Worchel, S.; V. V. Andreoli; and R. Folger. "Intergroup cooperation and intergroup attraction: The effect of previous interaction and outcome of combined effort." *Journal of Experimental Social Psychology,* 13, 2 (1977), 131–140.

Wright, T. L., and D. Duncan. "Attraction to group, group cohesiveness, and individual outcome: A study of training groups." *Small Group Behavior,* 17, 4 (1986), 487–492.

Wuthnow, R. *Sharing the Journey: Support Groups and America's New Quest for Community.* New York: Free Press, 1994.

Yalom, I. D. *The Theory and Practice of Group Psychotherapy.* 3rd ed. New York: Basic Books, 1985.

Young, B. L., Jr. "A whole-brained approach to training and development." *Training and Development Journal,* (Oct. 1979), 44–50.

Zald, M. "Organization control structures in five correctional institutions." *American Journal of Sociology,* 38 (1962), 305–345.

Zander, A. "The value of belonging to a group in Japan." *Small Group Behavior,* 14, 1 (1983), 3–14.

Zeigarnik, B. "Uber das behalten von erledigten und unerledigten handlunger." *Psychologische Forschung,* 9 (1927), 1–85.

Zigon, F. J., and J. R. Cannon. "Process end outcomes of group discussions as related to leader behaviors." *Journal of Educational Research,* 67 (1974), 199–201.

Author/Name Index

Subject Index

Reader Activities • Exercises • Individual Experiments

provide multidisciplinary applications

READER ACTIVITY

Below are two activities to help you understand the concept of norms.

1. One way to understand norms is to understand the difference between the "green" you and the "veteran" you. Select one of these situations, and using the situation you selected, list five things you found difficult (or were fearful of) as a new member.
   a. Being a first-year student and being a senior
   b. Being a new employee and being that employee a couple of years later
   c. Being a member and being an officer in the same group

2. As you became experienced in the group or organization, you learned what the real rules are. How do you handle these situations now?

For example, first-year students are very concerned with what to wear and often read magazines on the current college fashions; they are apprehensive about looking phony or too new and are eager to cultivate the "right" look. Seniors ridicule reading such magazines; they know what to wear.

Consider dealing with registration, meeting people, making friends, having a "crowd," picking the right teachers and the right courses, and, in the college situation,

The Concept of Group Norms 109

EXERCISE 1 **Toward Changing Group Norms**

OBJECTIVES

- To understand what is meant by group norms
- To recognize the difficulty in changing norms
- To offer an opportunity to examine and change norms at various levels
- To develop insight into how norms can be changed in organizations

When appropriate, this exercise can be used after a group has been working together for some time. It can be a work team, a task group, an organization, segment of a class group, or a seminar.

ACTION

Phase 1 *The facilitator presents a short lecture on norms—what they are, their influence on a group, and so forth. The material in the first part of the chapter might be the basis for development of such a talk. (Approximately 10 minutes)*

Phase 2 *The groups are asked to examine their norms. They list on paper as many as possible (dates, times, seating arrangements, order of meeting or work, typical behaviors, and so on). (Approximately 20 minutes)*

Phase 3 *The group is then asked to change some of its norms. The facilitator says, "Which norms can be changed?" He or she has the group change them and holds a brief session under the new conditions.*

Typically, groups change superficial norms: they will sit on the table instead of in chairs, they will shout rather than talk to one another, or they will attempt to conduct the session nonverbally. This encourages laughter and a reduction in inhibitions—perhaps even a party atmosphere. (Approximately 20 minutes)

(Usually a break is indicated here.)

Phase 4 *The groups are asked to examine which norms they changed and how relevant the changes were in helping to accomplish their goals. What impeded changing norms? What norms need to be changed? The group then goes into its work session on this basis. (The ensuing discussion is very different from the party atmosphere of the first change; it raises difficult issues and involves members in high-risk behaviors.) An observer might be assigned to watch for behavior that changes norms.*

Exercise 1 161

INDIVIDUAL EXPERIMENT

Choose a group of which you are a member, such as a class, club, sports team, committee, work group, or political organization. Make a list of the norms and informal rules of the group. Include such details as

Dress: formal, informal, or uniform

How people are addressed: title, last or first name, or nickname

Language: jargon, intellectual and formal, informal, or street language

Content of the meetings: serious and always work-related, mostly serious but a lot of socializing, mostly socializing and humorous but work gets done, intimate and personal discussions along with more superficial socializing and work

Process of the meetings: Who talks most and who talks least? Do people tend to agree and keep opposing opinions to themselves? Are different opinions debated openly? Who seems to influence the decisions of the group most often? Are decisions made strictly by the hierarchy of who is in charge or by the group leader? Who informally influences decisions?

Ask two other group members what they think the group's norms are. You will probably have to ask specific questions to help people think about the norms, because they probably have not consciously thought about them or talked about them before. It will be interesting to see what similarities and dissimilarities emerge in your lists.

The Diary of
JAMES C. HAGERTY

EISENHOWER IN MID-COURSE, 1954–1955

The Diary of JAMES C. HAGERTY

EISENHOWER IN MID-COURSE, 1954–1955

EDITED BY

Robert H. Ferrell

Indiana University Press Bloomington

Copyright © 1983 by Indiana University Press
All rights reserved
No part of this book may be reproduced or utilized in any form or by any means, electronic or mechanical, including photocopying and recording, or by any information storage and retrieval system, without permission in writing from the publisher. The Association of American University Presses' Resolution on Permissions constitutes the only exception to this prohibition.

Manufactured in the United States of America

Library of Congress Cataloging in Publication Data

Hagerty, James C. (James Campbell), 1909–1981.
The diary of James C. Hagerty.

Includes bibliographical references and index.
1. United States—Politics and government—1953–1961.
2. Eisenhower, Dwight D. (Dwight David), 1890–1969.
3. Press and politics—United States—History—20th century. 4. Hagerty, James C. (James Campbell), 1909–1981. I. Ferrell, Robert H. II. Title.
E835.H33 1983 973.921 82-48477
1 2 3 4 5 87 86 85 84 83

ISBN 0-253-11625-2

Contents

Acknowledgments

First of all I am indebted to the family of the late press secretary to the President, and especially his son Bruce C. Hagerty, whose encouragement and cheerfulness over the telephone has helped very much indeed. For some time there was a question as to whether James C. Hagerty might have kept an eight-year diary, and Bruce most kindly checked the storage room of his father's apartment. With the assistance of three former members of the White House staff, Lillian H. Brown, Marie McCrum, and William B. Ewald, Jr., I at last obtained the telephone number of Mary Caffrey Stephens, who confirmed what by then appeared almost evident, namely, that Mr. Hagerty kept a diary only for fifteen months.

In the course of telephoning Mrs. Stephens I spoke, to our mutual amusement, with her husband Thomas E. Stephens, appointment secretary to President Eisenhower, who upon learning that the call was from Bloomington, Indiana, remembered a time, years ago in the twenties, when in passing through Valparaiso he had pinch-hit in a vaudeville show and played a straight role to a magician friend; he sat on an orange crate, clad in a bedsheet, and presented himself as The Rajah.

My thanks also to the staff of the Dwight D. Eisenhower Library in Abilene—John Wickman, director; Martin M. Teasley, assistant director; James Leyerzapf, senior archivist; Thomas Branigar, David Haight, and especially Rod Soubers, archivists; and to Hazel Hartman, photo archives technician, who helped with illustrations for the book.

Marcia Gohlke of the Indiana University Law School explained the differences between the Bricker Amendment and the George Amendment, including the Bricker Amendment's "which" clause. William Z. Slany, Historian of the Department of State, set out the vicissitudes of the *Foreign Relations* series at the time of publication of the Yalta Papers.

John M. Hollingsworth drew the maps of the Quemoy-Matsu controvery, in part from military experience in the area at the time, and also from knowledge of the Chinese language. My learned friend Ssu-yu Teng spent several hours with gazetteers, searching out this problem.

George Juergens explained a point about a press secretary of the early seventies.

The staff of the Indiana University Press has been markedly helpful.

Fred J. Curtis of Logansport, Indiana, gave permission for the use of the photograph he took in November 1954 of President and Mrs. Eisenhower leaving the hospital.

My father, Ernest H. Ferrell, Sr., spent several patient days indexing the book. And a thank you, for many reasons, again, to Lila and Carolyn.

Bloomington, Indiana R.H.F.

A Note on the Editing

The temptation of editors is to fuss over prose, and I have saved my comments for headnotes or tailnotes or notes at the end of the book, not for bracketing in the text, and corrected without signs the few manuscript and typescript misspellings and the dropped words or commas, and likewise have changed dashes to commas, and written out abbreviations. Styling amounted to little more than lowering a few capitalizations. Ellipsis points appear in threes or fours, and if there are four points the first is the period of the preceding sentence.

Diary entries until April 13, 1954, were handwritten, in a small diary book in Hagerty's crabbed hand. For the most part I deciphered them after learning the author's peculiarities, such as trailing off of "ing" in a scrawl that looks like a single "g." For translation of words that proved impossible to figure out I am greatly indebted to Mary Caffrey Stephens, Hagerty's White House secretary, who dealt with his handwriting for eight years and knows every nuance.

The diary as published is not in full, and readers deserve an explanation as to why and how selections were made. The original diary, handwritten and typescript, runs to more than two hundred thousand words, and the published diary is around seventy-five thousand. Readers might think this a severe cutting, and wonder about principles of selection—how, in truth, anyone interested in the Eisenhower mid-course years could profit from so severely edited a diary. In actual fact, the cutting did not involve agonizing choices, for many parts of the diary are of slight historical interest. To have published everything would have wearied readers; it would have been an abdication of editorial responsibility. The following principles governed reduction of the diary: issues that no longer affect policy, foreign and domestic, such as raising the minimum wage a few cents; issues in which present-day readers have little interest (fine points of agricultural policy, or fiscal policy); repetitive issues (the Bricker Amendment); summaries of Cabinet discussions, if of routine matters; listings of people or issues that have little or no importance (lists of people present, issues of no interest for reasons mentioned above); office routine, or the routine of trips, of no historical importance. The full diary has been deposited in the Dwight D. Eisenhower Library at Abilene. Heirs of the Hagerty estate have dedicated literary rights to the public. The Director of the Library will arrange mechanical reproduction of parts or all of the diary, upon application, for a minimum fee.

Introduction

The late James C. Hagerty, whose White House diary appears in the pages that follow, may well have been the most successful press secretary ever to serve a President of the United States.

He served longer than any of his predecessors, and any of his successors into the 1980s, and although longevity may not be the best proof of success it surely is indication of ability, especially because he served a President who demanded much of assistants. President Franklin D. Roosevelt created the office of press secretary during the middle years of the New Deal, and gave the task of press relations to Stephen Early, who filled the post from 1939 until 1945 when Jonathan Daniels replaced him. Daniels had hardly taken over when Roosevelt died, and President Harry S. Truman passed the secretaryship to his boyhood friend and high school classmate Charles Ross, who held it until his death in 1950 and was followed by two other men. Then came Hagerty, who stayed through Eisenhower's two terms, from January 1953 until January 1961. After that, no President served two full terms, and press secretaries came and went. The prestige and importance of the office declined markedly and may have reached a low point during the last months of the Nixon administration when after a disagreement the President shoved his secretary, Ron Ziegler, in full view of reporters.

Hagerty was a better man than the others not simply because he served the longest, but because he organized the presidency for the single innovation in press relations that has itself almost changed the nature of the nation's highest office in recent decades, namely, national television. By the time of Eisenhower television had outgrown its initial proportions when it was a flickering exhibition of prizefights and quiz shows and the ever-present—or so it seemed to bored viewers such as the present writer—Arthur Godfrey who made patter and strummed his guitar and had nothing on his mind other than taking up the hours of the day that somehow needed filling. By the time of Eisenhower's inauguration television had, so to speak, come of age. Television people noticed how the Second World War had accustomed the nation to the evening news by radio, and they began to sense that the evening news, and perhaps news at other hours, might come equally, and because it would be visual it might be better, by television. For this grand purpose they conceived the possibility of invading the President's press conferences with their paraphernalia of cables and bright lights and big cameras, and bringing the presidential personality into focus before tens of millions of viewers.

The importance of television for the presidency was not for a moment lost on Hagerty, and as press secretary he adopted the new medium as if he had been brought up with it. For a lifelong newspaperman the introduction of newsreel and television cameras into press conferences in 1955 might have been unnerving and indeed it was to many members of the hitherto sacrosanct White House press corps—newsmen protested vehemently and at length against appearance of the camera people. Hagerty did not mind, for he knew that President Eisenhower's ability in front of an audience was an enormous asset for the Republican administration. For years, especially during the war when the President had been General Eisenhower and was accustomed to dealing with hordes of reporters, Hagerty's chief had been learning how to handle press relations, and had become highly skilled with reporters. He knew as well as any reporter when a question was a real one or a come-on, when it was from the heart or the head, when especially it had a lurking political meaning. And he knew also how to procrastinate during a press conference, and turn his remarks into a series of almost unintelligible, even ungrammatical, utterances. Eisenhower was a master of the public press conference, and Hagerty was proud of his boss's performances. He had every reason to believe that television would bring Eisenhower's personality so securely into the public mind that as the year 1956 approached, with another presidential election, the man who obtained all the free television time was certain of reelection.

Moreover, television could help Eisenhower with the task of unifying the Republican Party. The personality of the wartime general, the postwar chief of staff of the U.S. Army, the president of Columbia University beginning in 1948, Supreme Commander of the forces of the North Atlantic Treaty Organization beginning in

1951—all this had elected Eisenhower to the presidency in 1952. Meanwhile he had made the usual campaign promises. But once the "captive hero," as Marquis Childs later described him, became President, once he entered the Oval Office and began to stand apart from campaign oratory and had to make his own policies—once Eisenhower became President he had to set his course, and that was no easy task when the GOP had been in the wilderness for twenty years. The Republican Party contained two factions, center and right, and the latter may well have been dominant early in 1953. The right-wingers felt keenly the humiliation of the years of exile, and determined that if at all possible they would turn out the New Deal and the Fair Deal. Its leaders were the prominent personalities of the party, and dominated the Senate—by 1953 the senior Senator from Michigan, Arthur H. Vandenberg, was dead of cancer, and Senate leadership lay in the hands of Robert A. Taft of Ohio, no middle-of-the-roader. When Taft himself suddenly died of cancer, Senate leadership fell to William F. Knowland of California who had all of Taft's right-wingism and none of his general sensibility—Knowland was high-strung and given to outbursts, especially to the press, and President Eisenhower found him very difficult. But Knowland's confusions were also those of other right-wingers, and Eisenhower had to organize this group of people, if at all possible, so that they stayed within the Republican Party and did the President's bidding. Hagerty's task as press secretary was in fair part to help the President appeal to right-wing Republicans to follow the moderate Eisenhower policies, and not let national power slip back to the Democrats. The President had to use the organs of public relations, especially television, to secure his own position within the party, to make himself so attractive to voters that the GOP right-wingers would have to do what he asked.

Hagerty's job of assisting the President in remaking the Republican Party through White House public relations brings to mind a third aspect of the secretary's work that set off his tenure from that of predecessors and successors. In addition to the full eight years that he served Eisenhower, and his joyous welcoming of television to the White House, Hagerty quickly managed one accomplishment almost effortlessly. A remarkable closeness soon became evident between press secretary and President. Hagerty had not known Eisenhower well before the campaign of 1952, but he became

Eisenhower's confidant. If the President had a single close friend, a man whom he could trust, it was Hagerty. The President instinctively was attracted, and an almost father-and-son relationship developed, A near generation separated the two men, nineteen years, and when Eisenhower opened an explanation to Hagerty with an affectionate "Jim, my boy . . ." there was more than just words. The President trusted Hagerty to keep political secrets. No leaks ever occurred—unlike the President's experiences with Congressmen, Cabinet members, sometimes with his own assistants in the White House executive office. Moreover, the press secretary's political judgment was good, for Hagerty had served as press secretary to Governor Thomas E. Dewey of New York. Eisenhower could ask Hagerty for political hunches, and became accustomed to trying out political ideas on Hagerty.

The President trusted Hagerty far more than he might have trusted the usual press secretary, and Hagerty took on special assignments, such as dealing with the junior Senator from Wisconsin, Joseph R. McCarthy. In the crisis of McCarthy's relations with the administration in 1954, Hagerty became the President's go-between with the Senate. To change the figure, the press secretary helped orchestrate the downfall of McCarthy, through dealing with individual Senators as well as putting out press releases or talking to reporters in such a way that everything McCarthy did or insinuated was turned against him. Getting the Senate to censure McCarthy was no easy task, for Republican leadership in the Upper House was weak and unreliable. Knowland was no tower of strength, and was a right-winger, and the other prominent Republican Senators were conservatives—H. Styles Bridges of New Hampshire and Eugene F. Millikin of Colorado. Hagerty pacified them, encouraged the moderates, and helped bring McCarthy down, which was what both he and his boss wanted.

The great pity about the Hagerty White House diary is that it is fragmentary—it covers two years, and for those years, 1954 and 1955, it is partial. How wonderful if Hagerty had started his diary in January 1953 and continued to the end. Perhaps, however, that would have been too much to have asked of a busy man. At the outset of the Eisenhower era the press secretary may have been too busy to have kept a diary. When he started in January 1954, perhaps as a result of a New Year's resolution, he wrote everything in a scrawl not easy to read but in so much detail that it must have taken a half-hour each day. When he did this writing is difficult to say, presumably in evenings, for the mornings ("In at 8:15 . . .", entries begin) were too busy; the press secretary could not have brushed off callers, nor handled his work with the President of the United States (himself at his desk usually at 8:30, sometimes earlier), had it been necessary to begin each day by writing in a diary. Nor could he have kept a diary by taking out a pen and writing between appointments and telephone calls of reporters. In mid-April 1954 the secretary realized that the better way to handle his diary was to dictate it to his efficient secretary Mary Caffrey (later Mary Caffrey Stephens, wife of the President's appointment secretary, Thomas E. Stephens). Miss Caffrey took dictation as fast as Hagerty talked, and because she knew the personalities not merely in the White House but the Cabinet and Senate and House of Representatives, Hagerty did not have to spell names or reread what he dictated so as to sort out garbles. The team of Hagerty as dictator of diary entries and Mary Caffrey as taker-downer was perfect, and entries ran for pages in Mary's impeccable single-spaced pica typescript.

Once Hagerty dictated diary entries at the end of each day, the work of putting memory into statement was easy. The press secretary took reportorial notes, a scribbled shorthand, of Cabinet meetings and congressional leaders' meetings and colloquies with the President (these of course after he got out of the Oval Office), and he dictated from the scribblings. But he continued the diary barely into 1956; he dictated four inconsequential entries for the last week of January 1956, and from that time onward the diary stopped. Hagerty never told Mary Caffrey why.

President Eisenhower was a diarist* and one might have hoped for a sort of diary division of labor, whereby the press secretary recounted day-by-day happenings and the President dealt with the large issues. Instead, neither man seems to have told the other he was keeping a diary. Both press secretary and President concentrated their diaries in the same period, the first term. The Hagerty diary deals with 1954 and 1955. The Eisenhower diary is full for the opening of the administration in 1953, and thins out in the second term. In the case of the President the reason for less attention to the diary may have related to illness—the heart attack in 1955, ileitis in 1956, the stroke in 1957.

---

*Robert H. Ferrell, ed., *The Eisenhower Diaries* (New York, 1981).

One can only speculate on what might have been. So few holders of the nation's highest office have kept diaries—John Quincy Adams, James K. Polk, Rutherford B. Hayes, James A. Garfield, and in the present century Truman, Eisenhower, Richard M. Nixon, and Jimmy Carter (the Nixon and Carter diaries remain unknowns, the latter unpublished, the former still on tape in the National Archives). Next to diary-keeping by the President the best record would be a diary by a righthand man, and for President Eisenhower that man was Hagerty. If only Hagerty had kept up his dictation. One hardly dares think of the thousands of feet of presidential files the future researcher must traverse to capture this or that event or decision of the Eisenhower administration, happenings that the President or Hagerty could have epitomized in a few words.

James Campbell Hagerty was born on May 9, 1909, the son of James A. Hagerty, who for many years was chief political correspondent for the *New York Times.* The family moved to New York City from Plattsburg when he was three years old, and young Hagerty attended grade school in the Bronx and the Evander Childs High School before enrolling at Blair Academy in Blairstown, New Jersey. Upon graduation in 1928, he went to work on the New York Stock Exchange. The market crash sent him back to school and he received a B.A. from Columbia University in 1934. During his college years he became campus correspondent for the *New York Times,* and joined the paper after graduation. He worked for the *Times* as a member of the city staff and then as legislative correspondent and deputy bureau chief in Albany, resigning in 1943 to become executive assistant and press secretary to Governor Dewey. He handled press relations during Dewey's two campaigns for the presidency in 1944 and 1948. When General Eisenhower ran for the presidency in 1952, it was with Hagerty as spokesman and press adviser, which led to Hagerty's appointment as press secretary to the President beginning in January 1953. After the White House years Hagerty joined the American Broadcasting Companies as vice president for news, special events, and public affairs, and later was vice president for corporate relations. He retired from ABC in 1975 after suffering a stroke, and lived in retirement in Bronxville with his wife, the former Marjorie Lucas, until his death from heart failure on April 11, 1981, at the age of seventy-one.

The Diary of JAMES C. HAGERTY

EISENHOWER IN MID-COURSE, 1954–1955

In at 8 AM – Murray took press briefing at staff meeting – Pres. reworked statement over night – Morgan and I went over it with him in his office – also set up question on Dulles-McLeod-McCarthy with answer from Pres. that "appointment of administrative positions within a department, responsibility of Secretary – and no one else" – 10 A.M. briefing included 2,200; Indo-China; Mitchell letter on FEPC; Benson letter to railway referee; taxes and unemployment.

At press conference Pres. started off with short statement on House story – then read statement – went well with some reporters – New Dealers and fuzzy boys disappointed – wanted Pres. to call McCarthy names, crack him over head, etc – typical of reaction from these quarters was Reston in NY Times – "turning the other cheek" – and Doris Fleeson – "McCarthy can say Pres. didn't lay a glove on him" — nuts. All these people want is to have Pres. get down in gutter with Joe – personally think Pres. statement strong and dignified –

Particularly in light of Joe's intemperate rejoinder where he said in effect he'll go right on bullying etc – now it's up to our leaders in Congress – if they take the ball and run with it – if they force change in rules, then they can come out ahead – if they haven't got the guts, then, with Sen. Potter, will have to do it with Dem votes on Joe's Committee and let Dems take the credit. – Ferguson wobbly all around on this & so is Knowland, Millikin and Saltonstall – they have a chance now to make it good – my bet is they'll kick it over

January 1954

When the Eisenhower administration took office in January 1953 the moment was exhilarating beyond description, for after twenty long years the party at last was back in power. The national scene was far different than during the bleak last days of President Herbert Hoover early in 1933, and that fact too gave confidence. Businessmen, who for the most part were Republican, had proved their organizing abilities during the Second World War, and in the postwar years despite setbacks—bursts of inflation, and occasional labor troubles–had gone from triumph to triumph. The scene in 1953 was good, as the Eisenhower people came into the White House. And by early 1954 everything had become routine. A few problems had appeared, but they were not serious. The most pressing international difficulty, the Korean War, came to an end with the armistice of July 1953. Domestically all was rosy. Over the New Year's holiday the President and his assistants rested up in Georgia where the nation's chief executive enjoyed the course at the Augusta National Golf Club.

Friday, January 1, 1954

In Augusta. Worked on State of Union message at office at National. Adams, Lodge, Dodge, Martin, Harlow, Morgan, Jessup.[1] President worked in morning. Pictures at 8:00 A.M. Group rewrote until 1:30 A.M.

President golfed in P.M. Returned to Bon Air for press conference 1:00 P.M. and 6:00 P.M. Not much news.

• • • •

Saturday, January 2, 1954

In Augusta, Cutler met President at 8:30–9:30 for NSC briefing.[1] Speech group met at 9:30.

President got off definition of intelligence—"man who takes too many words to tell too many things he doesn't know."

Group worked 9:30 to 12:00. Returned to Washington 5:20 P.M.

Press conference at Bon Air. Gave statement I suggest to forestall stories on lack of detailed recommendations in State of Union message. Statement said additional messages would be going up to Congress on agriculture, Taft-Hartley, tax programs, health and production, and housing. Well received. Good stories except Belair in *New York Times* who had lousy piece on comparison of press treatment by FDR and President at Warm Springs and Augusta. Wants us to take press to bed.

• • • •

Sunday, January 3, 1954

In Augusta. Church at 11:15. Methodist. President of Augusta Ministerial Association.

Nothing doing in day. Left Bon Air at 4:00 P.M. President and Mrs. Ike, Mrs. Doud, Bill Robinson, Cliff Roberts, Douglas Casey arrived at airport 5:15 P.M.[1] Takeoff 5:20. President played bridge on way up. In good spirits. Took photos of crowds and photographers on leaving.

Arrived Washington MATS[2] 7:20 P.M. Home 8:15 P.M. Tired and bed early.

Accompanying the President on trips had its enjoyable moments, but Hagerty found life easier in his suite in the west wing of the White House, next to the Oval Office, where he could go in and out of the President's office and get decisions, and where frequently the President asked his advice on some problem. It was an easy arrangement, much assisted because the President kept regular hours, as he had been accustomed to do through long years in the military. Routines were punctuated by Cabinet meetings and sessions with GOP leaders of the Senate and House, and regular press conferences. There were frequent presidential radio and TV appearances.

Monday, January 4, 1954

Busy day. Meeting with Cabinet and GOP leaders on message in Cabinet room starting 8:30 A.M. Lasting until 1:00 P.M. Reviewed message. All seemed to go all right. Dan Reed objected to tax sections. Left to work out with Humphrey.[1]

T.V.-radio chat, 9:30–9:45 P.M. Montgomery handling; though Cabot tried to get in way.[2] Messed up talk, insisting on changing simple words to $2 ones. Big discussion on "no depression." Cabot argues not politically wise. Won out over my and Moore's objections.[3] Dave Lawrence panned points Cabot put in following day, saying not simple English.[4] Couldn't agree more.

Dress rehearsal 3:00 P.M. President using teleprompter, not cards, went fine. Talked him into doing same that night.

Used makeup for night. CBS gal did good job. So did President. After speech McCann, Montgomery, Cabot, Marge and self invited upstairs.[5] Ike in fine spirits. Talked about campaign, convention. Said he made up mind to run because he feared Taft wing of GOP and Truman incompetence. Said man who put most pressure on him was Jim Duff.[6]

White House staff members held meetings to be sure there were no loose ends of administration. The President demanded close staff work through his "chief of staff," former Governor Sherman Adams of New Hampshire, a scion of the famous New England family. Once in a while, as on the morning of January 5, the President met with members of Congress from both sides of the aisle, in bipartisan conference.

Tuesday, January 5, 1954

8:30 A.M. Staff meeting. Authorized timetable for subsequent messages to Congress as well as Red Cross and the Lincoln Day TV films.

10:30 A.M. Bipartisan congressional leaders meeting Cabinet room. Dulles, Stassen, and Wilson presentation.[1] Dulles and Stassen fine, Wilson as usual argumentative. Ike magnificent. Main Democratic questioning on why two divisions out of Korea, were we cutting back too much on defense plans and armed services.

Ike told them if Reds renew in Korea would "hit them with everything we got," including industrial plants in Manchuria. Said withdrawal of two divisions sign of strength, not weakness, of new weapons and air power.

On defense, Ike said we had no use for needless standing armies—"bottle washers and table waiters"—needed stronger trained armies, 3,000,000 in armed services, counting on reserves for buildup. In this age, if attack comes, retaliation by air hard. Have weapons and planes to do it. This can cut down ground forces.

Ike concluded by saying there were certain things in which all must as Americans agree—foreign policy and security. Hoped to have other such meetings and would want Democrats to come to see him on these problems. Good response.

Issued short statement on conference. Everybody agreed not to talk. Most kept word, except UP story on hitting Reds—suspect Wiley or Bridges.[2]

• • • •

Wednesday, January 6, 1954

8:00 A.M. Picked up President at White House at 7:45. Adams and I joined him for church services at National Presbyterian Church opening Congress. President considerably annoyed with Elson. . . .

In the years before the presidency Eisenhower never had joined a church, though Mrs. Eisenhower had been a Presbyterian since girlhood. He refused to join a church until after the election. The minister of Eisenhower's church, the National Presbyterian, was the Reverend Dr. Edward L.R. Elson.

Thursday, January 7, 1954

. . . Speech at 12:30. Montgomery changing height of rostrum so TV cameras don't just get top of Ike's head. Can't do much with lighting. Montgomery very good and easy to work with.

Daily News had "GOP senator" on bombing China if Korea resumes. Suspect Bridges.

President buzzed for me in middle of 10:30 press conference. Said he and Dulles wanted to insert paragraph on Bricker Amendment. Told him it would emphasize amendment. He said that's what he wanted. Was going to call Knowland. Agreed to give me paragraph if decided to put it in; if not, then I could put it out in answer to press? Later decided not to put it out. . . .

The so-called Bricker Amendment to the US Constitution was proposed by Senator John W. Bricker (Rep.) of Ohio, a conservative who believed that there was large danger in the possibility that a President might attempt to legislate by treaty. Bricker wanted treaties and executive agreements to deal only with international concerns, by which he meant matters that in no way affected issues within the United States. If a treaty or agreement did so, he maintained, it could be only after passage of domestic legislation. The Senator undoubtedly had in mind the international agreements of the late President Roosevelt, and upon taking office President Eisenhower sought to reassure him that a Republican President could be trusted. The Senator from Ohio was not sure of the liberal Eisenhower and insisted upon the letter of his proposed amendment.

Friday, January 8, 1954

In at 8:15. Press reaction to message good in general. Some confusion about Red citizenship revoke . . .

Noon—birthday party for Adams in Cabinet room. Complete surprise. Ike present and had chance to talk to him on spelling out citizenship thing. "I'm 'way ahead of you," he said, adding had asked Brownell for memo.[1] "Let 'em worry for awhile," meaning Reds. When I told him papers were concerned, he said call up AG and find out when getting it. Dodge came in. "Come in, Joe, we need more money," laughed President. Also talked to Martin and self about Bricker Amendment. Said "will fight to last ditch" any amendment seeking to usurp or cancel out presidential powers. ? [question mark in original] attempt to have states affirm treaties. . . .

2:45 P.M. Dulles meeting Zaroubin at State on Monday.[2] British have agreed to U.S.-Red bilateral talks on procedure.

Strauss called to tell about H-bomb Pacific test. Moving 10,000 troops and technical men to Pacific. Secret, no press. Simple announcement, saying only movement under way. Dulles called after meeting with Zaroubin. Brief announcement to effect they had met. Zaroubin promised to get in touch with Molotov with some suggestions so that he (Z) could talk further at Berlin meeting—preliminary discussion which must be kept secret. Agreed to this procedure for sake of possible working out with Reds of some form of arrangement on Tuesday UN.

The Atomic Energy Commission, of which Rear Admiral Lewis L. Strauss was chairman, was preparing a momentous test of a hydrogen device in the Pacific, in the megaton range, on the island of Bikini. The test came off on March 1, and proved an extraordinary success. In 1952 the United States had exploded a hydrogen device, but the package, the device, was so large that the wartime director of the Los Alamos nuclear weapons laboratory, the physicist J. Robert Oppenheimer, joked that it was so heavy it would have to be carried to its target in an oxcart. The task of American scientists was to miniaturize the device so that it could be carried by planes and by missiles of reasonable size. The test of March 1 hence was a crucial operation. It was indeed so much of a success that the United States abandoned its programs to produce large-thrust missiles, which no longer were necessary, and the result was that the Soviet Union sent up Sputnik in 1957, a satellite that startled people everywhere–though not officials of the Eisenhower administration who knew that Sputnik was a stunt, proof that the USSR had continued its large-thrust missile program because it was unable to miniaturize its H-bombs.

Monday, January 11, 1954

In at 7:45 A.M. Snow tied up town—four inches! . . .

Leaders meeting—Vice President, Knowland, Millikin, Saltonstall, Speaker, Arends, Halleck, Young, Brownell, Hall, Adams, Persons, etc.[1]

1. Patronage discussion. Need for each department to have patronage assistant. State, Defense and Agriculture still lacking. President agreed to bring up at next Cabinet meeting.

2. Bricker Amendment. President said if "which clause" stays in, "I'll go into every state to fight it." Can't abrogate power for foreign affairs conduct. Brownell reported Bricker, in phone call from Columbus Saturday, said had to back "which" clause. President said, "No president or secretary of state, sitting down with Malenkov or Molotov, can operate for forty-nine governments.[2] Only one United States of America in foreign affairs. Not going to surrender." Nixon, "basic difference." "Grave doubts" can be settled. Millikin, Saltonstall urge compromise. President "willing to go as far as possible, but no compromise with principle. Trustee for government and can't put future people in position where they can't act." Said Frank Holeman trying "made up his mind he's going to save United States from Eleanor Roosevelt, that's what he's doing."[3] . . .

The "which" clause of Senator Bricker's proposed amendment was a novelty to meet objections of members of the Senate, and provided that a treaty would not be effective as internal law except through legislation "which" would have been valid in the absence of a treaty.

Tuesday, January 12, 1954

In at 8:00 A.M. Decided to have press conference Wednesday. Went with President to Advertising Council opening at Red Cross. On way back discussed with him Korea situation, particularly as affected January 22 with release of POWs. Said everything possible had been done. Gave orders to military to carry it out and protect prisoners. Reports from Korea, ours and neutral, don't indicate trouble, but ready for any emergency. Will fight if any interference.

Dulles speech for night cleared with President. In effect, serve notice to Communists we'll counter revival of hostilities (anywhere) with instant retaliation, putting them on notice we won't stand for any funny business. . . .

• • • •

Thursday, January 14, 1954

In at 8:00 A.M. Release social security message at 8:30 A.M. Bricker Amendment fight broke open this morning. Bricker in interview for *Chicago Tribune, Times-Union* challenged Ike, stuck with "which" clause and called for Senate vote.[1] President had breakfast with Dulles and Brownell, agreed to fight up and down country. After breakfast, met in office with Adams, Martin and Persons and self; President mad and ready to go . . . President said "going to call names—say this was stupid, blind violation of Constitution by stupid, blind isolationists." . . .

• • • •

Monday, January 18, 1954

In at 8:10. Health message released for noon at 8:30 A.M. Legislative meeting . . .

1. Discussion of minimum wage. Halleck expressed doubts any wage increase could be passed at this session. President responded "labor leaders become stronger political leaders" if nothing done.

Mitchell recommended increase from 75 to 85 cents as well as increased coverage.[1] Nixon said South and rural areas would object, particularly if retail trades covered in, oppose present $1.25 bill. Knowland said 75–85 no objection. Left for further study Mitchell and committee chairmen. GOP reaction by leaders typical.

2. Bricker Amendment. Knowland turned up with substitute wording with "which" clause out. All agreed it was good and restated principle Constitution should not be infringed by treaty. "Button up gap in Constitution." Dulles said Senators who originally signed up for BA did so before "which" clause written in, so did not feel they would have to support it. President said Democrats told him they wanted "less than BA." Halleck said if B would take Knowland's words, let him introduce. All agreed. President read speech he had prepared for TV against BA. Federation "made country a laughing stock." "Can't afford making U.S. representatives mere pageant for forty-nine governments." "Futility of discarded Federation." Leaders not anxious to have President go on air. . . .

Montgomery and Moore and I went in at 2:15 to go over with President his Lincoln Day film—runs nine minutes. President asked us to "get . . ." for speech. In good spirits. Watched film taken in 1919 at a time when President was lieutenant colonel with motor caravan which took sixty days to go across country. When asked him his rank then, he laughed and said: "They used to call me the youngest lieutenant colonel. Hell, now younger men are generals." . . .

• • • •

Tuesday, January 19, 1954

In at 8:20. Not much doing today. Bricker broke with us on his amendment. Wouldn't accept our compromise. Sticking on "which" clause. Looks like good fight coming up. Must get over to public 49–1 idea. Good reaction to my campaign by columnists, editorials, and cartoons.

Senator Dworshak of Idaho screwed up Hawaii, by voting in committee to put Alaska statehood on as rider. Persons considerably disturbed. Looks to me like plot on part of our right-wing boys. Welker attacks Democrats; Dworshak does this. Bricker open upon his amendment. What's next. If have fight let's get on with it.

• • • •

Wednesday, January 20, 1954

First anniversary of presidential inauguration. . . .

Quotes at Cabinet meeting . . .

On patronage. President: "nothing has dogged or worried me as much as this patronage business, Ready to do anything ethical. Prefer good Republicans to good Democrats, but not going to break laws or destroy civil service."

On GOP who oppose us. President: "see no reason getting anyone elected who is trying to doublecross us." "Look upon him as prodigal son and kill fatted calf for him if he changes—if not, I have need for my own beef." . . .

• • • •

Friday, January 22, 1954

Snowstorm. In at 8:35 A.M.

CIA reported in morning air encounter off west coast of Korea, north of parallel. 16 F-86s escorting photo bomber, B-45, ran into "regiment" of 35 Migs on patrol. One Mig shot down. Pilot bailed out. When Snyder told President he said "This is something we don't want to know anything about. Let Reds announce it if they want." . . . [1]

Later in day in with President again on ticker story Bricker had sent letter to all Senators saying President giving "wide circulation to erroneous charges" in attacking "which" clause. "To hell with him," President said. Asked me to show story to Milton. Milton and I had long talk on need of publicizing our side of story in simple terms. . . . We're picking up votes against BA. Bush of Connecticut came out vs. it today. Sure we can beat isolationists on it. Persons working on problem. Plan is to get bipartisan sponsorship of substitute amendment and report it out. Senator George probably will help. Democrats want some credit for "saving the Constitution" and we'll give them that.[2]

• • • •

Saturday, January 23, 1954

In at 8:30 A.M. Winchell called last night to check story John and Barbara E on way with another baby.[1] Promised to check with Mamie.

Worked on draft of President's speech on Bricker Amendment. Good speech. Uses Baruch Plan as example of how states could stop inspection agreements of any atomic control plan. Cut it down some and put different ending on it. President accepted it. Hope he gives it, although in talking it over with him he said, "Bricker made big mistake in attacking me yesterday. Now if he loses amendment, I'm responsible for defeating it." . . .

• • • •

Monday, January 25, 1954

. . . Presidential quotes. On Yalta. "Nothing could have stopped Yalta. It was a meeting of three commanders-in-chief during war, but our c-in-c didn't have to be so indiscreet and crazy."

"I asked Roosevelt in Egypt if he had the right to make decisions on subjects that should properly be in the peace treaty and he replied, rather annoyed, 'Why yes—eh yes!' "

Millikin: "No one ever got to Heaven in one jump." President: "There's a lot of stairs."

Nixon on Bricker substitute. "As in any battle, you need second line of retreat." President: "No, Dick, you need two to go ahead, only one to retreat."

President on BA. "Let's win this once and for all. Let's not have it coming up every year."

President said he had been reading Federalist Paper No. 15.

President on Alaska. "It is one of the great tragedies to make Alaska a state at this time. It's really a national defense area. It's crazy to try to make it a state." . . .

• • • •

Thursday, January 28, 1954

. . . Our GOP boys on Hill still trying to compromise with Bricker's isolationists. George and Democrats now got jump on them with simple George Amendment. Ferguson, Millikin scared to death of fight.[1] Keep backing off as usual. Knowland inept in handling it. Fine mess, all of our own, because our people haven't got the guts to lick BA once and for all and then pass substitute Knowland

Amendment. Best they can do now is bipartisan approach on compromise, giving Democrats credit for saving Constitution. Now have to confer with George, in addition to Bricker. How dumb can we get? President getting really fed up with these tactics. . . .

February 1954

Monday, February 1, 1954

In at 8:10 A.M. Defense Department leaking like sieve. Adams called Wilson and raised hell on three leaks. (1) Defense order ending segregation at military schools which was supposed to have been held for President's press conference, but which was put out as Defense victory over Hobby's outfit. (2) Air Force announcement of Mig shot down ten days ago by US planes over China Sea. This was "top secret." (3) Pearson's column on technical advisers to Indochina. Wilson supposed to call me for help. Still think best way is to fire a general and admiral from Pentagon and send them to Greenland. . . .[1]

Meeting quotes. Ike, on postal employees. "Can't give way to every damn pressure group that bombards Congress. That's New Deal stuff." . . .

Ike, on Bricker A. "God, I'm getting so tired of the name. The time it's consumed."

On . . . case and Supreme Court, "Need wiser court—not Douglas writing decisions."

On BA. "Let's take the political side. You have all been yelping we must protect the Constitution. So have I. So what do we try to do. We try to change it. We are certain about what the Constitution does. That alarms me." . . .

In discussion with President we agreed that leaders could have defeated BA if they hadn't stalled so long over compromise. "Weak, awful weak," President said. Also said "I'm through with Bricker in any case." . . .

He seemed fully aware that many members of Congress would like to limit presidential powers, but added "as far as I know this is the first time anyone has tried to do it by amending the Constitution." Pointed out that Spanish bases would have been impossible to obtain under Congress sanction. Had to be done by executive action. "Only way to get it done was that way for good of country."

Brownell stayed with President for hour after. Decision made! Leaders going to submit amendment without executive agreement clause. President to write letter. Decision taken. Going to fight. Hurrah! . . .

• • • •

Tuesday, February 2, 1954

. . . President called me in at 2:30 and he and I went over proposed letter. Outlines his objections . . . and flatly says won't compromise with any plan to change Constitution. President: "Leaders admitted yesterday that they were trying to cut down on my powers through executive agreement plan." President quite exercised, strode around office while talking. Has pretty low opinion of GOP leadership right now. I urged him to put out letter from WH, or at press conference tomorrow, to get back our initiative again. Said "if it's true that when you die the things that bothered you most are engraved on your skull, I am sure I'll have there the mud and dirt of France during invasion and the name of Senator Bricker." President determined not to give in on this principle. Said "If our leaders had any guts this would all have been over last week." . . .

• • • •

Thursday, February 4, 1954

Prayer breakfast at Mayflower. President arrived at 8:20. Chief Justice, Veep and others joined. Conrad Hilton, the host, played breakfast for all it's worth. Carlson as usual fell in trap, praising Hilton as great Christian "who fell on his knees and prayed when he opened his new hotel in Madrid."[1] What a laugh. . . .

• • • •

Friday, February 5, 1954

In at 8:15 A.M. Cabinet meeting. (1) Public works program. President stressed need of getting real public works program ready. "Level of preparatory work up" so that if needed it could be used immediately to put people back to work. "If we don't move rapidly, we could be in terrible trouble. Could be wasteful, back to raking leaves." Urged road, school, thruway programs "to improve welfare of nation." . . .

Cabinet quotes. Nixon on security. "Under old loyalty program our friend, Hiss, would have been loyal. Under our program we could get rid of him."

President to Wilson on need for quick survey of employees. "Don't tell me you can't do it in Defense. I invented the system. You can ask for fat, bald-headed majors and they'll come tumbling out of the IBM machines." . . .

The above entry is the first reference to what became the interstate highway program.

Monday, February 8, 1954

. . . Saltonstall raised question about technicians to Indochina. President explained reasons carefully to Salty. Said he was "frightened about getting ground forces tied up in Indochina" and that we went through subterfuge of attaching them to MAAG.[1] Put them in back areas where couldn't get in a fight, to train French and Vietnamese. Said 200 would be there until June 15 and he would take them out at that date. Cut back from original French request for 400 men.

Leaders meeting quotes. Ike on Indochina technicians. "Don't think I like to send them there, but after all, we can go into Iran, Korea, Formosa, and Indochina with these technicians and not run a little bit of a risk. But we can't get anywhere in Asia by just sitting here in Washington and doing nothing. My God, we must not lose Asia. We've got to look the thing right in the face."

Halleck on pinks and New Dealers in regional offices. "They have loaded those offices with nits, bedbugs, and lice."

Ike on Bricker Amendment. "This Bricker business is now getting in the wisecrack stage. They are now saying that a U.S. Senator is engaged in tearing down the Constitution brick by brick by bricker."

Ike on Chiang. "I'd like to see Chiang's troops used in Indochina. But the political risk of Chinese Red moves would then be too great. We wanted to use them in Korea, but Rhee wouldn't have anything to do with them." . . .

The First Indochina War between the French and the Vietminh (Vietnamese Communist) forces of Ho Chi Minh began in 1946 when the French expelled

Ho's native government from Hanoi. Just before the Korean War the United States agreed to support the French forces in Indochina, in an arrangement that the Secretary of State of the time, Dean Acheson, considered blackmail, for the French insisted on arms support in Indochina as the price of their participation in NATO. Outbreak of the Korean War reinforced this decision, by giving it a kind of local logic—when the United States was battling Communism in Korea, it seemed sensible to fight it, through arms support of the French, in Indochina. By early 1954 events were moving downward in Indochina, French forces in deep trouble, and the Eisenhower administration tried to bolster them through sending technicians to give instruction in use of American weapons.

Tuesday, February 9, 1954

. . . Agriculture Department in soup again. Continued to publish "Dishwashing" pamphlet that Ike lambasted in campaign as "worthless." Ordered 15,000 more copies last July. Told them to lose 10,000 they still have and not to order any more. What dopes over in Agriculture.

Home early, and to bed.

• • • •

Wednesday, February 10, 1954

. . . At press conference, political questions foremost. . . . On way back President said, "You know that's what I mean when I say press conferences are really a waste of time. All these reporters are interested in is some cheap political fight. It's too serious a time to have that sort of stuff as the major problems of our times. What a life."

To WH this evening for a stag dinner with President. . . .

The President enjoyed the out-of-doors, and when he received an invitation from Secretary of the Treasury George M. Humphrey to visit Humphrey's estate in Thomasville, Georgia, to do a little game shooting, Eisenhower immediately accepted.

Friday, February 12, 1954

In at 8:15. President left for Lincoln Memorial at 10:55. Airport at 11:20. Airborne for Spence at 11:30. Arrived 2:30 P.M. Honors from training cadets of ten nations. Drove forty miles to Thomasville. Pleasantly surprised at town. Modern hotel and good golf course. President happy as boy. Arrived Humphrey's at 3:30. President dressed and ready to go out in fields at 3:40. Carried two guns. One 20 gauge, other 4–10 over-and-under. Kidded wire men briefly and then out in fields.

Back to hotel. Draper and I played nine holes in P.M., and stayed at hotel in evening.[1]

• • • •

Saturday, February 13, 1954

Out to Humphrey plantation for breakfast at 7:30 A.M.! President bubbling over with enthusiasm. This sort of stuff really does President good. Told good story about old general in army, "Shooting Jim," who drooled when talking to Ike as 1st Lt., and how Ike and others used to bet quarters, "a lot of money to us then," on whether drool would fall on left or right side of "Shooting Jim's" jacket. Also story of two officers, "Wonder what's become of the old guys who used to run the army?" "Old guys, we're them." . . .

• • • •

Sunday, February 14, 1954

Out to plantation at 8:30 A.M. President alone in room when I came in. Talked about hunting. President really in good shape. . . .

The President returned to Washington that Sunday afternoon.

Monday, February 15, 1954

In at 8:20. Leaders meeting. . . .

On Indochina, President said French wanted 25 planes and 400 technicians. Got 10 and 200, with warning 200 would be out of Indochina by June 15. Military situation not as bad as reported. Vietminh dispersing forces with political attacks, and forcing French to likewise disperse, but situation fairly favorable to French.

Leaders quotes. Ike on being told Wayne Morse went down to

Texas to attack Lyndon Johnson as not being a liberal. "Hell, Lyndon should pay him to come back and stay down there."

Ike on Warren nomination. "Is Senator Langer dragging his feet on this?[1] If he is, I'll have one of my slickers go down and see him. Damn it, he's casting grave doubts on the integrity of one of the greatest statesmen given to the Supreme Court in our times." . . .

On Wednesday afternoon, February 17, the President and Mrs. Eisenhower with Mrs. Eisenhower's mother, Mrs. Elivera Doud, left Washington by plane for Palm Springs, California, where they stayed at the Smoke Tree Ranch of a California bakery executive, Paul E. Helms.

Thursday, February 18, 1954

At Palm Springs. Palm Springs is quite a place. Beautiful. . . .

• • • •

Saturday, February 20, 1954

At Palm Springs. President broke cap off tooth. Had it fixed at local dentist, Dr. C.A. Purcell. AP, from Syracuse, flashed "President Eisenhower died tonight of a heart attack at Palm Springs." Someone fooling around with teletype. Move on open state wire. Caused some hell, but AP killed it two minutes later. Called AP New York offices for explanation and to demand a full report. . . .

• • • •

Tuesday, February 23, 1954

At Palm Springs. Before leaving had a flareup when Ray Scherer of NBC asked me at pool about "attempted assassination" of President. On checking found two drunks called at Smoke Tree in old car. Secret Service found 22 rifle in back. Arrested by Palm Springs police for vagrancy. Gave it out immediately in order to kill wild stories.

Left Palm Springs 8:30 P.M. and arrived MATS 7:30 A.M.

• • • •

Wednesday, February 24, 1954

Back in White House at 8:00 A.M. after 7:30 A.M. arrival at MATS. Busy schedule today. Legislative leaders meeting at 8:30 A.M. . . .

Quotes. Ike on pay raises. "Personally, I'm flatly opposed to any cross-the-board raise. All we would be doing would be rewarding mediocrity and not merit."

Ike on salary raises. "I've lived all my life with the Air Force. They got 50% more in pay than we did. That meant they were supposed to save some money or take out some insurance. They didn't. I've contributed more to funds to send an aviator's widow home, to set her up." . . .

Ike on applicants for his job. "It has been said here that there is no lack of applicants for federal service. I get $45,000 a year less than my predecessor. But I doubt, three years from now, that there'll be any lack of applicants for my job." . . .

McCarthy-Stevens row broke wide open today. Agree, after meeting with McCarthy, Dirksen, Potter, Mundt, and Stevens on "memo of agreement" giving Joe everything he wants, names etc.[1] Shouldn't have agreed. Stevens called me late at night (10:00 P.M.) to say he wanted to release his statement and then resign. Told him to cool off overnight. But we were sure dumb. Someone let Stevens walk right into a bear trap, and now I'll have to work like hell to get him out of it. What a job!

Senator Joseph R. McCarthy (Rep.) of Wisconsin first came out against Communists in the government in a speech before a Republican women's group in Wheeling, West Virginia, on Lincoln's Birthday, 1950, and soon his name was a household—one might better say television—word. He was constantly in the public prints, on radio and television. He moved so quickly, from one crusade to another, that it was impossible to keep up with him, a procedure that he enjoyed, for no one could check on his whereabouts, that is, what he really was investigating. There was fire behind McCarthy's smoke, for the Soviet Union had infiltrated the US government with spies, but McCarthy was a child in the business of ferreting out Communists and never managed to find a single one, save possibly an Army dentist who during an interrogation took the Fifth Amendment and who, alas, got out of the Army before the Senator could lay hands on him. In the course of investigating the dentist, the Senator, however, began investigating the Army, which he accused of trying to cover up the honorable discharge given to Major Irving

Peress of Camp Kilmer, New Jersey. Unimpressed by the Army's explanations, McCarthy went to the top, to the Secretary of the Army, Robert T. Stevens. The Secretary at first sought to placate McCarthy, which was impossible, and soon found himself involved in accusations that he could hardly deal with, short of resignation.

Thursday, February 25, 1954

In at 8:30. Stevens-McCarthy row really kicked up a mess. Staff meeting broke early so Adams, self, Persons, Martin, Morgan could have meeting with Nixon and Bill Rogers.[1] Later moved meeting to East Wing where Senator Dirksen joined us. Piecing together yesterday's mess seems that the Senator really jobbed up on Stevens, or else he didn't realize what he was doing. May have good results in long run, however.

Dirksen agreed to get Republican members of committee together and see if they could issue additional statement saying committee had complete confidence in Stevens' "integrity and ability." That he was pursuing proper course of action in dealing with problems arising from Peress case. Action to be taken by Stevens after completion of Inspector General's report made it evident may not be necessary to call any officers involved, and if called, would be treated with "proper respect."

Also Dirksen will work on Republican members and Democrats on committee to get Cohn fired, to stop one-man committee from meeting and to strip McCarthy of some of his powers by saying subpoena could be issued only by majority vote.[2] Dirksen couldn't deliver.

President very mad and getting fed up. It's his Army and he doesn't like McCarthy's tactics at all. Stevens and Kyes joined Nixon and all of us at 4:00 P.M.[3] Worked 'till 5:30 on statement. Cleared it with President who made it stronger and then released it in joint conference in my office.

Quotes. Ike on subject. "This guy McCarthy is going to get into trouble over this. I'm not going to take this one lying down." "My friends tell me it won't be long in this Army stuff before McCarthy starts using my name instead of Stevens. He's ambitious. He wants to be President. He's the last guy in the world who'll ever get there, if I have anything to say."

• • • •

Friday, February 26, 1954

In at 8:20. Papers looked better. Headlines "Ike supports Stevens." McCarthy's statement that he made no promise to stop "abusing" officers backfired. Press conference at 10:30 A.M. pretty rough. Even trying to get me to comment. Just declined to get involved, even on mail count, "not winning popularity contest." Everyone jittery around here, can't take gaff, when going is tough.

GOP policy committee started counteroffensive by announcing that they were going to "study" rules and procedures of investigating committees. Ferguson admitted "had something to do with McCarthy case." Eventual aim is elimination of one-man committee; subpoena powers in one man and place instead majority vote; protection of witnesses.

McCarthy, at later press conference, backed down somewhat. Said had "no differences" with Stevens. What a mess. Elliott Bell called from NY. Disturbed. Ike must be firmer and take initiative. Can't do business with guys who are trying to beat brains out.

Knowland voted with George Amendment. Defeated by one vote, 60–31.

In the course of maneuvers over the Bricker Amendment, Senator Walter F. George (Dem.) of Georgia announced his own amendment, which said that a treaty or international agreement that conflicted with the Constitution should have no force or effect, and that an international agreement other than a treaty should become effective as internal law in the United States only by act of Congress. Then at last the Bricker Amendment failed, 60–31, one vote short of the two-thirds majority required. It may well be that some Senators maneuvered to vote for the amendment in conviction that it would fail, and that the apparently close vote was largely a result of maneuver. Hagerty was unsure, and annoyed that two of the GOP leaders shifted their votes to Bricker.

Saturday, February 27, 1954

In at 8:45. Comparatively quiet day. Looks as if McCarthy-Stevens row quieting down somewhat. Believe President must take stronger lead though.

President not particularly concerned about Knowland-Millikin shift on Bricker vote. Told Ann hopes they keep in line on farm vote.[1] Hope he raises hell at legislative meeting Monday, but doubt it. . . .

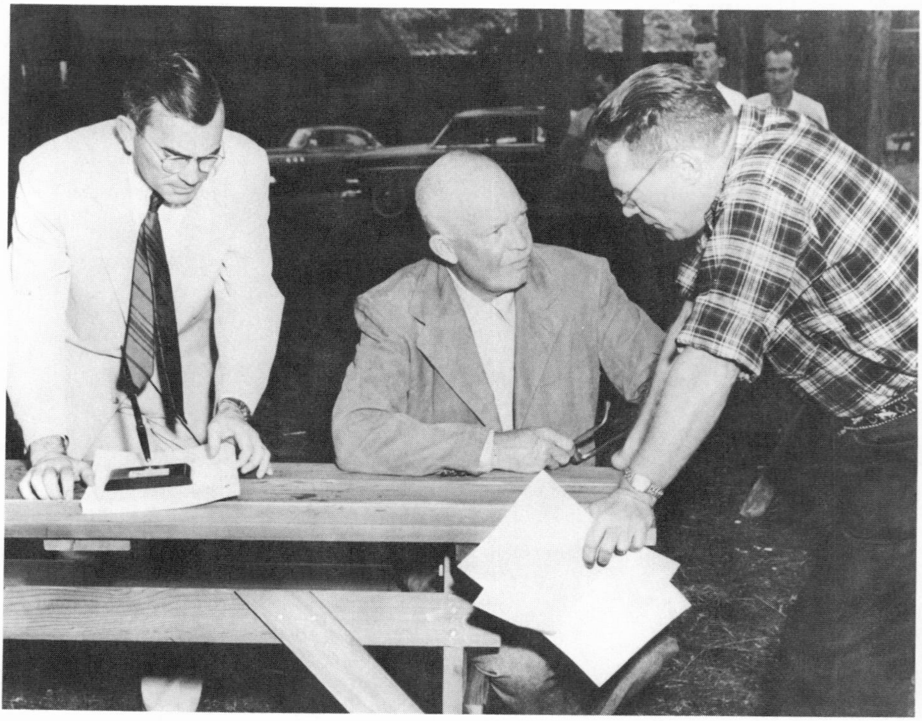

March 1954

Monday, March 1, 1954

In at 8:15. . . . Stevens-McCarthy. President said he would answer at press conference. "Can't defeat Communism by destroying America." President was tough and said he was going to speak his mind. Said leaders didn't protect Stevens. Knowland said they were trying to protect him from open TV hearing on Peress case.

Quotes. Ike on wetback bill. "I'm getting so tired of confusion and not knowing where people stand. I'm going to ask Congress for more money to build up Border Patrol. If we have to build fence down there, the Mexicans will be mad. That's too bad." . . .

Ike on Bricker and program. "That's over now. Let's get going. We've got a hell of a good thing to sell the country in our program. Let's get it going. I'll help any time you want me to, but don't want to keep talking all the time with my tongue chattering like a coffee mill."

Ike when told Allen would keep Alaska bill on shelf.[1] "Couldn't think of a better place for it. Can't understand Alaska statehood. It's an outpost."

Puerto Ricans shooting in House this P.M. Five members wounded. Congressional reception cancelled. Rowley and Baughman concerned. Had files on those in shooting. Stricter security laid on. Full shifts, without time off for a while.

VP, Adams, Persons, and I to lunch with President tomorrow on McCarthy row.

In the House of Representatives the Puerto Rican nationalists managed to get into the galleries with guns, and suddenly began shooting Representatives below. In the ensuing melee all the gunmen were caught, but the occasion was unnerving. In 1950 two nationalists tried to assassinate President Truman by approaching the President's residence, Blair House (the White House was being reconstructed), and bounding up the steps; one Puerto Rican was killed and the President, who had been resting upstairs, could easily have been killed. In 1954 the Secret Service—Special Agent James Rowley in charge of the White House detail, and the Service's chief, U.E. Baughman—was worried.

Tuesday, March 2, 1954

In at 8:15 A.M. Most of day spent working on President's statement for press conference on Stevens-McCarthy row. Luncheon at White House with President, Nixon, Adams, Persons, and self. Had preliminary draft to submit. President made suggestions on it and spent P.M. redrafting it for submission to him at 4:30.

President in angry mood (at Joe) all day. Relaxed and ready to fire back. Repeatedly said during day: "What's the use of trying to work with guys that aren't for you, and are never going to be for you." Other quotes from President during day. "You know, what we ought to do is get a word to put ahead of Republican. Something like 'new' or 'modern' or something. We just can't work with fellows like McCarthy, Bricker, Jenner, and that bunch."[1]

Morgan and I went over to WH at 6:30 P.M. to work over draft. Had memo from Nixon. Included some of it in draft, particularly part of it refusing to let witnesses be browbeaten. Nixon argues, and I agree, that many legislators ashamed of reaction to McCarthy flare-up. Trying to get our leaders to buckle down and force revision of procedures for committees.

Knowland came down privately to see President. Told him they were trying to work out something on bill. But at same time Senator Ferguson held meeting and then, in talking to reporters, said it would be up to individual committees. Senator Jenner characterized meeting as "much ado about nothing."

Senator McCarthy by this time was firing salvos in all directions, and tried to tell Secretary of State John Foster Dulles how to run his Cabinet department. This involved an answer by Dulles's appointee in charge of security, R.W. Scott McLeod, a conservative Republican and former member of the FBI.

Wednesday, March 3, 1954

In at 8:00 A.M. Murray took press briefing at staff meeting. President reworded statement overnight. Morgan and I went over it with him in his office. Also set up question on Dulles-McLeod-McCarthy with answer from President that "appointment of administrative positions within a department, responsibility of secretary, and no one else." . . .

At press conference President started off with short statement on House shooting. Then read statement. Went well with some reporters. New Dealers and fuzzy boys disappointed. Wanted President to call McCarthy names, crack him over head, etc. Typical of reaction from these quarters was Reston in *New York Times*—"turning the other cheek," and Doris Fleeson—"McCarthy can say President didn't lay a glove on him."[1] Nuts. All these people want is to have President get down in gutter with Joe. Personally think President's statement strong and dignified.

Particularly in light of Joe's intemperate rejoinder where he said in effect he'll go right on bullying etc. Now it's up to our leaders in Congress. If they take the ball and run with it, if they force change in rules, then they can come out ahead. If they haven't got the guts, then, with Senator Potter, we'll have to do it with Democratic votes on Joe's committee and let Democrats take the credit. Ferguson wobbling all around on this and so is Knowland, Millikin, and Saltonstall. They have a chance now to make it good. My bet is they'll kick it over.

• • • •

Thursday, March 4, 1954

In at 8:15 A.M. President upset at press reaction, particularly in *Washington Post* and *New York Times*. Both stories, in my book, really hit below the belt and were deliberately needled up by Folliard and Reston, both of whom know better, but can't forget to play their favorite side of the record—straight New Deal in thinking and in writing.[1] Other papers praised President for stand, for temperate language and for dignity. Believe as President's statement sinks in, coupled with his knockdown of Joe on State Department troubles with McLeod, real reaction will be favorable. That's why I'm glad we released tape of statement to radio, TV, and newsreels. To hell with slanted reporters. We'll go directly to the people who can hear exactly what President said without reading warped and slanted stories.

Secretary Stevens developing persecution complex. Highly irrational. Beginning to talk himself into position where he actually thinks he is big hero, did the right thing, and was only following orders from someone above. Who I'd never know.

• • • •

Friday, March 5, 1954

In at 8:20 A.M. Fairly quiet day. Ducked Cabinet meeting to catch up with mail dictation. Got rid of about 100 letters in day.

Rowley worried about Puerto Rican situation. Reports from sources hint at "second phase" by the crazy nationalists in revenge for arrests of Congress shooters. Protection tightened up, but good. Secret Service detail working round the clock, with no vacation or days off. . . .

• • • •

Saturday, March 6, 1954

. . . To White House correspondents dinner in evening. . . . Sat next to Bob Stevens at head table. Is he jittery. And is he talking. Talks about "Jim's the only one who stuck with me" and stuff like that in front of anyone and everyone. Very unstable and excited. Says "he's all alone in this fight." "Matter of principle." President had Donovan introduce him and he got a standing ovation.[1] Made him almost drunk with delight. Kept muttering to himself "They're for me. They're my friends." Quite a case. Someone better ride herd on him but good. . . .

One of Senator McCarthy's procedures was to insist upon equal time on the radio and TV, and the President was tiring of the Senator's attempt to dominate the media and become in effect the spokesman of the Republican Party.

Monday, March 8, 1954

In at 8:15 A.M. Leaders meeting. . . . Agenda (1) taxes, (2) Hawaii, (3) Freight Absorption Bill, (4) dairy support prices. . . .

After meeting President called leaders into his office and laid down the law. Said "Let's stop this nonsense and get down to getting program passed." Arrange to have Hall make request to NBC and CBS to answer with party spokesman. Not McCarthy who made request for time. Leaders all promised to be with President.

On request for time. Hall issued statement that he would designate spokesman, not "individual," to speak for party. Going to be Nixon. President wants it to be billed not as rebuttal but talk on "Republican leadership." President dead set against . . . McCarthy. Calls him "pimple on path of progress." Ike really made up his mind to fight Joe from now on in. All to good.

Shanley and I talked to President in gym, as he was changing clothes to go out on lawn to hit golf balls and it was agreed that I should sort of leak story on McCarthy action tomorrow, pointing out President's press conference statement, McLeod answer, and Hall action taken with WH and leaders' agreement. President wants Nixon remarks to be not answer to Adlai but talk on GOP leadership and party program.[1]

As the Army-McCarthy battle heated up, the presence of an Army enlisted man on the staff of Senator McCarthy, the scion of a theater family, G. David Schine, led to claims by the Senator that the Army was not making it easily possible for Schine to assist the Senator, and the Army countered by showing how many times Schine had obtained special passes and leaves, often by applying to his friend on McCarthy's staff, Roy M. Cohn.

Tuesday, March 9, 1954

In at 8:15 A.M. McCarthy still demanding time to answer "personal attack." Statement issued in NYC said "Networks will grant me time or learn what the law is. I guarantee that." Talked to Adams this A.M. He will call FCC chairman and get that nailed down. Adams tells me Potter is going to ask Defense for the Schine record tomorrow. That ought to kick up fuss and start ball rolling to get rid of Roy Cohn. Senator McClellan already publicly requested it. Potter's move to be made in executive session.[1]

Senator Flanders in speech on floor says McCarthy trying to break up GOP. Good speech. Joe getting reckless. Assails Flanders as "Republican hero." Also backtracks on threat to NBC and CBS. Says now have to have lawyer look up law. Refuses to let NBC and CBS into NY press conference. His pal, Lee, on FCC, says it's "square deal" to have Nixon make speech. Good day for us.[2]

Among other pursuits Senator McCarthy's staff investigated books at Army and other government libraries, at home and abroad.

Wednesday, March 10, 1954

In at 8:00 A.M. Press conference briefing at staff meeting. Topics included announcement of tax, TV-radio talk, Caracas, tax program, [Adlai] Stevenson speech, McCarthy on his books at Army libraries, Indochina, Senate rules, Hawaii, pay raises, etc.[1] At presidential briefing decided to go on air with tax speech Monday night, and to announce it at conference. As to Stevenson, agreed only to say "nonsense" to his charge GOP half-Eisenhower, half-McCarthy.

Good conference. President tough on Joe and backed up Flanders and networks. Authorized "nonsense," saying "You can use my influence on Mr. H to get him to release it." Also released about seven minutes of Q and A on McCarthy, Stevenson, and Indochina. President in fighting mood, has had it as far as Joe is concerned. "If he wants to get recognized any more," President told Persons, "only way he can do it is to stand up and publicly say, 'I was wrong in browbeating witnesses, wrong in saying the Army is coddling Communists, and wrong in my attack on Stevens. I apologize.' That's only way I ever welcome him back into fold."

C.E. Wilson threw monkey wrench in carefully prepared plans by sending his car to Senate today and picking up Joe for luncheon at Pentagon. Wilson didn't tell anyone in WH about luncheon. Just let it happen. When I told President he leaned back in chair, muttered a few "goddams" and then said "You know, Jim, I believe Cabot Lodge is dead right when he says we need acute politicians in those positions. They are the only ones who know enough to stay out of traps and the only ones who can play the same kind of game as those guys on the Hill." President greatly disturbed at Wilson luncheon and called me back several times to see if any announcement had been made from luncheon. "If they are cooking up another statement, then, by God, someone is going to hear from me—but good."

When Wilson-McCarthy interview finally broke on ticker, in which

Joe pulled in his horns, President read story and then said: "Just a lot of words. No use to have that luncheon at all."

President going to Sulgrave Club for dinner for Knowland and Ferguson. Asked who was calling for him, he was told Millikin and Saltonstall. Laughed and said "Looks like they want me to at least start out being seen with the liberals." On Knowland: "I used to think he was a good candidate for President and now I know he isn't."

• • • •

Thursday, March 11, 1954

In at 8:15 A.M. Finally caught up with Seaton on Wilson luncheon.[1] Seems McCarthy called Wilson after Wilson's press conference where he said "damn tommyrot" Army coddling Reds. Joe wanted to tell Wilson he wasn't against Army. Wilson asked him to lunch but didn't tell anyone over here. Went on his own. Bawled Senator out mildly. He said "Listen, if you think you have troubles, come over to the Pentagon." And I guess he's right. Doing good job.

President pleased by reaction to his press conference. Really got his back up. Not going to give in to Old Guard. Continue to fight them—but hard.

Army report on Schine-Cohn-McCarthy going up on Hill today. It's a pip. Shows constant pressure by Cohn to get Schine soft Army job, with Joe in and out of threats, really bad report that should bust this thing wide open. Eighteen copies to Hill. Started to leak out in evening, Donovan of *Herald Tribune* called me at home at 10:00 P.M. to see if I knew anything about it. Say "no" and didn't know where they could get copy. Cohn plenty worried, I hear. Senator Potter going to be tough on it and vote for Cohn's firing. If he doesn't resign. Really hemming Joe in. . . .

• • • •

Friday, March 12, 1954

. . . Knowland called President this A.M.—10:00—and threatened to resign as leader. Claimed he hadn't seen copy of Army report in advance, despite fact eighteen copies were sent to Hill, for committee chairmen. Knowland and leaders knew about report but apparently Knowland blew his top and wanted to sound off, let off steam. President calmed him down. Of course, Knowland never called meeting of Republican senators. In talking with President later, he said "You know, Jim, I suppose if those leaders had seen the report, it would never have gotten out in the papers." "They always want to play everything the hard way—compromise, compromise. Nuts." . . .

• • • •

Monday, March 15, 1954

In at 8:15. Leaders meeting. . . .

Meeting quotes. Millikin on Hawaii-Alaska: "I can come around to Hawaii after a lot of mental retching and vomiting, but I can't do it for Alaska." Ike on same subject: "Gene, you reflect my sentiments exactly. This linking of Alaska to Hawaii is just the old Democrat game of promising for years to give a compulsory FEPC.[1] What did they do? Nothing, not a damn thing." Millikin: "It will be a tin-cup state until all of us have humps on our back."

Ike, on Democratic tax moves: "Let them fight it. We'll tell the people that unless we get our tax program we will have to abandon or seriously curtail some of our program." "I'm getting sick and tired of having men, whom I have about as much political affinity for as a bull in a pen, saying they are for us. Hell, they're against us and always will be."

Talked to Foster Dulles about Normandy visit by President on tenth anniversary of D-Day. He characterized it as "a provocative idea" and said "he would think about it a lot." Mentioned French might have an objection and also question of what to do with Russians, who were our allies, and Germany and Italy, who were our enemies. Don't know what result will be, but it sure is worth studying.

Got out text of tax speech at 3:30 P.M. Cleared with President and released.

Sprung my Normandy idea on the President after TV-radio broadcast. Aksel Nielsen, Montgomery, and I went upstairs with him. He seemed pleased with the idea, didn't turn it down. Said "I could fly over to Cherbourg and fly back. I'm sure Coty would invite me." Asked me to check it out with C.D. Jackson and to follow up with Dulles. Said he wished he could do it within few weeks. "Think it might be helpful to EDC and French pride," Later in talking about difficulties with British during war used expression "The limitation of a common language." . . .[2]

• • • •

Wednesday, March 17, 1954

In at 8:00 A.M. . . .

At press conference, President did swell job. Most of questioning centered on retaliation theory of defense and, of course, questions linked to McCarthy. At President's briefing he said if questioned about "new look" he was going to "give the boys a lecture on fundamentals. They just don't seem to understand military tactics as applied to the times of nuclear weapons." Later released this "lecture" for radio-TV.

In evening Stephens and I went with President to Friendly Sons dinner. President made good, light speech.

Relations between the President and General MacArthur had gone back to the early 1930s when the then Major Eisenhower began work in Washington and soon was a subordinate in the office of the chief of staff, General MacArthur. When the general went to the Philippines in 1935, Eisenhower went along as his chief of staff, and remained in the Islands until 1939. Their paths crossed infrequently thereafter. In the new Eisenhower administration the general quite naturally looked for better treatment than under Eisenhower's predecessor at the White House, but the general was resident in New York at the Waldorf-Astoria, and Eisenhower in Washington, and a meeting was not arranged until 1954.

• • • •

Thursday, March 18, 1954

In at 8:16 A.M. General MacArthur in for 12:15 meeting with President and then luncheon at White House with Wilson, Kyes, Carney, Ridgway, Radford, Senator Saltonstall, and Representative Dewey Short.[1] Invitation was actually solicited by MacArthur men. Several wrote in to Adams that general would like to be invited down to visit with President on "anything." President decided to give him red carpet treatment, and did just that. . . .

• • • •

Saturday, March 20, 1954

. . . Indochina problem getting graver. Dulles, Radford, and Wilson met with President for 1½ hours this morning. French chief of staff Ely arriving in Washington this A.M. to see President with Radford Monday. Vietminh offensive serious. French need more light bombers (B-26s—25 of them) and more "volunteer" aviators to fly them. Change in weather for worse in Indochina aiding Reds and hampering airlift by French to Dienbienphu.

Dulles, Radford, and Wilson coming back to WH tomorrow for another meeting with President. . . .

In early 1954 the French forces in Indochina were getting into ever more trouble, and a garrison of 12,000 men was surrounded in north Vietnam in a place named Dienbienphu.

Monday, March 22, 1954

In at 8:00 A.M. At leaders meeting President had Radford and Dulles in for private briefing on Indochina. Only leaders at meeting. Radford stressed danger to French, said they needed more planes (B-26s) and that Vietminh were trying to win victory before Geneva.[1] Suffering heavy losses. Vietminh renewed attacks this P.M. Threatening Dienbienphu defenses. . . .

Ike on Empress of Ethiopia. "You know she personally owns all the bawdy houses in Ethiopia. It's all perfectly legal in E." . . .

• • • •

Tuesday, March 23, 1954

. . . Talked to President on McCarthy serving on committee investigating his row with Army. President all set to blast it as "inconceivable" at tomorrow's press conference. Question of ethics and morals. Hurrah! Also got him to hold off on any discussion of bombs at press conference until Admiral Strauss returns from Pacific in week to ten days.

In discussion with President on McCarthy matter, asked him if he had sent letter to Senator Mundt, as suggested by C.D. [Jackson] and Cutler, in which he opposed member of committee under investigation serving on same committee. President replied: "No I didn't send letter. I call Mundt. If I could trust him I'd have sent the letter. But you can't trust that fellow. He plays everything against the middle."

• • • •

Wednesday, March 24, 1954

In at 8:00 A.M. Had bitter argument with Persons on President's upcoming comment on McCarthy at press conference. Jerry bitter at taking any stand on question of whether Joe should stay or not stay on committee, or whether have right to cross-examine witnesses. . . . At President's briefing Cutler came in with Murray and I, also Persons, Morgan, and Martin. President stopped them dead in tracks by saying "Look, I know exactly what I am going to say. I'm going to say he can't sit as a judge and that the leadership can't duck that responsibility. I've made up my mind you can't do business with Joe and to hell with any attempt to compromise." . . .

On way over to conference President laughed and said "The two Jerrys didn't look very happy this morning."[1] When I ducked this, he said "I know, Jim, listen, I'm not going to compromise my ideals and personal beliefs for a few stinking votes. To hell with it." I told him "Mr. President, I'm proud of you."

Hill reaction good on press conference. Also good reaction from Len Hall who was in at 9:00 to recommend President praise House for their vote on tax bill. President did.

Senate cut excise taxes to 5%. Lot of our boys went over to Democrats. Yellow and couldn't stand heat like the House did. No guts in Senate leadership. How Halleck stands out.

• • • •

Thursday, March 25, 1954

. . . Mayor Wagner of NYC trying to dump ILA dispute on NY waterfront in our laps. Said last night it's President's responsibility after Dewey warned him and police commissioner to preserve order. Or be removed. Don't think governor should have used this language.

Went to lunch at Mark Trice's office in the Senate with Persons, Martin, and Morgan.[1] They said they didn't know who was going to be there. When I walked in, there was Joe McCarthy, Welker, Mundt, Malone, Hickenlooper, Butler (Md), Griswold, and Purtell.[2] Welker started in on me on McCarthy case. Knowland dropped in for handshake. McCarthy, Mundt, and Malone left right after social luncheon. Then Welker and Hickenlooper started in. Proposed both Cohn and Adams resign and case be dropped.[3] I kept quiet and just listened, as did other three from WH. Feel being jobbed by McCarthy boys. Hickenlooper criticized "those who advised President to get into row." Said "he should have kept out." Arrived at 12:45. Left at 2:20. On returning to House, heard that rumors floating around Capitol of "compromise luncheon." Called in Persons and Morgan and told them I was going to tell our wire men entire story. They agreed and told wires what happened.[4] No WH approval of luncheon. Only "social." Still think it was a put-up job and don't know whether our boys in on it. . . .

William Peer, Wagner's secretary, called me. Wanted to have mayor come down to see President tomorrow. Told him federal judge appointed to start contempt hearing Monday. Said would let him know. Shanley, Rabb, and I talked to President.[5] Reported Wagner just trying to throw waterfront situation in our laps. President said: "I'll see any mayor in a social visit, but, by God, I'll not see Wagner." President told me to tell Secretary Mitchell to have his assistant call Wagner back and say WH had referred labor question to Secretary of Labor. Tell him that court had acted, not interfere with court action, if wanted to come down to see Secretary of Labor that's okay. Wagner, of course, declined and later, 8:30 P.M., issued telegram saying he had been "rebuffed" in seeking appointment with President. Nuts to him!

• • • •

Friday, March 26, 1954

In at 8:15. Wagner telegram referred to Secretary of Labor for answer. Later NLRB examiner reported ILA "illegal" election.[1]

Cabinet meeting.

(1) Dulles reviewed Indochina situation. Said we must help French win in Indochina. If not, Reds would win that part of world and "cut our defense line in half." Predicted U.S. may have to take "fairly strong action," involving risks, "but these risks will be less if we take them now rather than waiting for several years." Said French should give political sovereignty to Associated States. French want our help, but not in any form they think might damage their prestige in area. We should train local troops and work for freedom for states. Fighting season to stop in about thirty days. But "serious situation." Cabot Lodge asked if couldn't turn Indochina into another Greece, where we trained and helped them. President said situation different. Greeks were sturdy people with will to win. Vietnam "backward people" who don't think French sincere in granting them freedom. "France presents difficult question everywhere you look." . . .

Cabinet quotes. Ike on fear speech: "Going to make a talk without text. The message of speech will be: For God's sake be reasonable, take a look at things." . . .

Ike on the French: "If we could only sit down and talk to them man to man like we can with the British when things get tough. But not the French. It sure takes a lot of patience."

Ike on supply lines in Indochina during the rainy weather. "You know in rainy weather, a pack train will eat up all its food in sixty days. There's no useful food after that time."

The Associated States were Vietnam, Laos, and Cambodia, making up Indochina.

Saturday, March 27, 1954

In at 8:30. . . .

Discussed with President at length "fear speech" he is going to make. Outlining fear of Kremlin, fear of Communism, fear of investigations, fear of depression, etc. Going to make it a "package deal" with Brownell following up with report on what administration has been doing and will do about Reds in America. President quite excited about deal. Has speech already outlined and on paper. Will speak only from notes and nothing else. 15 minutes. In talk will also say. Attorney General will follow up. Should take Red play away from McCarthy and put it back on decent level. . . .

• • • •

Monday, March 29, 1954

In at 8:00 A.M. Legislative leaders meeting. This was showdown day with leaders on (1) program and (2) foreign trade message, which most came ready to oppose. President started off meeting by saying he would like to make a few personal remarks. Speaking slowly and earnestly he said: "You know, boys, the Puritans thought they had to knock a lot of evil out of mankind. They even burned witches here in our country. Let's not look like witch-burners. Everyone on the opposite side is trying to show we don't care for the little fellow, and some of our people apparently don't. We have proposed a broad, liberal program—tax revision, housing, social security, hospitalization, highways, construction, and all the rest. . . . The finest, the only political speech I can make, is to show the people what the leaders of our party, working together, can accomplish. The faster you get the program through, the faster I can make purposeful speeches. Give me the ammunition I need to help you get reelected. . . ."

Ike to Knowland: "If the bill linking Alaska to Hawaii comes down here, I'll veto it. I just can't see Alaska as a state." . . .

Almost a month after explosion of the miniaturized H-bomb at Bikini the time came for a press conference on the subject.

Wednesday, March 31, 1954

In at 8:00 A.M. . . . Newsmen completely surprised when we walked into conference with Strauss. All except wire men whom I had tipped on confidential basis one hour ahead to allow them to set up machinery for fast coverage of Strauss statement. In answer to questions, Strauss said H-bomb could "knock out" any city, including NYC. On way down in elevator President said: "Lewis, I wouldn't have answered that one that way. I would have said: 'Wait for the movie.' But other than that I thought you handled it very well."

Strauss considerably upset. Thought President was mad. Actually President has habit of reviewing actions with people and expressing what he would have done in similar situation. Just like post-mortem on a bridge hand. . . .

April 1954

Thursday, April 1, 1954

In at 7:00 A.M. All hell broke loose last night and this A.M. on H-bomb release. Drew Pearson's column described in detail movie and *New York Times* then broke their story. . . . When told President about it, he, like I, was mad at Pearson. "Maybe you have to talk to his men, but as far as I'm concerned I wouldn't let him cover anybody in government, and if anyone was caught talking to him or his men, I'd fire them on the spot."

Indochina situation getting really hot. French want more help from us, but want it at their terms—refuse to let us train locals or send in American troops on long-term basis. Fear that would hurt what they call "French prestige." At luncheon at WH with President, Roy Howard, and Walker Stone, President expanded on problem.[1] Said U.S. might have to make decision to send in squadrons from two aircraft carriers off coast to bomb Reds at Dienbienphu. "Of course, if we did, we'd have to deny it forever." French very difficult to handle. Almost impossible. . . .

The so-called Lucky Dragon *affair, the catching of a Japanese tuna trawler in the radioactive fallout of the H-bomb test at Bikini on March 1, 1954, proved a tremendous embarrassment to the U.S. government. Fallout from the explosion was much greater than the AEC anticipated, and the trawler was caught. When it arrived back in Japan the men's hair was falling out, and after hospitalization and tests, including use of Geiger counters against their load of fish (which proved highly radioactive), they received such treatment as was possible for men who in effect had been under a gigantic X-ray machine. Eventually one of the crewmen died of secondary effects. Among results of the affair was a publicizing of the danger of radiation. Rumor of foul play meanwhile circulated among administration officials.*

Friday, April 2, 1954

In at 8:00 A.M. . . .

Here is good place to put down story on Japanese fishing boat who claims fishermen were "burned" by fallout of March 1 H-bomb explosion. Lewis Strauss and others suspect this boat was Red spy outfit. Here are the reasons: (1) The fish, supposedly radioactivized, were in refrigerators when the fallout occurred. (2) The Japanese government has refused to let our people examine the fishermen. (3) Their reported blood count same as those of our own weather station personnel who were also caught in fallout and who were not burned. (4) The "captain" is twenty-two years old, with no known background of seamanship. Suspect this part of Russian espionage system, but we don't want to say so publicly. Would tip our hand on other stuff we also know about. Interesting story and hope it will come out some day.

Indochina getting serious, more and more so. Our intelligence reports Chinese Reds moving into territory. Not in great numbers as yet but in special advisory and technical departments. Some antiaircraft and lots of material—trucks, ammunition, etc.

Went in evening to Charlie Willis party at Sulgrave Club.[1] Just after dinner received urgent call from Seaton. Could I come immediately to Struve Hensel's home.[2] Emergency. Marge and I went. Marge visited with Mrs. Hensel upstairs while I talked to Hensel, Seaton, and Joe Welch, the Army's new counsel in Stevens case. Welch accompanied by two young assistants, one of them Fred Fisher. Earlier in evening while going over each other's background, Fisher admitted that he had been a member of the Lawyers Guild (on Attorney General's subversive list) and had helped organize Suffolk County chapter in Massachusetts with assistance from a Mr. Greenberg, a Communist organizer. I first thought we should not give in on Fisher's membership, but Greenberg association was different story. It was decided Fisher to drop out and go back to Boston, too dangerous to give McCarthy opportunity to brand Fisher as Red and smear up Army defense, particularly in light of present controversy on Sears, attorney for Mundt and the subcommittee.[3] Tough decision, but necessary. . . .

What at first appeared a distressing inconvenience, discovery that Joseph N. Welch's assistant, Fisher, once had contact with an avowed Communist, and fear that Senator McCarthy might discover the fact, proved a blessing in disguise, for when McCarthy found out about Fisher and cruelly raised the issue in a hearing, Welch saw an opening and seized it. The hearings, which were being televised, by this time had become soap opera for millions of viewers, and before this huge audience Welch pounced upon McCarthy, said he never before had suspected how cruel the Senator could be, and so shamed him that McCarthy never recovered. Shortly afterward McCarthy's antagonists in the Senate roused themselves, and wavering Senators joined them, and the result was the Senator's downfall.

• • • •

Monday, April 5, 1954

In at 8:10. Legislative leaders. . . . Stassen opened meeting with discussion of Foreign Operations plan for coming year.[1] His requests total $3.498 billion, down 42% from two years ago. Of this, Indochina represented one-third or $1.133 billion. Indochina breakdown was $308 million for U.S. "hardware," $800 million to "back up war, pay French to keep forces there," $21.5 million for economic items, and $3.5 million for technical training—represented emphasis on East rather than West for first time. "More results for less dollars." . . .

On Indochina, President said: "If Dienbienphu had fallen two weeks ago we would be sitting here under tremendous tensions. If the French . . . come through this, I'll forgive them for a lot of things they caused me to worry about over the last four years." . . .

The President gave his "fear" speech that night over radio and TV, decrying fear of the Kremlin, fear of Communism, fear of investigations, fear of economic depression.

Tuesday, April 6, 1954

. . . President extremely pleased over his speech. Knew he had done a good job and wanted to hear all the reports. "That's what I've been telling you boys for a long time. Just let me get up and talk to the people. I can get through to them that way. I don't feel I do when I have to read a speech or use that damn teleprompter. It's not me and I feel uncomfortable."

NSC meeting in P.M. on Indochina. I announced it as just weekly meeting which was "more convenient" to hold on Tuesday this week. Situation getting crucial. French want 50 more bombers. And they are running short of pilots. Could use "American volunteers." Also considering use of troops eventually.

Talked several times with Strauss. He's getting more and more suspicious Jap fishing boat was Red spy ship. Also voiced unpleasant thought: "If I were the Reds I would fill the oceans all over the world with radioactive fish. It would be so easy to do"!!

• • • •

Wednesday, April 7, 1954

In at 8:00 A.M. Press conference day. Staff meeting included Indochina, H-bomb, Churchill debate including London visit, British planes, 1943 agreement, unemployment figures, Hawaii-Alaska Bill, etc. . . .

McCarthy, in charging last night that H-bomb development held up for eighteen months because of Reds in government, seems to be skating pretty close to Oppenheimer case. Hope we move fast, before McCarthy breaks it and it then becomes our scandal.

Robert Oppenheimer, director at the wartime Los Alamos nuclear weapons laboratory, thereafter head of the Institute for Advanced Study at Princeton, had opposed President Truman's decision announced early in 1950 to go ahead with an H-bomb, and the enmities among scientists, government and private, engendered by that controversy, which for the most part was a series of top-secret arguments within the upper reaches of the federal government, soon turned into public accusations. The more conservative scientists led by the Hungarian emigré Edward Teller and the mathematician Stanislas Ulam triumphed with design of a workable H-bomb. Flushed with success, these men turned on the anti-H-bomb scientists led by Oppenheimer, and perhaps to their delight discovered that the Princeton physicist had a long history of awkward association with Communists that at the least showed him to be indiscreet. The AEC held hearings on whether Oppenheimer should continue to possess top-secret clearance, and at that point it was necessary to notify Oppenheimer so that he might defend himself.

Thursday, April 8, 1954

. . . President called me in to his office at 10:00 A.M. He had just finished going over alone Brownell's draft. . . . Had deleted "Eisenhower" before word "administration" and made other such changes. He asked me to go over it also and report back to him. I made other changes, including giving Roosevelt credit for putting FBI into Red cells. No mention of Truman though. Also pepped up ending with emphasis on fact that this was the way to handle the Reds—by legal, orderly processes of fair play, etc. Deliberate crack at McCarthy. . . .

• • • •

Friday, April 9, 1954

. . . With Oppenheimer talking to Reston, and with Alsops knowing story already, it's just question of time before someone cracks it wide open and everything hits the fan. If this breaks it will be biggest news we've had down here yet. Real hot. Here's why: Oppenheimer who served as director of Los Alamos during war and high consultant in H-bomb staff has long record of association with Reds. His wife is a party member; his house guest for a while was Earl Browder's son; he tried to discourage Strauss testing of stratosphere right up to a week before we picked up first Soviet atomic blast; and a lot of other equally bad and shocking stuff.[1] . . .

• • • •

Saturday, April 10, 1954

In at 8:15 A.M. Oppenheimer business all the work did that day. Adams and I went in to tell President of our meetings yesterday. He listened gravely, asked "The record will be spelled out." . . . Strauss and Adams, with rest, went back to President at 11:30 A.M. to read him the statement. He looked serious, took off his glasses and chewed them throughout reading. . . . President insisted that we stick carefully to facts and to "orderly procedure." He likewise said: "We've got to handle this so that all our scientists are not made out to be Reds. That goddamn McCarthy is just likely to try such a thing." . . .

• • • •

Sunday, April 11, 1954

O case gets rougher and rougher. Herb [Brownell] and I went to Strauss farm and after luncheon had three-hour talk on case. . . . On way back, Herb said he would have to see President on this one. . . . Said only criminal action, at present, probably would be perjury. No one has proved any espionage. Just had associations. . . .

Albert M. Cole, administrator of the Housing and Home Finance Agency, was under pressure from a Senate committee chaired by Homer E. Capehart of Indiana. To the White House's embarrassment, Capehart was a conservative Republican and found paydirt in Cole's agency, which was giving out mortgages that were not going to be easy to collect upon. Combined with the inconvenient Oppenheimer affair it was almost too much.

Tuesday, April 13, 1954

In at 7:30 A.M. This was a rough day—*New York Times* broke Oppenheimer story last night . . .

FHA scandal getting hot and fear Cole's inability to handle it properly. Cole is jittery, knows the President is mad because he did not act sooner. Capehart Committee notified us they would also step into investigation and have asked for complete cooperation by government and for permission to get tax returns on property rental section. . . .

The President flew to Augusta, Georgia, that evening.

Thursday, April 15, 1954

In afternoon Murray called to tell me that statement would be coming down from State Department to be issued by President, giving American assurances to France and other NATO countries on EDC . . . I went out to National to clear it with the President. He gave approval saying, "I suppose this is necessary to give our French friends some guts." . . .

One of the warmest international questions in the early 1950s, and especially in early 1954, was the European Defense Community, a formula by which the United States and Britain hoped to persuade the French government to accept the rearmament of West Germany and thereby introduction of West German troops into NATO. At the time of the Korean War, Eisenhower had gone to Europe to galvanize NATO, and it soon had become apparent that France itself was unable to contribute much to NATO–because of involvement in Algeria and Indochina–and that if NATO was to have any strength at all (ideally strength enough to equal Russian troops in Eastern Europe) it would have to have German troops. The French could not decide what to do, and early in 1954 were procrastinating, even though EDC was their own suggestion. Early versions of EDC presumed the introduction of German troops into NATO in units smaller than divisions, a virtual brigading of troops into international divisions. The idea was difficult in practice because of language differences, but it was better than being without German troops. Whatever the version of EDC, however, it was not to French taste, a fact that was thoroughly apparent early in 1954.

Friday, April 16, 1954

As usual, Republican leaders in Senate sold us down the river on EDC assurance story. Saltonstall and Wiley said that they had not been informed on statement. Dulles told me later he had personally cleared statement with Saltonstall and Wiley and produced the original draft with changes made on it in their own handwriting. Clearance was made in March, and both Saltonstall and Wiley's only defense was "we forgot it." Democrats taking same line for political purposes despite the fact that they also were told about it in March. . . .

The French were tiring of the expense, human and otherwise, of their war with the Vietnamese Communists and were ready to find a convenient exit from their once attractive imperial possession of Indochina comprising the provinces of Vietnam, Laos, and Cambodia. They arranged a formula by which the Big Four foreign ministers–the United States, Britain, France, and the USSR–sponsored a conference over problems of Korea; the Korean War had ended in 1953 and it became an excuse to assemble a meeting over Vietnam. Parties to the Vietnam imbroglio were invited, including representatives of the People's Republic of China.

Monday, April 19, 1954

Dulles arrived at 12:10. Stephens and I met him at airport and rode in with him. . . . Russians now trying to have Geneva billed as five-power meeting which would mean virtual recognition of Red China and first step toward admitting them to UN. Dulles to discuss with the President possibility of United States refusing to start conference if Russian demands are followed through. . . . Going out in car to airport Dulles told me that President had left decision with him . . . Dulles is going to have a tough time with this one because both Eden and Bidault would like to give in to Russia on Red China question. England already recognizes Red China and has no objection to their sitting at the table as equals. France is scared to death and would do anything to try to appease the Soviets—all this despite agreement by United States, France, and Britain at Berlin.[1]

• • • •

Tuesday, April 20, 1954

Out at National in morning. Had long talk with President on international situation and situation on Hill. Told him that I was getting fed up with leaders not supporting us; that Knowland was trying to cut Dulles' heart out every time he had a chance and that our other leaders, with the exception of Halleck, didn't have the guts to come out of the rain. The President agreed and asked me to talk to him Monday morning. Pointed out to him that Congress has passed only 5 out of 245 recommendations that he has sent up—that they have stalled on McCarthy, the Bricker Amendment and other things and have just wasted time, that if they didn't get off their cans, they weren't coming back. He said, "Jim, I agree with you and I will tell them just that at the leaders meeting Monday. Will you come in and remind me of it Monday morning prior to the meeting?" We also discussed turning loose with a series of magazine articles and other publicity on this whole question. The President gave me a green light . . . I started out of office and he called me back, laid his hand on my shoulder, patted me, and said, "O.K., Jim, go ahead." As I was going out the door, he again called to me and said, "Jim, make it tough." Hurray!!!

Fred Seaton called in afternoon to inform me that Defense Department, with clearance by Adams, had prepared a statement on Indochina airlift to be used if story ever breaks. We have been carrying French personnel in American planes—more than has ever been reported. They do not land in war zones but airlift has been considerable, and sooner or later the Chinese Communists are going to break it.

• • • •

Wednesday, April 21, 1954

Comparatively quiet morning. President liked David Lawrence's column this morning and said it summed up our position on foreign policy very well indeed.

• • • •

Thursday, April 22, 1954

Left Augusta for Washington and New York City at 1:00 P.M. . . . Waldorf 5:20.

In talking to many of the publishers at the dinner, all had this to say: "You have to educate the people more on Indochina." They contended that the average citizen does not know where Indochina is, does not realize why we will have to move in eventually. All urged me to have the President explain more in detail the reason for Indochina and our interest in it.

Back home in Washington at 11:30.

• • • •

Friday, April 23, 1954

Kentucky Day. Left Washington at 9:00 A.M. for Fort Knox, Hodgenville, and Lexington. Tank review at Fort Knox and visit to Lincoln's birthplace at Hodgenville.

Secret Service considerably worried about Lexington. Several Puerto Ricans reported in city week before surveying airport and route of march. 3 were taken into "custody" but 4 were still at large. Used two follow-up cars throughout Lexington visit and military personnel along route of march from Hodgenville through Elizabethtown at noon. President knew about it, but took a completely fatalistic viewpoint—"If they're going to shoot me, they're going to shoot me—so what! There's nothing you can do about it." . . .

• • • •

Saturday, April 24, 1954

Staff on an hour's call to return to Washington because of Indochina. Situation getting very grave and it may be necessary to support French troops at Dienbienphu with two carrier aircraft we have off the coast. French would like us to send in these planes for a quick strike. Of course, if we do use them, we probably will never admit it, but decision to assist the French by use of American planes will be a very calculated risk and could lead to war. . . .

As affairs worsened in Indochina, a worrisome situation developed in the western hemisphere concerning a leftist regime in Guatemala under President Jacobo Arbenz Guzmán. When the Arbenz government stifled dissent and gave evidence of Communist leanings, the CIA sponsored a revolutionary invasion from Guatemala under Colonel Carlos Castillo Armas, which eventually was successful.

Monday, April 26, 1954

Legislative leaders meeting at 8:30 . . . The President started the meeting with a discussion of Guatemala and Indochina. On Guatemala, the President said that it was the usual Red penetration with a small minority which is gradually taking over the country. He said that he gave the present foreign minister, when he was ambassador here, "unshirted hell, but he's playing along with the Communists." . . . the Reds are in control and they are trying to spread their influence to San Salvador as a first step of the breaking out in Guatemala to other South American countries.

Indochina. The President said that the French "are weary as hell." He said that it didn't look as though Dienbienphu could hold out for more than a week and would fall possibly sooner. Reported that the British thought that the French were not putting out as much as they could, but that he did not necessarily agree with their viewpoint. "The French go up and down every day—they are very volatile. They think they are a great power one day and they feel sorry for themselves the next day." The President said that if we were to put one combat soldier into Indochina, then our entire prestige would be at stake, not only in that area but throughout the world. The President said the British are worried about Hong Kong and hope it will be left alone. They are fearful that if they move in Indochina the

Chinese Reds will move against Hong Kong and could take it easily. "My argument to the British has been that if we all went in together into Indochina at the same time, that would be fine but if they don't go in with us, they don't expect us to help them defend Hong Kong. We must have collective security or we'll fall." The President said the situation looked very grim this morning, but that he and Dulles were doing everything they could to get the free countries to act in concert. In addition, he said "there are plenty of people in Asia, and we can train them to fight well. I don't see any reason for American ground troops to be committed in Indochina, don't think we need it, but we can train their forces and it may be necessary for us eventually to use some of our planes or aircraft carriers off the coast and some of our fighting craft we have in that area for support." . . .

The President said he was also considerably disturbed by the fact that no "newsworthy piece of legislation had been passed by Congress for some time." He said that while he was confident Congress was eventually going to do so, in his judgment they had better get going and pass some of the program so that the people do not get the opinion that Congress consists of "nothing except McCarthy." . . .

The discussion then came back to the international situation, and the President said that what American policy was doing was "gambling thousands to save billions." . . . "Where in the hell can you let the Communists chip away any more. We just can't stand it." . . . Millikin said if our allies deserted, we would have to go back to Fortress America. President angrily ended the discussion by saying "Listen, Gene, if we ever come back to Fortress America, then the word 'fortress' will be entirely wrong in this day and age. Dienbienphu is a perfect example of a fortress. The Reds are surrounding it and crowding back the French into a position where they have to surrender or die. If we ever came back to the fortress idea for America, we would have, as I said before, one simple, dreadful alternative—we would have to explode an attack with everything we have. What a terrible decision that would be to make." . . .

• • • •

Thursday, April 29, 1954

. . . On Indochina the President said that . . . "The French have built up Dienbienphu as a symbol and are trying to hold it against impossible odds. They are losing seasoned troops and most of the green reinforcements they are trying to parachute in. Navarre wouldn't take our advice—why I don't know—on ways to relieve Dienbienphu."[1] President told me later that Navarre had sent only a small column for relief of Dienbienphu and that this column had been ambushed and cut to pieces. The French are also losing a lot of planes and paratroopers to Red antiaircraft by stupidly radioing their positions in French as they approach the place, instead of using code. . . .

• • • •

Friday, April 30, 1954

. . . At luncheon Bob Stevens came in jittery as the dickens. Everyone gave him a pat on the back and tried to bolster his morale. . . .

Rowley in this afternoon. Independent producer by the name of Bressler in Hollywood starting to make movie with Frank Sinatra on attempted assassination of a President of the United States. Do not name Eisenhower nor does "President" appear in the movie. Agreed with Rowley that nothing could be worse at this time, particularly with Puerto Ricans loose in this country. Informally called Eric Johnston and told him about it. He was horrified too but explained that Bressler was independent producer and not one of his Association. Said he would use whatever influence he could to get it called off and let me know the outcome.

Johnston was president of the Motion Picture Association of America.

May 1954

From Monday, May 3, 1954, through Sunday, May 9, Hagerty was on vacation.

Monday, May 10, 1954

In at 8:10.

Legislative leaders meeting. . . .

The President opened the meeting by bringing up the appropriation for the USIA. He said that the original $89 million appropriation had been "cut to the bone" before submission. Russians spent $2 billion on propaganda. House cut $13 million. . . . Bridges said that he was sure exchange program could be restored but that . . . "They are still distributing Acheson speeches overseas and Streibert himself told us he had not changed the policy and was proud of his predecessors."[1] The President said he made the USIA report to him personally and that he would ask Streibert to report also to the Senators. "We have cleaned it up a lot. It was a service founded by New Dealers and you couldn't expect to find Republicans there. It takes time to clean it up, but we are doing it." . . .

• • • •

Tuesday, May 11, 1954

In at 8:15.

. . . Comparatively quiet except for one thing—Army-McCarthy hearings. Great pressure by Republicans to try to take hearings into executive session after McCarthy's testimony. Legislative people here think it would be a good idea. I think it would be terrible. Discussed it briefly with the President, and he agrees with me. He called Charlie Wilson and told him not to put any pressure at all on Stevens along these lines but to tell Stevens to "do what you think is right." Stevens stuck to guns . . .

• • • •

Wednesday, May 12, 1954

. . . President getting pretty sick and tired of McCarthy, and I am sure one of these days he is going to sound off. . . .

• • • •

Thursday, May 13, 1954

In at 8:00 A.M.

The first order of business was the President signing the St. Lawrence Seaway Bill in ceremony held in conference room. . . .

After St. Lawrence ceremony, President asked Knowland to step into his office for a while and laid down the law to him on the program. Flatly warned Knowland that unless Senate stepped up and started to pass the program more rapidly, the President would go on the air and make his own fight for it. . . .

Attended part of NSC meeting for discussion of . . . dissemination within our country of Communist literature from abroad. Brownell outlined problem. Explained that Communist literature was coming into this country in increasing volume. President said that he was doubtful that a bill could do it. "It would be misunderstood and written that the administration was trying to impose censorship." After some discussion it was decided to do nothing about this at the time in the form of legislation. Instead it was left in the hands of the Post Office Department. Summerfield explained that his men, working in close touch with Customs, were keeping very close count of this material moving through the mails and that "you'd be surprised how much of the stuff gets lost and ends up in the dead letter office."[1] The President approved this plan and the matter was dropped for the time being. . . .

• • • •

Friday, May 14, 1954

The President asked me to play nine holes of golf at Burning Tree in the afternoon. On way out and back we had an opportunity in the car to discuss many things. . . . President is getting very impatient with Congress and repeatedly expressed the thought that all they were interested in was being reelected instead of working for the welfare of the nation. "How they fail to see that the best way they can get re-elected is by supporting the liberal program we have submitted to them is beyond me. If they don't pass a major section of this program, a lot of them, I am sure, are not coming back." . . . We also discussed the Army-McCarthy hearings and McClellan's threat to subpoena White House staff members and bring them before the committee.[1] The President said that he would not stand for this for one minute. . . .

• • • •

Monday, May 17, 1954

. . . "Any man who testifies as to the advice he gave me won't be working for me that night." "I will not allow people around me to be subpoenaed and you might just as well know it now." . . .

The Supreme Court in 1954 in what ever since has been justly described as a landmark decision reversed the "separate but equal" formula of Plessy *v.* Ferguson *(1896), by which black citizens were not necessarily entitled to attend the same schools or enjoy the same public facilities as whites.* Brown *v.* Board of Education of Topeka *may well have been the most important Supreme Court decision of the present century. When the court announced it, however, the Eisenhower administration was unsure of its benefits. The President privately felt it was too sweeping.*

• • • •

Tuesday, May 18, 1954

In at 8:15. Had conference with the President in the morning with Persons and Adams. Persons urging President not to have a press conference tomorrow because of McCarthy-Army situation and Supreme Court ruling on segregation. Adams and I did not agree fully, and President left it open pending decision after we returned from Charlotte.

Left White House for airport for Charlotte at 11:00. Rode out with the President after first announcing to newsmen that Secretary

Stevens would accompany us on the plane to Charlotte to take part in Armed Forces Week celebration in Charlotte. Newsmen, of course, did not believe this was the only reason—and they were right. President deliberately invited Secretary so he could give public support to him by having him as guest on plane and appearing with him on platform in Charlotte. At Charlotte, President pointedly said "we have confidence in our armed forces from their Secretaries and commanding officers down to the last private." . . .

When we returned to the White House at five o'clock Sherman Adams joined us, and we decided to go ahead with the press conference . . .

We also discussed with the President the question of the Supreme Court ruling, and he said that he would simply say the Supreme Court is the law of the land, that he had sworn to uphold the Constitution and he would do so in this case. The President is considerably concerned, as are all of us, on the effect of the ruling. There is a strong possibility that some of the Southern states will take steps to virtually cancel out their public education system and through legislative devices within their states place most of their schools on a "private" school basis, giving state aid to such "private" institutions. The President expressed the fear that such a plan if it were followed through would not only handicap Negro children but would work to the detriment of the so-called "poor whites" in the South. The state we are particularly afraid of in this instance is Georgia under Governor Talmadge. . . .

• • • •

Thursday, May 20, 1954

. . . Bill Lawrence dropped in late in the afternoon to tell me of an exclusive quote he had gotten just a short while ago from McCarthy. McCarthy, I think, made a mistake on this one, and I certainly hope the President will let me blast back at him tomorrow morning. What McCarthy told Lawrence was that the administration in refusing to let confidential advisors testify was "resorting to the Fifth Amendment." I would think that this charge of Fifth Admendment with its Communist connotation will really get the President mad. I hope he lets me burn McCarthy's ears off.

• • • •

Friday, May 21, 1954

In at 8:15.

Following staff conference had meeting with Adams, and we decided not to answer McCarthy Fifth Amendment charges but instead to have Stassen go after him on his foreign policy speech when Stassen held press conference later in afternoon. Decided that the President had spoken his piece and that we did not want to have daily arguments with McCarthy from the White House. That would just build him up and that would be what he would want. . . .

Cabinet opened by Hughes giving summary of budget situation for fiscal '56 and '57.[1] . . . The President said that he had at no time set an absolute date for balancing the budget but that we could establish trends away from needless spending. He pointed out that what we ought to do was project the Truman budget and compare our budget with that. For example, if the Truman budget were projected to '55 it would have ended up with a deficit of $15 billion. "Let us not use the words 'balanced budget' if we are at the same time going to pass tax cuts. It just can't be done." . . .

The Cabinet next turned to a discussion of legislation and the President warned all in the room that "the last thing we must ever mention is a 'must' list of legislation. We put in a program and we're for it—all of it." Persons then went over item by item a report on each bill in our program. The President said, "You know, it's a crazy thing the number of Republicans in an election year who are standing up in Congress and blocking us and then raising the dickens because we don't get the program through." Nixon said that the Democrats under Johnson were a united bloc and were deliberately trying to slow down all the President's program. He suggested that the President go on the air and point out that the program, specifically, the tax, housing, tanker, and health bills would provide more jobs and more opportunities. The President interrupted and said, "That is a little demagogic, but I am not above it." . . .

President on Millikin: "He's like the fellow who tries to put potatoes in two piles. How he hates to make decisions." . . .

President on 18-year-old vote: "I should think that this bill would give us a lot of political hay. Why, everyone under twenty-five should be on our side." . . .

• • • •

Monday, May 24, 1954

. . . Martin . . . said he did not know what would happen on the postal rate and postal pay increase bill but thought the House would go as high as $200 across the board but feared that the Senate would "double it." The President interrupted to say, "Can they pass it over my veto? Here we are cutting taxes and these fellows want to aid the Treasury some more. What the hell is going on? I'll veto the bill if it comes down for one simple reason. It is this: If we let them override my veto, then, gentlemen, believe me, every union will ask for additional pay increases. You will be opening up Pandora's box and the whole philosophy of our administration will go down the drain. I am going to stand up against this, and if it goes down the drain, I'm going down with my flag flying. Furthermore, it seems to me to be a terrible mistake to allow federal employees to unionize. Suppose you had an organized army reporting and responsible to union bosses. Wouldn't that be somthing! I am not going to be slick on this one. I am not going to run around the cabbage patch. I'm against it and I'll veto it when it comes down." . . .

President on bill to stop TV and radio ads about liquor and cigarettes: "What are we going to turn out to be—a police state?" . . .

President on Ferguson's proposal to insert words "under God" in pledge of allegiance: "Senator, I'm very much in favor of it. Why don't you get up a speech and say that the only one who would be opposed to this would be a Communist."

President on need for fringe benefits to military personnel: "These are prerequisites of army and military life. Let me tell you something of my own experience. In World War I, I was ordered away four days before the birth of my first son. You can imagine how Mamie, a young bride, felt when I had to leave. But the army doctor told her that it was OK, that she would have the best of care on the post and that everything would be all right, so I went away knowing that Mamie and my son would have the best of care. That's the way the army takes care of its own and that's the way it must be. We have got to give our military personnel these benefits." . . .

• • • •

Wednesday, May 26, 1954

. . . Ned Beach called in morning to give me first report of explosion and fire on aircraft carrier *Bennington.* First reports had 19 killed and 100 injured. Later reports brought the figures up to 79 and 220. Still later reports brought the death figure above 100. . . . As usual, Congresswoman Rogers issued her scare statement, blaming it on sabotage and saying there were too many Communists in the military establishments. I think she could at least wait for an investigation. . . . [1]

The explosion occurred when the carrier was seventy-five miles south of Newport, and the ship steamed back to the base as rapidly as possible. Eventually the death toll reached ninety-nine. Cause of the explosion was a faulty catapult.

Thursday, May 27, 1954

. . . Went to the Red Cross charity ball game in the afternoon between the Senators and the Yankees. Rowley told me Secret Service had a little flare-up on Puerto Rican situation about an hour before game time. Secret Service received anonymous telephone call from a person who identified himself as "Gomez" who said that two boxes of explosives had been planted in the ball park. He then hung up. Secret Service detail and Metropolitan Police went over park with fine-tooth comb but could find nothing. Secret Service also were on lookout for four Puerto Ricans, members of Nationalist Party, who are known to be at large but who have not yet been picked up in Attorney General's drive against Nationalist Party. All our agents had license numbers of the cars that these men were last known to be driving. License numbers also relayed to Metropolitan Police and very heavy police protection on way to, and back from ball park.

• • • •

Friday, May 28, 1954

In at 8:15. . . .

Following staff meeting drafted statement designed for President to issue regarding McCarthy's appeal at hearing yesterday to federal employees to disregard presidential orders and laws and report to him on "graft, corruption, Communism, and treason." . . . I gave out the statement at 11:00. A few minutes later the President called me in to his office and said he wanted to discuss this further. He was really mad at what he termed "the complete arrogance of McCarthy." Walking up and down behind his desk and speaking in rapid fire order he said the following:

"This amounts to nothing but a wholesale subversion of public service. McCarthy is making exactly the same plea of loyalty to him that Hitler made to the German people. Both tried to set up personal loyalty within the government while both were using the pretense of fighting Communism. McCarthy is trying deliberately to subvert the people we have in government, people who are sworn to obey the law, the Constitution, and their superior officers. I think this is the most disloyal act we have ever had by anyone in the government of the United States." . . .

The President then asked if it would not be possible to feed a speech to Senator Potter . . . I countered with the suggestion that maybe the best way to do would be to build up public opinion first. The President thought that was a good idea and after discussion we decided that it would be best for me on my own to call certain key people that I knew in radio, television, and the newspapers . . .

• • • •

Saturday, May 29, 1954

Admiral Strauss in this morning to discuss in detail the Oppenheimer case. Panel's report mailed registered special delivery to Oppenheimer last night. In outlining the procedure Strauss said Oppenheimer would have five days in which to appeal and he thought he would. . . . Strauss concerned that part of the panel's decision will be released and not the full text. The decision says that Oppenheimer is not disloyal but that because of his actions and companionships the revocation of his clearance should remain in effect. Oppenheimer could very easily leak the part that merely says he is not disloyal and then we would be handicapped trying to catch up. Strauss and I went in to see the President, and the President thought that the best thing to do was to obey all the rules without trying to put out the report in advance. "The Atomic Energy Commission must act decent on this and must show the people of the country that we are more interested in trying to find out the facts than to get headlines like McCarthy does." It was agreed, however, that should the panel's decision leak to the press, Strauss was to make it public immediately. . . .

• • • •

Sunday, May 30, 1954

At home in the morning President called me several times regarding his speech at the Columbia Bicentennial Dinner. . . . During our telephone conversation the President indicated that he was going to make this a finish fight with McCarthy. He believed the question was a fundamental constitutional one and was going to the people with it.

• • • •

Monday, May 31, 1954

In at 8:15.

President did not arrive at the office until 9:00 and we immediately started to work on several changes in the speech. . . . the President decided to leave in his speech all remarks aimed at McCarthy, particularly those dealing with "demagogues." . . .

The speech got wonderful reception at the dinner. . . . In the morning the President said he would not get much applause on this speech since he was speaking before an academic audience. He was pleasantly surprised when he was interrupted 25 times, particularly on those passages dealing with McCarthy, although he was not named.

On the way out to the airport with Bill Robinson and later in Washington the President expressed extreme satisfaction at reception of his speech.

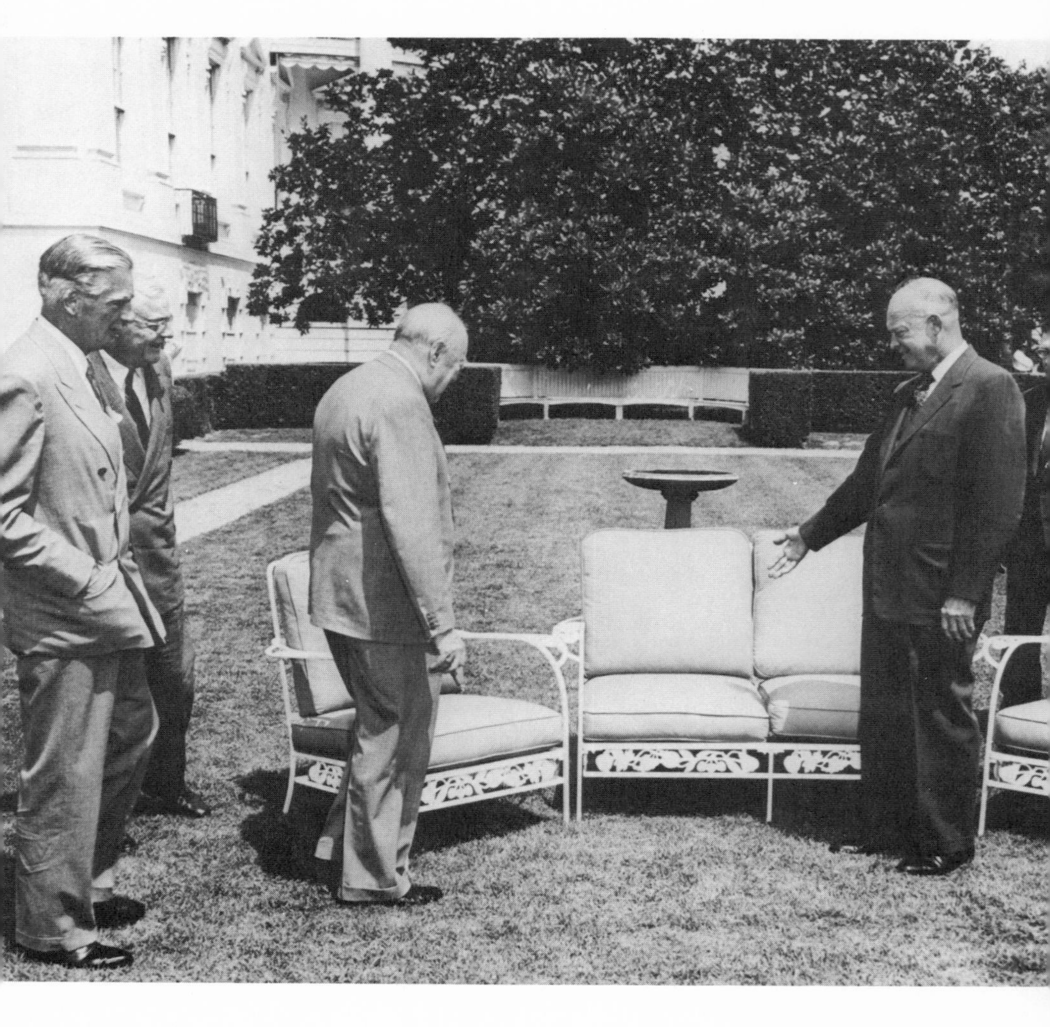

June 1954

Tuesday, June 1, 1954

. . . received a call from Nichols, general manager of the Atomic Energy Commission. He said he had just received a letter from Oppenheimer and his attorney informing the commission that Oppenheimer was going to make public the full text of the panel decision as well as his answer to the commission requesting an appeal. I told Nichols that a previous agreement reached with Strauss and the President called for us to immediately make public the panel report, saying we were doing so only because Oppenheimer himself had seen fit to do the same. The President was out on the putting green, and when I informed him of Oppenheimer's action, we had a long talk about Oppenheimer and the whole question of the case. The President said, "This fellow Oppenheimer is sure acting like a Communist. He is using all the rules that they use to try to get public sentiment in their corner on some case where they want to make an individual a martyr." The President and I agreed that one of the most damning things in the Oppenheimer testimony was his visit to Paris and his stay there with Chevalier after Oppenheimer had reported to the commission that Chevalier had tried to get secret information from him for the use of a foreign government.[1] "How can any individual report a treasonable act on the part of another man and then go and stay at his home for several days?", the President asked. "It just doesn't make any sense to me."

The President also expressed considerable concern about the mounting Democratic pressure against Strauss on the Atomic Energy Commission. He said he was more determined than ever to appoint a man who could work with Strauss on June 30th when the term of Eugene M. Zuckert expires. . . .

• • • •

June 11, 1954

. . . A colonel from the Defense Department called me at my home in the evening to clear a release announcing transportation by the Air Force of a thousand wounded French soldiers from Indochina across the Pacific, then across the United States and Atlantic to France. I made a recommendation, which was accepted, that the release stress that the pickup point in Indochina would be from noncombat areas. The Defense Department release did not have that in, and we would have been under serious criticism if we had given the impression that we were going to fly our planes into fighting areas to pick up French wounded. I'll never understand why the Defense Department can't think of those things and public reaction to them. . . .

When the city of Memphis sought to get the Tennessee Valley Authority to build a steam plant to generate electricity, and the plant would have had to burn coal, for the TVA had run out of sites for water power, the new Eisenhower administration thought it saw an opening to force a well-known government agency to give up its interference, the administration believed, with private enterprise—the plant at Memphis should be run by private industry. The result was a consortium of companies known as the Dixon-Yates syndicate. Unfortunately a member of the First Boston Corporation, Dixon-Yates' financial agent, sat in on Bureau of the Budget discussions of the issue, and when this information came to light in July 1954, President Eisenhower canceled the Dixon-Yates contract.

Monday, June 14, 1954

. . . Leaders meeting at 8:30. . . . Meeting opened with a discussion of the Atomic Energy [Commission's] pending contract for power with TVA. Hughes and Strauss gave advance briefing to leaders for presentation in committee tomorrow on the Hill. President's comments on it could be summarized in one statement he made as follows: "People come in to me and say that Memphis needs more power and the federal government will have to provide it. When I ask them why they don't provide it for themselves, they say because under the TVA contract the power must come from TVA. I tell them that if private enterprise can't bring more power into Memphis and they have to get it from a government agency, then something's wrong. I still feel that way and always will." . . .

The leaders meeting was curtailed this morning to permit the legislators to get back to the Hill before 10 o'clock so that they would not be caught here in the White House during the air raid drill.

The air raid drill went off as scheduled. The President and his immediate personal staff went to his bomb shelter with Mrs. Eisenhower. Office space has been provided in the shelter and the new secret two-way television between the bomb shelter and High Point [North Carolina], the civil defense headquarters, was used for the first time. It operates on microwave and worked perfect. I didn't, of course, report this to the newspapermen.

Late in the afternoon Allen Dulles called me to ask when the President was having his next press conference.[1] I said that he would have it on Wednesday morning, and Allen Dulles said that by that time it might be necessary for the President to make some statement on Guatemala. CIA sources indicate that the situation is rapidly coming to a head in Guatemala and a presidential statement may be in order. It may be necessary to have the United States take the lead in invoking the Caracas Resolution against the spread of Communism here on this continent.

The big important news of the day was, of course, the upcoming visit of Churchill and Eden to Washington on June 25th. There is quite a story that goes with the release which will be announced at 10:30 A.M. tomorrow Washington time and 3:30 P.M. British time. . . .

Churchill has been pressing for this meeting as he did with Bermuda and as he pressed off and on for a four-power meeting with Malenkov. We are not sure that anything good will come of it, but as the President says, "I've decided to let the old man come over for this visit." . . .

Churchill has been really pressing for this meeting, somewhat to the annoyance of the President. Foster Dulles has not planned to have a press conference at his usual 11 o'clock time, but the President urged him to do so in order that the proper note may be sounded from the American side as to the meeting. I talked to Foster later in the day and he told me that the President had urged him to hold the conference and stress the informality of the meeting. This is extremely important since world conditions and world affairs would give this meeting a stronger import than it will actually have.

With Geneva folding up, with the French government collapsing, and with the preannounced British decision on not making up their minds on any collective action in Indochina until Geneva is finished, there is every chance that unless carefully guided, this meeting will be another one of those things. Foster and I agreed that in addition to the two sentences which I would officially release, it would be an excellent idea if I were to say this is a visit between two old friends, that it is informal, that of course, many subjects will come up for discussion, but that there is no set agenda. I checked this with the President at 6 o'clock, and he agreed that that was exactly the right approach to take. "Winston really wants this conference although I don't know how much good will come of it, but I decided to go along with him once again and play it more or less by ear." . . .

As I was discussing the Churchill visit with the President in his office at six o'clock, a very amusing incident happened. His glass porch door was closed and a squirrel on the outside kept jumping up and hitting the glass. The President and I watched it for a few minutes. Then he laughed and said, "That just proves what I've been saying around here. This is a nuthouse. Oh well, that squirrel has a lot more sense than some of the visitors I have had lately."

• • • •

Tuesday, June 15, 1954

In at 8:15.

Much to my surprise the announcement on Churchill and Eden visit did not leak from London or our State Department overnight. Consequently it came as a complete surprise to the newsmen when I gave it to them at 10:20. Incidentally, this was the first joint Anglo-American announcement in many years that had not been broken in advance by the British or leaked to their correspondents for overnight purposes. . . .

Admiral Strauss called today. Having meeting of his commission to approve release of full testimony of witnesses in Oppenheimer case. Several days ago Zuckert told Strauss that he was reading the full testimony on a train going to New York and his manuscript was either "mislaid or taken." We suspect he gave it to some people friendly to Oppenheimer. Strauss told me that Gray, chairman of the Oppenheimer panel, urged publication of testimony and also that commission had checked with all of the witnesses and they agreed to have the testimony released. Strauss later called me to tell me that testimony would be released at 6:00 P.M. tonight for noon release tomorrow. It is a document of about 900 pages.[1] . . .

Also received this afternoon, from Rowland Hughes, memoranda on proposal by private utilities to furnish power to the Atomic Energy Commission for their plant on the Mississippi River. The present plan, which will meet considerable opposition by TVA Congressmen, is to have private power plant, built by private companies on the west bank of the river in Arkansas across from Memphis. This would be just outside of TVA territory and would save the government about $100 million over three years to build the steam plants if it were done under TVA sponsorship.

The President's representative at the Geneva Conference on Indochina, Under Secretary of State W. Bedell Smith, his wartime chief of staff, had an impossible task. Dienbienphu fell on May 7, and all that was left at Geneva was some sort of operation to pick up the pieces, an arrangement that the United States hoped would include a guarantee of peace in Indochina by the Geneva powers. The difficulty of such a guarantee was compounded by presence of representatives of the People's Republic of China, for any official contact between them and the Americans might be construed as recognition of the PRC.

Wednesday, June 16, 1954

. . . Dulles thought it would be a good idea to have the President hold a bipartisan meeting at the White House when Bedell Smith returns. He strongly urged that such a meeting be linked to a "report on Geneva" by Smith rather than an advance meeting with bipartisan leaders on Churchill visit. If the latter inference was given, Dulles was afraid this would "blow up" the Churchill visit and give the impression that the leaders were being called in in advance to give commitments to major decisions which would be made at the meeting between the President and Churchill.

. . . Allen Dulles and the CIA yesterday had prepared a brief memorandum for the President which was sent first to the State Department and which I actually did not see. Their memorandum, however, had the President backing "their form of activity in Guatemala." [John Foster] Dulles rejected this memorandum because he was afraid if the President supported the CIA, it would lead to charges that the President and this country were supporting revolutionary activities within Guatemala and would place the President in the dangerous position of appealing to citizens of a foreign country to revolt against their leaders. . . .

In briefing with the President, we decided not to have any opening statement other than to say he was going to speak for his program whenever he had a chance and he hoped they might ask him questions about it.

On Churchill visit, he said that he was going to use a bridge as an illustration of what this meeting was all about. "You take any one of these bridges here across the Potomac. Thousands and thousands of people use them every day without noticing it. But if the bridge collapsed or if it were impossible to use it, then everybody would immediately notice it and cause a lot of trouble. That's exactly the way it is between the British and ourselves. This visit is to strengthen the bridge between us and to prove to the world that it is being used everyday. The only ones who would get comfort out of any troubles we might have would be the enemy."

Press conference went off very well. It was a short one, about twenty minutes. On the way back the President made several comments:

He expressed some amazement that the newsmen had respected his warning of two weeks ago that he was not going to talk about McCarthy and had not raised any questions on that matter. When I told him that after all it was his press conference and he could lay the ground rules, he seemed a little surprised but also pleased.

The President also said that he was deliberately recognizing Ethel Payne, a Negro reporter, because he did not want to give anybody an excuse to write that he was overlooking or ignoring the colored press. While he thought many of her questions were foolish, he thought it was a good thing to give the Negro reporters recognition. "You know, Jim, I suppose nobody knows how they feel or how many pressures or insults they have to take. I guess the only way you can realize exactly how they feel is to have a black skin for several weeks. I'm going to continue to give them a break at the press conferences despite the questions they ask."

Ray Borst in *Buffalo News* story out of Albany reported that Dewey would not run again for governor, that Frankfurter would resign from the Supreme Court, that Foster Dulles would be raised to the

Supreme Court, and that Dewey would be named new Secretary of State. When I was queried on this, I at first laughed it off as ridiculous and "news to me." Later in the day, however, when British correspondents started to query me seriously about it, I decided that I had better bring it to the attention of the President. I told him of the story and said that the only reason I was bothering him with it at this time was because of the British queries. I thought that a stronger statement should be made by me in order that the British papers would not go off on the wrong tangent and weaken Foster's prestige in their country. The President agreed and said that I should say that the story was "absolutely untrue, that I had talked to him about it and that no one had even mentioned such a thing to him." The President also said this: "It's funny that they should mention the Supreme Court. I was considering only two men as Chief Justice. One of them was Earl Warren and the other was Foster Dulles. If Foster had been younger and therefore able to serve as Chief Justice for many years, I think I would have appointed him. However, I wanted a man to serve as Chief Justice who felt the way we do and who would be on the court for a long time. Therefore, I chose Warren. I am glad I made that decision because I believe that Foster Dulles as Secretary of State has the best training of any man I know for his job." . . .

• • • •

Thursday, June 17, 1954

. . . I called Dulles in the morning and relayed to him the nice things the President said about him last evening. He was highly pleased and said that he had at one time received a hint—but only a hint—that the President was considering him for Chief Justice. "This will make a nice story for my memoirs and my family sometime in the future." . . .

• • • •

Friday, June 18, 1954

In at 8:15.

Allen Dulles called early in the morning to tell me that his organization expected there would be an anti-Communist uprising in

Guatemala very shortly. Officially we don't know anything about it. The story broke late Friday night. . . .

Joe Welch and Jim St. Clair dropped in to say goodbye and I got them in to see the President.[1] The President congratulated Welch for a very fine job. Welch told the President that he thought that if the hearings had accomplished nothing else, the Army had been able to keep McCarthy in front of the television sets for quite a while, long enough to permit the public to see how disgracefully he acted. He said he was sure this would be helpful in the long run. The President agreed with him on this. The President also agreed with Welch that the only Senator who came out of the hearings with flying colors was McClellan. . . .

• • • •

Saturday, June 19, 1954

Allen Dulles called me—and later Pete Carroll dropped in—to tell me that the situation in Guatemala as reported by the American press is greatly exaggerated.[1] Press reports "bombing." As Pete Carroll said, "There are no such planes in that part of the world. There have been a few homemade bombs dropped by Piper Cubs but that is about all." Expect that the wire services have very poor men in Guatemala and that they are overplaying the story. However, the State Department and foreign ministers of the other American countries are watching the situation very closely.

I think the State Department made a very bad mistake, particularly with the British, in attempting to search ships going to Guatemala. This was done obviously in an attempt to stop arms shipment to the country, but somebody in the State Department (maybe Dulles) forgot that the right of search of neutral vessels on the high seas is one which we ourselves oppose. As a matter of fact, we were at war with the British in 1812 over the same principle. I don't see how with our traditional opposition to such search and seizure we could possibly have proposed it, and I don't blame the British for one minute for getting pretty rough in their answers. I don't see why we did not ask the British and other nations to cooperate and to clear cargo lists in their own ports rather than to have them suffer the indignity of a search of their own ships by a foreign power. . . .

Received a coast-to-coast telephone call from Dr. Gordon Watkins, provost of the University of California in Riverside. It was the first coast-to-coast long distance call put through under a new system which the telephone company calls "Magic Relay." It was put through by pushing a few buttons comparable to dialing locally.

The President arrived at Quantico at 11:40 and took review. . . .

In a short, off-the-record talk at the luncheon the President took the occasion to stress to the services the need to speak carefully in public about the military problems of the day. He urged that each general officer should be careful to "recognize the scope and limits of his authority" and gave a very good lecture against irresponsible statements or statements that had not been fully cleared. (While he did not say so, the President was speaking directly about recent statements by Admiral Carney and some officers in the Army in presenting a "go to war" attitude.)[2] . . .

The President said that his test of a good man was the man's honesty and imagination. He said that imagination would bring understanding of the problems of the day so that the military may keep the peace, "which is the only true answer today to any military problem—the keeping of the peace.

"No matter how well prepared for war we may be, no matter how certain we are that within 24 hours we could destroy Kuibyshev and Moscow and Leningrad and Baku and all the other places that would allow the Soviets to carry on war, I want you to carry this question home with you: Gain such a victory, and what do you do with it? Here would be a great area from the Elbe to Vladivostok and down through Southeast Asia torn up and destroyed without government, without its communications, just an area of starvation and disaster. I ask you what would the civilized world do about it? I repeat there is no victory in any war except through our imaginations, through our dedication, and through our work to avoid it."

After luncheon the President played golf with General Floyd Parks, General Collins, and General Twining and then went to the barbecue supper at night, returning to Washington at midnight.[3] . . .

After golf while we were waiting for the barbecue to begin at 8:00, we returned to General Cates' home and the President and Talbott got into a lengthy discussion about the Air Force Academy and its site.[4] While the President did not say so, the manner in which he discussed it proved to me at least that the President favored

Colorado Springs as the location. He urged Talbott to take a look at Fort Logan and two or three times said that he did not believe that the Air Force Academy should be in the Middle West; it was good to spread these things over the country. . . .

• • • •

Monday, June 21, 1954

In at 8:15.

Legislative leaders meeting. . . .

The President then in discussing foreign trade gave a little lecture using Japan as an illustration. Characterizing Japan as the "key to the Pacific," he said that he was amazed to see people on the Hill who would say one of four things: (1) that anyone who trades with the Reds should be cut off the American list; (2) let's not save Southeast Asia; (3) don't trade with Japan or let Japan trade with the Reds; (4) don't give Japan money. "If we don't assist Japan, gentlemen, Japan is going Communist. Then instead of the Pacific being an American lake, believe me it is going to be a Communist lake. If we do not let them trade with Red China, with Southeast Asia, then we are going to be in for trouble. Of course, we do not want to ruin our own industries to keep Japan on our side, but we must give them assistance. It is a delicate, difficult course we have to follow, but I am sure we can do it in the long run." . . .

The President on Dougherty, head of the postal employees union and his opposition to Summerfield's plan: "We're getting into a hell of a fix when old man Dougherty can come around and tell Congress what they can or cannot do. It's a disgrace in my book. After all, letter carriers are working for the federal government."

The President to Jerry Persons when Halleck said he had been trying to get $20,000 from the Corps of Engineers to survey a dam in his territory: "You tell that fellow Sturgis that I'm interested in getting $20,000 bucks for Charlie and he'd better find it."[1]

The President to Secretary Benson on wheat allotments: "Ezra, you'll be amazed to know that Governor Murray of Oklahoma called me yesterday. He said it was raining in Oklahoma, that they were going to get a lot more rain and that the wheat was going to be wonderful. He was very pleased but I know you will not be at this report." . . .

The President told me briefly about his meeting with Senator Potter this afternoon. Potter merely announced when he left the President's office that he "discussed legislative matters with the President." Actually, what they discussed was the McCarthy hearings and the upcoming report. Potter is fed up to the ears with the activity of Dirksen, Mundt, and McCarthy and told the President that there was a very good chance that he (Potter) would end up voting with the Democratic minority. The President said, "I told Potter to vote with his conscience and not to let Dirksen or Mundt or McCarthy put any pressure on him by saying that I wanted him to do otherwise. I think from what he told me that he will vote with the Democrats on many things and that's all right with me."

The President told me that Potter was sore as hell at Dirksen, and we discussed the double cross that Dirksen gave Potter on the day the Republicans on the committee outvoted the Democrats 4 to 3 to not have Hensel and Carr testify as witnesses.[2] At that time Potter was ready to vote with the Democrats and refused the motion made by Dworshak when Dirksen leaned over to him and whispered, "This is what the President wants." Potter took this at face value, did not bother to call the White House to check it, and voted with his colleagues. It was only after he left the hearings that he found out that Dirksen was not telling the truth. Dirksen had been down to see the President that day on other matters and in passing had merely said, "Mr. President, we are trying to shorten the hearings and we may not have Carr and Hensel testify." Dirksen did not ask the President for his opinion and it was done in passing conversation. Then Dirksen goes up on the Hill and pulls a fast one on Potter. Potter is still sore and promised the President that after that either he would call the President directly or he would have his man, Tom McIntire, call me any time any Republican represented as fact any view of the President.

The case of Alger Hiss was of course a cause célèbre to the new Republican administration, if only because of the large part played in Hiss's conviction by the then Representative Nixon of California. One of the bright young men of the New Deal period, a former State Department employee, president of the Carnegie Endowment for International Peace, Hiss had not been convicted for espionage because the statute of limitations had run out, and went to jail because of perjury—asserting that he did not know his principal accuser, Time *magazine editor Whittaker Chambers, when in fact he had. Or so the jury of the second trial (the first had resulted in a mistrial) decided. Whatever the uncertainty the Eisenhower administration wanted nothing to do with Hiss and was embarrassed when a technical issue arose in regard to his case.*

Tuesday, June 22, 1954

. . . Phil Young, chairman of the Civil Service Commission, and Roger Jones of the Bureau of the Budget pulled one of the boners of the year, if not of our administration. Last May, Young received a letter from Rees, chairman of the Civil Service Committee of the House, asking for Young's opinion on a series of eight bills, three of them directly concerning Alger Hiss, which in effect would stop pensions for people dismissed from government for perjury or Communist leanings.[1] Without telling anyone in the White House about it, Young and the Budget decided all on their own to answer him. Why anyone in government, when a question involves Hiss, would not bring it to us here at the White House is beyond me. . . .

On the way up to the Shoreham in the car I had a chance to talk to the President about the Hiss thing. He said, "Jim, my boy, let's not hurry into this. Let's wait and see how it looks in the papers tomorrow morning. Anyway, I am not going to turn on the Budget Bureau just because they made a mistake. I'm amazed that anyone would honestly think of giving Hiss a pension and why don't you get a question asked tomorrow and cite the military law which I have lived under all my life. Whenever we dishonorably discharged a man from the service, we specifically said that his pay and allowances due or to become due are forfeited. I think you can say that in just that way."

• • • •

Wednesday, June 23, 1954

. . . Had meeting with the President at 11:30 on upcoming Churchill visit. . . . When Dulles mentioned the communiqué, the President said, "Listen, Foster, the last time we met at Bermuda we agreed there would not be any communiqué, but we finally had to sweat one out. What we really want to do is talk about what is on each other's mind, and we want to hold such meetings so frequently that they will not be tremendous news events." The President asked me what I thought about a communiqué, and I said I thought it was necessary and that without one all sorts of wild interpretations would be given to the meeting. Dulles agreed. The President then laughed and said, "OK. You fellows draft the communiqué. I'll approve it, but I don't want to work on it." . . .

Ground rules. Dulles proposed, and the President agreed, that it would be very necessary to stress to Churchill right at the start that informal talks do not constitute any agreements unless they are specifically labelled as agreements. The President said, "That's right. I'll tell Winston right off that we are not here to make agreements and decisions but if we have to, we will write them out and initial them so we both know exactly what we are talking about and exactly what we are doing. Winston has a wonderful way of turning conversations at some later time into ironclad agreements. We surely want to avoid that." . . .

Dulles then turned to a discussion of Japan . . . Dulles then said that he had proposed quite some time ago with the British that the British and the United States set up study groups to discuss and work out mutual problems in Europe, the Middle East, and the Far East. The President said that he thought that was a very good idea and that he would bring it up with Churchill and tell him, "This is really your idea, Winston, and I am having trouble selling it to my boys. That's the way you have to work with Winston. You have to get him thinking it's his own idea."

North Africa. Dulles warned that Indochina will be repeated in North Africa very shortly and that North Africans are rising against French colonialism. The President interrupted to say he agreed to that but it could not exactly be an Indochina because the Red Chinese and Russians were not near North Africa and could not send troops or materials into that area. Dulles said that at present the United States was without policy on this upcoming question, that the British undoubtedly would back up the French but that he believed that nationalism would sweep through Africa within 10 to 15 years and the African continent would then be lost to the control of the West. The President said that it was a little difficult with Algeria, that the French had made Algeria part of metropolitan France. It was the same thing he said as Texas, which we took from Mexico by force of arms, and we would never expect or support a Mexican appeal for Texas to return to Mexico. He said the French have done everything possible for Algeria and have promised additional freedom to Tunisia and Morocco. Dulles said the French always promise to do things in the United Nations but never make good on them. If they had carried out their promises on Indochina, they wouldn't be in the position they are today. The President interrupted to say, "A typical French promise is only a basis for future discussion."

Dulles ended the session today by saying that the United States must have a long-range program of planning for Africa to meet contingencies that are going to arise. He said he thought we should side in the long run with the nationalist feeling in Africa and get them on our side. . . .

• • • •

Thursday, June 24, 1954

. . . The question of Sunday church then came up, and the President laughingly remarked that he had a letter from his "pusher pastor" inviting him to bring "your two friends to my church on Sunday." He said that he did not know Winston's desires about church but that he (the President) was going to go to church anyway. He said that if Churchill and Eden did not want to go to church it was all right with him and their responsibility. . . .

Dulles said he had Makins at his home last night for "a dry run" of some of the subjects discussed yesterday.[1] He said Makins had made notes of them and had brought up on his own the question of colonialism. Dulles said he was sure that meant that the British were going to make a plea for a differentiation between French colonialism and British colonialism. The President interrupted to say, "Sure, the British always think their colonialism is different and better. Actually, what they want us to do is go along to help keep their empire." Dulles then said that Makins had reminded him that on Sunday Churchill, unlike the Americans, always ate a "huge luncheon." The President was a little amused at this and said, "I suppose we have enough food in the White House to give Churchill his huge luncheon, but I'll be damned if I'm going to change my habits for the Prime Minister—I'll have a light luncheon."

Guatemala. The Guatemala question came up next with Dulles reporting that in many instances the differences between the United States and the United Kingdom were becoming almost unbearable. . . . The President interrupted to say that he thought we were "being too damned nice to the British on this" and said that as far as he was concerned to go ahead and use the veto and show the British that they have no right to stick their nose into matters which concern this hemisphere entirely. "The British expect us to give them a free ride and side with them on Cyprus and yet they won't even support us on Guatemala. Let's give them a lesson."

Southeast Asia. Dulles said that he had studied fully the text of the Eden speech on Southeast Asia and as far as he could see it contemplated a dual system—(1) the establishment of a Southeast Asian nonaggression pact (Southeast Asia Treaty Organization—SEATO including Australia, New Zealand, the United Kingdom, Thailand, Cambodia, Laos, Vietnam, and possibly the Philippines); (2) a Locarno-type mutual nonaggression pact guarantee to support the settlement on a cease-fire order to come out of Geneva. He said that he was not so sure that we could guarantee the latter point. The President said that it might possibly have some value—"In a cold war when people assert that they will not be aggressive and later it turns out that they are and we can prove it, then I would think we would help many other peoples throughout the world to see what kind of people they are—that they break their promises." He said that the Southeast Asia nonaggression pact probably would not hurt "but as to guaranteeing any settlement reached at Geneva that's something else." Dulles said that the settlement at Geneva would be something we would have to gag about—"I don't think we'll like the settlement." The President said he agreed and said that both he and Foster would look at any British proposals with a jaundiced eye. "There is one thing, however, we must recognize in all fairness to Eden. He was talking to his Parliament and trying to sooth the ruffled feelings within his country. I'll tell you what we'll do, Foster. Let's you and I listen and refuse to be committed and look bored at some times." Dulles said that as far as he was concerned, the United States had made its proposal on Southeast Asia in April when we asked for collective action to stop Communist aggression through allied intervention. The British had turned this down flatly. . . .

Congressional luncheon. Smith said that he had received reports that Churchill had preferred to have the Saturday lunch with the congressional leaders without having the Australian prime minister or the Pakistan prime minister in attendance—that Churchill wanted it purely as a United States-United Kingdom affair. . . . The President said it seemed to him . . . that any invitation to dinners and luncheons was up to the President since he was the host but that probably the best thing to do was invite the prime ministers to the Saturday night dinner. The President told the following story: "The only time I ever raised hell about who should be at a dinner was when DeGaulle invited me to a dinner to present me with Napoleon's sword. DeGaulle deliberately tried to keep the British out of the dinner and I had Bedell send word to DeGaulle that if the British weren't invited, I wouldn't come. DeGaulle let the British in." . . .

Atomic weapons. Dulles said he was somewhat at a loss to know exactly how Churchill was thinking on atomic weapons but that he was sure these points would come up:

1. An effort to get the United States to return to the terms of the Quebec Conference which held that the United States should consult with the United Kingdom before using atomic weapons anywhere any time. The President said that he didn't think he would agree with that but that he probably would be glad to agree if the British showed some common sense—"And what I mean by common sense is if they would agree to let us give the French a few arms and spray them around in Indochina." . . .

4. Arrangement for use of atomic weapons in an emergency. On this one the President said that we had already made some strides, that the British had been designing bombers for some time now to carry such weapons and that additional storage places for the bombs were being located so that we could give quick delivery of them to the British. "If we ever get into trouble when we need these bombs it is our duty to provide them as quickly as possible to the British air force. I don't want to see American crews and American crews alone take the punishment they will have to take to deliver those bombs." . . .

In the list of subjects to discuss with Churchill the Secretary of State mentioned a Southeast Asia Treaty Organization—SEATO—and also a Locarno-type pact. The latter, presumably patterned after the Locarno Pact of

1925 in which Britain, Germany, and Italy guaranteed France's border with Germany, would have been a clear-cut arrangement to underwrite the agreements of the Geneva Conference arrived at in July 1954 (a temporary border at the seventeenth parallel between the north and south of Vietnam, exchange of populations between the north and south of Vietnam, all-Vietnamese elections). The British evidently wanted to put steel in the Geneva agreements. But Dulles did not, and the message got through to the British. Churchill and Eden arrived Friday morning at 9:30 at the north portico of the White House, and by that afternoon a Locarno-type pact was out.

Friday, June 25, 1954

. . . One story that is particularly interesting was told to me by Ambassador Aldrich.[1] He also told the story to Dulles. He said that as the afternoon conference was breaking up, Eden turned to him and said, "You know, Mr. Ambassador, as far as I'm concerned I am going to drop this Locarno matter." . . .

• • • •

Saturday, June 26, 1954

In at 8:15.

The President was in his office at 8:30 and I had a half-hour talk with him on the progress of the conference. He said that it was awfully difficult to talk with Churchill, that he refused to wear a hearing aid and consequently the President had to shout at him all the time in conversation.

My own personal observations are that Churchill is considerably physically weaker than he was when I saw him in Bermuda, which of course is due to the fact that since Bermuda he has had two strokes. He is almost in the dotage period and gives the appearance at least of losing connection with the conversation that is going on in the room. However, when he speaks he still retains the forcefulness of delivery, the beautiful, ordered, and intelligent command of the English language although he doesn't seem to be able to stay on a point very long, He seems to get on one subject and repeat it many times. An example of this is the several talks that he has already given on the complexities of a central form of government, the advantages we have here with our 48 states taking much of the local load off our government and his thoughts on the restoration of the heptarchy. He said this to the staff in the President's office on Friday; he repeated it at the congressional luncheon today; and he stopped me in the hall on the second floor of the White House to give me a private speech on the subject. That was when the electric storm broke and the Prime Minister, like a little boy, rushed from the President's study to go to the solarium to watch the rain. Merriman Smith told me that Fisher, the UP man in London, had told him that the British had not given Churchill too much confidential information in the last month because of a speech he made in London spilling the beans on some confidential information without even knowing he was doing so.[1]

In the afternoon while I was waiting on the second floor for the meeting of the Big Four to break up in the President's study, the President came out to go to his room to get a copy of his "declaration release." He asked me if I was waiting to see him and when I said no, that I was waiting to see the Secretary of State after the meeting broke up, he invited me to come in to the meeting. Once again I was able to personally observe the Prime Minister's reactions. The President brought in the declaration and said that he and the Prime Minister had talked it over earlier in the morning, but the President addressed all his remarks to Eden and the British ambassador. The Prime Minister didn't seem to be able to hear the conversation or to follow it and constantly broke in with questions that had to be explained to him by either the President or Eden in a shouting tone of voice.

Of course, Eden treats the Prime Minister like a father with great deference and with great respect, but I am sure the entire British delegation realizes that the Prime Minister is a very feeble old man and that he has not too long to live. They are terribly proud of him naturally, but behind the pride and not too far below the surface you can always get the considerable strain of worry about the Prime Minister's condition and the fact that the leadership of the British Empire still rests in his hands. The President has told me of this more than once, and I had a chance to see it myself.

One thing that we were very successful on the very first day (although we had made no announcement of it) was on Guatemala. The President and Dulles talked cold turkey to the Prime Minister and Eden and told them that we would use the veto against them if they insisted on putting the Guatemalan question in the Security Council. Eden had a long talk with the President on this subject and later called the British representative of the UN. The result was that the American proposition to keep the Guatemalan situation in the American States organization was approved by the Security Council with England and France not voting. . . .

• • • •

Sunday, June 27, 1954

In at 10:00.

I met the President and Mrs. Eisenhower at the south portico upon their return from church at 10:10. The President invited me to attend the movie he was showing for Churchill and Eden on the royal tour of Queen Elizabeth made by British Movietone News. During the movie the President kept up a running conversation with Churchill. When a brook in Australia was shown, the President said, "That looks like a good trout stream." When an arch to train elephants in Ceylon was shown the President said, "Winston, there must be a lot of Republicans over there." When scenes of North Africa and Gibraltar were shown, the President remarked to Sir Winston, that they had visited those places sometimes together during the war. . . .

• • • •

Monday, June 28, 1954

In at 8:00 A.M.

Leaders meeting in the morning at 8:30. . . .

The President then turned the meeting over to Dulles who reported first on Guatemala and next on Indochina. On Guatemala, Dulles said that the resignation of Arbenz represented a "great triumph" for American diplomacy. . . .

On Indochina, Dulles said that the United States policy is aimed constantly at the creation of a defense line in the Far East. He said that it is too soon yet to get a clear picture of what the French will propose to the Vietminh and reported that the President had been prepared to recommend to the Congress that American troops intervene in Indochina if the French would go on with the fight and if the British would agree to come in with us. The French were not willing to make such a commitment and the British took a strong position that they were not going to send a single British soldier into the area. . . .

Churchill joined the President in his office at 11 o'clock. . . . It was agreed to meet again the following morning.

The President had a little fun with Churchill on the time of the meeting. He said, "Winston, I will be ready to meet you any time you want. I get up at 6:30 and will be available from seven o'clock on." The Prime Minister smiled and said, "Mr. President, as you know, I have a habit of getting up a little later than that." The President said, "10:30?" Churchill said, "A little later than that, please." The President: "11:30?" The Prime Minister: "That will be fine. That is more normal." . . .

• • • •

Tuesday, June 29, 1954

. . . As the Prime Minister left, I returned alone to the President's office with him and he told me that by and large he thought the meetings had gone off very well. As he had said on the first day, he repeated that it was very difficult to keep the Prime Minister on the beam in discussing any one subject for any length of time. The Prime Minister has moments when he does not seem to be entirely aware of everything that is going on. It is merely old age, but it is becoming increasingly more noticeable.

I asked the President if he had discussed the subject of Red China and its admission to the UN with Churchill, and he said that he had. "I just had one conversation on this subject. I told him that it was politically immoral and impossible for the United States to favor the admission of Red China to the United Nations, and surprisingly enough Churchill agreed. He pointed out that at the present time Britain was also at war with Red China and would remain so as long as Red China kept her military forces in Korea. According to the Prime Minister, that was that and we never discussed the situation again."

Later in the afternoon Lewis Strauss called me to report that his commission had voted to deny clearance of Oppenheimer by 4 to 1. When I reported this to the President, he was very pleased and personally called Strauss to congratulate him on the fine job he had done in handling a most difficult situation. The President expressed the hope that the handling of the Oppenheimer case would be such a contrast to McCarthy's tactics that the American people would immediately see the difference.

In the years just after the Second World War, when the Democrats were in charge of the White House and running foreign policy, the GOP never had extended bipartisanship to the Far East, only to Europe, although within the area of the Far East the Republicans did not criticize policy toward Japan as long as General MacArthur was supreme commander. China was another matter, and Republican doctrine had it that the Democrats lost China because of lack of support to Chiang Kai-shek. Just what sort of support they had in mind was unclear, and they never meant military support—American divisions in China—as leading GOP Senators related in the late 1940s. After the Republicans came into power the Chinese issue was lost—mainland China was Communist. But it was an irresistible issue and occasionally the Republicans' partisans brought it out, raised it up, and scolded the Democrats.

Wednesday, June 30, 1954

. . . At the staff meeting it was decided that the President must vigorously defend Nixon from Democratic attack. In his speech at Milwaukee, Nixon said that the loss of China was due to the Acheson policy and of course, the Democrats had a big crying towel out of it. All were unanimous that the President should not fall for this. . . .

At the presidential briefing the President agreed to follow these suggestions and to make a strong personal statement on the Vice President. At the press conference some of the left-wing press tried to trip him up on the Vice President, but he handled it very well and at his direction as soon as the conference was over, I called Nixon and gave him a full report. He was very pleased.

Left that afternoon at two o'clock and flew to New York for the dinner the *New York Times* men were giving for Dad on his retirement. It was a fine party and everyone had a good time.

July 1954

Thursday, July 1, 1954

In New York City. Went with Dad and Toots Shor to Giant-Dodger ball game and returned to Washington at ten o'clock. Home at 10:30.

• • • •

Friday, July 2, 1954

In at 8:15. The President left for Camp David at 12:30. . . .

• • • •

Tuesday, July 6, 1954

In at 8:15. The President returned from Camp David at 10:45.

During the morning Governor Adams called a meeting in his office which was attended by Carroll, Persons, Morgan, Hauge, Snyder, Martin, and myself.[1] The meeting was called primarily to discuss (1) the Knowland statement issued the day before in which the Senator said that he opposed admission of Red China into the United Nations, and if that happened, he would resign the majority leadership to wage a campaign within the Senate to get the United States to withdraw from the UN; and (2) the entire foreign situation, particularly Indochina and the upcoming French settlement with the Chinese Reds. Briefly, here is what we all are worried about.

First, although we are not in the French confidence and they are holding their talks with the Chinese Reds in secret, it looks as if the French are getting ready to almost completely capitulate to the Vietminh to partition Vietnam and withdraw from the entire north, leaving behind them many of the population of that territory who are Catholic and who have been strong anti-Red fighters. Of course, if that happens, these people will be brutally treated by the Communists and many will be liquidated.

Both the United States and the United Kingdom have urged the French government to make some arrangements to evacuate some of these people from the area, but we have no way of knowing whether the French are making such arrangements or whether the Chinese Communists will go along with such a plan. The partition of Vietnam, when it happens, will be badly received in this country and will be quite properly regarded as a tremendous triumph for Communism throughout the world. However, there is nothing we can do about this since the British would not agree to go into Indochina with us several months ago when we possibly could have saved the situation.

The more immediate problem before us is Knowland's speech and the fear that many of us have that it indicates a growing feeling in the country, fanned to life, of course, by the isolationists, that it would be better to wash our hands of the whole mess and even get out of the United Nations. Such a step would, of course, be tragic and would be a complete repudiation by the United States of its world leadership. We agreed that under no conditions should this viewpoint be taken as an administration viewpoint.

That afternoon at 3:30 we went in to see the President to discuss this whole situation. He was as concerned as we were about Knowland's speech, not the part dealing with opposition to admission of Red China into the UN (to which we all agree as that is the official American position) but to the part in which Knowland said he would resign from his leadership so that he would not cause the administration any embarrassment and lead the fight to get the United States out of the United Nations should Red China be admitted. The President pointed to this part of his statement and said, "What the hell did he have to say that for? That implies that we would favor the admission of Red China to the UN." Just at that point of the discussion Tom Stephens came in and said Knowland was calling and would like to see the President. The President said to send Knowland right down and he would have a talk with him on this subject and try to straighten him out. . . .

During the two meetings with the President that afternoon he made the following observation about Knowland: "He thinks he's Horatius at the Bridge. All he wants is attention and he acts like a little boy at times." The President also said that he wanted to discuss Red China at the press conference the following morning and asked me to make sure to have a question asked along those lines. I told him I was sure there would be one but that I would arrange it with Johnny Cutter.

Was called at home at eight o'clock by Shanley to tell me that he was going to have the President issue an executive order setting up a board of inquiry to investigate the wage dispute at atomic plants at Oak Ridge and Paducah, Kentucky. I came back to the White House at 8:30 and had a conference call with the wire services, releasing the President's order as well as two letters from Strauss which said that the strike was against the national interest and listed the operations and facilities at Oak Ridge and Paducah which might be interfered with as a result of the strike.

• • • •

Wednesday, July 7, 1954

. . . Later in the day Shanley and I kept in touch with Mitchell and Strauss on the board of inquiry for the atomic strike, but we were unable to pick the three members today. The AEC had sent over a list which was completely useless. It consisted mainly of men who had served in similar capacities under the New Deal and they were certainly not the type of men we wanted to appoint. Therefore, Jim Mitchell had to start from scratch to pick the board and we were not able to give it out today, although it was definitely tied down that we would be able to release it tomorrow.

• • • •

Thursday, July 8, 1954

In at 8:15.

Checked with Shanley on the board of inquiry and he told me that as soon as we got name clearance from the FBI we were going to appoint Glennan, Floberg, and Sanders. I left at ten minutes after ten with Ed Darby to fly to New York for a luncheon with the top staff of *Life* and *Time* magazines. I spent two hours with them in discussion and thought it was very worthwhile. Was able to set them straight, I think, on the President's attitude on Red China and the UN and on the results of the Churchill visit. Returned to the office at five o'clock.[1]

The President was out in the back yard hitting golf balls when I walked into Ann Whitman's office.[2] He stuck his head in while I was there and said to me, "Jim, I had my picture taken with those Spaniards. I couldn't help it. I was sort of on a spot." Later I learned from Murray that Franco's daughter had paid a visit to pay her respects to Mrs. Eisenhower. Murray had tried to fuzz up the requests for photographs, although some photographers were out at the north portico. Mrs. Eisenhower had sort of tripped the President into seeing Franco's daughter and as they left asked the President to walk out on the portico with them. Once they were out and the photographers were there, there was nothing the President could do. Actually, I don't think there was much harm done by the photographs. After all, as the President put it—"Spain is becoming one of our strong allies. We need her divisions."

I was able also to step out on the porch with him and talk about the Geneva Conference. I told him that I had been thinking about it and that I thought if Dulles or Bedell Smith did not return, America would look like a little boy sulking in his tent. We would be blamed for everything and would have no opportunity or forum to express our dislike for whatever settlement the French might make in Indochina. The President said that that was a viewpoint which he wanted to consider, adding, "The trouble, Jim, with this whole damn situation is that the French will try to get us, if we are physically there with Dulles or Bedell, to approve of the terms of the settlement. We don't think it's going to be a good one and it certainly isn't one we can support. Now, do we go and sit there and become a party to it, or do we express our disapproval by not sending our top men back to the conference?" I said that I thought we should make a fight against it or at least express our disapproval of it on the spot. If we did not have Foster or Bedell there, the Russians and the Chinese, together with a reluctant and ineffective France, could make quite a to-do about it. Eden, if he goes, would probably remain more or less quiet although undoubtedly he would be forced to hail the settlement as a step toward peace. "That's just the point," the President added. "If we do go and if we sound off against the settlement, as we should, then are we not dividing the free world and being put in the position of splitting publicly with France and probably with the U.K. It's a tough one to decide, but you have given me something to think over."

• • • •

Friday, July 9, 1954

In at 9:00.

At the Cabinet meeting Dulles gave a review of the international situation for the Cabinet and read a draft of a cable which he was going to send to Eden, declining to have either himself or Bedell Smith return to Geneva. The President interrupted Foster when he finished reading the cable and said that he thought probably we would have to study this question more fully before a definite decision was made. He repeated some of the arguments that I had presented to him the night before and told Foster that he wanted to talk to him further on this subject. . . .

It was decided later in the day that the board of inquiry in the atomic strike situation would call on the President and give him their report at noon tomorrow. The CIO union at Oak Ridge voted late this afternoon to return to work but the CIO union at Paducah has not done so. . . .

• • • •

Saturday, July 10, 1954

. . . The British moved to put on additional pressure for Geneva by releasing a story from London from the British Foreign Office saying that both Eden and Churchill hope that Dulles or Smith would return to Geneva. . . .

The day was further complicated by the very sad news that Milton Eisenhower's wife died that afternoon. Bob Schulz met the President at the golf course and told him about it, and I met the President when he returned to the White House.[1] Both he and Mrs. Eisenhower, of course, felt very bad about it although as the President said, "It was really a blessing." Milton was very broken up and of course the President and Mrs. Eisenhower planned immediately to go to the funeral on Tuesday. This raised the question of his scheduled trip to the Governors' Conference and he decided that he should cancel out.

The President called Tom Stephens and both Tom and I were on the phone for some time straightening out the program. Tom called Dan Thornton at the Sagamore Hotel at Lake George where the Governors' Conference was being held, and it was agreed to send the Vice President in the President's place.[2] . . .

The Governors' Conference address was important, for the President planned to propose the interstate highway program.

Sunday, July 11, 1954

I dropped down to see the President at ten o'clock after church to see if there was anything further he wanted me to do. He had nothing in particular that he wanted me to do with reference to the change of plans, but we did have an opportunity to talk about the international situation and the upcoming Geneva Conference. . . . "All in all it is going to be a tough situation, but I think you are dead right in urging us to have a high-level American representative at Geneva. Otherwise, the stories from Geneva will be entirely colored by Red propaganda and also by propaganda of our allies, particularly the French, who will then blame us for everything that goes wrong."

• • • •

Monday, July 12, 1954

In at 8:00 A.M.

Talked with the President briefly on the Governor's Conference and he agreed to send two wires—one to Dan Thornton and the other to Nixon to be used in connection with Nixon's visit to Lake George. Both wires expressed his disappointment at not being with the governors and consequently were very well received when they were read at the state dinner.

Took off from MATS at 9:15 and arrived at Glens Falls shortly after eleven. Nixon was met by Governor Dewey as the host governor . . .

On the way up in the plane Adams, McCann, and I talked over the upcoming speech with Nixon, and it was agreed to give emphasis to the $50 billion highway program that Nixon would announce, that we would take the unusual step of making public in advance the President's notes that he had prepared for the Governors' Conference.[1] . . .

I called Bruce and he came down about 5:30.[2] We had a visit and later he joined John Dewey and the young people for dinner. Seemed to have a nice time.

Nixon was in a terrible spot but did a good job, although Fine of

Pennsylvania immediately had to jump in with criticism of the $50 billion program.[3] Why he shoots off his mouth I'll never know except that he's all washed up in Pennsylvania and is just looking for headlines.

Left the Sagamore Hotel about ten minutes after eleven and arrived at MATS at 2:00 A.M., getting home at 2:30.

• • • •

Tuesday, July 13, 1954

In at 8:15 and left with the President, Mrs. Eisenhower, and Bob Schulz at 8:40 for the airport and then for State College to attend Mrs. Milton Eisenhower's funeral. Arrived at Altoona at 9:45 and State College at 11:00. Arrangements for the funeral were very good and everything went off with the minimum of grief although, of course, Milton, Bud, and Ruth were very broken up.[1] . . .

After we returned to the White House, the House on a surprise move and a surprise vote defeated the Health Reinsurance Program by a vote of 238 to 134. When I brought the ticker item in to the President, he asked me to get a complete breakdown of the roll call and to give him the names by the next morning of the Republicans who voted against it. "If any of those fellows who voted against that bill expect me to do anything for them in this campaign, they are going to be very much surprised. This was a major part of our liberal program and anyone who voted against it will not have one iota of support from me."

Dog tired. Home at six and to bed by about 8:30.

• • • •

Wednesday, July 14, 1954

In at 8:00 A.M. A particularly hectic day!! . . .

The President opened the leaders meeting by bringing up the House defeat of our reinsurance bill. Turning to Halleck, the President said: "Charlie, this is the first time I have had to bring out my crying towel to you and the House. What happened?" Halleck replied that the Democrats, of course, had ganged up almost solidly against the bill, the private insurance companies in Chicago had been effective on Midwest Congressmen, and united opposition of the American Medical Association had been reflected in the vote.

The President replied, "How in the hell is the American Medical Association going to stop socialized medicine if they oppose such bills as this. I don't believe the people of the United States are going to stand for being deprived of the opportunity to get medical insurance. If they don't get a bill like this, they will go for socialized medicine sooner or later and the Medical Association will have no one to blame but itself. Furthermore, I can't understand how any Republican voted against this bill. I am going to continue to speak my piece on this and continue to fight for it as long as I am in office. How is a Republican who voted against it going to support himself in his district?" . . .

When the story broke from Paris, I called in the newsmen and told them that Bedell was returning to Geneva, that the President had talked to Dulles on the transatlantic telephone and that Dulles was returning to Washington at 9:30 tomorrow morning and would report to the President on his conversations with Mendès-France and Eden.[1] . . .

Just before I went home the President asked me to come into his office again. The Postmaster General had just left his office and the President wanted to let me know what Summerfield had reported to him. "This is a very great secret at the present time. There are only a few people who know it—myself, the Attorney General, the Postmaster General, and yourself." The President told me that several days ago an official of the Post Office employees union had called at the office of Representative Broyhill to try to get him to support the postal employees raise bill.[2] As he left the office, the official handed Broyhill an envelope and told him that he would appreciate it if he would open it after he left the office. When the official left, Broyhill opened the envelope and found that it contained 25 – $20 bills. . . .

The following day Broyhill asked the official to return to the office without letting him know anything . . . As soon as Broyhill handed the money to him, the FBI jumped on him. . . . As the President told me this story, he was visibly shocked by the attempted bribe—"$500 for a vote! That's really something, isn't it? And to think they're handing out the funds of their own union which they get from their members. That $500 for one vote is more than any raise any postal employee expects to get in a year. What a business!"

. . . .

Thursday, July 15, 1954

In at 8:00 A.M.

The President knocked the cap off his favorite tooth in the morning and had to have a dentist come to the White House to fix it. Consequently he did not get over to the office until about 9:45. Dulles arrived at MATS terminal at 9:20 and was waiting for him. . . .

Prior to the time that the President arrived at the White House, Dulles and I had a rather long talk on the situation. He said that he thought that he had made the American position quite clear to the French and the British; namely, that we did not particularly like the idea of the partition of Vietnam but would go along with it if they agreed to support the American effort to form promptly in the Far East area a Southeast Asia Treaty Organization. . . .

• • • •

Friday, July 16, 1954

In at 8:15. Cabinet meeting at 9:30.

The first two items on the agenda at the Cabinet meeting were brought up by Adams and concerned (1) monitoring of telephone calls, and (2) organization for the development and coordination of foreign economic policy. . . .

On the monitoring of phone calls, Adams said that it was the recommendation of the subcabinet that such a matter was (a) not a subject for general directive by the President; (b) that the practice should be reduced in every way possible; and (c) it was the feeling that if calls are monitored the person on the other end should be notified that a record was being taken of his conversation.

The President said he had no opposition to this and "as a matter of fact, I cannot see where there would be any opposition if you tell the person on the other end that the calls are being recorded." . . .

On the coordination of foreign economic policy, the President said that . . . abroad as far as he was concerned he had always wanted to make the ambassador "the boss of American personnel in that country." . . .

The third subject discussed was the question of the St. Lawrence. . . . The President interrupted to say that he would much rather see the Attorney General and the Department of Defense work out the legal problems without having to go to the Senate for any treaty. He also said that he did not want to have additional expense on this subject. . . .

The President mentioned as one instance the demands that we would be bound to be getting from many cities on the Great Lakes who want their harbors deepened at federal expense—"I think we should get tougher about this. If we provide the main channel through the St. Lawrence, the cities on the Great Lakes will derive the benefits, so let them pay the cost for their own harbors. Let them do it themselves. Ever since I've been in this job I keep looking for someone other than the federal government to pick up the check once in awhile. You know, these fellows who get called to the phone just when the check comes to the dinner table really get my goat." . . .

Played golf with the President at the Congressional Country Club, leaving the White House at 12:30 for lunch at the club before the game. On the way out I had a chance to report to the President on the conversation I had with Chief Baughman of the Secret Service that morning. Baughman told me that he had a check made of Major John Eisenhower's new quarters at Fort Leavenworth and that while they were all right, he was worried about two or three things. (1) Leavenworth has the Army prison, has quite a few tough characters in the prison grounds, and some of them as trusties have almost a free run of the place. (2) Major John's quarters consist of a single-story home with the children's bedroom in the rear of the house. Baughman said that he would work out with the Signal Corps some photoelectric equipment on the windows and around the grounds. They would be put in privately and quietly; and he would put two Secret Service men with the family at all times. Baughman made one particular request to me, namely, that no photographs be taken of the quarters. I passed all this along to the President, and he agreed with Baughman and told me to send orders through to the Army that no photographs were to be made. . . .

On the way out to the golf club I also had a chance to talk to the President about the future of the Health Reinsurance Plan. . . . The President . . . told me to tell Mrs. Hobby to "get mad" at the legislative meeting on Monday. "You tell Oveta I said to let her Texas temper get the best of her on Monday, and let those fellows have it." When I returned home that evening, I relayed the information to Mrs. Hobby. She laughed and said, "Don't worry. I'll get mad." . . .

• • • •

Sunday, July 18, 1954

Played golf at Columbia Country Club with Bob Denton in the morning and then went out in the midafternoon and played ten holes with Bob and Marge.

We were just concluding the tenth hole when the phone at the refreshment shack rang and it was the President calling me. I told him where I was, but he said he thought it was all right to discuss the situation he wanted to with me over the phone. He said he was sitting in the White House with Dulles and that they both agreed that the situation in Geneva might get out of hand and that it might be necessary for him to go on the air Wednesday evening to make a full report to the American people. He asked me to get in touch with Bill Paley at CBS and General Sarnoff at NBC and tell them it might be necessary for the President to make a radio and television broadcast on Wednesday night.[1] He said that it was not definite, of course, and would depend upon developments at Geneva. He said that Foster would call me back and fill me in further on the situation when he got home. I gave the White House the number of the Columbia Country Club and told them I would come right in to await Dulles' call.

Dulles called back in about a half hour and explained that it might be necessary in the war of nerves game that we had to play in Geneva for the Communists to realize that if they turned down reasonable French demands the United States through the President would move dramatically through one or two possibilities.

The first possibility, which Dulles did not like himself, would be to have the President go to the Congress on Wednesday and ask for immediate wartime powers. This would cause anxiety here in the country, would scare everybody to death, and would be too drastic. The second was the possibility of a report to the people by the President, in which the President would end up by proposing that the United States would immediately take steps to bring the whole question of Indochina and the peace settlement there into the United Nations itself. Dulles explained that the second step was, of course, more likely than the first but what was more important was that the Communists had gotten the impression that we would not stand for much nonsense and were ready to move rapidly to counteract any stalling that they might pursue.

Of course, Mendès-France made a major political and diplomatic mistake in setting a deadline of July 20th. The Commies will never let the free world meet such a deadline and Mendès-France should have known that before he made it. . . .

Pierre Mendès-France, premier of France, had taken office on June 18 on the strength of his incautious pledge.

Monday, July 19, 1954

. . . Senator Knowland said that it was obvious that Mrs. Hobby ought to have money to run her own program. As to the Health Reinsurance Bill, he questioned the advisability of moving on that bill in the Senate since it was highly unlikely that it could be passed in the House. With that, the President broke in and said, "Listen, Bill, what do you think we're going to tell the people of the United States? We said during the campaign that we were against socialized medicine. One of the things we gave to Mrs. Hobby was her assignment to advance a program which would show the people of this nation that the Republican Party was interested in improving our people's health. As far as I'm concerned, the American Medical Association is just plain stupid. This plan of ours would have shown the people how we could improve their health and stay out of socialized medicine." Knowland said that he was recommending that we give the Health Reinsurance Bill top priority next year to permit the leadership to do a lot of work in the AMA during this upcoming year. Mrs. Hobby broke in to say that there was not any way they could do business with the top hierarchy of the AMA. She said that there was only a little group of reactionary men in charge "dead set against any change." . . .

I had a long and rather hectic session with Abbott Washburn in the afternoon on the USIA releases on the Oppenheimer case.[1] Washburn returned from vacationing in Minnesota at Adams' direction. I talked pretty frankly to him and told him that I thought it was a lousy job, that the people who had written the material were slanting it in favor of Oppenheimer and I could see no sense whatsoever in sending out Alsop columns on USIA wires attacking the chairman of the Atomic Energy Commission and the administration. The upshot of this discussion was that Washburn promised to check back on his department to watch the people that we suspected of being anti-administration and to report to me once a week. I told Adams that I thought it would be handled better and we will now await developments. When Streibert returns from his European tour, I will take it up with him. . . .

On July 21, one day late, Mendès-France signed an agreement with the North Vietnamese at Geneva that the signatories backdated to July 20 so he could meet his deadline. The accord's terms were those mentioned earlier. Its weakness was the lack of a Locarno-type pact. The guarantor powers at Geneva were Russia, the PRC, and Britain, but their divergence of interests worldwide ensured that they would not guarantee anything. The only Western response of any seriousness, and it was largely window dressing, was the Southeast Asia Treaty Organization, the treaty for which was signed later that year. In any event the President of the United States on July 21 did not have to make a speech to the American people.

Wednesday, July 21, 1954

. . . As a result of the way things have turned out in Geneva and the President's press conference statement, it was decided that it was not necessary for the President to go on the air and talk to the American people. . . .

• • • •

Thursday, July 22, 1954

In at 8:15.

In the morning papers there was a story that Knowland joined the attacks that the Democrats were making against the Indochina settlement. He characterized the settlement as "the greatest victory the Communists have won in twenty years." Why he has to make these statements is more than I'll ever know. When I arrived at the White House, I went in to see the President and asked him if he had seen Knowland's statement. He had and was as mad as I was. The President said, "The more I see of Knowland, the more I wonder whether he is a Republican leader or what."

I told the President that I had been thinking about this statement and thought it would be a good idea to have a Senator get up on the floor and ask the people who were talking about appeasement on the settlement and defeat for the free world if they had any alternative for the settlement and whether they would have voted to send American troops into Indochina. I recommended that Senator Potter would be a very good man to make such a statement. The President agreed with me and said that he had thought of doing it himself at his press conference but had changed his mind at the last moment. I told him that I knew John McIntire, Potter's assistant, and if he had no objection, I would call him. The President told me to go ahead, and as a result, Potter issued the following statement. I showed it to the President and he was very pleased.

> . . . I should like to ask my colleagues, particularly those who have talked about appeasement, if they would have voted to send American boys to fight in Indochina. . . . I for one am not ready to send American young men into Indochina in a fighting war and I believe that many of my colleagues who have seized upon this opportunity to speak of appeasement would not vote for armed intervention by the American military at the present time. There are features in the agreement which are not desirable but we must accept them. . . .

At 2:30 I went into the President's office with Malcolm Muir, publisher of *Newsweek.* Muir had just returned from a trip to Europe and Africa and the President was particularly interested in Muir's reaction to the feeling about America in Egypt.

Muir said he had a long talk in Cairo with Nasser and also talked with Naguib. He said that Nasser is the strong man in Egypt and Naguib is merely his messenger boy. He told the President that he had asked Nasser what he thought of the United States, and Nasser had replied that at the end of World War II, American prestige was at its highest in Egypt, but that it has been lessened for the following reasons:

American foreign policy had backed the French in Africa and Indochina and has sided with the British. In addition, the Roosevelt and Truman administrations had given full-hearted support to Israel as opposed to the Arab League states. Nasser told Muir that he did not see how America—which was founded after a war with England—could support the colonial ambitions of either England or France and said that if this word were circulated in the world to nationalist-inclined peoples, it would do a great deal of good.

The President said that he couldn't agree more with Nasser and told Muir that he had just finished dictating a letter to "a very important person." (It was Churchill and I am sure Muir knew that it was.) The President read a section of his letter to Churchill to Muir, in which the President told Churchill that on the question of colonialism the only way that England and the United States should work it was to encourage the independence of these countries and to encourage them also into joining a commonwealth similar to the present British Commonwealth. The President pointed out to Muir that in effect the Philippines were a part of a commonwealth with the United States. He said that despite the fact that we had given them independence they were now finding that they needed us badly, and the President reminded Mr. Muir that he had just signed a bill several days ago extending the trade agreements with the Philippines for two more years. "That's the way this situation must be handled. We must work with these peoples and then they themselves will soon find out that we are their friends and that they can't live without us. That's the way Britain must do with their colonial empire and that's the way the French must do. I will admit that the British have been smarter in dealing with colonial peoples than have the French. If the French are not careful, they will not have one single bit of territory left in Africa at the end of ten years." . . .

Marge won the CBS Cup in the Class B District Competition.

• • • •

Friday, July 23, 1954

Not much doing this morning. Marge still in a tizzy over winning the golf tournament and nice stories in both the *Post* and *Star.* Played golf with Roger in the afternoon.[1] . . .

• • • •

Monday, July 26, 1954

In at 8:15.

Leaders meeting at 8:30. . . .

The President then brought up the Southeast Asia situation and said that he had been hearing some talk that some of the people on the Hill wanted to save and cut out the $80 million in FOA funds presently allocated to Southeast Asia. He said that in his opinion this was a bad thing to do and added: "I don't know of any time when we need this money so badly to help build up Southeast Asia so that it can withstand further assaults. . . . As a nation, we just can't go around waving a pair of deuces in a man's face without risking being called some day."

The President then told the leaders that we had two airplane carriers in that vicinity and started to tell them about the Vietminh attack south of the seventeenth parallel when I had an urgent call from Dulles and left the meeting to take it. Dulles told me that he had just received word that two American search planes of the AD type from one of our carriers had been searching the waters near where the British commercial plane had been shot down by Communist fighters on Friday. Our planes were attacked by two Chinese Communist LA-9s, the same type of plane (and maybe the same two planes) which shot down the British airliner. Our planes were outside the territorial waters of China beyond the 12-mile limit. When the Chinese planes attacked, they found they weren't picking on an unarmed commercial plane and our planes immediately responded and shot down both Communist planes. . . . The meeting then broke up and I accompanied the President into his office while he called Dulles. . . . The President's opening words to Foster Dulles when he called him on the phone were, "Well, Foster, it didn't take long for something to happen over there, did it?" . . .

After the President finished talking to the Secretary, we discussed the situation briefly and while expressing concern over the incident, he also expressed himself in this way: "I wonder just what these people are up to. I saw the same thing in Europe during the war when the Hitler youth fanatics tried to rebel against our troops once they were taken prisoners. Of course, our troops shot them and that was the end of their resistance, but they knew they couldn't win and yet they tried it. What I'm concerned about is whether this is a deliberate move on the part of the Chinese Communists or whether it is an action of uncontrolled fanatics. It would seem to me that the Kremlin would not want the incident over the British plane and the incident today and would not want the incident of the Vietminh crossing the seventeenth parallel. Time will tell on this and we will have to watch it very closely."

The President told me that he had also received reports elaborating on the stories in the morning papers that Vietminh guerrillas had infiltrated south of the seventeenth parallel and had started guerrilla tactics against the French. . . .

John Eisenhower reported to work this morning and is presently assigned as aide in the White House. At Pete Carroll's recommendation and my own, John will wear a uniform while assigned here. That is his preference.

I also talked over with the President this morning Syngman Rhee's visit to Washington. We agreed that the Vice President should welcome Rhee at the airport before the sound cameras and that there should be no sound at the White House, mainly because we did not know whether Rhee might try to sound off publicly in the presence of the President on Korea and thus embarrass the President. To play it safe we will have no sound when the President and Mrs. Eisenhower meet President and Mrs. Rhee—just photographs. . . .

At four o'clock when I received the schedule for the following day, I found to my amazement that the legislative team had arranged to have a group of Congressmen come in to have their photographs taken with the President and that Paul Fino of the Bronx was one of those coming in "to pledge their support of the President's program." I asked Chesney and Morgan how come on this one since Fino had voted against us on the tax bill despite requests by Governor Dewey and Dean Taylor for him to go along. He told both the governor and Taylor in effect to go to hell and voted against the measure. I told both Morgan and Chesney that the New York State Republican organization would raise hell if it happened.[1]

The final result of this matter was that Chesney called Fino's office the next morning and told him that he had to cancel some of the people because the list has gotten too big. . . .

President Syngman Rhee and his wife arrived at the White House at 4:30 P.M., and President and Mrs. Eisenhower gave their visitors a dinner that night at 8:30. Next morning, anticipating trouble, Eisenhower called Hagerty early.

Tuesday, July 27, 1954

In at the White House at 7:15 A.M. The President called me up to his bedroom at 7:30. He said that he wanted me to stay with him throughout the morning so that he would have a record of any conversations that took place. He asked me also to sit in on the Korean-American talks with the same thing in mind.

The President told me that he was having considerable difficulty with Rhee: "I feel sorry for the old man. He wants to get his country unified, but we cannot permit him to start a war to do it. The consequences would be too awful. But he is a stubborn old fellow, and I don't know whether we'll be able to hold him in line indefinitely."

After the President dressed we went out into the living room section of the second floor and I had an opportunity to discuss quite a few things with him. . . .

1956. For the first time the President virtually told me that he would run again in '56. He put it this way: "A lot of people are urging me to run again for another term. They say that I should never discuss this or give any indication of which way I am going to decide until the very last moment in 1956. I suppose they're right. But when the time comes to make this decision, I will make it by myself after consultation with a few people in the White House, including yourself, Jerry Persons, and Sherm Adams. Right now I kind of think that the answer will be that I will run for another term, but I am telling everyone that they better not speculate on this and let me make the decision. After all, it is my life and it will have to be my decision."

Tension. The President told me that he was beginning for the first time to feel the tension of his office. He thought that that was only natural because of the closing weeks of the congressional session plus the very heavy burden of international decisions which he has had to make these days. "It's not the job particularly that bothers me or the title. It's the multiplicity of petty problems that many people bring to me. The selfishness of the members of Congress is incredible and the manner in which they try to put me on the spot and want me to decide questions that never should be brought to me are just about driving me nuts." The President said that he was trying to get away this weekend to Camp David with his family from Friday morning through Monday morning. The legislative leaders meeting has been postponed until Tuesday morning and he was sure if he could get three complete days away from the job, he would feel a lot better. Without his telling me all this I had noticed this same tension growing within [him] the last two weeks. Why he hasn't blown his top before this is something I'll never understand.

After the talks were over, Secretary Dulles and I went into the President's office with him.

The President said that he could not see how President Rhee could say that he wanted only to start a little war in Korea and could not recognize the danger of it rapidly spreading into an all-out global war. Dulles said that he had heard the same theme that Rhee had stressed today in his conversations with Rhee on other occasions.

My own personal observation from listening to President Rhee talk is considerably mixed. I feel sorry for him and his country but, of course, we cannot permit the danger of war and Rhee's actions, if taken, would very likely start one. Rhee is a zealous patriot who has worked all his life for Korean independence, who has been jailed, beaten, and tortured in that fight but who closes his eyes to the practical realities of the situation. I don't know whether he realizes that his Korean armies could not stand up for more than two or three weeks against the Chinese Communists, but I am sure that his advisers do, although they are deathly afraid of arguing with him on this subject. You have to admire his patriotism and his steadfast determination to bring about the unification of his country, but we cannot permit him to involve the United States in a war with Asia. It is a tough and somewhat tragic position to be in—but that's the way it is. . . .

Hagerty took down an account of the American-Korean talks that ran to more than six single-spaced-typescript pages, and it showed how Rhee, speaking in a low voice that was very difficult to follow, but speaking in fluent English, wanted to unify his country. The president of the Republic of Korea said that his nation "might propose to start some positive action at the front so that the United Nations forces would not have to remain there for a long time." In response, both the President and the Secretary of State did their best to make it clear that the government of the United States would do nothing in support of such an action. The President was at his best in this exchange, especially after Rhee with as much melodramatic description as possible sought to make a case for attack. Rhee said that his people to the north were crying for help, that his people in the south had heard their crying but kept quiet, that the children of the north had been sent to Manchuria, that many people had been slain. From that point he turned to rhetorical questions of a beseeching sort. The President of the United States answered with an eloquent statement of the danger of nuclear war: " . . . one thing is worse than winning any war—that's losing it. There is no disposition in America at any time to belittle the

Republic of Korea but when you say that we should deliberately plunge into war, let me tell you that if war comes, it will be horrible. Atomic war will destroy civilization. It will destroy our cities. There will be millions of people dead. War today is unthinkable with the weapons which we have at our command. If the Kremlin and Washington ever lock up in a war, the results are too horrible to contemplate. I can't even imagine them."

Wednesday, July 28, 1954

. . . Another question that did not come up at the press conference was the letter that the President had received from Joe Meek, Republican candidate for the Senate in Illinois, in which Meek publicly pledged his support of the President's program and policies. In return, the President answered him by saying that he welcomed such support and said he hoped Meek would be elected. This exchange culminated a long series of discussions between Governor Stratton and Governor Adams.[1] Originally Meek had been making noises about supporting McCarthy, but when he was nominated, he realized that he could not get elected without the President's support. The President and Adams were insistent that Meek publicly put his support of the President in writing before we went to Illinois for the state fair. Since the question was not raised at the press conference, it was decided that I release the letter several days later as an official exchange of correspondence—which I did.

On Wednesday evening the President and Mrs. Eisenhower attended a dinner at the Mayflower tendered by President and Mrs. Rhee, and Korean-American talks continued the next afternoon, Thursday, President Rhee being in attendance but not the President of the United States. This was the end of the conference.

Friday, July 30, 1954

In at 9:00. The President left for Camp David. Comparatively quiet day here at the White House with the exception of the final statement issued in connection with the American-Korean talks. . . .

The important thing about the statement is that President Rhee, who has been talking about restarting the Korean War, actually agreed to sign the statement, which in effect places the problem of Korea in the 9th session of the General Assembly of the United Nations which opens in New York on September 21st. . . . None of us can see how he can completely repudiate his signed statement and still save his face. . . .

• • • •

Saturday, July 31, 1954

Off today.

August 1954

Sunday, August 1, 1954

Quiet day.

Monday, August 2, 1954

In at 8:15. The President stayed overnight at Camp David, leaving the camp at 8:00 and arriving at the office shortly before 10:00. While awaiting his arrival, I called Dulles and Benson.

When I talked to Dulles, I asked him to send to me a full report from our chiefs of mission in the iron curtain countries pertaining to the President's offer last week to ship American food to people suffering from the Danube and other river floods in West Germany, East Germany, Austria, Czechoslovakia, Hungary, Rumania, and Yugoslavia. . . .

In the afternoon I received a memorandum from McCardle in the State Department to the effect that the President's offer was officially communicated by our chiefs of mission to the governments of those countries involved and that as yet no replies have been received from any country behind the iron curtain.[1] . . .

I called Secretary Benson and asked him what the drought conditions were this morning. . . .

My suggestions to the President on both the drought situation and the food situation in Europe led him to bring up again the question of freeing me for matters of this nature. "You just have to become free, Jim, to do more of this sort of work—to bring to me suggestions that you think are worthwhile. . . ."

I told the President that I would try to work it out and said that I thought if I could get Wayne Hawks assigned to my office, it would be very helpful.[2] Wayne knows the routine of the White House and we would not have to spend half our time breaking in a new man. The President thought this was a good idea.

The President also said one particularly significant thing to me. He stopped walking around the room, placed his hands on his hips and said: "I am convinced of one thing. The only right approach to take on all these domestic problems is a liberal approach. This party of ours and our program will not appeal to the American people unless the American people believe that we have a truly liberal program. Our hidebound reactionaries won't get to first base. Of that I am convinced." I told the President I could not agree with him more. He told me to aim all my thinking along that line and not to "pay any attention to anyone else in the White House, and I particularly mean our boys who are working with the Congress."

Later at the conclusion of the signing of the Housing Bill, the President let Senator Capehart have it when the Senator said he was fearful that the 35,000 units approved in this bill for next year were the last housing units that Congress would vote for. The President said: "Senator, I think you're one hundred percent wrong on that, and I want to tell you right here and now that next year in my State of the Union message I am going to ask for those 70,000 units for '56 and '57 which you cut out on me this year, and I am going to continue to fight for them until I get them. You might just as well know that right now." The Senator backed off fast and said nothing else to the President.

Later at two o'clock I went in with Secretary Benson and he reported to the President on the details of the feed program and recommended that the President declare Missouri and Oklahoma as disaster areas so that he could designate 76 counties in Missouri and 26 in Oklahoma as drought counties. We worked this out, and Benson held a press conference in my office to announce it and later went outside and did the same thing for the television cameras. Consequently we should get a good play on this, and this is the sort of thing we should do more often.

A hectic day on two or three major appointments. These appointments were: . . .

Announcements of Parkinson and Holder as new U.S. District Judges in Indiana. These announcements ended almost a year's fight within the organization in Indiana over these nominations. Holder was very much against us in Chicago but he was backed by Senators Jenner and Capehart. They could have held up all nominations if we had not finally agreed to send his name up. Parkinson is a Halleck man and is supporting both Halleck and Governor Craig. It was vitally important that we get his nomination through to strengthen Halleck's hand in Indiana and so we had to go through with Holder, although none of us here at the White House wanted to do so.

A particularly busy day on releases with a lot of routine postmasters and other nominations. At my afternoon press conference I had to knock down the story which Assistant Secretary of Defense Hannah gave to the newsmen on his last day in office before returning to Michigan State. Hannah deliberately took a secret document on military manpower, physically cut the "secret" off it with scissors and then gave it to the newsmen for publication in Sunday papers. He declared that the Eisenhower administration had adopted a sweeping new military manpower plan aimed at military duty for all qualified young men, followed up by compulsory service in a new reserve setup. "The whole thing is geared with the day of active war with the Soviet Union," Hannah said. Of course, this story raised the roof in the Defense Department and ODM and the President was as sore as the dickens. Consequently, at my four o'clock press conference I used the attached statement, knocking Hannah down, although not by name.

The statement related that the Hannah story did not "fully reflect" the attitude of the National Security Council, and there would be no decision or action until the Department of Defense and the Office of Defense Mobilization had reported back to the NSC in September.

Tuesday, August 3, 1954

In at 8:10. Leaders meeting at 8:30 . . .

The first subject to be discussed was the question of the postal rate increases and its companion measure, the postal pay increases. The President started off the discussion by saying that there were things that "so flatly violated what we are working for that it would be better for me to veto them if they came to me in the form of bills." "I am telling you right now that I am not going to approve any bill that does not provide for classification within the Post Office Department and postal rate increases to provide for pay increases. I will be the court of last resort on this and unless it comes down to me that way, I will veto it."

Halleck reported that the House was faced on Monday with the discharge resolution on the post office pay increases calling for a 7% raise or a minimum of $240.00. He expressed considerable doubt that the administration supporters could get enough votes to defeat it and that it probably would be passed, He and Martin urged the Senate to take this matter in hand and try to get it ironed out. The President asked how many Republicans had signed the discharge papers and when he was told by Arends that there were about 30, he turned to Jerry Persons and said, "Jerry, don't you ever let me get into the district of any one of those thirty." . . .

The President expressed the opinion that he was beginning to feel that a constitutional amendment was in order so that members of the House would have to run for election only every four years. Halleck replied that he believed the President's reasoning was good on this and he would like to see it, although the general feeling was that nothing could be done about it at this time. . . .

Later in the day I had a long talk with Governor Adams concerning the best way of getting out "an economic report at mid-year" from Burns.[1] Burns had presented this report to the Cabinet and it was so good that everybody thought it should be released. . . . I went over to Hauge's office to talk this over with Burns and Hauge, and they agreed to redo their memorandum within a week so we could announce it a week from tomorrow. They were being very careful on one point—on which I agreed with them—that the Economic Council not be brought into politics too much and that their memorandum and report be completely factual. I told them that was all right with us, that we would hand out a factual memorandum but that then the members of Congress and the Republican National Committee could use it as a political document to wallop fellows like Douglas and Humphrey who have been talking depression and who were the leading prophets of doom last winter.[2] The material in Burns' report will be excellent and will show a steady climb in the economic picture since last winter, with the prospects that 1954 will end up as the second or third best year economically speaking in the history of the country. . . .

In the later summer of 1954, Senator McCarthy was down but not out, for the processes of the Senate ground exceedingly slow, especially when Senators feared the man they were processing. Roy Cohn resigned on July 20, a good sign; but in August the Senate cleared McCarthy and his aides of the charge that they had exerted improper pressure on the Army. Meanwhile there was a great deal of life in the Senator and he produced testimony against President Eisenhower's onetime military superior General George C. Marshall, contributed by the maverick, cantankerous former governor of Kansas and erstwhile Secretary of War in the latter 1930s, Harry H. Woodring.

Wednesday, August 4, 1954

. . . Just before I went in to see the President, Eddie Folliard called me and told me he was going to ask a question on the letter from Harry Woodring which McCarthy had introduced into the record the other day which said that General Marshall would "sell his grandmother for personal advantage; sell out his policies, beliefs and standards to maintain his political and military position with the powers that be." I thanked Folliard for letting me know of the question and told him I was sure the President would have a very strong answer. . . .

In my briefing with the President, I brought up at the outset the question of the Woodring letter and he said: "Can you imagine that guy Woodring having the gall to write such a letter? He let everybody push him around when he was in government, never knew what he was doing and now he criticizes General Marshall. You may be sure I know exactly what I want to say and will repeat as I have many times in the past that I think George Marshall is and was a great American patriot. You don't have to brief me on this one. I know exactly what I am going to say."

On the way over to the press conference, the President told me that he still felt lousy—that Snyder had told him he apparently had some slight liver trouble which would take him about two or three days to get rid of.[1] He said he gets whoosy now and then and hoped he would not show any signs of how he felt at the press conference. He said he had about a quart of blood taken out of him last night and that he still felt the effects of that. He said he had been feeling so well lately that he was sort of beaten down that he had felt so bad these last two days, but he got through the press conference beautifully.

We released his remarks on General Marshall as well as his remarks in answer to Scotty Reston's question on his UN proposal, in which he said that he would continue to work for some sort of atomic plan to help undeveloped areas of the world. He likewise advanced for the first time publicly the new philosophy of "good partner" that the United States must take in its dealings with foreign nations. He warned that we could not beat our breasts demanding that other countries follow our lead regardless of the consequences but that we must work in cooperation with them and make them understand that we would [like] to be partners and not bullies.

When we returned to the President's office, he asked me to come in and said he wanted me to call up some of my friends and get them to write the "good partner" idea comparing it with the "good neighbor" policy which [we] have followed for many years in the western hemisphere. . . .

After several years of turmoil in Iran, the young Shah was securely in power and prepared to negotiate over his country's oil, which hitherto (that is, prior to the turmoil) had been in the hands of the Anglo-Iranian Oil Company, an adjunct of the British government. In the course of the Iranian confusion the CIA had operated in the country, and it seemed good to have peace and quiet.

Thursday, August 5, 1954

In at 8:15. Hectic day with a lot of appointments on my own schedule but not much really in the way of important news.

I went in to see the President about 8:20 to get his permission to release his message to the Shah of Iran in connection with the oil settlement. . . .

Tried all day to get the President's message to the Shah of Iran released and finally put it out at 6:30 P.M. without receiving formal notification from the State Department that Ambassador Henderson had officially delivered it to the Shah. . . This is just a surmise on our part but probably what happened out there was that the Shah, after signing the agreement, went out to celebrate and the ambassador was either cooling his heels waiting for the Shah to finish his celebration or trying to catch up with him someplace in the country. . . .

• • • •

Friday, August 6, 1954

In at 8:10. Attended Cabinet meeting.

The President opened the meeting by saying that he had been toying with an idea. "What would you think," he said, "if once a month we'd have a Cabinet meeting with agenda, sit over a table at the White House for luncheon, and have a high-powered bullfest. You all have to eat lunch anyway and why don't we do it in a social atmosphere. While the cooking at the White House might not be so good, I would try to provide good atmosphere." . . .

Humphrey said that he thought the one thing we should keep in mind was that Japanese business should be spread throughout the world and not concentrated only in American markets. He said that American industry could not compete with the intricate, delicate hand labor of Japan and their goods should not be permitted to come into America alone since if they were unloaded only on the United States, it would cause great unemployment here.

The President said that was right, but he warned: "Don't let us let Japan reach a point where they want to invite the Kremlin into their country. Everything else fades into insignificance in the light of such a threat." . . .

Debt limit. Secretary Humphrey reported that the Senate committee had recommended that the debt limit be raised only $6 billion. . . . The President said: "George, I am leery of this. We inherited deficit spending. We worked like dogs to get it down and we succeeded but the Congress wants to clamp down on us further. We must have a leeway. We have a record of honest administration, yet the Congress tries to clip us every time we talk about increasing the debt limit and I get very much annoyed." . . .

Summerfield. The Postmaster General said that it was the policy of his department to issue commemorative stamps for leading citizens and he recommended that an announcement be made that the administration was issuing a stamp for Senator Taft. Summerfield pointed out that this might be open to political attack but thought that the overall good to be obtained from it would counteract any such attack. With that the President said: "Listen, Arthur, any administration like the Democrats who wanted to change the name of Hoover Dam almost before President Hoover was out of office would have a tough time attacking this one. I think that situation stunk all around and I can see no room to apologize. Let them scream if they want to—but that's the way I feel about it."

Secretary Dulles argued, however, that Senator Taft was known as Mr. Republican and there may be political backfire. The question was left for further consideration and the Cabinet meeting was adjourned.

After the Cabinet meeting broke up, Murray Snyder told me he had just received word from Merriman Smith that East Germany had accepted our food offer and this would soon be on the ticker. . . .

• • • •

Monday, August 9, 1954

In at 8:15. No leaders meeting. That was postponed until tomorrow.

The *New York Times* had an irritating story on the Japanese situation with a considerable amount of statistics used at the Cabinet meeting of last Friday. I discussed this with the President and we agreed that it would be almost impossible to check to see what department is leaking out this sort of thing. I told him of the proposal I had to send to each department a Cabinet memorandum of some importance which would include 12 or 14 points. It would be a simple thing to renumber those points differently for each department and then if it were published, we could at least narrow down the department by the way the points came out in the paper. The President said: "Don't tell anybody about this, but we'll do it next time we have a message that has that many points in it. Talk it over with Ann Whitman and work it out."

I had luncheon with Scotty Reston at the Metropolitan Club and we got several things straightened out. Scotty was beefing that he had not obtained much background information from this administration and I asked him how many times he had called me. When he said only occasionally, I asked him to call me more often and I would try to keep him straightened out. This is very important to us because the *Times* is looked upon—rightly or wrongly—by the diplomatic corps here in Washington and abroad as more or less an official spokesman of the administration. They think that policy or reported policy positions on foreign affairs printed in the *Times* are the gospel truth. I think the luncheon was worthwhile and I think much good will come of the meeting.

Gabe Hauge told me that he was still having trouble getting the economic figures from the Council of Economic Advisors. I told him that if he would get them for me and send them over I would take care of them in my own way, even if I had to have them put out as a statement by the President. I told him I did not understand why the Council of Economic Advisors was making so much fuss about this. All I wanted was statistics which I could put out from the White House which showed the improving economic condition, and the Republican National Committee and Republican speakers could take the ball from there.

At four o'clock that afternoon the President decided to take the kids on a boat ride down the Potomac, using the old *Margie* which is still attached to the Potomac River Command since the original owner, Fisher of Detroit, had refused to buy it back. I had to tell the newspapermen that the *Margie* was still available for use and there was some puzzlement among them, but I think we straightened it out all right by saying the boat was attached to the Potomac River Command of the U.S. Navy rather than the White House.

The President and Mrs. Eisenhower had promised the children a boat ride and the kids were going to hold them to it despite a very heavy thundershower at four o'clock. Major John and I were in with the President when it started to rain and he grabbed up the phone and called Bill Draper to get an Air Force report on the weather right away. "I want to know what it's going to be one hour from now. I'm in a spot; I promised the kids I would take them for a boat ride, so find out what the weather will be and call me right back." Draper called back within a few minutes and said this was just a passing shower and the weather would be perfect if he left at five o'clock. On receiving this word, the President grinned, wiped some imaginary sweat off his forehead, clapped his hands, and said: "David and the girls would never have understood it if we hadn't gone this afternoon. Boy! I'm glad it's going to clear up."

The President and the family were out on the river for 4½ hours. They left from the Naval Gun Factory at 5:30 and returned shortly after 10 o'clock.

• • • •

Tuesday, August 10, 1954

. . . That evening at six o'clock I went over to the Carlton Hotel for a talk with Ambassador Luce.[1] She was very pessimistic on the situation in Italy and in Europe generally and said that as far as she could see, unless we did something to conquer it, Italy and Europe would drift into Communism within the next five years. . . .

Mrs. Luce . . . urged that the United States do something and do something fast to gain a political victory in the world and if necessary to gain a military victory. I asked her by military victory if she were actually suggesting that we attack somewhere in the world. She surprised me by saying—yes, she meant just that. I asked her where and she thought that Formosa and the Chinese mainland was the most likely spot. (This, of course, is a pet theory of the Luces and one to which I cannot agree.) I told her that I did not agree, but she asked me if she could send me an outline of her thoughts and I said I would be happy to get them and give them to the President. She will send me this outline next week.

• • • •

Friday, August 13, 1954

In at 8:00 A.M. Left for Camp David for Cabinet meeting with Stephens and Shanley at 8:15, arriving at Camp David at 10:30. Cabinet meeting held at Laurel Cottage. . . .

The following topics were discussed at the Cabinet meeting: . . .

Civil Service. The attached memorandum was issued by Phil Young. During the discussion the President professed the belief that he could not see why we would be put in the position of defending our steps in Civil Service. "These Democrats played ducks and drakes with the Civil Service system while they were in, and now they're kicking. I think the situation is funny. There is a simple thing we all should understand. I think if a man is qualified—and he must be qualified for a position—it is much better if he is a Republican instead of a Democrat." . . .

Indochina. Bedell Smith reported briefly that he expected that 250,000 refugees would have to be evacuated from Hanoi in the Tonkin Delta in Vietnam between August 10th and December 10th. He said that SIMPAC had already sent two vessels to Hanoi and could evacuate 3,500 in each ship. The French are airlifting 3,400 per day and the French Navy already is moving out the families of Vietnam troops and militiamen. He said that the whole problem is complicated by the fact that there is no government of Vietnam, that Bao Dai has sold out his office to a gangster who "paid $3 million for the job." Vietnam therefore is almost in a state of collapse with no government, and it is difficult to make arrangements to evacuate the people. . . .

I presented to the Cabinet the plan of the syndication of Cabinet articles by the New York *Herald Tribune* for use this fall and the participation of the Cabinet in the Herald Tribune Forum on October 19th. The President approved both of these wholeheartedly and urged the Cabinet to participate in them. . . .

The Emperor Bao Dai was head of state in Vietnam, established in that office by the French. He was known as the "nightclub emperor" because of well-publicized revels in his own country and on the French Riviera. As for point 9 above, the decision to syndicate "Cabinet articles" allowed the enterprising Herald Tribune *reporter Robert J. Donovan to use minutes of Cabinet meetings for a book,* Eisenhower: The Inside Story *(New York, 1956).*

November 1954

In the autumn of 1954 the offshore-island issue arose—tiny islands within a few miles of the mainland Chinese ports of Amoy and Foochow. The Nationalist Chinese controlled the islands, in September 1954 forces of the People's Republic of China had begun shelling them, and by November a crisis was at hand.

Monday, November 29, 1954

In Augusta.

Out to the office at the Augusta National at 8:15. Talked to the President about Dulles' speech in the evening in Chicago and recommended to him that I thought it would be a good idea if Dulles would take a firm stand against blockade of Chinese coast. The President thoroughly agreed and repeated his conviction that a blockade is an act of war which could at best lead only to serious consequences. "I am completely beginning to lose my patience with Bill Knowland. He has made the most irresponsible statements of late which are hurting us very much with our allies. Can't he see that this move by the Chinese is part of the general Communist plot to try to divide us from our Western allies and try to defeat ratification of the Paris agreements?"

The President thought I should call Dulles and I finally reached the Secretary at Chaumont, New York. He told me he had been thinking about the same thing, and that he wanted me to get approval from the President to say that the Russian Communists were deliberately talking peaceful coexistence for the benefit of the Western allies and that the Chinese Communists were deliberately trying to act provocative and cause incidents to cause trouble between the United Nations and the Western allies. I told him that the President wanted him specifically to mention the blockade as being an act of war, and he said he would be delighted to do so. He asked me to check back with the President and I did so—reaching him on the sixth green. The President thoroughly approved what Foster was going to say, and I so reported to the Secretary.

Earlier in the morning I also had a discussion with the President on what I believe was a need for him to speak out strongly against Knowland and those within the Republican Party who were engaging in this saber-rattling talk. The President did not say he would not but thought it would be better to have Dulles take the lead in his speech tonight . . .

Airborne from Augusta at 4:50. Into MATS terminal in the new plane in an hour and forty minutes.

• • • •

Tuesday, November 30, 1954

Back in Washington. In office at 8:15.

I saw the President at 9:10. He thought that the Dulles speech had received a good play in the newspapers and we both agreed that the lead quite properly featured the administration's objection to the blockade as an act of war. . . .

I also told the President that Dulles had expressed concern to me that Defense Secretary Wilson might take an opposite line at his press conference today. The President frowned for a minute and then said, "You call up the Defense Department and tell them that the Secretary is not to talk about anything dealing with this whole situation without getting it cleared in advance with the State Department. Tell them that that's an order directly from me." . . .

Bryce Harlow dropped in to see me to talk about the new setup we are trying to work out on the public relations side of the administration. He is going to take Rumbough's position and see what can be done to get people in Congress talking more about the Eisenhower administration than they have in the past.[1] Of course, the main decision on this has to await the opening of the session so that we can get down to Washington men like Senator Case, Bruce Alger of Texas, Senators Purtell and Bush of Connecticut, Saltonstall of Massachusetts, Allott of Colorado, etc., whom we are counting on to carry the load, bypassing almost completely the right wing. If they want to go along, all right. If they don't, we will have a nucleus of supporters who can do the job.

December 1954

Wednesday, December 1, 1954

In at 8:15. . . .

After the NSC meeting, I had rather a long talk with Allen Dulles about the 13 Americans held by the Communists. Dulles told me that these 13 had been held for at least two years and had been thoroughly brainwashed. He said he was convinced that this was part of the Communist conspiracy, with the Russian Communists giving the impression of acting softer in the West and the Chinese Communists acting tougher in the East. This is being done for two purposes—to try to defeat the formulation of SEATO brought about by the Manila Conference; and to try to divide the United States from its Western allies and consequently to lead to the defeat of the ratification of the Paris Agreements.

Dulles said that he could not understand why in the past Central Intelligence had permitted American civilians to be used on planes which were dropping information leaflets and men into Communist countries. Since he has taken over Central Intelligence, we have used Chinese civilians in Asia and Polish civilians in Europe for this purpose and not taken the chance of having American civilians shot down and being immediately classified (since they were out of uniform) as spies. . . .

Had another talk with Roscoe Drummond and told him I appreciated his column in this morning's paper in which he wrote that the President was going to attempt to get the Republican Party to become pro-Eisenhower and let the right wing go where it may.[1] The President knew I had talked to Drummond on this, and later in the day he said he thought it was a good column and one which he hoped would start some action.

Saw the President later in the day at three o'clock. Brought in ticker clipping which reported that Knowland had just announced that he was against censure of McCarthy because it would curtail the investigative powers of the Senate. When the President saw the story, he literally hit the roof and said he could not understand how Knowland could ever make such a statement. "What's the guy trying to do? Here, he personally picked the committee to draw up the censure charges, he vouched for their honor and integrity and then he turns around and votes against them, using this phony reason of investigative curtailment. If I am asked about it at my press conference, I will say it is entirely a Senate matter and that no one in the executive branch had any idea of any curtailment of investigative powers."

I told the President I thought it was a payoff by Knowland for the right-wing support of his "foreign policy" statements of recent weeks, particularly those dealing with diplomatic break with Russia and blockade of China. I said that as far as I was concerned, this was just another instance of Knowland being taken up on the mountaintop by the right wing and promised a lot of things, and the President agreed with me. I also told the President I thought it was vital to have a press conference tomorrow and speak out on this whole question of war or peace. I reported to him that the right wing as represented by Fulton Lewis was reporting that the administration was turning into cowards by refusing to take drastic action against the Chinese Reds and that I was sure that McCarthy would also jump into this as soon as the censure vote was finished.[2] The President agreed with this and went over some notes which I had prepared for his possible use. He liked them very much and inserted the first point in the two courses of action outlined in the notes. He talked over these notes with the Secretary of State while I was in his office, and both of them agreed that he should do this. The notes which I then prepared after our conversation were as follows:

. . . Two courses of action

1. To be belligerent and truculent; to goad both our people and their people into war by using the presidential office. This would be the easier course since once we moved toward war, nation becomes solidified behind leader and he has freedom to drive to war. This is the easy way.

I know about war. I have had to write thousands of letters of condolence to mothers and fathers. I don't want to do it again.

Break in diplomatic relations and blockade are actions to take us closer to war. Must think of consequences. Must think of the millions who would be killed.

What one bomb could do if dropped right now on Washington while we are having this conference.

2. Second course is one that requires more courage and more determination, more patience and more maturity.

It is to remain firm, to work for peace, to work for ratification of the Paris Agreements and the Manila Conference; to clear up tension spots like Korea, Iran, Suez, Guatemala.

To remain firm, insisting on our rights and those of our citizens.

To reject warlike acts.

UN action vs. Red China. . . .

• • • •

Thursday, December 2, 1954

. . . Following the staff conference, I had quite an argument with Martin and Morgan in Jerry Persons' office on the proposed opening statement by the President. Martin insisted that the President should merely say the Secretary of State had outlined the administration's viewpoint and that the President approved it. . . .

Apparently the legislative department is a little unhappy that this will be construed as a crack at Knowland—but so what!! If ever anyone has earned a crack from the President it has been Knowland with his break on foreign policy and his stand against McCarthy censure—and I know the President feels pretty much the same. Knowland can work with us if he chooses. If not, we will work with other more liberal and pro-Eisenhower members of the Senate once the session starts.

During the day talked to the Secretary of the Treasury, and he proposed two statements by the President at the press conference.

1. The Marshall Plan for Asia. He recommended that the President say that an interdepartmental committee has been studying this problem and that the committee is headed by Herbert Hoover, Jr., as chairman with representatives of State, FOA, Treasury, Commerce, and Agriculture on it.[1] Humphrey was particularly disturbed, as were Dulles and the President, that Stassen leaked out a story about increased aid for Asia while the Rio Conference was going on. This caused all sort of hell down there since our South American neighbors immediately put on the heat for more money. As Humphrey said, "Stassen couldn't have possibly pulled a worse boner if he had tried."

2. Humphrey recommended that the President issue a brief statement on the Rio Conference of ministers of finance which is ending today. He said that the President should say that reports he has received indicate that a great deal of good will come out of the conference and that the "good partnership" policy among the nations of the Western Hemisphere has been greatly strengthened by the work of the conference. . . .

In my preconference talk with Dulles, we went over the following matters: . . .

2. The question of Mr. Churchill and his statement on allowing Germany to fight the Reds which he made in 1945. Churchill first made the statement and later apologized for it, saying he had not done so. Actually, he did. When I went down on the plane to Augusta with Lord Montgomery, he told me that Churchill had first proposed the plan of making a cache of German arms to President Eisenhower who was then Supreme Commander. Eisenhower would have nothing to do with it so Churchill then ordered Montgomery, as a British officer, to do the same thing and Montgomery complied. Dulles recommended that the President merely say on this matter that that was a matter for Mr. Churchill and that he noted Mr. Churchill had retracted his earlier statement.[2]

3. Formosa Mutual Defense Treaty. Dulles said that the President could announce that Dulles and the Foreign Minister of the Republic of China, George Yeh, would sign the Mutual Defense Treaty in the Secretary's office at 4:00 P.M. As far as the offshore islands were concerned, Dulles said their position was the same as always. The treaty actually applies only to Formosa and the Pescadores, both of which were detached from China by Japan in 1895 and belonged to Japan during World War II.

As far as the other offshore islands were concerned, the Secretary said that they were not expressly covered by the treaty and recommended that the President merely say that their status was not changed and that if defense of those islands becomes involved in the defense of Formosa, we probably would help defend them. "Let's keep the Reds guessing on them, however, and not make any clear-cut statement about them." . . .

The President asked Chip Bohlen to come into my office after the President had seen him from 11:30 until 12:00.[3] Chip told me the President had gone over with him his proposed statement at the press conference and that he warned the President on one or two points, as follows:

1. The statement that there was "softness" from Moscow as regards Western Europe. Bohlen said he was a little bit afraid of that because the Soviets were holding a meeting now with their satellites in preparation of forming a Soviet NATO organization within those countries. He thought there was a good likelihood that the Soviet position would get a lot stronger in Europe and he did not want the President to be put in a position of having to eat his words within a week or two weeks.

Bohlen agreed with me that we could get around this by saying that the present Soviet policy seemed to be one that sought to create a softness towards Western Europe. We also agreed to recommend to the President that he say that if the Chinese Red action on the American prisoners was done with the concurrence of the Kremlin—and we believe it was—it made a mockery of their soft-talking words to Western Europe.

2. Bohlen and I also discussed the *Life* magazine article by Yuri A. Rastvorov, former Lt. Colonel in the MVD, who was in Tokyo and then deserted to our side. Bohlen thought the articles were greatly exaggerated (probably by *Life* writers). He said that Colonel Rastvorov was in Tokyo and was not in Moscow when Stalin died and that it appeared as if his pieces were written from bits of gossip, rather than facts, which he had been able to pick up in Tokyo.

One point which Bohlen was sure never happened was that Malenkov armed the members of the Central Committee prior to the arrest of Beria. "That just couldn't and didn't happen in the Kremlin," Bohlen said. "Malenkov could not trust that many members of the Soviet hierarchy to have guns in their possession while they were in his presence. Someone would be bound to shoot him if they were given a gun." . . .

Allen Dulles called after the conference to find out what the President had said on the prisoners and when I told him, that the President had made a very great distinction between the 11 uniformed men and the two civilians, Dulles thought that was correct. Actually, if the United States is to make a strong case on this subject to the world, we have to divide the uniformed men from the two civilians, who were members of the CIA. Dulles has stopped the practice which existed prior to the time we came in of sending American CIA members on such missions and it cannot happen again, but nevertheless the Chinese have a case against those two. That is why the President deliberately separated the 11 airmen in his press conference.

The above reference to Lavrenti Beria, first deputy chairman of the council of ministers and minister of internal affairs of the USSR, concerned Beria's death in the first months of the premiership of Georgi Malenkov, who succeeded Stalin in March 1953. According to a story that circulated widely in the West, Beria had entered a meeting of the presidium after leaving his bodyguards outside, and his fellow ministers thereupon executed him.

General Lucius D. Clay, retired from the Army after many years of service in the Corps of Engineers, and most recently U.S. commander in Germany, received the task from the President of putting together estimates and recommendations for the proposed interstate highway system.

Friday, December 3, 1954

In at 8:15. . . .

The second item I cleared with the President was the announcement that the first ship carrying feed grain to arrive behind the iron curtain had docked at the East German port of Rostock with 1,700 tons of barley for East Germany and 2,000 tons of corn for Czechoslovakia. This was in line with the President's policy of extending American aid to victims of last fall's floods in the Danube area and is good international propaganda.

In the afternoon conferred with Lucius Clay, Governor Kennon of Louisiana, and Jack Martin on the highway program and specifically with the recommendations of the Governors' Conference which Kennon submitted today to the President. This report recommended that the federal government spend $25 billion over the next ten years on the interstate highway system and feeder roads, leaving the states free to spend their money and the regular federal contributions they receive on primary, secondary, and urban roads.

Since the President had originally announced that the highway program would be $50 billion over the next ten years, it was important that we pointed out to the newsmen in the conference after the governor's appointment with the President that the governors' recommendation for $25 billion did not mean that the program had been cut in half or that it would be matched equally by the localities. Actually, what is going to happen is that the federal government will take over the responsibility for all the interstate highway systems and reimburse those states which have already built such roads. It is expected that this more or less pump-priming system will encourage the states to spend more money and that overall the expenditures over the next ten years will be well over $50 billion. . . .

The President called me in about six o'clock and said he had an idea that he would like to get my views on and also to have me check with Herb Brownell. He said: "Senator Watkins got quite a kicking around on the Hill from McCarthy and his side. I would like very much to do something which would show that I thoroughly approve of Senator Watkins and I am for him one hundred percent. What would you think if we invited him to the stag dinner Monday night? I have never had a Senator, but there is no reason why I shouldn't. Please call Herb Brownell and get his opinion on it. What I want from him is an opinion on whether he thinks that I would be starting the fight before I am ready for it. As you know, I don't mind having this fight but maybe by inviting Watkins to a stag dinner at this time it would be launching it before we want to." . . .

Brownell said that it was a very good idea, but he added that he thought that picking out Watkins at this time for the stag dinner would not be quite right since it would not seem a normal thing to do.

When I reported back to the President on my conversation with Brownell, he said, "Call him back and see if he would have any objection if I had Watkins in for an appointment tomorrow morning." Herb readily agreed that this would be the way to handle it and said that he would be very happy to see it happen that way.

On September 27 a committee headed by Senator Arthur V. Watkins (Rep.) of Utah had recommended unanimously that the Senate should censure McCarthy for contempt of a subcommittee and for unwarranted abuse of Brigadier General Ralph W. Zwicker, a combat veteran who was in command of Camp Kilmer during the Peress affair. On December 2 the Senate "condemned" but did not "censure" McCarthy, by vote of 67–22, and dropped the Zwicker count.

Saturday, December 4, 1954

In at 8:15.

Saw the President at 8:30 and reported to him my conversation with Brownell. He told me to have Tom Stephens invite Watkins in at ten o'clock and for me to release the appointment to the press in advance. In talking to me, the President said he was going to congratulate the Senate on a job well done. When Watkins came in, I chatted briefly with him and then brought him in to see the President. He was with the President about 40 minutes and I rejoined him in Stephens' office after he left the President's office. We agreed right there that I would issue a statement in which I would say that the President congratulated the Senator for a fine job in handling his committee with dignity and respect.

I went out with Watkins to the lobby and told this to the newspapermen and, of course, the political implications of the story were not lost on them. It was on the front page in both the afternoon and Sunday morning papers.

Golf in the afternoon with Bob Denton, Bruce, and Bob, Jr.

• • • •

Sunday, December 5, 1954

Quiet day. Played golf in the afternoon with Marge, Bruce, and Eleanor Finkel.

• • • •

Monday, December 6, 1954

In at 8:15.

The President called me in to his office at 8:30. He seemed to be a little amazed at the play the Watkins story had received in the papers. He had just come from a private breakfast with Knowland and Martin in which they set up machinery on having a Republican meeting on the program and a bipartisan meeting the next day on the international aspects of the program. Apparently Knowland said something to him about the Watkins statement that I had made, and the President forgot that he told me that I was to say he had congratulated the Senator. When I pointed this out to him, he laughed and said, "That's all right, Jim. As a matter of fact, I thought the stories looked good. I was just trying to refresh my memory on how this statement had got in the papers since I had told Watkins to tell the newspapermen what he had told me. I did not, however, authorize him to make a statement in my name, and when I first saw the stories, I thought that he had double-crossed me. Confidentially, I thought the stories were just exactly what I wanted to see in the paper, and I don't particularly care what the Old Guard thinks about it."

I had luncheon with Bill Robinson at the Hay-Adams, and we discussed in some detail the plan we have to step up the selling of the Eisenhower program during the next two years. Bill thought the President's press conference was the best thing he had ever done and urged that statements like this be continued and that the President continue to speak out on controversies that he is having with the right wing of the party. . . .

On December 8, 1953, in an address to the United Nations the President had urged that part of the world's nuclear stockpiles, which at that time meant those of the U.S. and USSR, be donated to an international "bank of fissionable materials" for the peaceful uses of mankind.

Tuesday, December 7, 1954

In at 8:15.

Saw the President in the morning and he decided to have a press conference tomorrow morning at 10:30.

I reminded him that tomorrow was the anniversary of his "Atoms for Peace" UN speech . . . He agreed that at the conference tomorrow all he would do would be to remind the newsmen that this was the anniversary of the speech and that while the progress had not been as speedy as we had hoped, much had been done. . . .

The inevitable happened this afternoon. McCarthy broke with the President in a speech before a hearing of his committee in which he made a statement in typical McCarthy fashion blaming the President for congratulating Watkins and Flanders and holding up the work of the investigation of Communism, while at the same time urging patience and niceties toward the Chinese Communists who were torturing American prisoners. McCarthy accused the President of "weakness and supineness" in ferreting out Communists here and said that he had been asked if he were going to apologize to the Senate for activities which led to his censure.[1] Instead McCarthy said he wanted to apologize to the American people for campaigning for the President in 1952 on the grounds that the President would be tough on Communists here at home. . . .

The President was alone in his office at the time and was reading the *Encyclopedia Britannica.* I asked him if he was reading the *Federalist Papers* and he said no he was looking up some information he wanted on the origin of the Jewish race. He said he was interested in finding out more about their history, that he had a breathing spell and was just reading about them.

I said I regretted that I would have to disturb his afternoon but that McCarthy had just let go with the expected blast against him. (The President and I had talked about this matter for the last two weeks, and we both fully expected that McCarthy, once the censure vote was out of the way, would take exactly the stand he did, trying to play on the sympathies of the American people, particularly as regards the 11 Americans held by the Chinese Communists.)

The President put down the *Encyclopedia* and carefully read the news stories. Then without any show of anger whatsoever he turned to me and said, "Jim, this is what we've been expecting and I am not at all sorry to see it come. I rather suspected that when I had Watkins in on Saturday, McCarthy would see in that visit an invitation to him to use it as a personal attack upon himself. But that's all right with me. I never had any use for him, as you know, and I am just as glad that he has made this statement now rather than waiting for a later time to do it. How do you suggest we handle this right now?"

. . . I recommended that he allow me to call in the newspapermen and tell them that as far as McCarthy's statement was concerned, the White House had this to say: On the international situation, I would refer them to the President's press conference of last Thursday. On the charge of weakness against Communism at home, I would refer them to the June 2nd statement which the President had made, say I had just talked to the Attorney General and that I had received up-to-date figures which I wanted to give them at this time. I urged that I be permitted to do this so that an answer from us would appear in the same stories as the McCarthy attack and so that we would not be forced into a position at the press conference tomorrow of waiting for 24 hours before answering him.

The President took off his glasses and bit the earpiece of them as he thought this out. He then said: "Go ahead, Jim. You put it out in your name." Then, getting up he started to walk back and forth behind me. As he did so, he started to talk. He said that as far as he was concerned, he was finished trying to work with the radical right wing of the Republican Party and that he would fight them from now on. "I've had just enough from the McCarthys, the Welkers, the Malones, and people like that. This party of ours has got to realize that they won't exist unless they become a party of progressive moderates—unless they can prove to the American people that they are a middle-of-the-road party and turn their backs on the extremes of the left and particularly the extremes of the right. If there is one thing that I am going to try to do during the next two years . . ." (I interrupted at this point to say "Don't you mean the next six years, Mr. President?" He laughed and said, "Right now, I'm speaking of the next two years. You and I will talk about the next four years one of these days.") "These next two years I have just one purpose, outside of the job of keeping this world at peace, and that is to build up a strong progressive Republican Party in this country. As you know, I have started working on it already and when the Congress comes back in January, I am going to get the people to think the way we do, to rally around and dig into this matter and see what we can do. If the right wing wants a fight, they're going to get it. If they want to leave the Republican Party and form a third party, that's their business but before I end up, either this Republican Party will reflect progressivism or I won't be with them anymore. And let me tell you one other thing. If they think they can nominate a right-wing Old Guard Republican for the presidency, they've got another thought coming. I'll go up and down this country, campaigning against them. I'll fight them right down the line."

The President then chuckled to himself and said, "Jim, you've heard this speech many times before, but I just wanted to get it off my chest today. Thanks for listening. Now go out and make your announcements." . . .

Later in the afternoon I went back to see the President alone, and we talked briefly about the upcoming press conference tomorrow. He said he was not going to engage in any personal attack on McCarthy and suggested if I so wanted, I could let the wire men know that this would be the case. Neither, however, would he retreat one iota and if he were to get a question on Watkins, he would repeat his congratulatory remarks. . . .

In the evening I went to the Motion Picture Association theater to see "Battle Cry." Roger who wanted to come could not get away from Quantico for the movie.

• • • •

Wednesday, December 8, 1954

. . . In my usual preconference briefing with the Secretary of State we went over the following subjects: . . .

UN resolution on American fliers held by the Chinese. Dulles said that Lodge yesterday in the UN had given the names of our other fliers and they would be placed in the same category by the American delegation of the United Nations as were the original 11. He said we had known in general that there was a possibility the Chinese were holding these men until the Canadian flier, McKenzie, had been released several days ago. McKenzie reported to our Central Intelligence that he had been in prison with the men. This was positive identification of them, and so we released their names. . . .

When I went in at ten o'clock to see the President, he was standing behind his desk with a grin on his face, He said, "You know how I am going to open this press conference. I'm going to urge every one of the reporters to get their newspapers and radio and television stations to put in a good plug on the 14th of December for Safe Driving Day, which is the 15th of December. I am going to ask them to feature safety in those two days in the hope that it will reduce accidents. I am sure that if the American people make up their minds on this, they can do just that."

I went over my notes with him, saving the McCarthy matter for last. On that he said, "You don't have to coach me on this one, Jim. I have been giving some thought to it overnight, and I am merely going to say that I am not going to indulge in vituperation. I hope they ask me questions about the role I believe the Republican Party must take in the future, and I'm going to give them quite a talk on progressive moderates."

The President was quite insistent that he handle this in his own way and when Jerry Morgan and Jerry Persons started to interrupt to suggest something, he leaned across his desk and said, "Listen, my boys, I'm glad this happened. I can never work with this fellow and I never thought I could. You asked me to try it and I did. But I'm glad the break has come because as far as I'm concerned, this fellow isn't ever going to get into the White House any more and don't any of you ever come to me with a proposal that he does. The McCarthys, the Jenners, the Brickers, and the rest of them can do what they want as far as I'm concerned, but I'm going to do one thing. I'm going to get this Republican Party of ours to be progressive or else—and that's that!" . . .

After the conference I talked to a few of the reporters—including Smitty, Marv Arrowsmith, Roscoe Drummond, and Eddie Folliard—and told them that I thought there was a good political story in the conference.[1] The President's use of the words, "progressive moderates," his insistence that any future nominee of the party reflect those views, and his turndown of McCarthy with the expression that if the right wing wanted to leave the party, that was their business, was a pretty good blueprint of the President's political thinking. They agreed with this, and all wrote separate stories to that effect. . . .

I'm tired—I'm going home!!!!!!

• • • •

Thursday, December 9, 1954

In at 8:15. Comparatively quiet day. . . .

After the NSC meeting broke up I attended a meeting at two o'clock in Jerry Persons' office with Fred Seaton, Jerry Morgan, Jack Martin, Andy Goodpaster, and Murray Snyder on the military plans which the NSC discussed this morning.[1]

What is going to happen is that the Army will be cut from its present 1.3 million strength to 1.1 million by June 1955 and to 1 million by June 1956. The Air Force will be slightly increased to 975,000 and the Navy and Marine Corps will be cut slightly. . . .

• • • •

Friday, December 10, 1954

Nothing particular doing. The President left for Gettysburg after the Cabinet meeting. Fairly quiet in the afternoon. I left early since Dad came in that afternoon for the Gridiron Dinner.

• • • •

Saturday, December 11, 1954

Down for a short time at the office at noon and had lunch downstairs with Murray and Bobby Cutler. Later went over to the Statler to visit Roy Roberts and he made one good suggestion.[1] He said he thought the best way to handle Knowland was to pay some attention to his father, and it might be a good idea when the elder Mr. Knowland was in town if we invite him over to the White House and give him good treatment, He said the Senator worships his father and often follows his suggestions.

Gridiron Dinner that night was pretty good, and the President made an excellent speech on the need for patience and strength in the world. Williams, the Democratic speaker, was an awful flop and after the dinner the almost universal crack was that the governor of Michigan laid so many eggs that the Secretary of Agriculture was getting worried about overproduction.[2]

Cliff Case was pretty good, although a little too serious.[3]

• • • •

Sunday, December 12, 1954

Went to Gridiron reception in the afternoon with Dad and Marge. Dinner at the Nanking with Bruce and Roger and the three of us.

The rush of work in the White House, including the offshore islands controversy and especially the Senate's condemnation of McCarthy, had prevented the President from thinking about the prospect in Congress as a result of the November elections. In exceptionally close contests the Democrats narrowly regained control of both Houses, with a 29-seat margin in the House and a 1-seat margin in the Senate. The Democrats won nineteen gubernatorial contests, including the Maine election (September 13), against fifteen victories for the Republicans.

Monday, December 13, 1954

In at 8 o'clock.

Republican legislative leaders meeting starting at 8:30 . . .

At the outset the President said that he had invited the leaders in because we have a lot to talk over. We have to decide how we are going to pick up the pieces and work on the Hill with the Democratic majority. A lot of the proposals we will make this year will not be new but we are going to carry through on them and complete the program which we started two years ago. The job this next session is going to be more difficult—let's not kid ourselves about this—but we will have to work together and be convinced that our program is in the best interest of all Americans. "I have called the bipartisan meeting tomorrow to discuss foreign affairs, mutual security, and national defense. I will talk more about this tomorrow, but I want to say one thing now. As far as defense is concerned, I feel that I have had a touch of knowledge on this subject, and I want you all to know the proposals we will make to you are ones which I have personally recommended and ones which I personally take responsibility for. In this world today we have got to keep up our guard and be strong but we have also got to use to the best advantage every single dollar that we spend. As you will soon hear, the budget outlook is not too healthy and that's all the more reason why we have to make our money work as hard as we possibly can for the United States. . . ."

The President then personally started a discussion of the national defense plan. He said that the controlling thought that the leaders must keep in mind was that the United States was really never frightened about enemy attack until the advent of atomic bombs and the long-range bomber. Until that time the United States had been separated by effective ocean barriers and traditionally we counted on a strong Navy and minimum essentials to protect us. No one ever thought that we would not be able, if war occurred, to change over our peacetime economy to a war economy and to outproduce very shortly any other nation or combination of nations in the world. But the invention of the A-bomb and nuclear weapons and the long-range bomber to carry them has caused us all to take a different look at the world. "It seems to me that the great emphasis that we now should put on national defense should be centered on two main objectives: (1) massive retaliation which simply means the ability to blow hell out of them in a hurry if they start anything and (2) a system of advance warnings developed through our radar system to minimize any such attack.

"But what we cannot do, and I want to make this very clear—speaking as commander-in-chief for a minute and not as President—is to plan deliberately for an attack on any given day or any given year. If we do so, and we build everything we have with the idea that war will occur in, let us say, two years and then it doesn't happen, we have a great letdown among our people and an utter weariness which would be as dangerous to us as if we were completely unarmed. Now, everything points to the fact that Russia is not seeking a general war and will not for a long, long time, if ever. Everything is shifting to economic warfare, to propaganda, and to a sort of peaceful infiltration. Now, we must be fully aware of these threats, but we must not sap our own strength by trying to build too much at the present time. Of course, we must maintain and even strengthen our air force and our continental defense. Actually, what I am going to propose will be a cutback on manpower. Right now the armed services, and particularly the ground forces, are only 300,000 men under the peak we had for the Korean War. What we want to do is to lessen the priority we have been keeping on Army ground troops and those parts of the Navy that do not deal with air and with submarines. I want you to know that this judgment is my own. It is taken after many long, long years of study on this problem. Of course, the land forces will try to find every reason to get more and more manpower and every land soldier wants more men. After all, that's what they deal with—manpower. The Air Force and the Navy deal primarily with machines. We will not have 100 percent concurrence on this program but when you link it with the powerful reserve program that we have in mind, I am convinced that it will do the trick."

(I had to go out of the meeting . . .)

When I returned, the meeting was discussing the so-called "fringe" benefits for military personnel, namely, increased medical care for dependents, pay raises for the military and better housing for their families. The President said, "I don't like the words 'fringe benefits.' Actually, they should be part of accepted assistance that we give to our military personnel and I urge very sympathetic consideration on all of these things."

Senator Knowland then asked if the Defense organization had any figures to show what the overhead was in the armed forces of maintaining a soldier in a combat unit. Secretary Wilson said, yes, that he could give him some. He said that in World War II only 43 out of every 100 members of the military were combat troops. In 1953 this had been raised to 52 out of 100 and they were aiming at raising it in 1955 to 62 out of 100.

The President interrupted to say that great progress had been made under Wilson in streamlining the Army and that more progress would be made in cutting out the underbrush.

Saltonstall asked what would be the increase in the Air Force as far as wings were concerned. Wilson replied that he expected to have 120 wings in 1955 and 130 in 1956. He said that these were actual wings and not paper organizations. At that the President interrupted and said, "If they're not, there's going to be some trouble around here. I'm tired of talking about paper wings. What I want is combat wings and we're going to get them."

Knowland then brought up the question of the Yalta Papers which had been raised earlier by Bridges. He told Wilson that as he understood it both State and Defense were working on this project and said he was anxious to have the publication as complete as possible and as soon as possible. The President asked Wilson, "Are you in on this Yalta business, Charlie?" and when Wilson said he was, the President continued, "This sounds like here's where I came in. When I was Supreme Commander and the Chief of Staff of the Army, I began to fight everyone on my staff to get out and make public all papers dealing with World War II. If we're still counting as secret anything that happened in World War II, I don't understand it. I'm in favor of getting the works out and I don't see how anything can hold them up. I pledge you that. Of course, there may be one or two little things that we would rather not make public. For example, when I was going over some papers, I came across something that on the face of it made the Prince of Wales appear to be a little indiscreet.[1] Actually, he was not, but the papers in question, not having the full story, made it appear that he was. I happened to personally know the answer to this one, so I ordered the papers on that case held up. But I'll tell you this, my boys, I'm on the side of opening up the books. More than that, if we get into trouble with Churchill about it, I'll conduct that fight." . . .

Clarence Randall was next on the agenda and had somewhat of a rough time.[2] The President had left the room to meet the Shah of Iran when Randall started to speak. . . . Halleck said that he had no doubt but that the Democrats would support the program and that he himself would support it. He said that he believed the Republican Party would have a hell of a time lining up a majority of the Representatives behind it but hoped that could be done so that the Democrats would not be able to claim credit for passing the President's program by themselves. . . . Knowland made the following priceless remark: "I don't want the Executive and Legislative Branches of the government to have different opinions. We are all interested in the Republican party and its success and it is necessary that we all work together." While no one said anything about this, there were quite a few raised eyebrows around the room, particularly from members of the staff. . . .

The afternoon session started about quarter of three, the President being delayed 15 minutes with the Shah. At the start of the meeting the President said that he had just come from a meeting with the Shah, that he was a fine little fellow who was working very hard. He said, "You know, I thought he had a very nice toast. He said, "Mr. President, except for your country I could not be here today to have this luncheon with you."

The President went right into the trade question and said that the program as outlined by Randall represents that part of the program which we did not get last year and for which I stand. Turning to a point that Millikin had raised about the GATT Convention, the President said that he was surprised that this should be open to question now since it had been agreed last year before this very same group that any agreements on GATT would be submitted to the Senate and would not go into effect unless approved by Congress.

He said that we were spending billions of dollars on mutual security, technical developments to help the economies of other countries, but that if we did not make some provision to permit them to trade, to make a living, then we would be in trouble. In effect, if we don't permit them to trade or make a living, we are saying they are helpless. That certainly would not serve to help the free world. "Let me make one thing clear, gentlemen. I am not looking for any means for giving away American strength. I am trying to make it stronger. That's why I'm for the Randall Report."

Halleck repeated his arguments that he believed it was important to get the majority of Republicans in Congress behind the Randall Report and said if a few minor adjustments were needed to get the votes, he was not above making them. The President, however, did not give any indication of going along with that, and the matter was dropped at this time.

The President then said that tomorrow at the meeting with the Democrats he would advise Randall to say that we were putting in the same recommendations as we did last year, that we were for it and were going to support it.

(This was the first attempted break by the Old Guard over liberal policies that the President stood for. It didn't work and they all knew it didn't. The President's strong approval of Randall and his report backed them right down.)

Adams reported on the highway program and said that the Clay committee report would not be in until the last week of December but that the President would give the details of his recommendations in a special message to the Congress late in January or February. He said in general terms the program would follow the Governors' Conference recommendations. The U.S. government would assume responsibility for the interstate highway system and this would be superimposed on the present federal-aid system for roads now in existence. In all, it would amount to about $27 billion in federal expenditure over the next ten years. So that this would not add to the national debt Adams said that we were thinking about using 30-year bonds to pay for the program. . . .

From what I observed today I do not think we will have any trouble in the House. Martin, Halleck, Arends, and Allen are for the President and his program and I'm sure they will work to carry it out.

The Senate, however, is another matter. Knowland, I am sure, is still smarting under the setback he has gotten and will not be entirely cooperative. Bridges and Millikin represent the thinking of the Old Guard section of our party and will be continually trying to stop what they call radical ideas. Saltonstall is 100 percent for us, but he is not a forceful individual by nature. Ferguson, of course, will not be with us in the new session,

The President is quite aware of the weakness of our side in the Senate and that is another reason why we are going to develop (particularly in the Senate) a group of Eisenhower representatives.

The question of the Yalta Papers, raised in the legislative leaders meeting, would come up again, and it had a long history. Many years before, during the Lincoln administration in the midst of the Civil War, the State Department under Secretary William H. Seward decided that American purposes abroad deserved more publicity than they were getting, and so Seward ar-

ranged to have the nation's diplomatic correspondence—instructions, notes, dispatches—published within the year of origin, in a series labeled variously at the time. His successors continued this practice, save for the year 1869 when no volume of diplomatic correspondence appeared, and by the end of the century the series had taken the name of Papers Relating to the Foreign Relations of the United States. *As years passed the custom of bringing out correspondence shortly after events, often within a year, lapsed, and the gap between events and documents lengthened, although only by a few years. As the twentieth century opened and the series continued, and American foreign relations became more complicated, and sometimes the role of the United States in foreign relations became central to European and world affairs, it proved necessary to omit documents, and once in a while a State Department editor from carelessness or instruction chopped out sentences and paragraphs. The series nonetheless marched on, year after year, an imposing publication of red buckram volumes produced beginning in the 1920s by the Historical Office of the department's Bureau of Public Affairs. When the Eisenhower administration came into office, Senator Bridges of New Hampshire got the idea of having the Department of State publish documentary volumes on the Second World War's diplomatic conferences, and believing that there was fire in the archives—that Republicans could expose Democratic wartime mistakes in negotiation especially with the Russians—he stipulated, in a rider to the 1953 appropriations bill for the Department of State, the order in which the conference series volumes were to appear. The first, he determined, should be the Yalta Papers.*

Tuesday, December 14, 1954

In at 8:00 A.M. Bipartisan leaders meeting at 8:30 . . .

The President called the meeting to order at 8:40 and said that he was gratified to see all of you here; that he had called them together to receive a review first of the fiscal situation and then have a discussion of foreign policy, foreign economic policy, national defense, and mutual security. . . .

Dulles then presented a review of foreign policy and said first that he considered the treaties which would be before the Senate as the first order of business in foreign affairs. In order of importance, in timing for ratification, he listed Manila first, then Formosa, and finally Paris. . . .

Russell asked what would happen to the $700 million in the present appropriation bill which was earmarked for France to carry on the war in Indochina.[1] Dulles reported that very little of that money would go to France. Some of it would go there to help the French maintain forces in Indochina, but that would not continue very long since he did not think it was desirable to have the French forces stay very long in those countries. The rest of the monies would go directly to the separate states of Vietnam, Cambodia, and Laos to help them directly in their own work.

Richards then asked if any European countries planned to help with Asian aid.[2] Dulles replied that some are already doing so and plan to do more. For example, he pointed out that many private German firms were actively engaged in economic activity in Asia with the approval and assistance from their government.

The President interrupted to say that he did not think that we had finally worked out the economic plan that we were proposing. He said that that was the reason he brought Joe Dodge in and that Dodge would soon prepare a plan which would later be sent to the Congress. "Incidentially, I think you will be glad to get this fact. Last year Congress appropriated $5 million to supplement the propaganda line of the U.S. Information Agency. That money was to be used as seed money to help get American industrialists to participate in fairs held throughout the world by arranging their own exhibits which would show the industrial skills and might of our country. That program has been overwhelmingly successful so far. Bangkok has a big fair. We've got Cinerama to put an exhibit into Bangkok and when the Russians found out that Cinerama was coming they moved out.[3] Cinerama was first used at the Damascus Fair and so many people flocked to see it, virtually deserting the Russian exhibits, that the Russians actually accused Cinerama of using unfair practices and being deceitful. Our exhibits have made a tremendous impact on the people who see them, and it is the best piece of propaganda that we can put out. The Russians have been building hand-built machines for exhibition to try to give a rosy picture. But it is catching up with them and they know it. . . ."

The President personally opened up the next discussion, national defense. He said: "I am going to speak to you now as commander-in-chief rather than the President. I am going to talk about national defense plans. It is a field where I believe I have some competence and some ideas. Even if you don't feel too kindly disposed toward them, I want to present them to you as my considered judgment.

"First, you must realize that there has been a basic change in the military picture. For the first time fear has been brought to the United States because we can no longer insure ourselves against attack. Previously, before the atom bomb and long-range bombers were invented, the oceans were our barriers, and as long as we kept a good solid Navy working there was really nothing much that could happen. There was really nothing much an enemy could do to attack us by surprise and overwhelm us. Today those barriers no longer exist and instead Germany and Japan have became the two great anchors in the defense of freedom, the two great prizes that the Communist world is seeking to attain. That means that the United States has great responsibility. We must do this: (1) we must keep on our side the great industrial potential of Japan and Western Europe. We must keep them from falling into Communist hands. We must make them strong outposts of our own defense, and (2) we must make a greater attempt to keep destructive attack from destroying us. We can do this, as I see it, in two ways: (1) by strengthening and working with our friends and our allies, and (2) by building our own strength to a posture so strong that no one will dare hit us. I believe the evidence today all points to the fact that Russia is less likely to attack us than at any time within recent years. We must do everything in our power to assure that the first blow by an enemy will not be a paralyzing one.

"Now, obviously, the security of the United States cannot be measured by a checkbook or a dollar sign. We have no D-Day to build for, but we must remain strong and keep a strong posture of defense. To do this we need an adequate and constantly modern defense establishment, backed up by strong reserves, and we must also keep our economy growing and strong. How do we get the greatest possible defense? We do this through building up our continental defense and our capacity to strike by air. We must make certain that we can't be destroyed by an attack. We must be certain that the enemy knows if he attacks we can hit him hard immediately. That is why we must keep a strong retaliatory power in our combat forces. Actually, it is good for our allies too even though they may shudder about it from time to time.

"Therefore, we must take our Air Force and build it to utmost combat efficiency. We must depend on our naval air arm through means of the big carrier. We need these carriers so that in time of any emergency we can establish floating bases anyplace in the world from which we can hit the enemy. We must, therefore, put emphasis on air and naval air — and of course, submarines. This means that if we are going to get our money's worth, we must cut down in some of the other armed forces. Today we are only 300,000 below the forces we had during the Korean War. Deployments in Korea and in Europe have actually kept our forces up beyond the point that we need. I think we can do this by backing up our combat forces with a strong reserve and, gentlemen, we need a strong reserve here at home. I think you all realize that if an atomic attack were made — for instance, on Gary, Indiana — it would be futile to think that the police or fire forces could handle the aftermath. We would need and need in a hurry trained, disciplined units which would have to come from a trained and disciplined reserve. The first blows of the next war will be hard ones, but I believe that if we have a good reserve at home they can get over that terrible spot and get us back to where our economy can outproduce anyone in the world.

"I am going to recommend that we cut back on all except our Air Force and the air branches of the Navy plus their submarines. I am going to recommend that we get a respectable posture of defense and I believe this is necessary. I believe it with all my heart. Nothing has engaged my attention so much since I entered the White House.

"Now, every specialist in the armed forces sees in his own department or group the ultimate need for victory so we will meet great arguments but what we have got to do is find the point beyond which we cannot go in reduction of force and then make up our minds to get the best possible combat force that we can."

At this point Rayburn interrupted to say, "Mr. President, I make the statement I made last year. I hope your figure is big enough." The President replied, "Well, Sam, this is my considered judgment. Look. We need research. We need to spend much more money and time on research. When an interceptor can't go as high as a bomber, all the ground forces in the world aren't going to stop that bomber from getting through. When a bomber can get through an adequate radar system, all the ground forces in the world aren't going to do you any good. You could take all the gold in Fort Knox and pour it into the ground forces and get nowhere. I hope no one would ever think I would be guilty of unnecessarily exposing this country to danger, and I will always be ready to discuss my beliefs with you any time and any place."

Cyprus long had been a British colony but the Greek government coveted it, and in postwar years when the government in London got rid of India in 1947 and Palestine in 1948, it seemed reasonable to the Greeks to put Cyprus under control of Athens. The trouble in Cyprus was twofold, a feeling on the part of many Cypriots that union with Greece would bring the mainland's troubles and perhaps a regime that would be almost colonial, and there also was the problem of the Turkish minority on Cyprus, a large and unassimilated group vociferous in support of Turkish rule, ideally from Ankara. The postwar cabinet of Clement Attlee, the Labor Party leader, might have given Cyprus to anyone who wanted it, but when Churchill came back into power in 1951 he determined not to be pushed around, least of all by the Greeks.

Wednesday, December 15, 1954

When I went in to see the President, he said as I came in, "The one question that I don't know how to answer is what do I say about Cyprus?" I told him that Hoover recommended that it was entirely a UN matter . . . he then put in a call to him. . . . "You know, Herbert, Churchill will be satisfied with nothing less than a statement from me that Cyprus is his own little private island. I am not going to give him that statement at any time, and if he wants to argue about it, tell him to argue it out with me. I'll take the responsibility for that one. We just can't side with colonial aspirations of Great Britain. The Greeks are our friends and we need them badly in that part of the world. I sincerely hope that the British can work this out agreeably with the Greek government."

We ran through the othe subjects quite rapidly and the President agreed with us that the State Department "no deal" statement was a mistake. However, he said, "Don't blame them too much. They probably wanted to spike the thing immediately, but I don't believe they closed the door irrevocably on any swap of students for flyers. Actually, I can't see where we can hold these students against their will and appear before the world and charge the Communists for doing the same thing to our flyers. True, these students are not in jail but if, as you say, 25 or 30 of them want to go back to China, I'm not so sure we shouldn't eventually try to swap them. But I'll duck on this if I get a question." . . .

The press conference went very well. As we were coming down in the elevator, the President expressed some surprise that no reporter had raised the question of the American flyers or of Cyprus. "I just don't understand it. It would seem to me that these were two important world questions and for the life of me I can't see why they weren't asked. I'm just as glad they weren't—but I can't understand it." I agreed with him one hundred percent.

Not long after entering the presidency Eisenhower began a series of stag dinners. The very word, implying an all-male invitation list, would have raised trouble in later years, but at the time, and whatever their privileged composition, they proved highly successful affairs. He was able to bring into the White House men of varied backgrounds who interested him for reasons of friendship or policy, and the dinners created an enormous amount of good will.

Monday, December 20, 1954

. . . The stag dinner at the White House was a very nice affair and quite successful from a political point of view. After having a drink in the President's study on the second floor, we all went down to dinner. The President set the tone of the dinner right at the outset by remarking, "I normally have a rule at these stag dinners that we talk about everything except politics. Tonight I want to revise that ruling and limit our discussions entirely to politics."

While we were at the dinner table the conversation, of course, was mostly limited to our right and lefthand neighbors or those across the table. However, toward the conclusion of the dinner the President took over and started the discussion of the future political strength of the Republican Party in the State of New York. . . .

The conversation actually didn't get down to real business until after we adjourned to the Red Room where the President continued the discussion of the New York situation with Clay, Stephens, Hall, McCrary, and Lodge. He asked me if I thought that Heck could work with Javits and I said I thought he could. The President then said that he could not, as President, interest himself entirely with the political situation in any one state but that he had deliberately raised the question of New York and that he now expected that the New York people in his administration—Brownell, Hall, Stephens, and myself in particular—should get it worked out. He said, "I'll do anything I can to help and I'm sure that my own staff members, Tom and Jim, have many friends up there and can do some good work."[1] . . .

Summerfield then gave a very interesting breakdown on Michigan, pointing out that Reuther and the CIO had actually scored a major political victory in Michigan, defeating Ferguson and gaining almost virtual control of Detroit and the state. He said that they had done this through unlimited expenditures of Union funds which resulted in television and radio broadcasts, "news" broadcasts by two paid CIO commentators and a continuing campaign of slandered exaggeration. He warned that Reuther was going to be a political power to be dealt with now not only within the state of Michigan but throughout the country. He recommended that the Republican Party and its spokesmen take means immediately to counteract slandered stories, reports, etc., issued against the administration by the CIO.[2]

Summerfield's statement led me to renew my often-repeated request for the formation of a team of carefully schooled pro-Eisenhower people, both in the administration and on the Hill. I pointed out and was seconded by McCrary that there were literally millions of dollars worth of free time available to us on radio and television through special programs such as Meet the Press, Face the Nation, Junior Press Conference, Man of the Week, and the like. I said that one of the reasons we were so effective in Chicago was that we were putting on the radio and television good-looking well-trained men . . . I said that I could not for the life of me see why we could not get such a team formed now, including men within the administration . . . , all of whom represent the progressive liberal Republican viewpoint and who by their appearances on the programs would attract to the Republican Party the young progressive liberal elements throughout the country.

The President said that he could not agree with me more, that he had been urging this himself and on the spot he told Len Hall that he thought it was his job to get up such a list, to hold coaching schools for the people on the list and to get going. . . .

The President then also said that he thought that the time had come to start the fight against the Old Guard within our party. He said that he would like to appoint right now an overall strategy committee, consisting of Herb Brownell, Len Hall, Cabot Lodge, Lucius Clay, and the Vice President, to call into operation all the brains we have within our country on this problem. He agreed with General Clay that it must be done, not only at a national level but also at the state levels, the county levels and down through the lowest precinct level. "It's going to be a tough fight, but let me remind you gentlemen that primaries start only a year and three months from now. We haven't got two years. We have only a little more than a year to do the job."

Adams then said that one thing which was needed, of course, in all of this was the leadership of the President and that it was necessary in this work to point out from time to time that the President was not going to back out of running in 1956, but on the contrary continually express the opinion that the President would be willing and ready to do his share if the party were built along the lines we were talking about tonight.

The President laughed and said, "Well, my boys, many of you people here in this room came to me before '52 and talked me into entering politics. I would say this. I will do everything possible to be of assistance to you, including running in 1956. But let me give you my philosophy a little further. This should not depend on one man. That would be disastrous because you never can tell when that one man whom you are counting on may become ill and may be taken out of the political picture by illness or even death. Now, I don't mind talking about Eisenhower policies and Eisenhower programs and Eisenhower progressives, but we have got to build up within the party many liberal men of promise in the future who can take over this job. That's why I want the young people to come into this party. Let me remind you that if everything goes well, I probably will vote in only two or three or four more presidential elections but a young man or woman of 21 who believes in our party and joins it is going to be able to vote in 15 or 20 more elections. So, let's go to work and build this thing up." . . .

The discussion about New York State politics, and the more private discussion in the Red Room about Michigan politics and especially the need to build a

Republican party not dominated by the Old Guard, displayed the President's political instincts. For a man who had spent forty years in the Army before he got into politics in 1952, Eisenhower showed political judgment of the highest order, far more so than most of his contemporaries, an ability to get to the center of political problems and find a solution that satisfied a majority. Unlike his military predecessors in office, he shifted to political issues as if he had been a politician all his life. One recalls the ineptitudes of William Henry Harrison, Zachary Taylor, and U.S. Grant. Harrison and Taylor never managed to understand the difference between the Army and their administrations, perhaps believing them the same for both words began with the same letter of the alphabet. Fortunately they were not long in office. Grant however clung to the presidency for eight long years and followed each political stupidity with an imbecility. When Eisenhower's predecessor Truman saw the general take up politics he, Truman, was sure Ike would be another Grant. The general proceeded to fool everyone.

Wednesday, December 22, 1954

In at 8:15. I went in to see the President on Augusta plans at 8:30 and we had a chance to have a discussion about several things.

The President opened the conversation by saying, "Do you think that I am surrounded by left-wing people?" I laughed and said no I did not—what was he referring to? He said he had been seeing in the papers of late mention of this fact and while he himself did not believe it, he was puzzled as to why some people should write that. I asked him if he was referring to George Sokolsky, David Lawrence, and Westbrook Pegler.[1] He said that he was and added that he was sure this was a deliberate counterattack by the right-wing forces of the Republican Party to try to smear the Eisenhower people in the party. Their usual idea is to call people who do not agree with them Communists, and I expressed the opinion that it wouldn't be too long before he would read that his press secretary or Sherman Adams or Cabot Lodge or Brownell were Communists. They haven't got quite to that point yet, but I think they will. . . .

At this juncture, the last ten days of December 1954, the scene shifted to international affairs, to the French Chamber where the European Defense Community issue in a new guise was up for a vote. What had happened was that on August 30 the Chamber had turned down EDC, to the consternation of statesmen in all the Western capitals save perhaps Paris, where there was almost unfeigned delight at this tweaking of the noses of other nations. Undaunted, though weary from the task of soothing the French, Secretary Dulles flew off to a series of consultations in Western Europe and managed a new formula. He converted an anti-German alliance negotiated in 1948 by Britain, France, and the Benelux countries, known as Western Union (at that time it also served as a preliminary to NATO, signed in 1949), to what became known as Western European Union, and invited West Germany into the treaty that a few years before the nations had devised against Germany. Dulles presented the new package with a flourish to the French Chamber, and then everyone watched, with bated breath, for the result.

Thursday, December 23, 1954

Left for Augusta at 11 o'clock. Arrived shortly after one.

Everything was comparatively quiet until late that evening when we received the news that the French House of Deputies by a vote of 280 to 259 had defeated German rearmament. This was only one of a series of test votes, however, and final action will not come until Monday or Tuesday. . . .

• • • •

Friday, December 24, 1954

I told the President about the vote at 8:15 in his office. His immediate reaction was, "Those damn French! What do they think they're trying to do? This could really upset the apple cart in Europe."

The President asked me to call Foster Dulles and have the Secretary call him back with a full report on the situation. This I did from the President's office at about quarter of 9. Dulles called back at eleven o'clock to tell me that he had just received reports from Ambassador Dillon in Paris. Dillon reported to Dulles that the situation was very serious and that he and the British ambassador to Paris thought that drastic action was necessary to impress upon the French deputies over the weekend, and the French people themselves, how concerned America and the United Kingdom were over the adverse vote. Dulles said that Dillon also proposed—although he, Dulles, did not agree, that a formal statement be issued jointly by the President and Churchill which would say in effect that despite French ratification or not, the United States and Britain were going ahead with the rearmament of Germany.

Dulles said that he did not think that was necessary but that he did believe that both the President and himself should issue statements expressing their grave concern about the matter. Dulles also said that the British ambassador to the United States, Sir Roger Makins, was coming to his house for a conference at noon, and he thought he should talk to the President prior to the arrival of Sir Roger. I told him I would have the President call back within fifteen minutes and went out to the club to get him.

The President was on the ninth green, practicing putting with Ed Dudley.[1] When I came over, he said to Ed, "Excuse me, Ed, but I've got to go to work. The French have not only disturbed the whole free world but they're cutting in on my lessons." . . .

When the Dulles call came through, the President and I were alone in his office. He opened the conversation with, "Well, Foster, they surely have gotten things in an awful mess, haven't they?" The President agreed with Foster that we should not issue a joint statement and gave Foster the task of relaying that to Churchill through Makins. . . .

When the phone call was concluded, the President briefly discussed this situation and said, "You know, here this plan like EDC was devised to protect all of Europe, the French included. They are really endangering the whole safety of Europe by such votes, but you see, I honestly believe what they are trying to do is this: They know we are going to have to keep bases and troops on the continent of Europe for a long time. They know we must work somehow or other to get a strong alliance of free nations of Europe. Now, what the French would like would be to act in that concert of Europe very much like we do and like the British do. . . . The French would like to be part of it without having the responsibility of being in it. It's the old French game of diplomatic doodling to see how much they can get out for themselves and never mind the rest of the world." . . .

Dulles reported that the British government had issued the strong note and was still requesting that we join them. The President firmly disagreed with that step . . .

• • • •

Saturday, December 25, 1954

The expected strong French reaction to the British statement developed today. On the other hand, the French were quite agreeably surprised with the mild tone of our statement. . . .

I gave out a story for Sunday morning which got a good play on the President's decision to send to the Congress on January tenth a special message on foreign economic policy. . . . It particularly emphasizes a split between the Eisenhower Republicans and the Old Guard, but we are very happy to have this happen.

• • • •

Sunday, December 26, 1954

Talked to Dulles early Sunday morning, and he reported that reports from Dillon indicated that Mendès-France was rallying his people and would probably have enough votes for passage of the various amendments. We cannot be too sure of this, however, since one adverse vote in any sitting would be a setback. I discussed the possibility with Dulles of what would happen as far as the President's plans were concerned, if the vote should be adverse. I told him that it was my belief that the President should return to Washington instead of remaining here in Augusta and having him and others, including the Secretary of Defense, come down. It would not be good publicity to have the President remain at a golf course when the safety of the free world had been placed in jeopardy. He agreed and I told him I would go out to see the President right away and have the President call him before going to church.

I went out to the President's cottage at 10 o'clock and found him in his little studio on the second floor, sitting in his pajamas and making a painting of Mamie's cottage. He agreed that it would be a good idea to talk to Dulles and put in a call to him. The President opened the conversation by saying that he himself had been thinking of what he should do if there were an adverse vote, and that he had decided to return immediately to Washington. . . .

• • • •

Monday, December 27, 1954

. . . It developed that today was really one of just waiting around and I called the Secretary again at 12:30. He told me that it looked now as if there would be no vote until at least six o'clock and that he thought I should tell the President about that. I went back to the club and told the President that I would not have anything for him until after he finished his golf game. . . .

I called the President once more in the evening to tell him that the Assembly had adjourned and closed up for the night and that the vote on German rearmament and the final vote on the whole package would not occur until Wednesday.

I was in touch several times during the evening with Dulles and he sent down to me a draft of two alternative statements for the President to issue, depending on which way the vote went. I did not particularly like the first one. It was too much like "peace in our time" and I rewrote it the next morning.

Reference to "peace in our time" was of course to the famous pronouncement of Prime Minister Neville Chamberlain after he returned from the Munich Conference in 1938, that he had received assurances from Hitler and they meant "peace in our time."

Tuesday, December 28, 1954

I went out to the President's office at 8 o'clock and gave him a copy of Eden's message and the Secretary's report. I also went over with him the two alternative statements from Dulles . . .

• • • •

Wednesday, December 29, 1954

This could be the big day for the United States and the free world.

I talked to Secretary Dulles this morning at 8:15 at his home, and he told me that the reports he had received overnight indicated that the vote by the French Chamber of Deputies would be very much closer. He said that London was very jittery over the outcome and that he was just sitting in Washington with his fingers crossed. The Secretary made changes in the drafts of the statements we had, the principal one being the elimination of the phrase "by an overwhelming and splended majority" in connection with the vote taken by the Italian Chamber last week. We changed it to "decisive."

An amusing thing developed in revising the draft of the Secretary's statement. As drafted, we had said that the French vote was particularly important because the Deputies "after initial hesitations against bringing Germany into Western Defense arrangements have now on sober second thought voted to ratify, etc." The Secretary laughed and said that even though he had suggested the phrase, "on sober second thought," he found that after looking at the French translation of it, it would give the impression that the Deputies had not been sober during their previous meetings or up until the time they had voted. So with the understatement of the year he said, "I think we'd better take it out." . . .

When I returned to the hotel I called Dulles . . . He then told me that in all probability the vote would not come until about 10 o'clock tonight at the earliest. He explained that under the French system of voting, the Deputies hand in their ballots and then they have to be counted in a close vote—and the Secretary expected it to be close. This procedure takes about two hours, so despite newspaper stories, at the conclusion of the vote we will have to wait for the final official tally. The Secretary and I also discussed my upcoming press conference at 10 o'clock. I told him that all I would do was merely tell the reporters that the situation was unchanged, that the President and the Secretary of State were just sitting by waiting for the results of the vote and that the *Columbine* was on the field here in Augusta.

The Secretary asked me to soft-pedal any dramatization of the *Columbine* standing by if I possibly could. He said it was a little point, but that the French were very emotionally upset today and even if they did vote favorably, they would do so only with the greatest of reluctance. He said that they recalled President Wilson's order when Wilson was at the peace conference at the end of World War I that the *George Washington* stand by for him and take him home right in the middle of the conference. Wilson was using this only as a threat, but it had an adverse effect in France at that time and the French still remember it—"I know this doesn't make any sense, but French logic and reasoning doesn't either. It is little things like this which might affect one or two votes, and we just can't lose one or two votes today." I told the Secretary that, of course, I would follow his advice, and the question of the *Columbine* was not raised directly although of course all the newspapermen knew it was at the airport. . . .

At about nine o'clock the French Assembly pulled a surprise and on a parliamentary procedure by the Communists delayed the vote on German rearmament for 24 hours. In talking with Dulles, he said that he was quite concerned over this postponement since it would allow the Communists throughout France to put pressure on the delegates and have mass meetings in every town, village, and city against rearming Germany. This, of course, is a very popular argument with the French since I don't suppose there is a French family who has not had a member killed or wounded by Germans in the three wars in the last eighty years. . . .

• • • •

Thursday, December 30, 1954

The French vote to rearm Germany really came fast today. . . .

By this time the President was on the practice tee, but when I called I sent word to him through Jim Rowley of what we wanted to do and a few minutes later Jim called back and said the President agreed and said by all means do so. I then made arrangements with Jim to have the Secret Service relay the vote to the President wherever he was, on the golf course, on the practice tee, in his cottage, or in the club dining room.

When the vote came through, I called the Secret Service and they relayed it to the President via shortwave on the golf course. When Jim Rowley told him of it, the President's only comment was "Good . . . That's fine." . . .

• • • •

Friday, December 31, 1954

With the tension off as a result of the French vote, today was a fairly quiet day. . . .

January 1955

Saturday, January 1, 1955

New Year's Day!

Went out to see the President at ten o'clock with the proclamation ending Korean benefits. He read over the press release and then signed the document . . .

Rainy day here. First rain since we arrived.

The proclamation ended benefits for the military as of January 31, 1955.

Shortly after the New Year, upon returning to Washington, an issue of public relations arose that annoyed Hagerty because, he thought, it was so unnecessary. Secretary of Agriculture Ezra T. Benson was without the slightest talent in dealing with newspapermen, always capable of raising a fuss, and this time it was over his department's charge that a respected specialist in agricultural economics, Wolf Ladejinsky, was a Communist. For a while Hagerty had his hands full.

Monday, January 3, 1955

Back in Washington. In the office at 8:15—and what a reception!

The Department of Agriculture, Benson, and his administrative assistant, Smith, have really fouled up the Ladejinsky case. In the first place, Benson is taking the advice of some of his security people and coming up with what I think are ridiculous charges against Ladejinsky, charges that are not upheld by either the State Department security clearance under Scott McLeod (who nobody could ever accuse of being soft) or the Federal Bureau of Investigation or the Attorney General.

Secondly, Smith made public a letter which the department had received from a White Russian by the name of Vitt in New York, which was full of anti-Semitic remarks. In releasing this to several newspapermen—one of them Clark Mollenhoff of the Des Moines *Register and Tribune* who is just out to needle us anyway—Smith classified the Vitt letter as typical of the thinking of right-minded people. All this was done without any notice to the White House, and it is sure causing quite a lot of hell. Snyder has been working with Adams ever since the story broke to try to keep the White House out of it and to try to get a solution. The one which looks the most likely is to have Ladejinsky go to work for FOA in his chosen field of land reform and send him to Southern Vietnam. The situation is more particularly screwed up since FOA made such a request from Agriculture three months ago and were told that Ladejinsky could not be spared from his work in Japan. They really fumbled the ball on this one in the worst way and we will try to help them put out the fire.

Snyder also filled me in on another one which he ran across and which deals with Agriculture. It seems that fifteen months ago Benson talked Mrs. Hobby into discontinuing the inspection under the Pure Food and Drug Law of surplus grain which we are sending abroad. Nelson Rockefeller tipped off Murray to this when he came over here, and this is another one we are trying to get straightened out.[1] Without inspection, there is mice and rat pollution quite normally in the grain. Under Adams' orders the Department of Health, Education, and Welfare is renewing the inspection. Of course, the millers themselves have a very strict inspection system, but nevertheless it would make a lousy story if it got out that we are not doing the same thing.

Bobby Cutler came in with Colonel Goodpaster early in the morning to discuss the need in their opinion for the President to make an additional statement on the cutback in the armed forces and the reason why. They are fearful, of course, that the Democrats will try to make this an issue in Congress and that Ridgway and the Army will try to make a case for a larger number of ground forces. . . .

At 2 o'clock the President had a joint meeting of the Cabinet and the Republican leaders . . . to discuss the State of the Union message. . . .

The question of manpower and the armed forces program came up almost immediately . . .

"It is a question," the President said, "of blunting the threat of attack by establishing an adequate continental defense and building up our guided missiles here at home, and secondly, to emphasize the retaliatory concept of warfare by putting more money into the air and developing a better early warning system. In the kind of war we are faced with, how long do you think it would take us to ship ten divisions to Europe or six to Japan? Enemy submarines would be swarming the seas, and troops at either the port of embarkation or debarkation would be sitting ducks for atomic aerial attack. What we have got to do in our new thinking is to realize that there will be a period when all we can do is to avert disaster. If we have time to do that job and hit back hard, then we can do the rest in time. But unless we do this, gentlemen, take my word for it we are going to be shot to pieces. As a matter of fact, Al Gruenther is very hopeful that we can set up our reserve program here in this country in a hurry so that he can then go to the European countries and appeal for them to do the same thing.[2] If we have an atomic attack, we will need those reserves here at home. Can you imagine what would happen in New York or Detroit, or Washington or Pittsburgh or any one of our big cities, if they got hit by an atomic bomb. The fire and police forces of those cities would be inadequate to cope with the panic and disaster that would result. That is why we need a disciplined reserve which could move in immediately to take over and preserve order. We have got to lay this whole program on the line and get the American people to realize what it is all about. . . ."

Toward the end of the meeting the President injected an entirely new idea—one which I had not heard him talk about in the past. He said that he thought it might be a good idea for this country to have some sort of an award similar to the British Order of Merit or the French Legion of Honor which we could award to outstanding civilians—scientists, scholars, doctors, etc. He pointed out that the British Order of Merit reserved twelve awards each year for civilians, while the French Legion of Honor mixed military and civilian awards almost 50–50. "This would be something that would allow our government to honor peaceful pursuits and if you think well of it, I think I will put a sentence or two about it into my speech." There was no objection although the congressional leaders expressed no wild enthusiasm about it. . . .

• • • •

Tuesday, January 4, 1955

In at 8:15.

The Ladejinsky case still continues to be an annoying one. Benson and his people really have messed this one up like nothing else has been messed up since I have been in Washington. . . . The trouble with him and his whole department is that they have absolutely no feeling for public relations. Actually, they should have been spanked publicly before this, but the President, of course, does not like to do this. . . .

Since the manpower cut was announced by the Secretary of Defense in December, the Democrats have been chewing at it. They think they have an issue—that they can make an argument to the American people that we are cutting our armed services just for budgetary reasons in an attempt to try to save some money. Of course, nothing could be farther from the truth and the reasons we are taking the steps we have is so that we can put more emphasis on nuclear weapons, guided missiles, and the Air Force. . . .

• • • •

Wednesday, January 5, 1955

At the White House at 7:45 to pick up the President to go to the National Presbyterian Church for the annual service commemorating the opening of the congressional session.

Sherman Adams also met us, and as we were driving in the car to the church, the question of Ladejinsky came up. The President said, "Why doesn't Benson admit he made a mistake and let it go at that." I told the President that it reminded me of the time LaGuardia, the mayor of New York, had made a mistake in the appointment of a magistrate. LaGuardia was under considerable pressure because of the appointment, and he merely laughed it off by saying to the newsmen, "When I make a mistake, it's a beaut." The President laughed and said, "That's exactly what I mean. Benson could end this once and for all by saying he was mistaken, but he is a stubborn man and I don't suppose we can get him to do that."

Adams filled in the President on the conversations he had had with Benson and expressed the opinon that there wasn't much chance that Benson would make such a statement.

Formal announcement from FOA on Ladejinsky to be made today at ten o'clock. . . .

The Bricker Amendment is kicking up again. I was in talking briefly with the President on the Ladejinsky case when Jack Martin and Sherman Adams came in to tell the President that Bricker was going to resubmit his amendment. I expressed the hope that we would take the same position against it and not give in. The President said that he certainly would take that attitude unless the Bricker Amendment merely confined itself to a restatement of the Constitution. . . . This amendment, of course, is a rallying ground for the Old Guard and should it be adopted, would represent a tremendous victory for them. This we cannot permit to happen. . . .

• • • •

Thursday, January 6, 1955

. . . The President was also somewhat annoyed at the length of his State of the Union message. His reading copy ran 86 pages and he had compared it with the one of last year which was only 72. "I don't see why I can't get somebody to cut out some of this stuff. Bryce Harlow is a wonderful fellow, one of the best I have ever had work with me, but he should learn how to say no to these various departments that insist on putting things into the speech. I'm going to cut out as many paragraphs as I can in order to cut down on the length."

During the morning the President called me back into his office quite a few times to show me some of the changes he had made in his speech. Two were important, and he asked me to get changes made in the text that was being moved on the wires. The first one dealt with the Army. In Point 3 of his summation of the need for cutting down military personnel, we had mentioned the Navy, the Air Force, and the Marines. "You can't mention three of the services and leave the Army out. Please get this included in all of the texts." . . .

The second point dealt with the report that he was going to make on school construction. As originally drafted, the text said that the federal government would act as a catalyst. The President said he did not believe the word "catalyst" was right since a catalyst was merely an element which was added to a chemical reaction to speed up the reaction but had nothing to do with the final result. "It may be necessary for us to put federal monies into school construction and therefore I want this word 'catalyst' changed to 'agent.' This is a more definite description of what we are going to have to do."

I picked the President up in his office just prior to the time he was scheduled to leave for the Hill, and his final words as he grabbed hold of his reading copy were, "The next time somebody gives me an hour's speech to read when I ask for a half-hour one, I'm going to tear the whole thing up and just speak for a half hour." He also told me that he was going to insert in his speech at the very beginning mention of Speaker Rayburn's 73rd birthday. With a grin he said, "I'm going to congratulate Mr. Sam for representing the district in which I was born. How do you like that?" I laughed and said I thought it would be very good and quite cute.

The President delivered his State of the Union message very well, taking 53 minutes to read it. He was 58 minutes on the air from the time he was introduced by Fishbait Miller and entered the House until the time he was finished.[1] The message was a good one covering a great many topics and it stole a lot of the Democratic thunder by proposing liberal action in many fields. . . .

• • • •

Friday, January 7, 1955

At Walter Reed and started a series of checkup examinations . . .

• • • •

Tuesday, January 11, 1955

Discharged from Walter Reed at 2:30. All the tests turned out fine. They told me what I already knew—that I had to have some teeth fixed, that I was overweight and had to take off 20 pounds, and I had some trouble and stoppage in my small intestine. . . .

• • • •

Wednesday, January 12, 1955

Press conference day. In at 8:10. . . .

In telephone conversation with Dulles the following points were covered: . . .

Chinese attack on Tachen Islands. Dulles said that these islands 200 miles to the north of Formosa, were not within the territory covered by the defense treaty with the Republic of China. He said we have no obligation to defend these islands but that it would be optional with us to take what action we deem necessary if such a time should come. He recommended that the President not take any definite stand one way or another on the defense of these islands but merely say that the United States was watching them very carefully. . . .

In the briefing conference with the President, I ran over rapidly the Dulles suggestions and he accepted all of them. He said that on both the Churchill and Nehru visits he would say that he would be willing to meet any time they wanted to see him. He also said he would be very strong on the Bricker Amendment should it come up at the press conference and make it clear that he was not giving in one iota. (None of these subjects came up at the conference, much to our surprise.)

Many questions at the press conference dealt with the security program and the Ladejinsky case. I personally thought the President tried to defend Benson too much . . .

• • • •

Thursday, January 13, 1955

In at 8:00 A.M. and gave out special messages to Congress on Army pay raises and reserve program. The President was a little unhappy about the details of the reserve program which was included in the message. Later in the day I had a chance to talk to him about this, and his reasoning was as follows: "It would seem to me, Jim, that it is going to the well too often for me to pose as an expert on details of every program that the administration is going to submit to the Congress. . . ."

Later in the day I had a telephone call from Foster Dulles who told me that Hammarskjold was meeting privately tonight at eight o'clock with Cabot Lodge to give him a report on his visit to Peiping.[1] This meeting is entirely off the record and no public notice has been given of the meeting. When Lodge gets Hammarskjold's report, he will call Dulles and Dulles will then call me. It may be necessary after talking with Dulles to inform the President of the conversation—either by myself or by Dulles. I will probably have to do it since Dulles will be at a dinner and will not be at liberty to talk too freely over the phone. When I received this call from Dulles, the

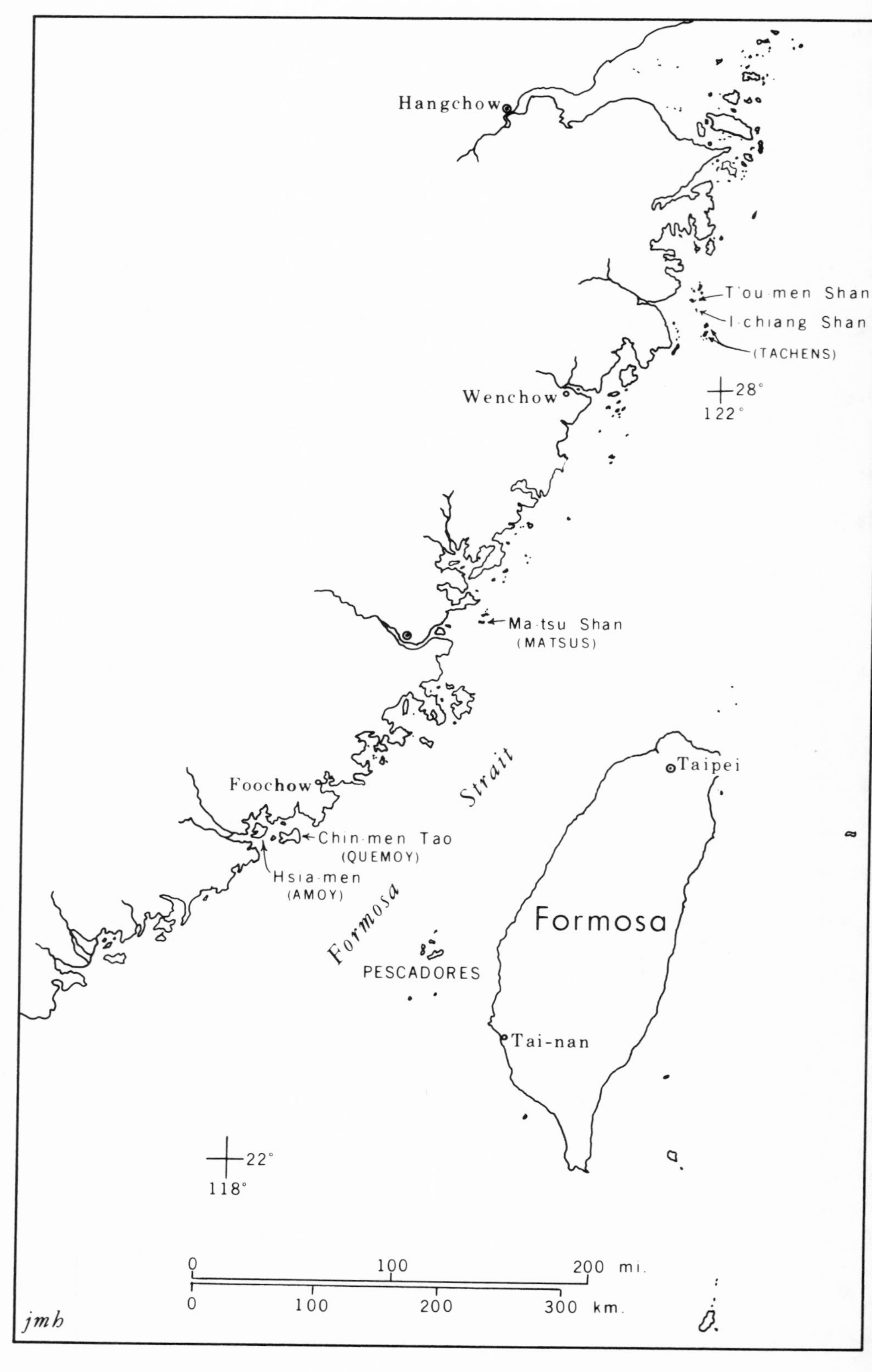
Hangchow
T'ou-men Shan
I-chiang Shan
(TACHENS)
28°
122°
Wenchow
Ma-tsu Shan
(MATSUS)
Taipei
Foochow
Strait
Chin-men Tao
(QUEMOY)
Hsia-men
(AMOY)
Formosa
Formosa
PESCADORES
Tai-nan
22°
118°
0
100
200 mi.
0
100
200
300 km.
jmh

President was in the White House and I went over to tell him about it. He was in his studio painting a scene of a watermill. I told him of my conversation with Dulles and he said, by all means, to give him a ring at any time if I thought it was necessary. He said he probably would not go to bed until 10:30 or 11:00, but if I thought it necessary, to wake him up.

The Secretary of State called the President at 9:45 and then the President called me. He said that Dulles had reported Hammarskjold's conversation with Lodge to him and that it added up to this: that Hammarskjold believed that the Chinese were going to release our airmen eventually but they would probably keep them in jail for several months and then commute their sentences. Of course, they are doing this deliberately to see how much trouble they can cause in this country, and the President said, "How we're ever going to keep those fellows on the Hill from shooting off their mouths for two months on this I don't know, but we've got to do it." . . .

• • • •

Friday, January 14, 1955

. . . The President told me to get in touch with Foster Dulles. He said that he believed Foster was now en route to Omaha for a briefing by the Strategic Air Command. . . . I could not help but feel that today was the worst possible time for Dulles and Lodge to be at a Strategic Air Command briefing. The implications, of course, would be that we were doing it deliberately to threaten the Communists, but actually it was nothing of the sort. This was an appointment which the Secretary had postponed for some time and which was on his schedule for six weeks.

However, I spent a good part of the morning in telling reporters there was no connection between Hammarskjold's return without our airmen and Dulles' visit to Omaha. . . .

One of the things about Hammarskjold's visit that was particularly worrisome to Foster Dulles and myself was . . . that Chou En-lai in conversation with Hammarskjold made the proposition that the Chinese Communists would grant visas to the families of our airmen to permit them to come to China and, as Chou En-lai said, "Permit them to see how well we are taking care of them."[1] This, of course, is a neat publicity and propaganda stunt and one which would cause us considerable trouble. The airmen were moved to better quarters only two or three days before Hammarskjold arrived in China and apparently are now being treated as model prisoners for propaganda use. . . .

There was a Cabinet meeting in the morning and I was in and out . . .

The President started the meeting by referring to the new lights in the cabinet room and laughingly remarked that Bobby Cutler said they made the cabinet room look like Peoples Drug Store.[2] He said he was inclined to agree but it would give more light and he thought it would be helpful.

I left the Cabinet room almost as the meeting started and returned in time to hear part of the presentation by Dr. Brownell, Commissioner of Education, on the proposals we are going to make for school construction. . . .

The President asked Mrs. Hobby how much exploration has been done on this program. He said that it was a modest one and while he was in favor of it, the question remains as to whether the introduction of such a program would start an avalanche of demagogic bills on the program. "Can we hold the line on this program or will we be forced off it almost before we get if off the ground?"

Dr. Brownell said there was strong support for direct federal grants . . . The President asked what would be the ultimate cost for a school construction program which would build the 340,000 schoolrooms that are needed. Dr. Brownell said between ten and fifteen billion dollars. The President then said that he was vitally concerned with this problem and that "if we don't hurry up and build schoolrooms, our whole level of education is going down. While you're frightened about what this is going to cost, I'm frightened about what the Congress will make us expend. As president of Columbia, I studied this problem quite fully and as a matter of fact, was looked upon as something of a reactionary. I was all in favor of helping the poorer states with federal monies but could see no reason why states like New York and California should be given federal monies when they are perfectly able to build schools themselves. That's why I wanted McGrath (former Commissioner of Education) fired as soon as I came down. He was for spending everything in a wild orgy of school construction." . . .

I left the Cabinet room again and missed Hughes' presentation of the budget and part of Burns' presentation of the economic report. One amusing thing happened when Weeks and Burns were talking about "EPT."[3] The President said, "What in the name of God is EPT?" Weeks said, "Mr. President, that's Excise Profits Tax." The President said, "Well, I'll be doggone. I sure get tired of using initials. Why don't you say Excise Profits Tax?" At the conclusion of Burns' presentation on the economic report, the President praised him and said, "Arthur, that's a brilliant effort."

• • • •

Saturday, January 15, 1955

. . . While I was in reporting . . . to the President, he asked me if I had seen Marie McNair's story in the *Post* this morning about the reception last night. He told me that he and Mrs. Eisenhower were very much concerned about a part of her story which said that Rayburn had been irritated at the treatment given his two sisters at the reception. Actually McNair blew this thing up. Rayburn's two sisters were guests of the President and Mrs. Eisenhower upstairs prior to the reception and went downstairs with Barbara Eisenhower. They got separated somehow and went into the East Room instead of going in the Red Room where the honor guests were.

The President called Rayburn in my presence and told him he was quite disturbed about the story, that of course he and Mrs. Eisenhower were delighted to have Rayburn's sisters present and regretted that they had become separated from the official party. Rayburn told the President to forget it—that he fully understood how those things could happen and that he had also seen the story but had paid no attention to it.

The upshot of this whole matter is that the story will probably result in newspaper women being kept out of the receptions. The President told me to look into the matter and report to him next week. I told him I thought it could be done very easily and while the girls might yell for a little while, that would be all there would be to it. . . .

• • • •

Monday, January 17, 1955

In at 8:15. Saw the President at 8:30 and reminded him that he had told me on Saturday that he wanted to talk to Foster Dulles about the 35 Chinese students who were being held here in this country and refused permission to return to their Red homeland. The President said that he had been thinking about this over the weekend and that he could see no reason why these students could not be pemitted to return. . . .

There is a first-class racial question brewing in the National Press Club. Louis Lautier of the *Afro-American* has applied for membership in the club. Some of the hotheads over there are drastically opposed to his admission, and it looks as if a full-fledged hassle is going to occur. Merriman Smith came in late in the afternoon to urge me to stay out of it. I told Smitty that I did not see how I could, that I was a voting member of the club and would have to vote on this question, and that I was going to vote for the admission of Lautier. . . .

• • • •

Tuesday, January 18, 1955

Chuck Von Fremd called me at 6:30 this morning at home to tell me that the Chinese Communists had launched a full-scale bombing and then invasion of the Nationalist-held island of I-Chang. This island is 220 miles north of Formosa but only 7 miles north of the largest Tachen island. He, of course, asked me for comment and I told him I would have none at that time until I could check out the story. . . .

The island of I-Chang had been under artillery fire from the Communist-held island of T'ou Men Shan, six miles to the north, for some time. Yesterday 60 Russian-built Communist bombers, escorted by Russian-built jets, made a series of raids on the island and then the Chinese Communists launched a sea invasion. The island is not fortified and is actually only a volcanic island. There are about 1,000 Chinese Nationalist guerillas on the island, but no regular troops.

The most impressive thing about the invasion was that there are no beaches on the island and that the Reds scaled the sides of the cliffs to land. As Andy Goodpaster said, "They're growing up and getting tougher." We also learned that recently during the Red bombing raids on the Tachen Islands, where there are 12,500 Nationalist regulars, the commanding general and his staff completely lost their heads. Their line of command fell apart. The

Chinese admiral, who was on the island at the time, left his ships in the harbor and they were clobbered with the resultant loss of one destroyer escort and 3 LSTs. The Nationalist commanding general claims he is not getting enough support from Formosa and things are in a terrible mess. . . .

Another subject which I discussed with the President the first thing this morning was the Knowland speech last night in Chicago. Knowland had gone against the President's warning of last week for restraint on the part of people in the government and had lashed out against Hammarskjold, declaring that his mission was a failure and saying the United States should take action, which Knowland did not describe, on its own to get our airmen back from Red China.

When I told this to the President, he was considerably annoyed and said: "I can't understand that fellow Knowland. He had a talk with Foster Dulles on Saturday about his speech but did not bring up any specific thing that he would say, other than that he expressed the opinion that he believed he should show objection to the failure to get our airmen released at this time. But as far as I'm concerned, this just confirms my opinion that Knowland is beyond the pale.". . .

The leaders meeting was attended by the President. . . .

Martin brought up the question of reciprocal trade and said that while the bill would be passed, he thought that there was some opposition . . .

The President interrupted to say that it was awfully hard for us to pass from a debtor to a creditor nation and assume our responsibilities. Martin replied that the textile people say that it is necessary to preserve their industry for national security purposes and argue why should they be asked to pay the bill for any lowering of trade barriers.

The President said that he had heard this argument before and that only recently he had been talking to a representative from Michigan who made the argument to him: "Why doesn't Canada take American beer? We take theirs." When the President laughed and told him he didn't think he could arrange that, the man from Michigan said, "I'm afraid you just lost one vote for your trade program." . . .

Knowland then brought up the question of standby controls . . .

The President said this brought him to another subject which he had wanted to discuss with the leaders for a long time. That was where Congress would relocate itself in case of attack. He said that of course in case of any attack, he would have to impose martial law throughout the country immediately but that he would want to get rid of this martial law as soon as possible. "The only attack we fear is a long-range atomic attack. As long as we can keep up our productive power, keep it in operation, we can lick anybody anytime. But we will need martial law at the start. You can imagine if we have 15 cities in ruin, that we will need every disciplined man we have in our country to restore order in those areas, but more particularly to restore production. We won't be able to ship divisions to Tokyo or to Marseilles. We will have to keep them here to get our production in operation. The weakness of dictatorships is that their troops fight because they have a gun stuck in their kidneys. But the day those dictatorships fear the gun in front of them more than the gun behind them, then the whole shebang blows up. So what we have to do is make sure we can keep up our production and then we have got to preserve free government in any war. The workings of free government will do more to preserve the morale of the nation than anything I know of. So, let's not let Congress do nothing about these relocation plans and just sit here in Washington and not be able to get out."

The President said that there was need for intelligent planning in this situation, and that he hoped that the congressional leaders of both parties would get together. He pointed out that in any case of attack, the roads would be so clogged up that it would be impossible to get the Congressmen out of Washington. "I've seen that happen in cities in Europe where the roads were piled full of refugees and where even military vehicles could not fight their way through. There is one other route that will not be jammed and that is the rivers here in Washington. It would be a comparatively simple matter to load the members of Congress on a naval craft and get them down the Potomac to, say, Mount Vernon or farther south so they could meet in regular session. I urge you to give consideration to relocation plans." . . .

At this point the President said that he wanted to talk to the leaders about one matter—namely, the invasion of I-Chang Island. . . . He said that the island which they had taken was an indefensible island and one which could not be construed as part of the Formosa defenses.

The discussion then turned to the question of the security program, and the President said that everyone in the administration was working like dogs to try to constantly improve the program and protect the best interests of the government and the people concerned. . . .

The President . . . then told the story of how on Labor Day of 1953 when Secretary of the Army Stevens asked him for advice on the Peress case, he told Stevens he had two fundamental rules in the Army which always worked very well. They were: one, if an error was made, admit it in detail and spell it out so that it told the complete story of the error, and two, to show a plan for preventing the recurrence of any such error. "Then stand your ground. Be dignified but tough. Say it was an error. Say it won't happen again and don't say anything else." The President then laughed and said, "I told that to Bob on Labor Day of 1953. Yet when I saw him after the Army-McCarthy hearings, I said, "Bob, why didn't you do what I suggested?" He responded by saying, "Mr. President, I thought I was doing you a service by not getting into the Peress case."

The President then added, "And then, I'll tell you gentlemen another story I learned a long time ago. Don't try to be cute or cover up. If you do, you will get so entangled you won't know what you're doing. I think the Secretary of the Army and his people tried to be cute and cover up with the result that they got just what was coming to them."

Knowland asked if there was any advice the President could give them on the foreign aid question—if there was any advance on the studies that Dodge was making in that field. The President replied that he had been studying the extension of FOA for some time and that as far as the question of foreign aid was concerned, the emphasis had been shifted from Europe to Asia. In Europe, he said, actual handout aid had just about reached its end. The European countries had responded quite well to economic recovery and all they needed would be that military aid be continued. Asia, however, was an entirely different question and the struggle there was developing into an economic one. He said that the Russians were fully aware of the economic struggle in Asia and were spending much of their time and money along this line. In several instances, notably the Bangkok Fair, we had licked the pants off them through our exhibits, but that was not enough. "Frankly, if we say we will not help the Asian countries economically, then I believe we are cutting off our own noses. We must do this for our own good." . . .

After lunch I met the President on his way back to the office and walked into his office with him. I told him that I had two matters to take up with him.

I reported that I had completed my survey on the question of having television and newsreel cameras cover the press conference, that I did not believe the lighting would bother him and he gave me the OK to go ahead and have the arrangement put into effect for tomorrow's conference. . . .

The second point I discussed with the President was the upcoming National Press Club election. I told him the situation and said that since I was a voting member, I did not see how I could duck it and was going to vote for the admission of Lautier. He took off his glasses, chewed them for a few minutes, smiled and then said, "Jim, if I were in your place, I'd do exactly the same thing. Go ahead and vote your convictions." . . .

Late that afternoon Governor Adams called me in to tell me that Howard Pyle would be coming to the White House on February 1st as an administrative assistant.[1] Actually, Pyle's job is going to be to work with the departments to get good publicity out of them and have the departments present their cases as forcefully as they can to the public. The departments' publicity is lousy and it will be up to Pyle to try to clean up that mess. Naturally, we are not going to say that in any release and the governor and I agreed to represent Pyle as one of the President's liaison representatives with the departments of government.

• • • •

Wednesday, January 19, 1955

Press conference day. In at 8:00 A.M.

There was considerable interest in the press conference today because of the fact that we were going to permit cameras in the room for the first time in history. . . .

At 3:30 I got a call from Charlie Shutt and went over to his studio with Murray and Art Minnich to see the films of the conference.[1] . . . We got a tremendous play on the film, of course. The news shows all carried excerpts from the film and gave a plug for the full running which would be held on their networks. NBC played the half-hour show on nationwide network from 11:30 to 12:00. ABC ran it nationwide 9:30 to 10:00 and CBS ran it nationwide 7:00 to 7:30, except for the local station which ran it 11:25 to 12:00.

All in all it was a good day!!!!

• • • •

Thursday, January 20, 1955

In at 8:15. Reception in the newspapers of the press conference was generally better than I expected. For example, while the *New York Times* story on the conference was sort of a snide one, Jack Gould, TV editor of the *Times,* and Arthur Krock had very favorable columns on it.[1] The general impression here among the White House correspondents and other reporters who have to cover the press conference every week was one of resignation to the inevitable. Practically all of them admitted that this was a very potent way of getting the President's personality and viewpoints across to the people of the country and they also admitted that they knew the Democratic National Committee was considerably concerned about it. The Democrats, however, can do nothing at all about it.

Actually, this manner of the President being on television is almost the same thing as the start of Roosevelt's fireside chats on radio. . . .

During the day a delayed story started on McCarthy not being invited to either the Vice President's or the Speaker's dinner. Pursuant to my conversation of yesterday with the President, I merely said that I did not check on people that the President and Mrs. Eisenhower invited to the White House. . . .

• • • •

Friday, January 21, 1955

. . . The Cabinet meeting was held at ten o'clock . . . The President said: "We have a man on the Hill, Senator Paul Douglas, who is chairman of the committee which will review the economic report. He is going to be just as troublesome as he can. Isn't he a professor of economics?" Arthur Burns interrupted with two words: "He was." The President laughed and said, "All right—was. But I expect that he is one of these fellows who is an expert in proving what is not true. He will try to be tricky and he will try to get into the same

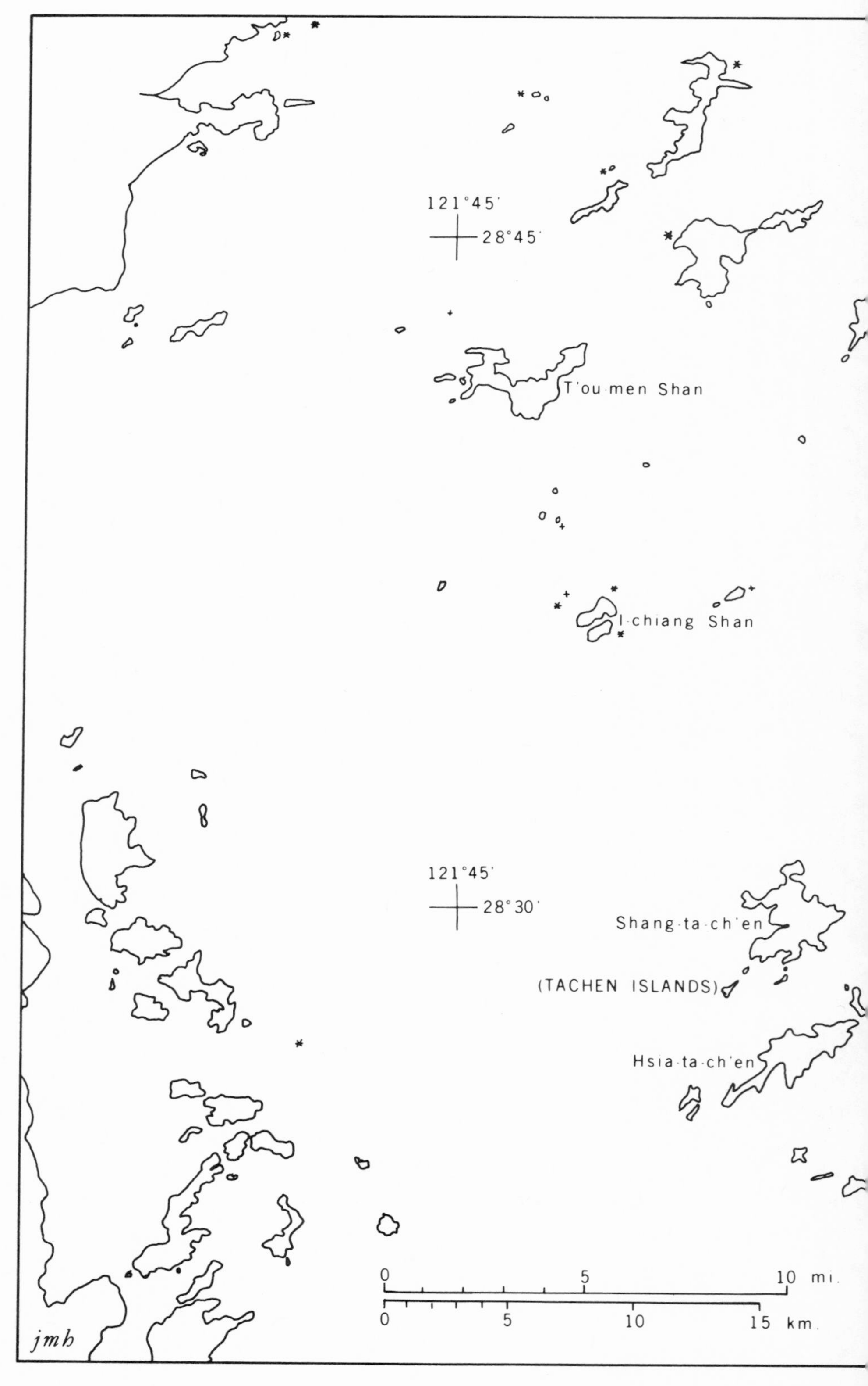

121°45'
28°45'
T'ou-men Shan
I-chiang Shan
121°45'
28°30'
Shang-ta-ch'en
(TACHEN ISLANDS)
Hsia-ta-ch'en
0
5
10 mi.
0
5
10
15 km.
jmh

hearing discredited members of the political world and by that I mean, former Democratic officeholders, and attempt to engage the Cabinet members in an open debate. I want you all to remember two things: first, I do not want any Cabinet officer to forget he is a Cabinet officer. I expect you to make a reasonable presentation of the program but I do not want you or expect you to jump through any Democratic hoops. If they try it, tell them to have experts who can discuss these technical matters but don't be drawn into their traps. Second, I do not expect or want the Cabinet members to engage in lengthy debate with people that Douglas brings in to needle you. I think a few smiles are in the common interest and I think if they try to needle you into debate, you should just sit back and listen. You can expect no good from any question they ask you."

The offshore islands controversy took a new turn early in January 1955, when on January 10 a hundred Communist planes raided the Tachen Islands two hundred miles to the north of Formosa and on January 18 the Communists seized the island of I-Chang, seven miles north of the Tachens, in a fight that lasted two hours. Next day Eisenhower decided to assist in evacuation of the Tachens but to help the Chinese Nationalists hold the Quemoy and Matsu island groups. On January 20 the President approved the wording of a special message to Congress asking authority to use American armed force to protect Formosa and the Pescadores and related positions (this latter portion of the request was suitably vague). He believed that the Korean War had been caused in part by the mistaken Communist notion that under no circumstances would the United States assist South Korea, and wanted no uncertainty about the American commitment to defend Formosa.

It is perhaps worth noting that the resultant congressional delegation of authority to the president was one of four such delegations after World War II. The second was the Eisenhower Doctrine of 1957, in support of any nation sensing itself endangered by communist aggression in the Middle East; the third was a resolution in regard to Cuba, just before the missile crisis in 1962, giving President Kennedy authority to act; the fourth was the Tonkin Gulf resolution of 1964, President Johnson's permission to widen the Vietnam War.

Saturday, January 22, 1955

. . . We are taking a big step in sending up this message. Actually, the President—as he himself put it—has made up his mind to not let the Chinese Communists get away with murder in the China seas. Three aircraft carriers from Pearl Harbor were sent to join the 7th Fleet Friday morning and are now on their way. Other forces are being quietly shuffled around the Pacific so that they can get to the area in a hurry if there is need for it.

The message will not draw any definite line as such but will serve notice that the President, if he sees fit, is going to use American strength in other areas outside of the treaty area, which includes just Formosa and the Pescadores . . .

If we get an overwhelming approval of the resolution—and I am sure we will—the Chinese Communists ought to know that we mean business. I am sure that they will know this and will think twice before starting any nonsense.

• • • •

Sunday, January 23, 1955[1]

I went to Foster Dulles' home at eleven o'clock and found him there with Bowie of the State Department. We went over the message and made some minor changes in it and some rearrangement of the paragraphs. . . .

As we finished up our work, Dulles walked to the front door with me and then outside. "I'm as nervous as a kitten. I feel just the same way I did waiting for my son to be born. It's a ticklish and very delicate question, and of course, none of us knows how the Chinese Communists are going to react." . . .

• • • •

Monday, January 24, 1955

. . . Dulles called me back at about 12 o'clock and said that he would urge very strongly that the President go before television and newsreel cameras to read sections of his message. . . .

I saw the President on this at one o'clock and he agreed to do it. This was somewhat of a change in the plans we had originally made in the presentation of the message. We had declined requests by Knowland and Clements to deliver the message in person because we thought it would scare people too much and give the impression that we were going to war tomorrow.[1] . . .

I went into Ann Whitman's office to wait for the President to bring him over to the broadcast room. He had General Collins in with him at the time, but after Collins left, the barber came in to cut his hair. The President asked me in and expressed considerable interest in the reactions received over the ticker from the Hill. I told him that for the most part the comments were good and he expressed gratification. . . .

Walking over with the President to the broadcast room, I asked him what he thought of Chou En-lai's statement. "Well," he said, "I don't know. You never can tell when the Communists are talking for propaganda purposes or when they mean it. I can remember when Truman sent me to NATO, the Soviets screamed all over the world that this was almost an act of war and they would so consider it. They even said that it would be an act of war the moment I stepped on French soil . . ."

Chou in effect warned the United States to take its forces out of the Formosa Strait and said the Chinese people were determined to liberate Formosa. "Taiwan is an inalienable part of Chinese territory. The liberation of Taiwan is a matter of Chinese sovereignty and internal affairs. No outside interference is allowed. . . . The government of the CPR absolutely cannot agree to a so-called cease-fire with the traitorous Chiang Kai-shek clique repudiated by the Chinese people."

Tuesday, January 25, 1955

In at 8:10. Leaders meeting at 8:30 . . .

Knowland, in reporting on the week's work before the Senate, said that the Senate Foreign Relations Committee was meeting today and that he was hopeful the committee would report the resolution out late this afternoon or this evening. . . . Saltonstall said that the questions he had received from Democrats on the Hill were: (1) will the resolution amount in effect to an advance declaration of war? and (2) that the title to Formosa was very much in doubt.

The President replied "You know, Senator, sometimes we are captains of history. Formosa is a part of a great island barrier we have erected in the Pacific against Communist advance. We are not going to let it be broken. If we accept the necessity for that, then I don't think we should worry about any cloudiness to any title. This is a military responsibility which we all must face. We just can't permit the Nationalists to sit in Formosa and wait until they are attacked, and we just can't try to fight another war with handcuffs on as we did in Korea. If we see the Chinese Communists building up in their forces for an invasion of Formosa, we are going to have to go in and break it up. Quemoy, for example, is only important because it guards the harbor and in Nationalist hands can be used to break up any offensive they may launch from that harbor at Formosa. It seems to me that it is foolish to try to strain to the limit my constitutional powers. Actually, no one has defined the President's constitutional powers in all the 175 years we have existed as a nation. What I am trying to do by the message and what you are trying to do through the resolution is to serve notice on the Communists that they're not going to be able to get away with it."

Knowland said that he was sure that when the chips were down, the President would have overwhelming Senate support for the resolution. He said that, of course, there would be some arguments against it, that he expected Langer would probably vote against it, but he didn't know who else. Bridges said Langer would vote against it and that Morse and Kefauver would make long speeches against it but would probably vote for it.[1] At that the President interrupted to say to Bridges and Knowland, "You sure got some strange characters up there on our side in the Senate. I can pick my boys here in the White House, but you fellows have to take what comes along."

Nixon said that the public reaction to the President's message was very good indeed, and Halleck pointed out that it was in tremendous contrast to Truman's action where many people in the United States thought that this country went to war in Korea through executive order only.

The President replied that of course the administration had talked this matter over with the leaders on both sides through bipartisan meetings and that he was proud that the reaction on the Hill seemed to be to act like a team in the interests of the nation instead of engaging in cheap political maneuvers. "You know, my boys, there is a hell of a lot of difference between a commander-in-chief having the authority to move the armed forces of our nation here and there throughout the world. But when you have to take action that may lead to war that has a risk attached to it, then I believe the President must go to the Congress and tell the people through them what it is all about. That is just what I have done."

The President then brought up the question of school construction and said that he was quite sure that most of the members in the room had been pestered to death by Mrs. Agnes Meyer.[2] "That woman wants to take $500 million to be applied as matching funds almost indefinitely each year to whatever state wants to build schoolrooms. If she had her way, what would happen would be that no state would build a school until they had matching funds from the federal government. I think this is terrible . . ."

The President concluded the meeting by asking the leaders if they had read the recent statement by Chou En-lai. He said, "That fellow is deliberately trying to provoke a war." (Later that afternoon the House, by a vote of 409 to 3, with Representatives Barden [Dem., N.C.] and Siler [Rep., Ky.] and Sheehan [Rep., Ill.] voting against it, approved the Formosa Resolution. The President authorized me to say he was highly pleased at the almost unanimous vote in the House of Representatives and he thought the vote represented a remarkable spirit of unity in the House in the welfare of the nation.)

At 12:00 I went with the President to the Natural History Building in the Smithsonian Institute where he received a bronze statue from the German ambassador as a token of gratitude from the German people to the people of the United States. The ceremony concluded with the playing of the German and American national anthems. I asked the President if he ever thought twelve years ago that he would hear both those anthems played together in a ceremony. He . . . said, no, that he did not. He then told me that after Germany was defeated, one of the most amazing things he saw in Germany was the way in which the people there seemed to be greatly relieved to be free of the Nazis and Hitler. "Maybe it was because my name was Eisenhower and they liked the German sound of it but they used to cheer me everywhere I went."

• • • •

Wednesday, January 26, 1955

In at 8:15.

Comparatively quiet day. I had to release the story on Tom Stephens's resignation as appointment secretary with Shanley going into his place, Morgan going into Shanley's place, and Fred Seaton taking Morgan's place.

Tom, of course, is going to New York to establish a law office and then in the fall start on the political business, building up the Eisenhower forces throughout the country. However, it was necessary to get him out of the White House and established as a lawyer right away, and that was the reason for his leaving now. . . .

• • • •

Thursday, January 27, 1955

. . . That afternoon Jim Rowley of the Secret Service and then later Goodpaster, through Central Intelligence, told me that the FBI had received a telephone call from an unidentified person to their New York office to the effect that he, the caller, was a foreign agent and had planted atomic bombs in Grand Central and Pennsylvania Station in New York City and unidentified places in Philadelphia, Baltimore and Washington. . . .

The military—particularly the Air Force—was taking no chances, since the caller had said the bombs would be detonated at midnight, and were manning the radar stations throughout the world and keeping strategic Air Force people fairly close to their home bases. The President listened to Goodpaster's report, then . . . told him that while he didn't believe it either, it was vital that we check this out all along the line. He laughed and said, "There's one thing I'm not going to do. You're not going to make me sleep in the bomb shelter tonight." . . .

• • • •

Friday, January 28, 1955

In at 8:15. Filled in the President on the bomb scare story and he . . . said, "Looks like you didn't get much sleep. I'll tell you though—I think you and I need a rest. I'm thinking of going down to Augusta over the weekend and will let you know shortly whether that will be possible. You come along with me and try to get away from this stuff for two days." . . .

In my talks during the last two or three days with the President, I am sure he has undergone a great strain in this Formosa crisis. He fully realizes that this could lead to war but is equally determined to do everything in his power not to have war come. His feelings on this matter showed up when Governor Lausche came in at 11:30 and I went in with him. When he told the President that the people of the country, particularly the people of the State of Ohio, supported him, the President was visibly affected and thanked Lausche . . .

During Lausche's visit the President . . . said to him that he had been reading some stories in the papers to the effect that Lausche might be the Democratic candidate for President. Lausche said that he had heard those rumors too but as far as he was concerned, the President was the best qualified man in America to lead this country through the present difficult situation. The President then said, "You know, they tried to get me to run as early as 1946. Twice in that year in this very room Truman personally asked me to run on the Democratic ticket for President with himself as the candidate for Vice President. I told him no both times and as a matter of fact, I never told anyone about our conversations until he (Truman) used it himself.[1] I frankly don't know yet about 1956 but the pressure is going to be very great. You're a younger man than I am and I find that as you get older, your reflexes slow down." Then he . . . asked Lausche how his golf was. Lausche said he plays a little in Ohio even during cold weather and the President slapped him on the back and said, "I'll tell you what we'll do, Governor. When I go down to Augusta in April would you come down and play golf with me a few days if I asked you?" Lausche said he would be delighted. The President laughed and said, "Let's do it. We'll confound all the political experts. They'll think we're trying to make up a combination ticket. OK?" Lausche agreed and left the President's office.

Just before the Cabinet meeting started, I talked with Herbert Hoover, Jr. He had called me last night to tell me that the Egyptian government had sentenced to death two of the Jews they had captured as spies and the others to hard labor for a long period of time. He was afraid that some of the American Jewish outfits would try to put pressure on us to interfere in this situation. He told me that the Secretary of State had sent a cable to the Egyptian prime minister, asking if possible they commute the sentence to life imprisonment. That is as far as we can go and that is as far as we are going to go.

Hoover in the morning and Dulles later in the day told me about another one that is really filled with dynamite.

Hammarskjold told Cabot Lodge yesterday—for the first time—that when he was in China, Chou had told him that he would release the American airmen to the families if the families came over to China. Why Hammarskjold, who has seen Cabot Lodge often and the Secretary of State here in Washington last week, did not mention this before is one we cannot figure out. It is a real rough one, particularly in view of the fact that our State Department has said that they would not let American families go there. It is probably only a question of time before the Chinese publicly announce this and then, of course, it will be impossible to stop any families from going. . . .

Mrs. Hobby came in after the cabinet meeting to tell me she was concerned about the way the school construction program was going. She said that Humphrey and Hughes were opposing putting any money into the plan and that she felt that she had to go directly to the President. I agreed with that and she made an appointment to see him this afternoon. This thing is filled with dynamite and we have to have a good plan or else the Hill Bill, calling for flat grants-in-aid up to $250 million a year, is going to pass, even over the President's veto. . . .

After the Formosa Resolution passed the Senate overwhelmingly, the President signed it on January 29. It gave him extraordinary authority "to employ the armed forces of the United States as he deems necessary for the specific purpose of securing and protecting Formosa and the Pescadores against armed attack, this authority to include the security and protection of such related positions and territories of that area now in friendly hands and the taking of such other measures as he judges to be required or appropriate in assuring the defense of Formosa and the Pescadores." The fall of Yikiangshan (I-Chang Island) made evacuation of the Tachen group a military necessity, but the Nationalists retained the two other island groups involved in the controversy, the Matsus and Quemoys. At the time or thereafter the United States government never made clear whether it would support Chiang Kai-shek in defending these islands, the theory being that it was good policy to keep the Chinese Communist regime guessing. In 1958, when the Communists again bombarded the Quemoys, they seemed to be trying primarily to embarrass the United States. At one point they were firing only on even-numbered dates; supplies could thus reach the garrison on alternative days. When Secretary Dulles visited Formosa in October 1958, shelling resumed during his stay, stopped after he left. No military decision was reached. In autumn 1960 the issue flared again during the presidential election in the United States, and in a television debate on October 7, Senator John F. Kennedy maintained that the United States had no obligation to defend the Quemoys and Matsus unless an attack on them appeared a preliminary to attack on Formosa and the Pescadores. His opponent, Vice President Nixon, said the United States should not abandon even one "island of freedom."

President and Mrs. Eisenhower left Washington for Augusta on Saturday morning, January 29, and arrived at Augusta National Golf Club at 11:40.

Sunday, January 30, 1955[1]

Lt. Billington called me at 12:30 last night at Camp Gordon, where I was attending a reception and dance, to tell me that his outfit had just started to receive two long coded messages for the President. . . .

I did not bother the President with these two messages so early in the morning but instead brought them out to him at about ten o'clock. He read them through very carefully and then said that as far as he was concerned, he had no intention of taking U.S. forces out of the area and letting the Chinese Reds have a free hand to walk in any time they wanted to. The President also told me that he would leave Augusta National at 4:30 and be airborne by 5:00, returning to Washington by 7:00 P.M. . . .

Actually, we stepped up our time of departure and flew back in a hurry—1 hour and 35 minutes. . . .

• • • •

Monday, January 31, 1955[1]

In at 7:50 . . .

Went in to see the President at 8:30 and he asked me if Goodpaster had filled me in on the meeting. . . . The President said what he had been worried about yesterday was that Chiang Kai-shek had made an official request for atomic bombs and weapons and that he was greatly relieved to learn, when he got to the White House, that this was not the case. . . .

In talking with the President, I asked him how he had enjoyed his Augusta weekend and he said he thought it did him a considerable amount of good. . . . Then the President pulled what I had been expecting ever since last week. He pointed out that Tom Stephens was leaving in the middle of February and asked me if I thought that, in addition to my regular job of press secretary, I could handle for him the details of telephone messages, etc., when he was on the road. I told him that I didn't see any reason why I couldn't and he . . . said, "I have a hunch that you were kind of expecting this anyway, weren't you?" I . . . said, "Yes." He then said, "Let's try it out. I'm used to working with you and you're used to my various moods and they don't seem to bother you. But if it gets too tough and you find that you are getting all jammed up, let me know." . . .

February 1955

General Matthew B. Ridgway had been a corps commander under Eisenhower during the fighting in France and Germany in 1944–1945, and during the Korean War had taken over the Eighth Army at a time of crisis, in December 1950, when the Chinese were forcing UN troops back down the peninsula and imperiled Seoul for a second time. At that precise moment, late in December when Ridgway arrived, the UN lines were in disarray, the forces spread out along a river line to the north of Seoul and in grave danger of being pinned against the river when the Reds attacked, which was almost certain to happen on New Year's Day. The doughty Ridgway went up to inspect the lines, found American troops surly, morale very poor, not usual for the U.S. Army. With dispatch he ordered a retreat and evacuation of the South Korean capital. Regrouping his lines to the south he then halted the Chinese and turned the war around by raking their lines with massive artillery fire, after which he moved the Chinese back up above the thirty-eighth parallel and stabilized the war. Ridgway's great achievement, in which he saved the Korean War, brought appointment as commander of NATO and then a term as U.S. Army chief of staff. In this latter role he clashed with his old superior Eisenhower, now President of the United States, over the proposed reduction of the Army, and let it be known not merely in administration circles but in testimony before Congress that he thought the administration's proposed "new look" for its military forces, known popularly as "more bang for the buck," was a crude reliance on nuclear weapons that would expose the country to a series of Koreas and hence was gravely against the national interest.

Tuesday, February 1, 1955

In at 8:15. Legislative leaders meeting at 8:30 . . .

Bridges started off a discussion when he asked the President how he would recommend the Senators handle the Ridgway testimony of yesterday when Ridgway said that the cuts in Army personnel would jeopardize to a degree the security of the United States.

The President, in reply, launched into a long and exceedingly emphatic discussion of this question which ran as follows:

"Gentlemen, Ridgway is Chief of Staff of the Army. When he is called up on the Hill and asked for personal convictions, he has got to give them. Each service has as its head and has traditionally had as its head, people who think that their service is the only service that can ultimately save the United States in time of war. They all want additional manpower and they always will. But we must realize that as commander-in-chief, I have to make the final decisions. I have to look at this whole question of the military establishment as one which must be kept in balance. I have to consider—which the heads of the services do not—the very delicate balance between the national debt, taxes, and expenditures. I have to decide what is necessary for adequate security. If I had all the money I wanted right now, I wouldn't use that money to keep 300,000 men in the Army. I would use it for other purposes. Why, even from the question of the defense of the United States I would much rather put that money into new highways and roads so that we could get around this country in a hurry in case of attack.

"You see, actually, the only thing we fear is an atomic attack delivered by air on our cities. Suppose that attack were to occur tomorrow on fifteen of our cities. God damn it. It would be perfect rot to talk about shipping troops abroad when fifteen of our cities were in ruins. You would have disorder and almost complete chaos in the cities and in the roads around them. You would have to restore order and who is going to restore it? Do you think the police and fire departments of those cities could restore order? Nuts! That order is going to have to be restored by disciplined armed forces. It's going to have to be restored by our military forces and by our Reserve. That's what our military is going to be doing in the first days of an all-out atomic attack. They are going to have to restore order and get our production going again. Anyone who thinks we are going to immediately ship out of this country division after division is just talking through his hat. It couldn't be done and if I tried to do it, you would want to impeach me. That's the trouble with Ridgway. He's talking theory—I'm trying to talk sound sense. He did the same thing at SHAPE. I was there before Ridgway went over and he tried to ruin it with the same sort of talk. We have to have a sound base here at home. We have got to restore order and our productivity before we do anything else. That's why in our military thinking today we have to put emphasis on two or three things first. One, we have to maintain a strong striking retaliatory Air Force and secondly, we have to build up our warning system so that we can receive as much advance notice as possible of any attack.

"What do you people think would happen if this city were hit today by an H-bomb? Do you think you would vote or ask me to send the troops at Fort Meade overseas—or would you be knocking on my door to get me to bring them in to try to pick up the pieces here in Washington? We have to do that. All our military plans are based really on two main things—one, to destroy the enemy's production and two, protect your own. To do that we need not just more men. We need more equipment, an expanded Air Force and an expanded warning system."

As the President was talking, you could hear a pin drop in the room. He pounded the table quite a few times for emphasis, and everyone in the room, I am sure, realized both the seriousness of the situation and the President's arguments.

Saltonstall then asked the President for his judgment on the situation on Quemoy. He said that Ridgway had testified privately that Quemoy could not be held without American foot soldiers on that island and that it was his understanding that at the present time there were no American foot soldiers on Quemoy and that none were expected to be placed there. The President said that that was true, that with the exception of a few technical advisers and observers there were no Americans on Quemoy and then he added: "They have 60,000 Nationalist troops on Quemoy and if Chiang can't protect that island with those troops, plus, if necessary, assistance from American air and naval power, then I don't think Quemoy would be worth holding. This question of sending American troops everywhere is one which I have to face and on which I have to make the final decision. I am not going to permit this country to send troops all over the world—to get all straddled out, to spread ourselves thin and consequently not be able to defend any area."

Knowland said that he thought Ridgway had gone beyond any reasonable basis in his testimony and then added: "The thing that amazed me was that Ridgway said that he hadn't any advance knowledge of the plans to reduce the Army until he had read it in the papers. It is my understanding that that wasn't true, and I told him that. I asked if General Bolté, the Vice Chief, was not at most of the meetings and if he had not reported these decisions to Ridgway. To my surprise, Ridgway said that was so, 'but Bolté can't speak for me.' In my opinion that's one hell of a way to run the Army—if the Vice Chief can't speak for the Chief when the Chief is out of Washington. It's inexcusable that Ridgway gave the impression that he was ignored."

The President replied that he agreed 100 percent with Knowland, that he has had Ridgway in several times before the National Security Council and the Joint Chiefs of Staff, that he had told the Chiefs that they were his military advisers and that he thought they should stick around Washington on the job and not go running off to inspect a fort. . . .

• • • •

Wednesday, February 2, 1955

In at 8:00. Press conference day. . . .

Governor Pyle and Nelson Rockefeller attended the presidential briefing for the first time at my request. At the briefing the President set the line immediately by saying that he was not going to be any more specific than he had been about the offshore islands. He said he had been thinking considerably about the question of hot pursuit and that while our airmen were under orders to engage in just that if they were attacked, he did not see at this time where any good could come from a specific announcement to that effect by him. All agreed to this decision. . . .

At the press conference the New York *Post* reporters, Spivack and Shannon, were the only ones who asked questions about my "censorship" of the television films of the conferences. This was obviously a straight ADA political move, and the President recognized it for just that. He referred Spivack's question to me and in a later question by Shannon dealing with the same subject, he dismissed it by saying we had received no objection from the television and radio companies on the way we had handled it. Later Spivack came in to see me and I told him that it was quite obvious that he was under orders, that if he wanted an answer, I would give it to him. I told him that the question of censorship was entirely phony since the full transcript was available to all media and all media were perfectly free to report what sections were given for direct quotes and what sections were not. With the *Post* objecting so strenuously to the filming of the press conferences, it was quite obvious to me that we are doing right and are hitting the opposition where it hurts the most. I am sure that the *Post* campaign has been deliberately inspired by the ADA and the left-wing boys. They realize the tremendous political capabilities of filming the conferences,

Released about half of the conference for direct quotes at 2:30 following a meeting in my office with Jack Martin, Gerry Morgan, Goodpaster, Pyle, and Snyder. When I went in to get the President's approval of it, I told him of the procedure I had followed. He said that he did not want to see the sections, that he would take my judgment for it. He seemed a little amused, as I was, about the *Post* questions and remarked, "If they don't like it, it must be good. Let's keep it up."

Left the White House at 3:30 to go to New York to appear on "Who Said That?" show in the evening. Had dinner with Mother and Dad before going on the air.

• • • •

Thursday, February 3, 1955

In New York in the morning. Back at the White House at 3:30.

Visited in New York in the morning with Frank Stanton of CBS, General Sarnoff of NBC, John Daly and Bob Kintner of ABC.[1] Dropped in to see them to find out how they thought the televising of the press conferences was going. Their reactions were all very favorable . . .

Returned to the White House at 3:30 and found out to my chagrin that Knowland had informed the President about an important statement made earlier that afternoon—carried on the ticker at 1:40—that Chou En-lai declined to come to the United Nations to engage in any cease-fire talks unless Nationalist China were thrown out of the UN and Red China put in their place. . . .

I took a copy of the Chou En-lai statement over to the President and he was in his studio painting a portrait of Winston Churchill. He was working from a photograph of a painting which showed Churchill seated in a chair with a cigar in his right hand. The Prime Minister was dressed in striped trousers and a Prince Albert jacket.

The President had a very good start on it but said he was having trouble doing the pin stripes in the trousers. . . .

I told the President that I had talked to Herbert Hoover and gave him the gist of the statement that Hoover would put out. He agreed with that and then said, "You know, they [the Chinese Communists] are certainly doing everything they can to try our patience. It's awfully difficult to remain calm under these situations. Sometimes I think that it would be best all around to go after them right now without letting them pick their time and the place of their own choosing. I have a feeling that the Chinese Communists are acting on their own on this and that it is considerably disturbing to the Russians. This Chou refusal must come as a great surprise to our British friends. You know, they were trying to get us in a position where they would solve the whole situation and stop the hostilities. Of course, they're not too interested in Formosa, but Hong Kong—that's another story. They'd do almost anything to retain that." . . .

• • • •

Friday, February 4, 1955

In at 8:15. Fairly routine but busy day. . . .

• • • •

Saturday, February 5, 1955

Came in late to dictate notes which were running about a week behind.

The two main news items today were that the French defeated Mendès-France and two Sabre jets shot down two MIGs off the Korean coast.

• • • •

Monday, February 7, 1955

Stayed home because of stomach raising hell.

• • • •

Tuesday, February 8, 1955

In at 8:15. . . .

The big story from Russia broke early this morning. I received a call at 7:30 at my house from Bob Clark of INS reporting that Malenkov had been replaced as Russian premier and issued a statement in typical Russian fashion claiming that he lacked experience to handle the agricultural program of his country. I called Foster Dulles as soon as I got to the office. He was at home, and the shocking thing was that no one in the State Department had called him despite the fact that the story had been out for several hours. (Dulles later raised all sort of hell in his department, and I don't believe such a thing will happen again.)

Dulles told me that while he had not anticipated these exact changes (it was later announced that Bulganin would succeed Malenkov) we had got wind of the fact that some big changes were coming up in Russia about a week ago. . . .

Throughout the day the President was informed of these reports by Goodpaster but neither the White House nor the State Department had any official comment. Actually, the President told me when he was in his office with Goodpaster that he believed the following:

1. That the Russian hierarchy had been having considerable trouble prior to Stalin's death. As Stalin was becoming weaker in health, the infighting and double-dealing for power had started. Actually, when Malenkov was named as his successor, it was in effect a compromise and the fighting still continued. This was, of course, evident when Beria was done away with and is more evident now with Malenkov in this post. The President also told me that this was just another reason why he had been resisting the British plea for a four-power conference. "It took an awful long time to get the British to realize that with the trouble going on inside of Russia, it would not be to the advantage of the free world for Churchill and myself and whoever the Frenchman would be to sit down publicly with any given leader of Russia. If we did that, it would serve notice, not only throughout the world but also within Russia, that we were recognizing Malenkov or Bulganin or whoever else it might be as the leader. That would give him a great advantage within Russia and would tend to minimize the struggles for power that are going on within Russia. We certainly don't want to do that and that's why I have

never wanted to meet with the Russian leader—at least for the time being."

2. I asked the President if he thought that Bulganin's appointment would mean that Russia was moving toward war. He said that he did not think so; that as a matter of fact, if the Army had more influence in Russia, it would probably be a conservative influence. "You know, if you're in the military and you know about these terrible destructive weapons, it tends to make you more pacifistic than you normally have been. In most countries the influence of the military is more conservative, and so while I do not know for sure, I would not be surprised if the army influence would be just that within the Soviet Union. They're not ready for war and they know it. They also know if they go to war, they're going to end up losing everything they have. That also tends to make people conservative."

Later in the day Molotov made a speech in Moscow when he really rattled the sword, saying that Russia was way ahead of the United States in the production of the H-bomb and also said if Russia were attacked, it would destroy Western civilization. I called Lewis Strauss on the H-bomb charge and he told me that we have no evidence at all that the Russians are as far advanced as we are on the H-bomb, although of course we know they have it and have exploded thermonuclear weapons on testing grounds within their country. Strauss said that he was sure this was merely a propaganda speech by the Russians. I told him to send me a memo to this effect so I could show it to the President, and he did the next morning. . . .

• • • •

Wednesday, February 9, 1955

. . . the press conference went off very well, I thought. A lot of intimate color was supplied when the President discussed his friendship with Marshal Zhukov who had just been named Defense Minister in Russia ten minutes before the press conference started.

The President went out to play golf in the afternoon and gave me authority to issue for television whatever parts I thought were right. We released about two thirds of the conference after the usual luncheon conference with Pyle, Martin, Snyder, Shanley, Goodpaster, and myself.

• • • •

Thursday, February 10, 1955

In at 8:15. Scheduled to leave for Thomasville at 12:45. . . .

• • • •

Friday, February 11, 1955

In Thomasville.

Cold and rainy when I went to see the President at Humphrey's plantation at eight o'clock. He slept late and did not get over to the dining lodge until shortly before nine o'clock. . . .

At the press conference on Wednesday, the President had been reminiscing about the invitation he had extended on behalf of our government to Marshal Zhukov in 1945. As he recalled it at the time, Zhukov had wanted to come to America and on one occasion the President's plane and the President's son had been assigned to Zhukov to come to America. The President laughingly remarked that at that time Zhukov had said, "With your plane and with your son I surely am going to be safe."

At the press conference Wednesday, Joe Harsch of the *Christian Science Monitor* had followed up this reminiscence with a question which read: "Mr. President, is that invitation to General Zhukov still open?" The President had replied that this was the first time it had been mentioned to him since he has been in his present position and added: "You can well imagine that I wouldn't stand here and suddenly issue an invitation without consulting with my advisers. So I would say this would be a remarkable thing in the present state of affairs. But I certainly wouldn't hesitate to talk it over with my people if we found it desirable."

Goodpaster told me Thursday morning Harsch had received a call from the third secretary of the Russian Embassy. The third secretary said he would very much like to talk to Harsch and they made a luncheon engagement at the Metropolitan Club. During the luncheon the third secretary tried to sound out Harsch on whether his question was one which was planted by the government or whether he had just thought it up himself. The third secretary also told Harsch that he was considerably interested in the wording of the President's answer to the question and that if Harsch thought the United States government was interested in this, it would naturally follow that the U.S. government might like to know in advance what the attitude of the Soviet government was.

This sounding out of Harsch by the third secretary was a very interesting development and, of course, Harsch confidentially reported it to the CIA. Goodpaster was sure that the President would want to hear of this and when I told him, he said, "Well, I'll be doggoned. Maybe Zhukov wants to come." The President then said:

"You know, this fellow Zhukov is a very independent citizen. I can remember several talks I had with him while we were both in Germany. On one occasion Vishinsky was with him and Vishinsky put on the darnedest performance I have ever seen anyone put on.[1] He sat directly behind Zhukov with his chin actually on Zhukov's shoulder. Zhukov does not speak English and while the interpreter was translating into Russian whatever I was saying, Vishinsky with his chin on Zhukov's shoulder was whispering suggested answers to Zhukov. It really was something.

"Another time when I saw him, however, he drew me aside to a corner of the room and announced through an interpreter that he wanted to talk to me alone and he did not want any political advisers around. Vishinsky was again in the room but stayed back after Zhukov gave those orders. That was the time we talked about Russian vs. American military tactics. At that time Zhukov told me the stories which I've told you several times about how the Russian Army cleared mine fields by marching a regiment through them and about how Zhukov had no concern about the German treatment of Russian prisoners since those Russian prisoners were captured by the Germans and were of no more use to him.

"Zhukov's a funny little fellow and very sensitive of his height. I remember on another occasion he made quite a point of telling me that he was taller than his wife and his two daughters. Several months later just before I left Germany, I made it a point to drop in on a reception he was having. As I came into the room Zhukov left the receiving line, grabbed his wife by the hand, and came rushing over. He turned his wife around and backed up against her and said, 'See, I'm taller than she is.' He had remembered that conversation for two months and was going to prove it to me firsthand."

As the President reminisced about Zhukov, he kept repeating the fact that he was considerably interested in the Harsch story. George Humphrey was present at the table at the time, and he also expressed considerable interest. Whether anything will come of it we do not know, but it certainly is an interesting move by the Soviets, although none of us believe that the Russians would let Zhukov out of Russia at this time.

It was a cold, wet, rainy day but nevertheless the President decided to go shooting this morning. He and George Humphrey and Clifford Roberts left at 9:15. Actually, they stayed out only an hour and a half and got no birds, although the President did pick up the start of a cold. It's a wonder he didn't get pneumonia. This raises in my mind the old question of how dangerous it is to travel without a doctor, and I am going to raise this question again with the staff when I get back to Washington. I believe it is criminal to have the President go traveling around the country without a doctor. Some day something serious will happen unless we change this tendency of the President to think that he does not need a doctor along.

That afternoon Andy Goodpaster called back to report that he expected the evacuation of the Tachens to be completed by ten or eleven o'clock, our time, that evening. . . .

Had dinner with the press boys at the Thomasville Country Club that evening.

• • • •

Saturday, February 12, 1955

Out to George Humphrey's by eight o'clock to find that the President had a cold and would not have breakfast until at least nine. When he did come to breakfast, it was obvious that he really picked up a beaut. His throat was very husky and he decided not to go shooting today but to stay in and loaf. . . . George C.C. Hayes, the Negro attorney, who had defended Mrs. Moss against McCarthy and who had handled part of the segregation fight in the Supreme Court, was appointed to the Public Utilities Commission.[1] The President was very pleased to be able to make this appointment and said, "If they construe this as another slap at McCarthy, so much the better."

Checked with the White House during the morning and everything was quiet. The rest of the day was very quiet also.

• • • •

Sunday, February 13, 1955

At Thomasville. . . .

Left George Humphrey's plantation at 1:30 and stopped to pick up Mr. and Mrs. Jock Whitney at Greenwood.[1] Took off from Spence Airfield about 3:00 and arrived in Washington at 5:45.

The President is still suffering from a cold.

• • • •

Monday, February 14, 1955

In at 8:15.

Sat in on the meeting with Len Hall, Brownell, Summerfield, Humphreys, Robbins, Adams, Pyle, and Stephens on a discussion of the time and place of the '56 convention.[1]

Hall reported that San Francisco had now come in with a bid and would pay as much as Philadelphia and Chicago, i.e., $250,000. . . .

The President then asked how this would affect television coverage. (I had told him that I would like to have him bring this up.) Humphreys said that he did not think it would be bad at all and as a matter of fact, that with the time differential he had been thinking of holding only one meeting a day at the convention, running it from two o'clock in the afternoon through six or seven in the evening. That would be 5:00 P.M. to 9:00 or 10:00 P.M. in the east and one hour earlier in Chicago and still another hour earlier in Denver. But it would be good television viewing time and would reach more people than a morning session or late session.

Throughout the meeting, the President gave absolutely no indication at all of his own personal plans, and no one asked him. It was a sort of sparring match by everyone concerned to deliberately not ask him anything. I think he realized the situation and got quite a kick out of it. . . .

The President's cold is still hanging on, and in the afternoon he called me into the office to tell me that he thought he would have to postpone the press conference . . .

I spent from 3:20 until a little after 6:00 in the dentist's chair.

• • • •

Tuesday, February 15, 1955

Had a long talk during the morning with Adams and Persons on the question of Cabinet members expressing their own opinions. We all agreed that despite the feeling by the President that Cabinet members had a right to express their own opinion, they should be stopped from so doing in the future. Actually, a Cabinet member, even though he is expressing his own opinion, is looked upon as talking for the administration. Recent examples of this have been Mitchell's plugging for a revocation of the right-to-work laws in some of our states and Benson's continual talking about the Ladejinsky case. We agreed that we would have a talk with the President and see if we could not get him to give orders to the Cabinet members to discuss only matters in public which have been agreed on and which represent administration policy. . . .

• • • •

Wednesday, February 16, 1955

In at 8:15. Leaders meeting at 8:30. . . .

The President said that he had asked Lucius Clay to join the meeting this morning to go over with the leaders the highway program which would be going to Congress next week. He said that this was in the form of a preview and would appreciate it if the leaders would not discuss it since Jack Martin had set up a bipartisan meeting with the chairmen and ranking members of the appropriate committees for Monday. All agreed to this.

Clay presented a brief summary of the program, in which he said that if all the highways throughout the country were brought up to standard, it would cost $101 billion within the next ten years. Presently the federal government is spending $900 million a year for state aid for highways, which is roughly equivalent to the gasoline tax collected by the federal government. He pointed out in 1944 the Congress had set up an interstate system. This system of main roads connecting main cities in the United States amounts to 40,000 miles. Funds to build this system had been appropriated on a 60–40 basis by the federal and state governments.

Clay said the cost of modernizing and bringing the interstate system up-to-date would amount to about $23 billion and that $4 billion more would be needed to build feeder roads into that system for a total expenditure of $27 billion over ten years. He said that at the present time there were 53 million motor vehicles in the United States and that it was anticipated that by 1965 there would be 80 million motor vehicles. He said that the federal government would assume this cost over a ten-year period and that he expected the states would put in an additional $2 billion. Furthermore, we will continue the federal aid to the states for primary and secondary roads, which has been amounting to about $622 million a year. He said that the soundest way to finance the federal monies for the highway program would be the issuance of $25 billion worth of highway bonds to be payable in thirty years. This would be paid off through earmarking the gas and diesel oil taxes over the $622 million which is given to the states each year for primary and secondary roads. All monies over $622 million would be paid for amortization and interest of the bond issue.

The President asked Clay to tell him why his committee had rejected the theory of a toll road system, and Clay replied that between 4,000 and 10,000 miles of the system could be used as toll roads but for the remainder he did not think it was feasible. We have taken the position that a toll road is actually a luxury transportation and that it is all right in sections of the country where the public have alternate roads to travel if they do not desire to pay the toll. That is all right in the East and Far West but there are many sections in the Midwest and West where this interstate highway system will be the only road. In that instance we do not think it should be tolled.

Bridges then said that he had received some arguments on the Hill that some states had received what had amounted to windfalls because they would get rebate from the federal government for those sections of the highways which they had built with their own funds. Clay replied that under the proposal certain states which have built some of the system would get a certain amount of rebate but that the monies that they got back could not be used for any purpose other than for road construction within the state. He said that if they had not agreed to do this, many states which had gone ahead and built such roads in the system would have waited until they received federal money, with the result that we would be just that much further behind at the present time.

Bridges replied that he was happy to know that the states must use the monies they get from the federal government in this matter on roads. The President then said that the physical layout of the United States was falling behind its needs. "There is no question in our minds, gentlemen, that unless we develop the road structure of our country, unless we develop new roads to handle increased traffic, we will have a terrible condition in this country. With our roads inadequate to handle an expanding industry, the result will be inflation and a disrupted economy. We must build new roads or else we will have an obsolete system. Let me remind you that almost every airfield built ten years ago in this country is now becoming obsolete and cannot handle the increased burden of traffic. We cannot let that happen on our roads." . . .

Knowland then asked the President if there were anything he could tell the leaders regarding the change in the Soviet government or anything he had to report on the Formosa situation. The President said that as far as the Russian change in government was concerned, there was nothing particularly significant as yet except that in our opinion it did represent dissatisfaction within the Soviet Union on the agricultural program and the general policies of Malenkov. As far as Formosa was concerned, he said the Tachen evacuation had been completed rapidly without incident and that he had nothing to add on that.

The President said, "One thing I would like to discuss is the problem we must face to get better understanding in the free world as to what we are trying to do. Many of our friends and allies, particularly the British, believe that the offshore islands rightly belong to Red China and they cannot see why we want to have the Nationalists keep them. They argue that as a military problem, the defense of Formosa and the Pescadores would be greatly simplified if Nationalist China would give them these small offshore islands and we withdrew to the Pescadores and Formosa. Militarily speaking, that would be the easiest way to handle it and we have enough naval and air strength in that territory to knock out any invasion of the Pescadores and Formosa, which would have to come from the mainland over a hundred miles of open sea. But what the British and our allies do not understand are the aspirations and hopes of the people on Formosa. As a nation, the United States has invested very heavily in Chiang Kai-shek. Any change in the Nationalists' morale from very good to very bad would be very bad for us. What we must do is get Europe to understand several things. Instead of believing only that the offshore islands should belong to the mainland they must be taught to realize that a free Formosa is a constant threat and a constant deterrent to Communist Chinese aggression anywhere in the Pacific. If, for instance, the Chinese Reds want to start some trouble in Korea or Indochina they can do so only with the realization that Formosa is unconquerable and that the Nationalist troops on Formosa are always a threat to them. They can't ignore this and we must keep this situation alive. In addition, Chiang Kai-shek looks upon the fighting between the Nationalists and the Reds as a civil war. We had the same problem in our own War between the States and when Great Britain started to give some help to the South our government said in plain language to them—keep out of this or there will be trouble. So we must keep up the Nationalists' morale to maintain two things—one, a free Formosa which is the very keystone of our island defenses in the Pacific and secondly, the morale of the Chinese Nationalists."

Knowland interrupted to ask if the British didn't realize the danger of the position they were taking on the offshore islands. If they carried it out to its logical extent, can't they realize that the Chinese Reds can also make the same claim to Hong Kong that they are trying to make to the offshore islands. The President replied that the British are laboring under the belief that Red China does not want Hong Kong. Furthermore, he said the British population is frightened about another world war, particularly an atomic one. "This is the time for us to move slowly and patiently. We must not be too quick to say what we want to do. We must exercise great patience and great coolness. I am corresponding right now with friends abroad to see if I can get them to see our way of looking at this problem."

The President revealed to the leaders that he was sending Assistant Secretary of State Robertson to Formosa. He said that Robertson was admired by Chiang Kai-shek and that he was sending him over there so he could sort of hold Chiang Kai-shek's hand throughout this difficult time. He said that if there was any change in the situation, of course he would notify the leaders. He also added that our British friends are firmer on the European situation than they have been in a long time. At long last, they are opposing any meeting with the Soviets until the Paris Accords have been carried through and agree with us that any meeting would serve no purpose at this time other than to make ourselves ridiculous and to give the Communists a world forum for their propaganda.

Then the President smiled wryly and said almost to himself, "But those damned little offshore islands. Sometimes I wish they'd sink." . . .

• • • •

Thursday, February 17, 1955

In at 8:15.

Today the President went to the Republican National Committee meeting and made a good speech following the notes that we had worked out the day before. Most of the National Committee finance members are convinced that the President will run again and are making their plans accordingly. The National Committee voted overwhelmingly for a San Francisco convention site and for short sessions from 2:00 to 7:00 in the afternoon. . . .

• • • •

Friday, February 18, 1955

Comparatively quiet day with not much doing.

• • • •

Saturday, February 19, 1955

Took the day off and played golf in the morning with Bob Denton.

• • • •

Monday, February 21, 1955

In at 8:15.

Most of the day was devoted to a discussion of the Highway Message, which we will send up to Congress tomorrow. In the morning Clay, Adams, Martin, and myself met in Adams' office, and it was agreed to have the President attend the meeting we were having in the afternoon at 2:30 in the Cabinet room with the Democratic and Republican members of the Public Works Committee and the Subcommittee on Public Roads of both the Senate and the House. . . .

The President opened the meeting by saying that he had always had a great interest in the road program and that he became aroused at the end of World War II when he saw the fine Autobahns and returned to this country to see the shocking condition of our roads. He said: "Gentlemen, highways have an influence on everything we do in our country. We will soon have more than 60 million vehicles traveling our roads and we will have to build up our highways to meet the traffic. Highways are vitally essential for our national defense since they permit quick exits from thickly populated areas and permit mobile columns to move over them in case of any enemy attack. From any standpoint, a ten-year road program will help our nation and will fulfill our great needs. It will help the steel and auto spare parts industry and I urge you to consider very seriously the plan we will propose. I've asked General Clay to come here today to tell you about it but before he does, I want to tell you that we plan to have a ten-year road program which will not add to our national debt. . . . Here is something that touches every person in the United States. It is good for America and I am sure our approach to it must be above politics." . . .

About the only good that came out of the meeting that I saw was that the President was on public record of asking for bipartisan consultation on the program. The only other good was this doodle which the President did while the meeting was going on.

• • • •

Tuesday, February 22, 1955

In at 8:00 A.M.

Legislative leaders meeting at 8:15. . . .

Although Speaker Martin was absent because of the death of his brother, the meeting was held because of Democratic maneuvering over the weekend by Sam Rayburn, McCormack, and some of the other House members. They moved Saturday to grant a $20 tax exemption starting in '56 for each taxpayer and $20 additional for each dependent. This will result in an annual loss of income of $2.3 billion. The President, Humphrey, and the leaders were all armed to give the Democrats a good political fight on this one if that's what they wanted. . . .

The President . . . said, ". . . I believe we should denounce the Democrats every step of the way. They are being completely political

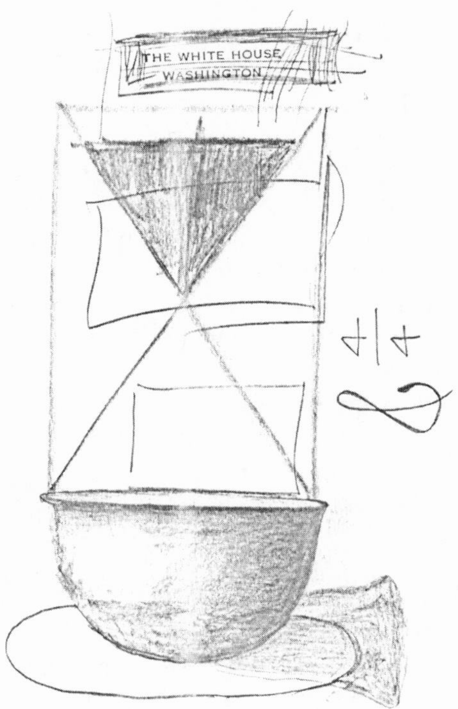

in this matter and if they are successful in their attempt, it will bring back inflation and will cause the cost of living to skyrocket up again. I'm going to have a press conference tomorrow and I am going to let them have it. This is fiscal irresponsibility at its worst and I am going to say just that. As to vetoing it, while I will not say so tomorrow, I would veto the bill if it comes down to me tied up with the excise and corporate taxes.". . .

The President then said, "You know, I think that I'll say publicly—although maybe not tomorrow—that the Democrats are seeking to buy votes with the public's money." . . .

Arends, in the absence of Martin, said that the House would be taking up shortly the Military Benefits Bill and the Pay Increases Bill in the Post Office and Civil Service. The President said that as far as the military was concerned, he believed everyone in the military was interested primarily in what they called "fringe benefits." "A man in the service wants his family to be taken care of. He wants to be assured of insurance, of survivors' benefits, of medical care and proper housing. If you give them that, you are taking a great step in helping them."

At the end of the meeting the conversation again got back to Rayburn's tactics and the President concluded with this thought. "You know, I think it's about time that I personally went after Rayburn. I know many of his constituents and have a lot of good friends in Texas. I think I should get those friends to go after him and ask him what the hell he is trying to do up here in Washington. I'll admit I can get after the Texas delegation better than I can Sam, but let's see what we can do. As one suggestion, let's see what we can do with him on this Natural Gas Report. Those are bills he wants very badly. I wouldn't mind if some of you fellows here would pass the word to him that he better think more than twice and stop his nonsense if he wants me to sign those natural gas bills." . . .

• • • •

Wednesday, February 23, 1955

In at 8:00 A.M. Press conference day. . . .

Knowland in a speech Monday night had said that the UN had been "tried and found wanting as an instrument of collective security." Hoover expressed the hope that the President would knock this down strongly and state his support of the United Nations. (Later in the briefing with the President, he [the President] said he was going to do just that if he got a question. "What's the matter with this fellow Knowland? Can't he ever keep quiet or doesn't he realize what he's saying? If I am asked a question, I am going to say that we do not give up our research laboratories here at home just because we have a few failures in research. Instead we would double our efforts to make them work. I just can't understand Knowland's popping off on this subject, and I am going to be quite forceful in my answer to the press.") . . .

In a telephone conversation with Lewis Strauss he told me that he had been to a subcommittee of the Armed Services Committee of the Senate yesterday and that Kefauver and Symington had tried to make quite a point of the fact that he had not gotten out his fallout report more promptly. He said that this was just nonsense and that the day after he got back from the first H-bomb blast in the Pacific, he had come with the President to the press conference in March of 1954 and publicly told the reporters all that we knew on the subject as of that date. He specifically discussed the fallout problem at this press conference and also made the statement that an H-bomb could "take out" an American city. . . .

A little hassle arose as a result of Sarah McClendon's question at the press conference about how we were distributing on the Hill copies of the President's messages to the Congress. Sarah, obviously reflecting Rayburn's feelings, at the press conference had told the President that there apparently was no coordination between Rayburn's office and the White House and that Rayburn had not seen copies of the messages until after they had been delivered to the floor. This, of course, was not true.

I told the President when we were coming back from the press conference that we had always sent up copies to McCormack's and Johnson's offices as well as to Arends and Knowland.[1] He told me to tell the newspapermen about this as soon as they finished up their press conference stories. I had a conference at 12 o'clock and told them that a check of our records had shown that on every one of the messages 250 copies had been sent to McCormack's office and Arends' office in the House and 100 copies to Knowland's office and Johnson's office in the Senate. I also gave them the time that the messages had left the White House, which averaged about 8:30. Later on in the day a rather embarrassed clerk, who was not identified, admitted that he had been receiving these copies in McCormack's office but he had not been told what to do with them and had merely left them on the table in McCormack's office and later on threw them in the wastepaper basket. Of course, this is a lot of nonsense but it just goes to show the bitterness and partisanship of Rayburn. He and McCormack are trying to do everything they can to play politics and to embarrass the President. . . .

• • • •

Thursday, February 24, 1955[1]

. . . In the afternoon went with Roy Howard to see the President. Roy is leaving in a few days for a trip around the world. . . .

Howard asked the President if there was anything he could do for him and for our country while he was traveling, and the President said that while he realized that Howard was going as a newspaperman and had to remain completely free to operate as a newspaperman he would think that Howard could be helpful in Formosa if in his friendly, informal conversations with the Generalissimo he would stress the following: "Someone—and it could be you—has got to get Chiang to see several things clearly. The first of these is that in holding Formosa and the Pescadores for the free world he must not permit his position to become a fixed one, one which is linked closely to those offshore islands. Secondly, he must realize that he is in a position of great opportunity and that he must keep up his Army and be ready to move if the Communists, as I expect they will sooner or later, make an attack either in Korea or in Indochina. Then Chiang is in a position to attack and to attack hard the center. That's the only way he's ever going to get back to the mainland and someone should tell him this."

The President discussed at great length with Howard the position of Quemoy and Matsu. In both instances he admitted that these islands were good for defensive purposes—that Quemoy controlled the harbor of Amoy and Matsu controlled the harbor of Foochow. But it would be extremely difficult since they were just off the mainland to defend them against an all-out Communist attack. Such an attack would endanger American fleet units which would have to be moved in close to the China mainland. The President said he was not saying that we would not defend Quemoy and Matsu, that he could think of many conditions where we would—but what he was impressing on Howard was that Chiang should not center his whole question of the morale of his people on those two islands. "If he does that and loses that eventually, he will be in exactly the same position as the French were when they tried to defend Dienbienphu, an impossible position, and then lost it. At the time we urged the French not to make a stand, that it could not possibly be defended—but they paid no attention."

Chiang must not make the same mistake. As to the position of opportunity which Chiang now holds, the President said that he hoped that Howard, in talking to him, would try to get it around so that this idea was Chiang's idea and not Howard's. He said that the Chinese Communists were getting arrogant and were being supplied with material of war by the Russians. We, in turn, are building up Chiang's forces, are building up their air force and are giving material to them. The President said that sooner or later he expected that the Chinese Communists would move either south or north and that that was the time when Chiang's great opportunity would come. "If he keeps up the morale of his troops, if he keeps up his army, he will always be a threat to the Chinese Communists. You know full well that he has 400,000 troops trained and equipped. Now, while Matsu and Quemoy are defensive positions, they certainly would not be used in an offensive by Chiang against the mainland. In an invasion of a mainland, you don't land on an island because if you do, you just have to get off of it and go forward. When I was in command during the war, we didn't land at Brest or Le Havre; we went around to the beaches of the mainland. That is what Chiang is going to have to do and that is the only way he is ever going to get back to the mainland."

The President also asked Howard if he was going to stop in India. Howard said he was not, that he did not particularly like Nehru and that he had no plans to do so. The President said that was all right but if he was writing stories from that area, to please not knock down the Indians too much. "After all, India is a vast continent of 350 million people. If they are ever added to the great populations that the Communists now control, the free world will be up against it, not only in the East but throughout the world. I don't trust Nehru. He thinks he is a kingmaker. But we have got to keep them at least on the neutral side if we can. So please, Roy, don't go slamming the Indians in any stories that you write." . . .

• • • •

Friday, February 25, 1955

In at 8:15.

The question of circulation of the President's messages on the Hill was still kicking around this morning, so I finally called Rayburn's office and talked to his administrative assistant. I told him that we had sent copies of the messages to McCormack's office and that I had assumed that the majority leader of the House would have enough sense to see that the Speaker's office received some copies. But notwithstanding that, I would be only too happy to see that a half-dozen copies were dropped in to the Speaker every time we made a delivery to McCormack's office. He thought that would be a good idea and as far as I'm concerned, that closed the case.

The President left for Gettysburg in the afternoon. Mrs. Eisenhower, Mrs. Doud, and Mrs. Moore had gone up on Thursday and the President will join them there today.[1]

The House voted on the Democratic $20 tax cut proposal, and Dan Reed's motion to recommit the Democratic section was lost by a vote of 210 to 205, when Republicans deserted the President and joined with the Democratic minority. 16 Democrats voted with us. The Republicans were: Fino, Radwan, and Pillion of New York, Edith Nourse Rogers of Massachusetts, and Fulton of Pennsylvania.

I called the President at Gettysburg to tell him about this and while he expected the outcome, he said, "You keep a list of those 5 Republicans and if you ever see at any time that anyone in the White House wants me to see any one of them, you bring it to my attention and I'll stop it. I've seen Mrs. Rogers for the last time. I don't know the others and I don't want to." . . .

• • • •

Saturday, February 26, 1955

Roger graduated from his basic course at Quantico today and Marge, Bruce, and I went down for the ceremonies.

March 1955

March 2, 1955

. . . In my telephone conversation with Herbert Hoover, Jr., Acting Secretary of State, we discussed the following subjects:

. . . The icebreaker *Atka*. The icebreaker is presently in the Arctic making initial explorations for providing logistical support for the scientific work that this country will do in that area as its contribution to the International Geophysical Year in '57–'58. The Communists in Latin America, notably Brazil, Chile, and Uruguay, have been using this *Atka* trip as propaganda, claiming that its real mission in the Antarctic is to find new testing grounds for thermonuclear weapons. These weapons are to be exploded in that area, and according to the Communists, the fallout will come drifting up through South America with disastrous effects. USIA is particularly interested in having this question asked and Bill Lawrence of the *New York Times* will ask it. . . .

The press conference was a very good one, with the President speaking on many subjects.

I released about three-quarters of the conference for direct quotes at 2:30.

• • • •

Friday, March 4, 1955

. . . Had luncheon with Lewis Strauss and discussed the following subjects: . . .

The proposal by the President that he visit the testing areas in Nevada to see a thermonuclear explosion. He has never seen one and wants to do so. He asked me to discuss this with Strauss and work out with him a legitimate news peg for his visit. Quite naturally, we are concerned about the international repercussions if the President merely went out there to watch an explosion without any explanation. It could be construed by the Communists as another aggressive act by the United States unless we had it nailed down satisfactorily. . . .

During the course of our conversation Lewis mentioned the fact that we had now made advances in nuclear warheads that were small and comparatively cheap to produce. These could be used defensively by exploding them in the air to destroy incoming enemy aircraft within a mile of the blast. Squadrons of attacking planes could be completely obliterated by one missile. I asked Lewis if he did not think that this was a better peg to hang it on if we could make a public announcement that the President was going out to see a new defensive device for the protection of our country against atomic aerial attack. . . .

• • • •

Tuesday, March 8, 1955

. . . Later in the day I issued a statement offering the Albanian people, who are faced with serious food shortages, help from the United States through the League of Red Cross Societies. This offer is being made deliberately with the belief that the Soviets will force the Albanian government to turn it down. But that is all right. If they accept it, they admit that their agricultural situation is in a mess. If they refuse it, then we can use it for propaganda value.

• • • •

Wednesday, March 9, 1955

Comparatively quiet day—since we did not have a press conference. . . .

The only thing of real interest during the day was a call I had from Paul Scott Rankin of Reuters. He dropped in to see me Monday to tell me that the Atomic Energy Commission was refusing to let British correspondents cover the atomic civil defense tests scheduled for April. After he left Monday, I called Lewis Strauss. . . .

For the life of me I cannot see why it is necessary for me to go through this hassle every time I get into this situation. . . . It is very simple to just admit British and Canadian correspondents and keep out all the others since America, Canada, and Great Britain are presently in an atomic arrangement.

• • • •

Thursday, March 10, 1955

. . . Last night Marvin Arrowsmith had told me that Butler, the Democratic National Chairman, had said that Mrs. Eisenhower's health was one of the reasons the President would not run again in 1956 and asked me for comment. I told him then that I would not have any comment at that time.

I went in to see the President at 8:30 and told him about the Butler remarks. I suggested that I thought it would be a darned good thing if we got our people on the Hill to let Butler have it. The President agreed and wryly shook his head, remarking, "Boy, politics is really a lousy business. This Butler thing is about as low as it can come, injecting Mrs. Eisenhower into my political plans. Actually, I suppose that Mrs. Ike would like to get up to that farm, but I am sure that she will not make the final decision but will leave that entirely to me." . . .

Marv Arrowsmith came in about 6:00 to tell me that a minister by the name of Reverend James A. Pike from the Cathedral of St. John the Divine, in a sermon at the Epiphany Church here in Washington, had criticized the President for issuing a July 4th Day of Prayer Proclamation in July 1953, and then instead of going to church that day, he went to Camp David and fished and played golf. . . .

Called Ken Crawford of *Newsweek* today on an item in Periscope which said that the budget included appropriations to build a bomb shelter for the Soviet embassy. I checked with the budget and they said embassies were foreign territory and we could not, even if we wanted to, appropriate federal money for them. . . .

The final mess in the evening was a UP story by Merriman Smith, which he had written after talking with Dr. Snyder about Mrs. Eisenhower's health. Smitty called Dr. Synder, who was caught off guard and talked to him, saying that Mrs. Eisenhower had a heart murmur caused by rheumatic fever and was easily fatigued. I told the doctor I would appreciate it if he would not give statements to the newspapermen and refer them to me instead of talking to them directly. He agreed to do so.

The administration's tendency to prayer was much remarked upon during the 1950s, and it may have produced more criticism than praise, although perhaps in the end everything cancelled out—some Americans praised Eisenhower, unbelievers continued to be irritated. President Truman, a devout Baptist, did not fail to notice that Eisenhower had joined no church until after the election. According to Truman, the incoming President in 1953 then committed the unpardonable sin of praying publicly at his own inauguration—Eisenhower opened his inaugural address with a prayer of his own composition. Under Eisenhower a movement succeeded in changing the pledge of allegiance to the flag to read "one nation under God . . ." And there were the prayers before Cabinet meetings, which unknown to outsiders were not as reverent, in any event not as lasting in results, as one might have expected.

Friday, March 11, 1955

In at 8:15.

Cabinet meeting at 9:00 . . .

The President, as usual, opened the Cabinet session with a request for silent prayer. At the end of the prayer he looked up at George Humphrey, smiled, and said to him, "George, I hope you are now more penitent. I've been reading in the paper where you have been calling some of the Democrats names lately, and I hope you are now feeling a little better disposed toward them." Humphrey laughed and replied, "Mr. President, not one damn bit! I still say their tax plans are irresponsible and silly." . . .

Attended a meeting of the Little Cabinet in the Cabinet room and briefed them on two subjects—(1) press conferences and (2) department leaks.

On the press conferences I recommended that they have some system of seeing that only legitimate working reporters attend the sessions. This would necessitate checking men in at the door and also asking reporters to identify themselves and their papers when they question the secretary. I was amazed last week to discover that in the Defense Department, for example, no check was made on those who were attending the conference and for all intents and purposes anyone, even a stranger, could get into one of Wilson's press conferences.

Secondly, I told them that until the President announced something it was extremely embarrassing to the White House and would be embarrassing to the department, if they leaked out in advance news of any appointments by the President, reports, etc. . . .

• • • •

Monday, March 14, 1955

. . . The President called me into his office about noon. Secretary Dulles was with him. He told me very confidentially that he and Dulles were exploring the possibilities of the President making a trip to Europe for V-E Day, May 7th, and that there was a very good likelihood that such a trip would come off. He would remain overseas for about ten days and would probably visit most of the NATO countries. . . .

Senator Watkins told me that he was considerably concerned about the Reciprocal Trade Bill and that he wanted to see the President to discuss with him the fact that he (Watkins) would have to be opposed to the bill unless it contained his amendment which held that the Tariff Commission decisions were supreme and could not be overruled by the President. I asked Watkins how come the Republicans were trying to cut down on the powers of the President, and he admitted quite frankly that he was forced to take this attitude as a result of pressure from home. I am sure he feels quite bad about it because he is a good friend of the President's. (I told the President about Watkins' conversation and he said he would send Randall up to see him tomorrow and then if necessary, would see Watkins himself.) . . .

• • • •

Tuesday, March 15, 1955

In at 8:15.

Leaders meeting at 8:30. . . .

Colonel Goodpaster returned from Honolulu today and went in to report to the President. He later came into my office and gave me a fill-in. He had a long talk with Admiral Stump and apparently it was a very profitable one.[1] As things now stand, Stump does not believe that the Chinese Communists can launch any all-out attack against Matsu for at least four weeks or any all-out attack against Quemoy for at least eight weeks.

The Chinese Nationalists are strengthening the forces on both islands and our military do not believe that those islands can be knocked out by any Communist attack. . . . Our military do not believe that any effective threat to the islands off Formosa can materialize until and unless the Chinese build airports closer to the coastline in the area between Quemoy and Matsu.

The President had a rather unusual visit at noon today from Menon, head of the Indian delegation to the General Assembly of the United Nations. . . .

When I went in to see the President with Sarnoff, he turned to me and said, "I had an interesting visitor—Menon of India. He just talked about how his country hated Communists and how they wanted to work with us. As he was leaving, he said, 'I hope to see you again.' So this may be the first visit on something they are trying to pull. I don't know about these Indians. They are funny people and I don't know how far we can actually trust them."

Eisenhower appreciated Menon less, the more he saw him, and wrote in his diary for July 14, 1955: "Krishna Menon is a menace and a boor. He is a boor because he conceives himself to be intellectually superior and rather coyly presents, to cover this, a cloak of excessive humility and modesty. He is a menace because he is a master at twisting words and meanings of others and is governed by an ambition to prove himself the master international manipulator and politician of the age. He has visited me twice (in company with Secretary Dulles) to talk about establishing some basis of mediation between Red China and ourselves. I have bluntly told him, both times, that the American people will not consider using the lives and freedom of their own citizens as a bargaining material. Since Red China, in violation of her solemn word given in the Korean armistice, unjustly held some of our men prisoners—men that China herself admits were in uniform when captured—we will not make important political concessions on the grounds that this would be recompensed by the return of some of these men." The Eisenhower Diaries, *p. 300.*

Wednesday, March 16, 1955

In at 8:00 A.M. Press conference day. . . .

Lewis Strauss. I asked Lewis for his recommendations on what the President should say if he got questions on Eden's statement that it was not necessary to explode any H-bombs. I recommended that the President refer that question back to the AEC and added "just for your own information, actually Eden did not have this right and made some mistakes. He did not know his subject fully or he would not have said what he did."

On the continuation of our atomic tests in Nevada, Strauss said that they would continue but that he had been very informative to date, that we had not had any trouble at all with any fallout, and that actually the tests were "low yield A-bombs."

On the Dulles statement that the United States would use atomic weapons if they got into a shooting war, Strauss said that Dulles had checked with him on this statement and he was all for it. Actually, he said, we wanted to show our enemies that we now deal with A-bombs as conventional weapons.

Foster Dulles.

1. Use of nuclear weapons in time of war. Dulles said that he had talked this over with the President before he had said it and repeated what Strauss had told me about deliberately impressing our enemies that these weapons were now conventional usage in our armed services.

2. Release of Yalta papers. Dulles said if the President were questioned on this, he should say it is entirely a State Department matter. Actually, we are trying to get them released and yesterday Dulles again cabled Eden to see if they would withdraw their objection but as yet has received no answer. The British opposition is based on two reasons: (a) some remarks in the minutes by Churchill which are rather disparaging of the French and (b) a rather terse comment by Churchill to Eden when Eden interrupted him. Churchill turned to Eden on that occasion and said, "Aw, shut up." . . .

Later in the day Joe McCarthy sounded off up on the Hill on Milton Eisenhower, accusing the President's brother of being a New Deal member of the palace guard, among other things. . . .

In line with these latest McCarthy moves, all of us on the staff, including the President, will make it a point not to have any comment whatsoever on anything McCarthy says or does. We have him relegated to the back pages of the papers and he knows he is not news any more. . . .

About three o'clock I caught one thing that could have been awfully embarrassing. Roscoe Drummond called me to tell me that he understood the *New York Times* had a copy of the Yalta Papers and was going to publish them tomorrow morning. This was the first time I had known that the *Times* had it and, of course, I agreed with Roscoe that, if possible, I would help him. I also told him that I thought the best thing to do under the circumstances was to get the State Department to release them for everybody.

I called Foster Dulles and told him that the *Times* had obtained a copy and was planning to run it tomorrow morning. This apparently did not come as a surprise to him, because he told me he planned to release it to the papers on Thursday and the *New York Times* was not going to publish them until Friday. I told him I had every reason to believe they were going to publish them tomorrow and I would strongly urge that the State Department get them out for morning release as fast as they could. Otherwise, the State Department would be holding the bag on this and would get it from every paper, radio and television station, and magazine in the country, to say nothing of the rest of the world. He said he would see what he could do on this and would have McCardle call me back. He said he would also let me know where I could get a copy for Roscoe Drummond. Carl called me back and said they were going to release the Yalta Papers to everyone and if Drummond wanted a copy, he could get one from the Vice President's office. . . .

Once the Historical Office of the State Department had finished compiling the Yalta Papers and had printed the papers in bound galleys prior to binding into books, question of their release arose, and because some documents were British in origin it was necessary to ask pemission of the British government to publish them. At this point it became clear that Eden did not want the papers released. Whether the reason was that mentioned above was difficult to say; probably it was concern for much of the casual conversation at Yalta, duly recorded in documents, not merely the comments about the French but such remarks as that Churchill did not care much for the Poles (apparently he meant he did not desire their opinion on an issue, but it was capable of misunderstanding) or jocular conversation between Roosevelt and Stalin about the disposition of 50,000 German officers captured by the Russians. The State Department offered confidential copies of galleys to leading members of Congress, and Republican members accepted and Democratic members declined. The New York Times *arranged with Assistant Secretary of State*

Carl McCardle to receive a copy, and at that juncture the department released the papers. Later that year the Department of State published them as a volume in the series Foreign Relations of the United States: The Conferences at Malta and Yalta, 1945 *(Washington, D.C.).*

Thursday, March 17, 1955

. . . Later in the morning the President called me in and gave me a statement which he asked me to clear with Stassen and the Secretary of State. This statement was the announcement by the President of Stassen as a special assistant to handle problems of disarmament but to continue for the time being at least as FOA chief and through the presentation of the Mutual Security Program to Congress. . . .

• • • •

Friday, March 18, 1955[1]

. . . The President said that he also had a talk with J. Edgar Hoover of the FBI on the same subject and that Hoover had told him that the Soviets had a far better intelligence system from reading the American press than we could have in Russia with 10,000 agents. . . .

Had luncheon in Herb Brownell's office with Justin Morgan, chairman of the judiciary committee of the New York State Assembly and chairman of the New York legislative committee on wiretapping. . . .

The meeting started at 12:30. Morgan reviewed briefly the background of the wiretapping investigation in New York which was brought to a head by indiscriminate tapping of wires by the New York police. He said that what had concerned him most was the fact that there were two persons whose names he did not give who wanted to testify publicly before his committee on the use of widespread wiretapping by the federal government. He said one of these was a man who was with the Internal Revenue Division until just recently, while the second was an individual who was with the CIA prior to the time Eisenhower was elected. . . .

Late in the afternoon Mary Caffrey told me that a Miss Lally of the Supreme Court library was on the phone and wanted to get an official Ward and Paul transcript of the President's press conference of this week. I talked to Miss Lally and told her that I would be very happy to give a transcript to her if she would tell me that the request came from a Supreme Court Justice and who the Justice was. She said that it was normal for her to make such a request and that Justices of the Court often asked her to do such things. However, she would not name the individual, and I was equally insistent that I could not give out the transcript without knowing who it was going to. I told her to explain to the Justice that I would be very happy to provide him with a transcript but that I had to know for my own protection who it was going to.

I have no idea who the Justice is, but I would not be surprised, if I ever find out who it is, if it turned out to be Douglas. That is typical of the way he operates. I do not think that any other Justice in the Court would hesitate to call me and ask me point-blank for a transcript, knowing of course that I would be only too happy to send it to him.

• • • •

Saturday, March 19, 1955

. . . After I had made the announcement of the Stassen appointment, I arranged with him to make a brief statement for camera and radio on his appointment. He did so and said, of course, he was happy to give this his full effort.

Mrs. Eisenhower in January 1954 christened the world's first nuclear submarine, Nautilus. *Its launching was an extraordinary development, marking a new turn in the arms race, as well as development of a virtually brand-new U.S. Navy.*

Monday, March 21, 1955

In at 8:15.

Over the weekend the stories on Stassen's appointment as "Secretary for Peace" were very fine and foreign reaction was good. . . .

Another newspaper hassle broke out in the afternoon—this time with the Navy Department concerning the atomic submarine, the *Nautilus*. The Navy permitted the commander of the submarine, Captain Wilkinson, to give the *Saturday Evening Post* an exclusive story on the ship. It was one of these "as told to" stories by Wilkinson, but he got paid for it—a figure that is being knocked about is $10,000—and the material has not been made available to any other news media. The story is due to be published soon, at about the same time as the Navy is planning to have a press conference with Wilkinson at New London. The *New York Times,* INS, and AP registered a complaint with me, and I told them I would look into it.

• • • •

Tuesday, March 22, 1955

In at 8:15.

Legislative leaders meeting. . . .

The next item on the agenda was the Postal Pay Bill. The President started the discussion by saying, "Boy! Did we take a licking!" referring to the House action of yesterday in refusing to vote a closed rule in considering the bill. . . . The President asked if Congress were helpless to do the right thing. He said that he did not see how he could accept any bill that was higher than 7.6% or that didn't carry reclassification with it. He also said that it was his understanding that "every postal letter carrier was going around telling his clients that he was underpaid, that his children were starving and were running around in raggedy-assed pants. . . ."

Knowland reported that in the Senate the Reciprocal Trade Bill was in for rough sledding . . .

Bridges then raised the question of a possible Big Four conference, and the President said that he had never discussed a Big Four conference with Senator George and that, as far as the United States was concerned, he could see a certain advantage to it . . . "As a matter of fact, 10 days ago Foster Dulles and I thought we saw a pretty good opening. We discussed it but we dropped it when we found there was considerable opposition to it abroad." . . . [1]

Senator Bridges asked if the President was familiar with some of the statements that former Senator Cain had been making as a member of the Subversive Activities Control Board. The President said he was not only familiar with them but had asked Brownell to call in Cain and have a Dutch Uncle talk with him, and if he didn't stop his talking, to make some move to get him out of there. "But I want to remind you gentlemen," the President said with a smile, "that he got into that job in the first place because some of my finest Republican friends—some of you in this room—urged me to nominate him." . . . [2]

In the afternoon I had a meeting with Commander Beach and Captain Selby of the Navy. We discussed the question of the *Nautilus* and the kick that I had received yesterday. Captain Selby told me that the *Saturday Evening Post* article was not going to be published until April 7th and that the Navy had agreed to make public on March 30th, when the Wilkinson press conference was scheduled in New London, the very same facts that were in the *Saturday Evening Post* story for general distribution . . .

The proposed summit conference became reality in the summer of 1955 when from July 16 to July 23 the President, Prime Minister Eden (who had replaced Churchill), Premier Nikolai A. Bulganin of the Soviet Union, and Premier Edgar Faure of France met to consider the state of Europe and the world. It was the first summit since the Potsdam Conference in July-August, 1945.

Wednesday, March 23, 1955

In at 8:00. Press conference today. . . .

In my telephone conversation prior to the briefing with the President, I discussed the following matters with the Secretary of State: . . .

Yalta Papers. On the Yalta Papers, Dulles pointed out that during the last two years the Senate Appropriations Committee, on its own initiative, requested that the papers be published and had appropriated money for that purpose. Dulles and the State Department had held up publication because of a British objection, but that objection was withdrawn by Eden prior to the release of the papers even though Eden did so rather reluctantly and looked upon the publication of the papers as the lesser of two evils, namely, having to come out piecemeal or having to come out all at once. As far as the President was concerned, Dulles said that he had discussed the problem of the Yalta Papers with him, and that the President was kept fully informed on the changing British position. The President knew they were in the process of preparation but never actually saw the galley proofs.

Dulles said that as far as other meetings were concerned, the Historical Section of his department is working on the Potsdam Papers but no date has been set for their release. He said that this is a normal procedure and that it normally takes the Historical Section many years to get the papers in shape for release.[1] . . .

In conversation with Lewis Strauss, we discussed two situations:

First, there had been a slight fallout on the city of Las Vegas but Strauss reported that it was nothing of any significance whatsoever and that the President could say that he had been assured by the Atomic Energy Commission and its medical advisers that no danger would occur to any of the citizens of that city.

The second matter I discussed with him was the story that several Senators on the Hill had appealed to the Navy following their visit to and trip on the *Nautilus* to build more atomic submarines. Strauss said that was a subject entirely for Navy decision, that we were building two additional submarines and others were on the drawing board. The *Sea Wolf* is nearing completion. . . .

• • • •

Friday, March 25, 1955

In at 8:15.

The only thing of note today was that I got the White House off the hook on the squirrels.

I talked to the President in the morning and told him that I thought we had better once and for all kill the squirrel story by saying that three squirrels were trapped and removed from the White House grounds, but the situation seemed to have cleared up and the putting green was no longer being dug up by our furry little friends. . . .

• • • •

Saturday, March 26, 1955

Roger took off for Sweden this morning. General Gruenther was kind enough to take him to Paris in his plane.

• • • •

Monday, March 28, 1955

In at 8:15. A rather hectic day!!

Went in to see the President at nine o'clock and discussed with him the rash of stories which broke out in the press and on radio and television over the weekend to the effect that the Chinese Reds would invade Matsu Island by April 15th and would invade Quemoy within a month after that. These stories resulted from an off-the-record dinner meeting which Admiral Carney had with some newspapermen Thursday evening at the Hotel Statler. They represented Carney's views and those of the Navy who, after all, are anxious to throw a blockade around the China mainland. As a result of the Carney dinner, the stories had gone somewhat hog-wild over the weekend and threats of use of atomic bombs, invasion of the mainland, and everything else were written and spoken. . . .

When I was talking to the President, he took off his glasses and characteristically chewed on the end of the earpiece. When I finished, he said, "I couldn't agree with you more. Are you sure that this came from Carney?" I told him that I was and that I had been so informed by several of my newsmen friends in Washington. He then exploded, got up from his desk, and walked around the room. As he walked, he talked rapidly and forcefully and said: "By God, this has got to stop. These fellows like Carney and Ridgway don't yet realize that their services have been integrated and that they have, in addition to myself, a boss in Admiral Radford who is chairman of the joint chiefs of staff. They are giving just their own service's viewpoint and presenting it as the entire administration viewpoint. I'm going to see Radford in half an hour, and I'm going to tell him to tell Carney to stop talking. I'm also going to see Charlie Wilson at 11:00, and I'm going to tell him the same thing." The President then said, "I think that you should tell the reporters you are meeting with tonight the following: Of course, there is always a danger in the Far East. The Chinese Reds are fanatical Communists and have publicly stated that they are going to try to take Formosa. But we are trying to keep the peace. We are not looking for war, and I think the stories like the ones they get from Carney, when published, are a great disservice to the United States. They're going to look awful silly when April 15th comes along and there is no incident, because honestly our information is that there is no buildup off those islands as yet to sustain any attack, and believe me, they're not going to take those islands just by wishing for them. They are well-equipped and well-defended, and they can only be taken, if at all, by a prolonged all-out attack. I would also tell them that you are not normally a betting man, but if any of them wanted to bet a thousand dollars that we would be in war on any of the dates they wrote about, you would be happy to bet them." I interrupted laughingly to say, "If you'll let me say a hundred dollars, I'll do it." He said OK. . . .

Admiral Robert B. Carney, chief of naval operations, had spoken indiscreetly, and thus put himself in the same boat of inconvenience as the Army's chief of staff, General Ridgway. Both officers' appointments were for two-year terms, followed perhaps by a second term. Eisenhower failed to renew the appointments.

Tuesday, March 29, 1955

In at 8:15. . . .

Leaders meeting. . . .

The next order of business was the Reciprocal Trade Bill, and Knowland asked Millikin to report on it.

Millikin reported that the bill was in a hell of a mess . . .

To that the President replied, "Actually, that's just what the President is concerned with—the international situation. A President has got to think of this world. . . . I wish someone would show me what we would do with Mexico and with our 1,500 miles of unprotected border if we would sit by and let Mexico go Communistic. It would be one hell of a mess and we would be in a terrible position. No one in this administration is trying to hurt the United States or United States business. It may be stupid, but our hearts are in the right spot and you can assure everyone that we do not intend to hurt American business, but we do have the world to think of." . . .

Halleck inadvertently touched off a mild explosion when he told the President that he had been reading some stories about the fact that the administration may ask for increased appropriations in the military to deal with the present situation. The President said: "Look, Charlie, I've read those stories and I'll tell you one thing. I think I know a little more about the military than some so-called experts who are sounding off on it. I'll ask you one question. If you had a bigger Army today, where in the hell would you put it? I don't know any problem that takes up more of my time than foreign affairs and national security—about 80% of my time. If anyone thinks I am trying to take unnecessary chances for the security of this country, they're just nuts. I get sick and tired of hearing about people who are trying to make politics out of something they don't know anything about." . . .

I got a call in the morning from Allen Dulles, and he came in to see me at 4:30. . . . He said . . . that he thought I should know that it would be possible for the Communists to build up virtually overnight air power for an attack on Quemoy and Matsu, although he did not think this was likely. He said he thought what would happen was this: The Chinese Communists had now gotten their gun embankments on the mainland around Quemoy and he thought that if they did attack, they would try to soften up the island for some time by a heavy artillery barrage. They could do this without any air power. They could pulverize Quemoy's beaches and raise a certain amount of disruption in the island's defenses. They could make it difficult to continue to supply Quemoy from the sea. They would do this in advance of an amphibious attack and would also do this to try to see what our intentions were. Matsu is a different situation and artillery fire that could reach greater Matsu could cause little, if any, real damage. We agreed that we did not think it was likely that the Chinese Communists would start anything prior to the Bandung Conference scheduled for April 18th. He showed me maps of the Quemoy area and pointed out that should an all-out attack occur, we would have to make a decision on whether we would use atomic weapons or not. The very nearness of Quemoy to the mainland would make it difficult to use these weapons without risking the result that Quemoy itself would be caught in the fallout pattern, if the winds were wrong. Likewise, if the winds were wrong, the fallout would endanger the city of Amoy with its several hundred thousand civilian residents. . . .

• • • •

Wednesday, March 30, 1955

In at 8:00 A.M. Press conference day. . . .

Following the press conference the President then held the first of his bipartisan luncheons for the Republican and Democratic leadership in the House. The meeting started at 12:30 and ran until quarter of three.

• • • •

Thursday, March 31, 1955[1]

. . . The President had the second of his bipartisan luncheons at the White House, this time for the members of the Senate.

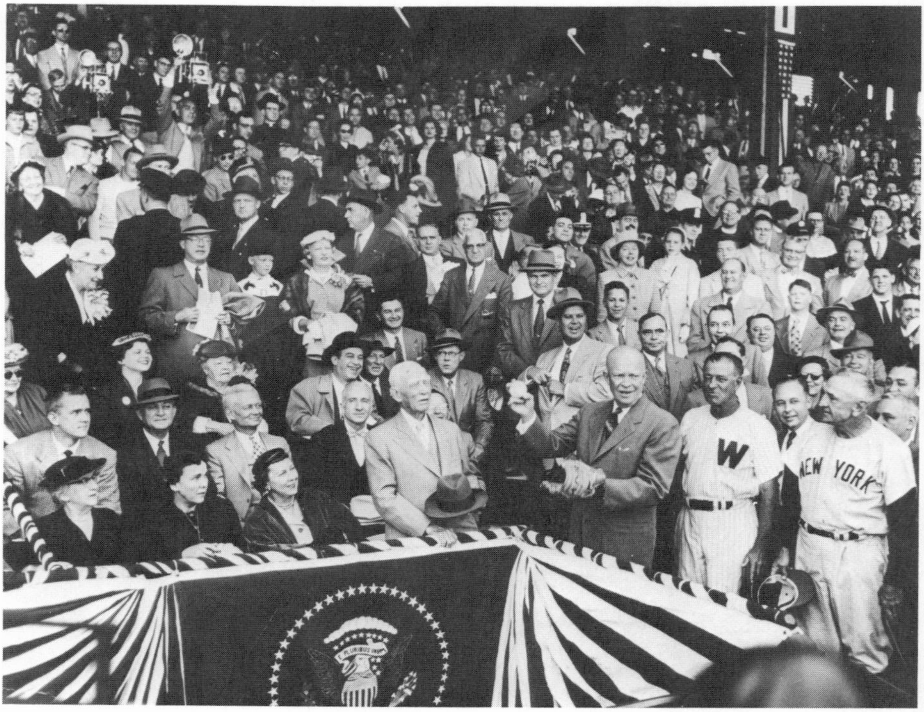
W
NEW YORK
E PLURIBUS UNUM

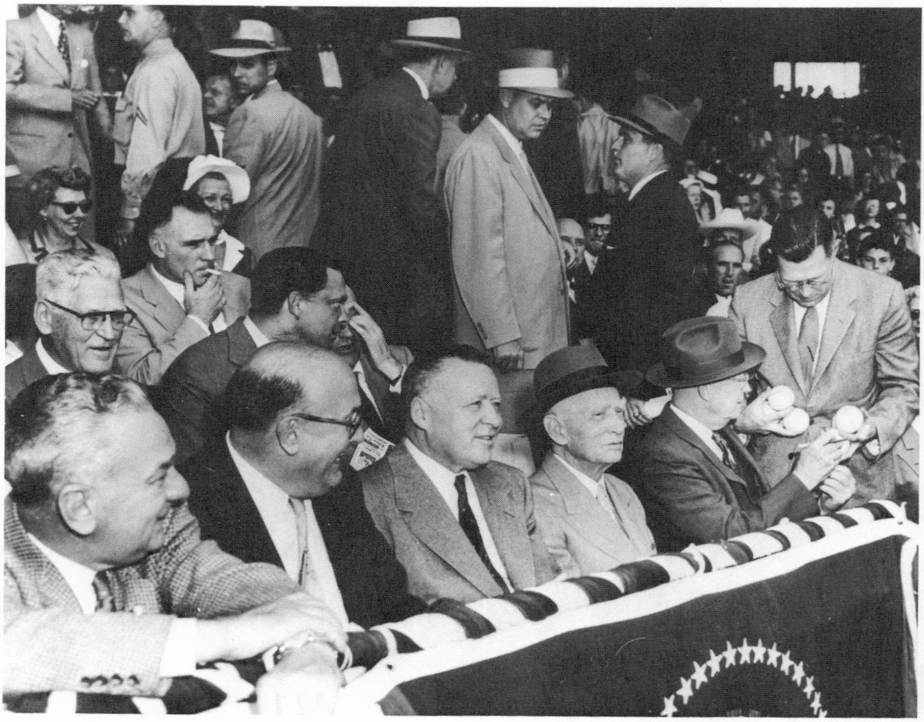

April 1955

Friday, April 1, 1955

In at 8:15.

The participants at the bipartisan luncheon yesterday all behaved themselves and issued short statements—with the exception of Alexander Smith of New Jersey.[1] He gave an interview with Telenews and there was a long story in the *Washington Post* and other papers to the effect that the President had told the participants yesterday that he did not believe Russia would come into any fighting off Formosa and that the Russians would not back up the Chinese. Smith phoned me early in the morning and tried to apologize for speaking out of turn. He said that he did not realize he was saying as much as he did, that he did not have any excuse for doing so, and that he wanted personally to apologize to the President. I told him the President was all tied up at the National Security Council meeting and that I would relay the information to him. This is about the fourth time that Smith has gone out of line in reporting presidential conversations or actions, and on the advice of Persons, Martin, and Shanley, we decided to let him stew in his own juice for a while.

Left the White House at 10 o'clock to fly to Pennsylvania State College to attend the seminar that evening of the Pennsylvania editors. . . .

• • • •

Saturday, April 2, 1955

Returned from Pennsylvania at 11:30. Arrived home at 12:00 and played golf in the afternoon with Bruce.

• • • •

Monday, April 4, 1955

In at 8:15.

Busy day on routine matters. The only thing worth reporting is a rather long conversation I had with the President alone in his office.

Our first topic of conversation was Mrs. Eisenhower, and the President said that he had received a report from Dr. Snyder this morning that her fever, which was about 102° last night, had completely broken and that Mrs. Eisenhower was just tired. . . .

The President said that in the past she had frequently just gotten "worn out" and was forced to take a rest from time to time. . . .

The second question we talked about was whether we would have a press conference this week. The President said he would prefer not to have one because if he did, the questions would center mainly around Formosa and would be merely a rehash of the Formosa situation. "Right now, the less anyone says about the situation, the better. Actually, we believe that the Russians are trying to discourage the Chinese Communists . . ."

The President then got back on the question of Formosa and said, "You know, Jim, if we could only get Chiang to realize certain things. If we could only get him to see it our way. Now, actually, those islands of Quemoy and Matsu are not defensible against an all-out prolonged large-scale attack. No force on earth could hold them for a long time, particularly if the Chinese Communists were willing to suffer enormous casualties to get them. We, of course, could slow them up with atomic weapons, but I do not think that it would be wise, unless we are forced to do it, to atomize the mainland opposite them. And even if we did, they could just wait for a while and start the attack over again. Actually, what Chiang should do would be to use those islands as outposts, as a defense outpost, and make it just as costly as possible if the Chinese Communists attempt to take them. But he should not make those two islands another Dienbienphu. He should not risk everything on holding them, because I don't believe they can be held over an indefinite period. Right now Chiang has 58,000 troops on Quemoy and 15,000 on Larger Matsu. That's just too many troops for those small islands. What he should do is leave about 5,000 crack troops on Quemoy and a correspondingly smaller detachment on Matsu. These troops should be supplied with every possible conventional defensive weapon and should be willing to die if necessary, but sell their lives very dearly. Then if the Communists attack, they would suffer very high casualties which would be inflicted on them by relatively few Nationalist soldiers. If in the long run the islands fell, Chiang could gain a great deal of morale for his people and for the free world from the fact that a small detachment of Nationalist troops inflicted such heavy casualties on the island. It would seem to me that this would be a much better way to handle the situation, but to date we haven't had much luck in selling this to Chiang." . . .

• • • •

Tuesday, April 5, 1955

In at 8:15.

Went in to see the President at 8:30 to ask him how he intended to handle the upcoming Churchill retirement. He said he would send a personal message to Churchill but asked me to get up a message which I would release from the White House. . . .

Later in the day I had a meeting . . . on a very hot problem which has been raised within the Defense Department by General MacArthur.

When the Yalta Papers were published, the Democratic high command, of course, trying to get Roosevelt out from under the political decisions that were made at Yalta, embarked on a campaign to blame the Yalta decisions on our military. This, of course, is completely ridiculous and Yalta was a political conference, not a military conference. It is the same sort of Democratic defense that they made about Roosevelt's Boston speech in 1940 when he said, "And I tell you mothers again and again and again that your sons shall not fight on foreign soil."[1] In this case the Democrats tried to add the words "unless we are attacked" which, of course, Roosevelt never said.

The Democratic speakers on the floor of the Congress, after publication of the Yalta Papers, have been saying that the decisions taken at Yalta were urged by the military. Sunday, General MacArthur issued a statement in which he said that this was not true, that he was opposed to the entrance of Russia into the war in the Pacific, and that he urged the Defense Department to publish all the papers dealing with the conduct of the war in the Pacific to prove his point.

The *New York Times* claims that many of the papers were not classified in any of our three classifications—Top Secret, Secret, or

Confidential—but were merely "Restricted." And the issuance of our Executive Order in 1953 on classifications made that "Restricted" classification one which was of a public nature. They asked me to look into the situation and I told them I would.

In the meeting today it was pointed out . . . that any complete handing out of the reports would of necessity entail publication of intelligence reports and evaluations from many sources and also complete planning of strategy on invasion plans for Japan, Okinawa, etc., which are still the same type of plans which would be followed out if we were to become involved in a war in China, and the enemy reading these reports would receive a pretty good indoctrination on just how we would act, how we would move, and how and to what extent we use intelligence among local populations. I agreed, of course, with Goodpaster that we could not give out such documents but also said that I thought Ross should make an attempt to get in touch with MacArthur or his spokesman to find out if he himself planned to release intelligence and planning documents.[2] I said I thought the call should be made if only to establish a record that it was. Ross said he would do that and would let me know further about it tomorrow. . . .

• • • •

Wednesday, April 6, 1955[1]

. . . Dulles believes that both in Russia and China the eventual internal trouble in those two countries will come through a complete breakdown in their agricultural production. When people start to starve, that is when they are most likely to rebel against their government. . . .

• • • •

Thursday, April 7, 1955[1]

. . . After the National Security Council meeting, the President in the company of the Secretary of State signed the protocols carrying out the Paris Agreements, admitting Germany to the NATO organization and granting that nation sovereignty. . . .

I had another meeting in the afternoon with Bob Ross and Mr. Winnacker of the Defense Department with Fred Seaton and Andy

Goodpaster. They had finally gotten up a release which they proposed to put out which said in effect that the Defense Department had decided not to release any part of the records of the Defense Department on the closing phases of the Pacific War. . . .

The President listened to my explanation and then read the release—then he mildly exploded. "I cannot see why the Defense Department has to wait until these things develop and then try to reach a solution. Something must be very wrong over there if they have not already gotten World War II papers in shape. I admit that I would be worried a little about the intelligence reports from many sources being made public. That I do not think is in the best interest of our country. I can understand the argument made on the planning papers, but I do not think they are too valid, although I suppose some of the material in them should not be given out. But as for the rest, I do not see why it is not made public. I can remember when I was assigned in Washington in the '30s going down to a building here and looking through World War I reports. They were all available and anyone who wanted to could come in and study them. That's what I think we should do on World War II. We should not release the documents but tell anyone who is interested in them that they are available for their inspection." . . .

Fred Seaton and I came back into my office and told Ross of our decision. Later Fred went over to the Pentagon to work out a short statement saying the Department was giving its full attention to a study of these papers and after eliminating some intelligence reports and some planning reports, they would be made public.

The Department of Defense's publication was The Entry of the Soviet Union into the War Against Japan: Military Plans, 1941–1945 *(Washington, D.C., 1955).*

James F. Byrnes, Secretary of State in 1945–1947, had enjoyed a long career in politics, first as a member of the House of Representatives during the Wilson administration, then as a Senator, and after appointment as Associate Justice of the Supreme Court just before American entrance into the Second World War, he resigned to enter the White House where he became virtual "Assistant President" in charge of the home front. He was a candidate for the Democratic nomination for the vice presidency in 1944, and lost out when President Roosevelt decided upon the nomination of the then Senator Truman. During the so-called Dixiecrat rebellion against Truman's postwar leadership of the Democratic Party, Byrnes went over to this fragment of the party that favored Southern rights, and in the early 1950s he was very friendly with Eisenhower. The President found Jimmy Byrnes engaging although he was not completely in favor of Old Guard Democrats, who were not much different from Old Guard Republicans. The chance to divide the Democratic Party was, however, too good to pass up.

April 12–April 20, 1955[1]

Left for Augusta the morning of April 12th. The President, myself, Ann Whitman, and Betty Allen. . . .

Very busy press time in Augusta. . . .

From the time the President arrived in Augusta we jumped right into the middle of a hot pressure campaign by friends of Jimmy Byrnes to get the President—or in his absence myself—over to the Byrnes dinner at Aiken on Saturday night. This dinner was being held on the same evening that the Democratic National Committee was holding a dinner for Rayburn in Washington with Truman and Stevenson attending. The Byrnes dinner was a strict Dixiecrat affair, and we could do nothing but lose by injecting ourselves into a Democratic Party fight.

The President talked to Byrnes at the Citadel and told him he would be unable to get to Aiken, and Byrnes fully understood and appreciated the President's insistence on not accepting any invitations while he was in Augusta. However, the people running the dinner kept the pressure on me right up until the time of the dinner. The President and I finally agreed that the least we could do was to send a message . . . it turned out to be a good solution. . . .

There were several important developments during the week in the international field. They were:

Admiral Stump's visit. . . .

Stump flew down to Augusta . . . Stump was accompanied by General Loper who came down to see the President on a secret matter and whose presence was not reported or was not known. The newspapermen and photographers met us at the club when we arrived and when they asked me who Loper was, I said he was merely a security person who was with the general. He was in civilian clothes and was not recognized.

Loper brought down with him a paper which the Defense Department wanted the President to see. The Defense Department had been asked by the Joint Committee on Atomic Energy about just what kind of information we were going to exchange with our NATO allies on atomic energy. The President approved the decision of the Defense Department to tell the committee that under no conditions at this time would we give the NATO countries any knowledge of the manufacture or production of atomic weapons, nor would we give them live weapons to practice with. . . .

General Collins. General Collins is returning to Washington on the 22nd of April. The excuse we are giving is that Collins is going to return so that he can testify before the Congress in the hearings that will be held on the Mutual Security Program. Actually, Collins is coming back to report in detail to the President on the deteriorating situation within Vietnam. The situation there is getting worse. The present government is weak and is being constantly attacked by the Binh Xuyen, which is a gambling syndicate, as well as two of the religious sects—the Hoa Hao and the Cao Dai.

The French are trying to bring back Bao Dai, and we would not have any objection to that if we could get an advance commitment from Bao Dai that he would settle down and do some work instead of fooling around in Paris and Cannes. A decision on this will probably be upcoming within the next few weeks.

While I was more busy than ever down there—the Western Union moved more than 200,000 words with an all-time record for us of 42,000 words on one day—I think the President was able to get some rest and a great deal of relaxation. When we arrived down there, he was particularly jumpy and tense, but as the days unfolded, he relaxed and seemed to be thoroughly enjoying his stay. Bill Robinson stayed with him and he had Cliff Roberts, Jock Whitney, Slats Slater, Clarence Schoo, Bob Woodruff, and Bobby Jones to visit with, play golf and bridge with, so all in all he had some good rest.[2] . . .

General J. Lawton Collins, former Army chief of staff, Eisenhower's best corps commander (so Ike had said) in Europe during the Second World War, had gone out to Saigon as special ambassador in an effort to bring the President's point of view to the weak Saigon government, and his report to the President was one of the first signs that after the exit of the French in 1954, following the debacle at Dienbienphu, the situation in Vietnam was anything but heartening. Collins spoke frankly to the President.

Monday, April 25, 1955

In at 8:00 A.M.

The President was scheduled to leave for New York and the AP luncheon at 9:30. . . .

The President's speech went off very well and as expected, the announcement on the atomic merchant ship received worldwide headlines. It tied in very nicely with the President's insistence on the passage of the reciprocal trade treaty, and all in all, I think it was a very worthwhile trip for the President.

Remained in New York overnight to see Mother and Dad. Dad has a very heavy cold and virus, but in addition to that, Mother told me that he is getting to be sort of blue over retiring. He does not know what to do with himself and it is a reaction that I have been expecting for some time. When he gets over the cold, I want to talk to him about serving on a consultant basis with either the USIA or some organization like that in the government which is completely divorced from politics and in which he could give a considerable amount of advice. I don't know what he will say, but I am going to try it.

The President announced that the United States would construct the world's first nuclear-powered merchant ship, the Savannah.

Wednesday, April 27, 1955

In at 8:00 A.M. Press conference day. . . .

I thought the press conference went off very well and the President did a good job as usual. . . .

When I came back with the President from the press conference, he himself had thought he had done a good job and said that as far as he was concerned, I could offer all the conference in direct quotes to the newsreels and radio.

With the exception of an entry for Thursday, April 28, 1955, which was inconsequential, the diary stopped until the following account for Saturday, September 24.

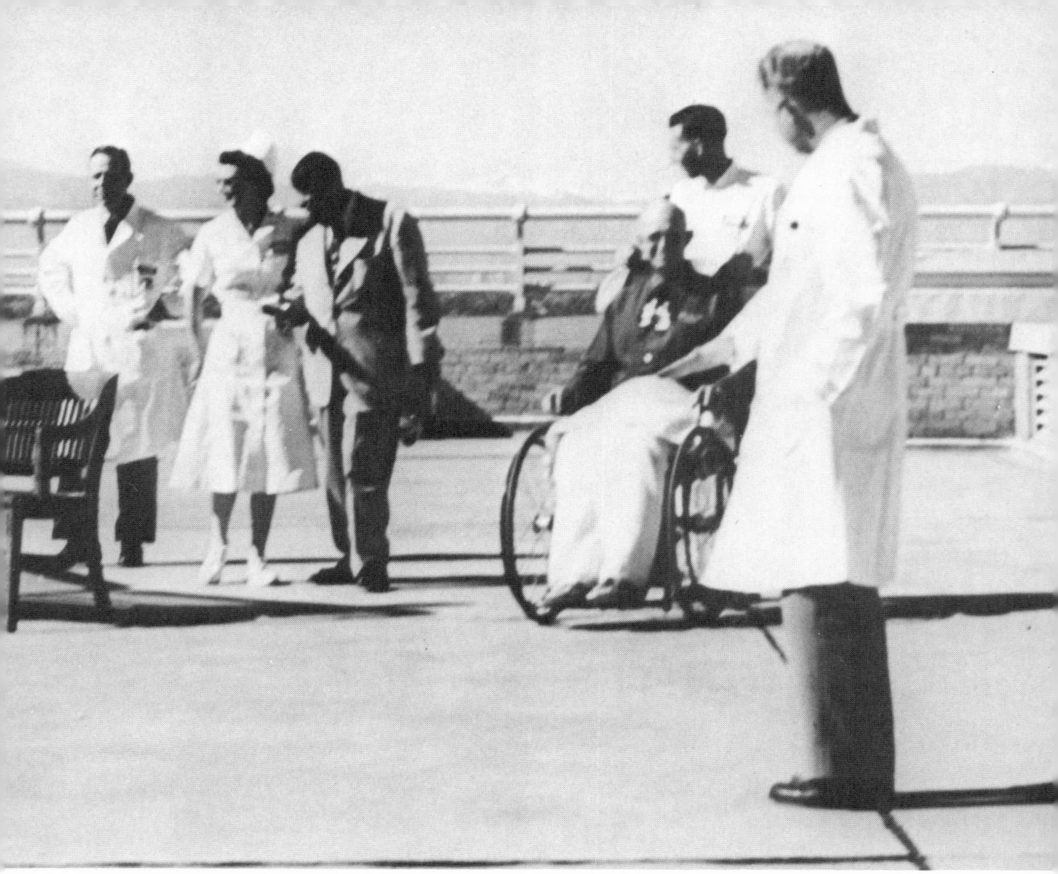

September 1955

Saturday, September 24, 1955

It was raining in Washington, but despite that, Bob Denton, George Dorsey, Wally Gardella, and myself decided to play golf at Columbia Country Club. I was on vacation from the Denver White House and Murray Snyder was taking my place out there. We played golf in the morning and I then had lunch at Columbia and watched the final half of the Maryland-UCLA game on television.

I got home about four o'clock and picked up a copy of that afternoon's edition of the *Washington Star.* A two-column box on the bottom of the page said that the President had suffered a digestive upset and had not come in to work. I did not think anything particularly of the story at the time except that I do remember saying to myself that the President must have gone in for a lot of fancy cooking at Fraser.[1] He had just returned from there the day before after a five-day fishing trip.

I decided to take a nap and went to sleep in the den. At 4:30 P.M. Washington time the White House phoned, awakening me. When I answered it, the operator said that Mr. Snyder was on the phone and wanted to talk to me immediately. I said, "Hello, Murray" and he said: "Jim, Dr. Snyder has just called me and told me that the President has suffered a heart attack and that they are taking him to Fitzsimons Army Hospital. I am going to tell the press that the President has had a mild coronary thrombosis and, of course, I wanted to let you know first."

I could not believe it at first, and Murray was as shaken as I was. He told me that Dr. Snyder had told him earlier in the day that it was a digestive upset. I asked Murray how come the change in the diagnosis, and he told me that Dr. Pollock and General Griffin had taken a cardiogram of the President at one o'clock Denver time and that it showed the heart attack. I told him that, of course, he would have to put the story right out, and he said that he was planning to do that and that he had called the Brown Palace to tell the newsmen to come right out to the Lowry Air Force Base press room. I said that was the only thing he could do and that I would be out as soon as I could get a plane from the Air Force.

Murray then said that Ann Whitman was trying to get General Heaton at Walter Reed to get him to send Dr. Thomas W. Mattingly out immediately. Mattingly had done all the President's physical examinations since he has been President and was therefore thoroughly familiar with the President's condition. After telling Murray to go ahead, I asked to speak to Ann Whitman and I got her on the phone. She was crying and quite upset, of course. She told me that she had put in a call for General Heaton, but I told her to forget it, that I would handle it from this end and that I would be out as soon as I could that night. She said, "Please hurry and get out as soon as you can. Both General Snyder and I need you out here."

I called Marge into the den and told her what had happened and told her I was leaving as soon as possible. We had a date to go to the annual golf dinner at Columbia Country Club that night, but of course that went by the board.

I then picked up the phone and told the telephone operator confidentially that the President had suffered a heart attack—that I would be calling a lot of people and to stand by and watch both my White House phone and my Kellogg telephone number. I said I wanted to speak to the Vice President immediately and then to General Heaton and Jerry Persons.

From then on the telephones were ringing all the time—both the White House phone and the Kellogg number. If I was on the White House phone, Marge would answer the Kellogg one and ask the individual who was calling in to just wait a minute, that I was on the other phone and wanted to speak to him on an urgent matter.

The first call I got back was from the Vice President. He was at his home. I said, "Dick, sit down. I have something serious to tell you. The President has just suffered a heart attack in Denver and has been taken to Fitzsimons Army Hospital. I do not know any other details and have just been informed of this by Murray Snyder in Denver, who is announcing this to the press within the half hour."

Nixon replied, "My God! That's awful. Is there anything I can do?" I told him that, of course, I would keep him fully informed, that I was going to get out to Denver as fast as I could, and that I would keep him informed of developments as they occurred, both while I was in Washington and when I got to Denver. He said that he would stay by the telephone throughout the day and night and wanted me to call him whenever possible. I told him I would call him back before I left Washington with any additional information.

The next call came from General Heaton, who had gotten through to Ann Whitman and knew the story. He said that he was getting in touch with Dr. Mattingly and would have him stand by, and if I would let him know when I was going to get a plane, he would have Mattingly at the airport to go out with me. I told him I would let him know just as soon as I got in touch with the Air Force.

The next call I made was to Jerry Persons. I said, "Jerry, Murray has just called me from Denver and told me that the President has had a heart attack and is on the way to Fitzsimons Hospital. I do not know all the details as yet but it's a real attack and you are the first one I have talked to on this with the exception of the Vice President and General Heaton, who is sending Tom Mattingly out with me. I want to know the answer on two things right away. Who do I call in the Air Force to get a plane?—and—"It's up to you to take over on the staff in the absence of Sherman Adams" (who was in Europe and not due back until Monday morning).

Jerry was as shocked as I was at the news, but said that he would immediately notify as many members of the Cabinet as he could get on the phone. He told me that, of course, he would take over in Adams' place and that I should call either General Twining directly or General Tommy White, Twining's deputy. He asked me how long it would be before the story would break publicly and I told him it was a matter of minutes, that Murray had the men coming to the Lowry Air Force Base press room now and I expected it momentarily. . . .

Tommy White called me back to tell me that a Constellation would be standing by within the hour to get Dr. Mattingly and me out to Denver. . . .

On the flight out, Dr. Mattingly and I talked about the President's physical condition. He told me that on August 1st, the last time the President had had a thorough examination at Walter Reed, there had not been any slightest trouble with his heart, and with the exception of bursitis in his right shoulder, the President's condition had been first-class. He said that previous examinations had also never revealed any sign of heart disorders, and he was just as mystified as I as to what might have caused it, although he said that such attacks can happen to anyone at any time. . . .

We arrived at the hospital about 10 minutes until 12, and Dr. Mattingly and I went directly to the eighth floor where we were met by Dr. Snyder, who introduced me to General Griffin (Martin E.) and the Fitzsimons doctors on the case—Colonel Byron E. Pollock, Colonel George M. Powell, and Lt. Col. John A. Sheedy. All of these doctors, as I soon found out, were competent, fine physicians, but there was understandably an air of concern which you could almost cut with a knife. The President of the United States was in their charge . . .

The President's physician, Dr. Snyder, asked the eminent specialist Dr. Paul Dudley White of Boston to come out, and Hagerty was pleased, for Army doctors surrounded the President and the public would have confidence in White's appearance.

Sunday, September 25, 1955

Arrived at the hospital at 6:30 A.M. . . .

I met Dr. White on his arrival at Lowry at 1:30 and took him immediately to the hospital. I liked him from the minute he came off the plane, which, incidentally, blew a front tire as it was landing, and it was a fine way to welcome the doctor to Lowry. On the way to Fitzsimons he asked me to give him a fill-in and I started to do that when I realized I was trying to tell Dr. White, the eminent heart specialist, about a heart attack. I apologized to him and said I was talking only as a layman and he said, "Go ahead. You're doing all right. I just wanted to see how many medical terms you knew."

Dr. White and I arrived at the hospital at two o'clock and he immediately went into consultation . . .

They brought Dr. White up-to-date on the case, and then Dr. White went in with Dr. Pollock to the President's room to see him briefly. When he came out, he went back to the doctors' room and we talked for a while. Dr. White said as far as he could see right away, the President had had a slightly more than moderate attack. As he put it, "I would say Grade 3 out of five grades." I told Dr.

White and the other doctors that I had been questioned by the press as to how acute an attack the President had had and thought this would be the time to answer it. They agreed . . .

During the day I also called the Vice President several times and talked personally to all four of the President's brothers, filling them in on the way things stood at that time.

We also announced during the day that the President's Conference on Physical Fitness had been postponed, and that the Vice President, who was going to preside at the meetings, consequently would not come to Denver.

• • • •

Monday, September 26, 1955

Got out to the hospital at 6:30 A.M. and reported my 7:00 A.M. bulletin that the President had had a comfortable night . . .

Dr. White did a marvelous job at his press conference, one of the best I have ever attended, and it did much to clear the air on the President's illness. . . .

I saw the President this morning in his room at the hospital for the first time. Dr. Pollock and Dr. White told me that they thought it would be good for the President if I just walked in and said hello. I went in and said, "Good morning, Mr. President. I'm glad to see you." The President was lying down in his bed with his head slightly elevated. He smiled weakly and said, "Hello, Jim, when did you get out?" I told him I arrived at 11:30 Saturday night, and he replied, "Oh yes, that's right. Howard Snyder told me you were coming out."

He then asked me how everything was going. I said, "Fine, Mr. President. The government is well in hand and there is nothing to worry about. Governor Adams got back from his trip this morning, and he and all the members of the Cabinet wanted me to tell you this. They also wanted me to give you their best." The President said, "Thanks for that" and I left the room.

Actually, I thought the President looked surprisingly good. I thought he would look a lot worse. He was under narcotics and sedatives and could only engage in trivial conversation. But he looked all right to me. Of course, I was deeply shocked to see him in bed as was only natural, but was greatly pleased by the way he looked. . . .

Recovery in the Army hospital in Denver required nearly seven weeks; the President was not discharged until November 11. Meanwhile he rested and for the first five weeks saw virtually nothing of a public sort—he later said he had not seen a newspaper. Upon leaving the hospital, Eisenhower flew back to Washington, and on November 14 he and Mrs. Eisenhower drove up to Gettysburg to continue his convalescence. On November 22 he attended his first Cabinet meeting since his illness, held at Camp David, and by the end of the year he felt well again.

December 1955

The diary had no more entries from September 26 until a dictation of December 14: "Since Saturday I have had the opportunity to be alone with the President quite a few times, and it is obvious to me from his conversations that he is thinking more and more about politics and 1956. Here, chronologically, is a report of our discussions."

Saturday, December 10, 1955

The President went to Walter Reed for his monthly X-ray and fluoroscopic examinations, and I left Ward 8 with him and rode down alone with the President to the White House in the car. As we were going down on the elevator, he asked if Dr. Snyder were coming with us. I said, no, that Dr. Snyder had to remain at the hospital to look at the X-rays with Dr. Mattingly and General Heaton and was then coming down to my office to give a statement to the press. The President laughingly said, "Can't you just tell them that I'm not dead and let it go at that?" I told him I thought we would have to make a medical statement, and he said he would like to talk about it going down in the car.

Once we got in the car, the President said he thought it would have been better if the doctors had given me a statement to read and I handled the press rather than to have Dr. Snyder come down for a press conference. "He doesn't know how to handle the press. He is liable to talk too much, and he certainly can't handle the political questions that will be asked. I don't want him to give any indication of my plans at all, and I want you to give him a good talking to on this point before he has the conference."

I promised to do so, and then the President brought up the question of 1956 himself. He said that he had been giving a great deal of thought to it ever since he had become ill, and that he was deeply concerned with the welfare of the country, particularly in the foreign field. He said that he was appalled by the lack of qualified candidates on the Democratic side and particularly pointed to Stevenson, Harriman, and Kefauver as men who did not have the competency to run the office of President.

The President said that he would like to continue to have a series of talks with me on this, but that he wanted it to be confidential and did not want me to tell anyone of these talks. He said that when we got to Gettysburg next week, there would be ample time to sit down occasionally for such talks. I told him that I would be happy to talk to him about this situation at any time, and he said, "OK, that's a date." . . .

• • • •

Sunday, December 11, 1955

I met Governor Adams in his office at 9 o'clock, and we called over to the house to ask the President if he could see us. He said to come over and we met him in his upstairs office on the second floor. . . .

While we were still with the President, he said that he wanted particularly to talk with Governor Dewey about the political situation. Then he grinned and said, "You know, boys, Tom Dewey has matured over the last few years and he might not be a bad presidential candidate. He certainly has the ability and if I'm not going to be in the picture, he also represents my way of thinking."

Neither Governor Adams nor myself said anything at that time, and we left the President.

• • • •

Monday, December 12, 1955

During the Republican legislative meeting Harriman's name came into the conversation during a brief preliminary discussion of some of our foreign policy questions which would, of course, come up at the bipartisan meeting the following day. The President declared that as far as he was concerned, Harriman was a complete nincompoop. "You know," he said, "he's nothing but a Park Avenue Truman." There was no further discussion of politics or the President's position at the meeting.

• • • •

Tuesday, December 13, 1955

Following the bipartisan meeting Tuesday morning, the President decided to fly to Gettysburg and I went with him and Jim Rowley in the Aero Commander. As we left the White House and were driving to the airport, the President himself brought up the question of '56. He asked me if I had been doing some thinking on this subject, and I said I had. He said he had also, and he just could not see or go for turning the country over to any of the so-called Democratic candidates—Stevenson, Harriman, or Kefauver. I asked him directly, "Mr. President, do you know what you're going to do yet in 1956?" He replied this way: "Jim, you've always known that I didn't particularly want to be President, and that I had always thought that while I was in the White House the Republicans would have an opportunity to build up men who could take my place and who could successfully keep out of that office the crackpot Democrats who were seeking it. I don't want to run again, but I am not so sure I will not do it. We have developed no one on our side within our political ranks who can be elected or run this country. I am talking about the strictly political men like Knowland. He would be impossible and so in answer to your question, I don't want to, but I may have to."

By this time we had reached the airport and we got aboard the Aero Commander. As we were taking off with two other Aero Commanders, the President reminisced about his flying in the Philippines and said that in taking off with three small planes it reminded him of how they used to fly in the Philippines in much the same way except their taking-off strip was much narrower and they had to watch for the backwash of the other planes or else they would crash.

Once in the air he came back to '56. "What do you think about my suggestion on Tom Dewey? You're a friend of his. Do you think it would work?"

I told him that I did not think that it would. I said that rightly or wrongly Dewey was looked upon by the Midwest Republicans as an Easterner who represented all the views of Easterners. I said that I thought it would split the party badly and give encouragement to the Midwest, determined to defeat Dewey, to rally around someone like Knowland whom they wouldn't really be for. The President listened to me and then said, "Yes. That makes sense. I guess you're right."

The President then said, "What do you think about Nixon's chances?" I told him that I thought Nixon was a very excellent vice presidential candidate on the ticket of Eisenhower and Nixon, but that I did not believe that Dick on his own could get the nomination even though the President himself would actively support his candidacy. The President interrupted. "That is one thing that I must watch very carefully if I'm not going to run. I think I can control the convention and get someone nominated that we want, but it has to be done very delicately and cannot be done through any show of force or stubbornness." I laughed and said, "Mr. President, have you changed your mind from yesterday that you may have to run." He laughed in return and said, 'No, I was just asking you some questions. Just trying to get some of your ideas."

By this time we were nearing Gettysburg and Bill Draper circled over the President's farm so he could see it, and the conversation was concluded and was not resumed on the ride from the airport to the farm. Instead we talked about the Battle of Gettysburg, and the President pointed out an English rifle cannon that the Confederates used that could shoot four miles with a great deal of accuracy. These cannons were far superior to any on the northern side. "Unfortunately for the South," the President said, "they only got a few from the British. The British, you know, were trying to help the South with arms but could get only a very few through the Union blockade. If they had been completely equipped with those British guns, the Civil War might have been a different story."

When we came to the farmhouse, the President got out and I said I would drop out tomorrow. The President said he would like for me to come out shortly after nine, because he would like to continue our private discussion. I told him I would be there.

• • • •

Wednesday, December 14, 1955

I arrived at the farmhouse shortly after 9, and the President was alone on the front porch. He told me he was glad to see me and to sit down. We discussed briefly the stories in the paper and in particular the attitude of Senator George and Sam Rayburn on tax cuts with Rayburn being quoted as being not so sure that tax cuts would come through this session and George being quoted in favor of tax reductions. The President said that he expected nothing but politics from Mr. Sam and would take everything he said during this session with "six grains of salt." As to Senator George, he said, "I wonder why George is being for tax cuts." I said I thought it was probably for local consumption in Georgia since George was faced with a very tough race with Talmadge for his reelection. I said the newspaper reporters who I trusted in Georgia had said that Senator George would be licked probably. The President said his friends had said the same thing . . .

Then the President got up from his chair and started to walk around the porch. "Now, getting back to 1956," he said, "I have some more thoughts I want to talk to you about. I've been thinking about this more than ever."

I asked him if he had read David Lawrence's column in the *Herald Tribune* and when he said he had not, I handed it to him with a comment that David Lawrence could very easily have been sitting in the car the other day. The gist of Lawrence's column was that the President's basic attitude toward public service is not one of health and convenience of an individual but the needs of one's country. Then David Lawrence had the following paragraph: "The opinion is crystallizing that, in the event that the doctors give Ike advice saying he is physically able to continue in office if he so desires, the President will not seek to be a candidate but will tell the American people something to this effect: 'I had no desire to come to public office in the first place. I think there are able men to be found to succeed me. But if the people want me to serve, I shall obey their wish and serve if elected.' " The President read it, then laughed and handed the paper back to me, saying "Well, I'll be goddamned." Then he turned serious and said, "Jim, you would think he was sitting in that car. That's almost exactly the words that are forming in my own mind should I make up my mind to run again. But let me ask you some more questions. Do you still feel the same about Dewey's chances?" I told him that I did, and he said, "Well, I guess you're right on that, but let me try you out on some more. I've been trying to think of a ticket that could gain widespread support and could be elected. Let me try out this one on you—George Humphrey for President and my brother for Vice President. Let me tell you why. George is one of the ablest men I know. He is a fine administrator and could rally the conservatives, particularly in the Midwest, to his support. Now George really isn't a conservative because every time we have an argument along these lines and the facts are presented to him,

George usually ends up going along with the liberal point of view or my point of view, which I think is fairly liberal. Now, my brother would lend the Eisenhower name to the ticket and I of course could give my support completely." I asked the President if he thought George Humphrey could get the nomination. He grinned and said, "Well, that's the trouble. I don't know. But if he could, I think he could be elected." I said that I thought it would be difficult to get the nomination for Humphrey, but that it would not be impossible.

The President by this time was really throwing ideas out fast. He was walking up and down the sun porch, sitting down in the chair, getting up again as he always does when he is talking about something he has had on his mind for a long time and is getting off his chest with somebody who has his confidence. "You know, I just hate to turn this country back into the hands of people like Stevenson, Harriman, and Kefauver. Let me ask you another question. Two of the Democratic candidates are divorced men. In this country up until recently there has been a political axiom that no divorced man could ever be elected President of the United States. Well, apparently that's changed, and the old feeling doesn't cut much ice any more. Now, if that's the case, what do you think about a Catholic being nominated and elected? Do you think Lausche could get the nomination?"

I told the President I did not know whether a Catholic could be nominated or not, let alone elected. "Well," he said, "let's continue this further. I think that in Congress Sam Rayburn and Lyndon Johnson are going to be politically important. It seems to me, and from what I know from my Texas friends, that they don't care much for Stevenson or Harriman and, of course, despise Kefauver. That being the case, it might be possible that they might get behind someone like Lausche. (Neither the President nor myself knew about it at the time, but while we were having this very discussion, Lausche issued a statement from Columbus permitting his name to be entered in the Ohio primary for delegates to the convention as a favorite son candidate. At the same time Lausche ducked the question as to whether he would permit his name to be entered in contests in other states.)

I told the President that I was afraid that Lausche as a Catholic would get hurt in many Southern states as did Al Smith, and that the only man I knew in politics who thought he could get the nomination was Jim Farley. At one time Jim had argued with my father and myself that his religion would not work against him for the nomination because he was on such friendly terms with the Democratic leaders, even district leaders, in the South. The President said, "Well, if Farley thought that, Lausche could think it now, and maybe Lausche will be the candidate to whom Rayburn and Johnson will ultimately turn. Look, Jim, Lausche would be a natural. In 1952 many Democrats voted for me because they didn't like Stevenson and the Truman Fair Deal-New Deal boys. Furthermore, despite all we have done in four years, I'm the only Republican that the young folks will support. With me out of the picture, they will support a Democrat. Lausche would appeal to the youth and hundreds of thousands of Democrats who left their party to vote for me would go back to their party, I am convinced, to vote for Lausche."

I told the President he might very well have a point there, and I could not disagree with him. He continued: "Now that we have talked about the Democrats, let's go back to the Republican Party and assume I am not going to be a candidate. I can't see Knowland from nothing. Who else have they got?"

"Mr. President, what about Warren?" I asked.

"Not a chance," the President snapped back, "and I'll tell you why. I know that the Chief Justice is very happy right where he is. He wants to go down in history as a great Chief Justice, and he certainly is becoming one. He is dedicated to the Court and is getting the Court back on its feet and back in respectable standing again. I believe that is his life's work and I do not believe he will run. Furthermore, I do not think I would approve of a Chief Justice stepping down from the bench to run for office. Earl is one of those fellows who needs time to make decisions, and his present spot is the best spot in the world for him. He is perfectly happy where he is. He has a lifelong job and I think he means it when he says he will not enter political life again."

"Who else have we got?" I asked.

"Well, we have four people that I think are mentally qualified for the presidency. Three of them are in the executive branch of the government. One is George Humphrey, one is Herb Brownell, and the third is Sherman Adams, but I don't think either Herb or Sherm can get the nomination, but I do think there is a chance for George. I would also like to see Bob Anderson in there, but I don't think he can be built up for the presidency, maybe Vice President.[1] Actually, I can't see anyone in the Senate who impresses me at all on both sides of the aisle."

I told the President I fully agreed on that statement and said that the greatest blow we suffered as far as the Senate was concerned was the death of Bob Taft. When I mentioned Taft's name, the President stopped mentally in his train of thought and said, "Let me tell you a piece of history about Bob Taft. . . ."[2]

While the President was telling me the Taft story, he was sitting on the sofa right next to me. Then he jumped up again and started pacing.

"Let me try you on something else. I think my brother would do anything I wanted him to. I think he would run for President, if I wanted him to. I think, if I approved, Pennsylvania would go to the convention with Milton as a favorite son. They could say they were for Milton Eisenhower, or the Young Ike or just Ike. I would, of course, do everything I could to help him. What do you think of that?"

"Well," I said, "as long as we're talking this way, I think one of the great hurdles Milton would have to get over would be an Eisenhower dynasty. The people of our country don't like dynasties, and that would be a hurdle." "That's right," the President replied, "but they elected two of Roosevelt's sons to Congress in New York and California." "Congress, Mr. President, is not the office of the President, but anything that would send Pennsylvania solidly committed to a favorite son would be a help to us if you're not going to be the candidate."

Once again the President laughed and said, "Listen, Jim, I haven't said I'm not going to be a candidate. I'm just trying to get some thoughts. Let's see what we have done so far. You have said that you thought Tom Dewey couldn't get the nomination, and I'm inclined to agree with you. You sort of like the Humphrey-Milton ticket, and you have no objection to the Young Ike ticket."

"Yes, sir," I said, "but I still have my own opinion—Eisenhower-Nixon."

The President laughed and said, "Well, I guess that's about all we should talk about now, but we'll be up here for a week and we'll talk about it some more. You drop in about nine in the morning. It helps to have someone to listen to me sound off. Now call Ann Whitman and tell her to come out." . . .

Typically, having enjoyed political talk with his friend Hagerty, the President called for his secretary and began to dictate, probably letters to the host of friends and acquaintances and officials, domestic and foreign, who had inquired during his recent illness. And after this long discussion with the President over the political prospects for 1956, Hagerty's diary virtually ends. He picked it up for January 24–27, 1956, and dropped it. The accounts during those four days are quite uninteresting, about a Soviet proposal of a twenty-year treaty of friendship, a nonaggression pact, which the Eisenhower administration did not take seriously, believing it a propaganda move. In this manner one of the most interesting diaries in the entire course of American politics stopped, without ceremony, no rumination or afterthought, as abruptly as it began.

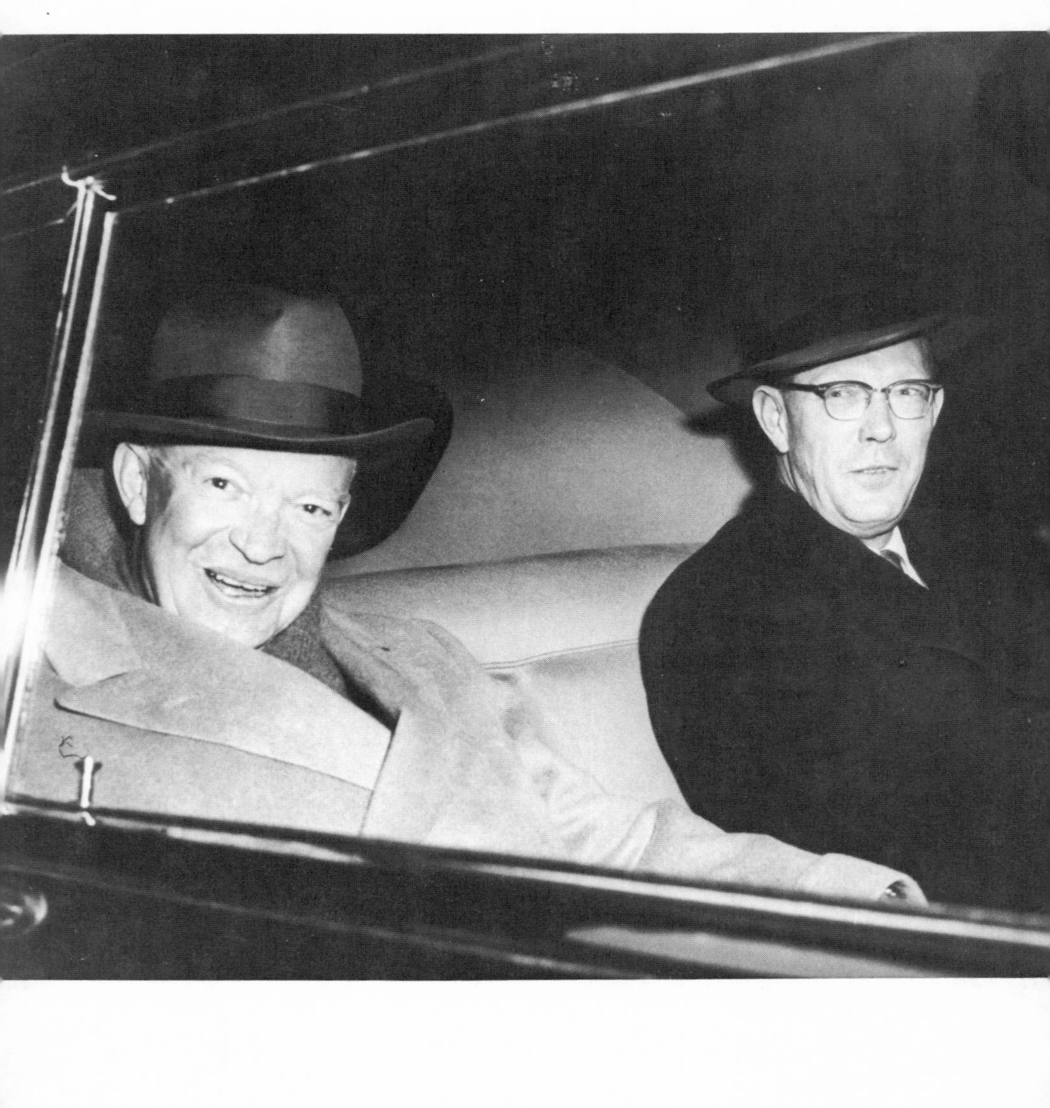

Notes

January 1, 1954

1. Sherman Adams, former governor of New Hampshire, the assistant to the President, 1953–1958; Henry Cabot Lodge, Jr., ambassador to the UN; Joseph M. Dodge, director of the budget, 1953–1954; I. Jack Martin, administrative assistant; Bryce N. Harlow, White House liaison with Congress; Gerald D. Morgan, administrative assistant; John K. Jessup, chief editorial writer for *Life* magazine.

January 2, 1954

1. Robert T. Cutler, administrative assistant, later special assistant for national security affairs.

January 3, 1954

1. Mrs. Elivera Doud, mother of Mrs. Eisenhower; William E. Robinson, an official of the Coca-Cola Company; Clifford Roberts, New York financier, leading figure in the Augusta National Golf Club; Douglas Casey, Chicago investment banker and member of the Augusta Club.
2. Military Air Transport Service.

January 4, 1954

1. Congressman Daniel A. Reed (Rep.) of New York; George M. Humphrey, Secretary of the Treasury.
2. Robert Montgomery, actor, was advising the President on radio and television appearances.
3. Charles Moore, administrative assistant.
4. David Lawrence, president and editor of *U.S. News and World Report;* Henry Cabot Lodge.
5. Kevin McCann, special assistant.
6. Senator James H. Duff (Rep.) of Pennsylvania.

January 5, 1954

1. Harold E. Stassen, director of the Mutual Security Administration; Charles E. Wilson, Secretary of Defense.
2. Senators Alexander Wiley (Rep.) of Wisconsin; H. Styles Bridges (Rep.) of New Hampshire.

January 8, 1954

1. Herbert Brownell, Attorney General.
2. Georgi N. Zaroubin, Soviet ambassador to the United States.

January 11, 1954

1. Vice President Richard M. Nixon; Senator Eugene D. Millikin (Rep.) of Colorado; Senator Leverett Saltonstall (Rep.) of Massachusetts; Representative Joseph W. Martin, Jr. (Rep.) of Massachusetts; Representative Leslie C. Arends (Rep.) of Illinois; Representative Charles A. Halleck (Rep.) of Indiana, majority leader of the House; Philip Young, chairman of the Civil Service Commission; Leonard Hall, chairman of the Republican National Committee; Wilton B. Persons, aide.
2. Georgi Malenkov was chairman of the council of ministers of the USSR; Vyacheslav Molotov was foreign minister.
3. Frank Holeman, reporter for the *New York Daily News.*

January 14, 1954

1. The *Times-Union* of Albany, New York.

January 18, 1954

1. Secretary of Labor James P. Mitchell.

January 19, 1954

1. Senator Herman Welker (Rep.) of Idaho.

January 22, 1954

1. Murray Snyder, assistant press secretary.
2. Milton S. Eisenhower, president of Pennsylvania State University; Senator Prescott Bush (Rep.); Senator Walter F. George (Dem.) of Georgia.

January 23, 1954

1. Walter Winchell, columnist.

January 28, 1954

1. Senator Homer Ferguson (Rep.) of Michigan. For the George Amendment, see below, p. 20.

February 1, 1954

1. Oveta Culp Hobby, Secretary of Health, Education and Welfare; Drew Pearson, columnist.
2. Associate Justice William O. Douglas.

February 4, 1954

1. Chief Justice Earl Warren; Senator Frank Carlson (Rep.) of Kansas.

February 8, 1954

1. Military Assistance Advisory Group.

February 12, 1954

1. William G. Draper, presidential pilot.

February 15, 1954

1. Senator Morse (Rep.) of Oregon; Johnson was Senate minority leader; Senator William Langer (Rep.) of North Dakota.

February 24, 1954

1. Senator Everett McK. Dirksen (Rep.) of Illinois; Charles E. Potter (Rep.) of Michigan; Senator Karl E. Mundt of South Dakota.

February 25, 1954

1. William P. Rogers, Deputy Attorney General.
2. Roy Cohn, assistant to Senator McCarthy.
3. Roger M. Kyes, Deputy Secretary of Defense.

February 27, 1954

1. Mrs. Ann Whitman was private secretary to the President.

March 1, 1954

1. Leo Allen, chairman of the House Rules Committee.

March 2, 1954

1. Senator William E. Jenner (Rep.) of Indiana.

March 3, 1954

1. Doris Fleeson, columnist.

March 4, 1954

1. Edward T. Folliard was a reporter for the *Washington Post.*

March 6, 1954

1. Robert J. Donovan, correspondent of the *New York Herald Tribune.*

March 8, 1954

1. Bernard M. Shanley, special counsel to the President; Leonard Hall, chairman of the Republican National Committee; Adlai E. Stevenson, leader of the Democratic Party.

March 9, 1954

1. John L. McClellan (Dem.) of Arkansas.
2. Senator Ralph E. Flanders (Rep.) of Vermont; Robert E. Lee, commissioner of the Federal Communications Commission.

March 10, 1954

1. The Tenth Inter-American Conference of the Organization of American States met at Caracas in March 1954.

March 11, 1954

1. Fred A. Seaton, Assistant Secretary of Defense.

March 15, 1954

1. The Fair Employment Practices Committee of 1941 sought to curb discrimination in war production and government employment.
2. Aksel Nielsen, Denver financier, friend of the President; C. D. Jackson, special assistant; President René Coty of France. For EDC, see below, pp. 44ff.

March 18, 1954

1. Admiral Robert B. Carney, chief of naval operations; General Matthew B. Ridgway, chief of staff of the U.S. Army; Admiral Arthur W. Radford, chairman of the joint chiefs; Representative Short (Rep.) of Missouri.

March 22, 1954

1. See below, pp. 45, 76–77, 95.

March 24, 1954

1. 1. The two Jerrys were Persons and Morgan.

March 25, 1954

1. Mark Trice was secretary of the Senate.
2. Republican Senators Herman Welker of Idaho, George W. Malone of Nevada, Bourke B. Hickenlooper of Iowa, John Marshall Butler; Dwight Griswold of Nebraska; William A. Purtell of Connecticut.
3. John Adams was Army Counsel.
4. "Wires"—wire men.
5. Maxwell M. Rabb, associate counsel.

March 26, 1954

1. National Labor Relations Board; International Longshoremen's Association.

April 1, 1954

1. Roy W. Howard, chairman, and Walker Stone, editor-in-chief, of Scripps-Howard Newspapers.

April 2, 1954

1. Charles F. Willis, Jr., was a White House assistant.
2. H. Struve Hensel, Assistant Secretary of Defense.
3. Samuel P. Sears, Boston attorney.

April 5, 1954

1. Stassen had become director of the Foreign Operations Administration.

April 9, 1954

1. Stewart J. and Joseph Alsop, columnists; Earl Browder, wartime head of the Communist Party, U.S.A.

April 19, 1954

1. Georges Bidault, French foreign minister. At a Berlin foreign ministers conference early in the year, the three Western ministers refused a Soviet proposal on reunification of Germany.

April 29, 1954

1. General Henri Navarre was the French commander in Indochina.

May 10, 1954

1. Thomas C. Streibert was director of the United States Information Agency.

May 13, 1954

1. Arthur E. Summerfield, Postmaster General.

May 14, 1954

1. Senator John L. McClellan (Dem.) of Arkansas.

May 21, 1954

1. Rowland R. Hughes succeeded Joseph M. Dodge on April 15, 1954, as director of the budget.

May 26, 1954

1. Commander Edward L. Beach, naval aide; Congresswoman Edith Nourse Rogers (Rep.) of Massachusetts.

June 1, 1954

1. Haakon M. Chevalier, longtime professor of French at the University of California, translator of many books, lived in Paris. For his side of the Oppenheimer affair see *Oppenheimer: The Story of a Friendship* (New York, 1965).

June 14, 1954

1. Allen W. Dulles, brother of the Secretary of State, was director of the CIA.

June 15, 1954

1. *In the Matter of J. Robert Oppenheimer: Transcript of Hearing before Personnel Security Board* (Washington, 1954).

June 18, 1954

1. The lawyer James St. Clair assisted Welch in defending the Army against McCarthy.

June 19, 1954

1. Brigadier General Paul T. Carroll, staff secretary and defense liaison officer at the White House.
2. Admiral Robert B. Carney, chief of naval operations.
3. Lieutenant General Floyd L. Parks was commanding general of the Second Army, General J. Lawton Collins the former U.S. Army chief of staff, General Nathan F. Twining chief of staff of the Air Force.
4. General Clifton B. Cates, commandant of Marine Corps schools at Quantico; Harold E. Talbott, Secretary of the Air Force.

June 21, 1954

1. Major General S. D. Sturgis, Jr., was chief of the Corps of Engineers.
2. Francis P. Carr was staff director of the McCarthy subcommittee.

June 22, 1954

1. Edward H. Rees (Rep.) of Kansas.

June 24, 1954

1. Sir Roger Makins, British ambassador.

June 25, 1954

1. Winthrop Aldrich, ambassador to Great Britain.

June 26, 1954

1. Smith was a veteran White House reporter and dean of the press corps, whose task at the end of press conferences was to say "Thank you, Mr. President."

July 6, 1954

1. Gabriel Hauge, special assistant for economic affairs.

July 8, 1954

1. T. Keith Glennan, president of Case Institute of Technology; John F. Floberg, Washington lawyer.
2. Private secretary to the President.

July 10, 1954

1. Robert L. Schulz, military aide.
2. Thornton was former governor of Colorado.

July 12, 1954

1. Kevin McCann, president of Defiance College, consultant and special assistant.
2. Hagerty's younger son Bruce.
3. Governor John S. Fine.

July 13, 1954

1. Mr. and Mrs. Eisenhower had two children, Milton S., Jr., and Ruth.

July 14, 1954

1. Pierre Mendès-France, French premier.
2. Joel T. Broyhill (Rep.) of Virginia.

July 18, 1954

1. William S. Paley was chairman of the board of CBS; David Sarnoff was president of NBC.

July 19, 1954

1. Washburn was deputy director of the United States Information Agency.

July 23, 1954

1. Roger was Hagerty's elder son.

July 26, 1954

1. Earle D. Chesney, presidential assistant; Representative Dean P. Taylor (Rep.) of New York.

July 28, 1954

1. Governor William G. Stratton of Illinois.

August 2, 1954

1. Carl W. McCardle was Assistant Secretary of State for public affairs.
2. A. Wayne Hawks was chief of White House records.

August 3, 1954

1. Arthur F. Burns was chairman of the Council of Economic Advisers.
2. Democratic Senators Paul H. Douglas of Illinois and Hubert Humphrey of Minnesota.

August 4, 1954

1. Major General Howard M. Snyder was personal physician to the President.

August 10, 1954

1. Clare Boothe (Mrs. Henry R.) Luce was ambassador to Italy.

November 30, 1954

1. Stanley M. Rumbough, Jr., was a special assistant.

December 1, 1954

1. Drummond was Washington correspondent of the *Christian Science Monitor.*
2. Fulton Lewis, Jr., was a radio commentator and columnist.

December 2, 1954

1. Hoover was Under Secretary of State.
2. Churchill's long-time hatred of the Soviet regime was well-known; at the end of the First World War he had spoken openly of "the foul baboonery of Communism." During the Second World War his relations with Stalin were necessarily awkward. According to Dulles he was willing in 1945 to accumulate a cache of German arms in case it became necessary to enlist Germans to fight the Reds.
3. Charles E. Bohlen was ambassador to Russia.

December 7, 1954

1. Here Hagerty of course meant "condemnation" rather than "censure."

December 8, 1954

1. Smitty was Merriman Smith.

December 9, 1954

1. Andrew J. Goodpaster, Jr., staff secretary.

December 11, 1954

1. Roy A. Roberts was president of the *Kansas City Star.*
2. Governor G. Mennen Williams of Michigan.
3. Senator Clifford Case (Rep.) of New Jersey.

December 13, 1954

1. After his abdication, Edward VIII became Edward Windsor.
2. Clarence B. Randall was chairman of Inland Steel.

December 14, 1954

1. Senator Richard B. Russell (Dem.) of Georgia.
2. Representative James P. Richards (Dem.) of South Carolina.
3. A spectacular wide-angle color film process that used a huge semicircular screen and gave viewers the feeling of standing within what they watched.

December 20, 1954

1. General Lucius D. Clay, postwar military governor of Germany; Tex McCrary, New York public relations counsel; Oswald Heck, Republican leader of New York State; Representative Jacob K. Javits, elected attorney general of New York.
2. Walter P. Reuther, president of the CIO.

December 22, 1954

1. Columnists.

December 24, 1954

1. Golf pro.

January 3, 1955

1. Rockefeller was a special assistant to the President.
2. General Alfred M. Gruenther, supreme allied commander in Europe.

January 6, 1955

1. Miller was minority doorkeeper of the House.

January 13, 1955

1. Dag Hammarskjold was secretary general of the UN.

January 14, 1955

1. Chou En-lai was foreign minister of the People's Republic of China.
2. Chain of Washington drugstores.
3. Sinclair Weeks was Secretary of Commerce.

January 17, 1955

1. Pyle was a former governor of Arizona.

January 19, 1955

1. L. Arthur Minnich was assistant staff secretary.

January 20, 1955

1. Krock was Washington correspondent for the *New York Times.*

January 23, 1955

1. Portions of this entry have been closed by Executive Order 12065, Sec. 1–301 (b) (d), governing access to national security information.
2. Robert R. Bowie was director of the policy planning staff.

January 24, 1955

1. Senator Earle Clements (Dem.) of Kentucky.

January 25, 1955

1. Senator Estes Kefauver (Dem.) of Tennessee.
2. Mrs. Meyer was the wife of Eugene Meyer, publisher of the *Washington Post.*

January 28, 1955

1. Former President Truman always denied that he had asked Eisenhower to take the Democratic presidential nomination, although talk to this effect circulated for years. One story had it that Truman proposed the nomination to Eisenhower at the end of the war when he met the general at Brussels en route to the Potsdam Conference. Another that banter during a Pentagon meeting while Ike was chief of staff of the Army led Truman to say jokingly that there wasn't anything within his power that he would deny Eisenhower. Secretary of the Army Kenneth Royall years later said that he was Truman's go-between to try to get Eisenhower to accept the Democratic nomination in 1948.

January 30, 1955

1. Portions of this entry closed by Executive Order 12065, Sec. 1–301 (b) (d), governing access to national security information.

January 31, 1955

1. Portions of this entry closed by Executive Order 12065, Sec. 1–301 (b) (d), governing access to national security information.

February 3, 1955

1. John Charles Daly was radio news correspondent and analyst and vice president of ABC; Robert E. Kintner was a columnist and president of ABC.

February 11, 1955

1. Andrei Vishinsky, an official of the Soviet foreign office and sometime deputy foreign minister, was then political adviser to Zhukov.

February 12, 1955

1. Mrs. Annie Lee Moss was a timorous, pathetic widow, suspended from her job with the Signal Corps, who appeared during the McCarthy hearings. Her case demonstrated the slipshod work of McCarthy's counsel, Cohn, who confused Mrs. Moss with other individuals of the same name and who at one point confused her supposed knowledge of a *Daily Worker* correspondent, Robert Hall, with another Robert Hall. Mrs. Moss obviously was no Communist. "Do you know who Karl Marx is?" asked Senator Stuart Symington (Dem.) of Missouri. "Who's that?" she asked blankly.

February 13, 1955

1. John Hay Whitney was a New York financier.

February 14, 1955

1. Robert Humphreys, staff member.

February 23, 1955

1. Congressman John W. McCormack (Dem.) of Massachusetts.

February 24, 1955

1. Portions of this entry closed in accordance with restrictions contained in the donor's deed of gift.

February 25, 1955

1. Mrs. Gordon Moore was the sister of Mrs. Eisenhower.

March 15, 1955

1. Admiral Felix Stump was commander of the Pacific Fleet.

March 18, 1955

1. Portions of this entry closed in accordance with restrictions contained in the donor's deed of gift.

March 22, 1955

1. The French government was less than enthusiastic.
2. Former Senator Harry S. Cain (Rep.) of Washington had been a conservative, but after taking a post on the board he turned liberal. The issue, of course, was the administration's rigorous measures, many of which involved guilt by association—Cain rightly saw that they skirted constitutionality.

March 23, 1955

1. The Potsdam Papers appeared in *Foreign Relations of the United States: The Conference of Berlin (The Potsdam Conference), 1945* (2 vols., Washington, D.C., 1960).

March 31, 1955

1. Portions of this entry closed in accordance with restrictions contained in the donor's deed of gift.

April 1, 1955

1. Senator Smith was a Republican.

April 5, 1955

1. The President's words were: "I have said this before, but I shall say it again and again and again. Your boys are not going to be sent into any foreign wars."
2. Robert R. Ross, Deputy Assistant Secretary of Defense.

April 6, 1955

1. Portions of this entry closed in accordance with restrictions contained in the donor's deed of gift.

April 7, 1955

1. Portions of this entry closed in accordance with restrictions contained in the donor's deed of gift.

April 12–20, 1955

1. Portions of this entry closed by Executive Order 11652 governing access to national security information.
2. Ellis D. Slater was president of Frankfort Distillers. Robert Woodruff was president of the Coca-Cola Company; Robert Tyre Jones was the well-known golfer.

September 24, 1955

1. The President was spending a vacation in Denver at the house of his mother-in-law, Mrs. Doud, and after arriving in Colorado he headed for the Rockies, for Byers Peak Ranch on the western slope of the Continental Divide, some eighty miles from Denver, at Fraser, Colorado.

December 14, 1955

1. Robert B. Anderson was Deputy Secretary of Defense.
2. The President in telling this story said to Hagerty that he never had mentioned it to anyone before. But he did discuss it in *At Ease* and it is now fairly well-known, namely, that before going to Europe as NATO commander he met privately with Taft in the Pentagon and asked for support in trying to build up Europe. Taft refused to offer support, saying only that he did not know how he would vote in favor of additional divisions for NATO. Eisenhower had determined to take himself out of the 1952 presidential race, irrevocably, with a public statement, in event Taft promised support. Because he did not get an answer, he did not make the statement. "It's funny," he told Hagerty, "how little things can change your life."

Index

COLLEGE LIBRARY